Excavations in the Santa Cruz Floodplain: The Early Agricultural Period Component at Los Pozos

Edited by
David A. Gregory

Contributions by

Jenny L. Adams
Michael W. Diehl
Alan Ferg
David A. Gregory
James M. Heidke
Lorrie Lincoln-Babb
Penny Dufoe Minturn
M. Steven Shackley
R. Jane Sliva
Arthur W. Vokes
Jennifer A. Waters
Helga Wöcherl

Submitted to

Arizona Department of
Transportation
Environmental Planning Services
Phoenix, Arizona
Contract No. 94-46
TRACS No. H380601D

Anthropological Papers No. 21
Center for Desert Archaeology
3975 North Tucson Boulevard, Tucson, Arizona ● February 2001

ACKNOWLEDGMENTS

Many individuals contributed their efforts to the successful completion of this project. Alternately scorched by the late summer sun and drenched by monsoonal storms, the field crew met all challenges with equanimity and high spirits. The names of individuals who served on the field crew in various capacities are listed below; their substantial contribution to the success of the project is greatly appreciated.

Assistant Project Director:
Helga Wöcherl

Crew Chiefs:
Sam W. Baar IV
Noreen Fritz

Archaeologists:
Lisa Armstrong
Dale Brenneman
Rob Caccio
Allison Cohn
Michael Diehl
Alan Denoyer
Andrew Dutt
Lambert Jose
Josh Miller
Dominique Rampton
Ellen Ruble
Jon Shumaker
Michelle Stevens
David Tucker

Laborers:
John Arnold
Richard Arnold
Jaylon Conde
Loren Conde
Arnold Miguel
Janice Moristo
Gary Narcho
Joe Ortiz
Tommy Sam
Catherine Treat
Jennifer West
Patricia Wilson

Geomorphologists:
Andrea K. Freeman
Gary Huckleberry (testing)

Public Tours:
Catherine Gilman

Backhoe Operators:
Dan Arnitt
Paul Giaccomino
Eugene Norstadt

As with any such project, the in-house support staff also made a critical contribution. Dr. William Doelle, President of Desert Archaeology, Inc., was unstinting in his interest and support both during and after the field work. In addition, Trish Castalia (Project Manager), Jean Kramer (logistics), Lisa Eppley (Laboratory Director), Dylan Cooper (computer systems management), and Sara Lely (data entry) all contributed their particular skills.

The line drawing presented in Figure 2.9, all the drawings in Chapter 7, and those in Figures 8.7 and 8.10 were executed by Rob Ciaccio. The drawings in Figures 4.1, 4.2, and B.2 were rendered by R. Jane Sliva. All the photomicrographs illustrated in Chapter 5 were taken by Jenny L. Adams. Greg Berg produced the photographs shown in Figures 6.1, 7.6, 8.15, and B.3.

Bettina Rosenberg, Robert Gasser, and Owen Lindauer of the Arizona Department of Transportation provided input and support during the project, and Lindauer read and provided critical comments on this volume. The continuing involvement of the Arizona Department of Transportation in the study of Arizona archaeology is gratefully acknowledged.

Adams wishes to acknowledge the dedicated staff of Desert Archaeology, Inc., for their assistance in completing Chapter 5. Lisa Eppley, Desert's laboratory director, and her crew did a remarkable job of processing the materials and getting them ready to be analyzed. Chip Coldwell created the line drawings. Dominic Oldershaw photographed the artifacts. Dena McDuffie, head of the Production Department, and her staff, Andrea Mathews and Laura Orabone, edited and formatted the chapter—no easy task considering all the tables and figures. Thank you to everyone for your help.

With respect to Chapter 8, Heidke and Ferg would like to thank Marci Donaldson and the Central Arizona Project Repository staff for making the Coffee Camp collection available for reanalysis. Similarly, we would like to thank Mike Jacobs and the Arizona State Museum for assisting us in our examination of the

Snaketown collections. We would also like to acknowledge the important contribution that Project Directors Michael Diehl (Clearwater), Andrea "Max" Freeman (Wetlands), and Jonathan Mabry (Santa Cruz Bend) made in supporting the research leading up to the synthetic discussion of incipient plain wares presented here, as well as the support provided by Bill Doelle and the Center for Desert Archaeology. Miriam Stark and Jonathan Mabry furnished useful comments on an earlier draft of the material presented here. Preliminary results of this study were presented at the 29th Annual Chacmool Conference, "Eureka!! The Archaeology of Innovation and Science," in the session, "Technological Innovation in Social Context: The Development and Change of Pottery-Making Traditions," organized by Michelle Hegmon; Miriam Stark coauthored that paper.

TABLE OF CONTENTS

LIST OF FIGURES

LIST OF TABLES

PREFACE

Archaeological research reported in this volume was conducted under an on-call contract between Desert Archaeology, Inc. and the Arizona Department of Transportation (ADOT; Contract 94-46). This contract provides for documentation and appropriate treatment of cultural resources encountered during long-term implementation of proposed ADOT improvements to the Tucson area segment of the Interstate 10 corridor between the Interstate 19 interchange on the south and Tangerine Road on the north (Mabry 1993a). Several archaeological sites along this corridor have been previously investigated under this contract (Baar 1996; Clark 1993a, 1993b; Jones et al. 1994; Mabry 1993b; Mabry et al. 1997; Mabry, ed. 1998; Swartz 1997a).

The present report deals with investigations in that segment of the corridor falling between Prince Road on the south and Ruthrauff Road on the north and along both sides of Interstate 10. Following a records search and pedestrian survey of the project right-of-way, a plan for archaeological testing was prepared and subsequently carried out during January and February of 1995. Subsurface testing revealed an extensive component dating to the Early Agricultural period, as well as a much more spatially restricted and deeply buried Middle Archaic component.

Based on results of the testing program, a data recovery plan was prepared (Gregory 1995) and, between 7 August and 24 October 1995, excavations were carried out at the site later named *Los Pozos* (AZ AA:12:91[ASM]). The current volume reports investigation of the Early Agricultural period component at the site, while a companion volume documents work in the Middle Archaic component (Gregory, ed. 1999). The site name acknowledges several Early Agricultural period wells discovered during work at the site (see Chapter 3).

A word on the site number used for Los Pozos is in order. The records search conducted prior to pedestrian survey revealed that several Arizona State Museum numbers had been previously assigned to sites whose boundaries overlapped the project area (Gregory 1995). However, aside from two canal segments identified during the investigations and given new numbers in accordance with ASM guidelines (AZ AA:12:789 and AA:12:790), all materials recovered during the 1995 work have been described and documented under the AZ AA:12:91 (ASM) designation. Although some features discovered during the testing phase fell within the boundaries of site AZ AA:12:19 (ASM) as shown on ASM maps, and some fell outside of *any* previously described sites, but near the boundaries of site AZ AA:12:11 (ASM), it was clear that the discovered features formed a more or less continuous distribution most appropriately treated under a single site number (Gregory 1995:Figure 2). The most logical grouping was under AZ AA:12:91 (ASM), the largest of the several previously recorded sites and the one whose boundaries most closely approximated the overall distribution of materials documented during testing. Use of a single site number greatly facilitated investigation and documentation of the remains, and in particular, circumvented potential problems associated with use of two similar site numbers (19 and 91). It may be noted that the original site card (1937) for AZ AA:12:19 (ASM) shows it entirely east of the Southern Pacific Railroad tracks; when these boundaries were extended to the west of the tracks–and thus into the current project area–is uncertain (but see Adams and Macnider 1992a, 1992b).

The chapters that follow present descriptions and analyses of the Early Agricultural period materials recovered. Chapter 1 reviews the research goals that guided the investigations, discusses the methods employed, and summarizes general results. Chapter 2 discusses the characteristics of investigated architectural features, while Chapter 3 covers extramural features. The next five chapters deal with the substantial artifact assemblage recovered, including flaked stone (Chapter 4), ground stone (Chapter 5), shell (Chapter 6), bone (Chapter 7), and artifacts of clay (Chapter 8). Chapters 9 and 10 report on the paleobotanical and faunal remains, respectively. Chapter 11 evaluates the current Early Agricultural period chronology for the Tucson Basin, in light of the new data from Los Pozos; the effects of calibration on the clustering of radiocarbon dates during this period are also considered. Chapter 12 presents a synthesis of what has been learned in a comparative framework and reviews prospects for future research.

As the chapters in this volume attest, the investigations at Los Pozos have resulted in a wealth of new data relating to the latter centuries of the Early Agricultural period in southern Arizona. However, while much has been learned, a great deal remains to be discovered and major research issues remain unresolved. As new discoveries are made, and as existing information is continually reanalyzed and reassessed, the data from Los Pozos will continue to be an important component in the investigation of this lengthy and fascinating interval in Southwest prehistory.

David A. Gregory
Project Director
February 2001
Tucson, Arizona

CHAPTER 1

GOALS, METHODS, AND GENERAL RESULTS

David A. Gregory

The Early Agricultural period remains reported here represent a component of the distribution designated as AZ AA:12:91 in the Arizona State Museum Site Survey system and named Los Pozos. The site was investigated in anticipation of impacts from proposed Arizona Department of Transportation (ADOT) improvements to the Interstate 10 corridor in the Tucson metropolitan area (Mabry 1993b; see Preface to this volume). In addition to the spatially extensive Early Agricultural period component, a Middle Archaic component of much more limited extent was discovered and investigated, and is reported on in a companion volume (Gregory, ed. 1999). The site name derives from several wells associated with the Early Agricultural period component (see Chapter 3).

The project area is located between Prince Road on the south and Ruthrauff Road on the north and along both sides of Interstate 10 (Figure 1.1). On the east side of the interstate, the area extends for this entire distance (approximately 2.4 km), but practical constraints reduced the area examined to the northern 1.6 km of this reach. Also due to practical constraints, the area available for study on the east side was restricted to the narrow strip (approximately 16 m) between the interstate and the frontage road. On the west side, the project area was defined by an approximately 20-m right-of-way for a large temporary drainage facility associated with east side frontage road construction. This alignment runs immediately west of the interstate right-of-way fence from a point just north of Sweetwater Drive to a point approximately 402 m south of Ruthrauff Road, where it turns and runs west along an existing ditch for some 250 m. The total length of the west side right-of-way segment is approximately 1.6 km.

With reference to the natural landscape, Los Pozos is located in the north-central part of the Tucson Basin, on the southwest side of the southeast-northwest trending point of land that separates Rillito Creek from the Santa Cruz River above the confluence of these two drainages (Figure 1.2). The large multicomponent Hohokam settlement known as the Hodges site later occupied an extensive area atop this point of land (Kelly 1978; Layhe 1986; Swartz 1995, 1997b). Los Pozos is situated between 402 and 804 m east of the present-day channel of the Santa Cruz, and approximately 3.2 km upstream from the Rillito-Santa Cruz confluence; to the northeast, the straight-line distance from the site to the floodplain of Rillito Creek is approximately 1.6 km. The entire project area lies within the Holocene floodplain of the Santa Cruz, on the T2 terrace as defined by McKittrick (1988:4), and the site is roughly midway between the present channel of the Santa Cruz and the western margin of the older T3 or Jaynes Terrace as currently mapped (McKittrick 1988:5; Smith 1938; see also Chapter 2). Although much modified by modern activities, the present ground surface retains the naturally gentle south to north and east to west floodplain gradients. Elevation within the project area ranges from approximately 686 m to 690 m over a north-south transect of roughly 1.6 km (a .3 percent gradient).

TESTING PHASE RESULTS

At the inception of the project, pedestrian survey of the project area was conducted and followed by a systematic testing program designed to determine the nature and extent of subsurface remains within the right-of-way (Gregory 1995). Testing phase exposures revealed that the upper 2 m of natural strata in the project area consist primarily of overbank deposits derived from the Santa Cruz River, all clearly Holocene in date and variably modified by erosion, bioturbation, pedogenesis, and modern activities. These stratigraphic units proved to be quite uniform across much of the project area, and are discussed and illustrated in detail in the report on the Middle Archaic component at the site (Gregory and Baar 1999; Gregory et al. 1999). The younger features of concern here were consistently encountered near the top of this sequence of strata, lying immediately below and truncated by a 30- to 50-cm zone of modern disturbance, in most cases a plow zone. Owing to this truncation, the actual surface from which these features were originally intruded appears to have been completely removed, and no evidence was found of any preserved extramural surfaces. Figure 1.3 represents a typical exposure showing the relationship between features and natural strata.

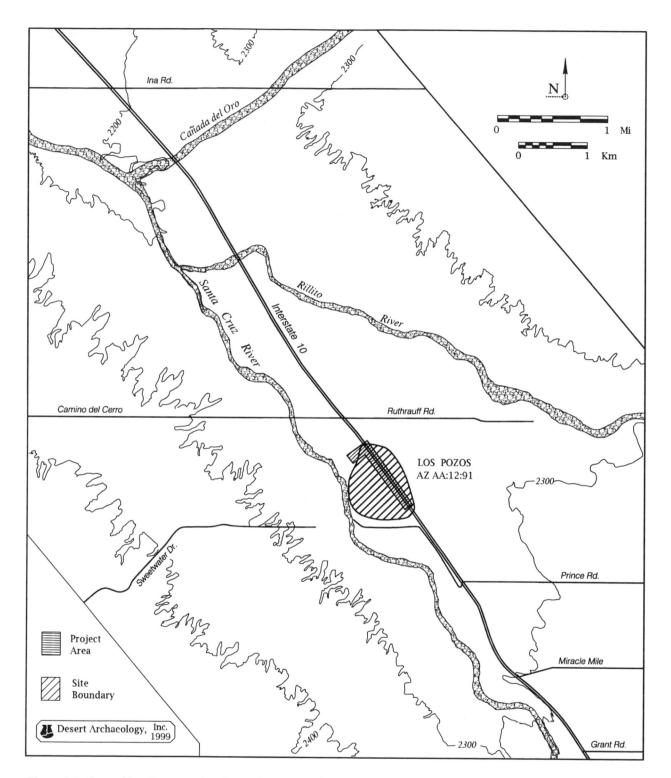

Figure 1.1. General location map showing project area and site boundaries.

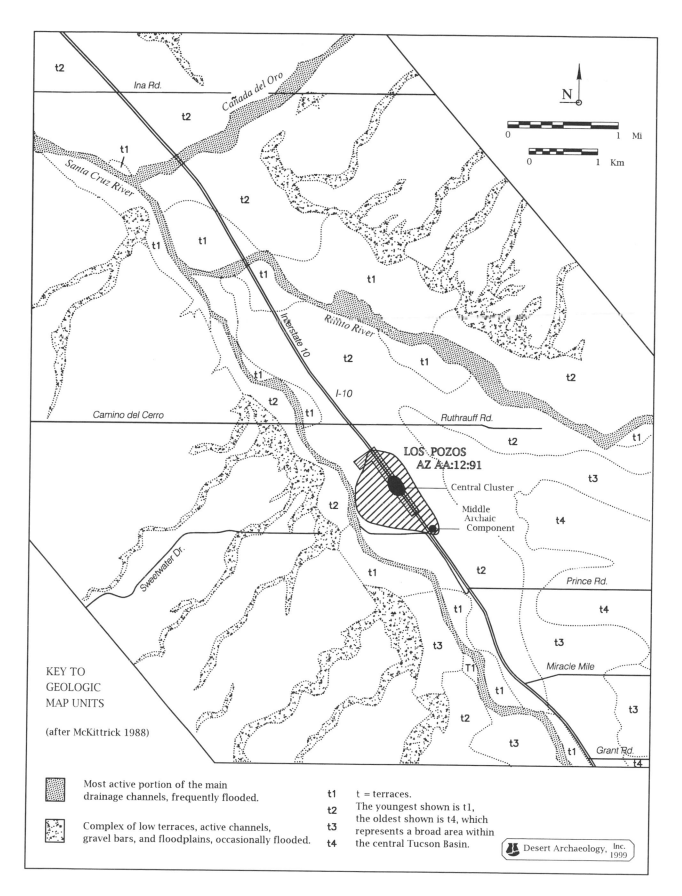

KEY TO GEOLOGIC MAP UNITS

(after McKittrick 1988)

Most active portion of the main drainage channels, frequently flooded.

Complex of low terraces, active channels, gravel bars, and floodplains, occasionally flooded.

t1
t2
t3
t4

t = terraces.
The youngest shown is t1, the oldest shown is t4, which represents a broad area within the central Tucson Basin.

Desert Archaeology, Inc. 1999

Figure 1.2. General location map showing site boundaries and terrace designations.

Table 1.1. Early Agricultural period and Early Ceramic period chronology.

Period	Phase	Dates
Early Agricultural	San Pedro	1200-800 B.C.
	Cienega	800 B.C.-A.D. 150
Early Ceramic	Agua Caliente	A.D. 150-550
	Tortolita	A.D. 550-650

developing. Although analyses of materials from these sites and preparation of resulting reports were still under way when the Los Pozos data recovery plan was formulated, information from these sites was incorporated into the design of research for Los Pozos to the degree possible. The general problem domains were retained in unmodified form, but additional research questions were posed under each of them. Each of the problem domains is reviewed briefly below, with emphasis on the supplementary questions generated specifically for the Los Pozos investigations. Editorial changes have been made in certain instances, but along with the queries contained in the Treatment Plan, these questions are in essence those posed to guide data recovery at Los Pozos (compare Gregory 1995:23-29).

Holocene Floodplain Development and the Archaeological Record

Owing to the discovery of deeply buried Middle Archaic deposits and a sequence of paleo-channels of the Santa Cruz River, several additional research questions were posed under this problem domain, as follows:

- What are the ages of the principal natural stratigraphic units represented at the site?
- What may be inferred about changing environmental conditions represented by the natural strata present in the project area? Specifically, what can be inferred about the position of the Santa Cruz channel during these intervals?
- What can be inferred about specific environmental conditions that obtained during the intervals represented by the natural stratigraphic units documented at the site?
- What can be demonstrated or inferred about the relationship between settlement location, duration, and intensity and the changing floodplain environment for the periods of occupation represented?

Table 1.2. Research issues and questions from the Interstate 10 corridor improvement treatment plan (after Mabry 1993b).

Holocene Floodplain Development and the Archaeological Record
- What are the spatial patterns of alluvial surfaces and landforms of different ages?
- Can the current model of floodplain development during the span of human use of this environment be improved?
- Can the probable locations and states of preservation of archaeological sites of different ages be predicted?
- What do the sedimentological and structural contexts of archaeological sites tell us about stream behavior and floodplain processes before, during, and after site occupations?
- What are the relationships between alluvial processes and regional shifts in strategies and settlement systems?

Resource Variability and Prehistoric Subsistence Adaptations
- How did changes in hydrology and landscape characteristics alter opportunities and constraints on prehistoric subsistence?
- Is there evidence of changes in the variety, abundance, and seasonality of plant and animal resources exploited for subsistence through time?
- What was the timing of major shifts in prehistoric subsistence technologies, such as hunting and butchering tools, plant processing equipment, food storage facilities, and soil and water control devices, and what were the factors involved in these adaptive changes?

Regional Shifts in Prehistoric Settlement Patterns
- What are the regional patterns and trends in site occupational histories, village plans, and settlement systems?
- What were the timings of regional interruptions and reorganizations in settlement?
- Which model, or combination of models, best explains the new sum of evidence for different phases of regional settlement and abandonment?

Prehistoric Community Organization and Interaction
- What was the internal organization of prehistoric riverine communities?
- What groups of sites were socially and functionally related?
- What kind of production and exchange relations developed between communities?

Historic Patterns of Floodplain Use and Effects of Urbanization
- What traces of historic canals and diversions are preserved along the river, and how did long-term plowing and irrigation affect floodplain soils?
- How have private industrial operations utilized the natural resources of the floodplain?
- What traces of the early-twentieth-century Yaqui refugee settlements are preserved along the railroad right-of-way?
- How have historic and modern irrigated agriculture, industrial uses, residential development, municipal landfills and sewage treatment, and county bank stabilization efforts affected the floodplain environment and the preservation of its archaeological resources?

Results of investigations relating to this problem domain are dealt with primarily in the volume documenting the Middle Archaic occupation at Los Pozos (Gregory, ed. 1999). These findings are reiterated and expanded upon in subsequent chapters of this volume as they relate specifically to the Early Agricultural component.

Resource Variability and Prehistoric Subsistence Adaptations

Because the presence of a Middle Archaic occupation was recognized during testing, additional questions included under this problem domain were designed to facilitate temporal comparisons at two different scales: first, those incorporating the long-term perspective provided by the presence of both Middle Archaic and Early Agricultural components at the site; and second, analyses and comparisons focused on variability *within* the intervals represented by the two components.

As data concerning the Early Agricultural period have accumulated, it has become clear that maize cultivation was a consistent aspect of subsistence strategies practiced by groups occupying the Santa Cruz River floodplain during this interval. However, much remains to be understood about the overall subsistence strategies employed by these groups, and in particular about the relative contribution of maize cultivation as against hunting and gathering of wild plant foods, and how these relationships may have changed over this rather lengthy interval. Thus, the following questions were added to those identified in the Treatment Plan under this problem domain:

- What may be inferred about changing subsistence patterns during the span of occupation represented at the site?
- What was the suite of plants and animals exploited at various times in the cultural sequence represented at the site? What may be inferred about changes in prehistoric subsistence patterns from similarities and differences in these inventories?
- If domesticated plants are present throughout the sequence, what evidence exists for changes in the importance of these plants in the overall subsistence base?
- What may be inferred from artifact assemblages related to food procurement and processing about similarities and differences in subsistence practices through time?

Regional Shifts in Settlement Patterns

This problem domain is concerned primarily with data that transcend individual sites, focusing on settlement relationships at a larger geographic scale. A concern with the regional referent implies the need to examine data on an areal scale as well, in this case the distribution of settlements along the middle Santa Cruz River and in the Tucson Basin more generally. Similarly, a concern with shifts in patterns implies that basic patterns have or can be established for various intervals in the prehistoric sequence. The latter must include consideration of several issues: the absolute contemporaneity of individual settlements; the nature of those settlements, including the relative permanence and intensity of the occupation–sedentism and site function; and the number of people in residence at any given time–demography. Thus, this general problem domain is closely related to that of prehistoric community organization and interaction, discussed below.

One aspect of this problem relates to the distribution of Cienega phase settlements along the middle Santa Cruz River (Figure 1.4). Los Pozos is approximately 3.6 km north of the Santa Cruz Bend site, while Santa Cruz Bend is only some 1.8 km north of the Stone Pipe site. Investigations at the Clearwater site below A-Mountain have documented another substantial Early Agricultural period settlement in that area (Diehl 1997a; Elson and Doelle 1987), lying 3.4 km south of the Stone Pipe site and thus 5.2 km south of Santa Cruz Bend. Another Early Agricultural period component of at least moderate size has been discovered recently at the Julian Wash site (Swartz 1997a), lying approximately 2.0 km south of the Clearwater site.

Thus it has now been demonstrated that the Santa Cruz River floodplain was regularly occupied and exploited during the Early Agricultural period, and during the Cienega phase in particular. However, the degree of permanence of the occupations represented and their temporal relationships have yet to be established with certainty. If it is assumed that occupations at Stone Pipe, Santa Cruz Bend, Los Pozos, Clearwater, and Julian Wash represent contemporaneous loci of permanent settlements sometime during the Cienega phase, then relatively dense settlement and population would be indicated. At the other extreme, it is theoretically possible that these sites could have been produced by one or two band-sized groups shifting their preferred settlement location over this millennium-long interval (see Chapter 12).

With respect to the following Early Ceramic period, one occupation is represented at Stone Pipe and another, possibly smaller, at the Square Hearth site, located some 2.3 km north of Stone Pipe. Both sites show a lower density of pit structures and other features than at any documented Cienega phase floodplain site. Further, no evidence of Early Ceramic occupation has been found at Santa Cruz Bend, Clearwater, or Los Pozos, and none is yet apparent at Julian Wash. If these data are at all representative, then it appears that the floodplain was less frequently and perhaps less intensively occupied than during the Cienega phase, and a shift in settlement location may have occurred between the Cienega phase and the Agua Caliente phase of the Early Ceramic period. Alternatively, the period of occupation represented at the Cienega phase sites is clearly much longer, and the duration and intensity of Cienega phase use for any particular point in time may have been similar to that documented for Agua Caliente phase sites.

While it was anticipated that these issues could not be fully resolved in the context of the project, Los Pozos represents another extensive Early Agricultural period settlement along this reach of the river and thus an additional data point with which to explore this general problem. The following questions bearing on this issue were appended to those contained in the Treatment Plan:

- How does the period of occupation at Los Pozos compare with that documented for the nearby sites of Santa Cruz Bend and Stone Pipe?
- What may be said about the possible historical and socio-cultural relationships among the populations represented at these different sites?
- What may be inferred from existing data about differences in Late Archaic and Early Ceramic settlement location and density; what factors may be inferred to be responsible for these differences?

Prehistoric Community Organization and Interaction

Among the most striking and surprising features of recently investigated Early Agricultural period sites in the Santa Cruz floodplain are the large numbers of pit structures present and the great horizontal extent of their distribution. However, as noted above, questions remain regarding the manner in which these settlements developed and the interval of time over which that development occurred, and a principal focus of the research at Los Pozos was on elucidation of these problems. This problem domain is closely related to the issues of regional and areal settlement patterns raised above, in that the composition (demographics) and duration of individual settlements (sedentism) and the

purposes for which they were established (site function) are critical issues in establishing areal and regional settlement patterns.

An important issue involves the kind and number of social groups in residence at any given time. Several circular clusters or groups of structures have been recognized at Santa Cruz Bend, composed of a ring of up to 11 or 12 structures surrounding a single larger feature that has been interpreted as a storage facility (Mabry, ed. 1998; see also Gregory 1995:Figure 7). These rings measure approximately 30 to 35 m in diameter and thus the groups encompass an area of between approximately 700 and 960 m². Another ring of houses may have been present at the Stone Pipe site, but the narrowness of the area available for investigation there precludes positive identification. Although arranged differently, house clusters or courtyard groups of similar areal extent are characteristic of later Hohokam settlements, and define the former spatial domains of basic residential groups within settlements. If such clusters are a consistent feature of Early Agricultural period site structure, they would constitute an important avenue into the closely related issues of demography and organization.

However, most houses at both Santa Cruz Bend and Stone Pipe *cannot* be interpreted as being a part of such groupings, and why it should be that some houses are parts of formal arrangements while most are not is an interesting and important problem. Do the clusters represent a period of continuous occupation by larger social groups while the more (apparently) randomly scattered houses represent more limited occupations by smaller groups that occurred over a long period of time? Or, does the formal versus non-formal arrangement of houses represent a contemporaneous dichotomy that reflects functional differentiation of space within the settlements? These are only two of the more obvious possibilities.

Given the relatively narrow right-of-way available for investigation at Los Pozos and the size of documented house clusters, it was anticipated that recognition of such arrangements would be a hit-or-miss proposition. However, two related issues were considered to be fundamentally important, whether or not formal arrangements could be identified: 1) the function of individual structures (residential or non-residential), and 2) the use-life of structures. Both of these issues have obvious implications for reconstructions of demography and organization, and both dictated an emphasis on documentation and interpretation of the depositional histories of structures and intramural pits. Given these perspectives on settlement organization, several questions were added to those contained in the Treatment Plan:

- What may be inferred about the use-life of pit structures represented in the sample?
- What may be inferred about functional differentiation of houses, based on size, floor features, and other criteria?
- Can formal arrangements of houses with consistent compositions be identified? If so, what may be inferred about the character (size, composition) of the residential units represented by such groupings? What may be inferred about the number of such units present during a given interval? What are the implications of these inferences for interpretations of settlement size, composition, and duration?
- What may be inferred about the overall character of the settlement represented at any particular time?
- What was the magnitude of population aggregates present at any given time?

Historic Patterns of Floodplain Use and Effects of Urbanization

No historic-period features or deposits were encountered during the testing program. It was anticipated that the contribution of the project to this problem domain would be at best modest and general in nature, possibly involving archival documentation of the historic-period use of the project area. One possible exception is a relatively recent flood channel discovered on the west side of the freeway, interpreted as possibly representing the former course of a canal that was washed out by a flood event (Gregory et al. 1999:Figure A.5). An archival search was proposed to explore the possibility that a historic canal was present in this area and that one or more of several recorded historic-period floods may have been responsible for this channel. The proposed archival research was to be guided by the following general questions:

- What may be demonstrated or inferred about the character of historic-period use of the project area?
- What have been the effects of floodplain development on archaeological resources in the project area?

DATA RECOVERY STRATEGIES

In order to address the research issues and questions outlined above, the data recovery plan called for intensive excavation within selected portions of the project right-of-way (Gregory 1995). Proposed data recovery strategies, modifications to those strategies made during fieldwork, and excavation methods are discussed below.

Coverage

Based on the density of pit structures and other features present in the identified clusters, and on data from machine stripped areas at the Santa Cruz Bend and Stone Pipe sites, estimates of pit structure density were derived using several different formulas. The resulting estimates indicated that between 240 and 530 pit structures could be wholly or partially contained within the right-of-way at Los Pozos, with five of six estimates falling between 240 and 330 structures (Gregory 1995:Table 5). It should also be noted that Mabry's (ed. 1998) recent estimate of over 500 structures for the Santa Cruz Bend site is based on an estimated site area that extends well beyond the area stripped by machine. If a similar approach was applied at Los Pozos, the estimated number of structures would be well over 1,000.

Horizontal coverage proposed in the data recovery plan was ambitious, calling for machine stripping and subsequent excavation within six of the clusters of features. A raw sampling fraction of 25 percent or more of the structures present in each cluster was projected, and excavation of the equivalent of 30 whole structures was proposed. Given strategies for sampling of individual structures (see below), this figure translated into proposed sampling of an estimated 50 to 90 structures and a raw sampling fraction of between 17 and 45 percent of all structures in the right-of-way, depending upon the actual number of structures discovered. Initial efforts were to be focused on the densest portion of the central cluster of features (Cluster B_2), with work in other clusters beginning as feasible.

Several practical impediments arising during fieldwork resulted in reduction of originally proposed horizontal coverage. As was the case with excavations in the Middle Archaic deposits at the site, the early stages of work in the Early Agricultural component were plagued by unusually heavy rains (Gregory and Baar 1999). Both in recognition of a potential drainage problem and to provide a more accurate picture of feature distribution, a continuous trench (Trench 95) was excavated along the eastern margin of the right-of-way at the start of excavations in the central cluster. Reopening of trenches dug during the testing phase also provided drainage in the central portion of the right-of-way. Large sheets of plastic had to be positioned over ongoing excavations each day, with the dual goal of protecting the exposed features and directing the water into open trenches. Nonetheless, heavy storms occurring during the first three weeks of excavation completely filled and overflowed the trenches on two occasions and eroded trench walls in places and portions of some features were clearly lost. Accompanying these more obvious effects was a general slowdown in progress.

Another particularly difficult problem was encountered in the portion of the right-of-way traversed by an informal access road created by vehicular traffic moving between Ruthrauff Road on the north and Sweetwater Drive on the south. Owing to a long period of use–probably several decades or more–and the high clay content of the underlying sediments, the 40 to 50 cm of deposits lying immediately beneath the surface of the road were extremely compact and exhibited a massive, blocky structure (Figure 1.5). The road occupied approximately the west half of the right-of-way, and compaction extended through the plowzone and into the undisturbed deposits below. It quickly became apparent that when backhoe was employed in the usual manner to strip off the plowzone, the requisite control was not possible. Rather than being able to shave off centimeters at a time, the edge of the backhoe blade caught the edge of the massive prismatic blocks and tore them out as chunks, along with the contents of any features lying below.

This problem was ultimately solved by the application of large amounts of water, something of a paradox given the problems caused by rain during the early stages of the excavation. First, the portion of the right-of-way taken up by the modern road was surrounded by embankments of dirt to contain the water and to prevent wetting of the unaffected areas lying east of the road. This was accomplished in a north-to-south sequence of segments roughly 60 to 80 m in length. The road surface within these banked segments was scarified with the backhoe, and water was applied and allowed to soak in over a period of several days. This expanded the clays and closed gaps between the prismatic blocks, and allowed the backhoe to be used in the desired manner to remove the plowzone. Some 300,000 gal of water were required to create conditions under which effective stripping could be accomplished. Once again, however, a general slowing of progress on the excavations was experienced.

As the first few weeks of fieldwork elapsed, it became apparent that it would not be possible to execute the broad horizontal coverage originally proposed. By this time, it was apparent that the compaction problem noted above would have to be dealt with in all of the identified clusters on the west side of the interstate. In addition, the substantial difficulties involved in working within the extremely narrow right-of-way on the east side of the interstate had manifested themselves during the initial weeks of work in the Middle Archaic component. As a result, the decision was made to concentrate more intensively on excavations within the large B_2 cluster, and to abandon exploration of the smaller, outlying clusters. The targeted sampling fraction was increased to include half of the pit structures discovered in this area.

Figure 1.5. Blocky prismatic structure resulting from compaction by vehicular traffic.

Selection and Sampling of Individual Features

Four criteria were established for selecting pit structures for excavation: size, membership in perceived house clusters, preservation, and superposition (Gregory 1995:34-35), with the primary criterion being size. Assessment of floor areas of excavated Cienega phase structures at the Stone Pipe and Santa Cruz Bend sites revealed four general size classes: those with floor areas less than 6 m², those with floor areas ranging from 6 to 10 m², those with floor areas ranging from 10 to 16 m², and very large, probably communal structures having floor areas in excess of 30 m² (Gregory 1995:Tables 3 and 4). The frequencies of houses in the first three size classes have similar distributions within the two sites, and it was anticipated, on the basis of measurements from trench exposures, that the size of structures at Los Pozos would follow a similar pattern. Previous excavations at Santa Cruz Bend, Stone Pipe, and Square Hearth also showed that the stains revealed by machine stripping of the plowzone were a relatively accurate indicator of floor area as measured after excavation. Based on data from these sites, a formula was derived to describe the relationship between the area of stains and floor area revealed by excavation (floor area = .83 × area of stain).

Given these previously documented patterns, and since size was thought likely related to function, the stains revealed by machine stripping and marking the presence of individual structures provided a primary basis on which to stratify the sample of houses to be wholly or partially excavated. After stripping, the areas of these stains were measured and estimated floor area was derived by applying the stain/floor area formula. The number of sampled structures in the three size classes was kept proportional to the total number of structures in any given size class found in the stripped area. The sample was adjusted as more features were exposed by stripping, and once the entire targeted section of the right-of-way had been stripped and all features mapped and measured, the entire sample was reassessed and adjusted within size classes. No circular clusters of structures were definitively identified, and the other two selection criteria were accommodated within the primary emphasis of obtaining a representative sample of structures based on size.

The minimum fraction of a pit structure excavated was one-quarter. It was anticipated that most if not all of the houses would be round in shape [which proved to be the case], and a quarter-section not only provides a volumetrically controlled sample, but exposes the stratigraphy in such a way as to provide relatively complete data concerning the depositional history of the feature. A quarter is also usually sufficient to reveal any characteristics of a particular house that might warrant a greater portion being excavated (e.g., de facto floor assemblages).

Extramural features were selected for excavation on the basis of size and presumed function. Data from previously excavated sites suggested three basic categories of extramural features: roasting pits, identifiable on the basis of abundant ash, charcoal, and fire-cracked rock; pits with a circular plan; and pits having non-circular or irregular outlines. These three basic categories could be further subdivided on the basis of size, and selection of extramural pits for excavation was also generally proportional to their distribution across the size classes. Pits having diameters of less than 50 cm were completely excavated, while only one-half of larger pits was excavated. Two pits targeted for excavation proved to contain inhumations and were completely excavated, and one of the two wells discovered in the stripped area was also completely excavated.

Excavation Methods

Horizontal control for the excavations was established with reference to a metric grid system projected to include the entire project area, with the 0/0 point located well outside the project area to the southwest. Vertical control was maintained with reference to an arbitrary site datum that corresponds to 691.22 m above mean sea level. The plowzone had been shown to be relatively uniform in thickness across the area and was removed by machine stripping with a backhoe. All features revealed by stripping were mapped and measured as a basis for selecting features for excavation as described above. In cases where features selected for excavation had been cut by trenches during the testing phase, these trenches were reopened to provide a stratigraphic cross section as a starting point for excavation; in cases of features not intersected by trenches, new trenches were sometimes cut for this same purpose. In order to provide more complete data on floor plans, the fill remaining in a number of structures after a portion of the feature had been subjected to controlled excavation was removed without screening. In these instances, artifacts resting on the floors were mapped and collected.

In the absence of visible natural or cultural stratigraphy within features, the standard vertical unit was a 10-cm level. With few exceptions (see below), all hand-excavated materials were screened through ¼-in mesh. Composite pollen samples were taken from the floors of all excavated structures, with individual samples making up the composite distributed more or less evenly over the exposed floor. Flotation samples were taken from all identified strata within features, and from near the tops and bottoms of large intramural pits in which only one stratigraphic unit was recognized. Pieces of charcoal were collected for species identification, and large numbers of charcoal samples were taken in particular from several burned, well-preserved structures (see Chapter 2). Detailed records were kept using standard forms and supplemental notes, and all excavated features and deposits were mapped in detail by triangulation from grid points established via all station EDM. All features were photographed after excavation.

GENERAL RESULTS

Following the procedures outlined above, the plowzone was machine stripped from an area some 270-m long and averaging 15-m wide (approximately 4,100 m²). One hundred and eighty-three features were revealed, including 84 pit structures and 99 extramural features of various kinds. Another nine features were observed only in the walls of Trench 95, a continuous exposure dug along the eastern margin of the stripped area; these included two pit structures and seven extramural pits. Figures 1.6 through 1.14 illustrate the distribution of excavated and unexcavated features across this area, while Table 1.3 lists all recorded features, their respective coordinates within the site grid, and their excavation status.

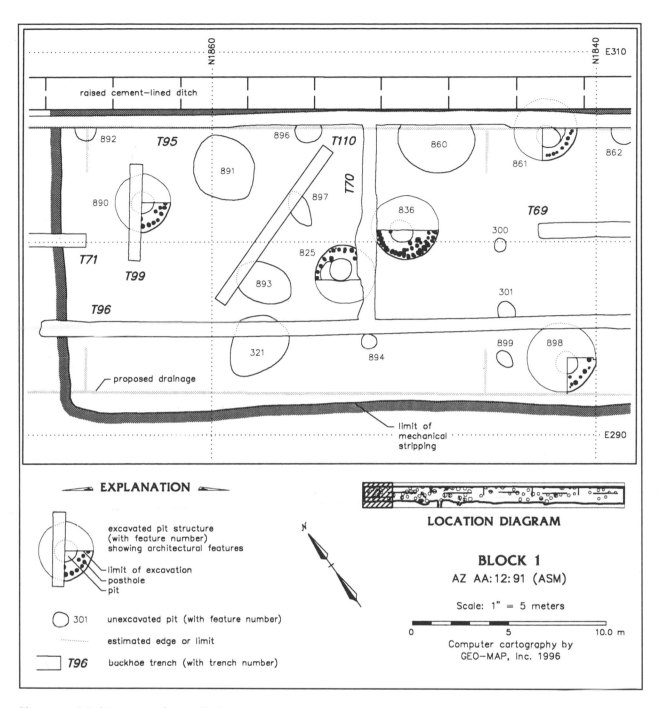

Figure 1.6. Machine stripped area: Block 1.

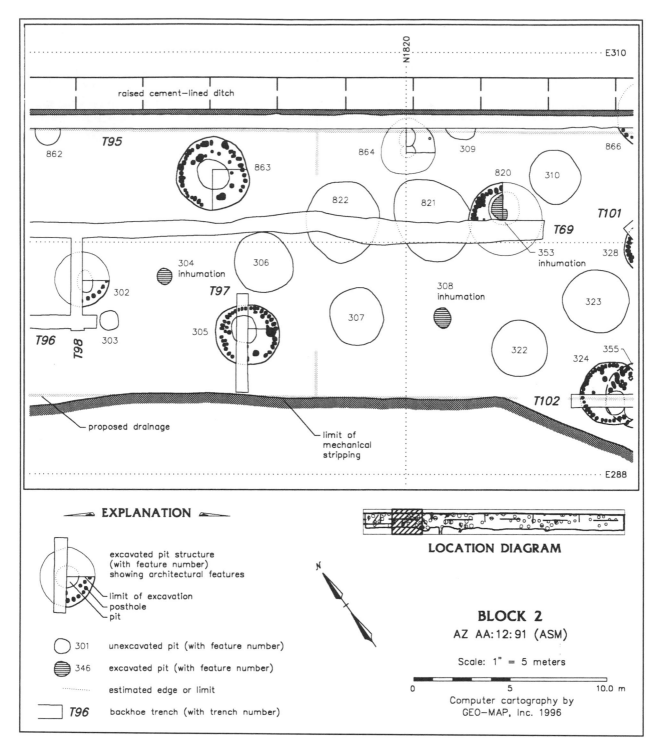

Figure 1.7. Machine stripped area: Block 2.

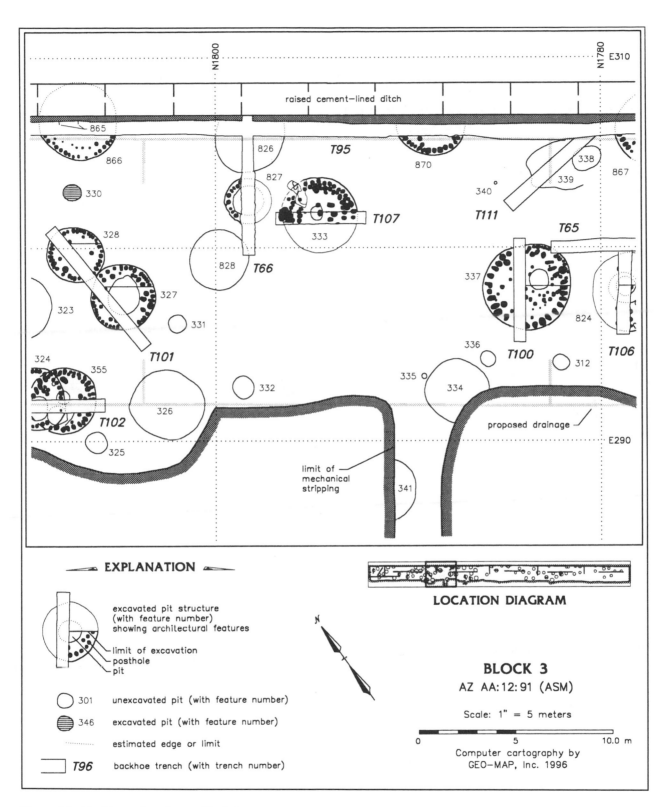

Figure 1.8. Machine stripped area: Block 3.

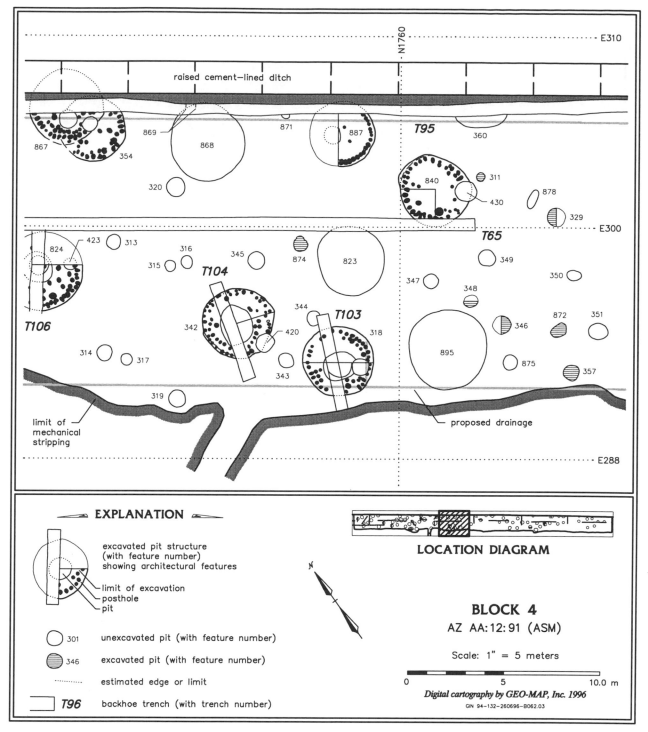

Figure 1.9. Machine stripped area: Block 4.

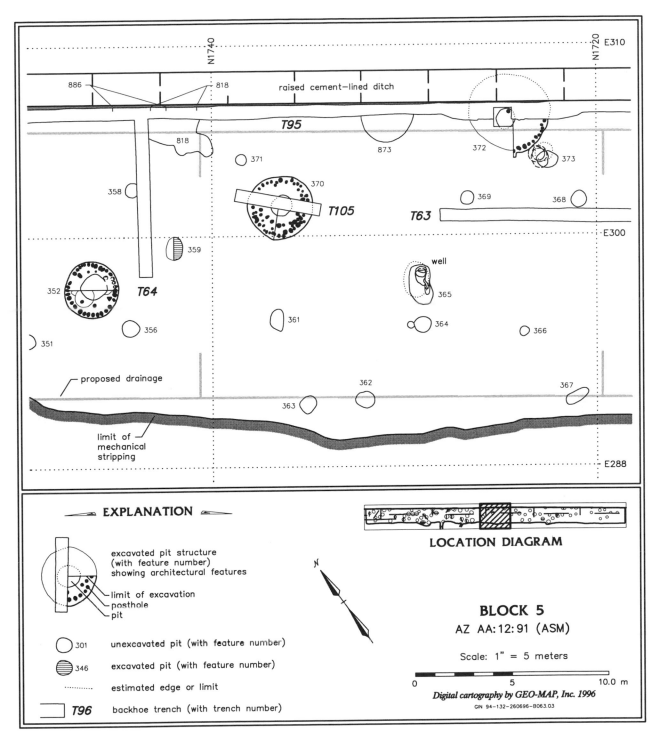

Figure 1.10. Machine stripped area: Block 5.

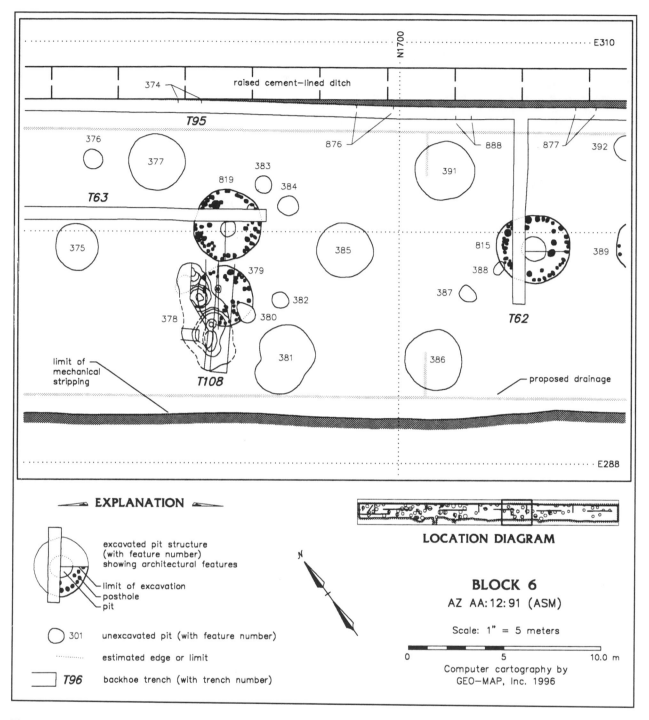

Figure 1.11. Machine stripped area: Block 6.

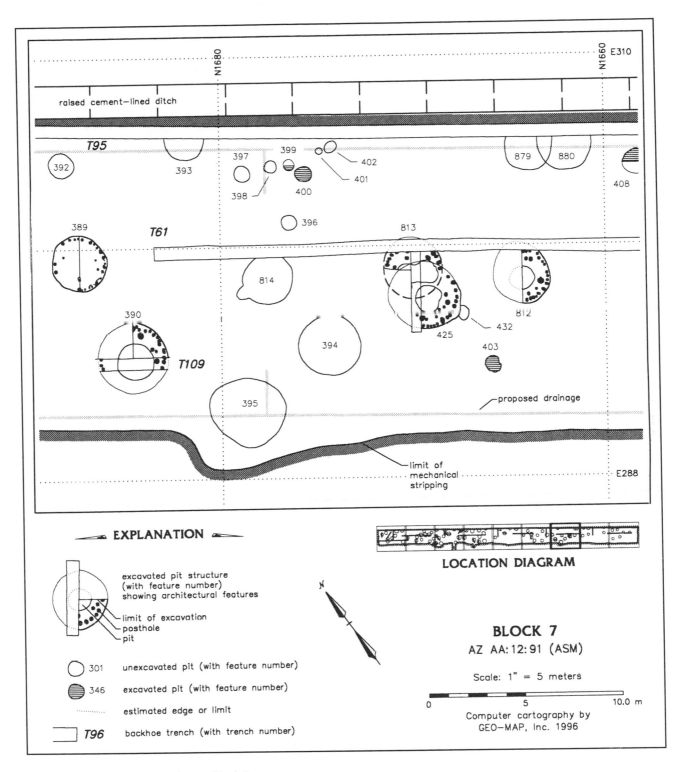

Figure 1.12. Machine stripped area: Block 7.

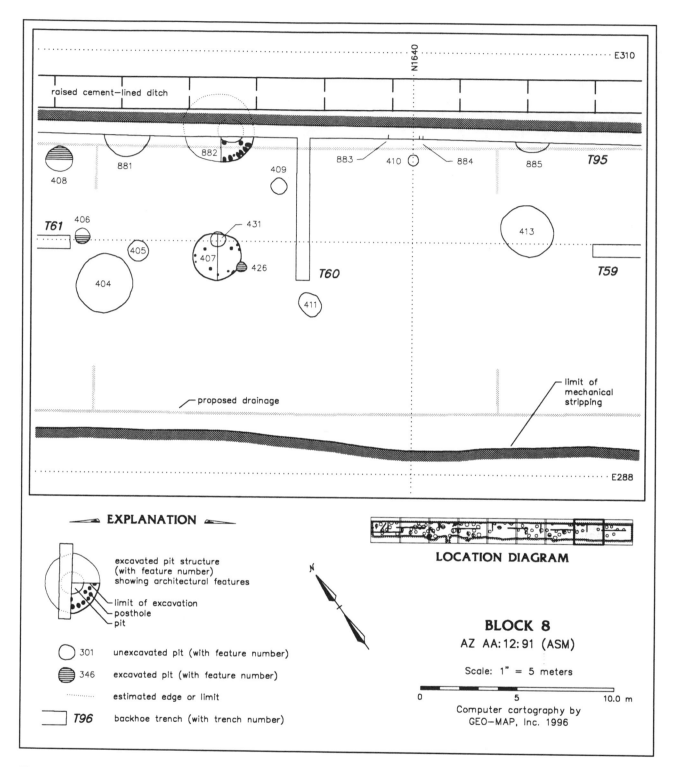

Figure 1.13. Machine stripped area: Block 8.

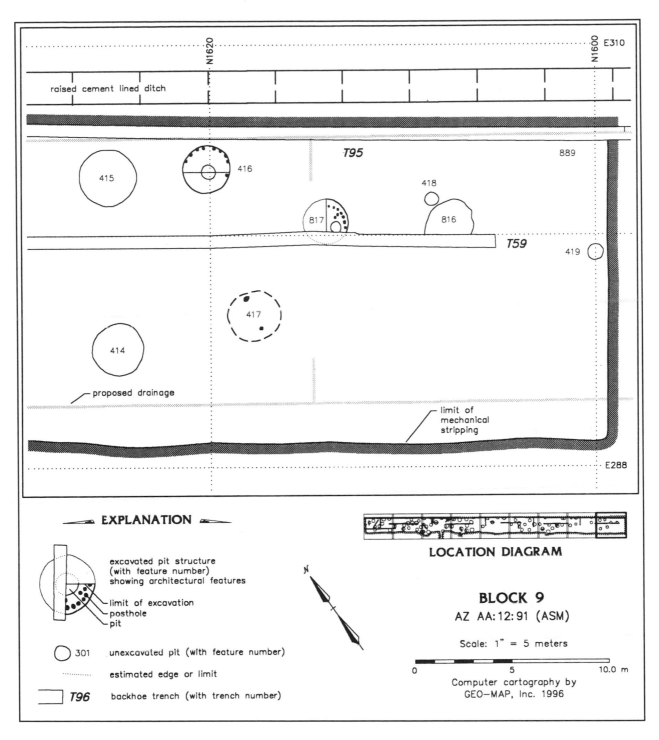

Figure 1.14. Machine stripped area: Block 9.

Table 1.3. Summary data for features identified in the machine stripped area.

Feature	Type	Coordinates	Excavated	Feature	Type	Coordinates	Excavated
302	Pit structure	N1835.20-1836.70 E296.70-298.00	●[a]	385	Pit structure	N1701.35-1704.25 E297.50-300.30	–
305	Pit structure	N1826.53-1829.83 E293.68-296.24	●	386	Pit structure	N1696.80-1699.70 E291.80-294.95	–
306	Pit structure	N1825.80-1828.90 E297.40-300.50	–	389	Pit structure	N1685.85-1688.71 E297.85-300.75	●
307	Pit structure	N1821.20-1824.00 E294.70-297.60	–	390	Pit structure	N1682.77-1686.40 E292.40-296.30	●
309	Pit structure	N1816.40-1817.95 E305.40-306.00	–	391	Pit structure	N1696.10-1699.20 E301.60-304.70	–
310	Pit structure	N1810.95-1813.60 E302.00-304.85	–	393	Pit structure	N1680.60-1682.80 E304.60-305.80	–
318	Pit structure	N1761.35-1765.00 E291.30-294.85	●	394	Pit structure	N1672.80-1676.00 E293.40-296.40	–
321	Pit structure	N1856.00-1859.10 E293.00-296.20	–	395	Pit structure	N1676.70-1680.72 E289.70-293.20	–
322	Pit structure	N1812.70-1815.60 E293.10-296.00	–	404	Pit structure	N1654.70-1657.40 E296.20-299.30	–
323	Pit structure	N1808.40-1811.90 E295.35-298.60	–	407	Pit structure	N1648.85-1651.40 E297.96-300.37	●
324	Pit structure	N1807.79-1811.02 E290.63-293.82	●	413	Pit structure	N1632.70-1635.40 E299.30-302.00	–
326	Pit structure	N1800.60-1804.40 E290.20-293.70	–	414	Pit structure	N1623.50-1626.10 E292.80-295.50	–
327	Pit structure	N1803.05-1806.41 E295.78-299.14	●	415	Pit structure	N1623.80-1626.80 E301.60-304.50	–
328	Pit structure	N1805.70-1807.50 E298.60-300.25	●	416	Pit structure	N1619.02-1621.48 E302.02-304.52	●
333	Pit structure	N1792.60-1796.73 E299.75-303.67	●	417	Pit structure	N1616.43-1619.22 E294.53-297.15	●
334	Pit structure	N1775.80-1778.10 E290.90-294.20	–	425	Pit structure	N1667.52-1671.50 E295.68-298.43	●
337	Pit structure	N1781.57-1786.11 E295.72-300.15	●	812	Pit structure	N1662.86-1665.80 E295.68-298.43	●
339	Pit structure	N1781.00-1783.80 E301.80-305.00	–	813	Pit structure	N1667.20-1671.50 E295.60-300.30	●
341	Pit structure	N1789.60-1790.70 E285.90-289.00	–	814	Pit structure	N1676.30-1679.20 E297.10-299.40	–
342	Pit structure	N1766.50-1770.17 E293.17-296.79	●	815	Pit structure	N1691.14-1694.95 E297.35-300.87	●
352	Pit structure	N1744.87-1747.65 E295.85-298.78	●	816	Pit structure	N1606.30-1608.80 E300.00-301.80	–
354	Pit structure	N1774.25-1777.40 E303.39-306.00	●	817	Pit structure	N1612.50-1615.20 E300.00-302.00	●
355	Pit structure	N1806.18-1809.62 E290.40-293.83	●	818	Pit structure	N1739.80-1743.10 E304.00-306.06	–
360	Pit structure	N1754.40-1757.00 E305.30-306.00	–	819	Pit structure	N1707.10-1710.65 E298.45-302.18	●
370	Pit structure	N1734.76-1738.17 E299.81-303.12	●	820	Pit structure	N1812.95-1816.80 E301.15-303.15	●
372	Pit structure	N1722.40-1726.60 E303.98-306.68	●	821	Pit structure	N1816.80-1820.60 E299.00-303.25	–
375	Pit structure	N1715.40-1717.70 E297.75-300.20	–	822	Pit structure	N1821.40-1825.10 E298.90-303.10	–
377	Pit structure	N1710.95-1713.90 E301.90-304.85	–	823	Pit structure	N1760.80-1764.20 E296.50-299.80	–
379	Pit structure	N1707.57-1710.40 E295.12-298.23	●	824	Pit structure	N1776.45-1780.40 E295.62-299.80	●
381	Pit structure	N1704.30-1707.30 E291.50-295.05	–	825	Pit structure	N1852.23-1854.57 E297.00-299.83	●

Table 1.3. Continued.

Feature	Type	Coordinates	Excavated	Feature	Type	Coordinates	Excavated
826	Pit structure	N1796.40-1800.00 E304.00-306.70	–	303	Extramural pit	N1834.90-1835.90 E295.50-296.40	–
827	Pit structure	N1796.80-1799.55 E301.10-304.00	●	311	Extramural pit	N1755.64-1756.07 E302.41-302.86	–
828	Pit structure	N1798.30-1801.30 E297.80-300.90	–	312	Extramural pit	N1781.60-1782.50 E293.65-294.45	–
836	Pit structure	N1848.15-1851.50 E299.07-302.44	●	313	Extramural pit	N1774.50-1775.20 E298.85-299.60	–
840	Pit structure	N1756.32-1760.10 E300.45-303.80	●	314	Extramural pit	N1774.90-1775.60 E293.10-293.90	–
860	Pit structure	N1847.64-1849.40 E303.60-306.00	–	315	Extramural pit	N1771.60-1772.10 E297.70-298.25	–
861	Pit structure	N1840.95-1844.30 E303.80-306.00	●	316	Extramural pit	N1770.70-1771.25 E297.85-298.50	–
863	Pit structure	N1828.05-1831.88 E301.80-305.55	●	317	Extramural pit	N1773.80-1774.40 E292.90-293.45	–
864	Pit structure	N1818.50-1821.30 E303.57-306.00	●	319	Extramural pit	N1771.00-1771.85 E290.65-291.60	–
866	Pit structure	N1805.10-1808.97 E304.60-305.99	●	320	Extramural pit	N1771.10-1772.05 E301.60-302.60	–
867	Pit structure	N1775.40-1779.25 E304.47-306.00	●	325	Extramural pit	N1805.60-1806.70 E289.40-290.45	–
868	Pit structure	N1768.00-1771.80 E302.40-306.00	–	329	Extramural pit	N1751.43-1752.30 E300.07-301.03	●
870	Pit structure	N1787.08-1790.42 E304.82-305.86	–	330	Extramural pit	N1806.88-1807.83 E302.50-303.36	–
873	Pit structure	N1729.20-1732.00 E304.50-306.00	–	331	Extramural pit	N1801.55-1802.40 E295.60-296.55	–
876	Pit structure	N1700.40-1702.20 E306.40—	Trench only	332	Extramural pit	N1798.10-1799.15 E292.20-293.40	–
879	Pit structure	N1662.60-1665.10 E303.80-305.60	–	335	Extramural pit	N1789.00-1789.25 E293.30-293.55	–
880	Pit structure	N1660.60-1663.40 E303.80-305.60	–	336	Extramural pit	N1775.50-1776.25 E293.85-294.60	–
881	Pit structure	N1653.60-1654.00 E304.40-305.60	–	338	Extramural pit	N1780.00-1781.40 E304.00-305.30	–
882	Pit structure	N1648.20-1652.00 E304.10-305.50	●	340	Extramural pit	N1785.35-1785.42 E303.35-303.42	–
885	Pit structure	N1633.00-1634.70 E304.80-305.30	–	343	Extramural pit	N1765.40-1766.20 E292.70-293.50	–
886	Pit structure	N1742.20-1745.00 E306.70—	Trench only	344	Extramural pit	N1764.10-1764.70 E294.90-295.70	–
887	Pit structure	N1761.35-1765.00 E303.20-305.95	●	345	Extramural pit	N1766.95-1767.80 E297.80-298.85	–
889	Pit structure	N1595.40-1598.50 E306.00—	Trench only	346	Extramural pit	N1754.21-1755.20 E294.48-295.44	●
890	Pit structure	N1862.15-1865.00 E300.55-306.00	●	347	Extramural pit	N1758.00-1758.70 E297.05-297.75	–
891	Pit structure	N1857.80-1861.00 E302.40-305.60	–	348	Extramural pit	N1756.69-1756.95 E295.89-296.52	●
893	Pit structure	N1855.80-1858.70 E296.80-299.00	–	349	Extramural pit	N1755.10-1755.90 E298.10-298.95	–
895	Pit structure	N1755.60-1759.60 E293.80-295.80	–	350	Extramural pit	N1750.60-1751.30 E297.30-297.80	–
898	Pit structure	N1840.00-1841.50 E292.00-294.00	●	351	Extramural pit	N1749.30-1750.30 E294.20-297.00	–
300	Extramural pit	N1844.70-1845.25 E298.50-299.15	–	356	Extramural pit	N1743.95-1744.80 E294.70-295.50	–
301	Extramural pit	N1844.20-1845.10 E295.10-295.90		358	Extramural pit	N1743.62-1744.40 E301.90-302.65	–

Table 1.3. Continued.

Feature	Type	Coordinates	Excavated	Feature	Type	Coordinates	Excavated
359	Extramural pit	N1741.54-1742.39 E298.81-300.00	●	410	Extramural pit	N1639.80-1640.30 E304.00-304.60	–
361	Extramural pit	N1736.20-1736.80 E294.80-295.85	–	411	Extramural pit	N1644.60-1645.90 E296.18-296.94	●
362	Extramural pit	N1731.30-1732.40 E290.70-291.50	–	418	Extramural pit	N1608.20-1608.80 E301.50-302.20	–
363	Extramural pit	N1734.50-1735.30 E290.40-291.35	–	419	Extramural pit	N1599.60-1600.40 E298.70-299.50	–
364	Extramural pit	N1728.40-1729.30 E294.60-295.40	–	420	Extramural pit	N1766.45-1767.40 E293.52-294.50	●
366	Extramural pit	N1723.35-1723.80 E294.40-294.85	–	422	Extramural pit	N1795.21-1796.25 E302.10-303.58	●
367	Extramural pit	N1720.30-1721.40 E290.80-291.60	–	423	Extramural pit	N1776.74-1777.45 E297.75-298.00	●
368	Extramural pit	N1720.30-1721.10 E301.00-301.90	–	424	Extramural pit	N1830.00-1830.73 E302.75-303.93	–
369	Extramural pit	N1726.20-1726.80 E301.20-301.95	–	426	Extramural pit	N1648.51-1649.10 E298.43-298.92	●
371	Extramural pit	N1738.10-1738.60 E303.40-304.00	–	428	Extramural pit	N1684.60-1686.22 E294.37-295.93	–
373	Extramural pit	N1721.89-1723.30 E303.43-304.55	–	429	Extramural pit	N1684.60-1685.31 E294.36-294.85	–
374	Extramural pit	N1710.20-1711.40 E306.65—	Trench only	430	Extramural pit	N1756.05-1757.18 E301.37-302.41	●
376	Extramural pit	N1715.25-1716.25 E303.00-304.00	–	431	Extramural pit	N1649.67-1650.46 E299.70-300.52	●
382	Extramural pit	N1705.65-1706.50 E295.90-296.70	–	432	Extramural pit	N1666.60-1668.00 E304.00-304.50	–
383	Extramural pit	N1706.55-1707.35 E301.75-302.60	–	433	Extramural pit	N1683.68-1685.40 E293.74-294.37	–
384	Extramural pit	N1705.20-1706.20 E300.65-301.60	–	434	Extramural pit	N1707.50-1707.85 E301.10-301.35	–
387	Extramural pit	N1696.00-1696.90 E296.30-297.20	–	862	Extramural pit	N1838.00-1839.20 E305.10-306.00	–
388	Extramural pit	N1694.50-1695.10 E297.70-298.45	–	869	Extramural pit	N1770.60-1771.10 E306.50—	Trench only
392	Extramural pit	N1687.50-1688.80 E303.70-305.05	–	872	Extramural pit	N1751.34-1752.17 E294.34-295.09	●
396	Extramural pit	N1676.00-1676.70 E300.90-301.60	–	373	Extramural pit	N1721.89-1723.30 E303.43-304.55	●
397	Extramural pit	N1678.40-1679.20 E303.40-304.30	–	875	Extramural pit	N1754.00-1754.70 E294.34-295.09	–
398	Extramural pit	N1676.00-1676.70 E303.90-304.60	–	878	Extramural pit	N1752.75-1753.35 E301.00—	Trench only
399	Extramural pit	N1676.08-1676.66 E304.00-304.60	●	883	Extramural pit	N1641.30— E305.40—	Trench only
400	Extramural pit	N1675.20-1676.06 E303.40-304.19	●	884	Extramural pit	N1639.60— E305.50—	Trench only
401	Extramural pit	N1674.60-1674.90 E304.80-305.20	–	888	Extramural pit	N1696.60— E305.80—	Trench only
402	Extramural pit	N1673.80-1674.50 E304.90-305.50	–	892	Extramural pit	N1866.00-1867.10 E305.30-306.00	–
405	Extramural pit	N1653.70-1654.70 E298.90-300.00	–	894	Extramural pit	N1851.40-1852.20 E294.50-295.20	–
406	Extramural pit	N1656.75-1657.52 E299.82-300.60	●	896	Extramural pit	N1854.30-1855.60 E305.20-306.00	–
408	Extramural pit	N1657.65-1659.17 E303.57-304.92	●	899	Extramural pit	N1844.30-1845.20 E292.50-293.40	–
409	Extramural pit	N1646.50-1647.30 E302.50-304.92	–	357	Roasting pit	N1750.65-1751.49 E292.09-292.90	●

Table 1.3. Continued.

Feature	Type	Coordinates	Excavated
403	Roasting pit	N1665.48-1666.31 E293.36-293.76	●
421	Roasting pit	N1817.68-1818.56 E295.57-296.59	●
427	Roasting pit	N1662.80-1664.30 E297.65-298.75	–
865	Roasting pit	N1807.00-1808.00 E306.70—	Trench only
871	Roasting pit	N1765.80-1766.12 E305.75-306.00	–
874	Roasting pit	N1764.75-1765.51 E298.73-299.55	●

Feature	Type	Coordinates	Excavated
877	Roasting pit	N1689.80-1690.80 E306.50—	Trench only
365	Well	N1728.43-1729.68 E296.39-298.46	●
378	Well	N1710.60-1711.50 E296.60-297.50	●
380	Well	N1707.60-1711.50 E294.50-297.50	●
304	Inhumation	N1832.79-1833.64 E298.12-298.88	●
308	Inhumation	N1817.68-1818.56 E295.57-296.59	●
353	Inhumation	N1815.00-1815.75 E301.20-302.60	●

[a] ● = Excavated feature.

Forty-two pit structures were wholly or partially excavated, constituting 50 percent of all structures discovered by stripping. Detailed descriptions of them are presented elsewhere (Gregory 2001a). Thirty-one extramural features were wholly or partially excavated, constituting 31 percent of the total number discovered by stripping. Excavated features include 3 inhumations, 2 wells, 5 features classified as roasting pits, and 21 pits of unspecified function. Detailed descriptions of them are also presented elsewhere (Gregory 2001b). The artifact assemblages resulting from these efforts include some 6,000 flaked stone items (Chapter 4); 300 ground stone artifacts (Chapter 5); 166 pieces of shell, predominantly including marine genera (Chapter 6); 122 bone artifacts (Chapter 7); and a number of fragments of small ceramic containers and miscellaneous objects of clay (Chapter 8). A large complement of flotation samples and a suite of pollen samples from structure floors were examined, and numerous charcoal samples were identified as to the species represented (Chapter 9). Over 17,000 whole and fragmentary animal bones were also recovered (Chapter 10).

Nineteen radiocarbon determinations were obtained on materials collected during the excavations. All are Accelerator Mass Spectrometry (AMS) determinations and all are from samples representing annual plants. Most of the dated materials were recovered from flotation samples taken from the fill of structures or intramural pits, and include maize kernels and cupules, mesquite seeds and pods, and grass stems. In one case, mesquite seeds recognized during excavation and collected specifically for purposes of dating are represented, and two of the dated samples are from burned structural remains (grass thatching). Table 1.4 summarizes data for the dated samples, while Table 1.5 presents calibration results obtained using the CALIB 3.0 program (Stuiver and Reimer 1993). Calibrated dates are represented in Figure 1.15.

As is apparent from Tables 1.4 and 1.5 and from Figure 1.15, the samples produced a consistent and relatively tightly clustered suite of dates. Based on the test for statistical differences provided by the CALIB 3.0 program, the oldest date (2240 ± 60) is a statistical outlier to the other 18. Averaging of these 18 dates produces a date of 2097 ± 15 (T = 19.86; Xi^2 = 27.60), which produces a calibrated 2 sigma range of 169-3 B.C. The south-north distribution of dates across the excavated area shows a slight tendency for earlier dates to occur toward the south end of the stripped area and for later dates to be toward the north end. The chronology of materials represented at the site is given further attention in Chapters 11 and 12; for the present, it may be noted that a tightly clustered suite of dates brackets a general occupation occurring primarily in the last three centuries B.C. With reference to previously investigated Cienega phase sites, Los Pozos is clearly later than Clearwater (Diehl 1997a) and Wetlands (Freeman 1998), and is somewhat later but overlaps with Santa Cruz Bend and Stone Pipe (Mabry, ed. 1998).

Table 1.4. Radiocarbon dates from the Early Agricultural component.

Sample No	Feature No	Sample Context	Dated Material	$^{13}C/^{12}C$	Conventional ^{14}C Age
B-88139	825.00	Burned structural elements	Grass stems	-25.2	1940 ± 60
B-88140	866.26	Intramural pit fill	Mesquite (?) seed	-21.4	1980 ± 60
B-88141	327.01	Intramural pit fill	Mesquite pod	-24.2	2020 ± 50
B-91143	318.01	Intramural pit fill[a]	Maize cupule	-7.5	2050 ± 50
B-95631	815.00	Pit structure fill[a]	Maize cupule	-11.6	2060 ± 80
B-91146	389.00	Pit structure fill[a]	Maize cupule	-8.3	2090 ± 60
B-95632	861.01	Intramural pit fill[a]	Maize cupule	-11.3	2090 ± 80
B-91145	333.01	Intramural pit fill[a]	Maize cupule	-11.6	2110 ± 50
B-95630	840.00	Pit structure fill[a]	Maize kernel	-10.7	2110 ± 80
B-91141	305.01	Intramural pit fill[a]	Maize cupule	-8.2	2120 ± 60
B-91140	898.00	Pit structure fill[a]	Maize cupule	-2.5	2140 ± 60
B-91148	417.00	Pit structure fill[a]	Maize cupule	-9.6	2140 ± 50
B-88142	407.00	Burned structural elements	Grass stems	-17.2	2150 ± 50
B-91142	337.14	Intramural pit fill[a]	Maize cupule	-7.6	2150 ± 50
B-91149	812.23	Intramural pit fill[a]	Maize cupule	-6.7	2150 ± 60
B-95629	819.00	Pit structure fill[a]	Maize cupule	-11.0	2150 ± 80
B-91144	355.10	Intramural pit fill[a]	Maize cupule	-8.2	2170 ± 60
B-95628	352.01	Intramural pit fill[a]	Maize cupule	-11.3	2190 ± 80
B-91147	416.01	Intramural pit fill[a]	Maize cupule	-8.0	2240 ± 60

Note: All samples dated by AMS analysis.
[a]Material recovered from flotation samples.

Table 1.5. Calibrated radiocarbon dates and calibration data.

Sample No	Feature No	Conventional ^{14}C Age	Cal Intercept(s)	Cal 1 Sigma Range	Cal 2 Sigma Range	Cal 1 Sigma Segment(s)	Cal 2 Sigma Segment(s)
B-88139	825.00	1940 ± 60	A.D. 70	A.D. 3-A.D. 30	A.D. 47-A.D. 237	A.D. 3-A.D. 10 A.D. 20-A.D. 130	A.D. 47-A.D. 237
B-88140	866.26	1980 ± 60	A.D. 30 A.D. 40 A.D. 50	41 B.C.-A.D. 114	160 B.C.-A.D. 216	41 B.C.-26 B.C. 24 B.C.-9 B.C. 1 B.C.-A.D. 81 A.D. 103.-A.D. 114	160 B.C.-143 B.C. 110 B.C.-97 B.C. 94 B.C.-A.D. 134 A.D. 141-A.D. 172 A.D. 201-A.D. 216
B-88141	327.01	2020 ± 50	40 B.C., 30 B.C., 20 B.C., 10 B.C., A.D. 1	50 B.C.-A.D. 54	166 B.C.-A.D. 121	50 B.C.-A.D. 31 A.D. 38-A.D. 54	166 B.C.-127 B.C. 122 B.C.-A.D. 84 A.D. 101-A.D. 121
B-91143	318.01	2050 ± 50	40 B.C., 10 B.C., 1 B.C.	158 B.C.-A.D. 24	196 B.C.-A.D. 67	158 B.C.-146 B.C. 109 B.C.-99 B.C. 93 B.C.-66 B.C. 64 B.C.-A.D. 4 A.D. 8-A.D. 24	196 B.C.-191 B.C. 172 B.C.-A.D. 67
B-95631	815.00	2060 ± 80	50 B.C., 10 B.C., 1 B.C.	169 B.C.-A.D. 51	351 B.C.-A.D. 127	169 B.C.-A.D. 29 A.D. 40-A.D. 51	351 B.C.-296 B.C. 229 B.C.-219 B.C. 211 B.C.-A.D. 91 A.D. 97-A.D. 127
B-91146	389.00	2090 ± 60	90 B.C., 80 B.C., 60 B.C.	195 B.C.-0	349 B.C.-A.D. 55	195 B.C.-193 B.C. 171 B.C.-38 B.C. 30 B.C.-20 B.C. 11 B.C.-0	349 B.C.-300 B.C. 228 B.C.-221 B.C. 209 B.C.-A.D. 32 A.D. 37-A.D. 55
B-95632	861.01	2090 ± 80	90 B.C., 80 B.C., 60 B.C.	200 B.C.-A.D. 16	357 B.C.-A.D. 77	200 B.C.-186 B.C. 174 B.C.-A.D. 3 A.D. 14-A.D. 16	357 B.C.-271 B.C. 259 B.C.-239 B.C. 234 B.C.-A.D. 77
B-91145	333.01	2110 ± 50	160 B.C., 140 B.C., 110 B.C.	198 B.C.-4 B.C.	349 B.C.-A.D. 18	198 B.C.-189 B.C. 177 B.C.-47 B.C. 6 B.C.-4 B.C.	349 B.C.-299 B.C. 228 B.C.-220 B.C. 209 B.C.-A.D. 3 A.D. 12-A.D. 18

Table 1.5. Continued.

Sample No	Feature No	Conventional ¹⁴C Age	Cal Intercept(s)	Cal 1 Sigma Range	Cal 2 Sigma Range	Cal 1 Sigma Segment(s)	Cal 2 Sigma Segment(s)
B-95630	840.00	2110 ± 80	160 B.C., 140 B.C., 110 B.C.	345 B.C.-0	362 B.C.-A.D. 66	345 B.C.-322 B.C. 204 B.C.-38 B.C. 30 B.C.-20 B.C. 11 B.C.-0	362 B.C.-266 B.C. 264 B.C.-A.D. 66
B-91141	305.01	2120 ± 60	170 B.C., 130 B.C., 120 B.C.	338 B.C.-47 B.C.	354 B.C.-A.D. 46	338 B.C.-329 B.C. 202 B.C.-47 B.C.	354 B.C.-287 B.C. 278 B.C.-274 B.C. 258 B.C.-246 B.C. 232 B.C.-215 B.C. 214 B.C.-A.D. 4 A.D. 7-A.D. 25 A.D. 44-A.D. 46
B-91140	898.00	2140 ± 60	170 B.C.	347 B.C.-53 B.C.	360 B.C.-A.D. 2	347 B.C.-317 B.C. 226 B.C.-223 B.C. 206 B.C.-86 B.C. 83 B.C.-53 B.C.	360 B.C.-268 B.C. 262 B.C.-35 B.C. 34 B.C.-17 B.C. 13 B.C.-A.D. 2
B-91148	417.00	2140 ± 50	170 B.C.	345 B.C.-56 B.C.	355 B.C.-1 B.C.	345 B.C.-321 B.C. 205 B.C.-89 B.C. 78 B.C.-56 B.C.	355 B.C.-287 B.C. 280 B.C.-273 B.C. 258 B.C.-245 B.C. 233 B.C.-215 B.C. 214 B.C.-40 B.C. 28 B.C.-22 B.C. 10 B.C.-1 B.C.
B-88142	407.00	2150 ± 50	200 B.C., 190 B.C., 170 B.C.	347 B.C.-62 B.C.	357 B.C.-3 B.C.	347 B.C.-317 B.C. 226 B.C.-223 B.C. 207 B.C.-107 B.C. 103 B.C.-92 B.C. 71 B.C.-62 B.C.	357 B.C.-270 B.C. 260 B.C.-238 B.C. 234 B.C.-43 B.C. 8 B.C.-3 B.C.
B-91142	337.14	2150 ± 50	200 B.C., 190 B.C., 170 B.C.	347 B.C.-62 B.C.	357 B.C.-3 B.C.	347 B.C.-317 B.C. 226 B.C.-223 B.C. 207 B.C.-107 B.C. 103 B.C.-92 B.C. 71 B.C.-62 B.C.	357 B.C.-270 B.C. 260 B.C.-238 B.C. 234 B.C.-43 B.C. 8 B.C.-3 B.C.
B-91149	812.23	2150 ± 60	200 B.C., 190 B.C., 170 B.C.	349 B.C.-56 B.C.	363 B.C.-0	349 B.C.-303 B.C. 228 B.C.-221 B.C. 208 B.C.-89 B.C. 78 B.C.-56 B.C.	363 B.C.-38 B.C. 31 B.C.-19 B.C. 12 B.C.-0
B-95629	819.00	2150 ± 80	200 B.C., 190 B.C., 170 B.C.	352 B.C.-50 B.C.	389 B.C.-A.D. 49	352 B.C.-293 B.C. 231 B.C.-217 B.C. 212 B.C.-50 B.C.	389 B.C.-A.D. 27 A.D. 42-A.D. 49
B-91144	355.10	2170 ± 60	200 B.C., 190 B.C., 170 B.C.	352 B.C.-113 B.C.	385 B.C.-3 B.C.	352 B.C.-292 B.C. 231 B.C.-217 B.C. 212 B.C.-159 B.C. 139 B.C.-113 B.C.	385 B.C.-43 B.C. 8 B.C.-3 B.C.
B-95628	352.01	2190 ± 80	350 B.C., 320 B.C., 200 B.C.	362 B.C.-113 B.C.	397 B.C.-0	362 B.C.-267 B.C. 263 B.C.-159 B.C. 138 B.C.-113 B.C.	397 B.C.-38 B.C. 31 B.C.-20 B.C. 11 B.C.-0
B-91147	416.01	2240 ± 60	350 B.C., 290 B.C., 260 B.C.	387 B.C.-174 B.C.	399 B.C.-118 B.C.	387 B.C.-201 B.C. 185 B.C.-174 B.C.	399 B.C.-163 B.C. 133 B.C.-118 B.C.

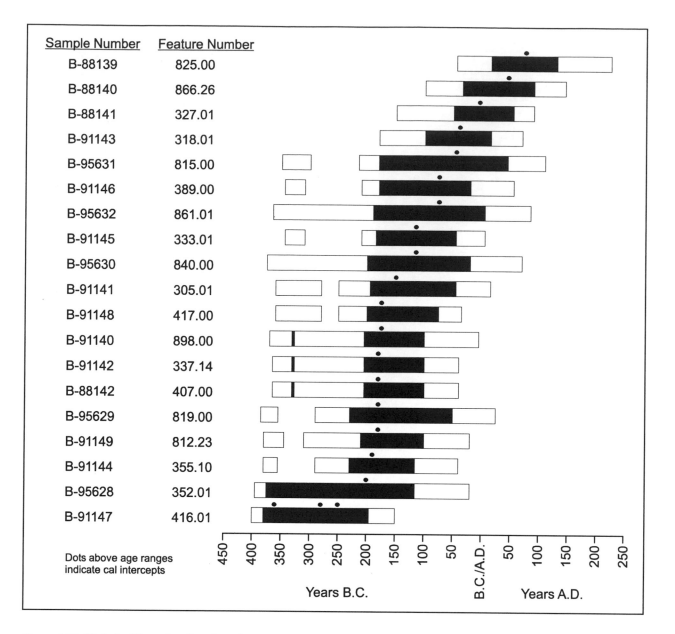

Figure 1.15. Plot of calibrated radiocarbon dates.

CHAPTER 2

ARCHITECTURAL FEATURES
AND THEIR CHARACTERISTICS

David A. Gregory

As described in Chapter 1, 42 structures were wholly or partially excavated during data recovery at Los Pozos (AZ AA:12:91 [ASM]). Detailed descriptions of these features and associated deposits are presented in Gregory (2001a) and provide the basis for summary and analyses of architectural data presented in this chapter. As also noted in Chapter 1, floor plans of 20 structures were completely exposed, while the remainder of the investigated structures was only partially excavated. The dichotomy between completely exposed and partially excavated structures is apparent throughout the following discussion. Completely exposed examples obviously provide the best data set for inferences concerning most aspects of architectural form and variation; data from partially exposed structures are used to the fullest extent possible, depending upon the attributes and topics being considered.

The architectural features at Los Pozos are considered here in terms of the use-life sequence of individual structures and associated features. This sequence begins with all aspects of initial construction and follows through the use and transformation of interior space over the use-life of individual structures. Consideration is then given to the amounts of labor and materials invested in these structures. Finally, processes following the abandonment and demise of individual structures are considered, including use of the remaining depressions as receptacles for domestic refuse. Data tables and equations used in calculations reported here are included in Appendix A.

CONSTRUCTION TECHNIQUES
AND MATERIALS

The remarkably well-preserved remains at Los Pozos provide significant new details of and perspectives on architectural form and variation during the latter half of the Cienega phase as it is currently defined (see Chapters 11 and 12). The probable sequence of construction for individual structures is employed below to organize a discussion of construction techniques and materials used to build these structures.

Pits Dug to House the Framework

Construction began in all cases with excavation of a roughly circular, relatively straight-sided pit. Measured pit depths range from 5 to 54 cm (Figure 2.1), while excavated volumes range from less than .5 m³ to over 4.5 m³ ($x = 2.57$, $\sigma = 1.48$; see Labor and Materials Investment below). Given at least some truncation by the plowzone, measured depths and volumes of structures must be considered minima, and actual values for these variables were originally somewhat greater. When the pit had been dug, a framework of perishable materials was erected entirely within it. The pit walls did not serve as the walls of the structure in most cases, and these constructions were thus houses-in-pits rather than true pithouses (Mabry et al. 1997:6-12).

Roof Support Systems and Roofs

The available evidence suggests that most structures had roofs supported by interior support posts, and it is likely that this was the first part of the structural framework erected once the pit was dug. Four completely exposed floor plans provide the most direct evidence for the layout of roof support systems (Figure 2.2). In these structures, the number of interior postholes is few, all or most of them are reasonably accounted for by the assumption that they housed roof support posts, and in one case a burned post was found in situ in one of the postholes (Feature 389). However, some extrapolation is necessary even in these best cases: in one instance (Feature 328) a post removed by a trench has to be assumed to complete the pattern, and in another (Feature 389) a former post without a discernable posthole must be assumed. In this instance, all of the postholes in the structure were extremely shallow (mean depth = 6 cm), providing some support for the assumption. In addition, alternative support patterns are possible in each case. Two support posts found in situ (Features 389 and 825) are of mesquite and originally measured between approximately 8 and

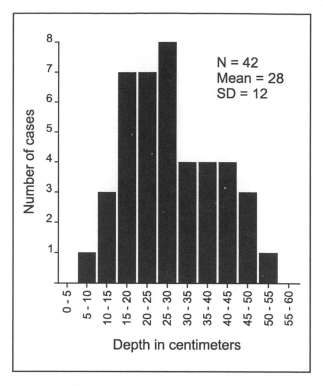

Figure 2.1. Histogram of structure pit depths.

12 cm in diameter. Mesquite seems to have been the favored wood for support posts, and possibly for the rafters that connected them (see below).

As shown in Figure 2.2, the shape of polygons defined by possible interior support posts is variable in each of these four cases. In three structures (Features 389, 407, and 840), either a four-sided or five-sided polygon may be discerned. In the case of four-sided shapes, a trapezoid is defined by four posts in two cases and six posts in the third. In the five-post alternative for these same structures, a pentagonal or "home plate" shape is defined–essentially a box with a triangle attached to one side–and is represented by five posts in two cases and seven in the third. As with the quadrilateral options, the pentagonal or home plate shape is variably distorted in these examples and none is completely symmetrical. The fourth structure (Feature 328) probably had six interior postholes from which either a hexagonal, pentagonal, or quadrilateral polygon can be derived by assuming that all postholes represent former roof supports, or that one or both of the two postholes forming triangles on the ends of the box did not house posts.

For most other structures, the issue of roof supports is muddied by the large number of interior postholes, by the fact that some interior postholes may relate to earlier features or to earlier incarnations of the same structure, and by incomplete excavation. Nonetheless, some attempt to reconstruct roof support patterns is

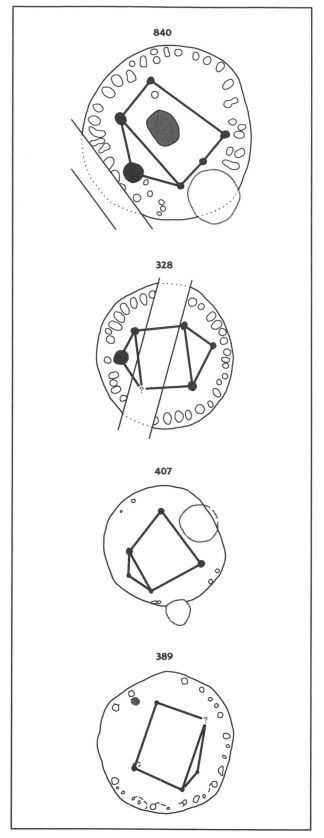

Figure 2.2. Reconstructed roof support systems for Features 328, 389, 407, and 840.

warranted for those structures whose floors were fully or largely exposed. A quadrilateral (rectangular or trapezoidal) or a pentagonal pattern can be coaxed from the more complex arrays of interior postholes in 11 of these structures, as illustrated in Figure 2.3. The seven-post pentagonal arrangement represented in Features 840 (Figure 2.2) and possibly in Feature 815 (Figure 2.3) shows similarities to possible patterns seen in the Agua Caliente phase Feature 337 at the Stone Pipe site (Swartz and Lindeman 1997:Figure 4.48) and the Cienega phase Feature 186 at the Santa Cruz Bend site (Mabry and Archer 1997:Figure 2.79).

There is no direct evidence that the postholes selected for these reconstructions actually housed roof support posts. Alternative arrangements are possible in several cases, none account for all of the interior postholes in a structure, and postholes taken out by trenches have to be assumed in several cases. In addition, some of the same postholes identified here as possibly relating to roof support are also interpreted as being part of earlier constructions (see below), and thus require the assumption that earlier postholes were reused.

If one mode of roof support was employed on a regular basis, it can be expected that the proportion of the floor area covered by the roof would have been relatively consistent, regardless of the size of the structure. Comparison of the areas of the polygons and the proportion of the floor area taken up by the roof shows that the proportion of floor area included is somewhat more consistent for the pentagonal or home plate option ($x = 34.4$, $\sigma = 5.29$, cv = .154) than for the quadrilateral or box arrangement ($x = 27.31$, $\sigma = 5.7$, cv = .209) (see Table A.1). Additional support for the pentagonal reconstructions may be provided by the fact that the point of the pentagon is near possible entries and/or hearths in eight of the 11 reconstructions. A roof support in this position might provide additional headroom near the entry, and in some cases could have also served as an anchor for jambs or other structures to reinforce the entry.

Three of the remaining five completely exposed floors and several of the partially exposed structures have interior postholes that probably housed roof supports, but no patterns are readily apparent. Two definite roof support posts were present in Feature 825, and given the position of these supports in relation to the unexcavated portion of the structure, both pentagonal and quadrilateral support systems are feasible (Figure 2.4). A burned mesquite post was present in the southernmost of these two postholes. Although a large part of Feature 354 was removed by the later construction of Feature 867, three postholes potentially forming the point of a pentagon are present (Figure 2.4); once again the point would have been near the possible entry and one of the hearths. Given the incomplete exposure of the structure, a four-post pattern is also possible.

In sum, most of the structures at Los Pozos probably had interior roof supports, and a four- or five-post pattern is supported by the available data. Intuitively, a four-post, quadrilateral roof support system would seem the most logical alternative, and this is the dominant pattern for ethnographically documented groups occupying southern Arizona (Russell 1975:155; Spier 1933:83-88, Figure 6). However, the data from Los Pozos suggest that there may have been considerable variation in roof support systems, and no consistent, symmetrical placement is definitely represented and clearly defined. Much additional data are needed to clarify this important aspect of construction.

Once the roof support posts were in place, rafters would have been secured between the tops of them to form the frame or box for roof construction. The best evidence for the relationship between rafters and primary roof elements comes from Feature 407, where a box formed by the rafters and the closely spaced roof members may be discerned in the structural debris that collapsed inward (Figure 2.5). Based on this example and on other fragments observed in Feature 825, it appears that rafters were pieces of mesquite or cottonwood approximately 4 to 6 cm in diameter. Data from these same structures indicate that primary roof elements were of lengths of wood with diameters of approximately 1 cm, placed side by side and resting on the rafters at right angles rather than obliquely. Species represented by in situ examples of primary roof elements are exclusively cottonwood or willow.

Wall Framing

In the majority of structures, a continuous series of evenly spaced postholes was excavated along the interior margin of the pit to accommodate the poles that formed the principal structural elements of the walls (Figure 2.6). Fourteen of 20 completely exposed structures exhibit this pattern, and 21 of 23 partially excavated structures were also probably constructed in this manner. Structures 12, 17, 26, 310, and 570 at the Santa Cruz Bend site show this same kind of wall posthole pattern (Mabry and Archer 1997:Figures 2.15, 2.20, 2.23, 2.82, and 2.91).

Five completely exposed structures show variations in this basic pattern: in two cases, the continuous distribution of postholes is interrupted by lengthy arc segments where none were present (Features 389 and 863), and in another similar instance (Feature 416) there are two postholes centered on the arc segment otherwise lacking postholes. These may represent entries (see below), and these examples recall several structures at the Santa Cruz Bend (Mabry and Archer 1997;

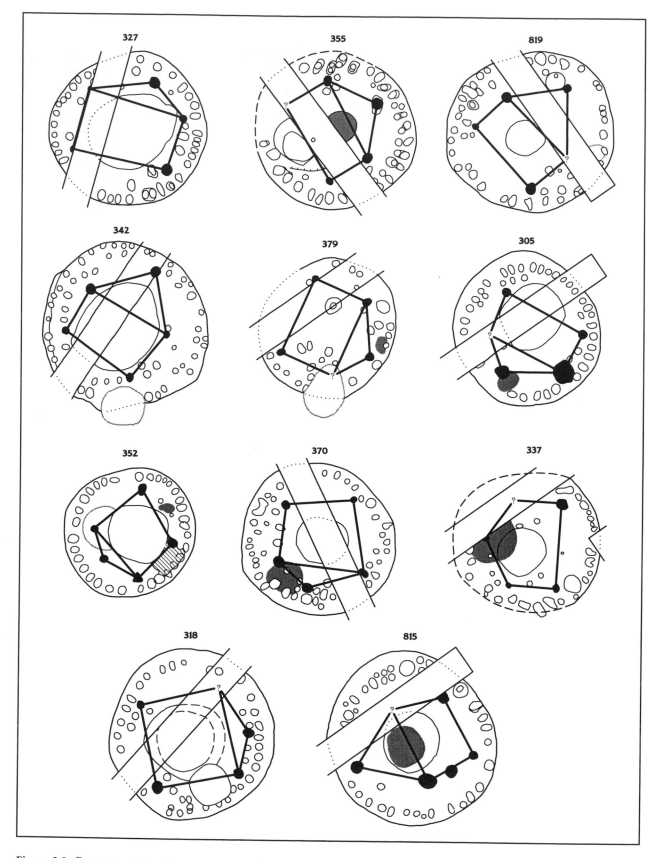

Figure 2.3. Reconstructed roof support systems for other structures.

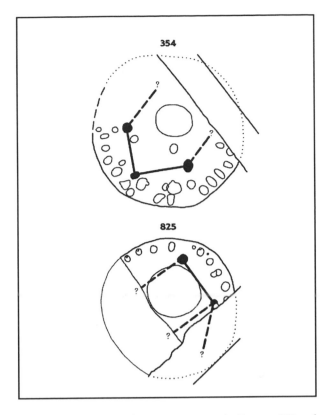

Figure 2.4. Partial roof support systems in Feature 354 and Feature 825.

Figure 2.6. Photograph of Feature 328 showing typical wall posthole pattern.

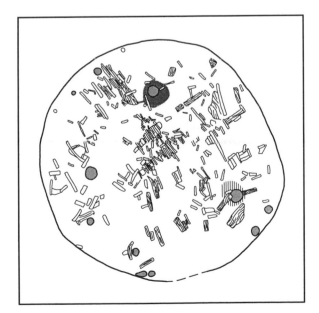

Figure 2.5. Collapsed roof and stringers in Feature 407.

Features 1, 43, 77, and 90) and Stone Pipe (Swartz and Lindeman 1997; Feature 364) sites, where similar large breaks in floor grooves or posthole distributions are seen. The array of wall postholes in Feature 416 is very similar to that in the larger Feature 127 at Santa Cruz Bend (Mabry and Archer 1997:Figure 2.71).

In one completely exposed structure (Feature 407), only six wall postholes were present. These were distributed in three pairs that formed a roughly equilateral triangle within the structure pit. One completely exposed structure (Feature 417) showed no evidence of wall postholes at all. The latter was poorly preserved, which may have influenced the discovery of postholes, but one of the partially excavated structures also showed no evidence for wall postholes in the excavated quadrant (Feature 864).

Figure 2.7 illustrates examples of the typical pattern and the variations described above. As is apparent in this figure, the circular shape defined by the wall postholes is in many cases more regular than that of the pit itself.

Several variables were recorded for each wall posthole, for purposes of comparing construction techniques and materials and labor investment, and as a basis for inferring the location of entries (see below). The minimum and maximum diameters of each feature were recorded (whether excavated or not; 828 postholes), as was the perpendicular distance from the back of the posthole to the margin of the pit and the on-center distance between each contiguous pair of wall

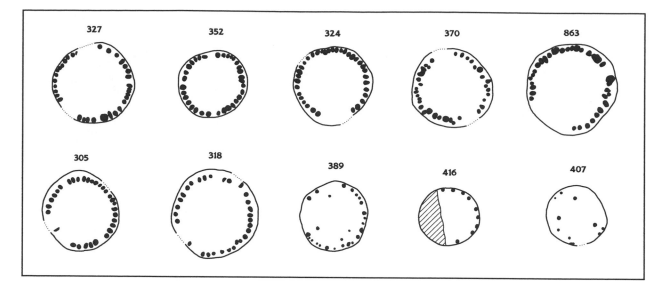

Figure 2.7. Typical wall posthole patterns and variations.

postholes in each structure. Estimates of the number of wall postholes found in completely exposed structures were derived when necessary by adding the number of postholes actually recorded to an estimate of the number removed by trenches and intrusive features. Estimates of the number of wall posts in partially excavated structures were derived by dividing the circumference of the estimated floor area (see below) by the mean distance between exposed wall postholes.

Based on the entire sample of measured examples (828 postholes), the average wall posthole was 18 cm long (σ = 4 cm) by 13 cm wide (σ = 6 cm), and was placed 12 cm inside the margin of the pit (σ = 6 cm) and 28 cm from its nearest neighbor (σ = 4 cm). Based on the sample of excavated features (469 postholes), wall postholes were typically 20 cm deep (σ = 9 cm) (see Tables A.2 and A.3). Histograms of these measurements (Figure 2.8) illustrate documented variability in each. The average number of estimated wall posts per structure is 38 for completely exposed structures and 36 for partially excavated structures. The average spacing of 28 cm between wall postholes is somewhat greater than the 20 cm given by Russell for the average Pima *ki* (1975:155; the number of observations on which this figure is based is unknown).

Burned poles found in situ show that flexible saplings of willow or cottonwood typically measuring between 2 and 4 cm in diameter at their base were used for wall poles. These examples and presumed wall poles found within several burned structures indicate that wall postholes were much larger than they needed to be to accommodate the poles. Although no definite examples of the practice were found, it is possible that each posthole could have housed paired rather than

single poles (see Cressman 1943). In situ poles also show that they were placed against the outside of the posthole (toward the pit wall), probably to provide leverage for bending them in toward the center of the structure. The use of rocks to wedge or stabilize posts was not a common practice, perhaps because–given the tension created by the bent pole against the posthole wall–further stabilization was unnecessary.

Once the wall poles were in place, they were tied together and stabilized with horizontal stringers in a series of hoops of decreasing diameters up the wall poles. A pattern of fallen wall poles and associated stringers could be discerned in the collapsed structural debris of Features 825 and 407. The spacing of these stringers is unknown, but three or four per structure is probable. Russell gives 30 cm as the average distance between horizontal stringers for a typical Pima house (Russell 1975:155). Evidence from Feature 825 suggests that the first of these stringers was placed quite low on the wall poles, perhaps to provide additional stability once the poles were in place and before they were bent over in the process of framing.

In structures with interior roof supports, the wall posts would have been bent over and lashed to the rafters. However, one fully exposed structure (Feature 417) and several partially excavated structures (Features 827, 302, 372, 861, and 864) show no evidence of having had interior roof support posts; all but one of these features (Feature 864) have the typical alignment of wall postholes. In these cases, the roof could have been constructed in one of two ways. The first would involve the wall poles being bent over and encircled by a series of stringers as described above, with the last and smallest of these forming an open hole at the top of

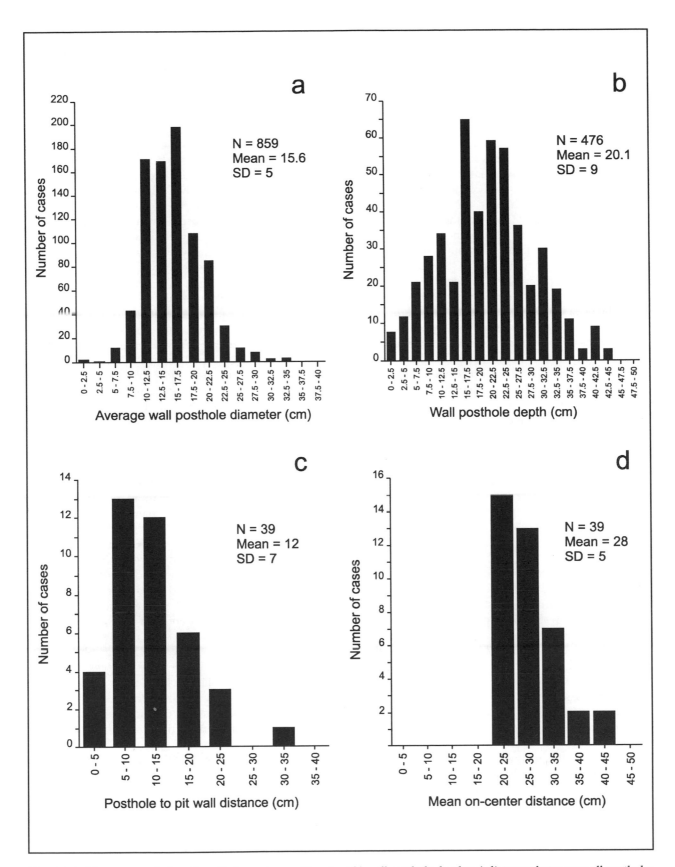

Figure 2.8. Histograms of: a) wall posthole maximum diameters; b) wall posthole depths; c) distances between wall postholes and pit margins; and d) on-center distances between wall postholes.

the framework that served as the platform for the roof members. The second possibility is that wall poles on opposing sides of the structures were bent over and tied to one another, thus creating a dome-shaped rather than a flat-roofed structure.

Presuming that structures in which wall postholes were not discerned actually did not have them originally, wall frames could have been erected in one of two ways. First, they may have been constructed in a manner similar to those features having wall postholes, but with the wall poles simply braced up against the margin of the pit. In such cases, the tension created by the bent poles, joined to one another directly or via stringers, would have functioned in a manner similar to that of graphite tent poles in modern camping tents in creating the basic frame of the structure. It is also possible that wall poles may have been leaned over and tied to one another at the top rather than being secured in postholes and bent over. In such an arrangement, poles would have been simply braced against the interior base of the pit, and a conical or tepee shape rather than a truncated dome would have been created. Wall postholes would not have been necessary in either of these alternatives, and the structures would not have had true roofs. Such structures may have been somewhat less substantial and would have involved less materials and labor investment in their construction. Although structures showing no evidence for wall postholes are in the minority at Los Pozos, structures with no wall postholes or having only a few, irregularly spaced examples are common in Cienega phase structures at the Santa Cruz Bend and Stone Pipe sites (Mabry and Archer 1997).

Thatching, Roof Coverings, and Embankments

Several well-preserved structures at Los Pozos indicate that the wall framework described above was covered with grass thatching. The position of large patches of thatch in burned structures, as well as fragments found in place against pit walls, indicates that the thatch was laid vertically. Although broken up, these patches show that the individual grass stems were quite long, perhaps up to 60 or 70 cm. All identified specimens of thatching belong to the family *Gramineae*, but the species could not be determined. It is probable that the grass was collected into bunches or sheaves, although no direct evidence for this was found. The thatch was held in place by horizontal stringers tied over it, in the same fashion represented in documented examples of Pima, Gila River Yuman, and even Great Basin Paiute houses (Fowler and Fowler 1971; Russell 1975:Plate XXXVc, d; Spier 1933); once again, three or four outer stringers to hold the thatching in place may be surmised.

There is no evidence to suggest that mud or daub was applied over the thatching. In none of the burned and well-preserved houses were impressions of perishable construction materials found, and chunks of burned earth present among the structural debris were crumbly and retained little integrity. Given the position within the collapsed construction debris, these materials probably represent elements of roofs or possibly collapsed embankments (see below) rather than walls. By virtue of the relatively high clay content of the natural strata into which the structures were excavated, and given the temperatures probably reached during the burning of some houses, it would be expected that daub would have been fired sufficiently to retain impressions. The available evidence thus supports the conclusion that daub was not an element of construction.

The addition of sequential layers of brush and earth completed the roof. This may have occurred after the outer wall thatching was in place, to allow for overlap with the wall thatching and more effective waterproofing. Burned twigs from 1 to 4 mm in diameter were found in two structures and probably represent the remains of brush used for secondary roof elements; the species could not be identified, but creosotebush is a possibility. As with the walls, there is no evidence that the layer of earth on the roof was wet when put in place.

Probably one of the final tasks in construction was the packing of earth around the outer base of the thatched walls to create an embankment, in the manner seen in ethnographically documented Pima, Papago, and Gila River Yuman houses (e.g., see Haury 1976: Figure 3.29; Russell 1975:Plate XXXVb, c; Spier 1933:86-87). This process would have filled in the space left between the pit wall and the wall of the structure built inside the pit, and provided for drainage away from the base of the structure. Owing to truncation by the plowzone, no direct evidence for embankments was found at Los Pozos, but the remnant of such a feature may have been associated with a Cienega phase structure at the Stone Pipe site (Feature 251; see Swartz and Lindeman 1997:4-60, Figure 4.45). Even in the absence of direct evidence, the semisubterranean character of the structures and other documented features of construction make it likely that embankments were a necessary feature. As with the roof and walls, no evidence was found that earth forming embankments was wetted before being packed in place.

The height of this embankment up the wall and away from it was probably variable, depending in part upon the size of the structure (see Labor and Materials Investment below). For houses with approximately similar superstructures (but not constructed within pits), Spier notes that the Gila River Yuman tribes packed earth "as far up the wall as its curvature would permit" (1933:86). It is also possible that embankments were continued in attenuated form across the entries to prevent water from draining in through them; once again, however, no direct evidence for such a practice was found.

A cut-away reconstruction of a typical structure is presented in Figure 2.9.

Additional Observations Concerning Plant Species Used in Construction

The size of structural elements and the species identified in cases cited above represent largely unambiguous examples in which specimens were found in situ and could be argued with some confidence to represent a particular element in the framework. However, most of the burned structural remains found in several well-preserved structures could not be confidently assigned to a particular element. One hundred and fourteen pieces of wood and other plant remains from seven structures were collected, identified, and measured. It is useful to look at this data set to further elucidate the principal species used in construction and as a reflection of the technology used to collect those materials.

Based on this overall distribution and examples of in situ elements, the following can be inferred about the size of various structural elements and the species used: the roof support posts and the rafters were the largest structural elements; mesquite posts from approximately 8 to 12 cm in diameter were most commonly used for these purposes, and cottonwood may have been used occasionally as well, with the rafters being slightly smaller pieces. Cottonwood or willow saplings measuring approximately 2 to 4 cm in diameter were used almost exclusively for wall poles and horizontal stringers, and smaller pieces (.7-1.2 cm) of these same species served as the primary roof elements. Small brush of one or more unidentified species served as the secondary roof layer (creosotebush?); the twigs representing this brush measure between 1 and 3 mm. Grasses of the family *Gramineae* were used to thatch the structures.

Given the flexibility necessary for use as wall poles and stringers, it is not surprising that several specimens of cottonwood or willow with the bark remaining were identified, indicating that they were obtained when green. A few unidentified specimens show that other woods (perhaps paloverde and/or oak?) were occasionally used in construction; the characteristics of these species suggest that they were probably used as roof supports and/or rafters rather than for the necessarily more flexible wall poles and stringers. One specimen of *Phragmites* was identified, indicating that reeds too were occasionally used, perhaps as secondary roof elements.

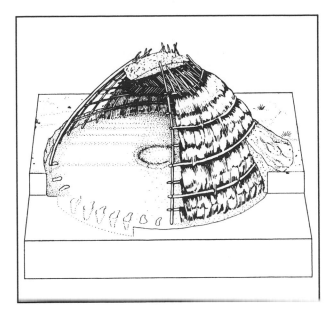

Figure 2.9. Artist's reconstruction of typical Los Pozos structures.

It is probable that the use of mesquite was largely restricted to dead and down wood or driftwood that could be easily collected, or to lower limbs of moderate size that could be easily broken off from living trees. This inference is supported by a significant absence in the stone tool technology of these populations: thus far axes have not been found in any Early Agricultural period or Early Ceramic period sites, and it would appear that this tool did not become a part of the technological inventory until later times. Cottonwood and willow saplings or shoots that made up the bulk of construction materials for individual structures could have been cut and trimmed easily with flaked stone knives, but to saw off a limb of mesquite 10 or 12 cm in diameter would have been an extremely labor-intensive activity and seems an unlikely prospect.

These data also indicate that willow and cottonwood saplings were readily available in some quantity at any given time during the occupation at Los Pozos, a fact consistent with the presence of a nearby riparian environment (see Chapter 9 and Labor and Materials Investment, below). Notably absent from the inventory of species used in construction are saguaro ribs and ocotillo branches, materials which were probably not abundant in the immediate area of the settlement. Once again, consistent reliance on and the requisite abundance of locally available construction materials is indicated.

Finally, composite pollen samples recovered from the floors of structures provide interesting perspectives. Although it is difficult to account for all of the means by which pollen grains may have entered the structures and been deposited on the floors (see Chapter 9), one possible source would have been from construction materials. Of the 30 productive floor samples, all produced *Gramineae* pollen, 23 of 30 produced cottonwood pollen, and seven produced willow pollen. Oak also occurred seven times, and mesquite pollen is absent altogether.

Entries

The later practice of incorporating or attaching an extension to the structure to form an entryway or vestibule is not in evidence at Los Pozos, and access to the interiors of structures was apparently provided simply by a break left in the wall frame and covering. Distance measurements between individual wall postholes show that there is often one place in each structure (and sometimes two or even three places) where this distance is greater than the mean for the structure, sometimes substantially greater. In cases where two or more possibilities are revealed, two are often adjacent to one another. An examination of these measurements for individual structures thus provides a means for identifying possible entries. Possible entries identified in this manner are indicated as such on the illustrations of individual structures provided in Gregory (2001a), and a summary of metric and other data is provided in Table A.4. The mean width for all possible entries (55 cm) is similar to that recorded by Russell (1975:155) for the average early twentieth century Pima house (61 cm).

Taking all possible entries identified, including those cases of more than one possible location per structure, the direction in which the entry emerged is plotted in Figure 2.10a. Figure 2.10b shows the orientations of possible entries from the Cienega phase components at the Santa Cruz Bend, Stone Pipe, and Clearwater sites (Diehl 1997a; Mabry and Archer 1997) while Figure 2.10c shows those from Agua Caliente phase structures at Stone Pipe, Square Hearth, and Houghton Road (Ciolek-Torrello 1995; Mabry et al. 1997).

The Los Pozos entries cluster loosely in the north part of the northeast quadrant, the south part of the southeast quadrant, and the south part of the southwest quadrant; the north portion of the southwest quadrant, and the northwest quadrant were largely avoided. The small sample of entries at other Cienega phase sites shows some preference for the northeast quadrant. By Agua Caliente phase, a definite pattern had crystallized, with the south part of the northeast quadrant and the south part of the southeast quadrant dominating; entries are essentially absent from the northwest semicircle of the compass in Agua Caliente structures.

Of interest is the fact that the strong pattern among the Pima and Gila River Yuman tribes of east-facing

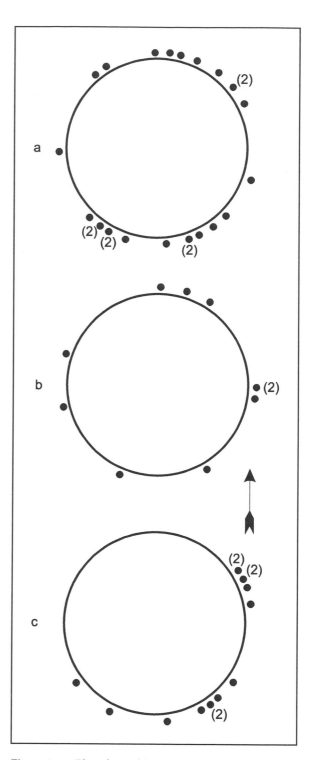

Figure 2.10. Plot of possible entry directions at Los Pozos.

entries (Russell 1975:154; Spier 1933:87) is not in evidence. Although symbolic import was assigned to this placement, Russell notes that it also served the practical function of avoiding the prevailing southwesterly winds (Russell 1975:154). Given the number of entries in the southwest quadrant, this was clearly not an overriding consideration for the inhabitants at Los Pozos; however, the majority of possible entries would have indeed been away from the prevailing southwesterly winds.

In most cases entry would have involved a short step down to the floor of the structure. But in the deepest structures (e.g., Feature 815), it is difficult to see how entry was afforded without some sort of physical step–perhaps a log or a large rock later removed for reuse. However, none of the latter have yet been found in place, and the specific means of vertical access into structures remains unknown.

Floors

No evidence was found of plastering or any other formal preparation of floors. All floors appear to have been created in large part by pedestrian traffic over the probably sometimes damp natural deposits into which the house pits were excavated. Sometimes bits of charcoal and ash had been ground into the floor by this process, giving the floor a grayish or whitish cast, but in cross section the floors appeared as a thin layer of more compact material rather than a distinct unit of different material. Even in the two definite cases where two sequential floors were present (Features 825 and 866), creation of the second appeared to have been accomplished simply by emplacement of fill over the older floor, with subsequent compaction of the new floor surface in the same manner. In only one case was the level of the floor raised significantly by creation of a new floor: some 15 cm of fill was deposited to create the second floor level in Feature 866.

Possible Votive or Dedicatory Deposits

Five worked artiodactyl femur heads were found in a wall posthole in Feature 812, three of which had red ochre on or embedded in their surfaces (see Chapter 7). This discovery suggested that these artifacts may have been interred as a dedicatory or votive deposit at the time the structure was constructed. Recognition of this possibility led to a search for additional evidence of such behaviors, which resulted in identification of a number of similar occurrences. Placement of unusual or special items in wall postholes at the time of construction now appears to have been a relatively common practice during the occupation of Los Pozos, favoring the hypothesis that votive or dedicatory deposits are indeed represented–rather than simple loss or displacement from other contexts by various agents.

Ultimately, 12 instances of artifacts recovered from postholes and possibly representing such behaviors were identified (Table 2.1). Shell is by far the most common of the items included (six cases), followed by artifacts of animal bone (three cases), the latter including two interments of the femur heads that prompted the original search (see Chapter 7). The three remaining cases include a triangular pendant fashioned from an obsidian flake, a projectile point, and a clay bead. The pendant was made of obsidian from an unidentified source.

Also shown in Table 2.1 is the location of the respective postholes with reference to the cardinal directions. Six are located in the south quadrant, four in the north, and one each in the east and west. Although the nature of the sample of excavated postholes precludes identification of definite patterns with respect to direction, this feature of such items should be given attention in the future.

Table 2.1. Possible dedicatory or votive items recovered from postholes.

Items	Feature	Direction	Possible Votive Items Also in Pit
5 femur heads	318.03	SW	●
1 femur head	337.28	NW (interior)	●
Obsidian pendant, triangular	812.22	S/SE	●
Projectile point	354.02	NW (interior)	●
Bone bead	333.48	N	N/A
Clay bead	324.18	SE	●
Cut shell pendant, triangular (*Laevicardium elatum*)	863.02	SW (interior?)	–
Shell disk bead (marine, nacreous)	337.08	S	●
Whole shell bead (*Olivella dama*)	355.46	W	●
Whole shell bead (*Olivella* sp.)	425.11	S/SW	●
Shell disk bead (*Spondylus* sp.)	867.04	NW	●
Whole shell valve (*Trivia solandri*)	390.15	E/NE	●

It is also noteworthy that the other common context of recovery for similar items was from the fill intramural pits, and Table 2.2 provides a listing of items from 16 pits. Femur heads with ochre occurred four times, while cut shell pendants were recovered from six pits and shell beads from four. Projectile points occurred four times. A cruciform was recovered from each of the two filled pits in Feature 318, accompanied in one case by a femur head and in the other by a rectangular cut shell pendant of *Haliotis*.

Of particular interest is the fact that in all of these cases but one, the pits had been intentionally filled during the use-life of the structure while the structure continued in use (see below). Further, only one of the seven intramural pits left open at the time of abandonment produced a similar item (Feature 812.23), an unworked fragment of shell. Thus the idea that such items were deposited in intramural pits with the same intent hypothesized for the materials recovered from postholes should be considered. The case for this interpretation is perhaps strengthened by the repetition of artifact types and groups of types in the pits and postholes.

Whether or not the items in intramural pits represent similar behaviors, the posthole dedications may be interpreted as representing a consecration of space and a kind of claim of ownership when the structures were built. This, in turn, may suggest that ties to this particular settlement location were formally and consistently recognized.

INTERIOR SPACE AND ITS USE

We now turn to consideration of the use and modification of structures during the interval from completed construction through abandonment, focusing on the interior space created by construction and subsequently modified according to the needs of the inhabitants. A number of simple questions guided investigation of the use of interior architectural space: 1) What was the amount of available floor area inside the structures at any given time? 2) What types of intramural features were present, what are their characteristics, and how was interior space structured by these features? 3) What is indicated by floor assemblages of artifacts about activities carried out inside the structures? and 4) What may be inferred more generally from these and other lines of evidence about the use of interior space by the former inhabitants?

In the discussion that follows, the guiding concept of *effective floor area* is first presented. Intramural features and their characteristics, floor assemblages of artifacts, and evidence relating to artifacts inferred to have been stored in the ceilings or walls of the structures are then discussed, and instances of refurbishing,

Table 2.2. Possible dedicatory or votive items recovered from filled intramural pits.

Feature	Items
302.01	Femur head (2)
	Projectile point
	Whole shell bead, *Olivella* sp.
	Cut shell pendant, rectangular, *Haliotis* sp.
318.01	Cruciform
	Femur head
318.02	Cruciform
	Cut shell pendant, geometric, *Spondylus* sp.
327.01	Figurine fragment (?)
	Projectile point
337.14	Bone tube
	Cut shell pendant, geometric, *Haliotis* sp.
	Shell disk bead, *Haliotis* sp.
	Shell disk bead, *Haliotis* sp.
390.16	Cut shell pendant, rectangular, unidentified marine-nacreous
	Cut shell pendant, geometric, unidentified marine-nacreous
	Whole shell valve, *Trivia solandri*
	Worked shell fragment, unidentified marine-nacreous
	Projectile point
342.01	Femur head
	Projectile point
355.09	Whole shell bead, *Olivella* sp.
425.01	Whole shell bead, *Columbella aureomexicana*
898.01	Femur head
352.01	Bone tube
825.01	Bone pendant (?)
867.01	Projectile point
	Worked shell fragment, unidentified marine-nacreous
372.01	Cut shell pendant, geometric, *Anodonta californiensis*
812.23	Unworked shell fragment, *Olivella* sp.
813.01	Cut shell pendant, geometric, *Anodonta californiensis*

remodeling, and superposition of structures are reviewed. Based on these considerations, the dimensions, organization, and use of interior space are examined, resulting in morphological and functional differentiation of structures.

Effective Floor Area

Quantification and analyses of interior space presented here are based on the concept of *effective floor area*, or the actual amount of useable floor area within a structure at any given time. The concept is operationalized by starting with the area of the pit dug to accommodate a structure, and then subtracting from that figure the space taken up by the walls and by excess pit area falling outside the walls. An estimate of the actual floor area contained within the walls of the structure is thus produced.

Evidence presented above indicates that wall poles were positioned at the outer margins of the holes dug to accommodate them–that is, against the side of the posthole nearest the pit wall. The grass thatching and the stringers to secure it were attached to the outside of the frame, and most of the area of the filled postholes would have been toward the interior of the structure. Once the wall poles were in place and the holes filled in, most of the area taken up by the postholes became useable floor space. This fact is confirmed by instances of floor artifacts found sitting near or up against the former walls and over the inner portions of postholes and several hearths found in similar positions (see Floor Assemblages and Hearths, below).

To provide a reasonable estimate of the actual floor area within the walls of the structures, measured distances from the outer margin of each wall posthole to the pit wall were used. The mean of these values for each structure provides an approximation of the area between the floor and the pit wall, which is then subtracted from the area of the pit to provide a measure of the floor area within each structure. Table A.5 presents estimates of floor area based on these calculations; in the case of partially excavated structures, the area of the stain apparent after machine stripping is used to determine the pit circumference, and some overestimation of pit area may be involved in these cases. All previous references to floor area have been to the within-the-walls areas included in this table.

Once the within-the-walls floor area has been established, the area taken up by any intramural features is subtracted to provide *effective floor area*. As will be shown below, this figure could and did change over the life of individual structures. Many intramural pits probably dug at the time of initial construction were filled in during the use-life of the structures, with the floors then extending over the former pits or in some cases all or part of the area of the former pit being used as a hearth. In these instances, at least two effective floor areas are represented in a single structure: the area available while the pit was open and the area available after the pit was filled. In addition, some structures were enlarged or remodeled, also changing the amount of available interior space; intramural pits were variably involved in these remodelings, adding to the complexity of the sequence in particular instances.

Thus, the areas of pits open during the occupation of a structure, space added by remodeling, and the areas of pits filled while the structures were still in use must be selectively added or subtracted from the floor area to create an accurate sequence of effective floor area over the life of the structure. Inferences concerning the constellation of features present at any given time are made primarily with reference to the depositional history of structures and associated intramural pits as revealed in stratigraphic cross sections. Following discussion of intramural features, artifact assemblages, and instances of remodeling and superposition, sequential configurations of effective floor areas are presented and analyzed.

Intramural Pits

Intramural pits were definitely present in 33 of the 42 investigated structures, and could have been present in two other cases where the portion of the structure excavated was not sufficient to rule out their presence. Three structures had two pits each, bringing the total number of intramural pits investigated to 36.

Morphology and General Characteristics

Figure 2.11 provides a synoptic view of pit shape and size, while Figure 2.12 provides a histogram of pit volumes (a) and diameter to depth ratios (b) (see also Table A.6).

The shapes of pit openings at the floors varied from circular to oval to irregularly oval. Some asymmetry may have resulted from crumbling of pit edges during use and consequent reduction and smoothing of the pit margins at the floor. Particularly in features with more pronounced belling, diameters may have originally been somewhat smaller and the mouths more regular. In several cases, there was a secondary, shallower portion of the pit that partially encircled the deeper portion (Features 824.02 and 812.23; possibly Features 825.01, 863.01, and 318.01). The pits represented are some of the larger ones, and this feature may have been created to provide greater ease of access.

As Figure 2.14 shows, pit cross sections also vary considerably. Attenuated belling of pit walls, in some cases only toward the bottoms of the features, tends to be a characteristic of the larger pits. However, not all are symmetrical and uniform, and in several cases one side is undercut while the other is relatively straight. Many of the pits are approximately cylindrical, while some have slight inward slopes to their walls. Regardless of size or shape, all have relatively flat bottoms. Diameter to depth ratios all exceed 1:1, and pit volumes vary from less than .1 m^3 to over 2.5 m^3. Volumes show a weak bimodal distribution, with one set falling between .1 and .9, and the other over .9 m^3, with 12 pits having volumes greater than 1 m^3. The largest of the Los Pozos examples are some of the largest Early Agricultural period intramural pits yet documented (see Chapter 12).

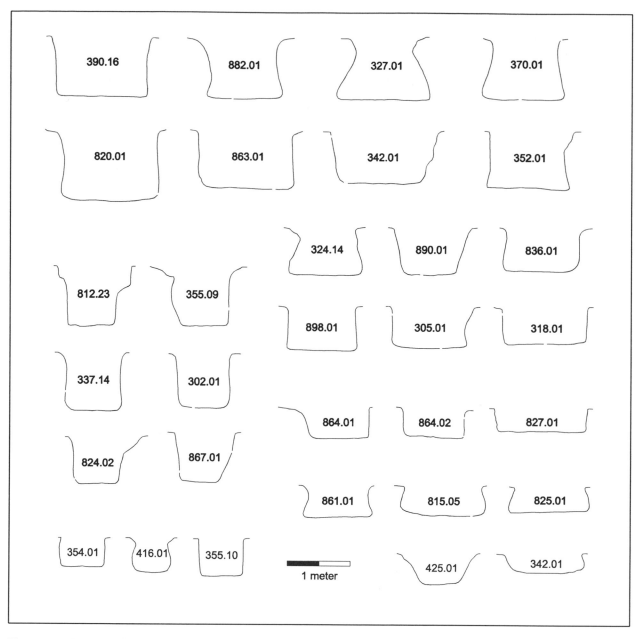

Figure 2.11. Intramural pit size and shape.

Creation of the pits was largely a matter of excavating a hole of the desired shape and size, and there was no indication that any of the pits had been intentionally fired to dry and harden the sides. Seven pits had a 2 to 3 cm lining of clean, well-sorted sand at the bottom of the pit, presumably emplaced when the features were originally dug. Linings tended to occur more frequently in the larger pits (Table A.6). Small postholes were found in three pits (Features 355.09, 372.01, and 824.01), all located near the south wall of the respective features. The function of these postholes is unknown, but perhaps small posts from which to hang various objects are represented (skin or woven bags?). In two cases the pits are quite deep, and the association of the posthole with the pit is not in doubt. The other pit is relatively shallow (Feature 372.01), and the posthole could have been for a roof support post and not directly related to pit function.

One pit differs from all others in its morphology and contents. Feature 817.01 was a small, shallow basin-shaped pit that contained a layer of unworked cobbles and cobble fragments at the bottom (Figure 2.13). Some of the cobbles and fragments had spalled, and it is possible that the structure served as a

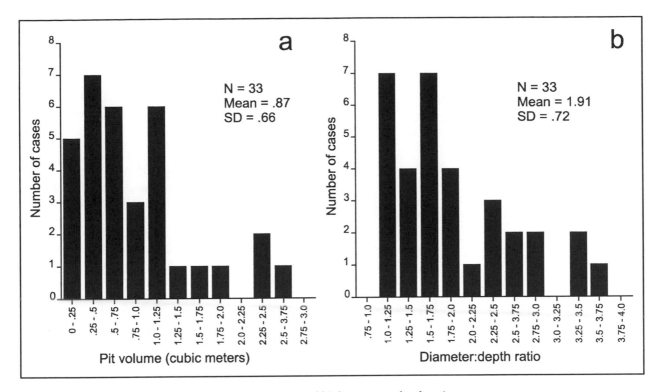

Figure 2.12. Histograms of intramural pit: a) volumes; and b) diameter-to-depth ratios.

Figure 2.13. Photograph of Feature 817.01.

sweathouse, with heated stones placed in this pit and water applied to them to supply the steam. This interpretation is consistent with the small size of the structure as well as with the unique nature of this pit (see below). Although the structure itself is much larger and has multiple intramural pits, a similar feature may be represented by a pit in Feature 102 at the Santa Cruz Bend site (Feature 102.02; Mabry and Archer 1997: Figure 2.56).

Finally, several features may be noted that have been interpreted as postholes but could conceivably represent pits of unknown function. In seven structures

there was one interior posthole considerably larger than all the rest (Features 305, 328, 337, 379, 812, 819, and 840), and a similar feature can be tentatively identified in five other structures (Features 333, 354, 815, 824, and 863). Most tend to be quite round and all are located near one of the walls. Several of these features have been included as elements in reconstructions of roof support systems presented above. Two of these features were excavated (in Features 305 and 812), and there is nothing about them save their size to distinguish them from other postholes. For the present they are treated as such, but future research should consider possible alternative functions in the case that similar features are found.

Pit Floor Assemblages

Artifacts were recovered directly from the floors of seven intramural pits (Table 2.3). None of these assemblages may be considered complete, as all of these pits were either only partially excavated or portions of them had been removed by trenches.

In one case (Feature 861.01), the artifacts were clearly in place and the pit was open when the associated structure burned and collapsed (see below). In another instance (Feature 342.01), the pit was open when abandoned and subsequently filled entirely with water-lain deposits. Thus, the first case probably

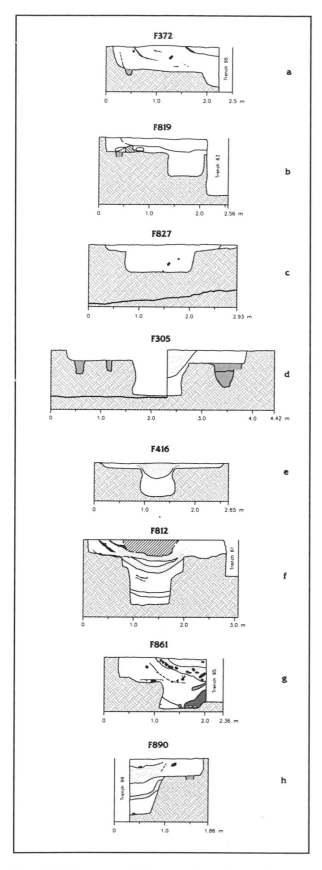

Figure 2.14. Intramural pit cross sections showing the open pit signature.

represents a storage context, while in the second an abandonment assemblage is indicated. In the other five cases, the pits had been intentionally filled with domestic refuse, and the artifacts could simply have been included in the bulk of refuse used to fill the pits. Thus, these artifacts may have been discarded elsewhere and came to rest on the pit floors fortuitously.

The assemblage from the floor of Feature 342.01 is of interest, because of the subsequent depositional history of the pit (see below), the nature of the artifacts, and the fact that all had been coated to varying degrees with ochre. The projectile point and the femur head recall the possible votive deposits in wall postholes described above, and similar behaviors may be represented in the case of this pit. Once again, the fact that these artifacts were left in place when the feature was abandoned for some period of time may suggest an expression of ties to this particular settlement location and perhaps an intention to return. The assemblage from Feature 361.01 suggests that some intramural pits were probably used for the storage of artifacts as well as foodstuffs.

Sequence of Use as Revealed by Depositional Histories

Examination of stratigraphic cross sections shows two principal modes in the relationship between pits and the structures in which they were found: either the pits were open when the structures were abandoned, or the pits had been filled in while the structures were still in use. These cross sections also reveal that the depositional sequence represented in filled pits can be quite complex and potentially informative.

Open Pit Signatures. Eleven pits show stratigraphic signatures indicating that the pits were open when their respective structures were abandoned (Figure 2.14a-c). In these cases, there is stratigraphic continuity between the fill of the pit and the fill of the structure, with two basic variations.

In the first instance, the fill of the pit and that in at least the lower portions of the structure consists of domestic refuse, uniform in appearance and lacking any stratigraphic variation that would reveal a hiatus or change in deposition. This indicates not only that the pits were open, but that the pits and structures were filled in relatively rapid fashion.

In the second instance, more than one depositional unit may be recognized, including both intentional deposits of domestic refuse and natural water-lain sediments that washed into the pits, sometimes in alternating fashion. These cases show a characteristic inverted parabolic shape to the strata, created by the much deeper, smaller hole left by the open pit in the interior of the structure (Figure 2.14d-h). Alternating cultural and natural deposits indicate intermittent deposition of domestic refuse separated by intervals during which natural sediments washed into the pit,

Table 2.3. Intramural pit floor assemblages.

Feature	Mano	Handstone	Pestle	Lapstone	Core	Core Fragment	Core Hammer	Flakes	Projectile Point	Other Flaked Stone Tool	Femur Head
342.01	–	–	●	–	●	●	–	●	●	●	●
352.01	–	–	–	●	–	–	●	–	●	–	–
324.14	●	–	–	–	●	–	–	–	●	–	–
861.01	●	●	–	–	–	–	–	–	–	–	–
370.01	–	●	–	–	–	–	–	–	–	–	–
815.01	–	–	●	–	–	–	–	–	–	–	–
864.01	–	–	–	–	●	–	–	–	–	–	–

and thus provide evidence of discontinuous refuse deposition.

Water-lain deposits observed in the pits and structures are themselves of more general interest, since all consist of small sands, silts, and clays, and all exhibit tiny alternating laminae of these materials. These deposits suggest relatively slow and intermittent deposition rather than emplacement by single or multiple large flood events and inundation.

Filled Pits. At least 24 and possibly as many as 26 intramural pits were filled to the approximate level of the house floor while the structure was still in use, and a clearly different stratigraphic signature is represented (Figure 2.15). In these cases, there is always a clear stratigraphic break at the approximate level of the floor, with the materials in the pit differing from the fill of the structure above the floor; the uppermost stratum in the pit is either horizontal and level with the floor or shows a slight depression at the top of the pit.

Whether some depressions were left intentionally when the pit was filled or are a function of post-abandonment settling cannot be determined in every instance, but it is likely that settling played a role in creating them. In five cases, however, the depression left by filling of the pit subsequently served as a hearth (see below), confirming that use of the structure continued after the pit had been filled and was no longer a feature of interior space. In these instances, a depression may have been purposefully left. In three other cases (Features 337, 825, and 836), a later hearth partially overlapped the top of the filled pit, confirming the continued use of the structure after the pit had been filled.

Several of the filled-in pits exhibit humped-up deposits or features such as large, discrete ash lenses within the fill (Features 302, 352, 836, and 898; see Gregory 2001a). The shape of these deposits suggests individual loads dumped into the features during the filling process and provides evidence that the filling was not intended to produce a refreshed, flat pit floor as appears to have been the case in other filled pits (see below).

Water-lain deposits void of artifacts almost completely filled Feature 342.01 to the floor level, while the fill of the structure was composed of domestic refuse. The water-lain sediments show several internal breaks and indicate a relatively lengthy period of deposition. This feature is interpreted below as having been a feature of an earlier construction and not directly associated with the later structure within which it was found and which was filled entirely with refuse (see below). Regardless of its prior history, it is clear that the pit was open when it was abandoned and began to fill with water-lain sediments.

Two cases were observed in which pits were filled and then replaced by another pit, which was then also filled while the structure was still in use (Features 864.01 and 864.02, and Features 355.9 and 355.10). In the case of the pits in Feature 864, sequential use is demonstrated by the fact that one intrudes the other. The two pits in Feature 355 are not directly related stratigraphically, but the structure was enlarged, and an argument is made below that one of the pits belongs to the earlier configuration of the structure and one to the later (see Remodeling, Refurbishing, and Superposition of Structures).

Evidence for Refurbishing of Pits. Intentionally filled pits were not always filled in one episode, and there is some evidence to suggest that partial filling of them during their use-life may have been a means for refreshing features that had become either too damp, infested with vermin, or both. A number of pits show one or more depositional episodes that may represent refurbishing or refreshing of pits, after which they appear to have continued in use for some period of time (Figure 2.16). In these cases, the first unit deposited in the pit is between 10 and 20 cm thick, and would not have substantially reduced pit volume. This initial episode is sometimes associated with a thin layer of charcoal at the bottom of the deposit, perhaps representing the remains of live coals dumped in to rid the pit of vermin and/or dry it. The tops of these first depositional units are all flat, and in one case a deer cranium was present on the surface of the unit (Feature

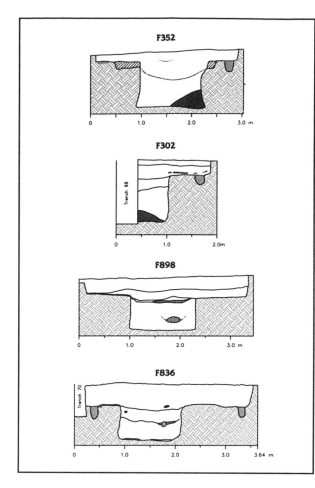

Figure 2.15. Intramural pit cross sections for filled pits.

863.01), suggesting that the cranium rested on a new, intentionally created pit bottom.

Function

Given their respective morphologies and contents, it is difficult to envision most of the intramural pits as being used in food processing or preparation. With the exception of Feature 817.01 (discussed above), most are probably appropriately interpreted as containers or vessels for storage of materials including foodstuffs. As noted above, none show evidence of having been used in conjunction with fires or coals. Pollen samples from the floors of seven large pits were analyzed (Features 863.01, 327.01, 342.01, 352.01, 815.01, 824.24, and 812.23; see Diehl 1999). Only three produced recoverable pollen (Features 863.01, 815.05, and 824.24) and all three show similar profiles. Chenopods dominated the samples, accounting for over 90 percent of the grains counted. All had small numbers of *Gramineae* and *Typha* grains, and two produced *Zea* pollen; two grains of arboreal pollen were present in each of the samples,

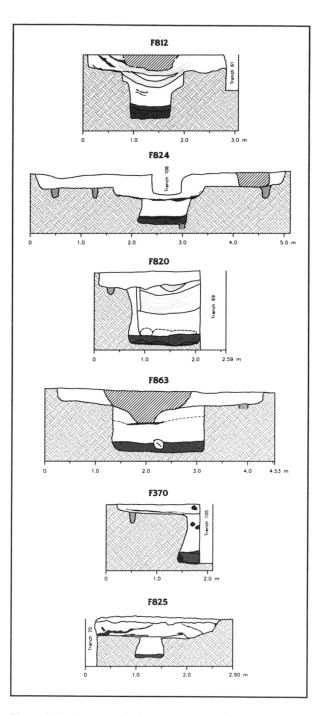

Figure 2.16. Intramural pit cross sections showing possible refurbishing.

Populus in two cases and *Quercus* in the other. While not in any way definitive, these results are not inconsistent with an inferred storage function.

There is some evidence that the larger pits were used to store artifacts, probably in addition to foodstuffs. This suggests that the vision of large pits as being brim-full of ears of maize may be erroneous in some cases. The belled shape and size of the larger pits may support the inference that they were essentially used as grain bins, and it will be shown below that these large pits were often contained in structures whose principal function was to shelter the pits rather than to create useable intramural space. However, some of the smaller pits, and in particular the relatively straight-sided, deeper ones, may have been used somewhat differently.

Some pits may have served as more general-purpose features, with seeds and other foodstuffs which had undergone some processing (winnowing, parching?) contained within baskets or bags that were themselves placed in the pits (hung from poles represented by the postholes mentioned above?) along with tools and perhaps other personal items. Better air circulation and presumably preservation would have been fostered if pits were used more like closets or pantries than grain bins. Many of these pits were filled in during the use-life of the structures, indicating that whatever function they originally served had become unnecessary while the structure was occupied (see below).

Hearths

Hearths were present in 23 (55 percent) of the investigated structures and definitely absent in seven of them (16.3 percent). Because of trenches or incomplete exposure of floor plans, hearths may or may not have been present in another 14 structures. Of the 21 structures whose floor plans were completely exposed, hearths were present in 13 (61.9 percent), absent in four (19 percent), and possibly present in the remaining four structures. Five structures had two hearths, bringing the total number of hearths discovered to 28. It is of course possible that some of the partially excavated structures with identified hearths had more than one. Table 2.4 summarizes data for these features.

In 19 cases, hearths consist simply of an oxidized patch of floor, variable in size and shape. The degree of oxidization varied from light to moderately heavy, and hearths were often marked by an overlying lens of the fine white ash typically found in chronologically later hearths; the associated ash lens occasionally extended well beyond the oxidized area. Similar features were discovered within several structures at the Santa Cruz Bend site and identified as hearths (Mabry and Archer 1997).

Six hearths occupy the area at the tops of filled-in pits (Features 327, 352, 355, 815, 824, and 898). In four cases, the fill of the pit produced a flat or slightly depressed area, while two of these hearths occupy shallow basins at the tops of the former pits (Features

Table 2.4. Data relating to hearths.

Feature	Type[a]	Location
Completely exposed structures		
305	Ox	S/SW
324	Ox	N
327	Fp	C
337	Ox	C
352(2)	Fp; formal pit	C, NE
354(2)	Ox; ox	S/SE, W
355	Fp	C
370	Ox	S/SW
379	Ox	E
389	Ox	NW
815	Fp	C
840	Formal pit	C
863(2)	Ox; ox	S, N
Partially excavated structures		
333	Formal pit	C
425	Ox	W/SW
812	Ox	SE
824	Fp	C
825(2)	Ox; ox	C, NE
836(2)	Ox; ox	S, N/NW
866	Ox	S
870	Ox	W
882	Ox	S/SW
898	Fp	C

[a]Ox = Oxidized patch; Fp = Top of filled floor pit.

352 and 824). Hearths above filled pits tend to be somewhat larger than the two formally prepared features described below. The hearths in Features 327, 352, and 824 also differ from other documented examples in that the bottoms of the features were marked by lenses of small pieces of charcoal rather than or in addition to the fine white ash mentioned above.

Three examples show evidence of formal preparation. One of these (in Feature 352) exhibited a slightly raised border of earth around most of its perimeter, and had been excavated just barely into the floor of the structure. Preparation involved only minimal excavation and the packing of earth around the perimeter, and there was no evidence that the earth was purposefully wetted when this simple feature was created. Two small postholes were located immediately outside the raised margin to the north and south, and may have been associated with it (a spit or rack?).

Two other features (in Features 333 and 840) are simply shallow (25 and 20 cm, respectively), roughly oval pits with sloping sides, excavated in the approximate centers of the two structures. In the case of the hearth in Feature 333, it was definitely present in the last of three remodelings of the structure and could have been there during the earlier incarnations as well (see below). Both measure approximately 60 by 70 cm in their maximum dimensions, and are similar in overall size and shape to hearths found in San Pedro phase structures at Milagro (Features 15 and 23; Huckell and Huckell 1984; Huckell et al. 1995), and to Cienega phase features found at the Santa Cruz Bend site (in Features 201 and 570; Mabry and Archer 1997:Figures 2.80 and 2.91), the Donaldson site (in Feature 11; B. Huckell 1995:Figures 3.6 and 3.7), and the Valencia site (in Feature 5; Bradley 1980).

The powdery white ash associated with most of these features and the absence of any but the smallest flecks of charcoal indicate that most were probably created by repeated import of live coals from the outside for purposes of heating the interior of the structure, warming or cooking food, or both of these, and possibly for other as-yet unimagined purposes. Perhaps the interior heating function is most likely, and the presence of hearths in a large proportion of the structures may support the inference of use during the late fall, winter, or early spring, when nights were cold enough to warrant interior warming. The three formally prepared hearths show evidence for the same kind of use–the import of live coals without a live flame. No trivets were found in association with any hearth.

The small pieces of charcoal present in the hearths in Features 327, 352, and 824 and the shape and size of these examples may suggest a somewhat different use: the depressed or basin shape of these features would have been suitable for parching of seeds using hides or large basketry trays worked over coals.

Despite the informal character of most examples, a review of the locations of hearths within interior space indicates that their placement was not haphazard. Hearths consistently occur in one of two locations within the structures: 1) very close to one of the walls–often with the disquieting impression that the bed of coals would have been very near one or more of the outer wall support posts and the highly flammable grass thatching; and 2) in the approximate center of the structure.

Considering first those structures whose floor plans were completely exposed, two positions account for 9 (64 percent) of the 14 cases: six examples occupy a central position within the structure, and another three fall along the south wall (Figure 2.17a). For partially excavated structures, the pattern is similar (Figure 2.17b), with four of the 12 hearths being in a central position and another five along or near the south wall.

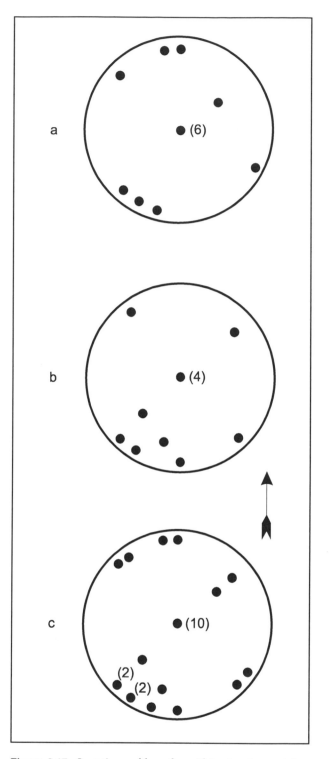

Figure 2.17. Locations of hearths within structures at Los Pozos and selected Cienega phase and Agua Caliente phase sites.

If all hearths are included, the central (10 cases, 38 percent) and south wall (7 cases, 27 percent) positions account for 65 percent of the cases (Figure 2.17b). Four of the remaining 10 examples fall in the northwest quadrant, representing a third, more diffuse emphasis. As previously noted, two of the central hearths are formally prepared. In all but one of the other instances of central position, the hearths occupied the tops of filled floor pits and, as noted above, four of these are slightly depressed or basin-shaped. Thus, while not formally prepared, they were located in a depression in the center of the floor. For hearths positioned near walls, it is of interest that in six cases, the placement is either immediately left (Features 825 and 389), right (Features 866, 863, and 354), or approximately in line with (812) possible entries as determined by spacing of wall posts described above. In one case (Feature 370), the hearth is directly opposite a possible entry.

Of the five cases where two hearths were present, two (in Features 825 and 352) represent features that were more or less immediately adjacent to one another–with one of the two in each case located over a filled pit in the center of the structure and the other lying immediately to the northeast and not as close to the wall as are other examples. In the other three cases (Features 354, 836, and 863), the two hearths are both near or against the walls and on opposing sides of the structures, with one along the south wall in all three cases and the other variably placed along the west, northwest, or north wall. Whether these features witnessed simultaneous or sequential use is not known.

Tendencies in hearth placement at Los Pozos foreshadow in several respects the rigidly consistent pattern that emerged during the Agua Caliente phase (Ciolek-Torrello 1995; Swartz and Lindeman 1997; Wöcherl and Clark 1997). In all documented cases, Agua Caliente phase hearths are positioned along the axis of the entry and located at varying distances between the entry and the center of the structure, often immediately inside the entry. This position can be seen as an amalgam of the two dominant placements at Los Pozos: near possible entries and in the center of the structure.

Other Possible Intramural Features

In several structures, interior postholes are present that do not appear to represent roof support posts or the remains of earlier constructions. Although no patterning in these features could be discerned, it is possible that they represent the remains of interior features such as screens or posts on which items were hung (e.g., in Features 379 and 824). Cited examples of such unaccounted for postholes may be seen in the maps of structures included in Gregory (2001a).

Floor Assemblages

Artifacts were recovered directly from the floors of 20 structures and thus may have been in their primary use, temporary storage, or abandonment contexts. This total includes 11 structures whose floors were completely exposed and nine partially excavated structures. Eight of the structures burned while in use, and the artifacts from these floors may be presumed to have been in place at the time of the fire. However, many of these features served as a place for discard of domestic refuse following abandonment (see below). Thus, it is difficult in the case of unburned structures, partially excavated structures, and/or single floor artifacts to determine whether the items were actually in their use, temporary storage, or abandonment contexts, or were elements of refuse that came to rest on the floor fortuitously. The floor assemblages exhibit considerable variation, ranging from single items to a spectacular array found on the floor of Feature 819, which is discussed separately below. Table 2.5 summarizes the items present on floors.

The floor of Feature 416 produced the greatest number of items, including pieces of fire-cracked rock, apparently unburned cobbles and fragments of cobbles, flakes, cores, fragments of an eared tray, other fragments of ground stone, and fragments of a bone awl. Unfortunately, approximately the west third of the structure had been disturbed by a later irrigation ditch, and while the outline of the structure could be traced, the floor was disturbed and additional artifacts were probably once present there. The small central pit in this structure was open when the structure was abandoned, and the distribution of floor artifacts inscribes a rough arc around this feature.

The partially exposed floor of Feature 861 revealed five unworked cobbles positioned around the margin of a large floor pit that was open at the time the structure burned. Possibly these cobbles served to anchor a hide or woven cover for the pit. As described above, several ground stone artifacts were found on the floor of this pit.

A whole mano and a complete stone tray were found against the wall of Feature 333, along with a large piece of fire-cracked rock that may have served some unknown function. It is clear that this structure burned and that the above-mentioned objects were on the floor at that time. Seventy-five flakes representing 18 different raw material types were also recovered from the floor. The number and diversity of flaked stone raw materials and the absence of any hammers perhaps indicate that many of these flakes were in refuse deposited in the structure after it burned and collapsed.

Unworked animal bone was largely absent in floor contexts, with one notable exception. Two hundred and

Table 2.5. Floor assemblages from structures.

Feature	Fire-cracked Rock	Cobble	Mano	Tray	Other Ground Stone	Core	Hammerstone	Other Flaked Stone Tool	Flakes	Flake Cluster	Projectile Point	Bone Awl	Antler	Other Animal Bone
Completely exposed structures														
324.00	–	–	–	–	–	–	●	–	–	–	–	–	–	●
355.00	–	–	–	–	–	–	–	–	●	–	–	●	–	●
379.00	–	–	●	–	●	●	–	–	–	–	●	●	–	–
389.00	–	–	●	–	●	–	–	–	–	–	–	●	–	●
407.00	–	–	●	–	●	–	–	●	●	–	–	●	–	●
416.00	●	●	●	●	●	●	–	–	●	–	–	●	–	–
417.00	●	–	●	–	–	–	–	–	●	–	–	–	–	–
819.00[a]	–	–	●	–	–	–	–	–	–	–	–	–	–	–
840.00	–	–	–	–	–	–	–	–	●	●	–	–	–	–
Partially excavated structures														
333.00	●	–	●	●	–	–	–	–	●	●	–	–	–	–
867.00	–	–	–	–	–	●	–	–	–	–	●	●	●	–
825.00	–	–	●	–	–	–	●	–	●	●	–	–	–	–
836.00	–	–	–	–	–	●	–	–	●	–	–	–	–	–
861.00	–	●	–	–	–	–	–	–	–	–	–	–	–	–
866.00	–	–	–	–	–	–	●	–	–	–	–	–	–	–
870.00	–	–	●	–	–	–	–	–	–	–	–	–	–	●

[a]Items in the ritual floor array not included in this tabulation; see Appendix B.

thirty-five fragments of bone were recovered from the floor of Feature 355 (NISP = 78). Mountain sheep and artiodactyls (including some identified as deer) are disproportionately represented in this assemblage as compared to that for the site as a whole, and are perhaps the remnants of butchering activities following a hunting foray are represented. However, it is uncertain whether these remains were on the floor when the structure was abandoned or whether these materials were included in the first refuse deposited in the abandoned structure.

Several tendencies in the kinds of artifacts present and their position within the structures may be noted. If pieces of fire-cracked rock and unworked cobbles are included, then up to eight different kinds of items were present on floors; if only artifacts are considered, six different classes are present. Manos are the most commonly occurring floor artifact (nine cases), and were often found up against or near a wall. Flakes form the next most common artifact class (seven structures), and in four cases clusters of flakes were recognized; three of these were near hearths. Other ground stone artifacts (including stone trays on two floors), cores, bone awls, and other animal bone each occurred on four floors, while fire-cracked rock and hammerstones

were found on two floors each. The relatively common occurrence of bone awls parallels the storage of such artifacts in the walls and ceilings of structures (see below).

A remarkable ritual array of artifacts from the floor of Feature 819 stands apart from other floor assemblages and is reported in detail in Appendix B.

Use of Interior Walls and Ceilings

Evidence from several burned structures indicates that some items were routinely stored inside structures by being stuck into or hung from the thatch or framework of the superstructure of the interior walls and/or ceiling. The most consistent pattern is apparent with respect to bone tools.

Whole and reconstructible bone tools were recovered from within the burned structural debris of eight structures (Features 379, 389, 407, 417, 819, 825, 836, and 861), indicating that these items were stored in the walls or ceilings of the respective structures at the time they burned (see Chapter 7). Various awl forms were most commonly recovered from these contexts, but spatulate tools, chisels, and other forms are represented

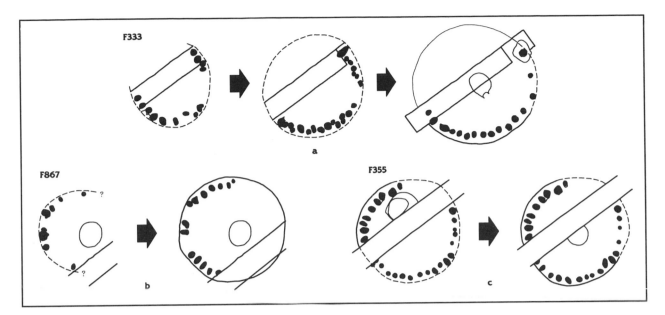

Figure 2.18. Examples of remodeling of structures.

as well. As many as six different tools were recovered from a single structure (Feature 379), multiple tools were represented in six of the seven structures, and multiple tool types were recovered from three of them. Taken together, these items constitute an extremely high proportion of all whole bone tools recovered from the site (see Chapter 7).

In another probable case, 64 shell beads were recovered from within the fill and strewn about the floor of Feature 836. These materials have been interpreted as representing a shell necklace that may have been hanging from the ceiling or interior wall of the structure when it burned (see Chapter 6).

Remodeling, Refurbishing, and Superposition

Remodeling and refurbishing of structures was accomplished with some regularity during the occupation at Los Pozos. Such modifications variably altered the effective floor area of the structures involved and are thus important to the current discussion. Also considered are instances of structure over structure superposition, including a number of special cases that represent a consistent pattern of features enlarged from or built completely over earlier, functionally specialized structures.

Remodeling and Refurbishing

Four structures show evidence of having been remodeled via construction of partially or wholly new walls or wall segments which added substantial amounts of interior space. Features 333, 354, 355, and 867 all witnessed such a sequence of events. A number of other structures show possible evidence for minor remodeling or refurbishing.

The most complex example of remodeling is represented by Feature 333, which was enlarged at least twice after its original construction with the center of the structure remaining in approximately the same position (Figure 2.18a). These episodes involved expansion of the structure pit and probably a largely if not completely new set of perishable materials. Although only half of the structure was excavated, estimates of floor area for the first two incarnations of the structure were made under the assumption of symmetry for the posthole patterns represented in the excavated portion of the structure. Each remodeling episode essentially doubled the amount of effective floor area: the original floor area is estimated to have been approximately 4.83 m^2, and the first enlargement increased the area to 6.97 m^2, a 44 percent increase; the second and final remodeling resulted in a floor area of 10.99 m^2, a 58 percent increase. Any earlier fill was completely removed with each enlargement, so it is impossible to determine if the structure was abandoned between construction episodes or whether continuous use is represented. There is no evidence that the structure pit was deepened during either of the remodelings. The central hearth was definitely a feature of the last configuration, and may have been present in one or both of the earlier versions of the structure.

Another complex sequence of remodeling, superposition of structures, and further remodeling is represented by Features 867 and 354. Portions of both were removed by Trench 95, and both extended slightly beyond the project right-of-way to the east. Thus, neither was completely exposed and no attempt has been made to quantify the proportional increase in floor space represented by the respective enlargements. Nonetheless, both show evidence of having been remodeled and are considered here. Feature 354 was the first constructed. Evidence for remodeling is represented by an incomplete but relatively clear line of postholes lying immediately inside the continuous series that marks the second incarnation of the structure (Figure 2.18b). Because Feature 867 later removed the upper portions of the pit within Feature 354, the relationship of the pit to the floor is unknown; as with Feature 333, it was not possible to determine the temporal relationship between the earlier and later versions of this structure.

Feature 867 was later constructed over approximately the northeast half of Feature 354, and also appears to have been remodeled at least once (Figure 2.18b). The earlier construction is represented by an arcing line of postholes that encircles the large floor pit present in the structure. The second is represented by the typical continuous line of wall postholes immediately inside the pit. It is possible that remodeling of Feature 867 represents another example of the special cases of superposition discussed below. In any case, it is clear that the structure was substantially enlarged at some point, with a resulting increase of floor space that likely exceeded 50 percent. Once again, the temporal relationship between the two construction episodes could not be determined.

Feature 355 was enlarged somewhat by an expansion of the pit and emplacement of a new line of wall posts along the south and east sides of the structure (Figure 2.18c). Two pits were discovered within the structure, with the larger of the two (Feature 355.09) offset from the center of the structure, and the smaller one (Feature 355.10) centrally located. Water-lain deposits at the top of the larger pit may indicate a hiatus in use, and it is reasonable to infer that this larger pit went with the earlier configuration of the structure while the smaller one was dug when the structure was enlarged. The original floor area of 6.97 m^2 was increased to 8.45 m^2, a 21 percent increase. The smaller pit was intentionally filled during the use-life of the second incarnation of the structure, and the area atop the filled pit served as a hearth. There is no evidence that the structure pit was deepened appreciably during remodeling.

Variations in wall posthole patterns in several other structures hint at some refurbishing or slight enlargement, but are not sufficiently clear to warrant definitive conclusions. Some irregularities or partial overlap in wall posthole alignments may be noted (e.g., in

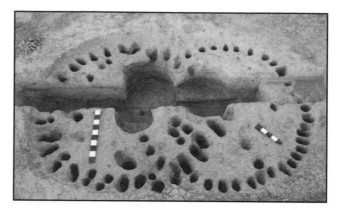

Figure 2.19. Photograph of Features 324 and 355 showing superposition.

Features 342, 370, 840, and 863), and other possible examples involve the doubling up of wall postholes, with the second feature immediately adjacent to the first but positioned toward the interior of the structure (e.g., in Features 815, 819, and 840). While some of these examples may simply illustrate variation in wall posthole placement during original construction, occasional repairs to or reinforcement of walls could also be represented.

Superposition of Structures

Undoubtedly recognizing that the trash fill of abandoned structures provided easier digging than virgin deposits, and possibly with the purpose of occupying the same area of the settlement after a period of absence, the inhabitants of Los Pozos sometimes built new structures that overlapped significantly with older ones (Figure 2.19). Feature 324 cut through the remains of Feature 355; Feature 813 intruded Feature 425; an earlier version of Feature 337 was almost completely subsumed by construction of a later, much larger structure; and Feature 867 cut through Feature 354 as discussed above. The unexcavated Features 879 and 880 undoubtedly represent another instance of superposition, and it is also likely that the unexcavated Feature 381 represents another case of two superimposed structures (see Figures 1.12 and 1.13). Interestingly, the overlap between the older and younger structures is approximately the same in four of the definite cases cited above, and it appears that it would have been similar in the case of unexcavated Features 879 and 880. Later extramural pits, wells, and one inhumation pit were cut into the fill of nine structures, and in three cases the structures themselves were cut into or completely overlay earlier extramural pits (see Chapter 3).

Feature 337 represents two sequential structures, with the earlier, smaller structure almost entirely

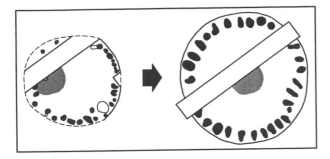

Figure 2.20. Earlier and later versions of Feature 337.

subsumed within the pit and walls of the second (Figure 2.20). The first structure had an intramural pit that was filled during use of the structure, and the centrally located hearth of the second structure partially overlay this filled pit. Although it is not possible to be absolutely certain about the amount of time that passed between the two constructions, it appears that the earlier feature did influence construction of the later one. Along the southeast wall of the second structure, four of the wall postholes seem to bend around a large posthole interpreted as being part of the earlier structure. The reason for this diversion in the wall posthole alignment is unknown, but it is possible that some elements of the earlier feature were somehow incorporated into the later one. The second of the two features is the largest structure discovered and differs from all other investigated structures in a number of other ways as well (see below).

Eight Special Cases

With the possible exception of Feature 337, all of the above-cited instances of superposition involve a sequence in which the older structures had clearly been abandoned and filled prior to intrusion by the younger ones. In another set of cases, however, it appears that later structures having a new configuration of functional attributes were consistently built entirely over earlier ones that may have been razed at the time to make way for the new constructions. Thus, both remodeling and superposition are involved.

It was observed during the excavations that a number of structures having large intramural pits also had a relatively large number of interior (non-wall) postholes that partially encircled the pits (Figure 2.21). The hypothesis that these postholes represented anchors for some sort of covers for the pits was initially considered. However, a number of factors argued against this interpretation, while other data pointed the way to an alternative formulation: that these cases represent a sequence in which small structures with large intramural pits were replaced after some period of use by entirely new, larger structures in which an interior pit was in most cases not a feature. Such an

Figure 2.21. Photographs of Features 342 (top), 863 (center), and 327 (bottom); dotted line highlights line of interior posts encircling large intramural pits.

interpretation has obvious implications for considerations of the use of interior space, and the evidence in support of this hypothesis is reviewed and discussed below.

Seven structures whose floor plans were completely exposed show interior posthole patterns of the sort described above. In all but one case (Feature 305), the large pits were filled to the level of the floors of later constructions. As noted above, the partially excavated Feature 867 was sufficiently exposed to indicate that it too may have witnessed a similar sequence. Figure 2.22 illustrates the proposed sequence for the seven completely exposed structures. The earlier configuration in each of these cases is referred to here and subsequently with an "r" suffix, to indicate that they represent reconstructed versions of the respective structures (e.g., 352r). In all cases, the pit dug to house the earlier structure would have been entirely removed or enlarged through construction of the later one.

Several particulars of these reconstructed features are of interest. The alignments of wall postholes are neither as regular nor as complete as those for other structures, with only a partial circumference of postholes represented in most cases and the separation between postholes being quite variable. In two cases, there are two larger postholes inside the obvious encircling alignment and on opposite sides of the pits (Features 327r and 342r; Figures 2.22c and 2.22d), and a similar configuration may be represented in the partially excavated Feature 867. In another instance, two large postholes on opposite sides of the pit are a part of the encircling arc (Feature 863r; Figure 2.22e). In two cases, there is a large posthole roughly centered on a large break in the overall posthole alignment (Features 342r and 305r; Figures 2.22d and 2.22f). These features suggest that these earlier structures may have been constructed somewhat differently than those previously described, and perhaps were less substantial overall. Clearly it is unlikely that any of these features would have had interior support posts, and lower ceilings are likely.

The pits involved include some of the largest in the sample (see Table A.6), and in one instance (Feature 318), two pits appear to have been present within the earlier structure–a shallow one and a more typical large, deep one. The smaller feature may have served to facilitate access to the deeper one. In two cases, the top of the filled pit served as a hearth for the later structure (Features 327 and 352). In the single instance where the pit was left open after the hypothesized rebuilding (Feature 305), enlargement of the structure resulted in an effective floor area of 5.49 m², even with the large pit. This is well within the range of effective floor areas for structures which were built without pits; in addition, expansion of this structure resulted in the pit being offset from the center of the structure toward the north wall and opposite a hearth (see The Dimensions and Organization of Interior Space, below).

Four partially excavated features represent small structures with large pits that were *not* overlain by

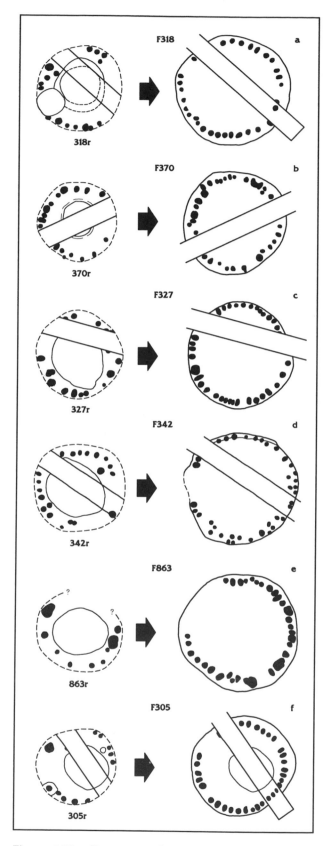

Figure 2.22. Reconstructed sequences involving small structures with large intramural pits.

subsequent constructions, and thus provide support for the hypothesis presented here. Features 827, 861, 890, and 302 have estimated floor areas of 3.73, 5.23, 5.23, and 4.45 m², respectively; when the estimated areas of the large pits contained within them are subtracted, the resulting effective floor areas are 1.76, 4.11, 4.17, and 3.70 m² (see Gregory 2001a). Importantly, three of these structures (Features 827, 861, and 890) have stratigraphic signatures indicating that the pits were open when the structures were abandoned, and in the case of Feature 861, burned structural debris fell directly into the open pit. This demonstrates that small structures with proportionally large pits were created, used, and abandoned without further modification and thus represent a particular configuration of interior space that differs from all others.

In the case of Feature 302, the pit was filled to floor level and the structure used thereafter; as was the case with the completely exposed Feature 305, the estimated effective floor area even with the large pit present is 5.53 m², somewhat larger than the effective areas of the smallest investigated structures that lacked any intramural pits (see below).

Table 2.6 includes the estimated floor area, the area of the respective pits, the effective floor area, and the proportion of the floor area taken up by the pit for each reconstructed feature and for the four partially excavated structures discussed above. Floor areas for reconstructions of storage structures have been estimated by drawing the smallest circle necessary to enclose the postholes hypothesized to be part of the earlier constructions (as shown in Figure 2.22). Since it is not certain that the features were originally circular, floor areas may be overestimated in some cases. As may be seen, the dimensions for the reconstructions are quite similar to those for the four partially excavated structures, while the proportion of floor area taken up by the pits is, in all but one case (Feature 827), greater for the reconstructions than for the partially excavated structures. It is possible that the areas of pits in the partially excavated structures have been under-estimated and that the effective floor areas have been over-estimated.

Given the reconstructions presented above, a number of other structures may represent the same sequence. Although no clear encircling line of posts was observed, Feature 815 is quite deep (50 cm), and an earlier small structure with a large pit could easily have been truncated by construction of the later feature. The former wall postholes for the earlier structure may have been entirely removed because of the depth of the pit dug to house the later structure. In this case, then, the earlier structure as well as the upper portions of the large floor pit may have been removed. Based on the size of the intramural pits present, the interior postholes visible in the excavated portion, and the stratigraphic sequences represented in cross sections,

Table 2.6. Metric data for reconstructed structures and actual structures with large intramural pits.

Feature	Floor Area	Pit Area	Effective Floor Area	Proportion of Floor Area Taken Up by Pit (%)
Completely exposed structures				
305r	4.91	1.48	3.43	30.1
318r	6.16	2.75(2)	3.41	44.6
327r	5.73	2.35	3.38	41.0
342r	6.16	2.65	3.51	43.0
352r	3.80	1.32	2.48	34.7
370r	4.91	.83	4.08	16.9
863r	5.73	2.11	3.62	36.8
Partially excavated structures				
867r	3.14	.71	2.33	22.6
302	4.45	.75	3.70	16.9
827	3.73	1.97	1.76	52.8
861	5.23	1.12	4.11	21.4
890	5.23	1.06	3.70	20.3

Features 390, 425, 812, 824, and 836 may have also witnessed the transformation of a small structure with a large pit into a larger structure with or without a pit (see Gregory 2001a).

Other possible but less secure candidates include Features 337(1), 813, 820, 882, and 898. If even half of these possible examples represent the same kind of sequence, the process represented was a common one during the occupation of Los Pozos. It may also be noted that several structures at the Santa Cruz Bend site appear to represent similar small features with relatively large pits (Features 85, 109, and 122; Mabry and Archer 1997:Figures 2.40, 2.61, and 2.69).

Based on their size and the relative amounts of interior space taken up by the pits, it is reasonable to infer that the primary purpose of the reconstructed features and the four partially excavated structures discussed above was to shelter the large pits and materials placed in them. The effective floor areas of the structures would have been quite small and, as will be shown below, they form a size category that contrasts with effective floor areas represented in other structures.

The Dimensions, Organization, and Use of Interior Space

Having examined the characteristics of intramural features and artifact distributions, and having sorted out some of the complexities of sequential use of interior space within individual structures, it is now possible to examine the characteristics of interior space more generally. The amounts of available interior space and the manner in which that space was structured by intramural pits and hearths are first explored. The range of intramural activities as revealed by floor assemblages and other lines of evidence is then dealt with. Finally, functional categories of structures derived on the basis of these considerations are presented and discussed.

The Dimensions and Organization of Interior Space

Quantitative analyses presented here are based on 49 different configurations of interior space. These include those represented in the completely excavated structures, including the eight reconstructed features inferred in the preceding section to be storage structures; by the four partially excavated structures also cited above as probably representing storage structures; and in the partially excavated Features 333, 354, 825, 867, and 887, where their dimensions have been estimated. In the latter case, more than half of each structure was excavated, their depositional histories are well-documented, and estimates based on exposed portions of the structures may be taken as reasonably accurate. Sequential configurations within the same structure are designated with an appended arabic numeral in parentheses (e.g., 324[1], 324[2], and so on), or with the "r" indicated above for the reconstructed and inferred storage structures. Data from other partially excavated structures are referred to as appropriate.

In all illustrations that follow, the outlines of effective floor areas are based on the proposition elaborated above that the outer margin of the postholes defines the available floor area within the structures. This method better represents the configurations of available floor space and the manner in which that space was structured by intramural features.

Two basic variations with respect to the use of interior space are already obvious: those configurations which included intramural pits as a feature of interior space and those that did not. The latter include those structures originally constructed without pits as well as those in which pits originally present were filled while the structure continued in use. A histogram of effective floor areas for all 49 configurations is presented in Figure 2.23.

Although no attempt has been made to account for the influence of interior support posts in structuring interior space, they clearly would have defined a central area having the greatest amounts of headroom in all structures where they were present. Curvature of the walls would have made areas closer to them more awkward for some activities but perhaps suitable for others, including sleeping and temporary storage of items not in use (see below).

Configurations without Pits. Figure 2.24 graphs effective floor areas for the 25 configurations lacking

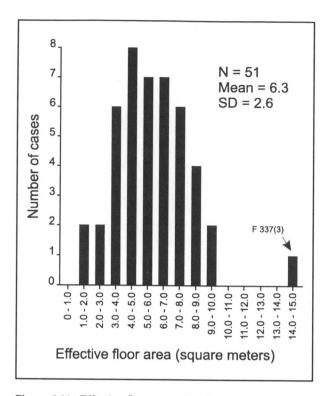

Figure 2.23. Effective floor areas for all structures.

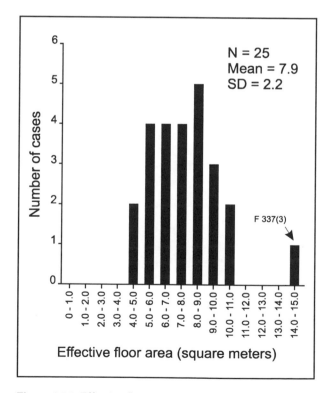

Figure 2.24. Effective floor areas for structures without pits.

intramural pits, and Figure 2.25 illustrates them. Locations of hearths and possible entries are indicated. As these graphics show, effective floor areas in configurations lacking pits are quite variable, ranging from 4.08 to 14.25 m². All but three structures fall between 5.5 and 10.99 m², with the very large structure 337(3) and two very small structures–Features 407 and 333(1)–representing outliers in the distribution. Two general size classes may be recognized in the remainder of the distribution, one including structures with effective floor areas falling between 5.5 and 7.5 m² and one including structures with effective floor areas between 7.5 and 11 m².

At least 12, and possibly as many as 18, of the 25 configurations without pits had hearths. Central placement of hearths tends to be a feature of structures with greater amounts of floor space: only one structure with an effective floor area of less than 8 m² shows this hearth location (Feature 352). Conversely, placement of hearths near the walls tends to be characteristic of structures with lesser amounts of available floor space: only one structure with an effective floor area greater than 8 m² has the hearth placed near the structure wall (Feature 863).

Configurations with Pits. Figure 2.26 graphs effective floor areas for all structures with pits (a), for inferred storage structures (b), and for other structures with intramural pits (c). Figure 2.27 illustrates the 13 non-storage configurations including intramural pits, and Figure 2.28 illustrates the storage structures; locations of hearths and possible entries are shown. Effective floor areas for storage structures and other structures with pits show little overlap. The non-storage structures with pits exhibit an effective floor area range quite similar to that represented in configurations without pits, between 4.0 and 9.5 m².

Figure 2.29 plots effective floor area against the proportion of floor area taken up with pits. Once again, storage structures and other structures with pits form distributions that are almost mutually exclusive. Pits in identified storage structures account for between 17 and 47 percent total floor area, leaving effective floor areas that are all less than 4.2 m². In other structures, pits most often occupy less than 15 percent of available floor area, leaving effective floor areas that exceed 4.5 m² in all but one case (Feature 416); six of these structures also had hearths, which were not present in any of the inferred storage structures.

In the non-storage structures, most pits tend to be offset rather than central within the structures (see Figure 2.27), and two structures with offset pits have hearths opposite the pits. Three pits are opposite possible entries. A sufficient amount of 10 partially excavated structures was revealed to indicate that pits in these structures were also substantially offset from the center toward one wall (Features 372, 817, 820, 824,

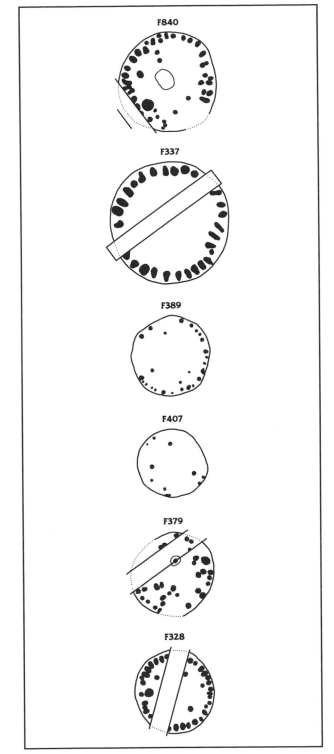

Figure 2.25. Structures without pits.

825, 836, 864[1], 867, 882, 887, and 898; see Gregory 2001a). These arrangements suggest that pits often may have been positioned toward the backs of structures, leaving a wide crescent of useable floor space toward the front.

As previously noted, most pits in non-storage structures were filled during the use-life of the structures and converted either to hearths or useable floor space. As shown in Figure 2.29, the proportion of the floor area taken up with these pits was relatively small in most cases. Thus, the absolute amount of space gained by their filling was not great, and the principal advantage may have been in altering the structure of interior space in a way that made more of it more easily accessible. The filling of pits also implies that they were no longer considered necessary features of intramural space and, by extension, that their function was important during the early part of the use-life of the structure but not later.

Intramural Activities

Based on floor assemblages and features described above, a tentative list of activities carried out within the structures may be constructed. There is little direct evidence for specific activities, however, and it is important to acknowledge the distinction between the possible temporary storage of artifacts versus the actual conduct of activities involving them.

Perhaps the strongest case can be made for flintknapping, with evidence in the form of cores, hammers, an antler flaker, and several clusters of flakes located near hearths and representing a limited number of raw material types. Heat treatment of materials to improve flaking qualities could be indicated by the association of these clusters with the hearths, but few heat-treated specimens were identified (see Chapter 4). Proximity of flake clusters to hearths may simply represent a general focus of activity within the structures.

Storage of awls and other bone tools in the walls and ceilings of the structures and the occurrence of a spatulate tool and an awl on floors may indicate that basketmaking, hide working, and sewing occurred in the structures; however, these items could simply have been stored inside and used elsewhere. A whole, unmodified Artiodactyla long bone recovered from one floor was interpreted as stock for awl manufacture (see Chapter 7), and suggests the possibility that bone tools may have been manufactured as well as stored inside structures.

The consistent occurrence of manos and other ground stone artifacts up against the walls of structures probably represents artifacts in temporary storage contexts rather than use contexts, but some manos were also found in the central areas of structures. However, no whole metates were found and metate fragments occurred infrequently on floors; it is also

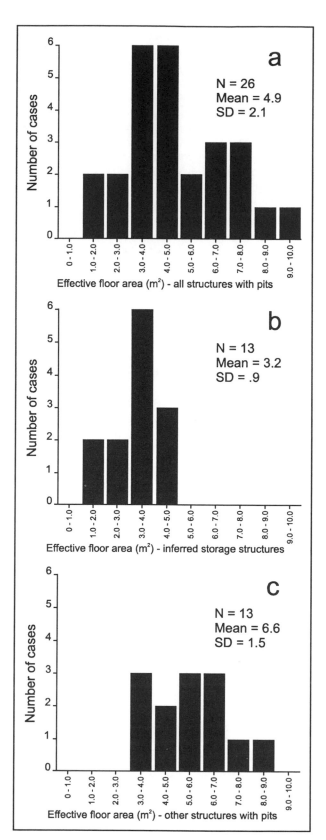

Figure 2.26. Effective areas of structures with pits.

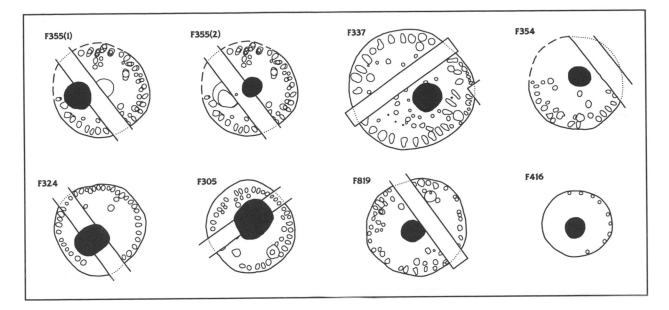

Figure 2.27. Structures with pits.

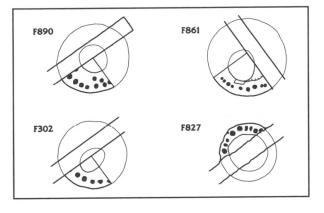

Figure 2.28. Storage structures.

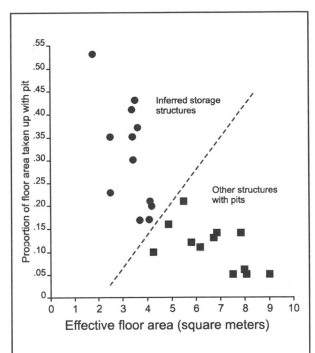

Figure 2.29. Plot of effective floor area against proportion of floor area taken up with pits.

possible that metates were sufficiently valued to have been curated whenever possible, even to the extent that they were removed from the remains of accidentally burned structures.

The possibility that some large hearths at the tops of filled-in pits may have been used in parching has been noted, and this activity may also be added to our tentative list. If a spit or rack is in fact represented by the two postholes astride one of the hearths in Feature 352, cooking or food preparation may be inferred. Finally, the remarkable floor array of artifacts in Feature 819 indicates that esoteric or ritual activities were at least occasionally undertaken within the structures.

Going beyond the evidence from artifacts and features, it is logical to assume that one function of interior space would have been to provide shelter for sleeping. Figure 2.30 shows the floor plans of selected structures of varying sizes and with and without pits, with scaled figures in sleeping positions. These include the smallest structure without intramural pits, the structure with the largest open intramural pit, and an average structure with a central hearth but lacking intramural pits. A stature of 1.68 m (5 ft 6 in) has been assumed, possibly a slight over-estimation (Minturn et al. 1998:Table 17.1; Snow and Sanders 1954; Woodbury and Woodbury 1955). As may be seen, two or three individuals could have slept in even the smallest structures as well as those having the largest open pits.

These simulations do not take into account cultural practices such as described by Powell for Paiutes in Utah, whose structures were similar in size to or smaller than those represented at Los Pozos: "In cold weather the family will crowd about the fire, and sleep at night in a common huddle or heap" (Fowler and Fowler 1971:53, Figures 19 and 22; see also Wheat 1967:103-111). Thus, the Los Pozos structures may have provided sleeping space for a greater number of individuals than illustrated in Figure 2.30.

It is also appropriate to raise the issue of gender with reference to the use of interior space. Once again, there is no basis for direct inferences, but if we assume that most or all of the activities suggested above may have been gender specific (women: basketmaking, plant food processing and preparation; men: flintknapping, animal food processing, shamanistic activities), then it is likely that both men and women carried out various intramural activities. There is as yet little evidence to suggest structures dedicated to particular and gender specific activities such as those represented by the *huki* of the Pima Bajo; these small, semisubterranean structures were specifically constructed as places where women engaged in basketmaking and where basketry materials were stored (Brugge 1961:10-12; but see discussion of Feature 817 below).

Taken together, the evidence suggests that the following activities may have occurred within the structures: sleeping, eating, food preparation, plant processing, flaked stone tool manufacture, and temporary storage of a variety of items including foodstuffs. Inferences of more specific activities are yet more tenuous, but basket weaving, hide working, and bone tool manufacture are other possibilities.

Functional Classes of Structures

On the basis of the amounts and configurations of interior space, two general functional classes of structures and two specialized structures are identified. *Storage structures* have already been discussed. These features had a large proportion of interior space taken up with pits (> 17 percent; x = 31 percent) and effective floor areas most often less than approximately 4 m² (x = 3.3 m²). Their primary function was to provide shelter for the pits they covered rather than to create useable interior space, and there may have been substantial differences in the construction techniques used to build them.

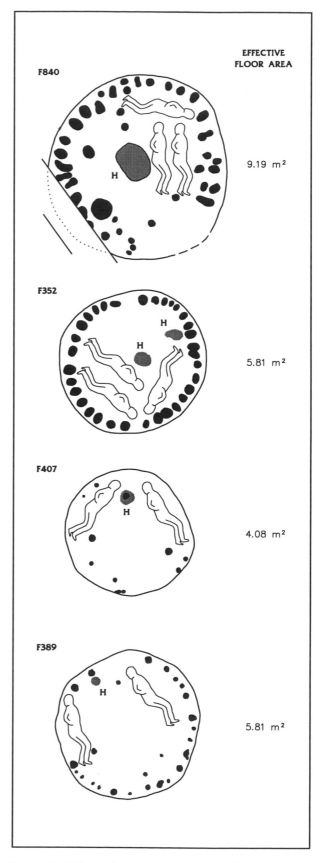

Figure 2.30. Floor plans of structures with sleeping figures.

It appears that the replacement of storage structures with later habitation structures built entirely over them was a relatively common pattern. It is possible that these cases represent a sequence that occurred on an annual basis, with large, covered storage pits built to contain excess harvest at the end of the growing season when the population shifted their locus of residence away from the floodplain settlement. Returning the following spring, the stored materials were removed for use, and the structure was enlarged to accommodate the social group during planting, cultivation, and harvest. This hypothesis is entirely speculative and would be difficult to test, but it should be kept in mind as additional data accumulate and different approaches to the problem can be developed.

With two exceptions noted below, the remaining configurations may be identified as *habitation structures*. Their principal function was to provide shelter, warmth, and sufficient interior space to accommodate a variety of activities. Effective floor areas of configurations representing habitation structures range between approximately 4 and 11 m², and three general size classes may be discerned within this distribution (Figure 2.31): those structures having effective floor areas less than 5 m², those falling between 5.5 and 7.5 m², and those falling between 7.5 and 11 m². Summary data for each of these size classes is presented in Table 2.7, with the classes designated from smallest to largest with arabic numerals.

Hearths are evenly distributed across the three size classes, with hearths present in two of five Class 1 configurations (40 percent), seven of 14 Class 2 configurations (50 percent), and nine of 18 Class 3 configurations (50 percent). Intramural pits were included as elements of interior space in two of five Class 1 configurations (40 percent), five of 14 Class 2 configurations 36 percent), and five of 18 Class 3 configurations (28 percent).

Remodeling of structures resulted in a change from one size class to another in three cases. Enlargement of Feature 333 moved it from Class 1 to Class 2 and then to Class 3, while remodeling of Feature 355 resulted in a Class 2 to Class 3 transformation. The filling of the pit in Feature 825 turned it from a Class 1 to a Class 2 structure; interestingly, this is the only case where the filling of pits while the structure was still in use produced a change in size class.

Using the mean effective floor areas for the three classes, the proportion of increase from one to another is the same: Class 2 configurations are on average 1.4 times as large as those in Class 1, and Class 3 configurations are 1.4 times as large as those in Class 2. The fact that configurations representing some of the smallest effective floor areas (Class 1) also had hearths and floor assemblages of artifacts is significant, since it allows the inference that these features approximate the minimum

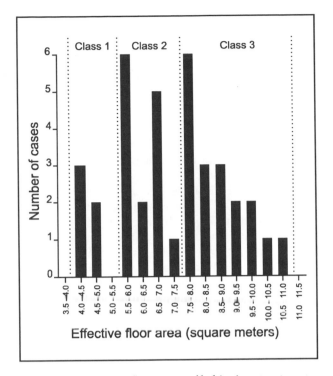

Figure 2.31. Effective floor areas of habitation structures.

space required for intramural activities not involving intramural pits. Similarly, the fact that the three size classes each include structures with and without intramural pits indicates that there were relatively consistent requirements for intramural space regardless of whether or not pits were present.

Observed variation between the size classes may be accounted for in one of three general ways. First, the activities carried out were essentially similar in all cases, but the size of the social groups using the space was variable. Second, it is possible that the sizes of social groups were essentially similar in most cases, but that the range of intramural activities and their spatial requirements varied. Finally, some combination of these two alternatives could be represented. For the moment, there is no basis for selecting among these hypotheses. However, it may be noted that documented variation in the size of families among hunters and gatherers could easily account for observed differences in the dimensions of interior space (Yellen 1977). In this regard, it is tempting to see the three size classes as representing groups of different sizes, perhaps a basic nuclear family on the smaller end and a small extended family on the other, with the variation accounted for by the growth cycle of domestic groups. However, this is purely speculative, and much additional data are needed with regard to the issue of Cienega phase site structure before this question can be fully addressed.

Table 2.7. Summary data for size classes of habitation structures.

Class	n	Mean	Standard Deviation	Minimum	Maximum	Hearths	Pits
1	5	4.50	.35	4.08	4.89	2	2
2	14	6.29	.55	5.51	7.16	7	5
3	18	8.70	.95	7.50	10.99	9	5

Two examples of apparent overlap between the storage structure and habitation structure categories are represented by Features 302 and 305. As described above, Feature 305 began as a storage structure and was expanded; however, the large pit remained open after the remodeling and a hearth was present. Even with the large pit open, the effective floor area (5.49 m²) was 1.5 m² larger than the smallest structure without intramural pits. As previously noted, the remodeling appears to have placed the pit against the back wall of the structure, leaving full access to all useable floor space. With respect to the partially excavated Feature 302, the pit was filled but there was no apparent enlargement of the structure. The estimated effective floor area after filling of the pit was 4.45 m² and the pit would have been offset to one side of the structure. Both of these features are classified as habitation structures.

Two features stand out from all others by virtue of their size and other attributes and are treated here as *specialized structures*. These include the very large Feature 337(3) and the very small and only partially excavated Feature 817.

With an effective floor area of 14.25 m², Feature 337(3) has 30 percent more area than the next largest habitation structure (see Table A.5). The wall postholes of this structure were substantially larger and deeper than all others (see Table A.2), and it required 30 to 50 percent more labor and materials to construct than the next largest habitation structure at the site (see below). One of the wall postholes and one interior posthole contained possible votive deposits (a femur head and a shell pendant). The structure lacked interior pits, but had a large central hearth and a number of interior postholes (including some extremely small ones) that may suggest interior features of unknown character. Based on the amount of effective floor area alone, it may be inferred that activities associated with this structure involved more than one social group of the size that occupied habitation structures.

While not nearly as large as the so-called big houses at Santa Cruz Bend and Stone Pipe, this structure is clearly something out of the ordinary within the current sample of structures from Los Pozos. However, given the differences in size between Feature 337(3) and the large structures at Santa Cruz Bend and Stone Pipe, it is probably premature to label this feature as communal. Similarities may be noted between Feature 337(3) and a large structure at the Coffee Camp site (Feature 315; Halbirt et al. 1993:87-91, Figure 3.14). The Coffee Camp feature is similar in size (16.1 m²) and had a central hearth represented by an oxidized patch of floor. Conversely, the unusual floor artifact assemblage from the Coffee Camp structure is not duplicated in Feature 337(3), and Feature 337(3) was not burned as was the feature at Coffee Camp.

The unique nature of the pit lined with unworked, spalled cobbles in Feature 817 has already been mentioned. This pit and an estimated effective floor area of 2.48 m² make this feature unique in the sample. Although the structure was not fully excavated, it is reasonable to suggest that it may have been a sweathouse or perhaps a menstrual hut; clearly it represents a functionally distinctive configuration of interior space.

The dimensional aspects of these functional classes and subclasses and specialized structures are represented in Figure 2.32 as box plots indicating the range, mean, and one standard deviation of the values. Data for Feature 817 are estimated on the basis of the excavated portion of that structure.

LABOR AND MATERIALS INVESTMENT

It is now possible to examine data relating to the labor and materials investment involved in initial construction of the structures at Los Pozos. The construction sequence discussed above indicates that there were three relatively discrete tasks involved in construction: excavation of the pit, postholes, and any interior pits created at the time of construction; collection and transport of perishable materials with which to build the framework and cover it; and assembly of the structural elements and emplacement of earth on the roof and around the base of the completed structure. Estimates of labor and materials investments are made for all of the completely exposed structures. Assumptions made and equations used to generate these estimates are presented in detail, in anticipation of controlled comparisons with future data sets.

Volume of Excavated Earth

A substantial portion of the labor involved in construction would have been expended in excavation of the pit to house the structure, the postholes that housed the principal structural members of the walls and roof, and any floor pits created at the time of initial construction. Thus the volumes of these features taken together provide an estimate of the volume of earth excavated. Since all structures were truncated by the plowzone, estimates of the volumes of pits dug to house the structures must be considered minima.

Estimates of posthole volumes are based on the mean for all wall postholes and interior postholes within each structure. In the case of those larger structures inferred to have been built over smaller ones with large storage pits, the estimated volume of the earlier pit has been subtracted from the estimated excavated volume for the later structure, since this material had already been removed. Equations used to arrive at these estimates are given in Table A.7, while Figure 2.33 plots the results. Assuming a figure of 1 m³ of earth excavated per person per day, most structures involved between one and four person-days of excavation.

Perishable Materials

Another large portion of the time and labor expended in construction would have been invested in the collection and assembly of the perishable materials used to construct the framework and most of the exterior covering. Estimates of the amounts of the various elements needed for construction have been made for both four- and five-post roof support patterns in those cases where these patterns have been inferred or reconstructed. Estimates for the few structures lacking interior roof supports have been made on the assumption that a flat roof was present. A number of other assumptions have been made in order to produce these estimates, as follows:

1) It has been assumed that the interior height of ceilings was 1.5 m. The length of roof support posts is estimated by adding 1.5 m to the average depth of excavated interior posts on a structure-by-structure basis.

2) It has been assumed that there would have been rafters connecting each of the four or five interior support posts. The length of the rafters is determined by the measured lengths between support posts in the reconstructions offered above; or by the mean of these measured values in cases where no support post pattern could be reconstructed; or is equal to zero in cases where there is no evidence for roof supports.

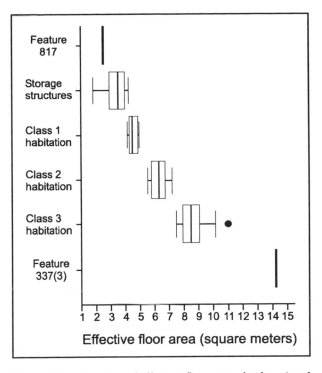

Figure 2.32. Box plots of effective floor areas for functional classes.

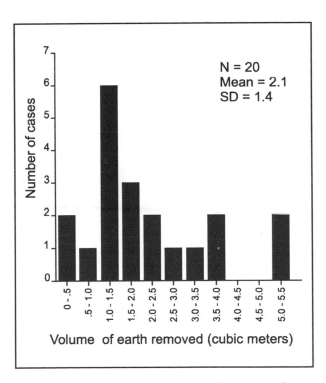

Figure 2.33. Plot of estimates of earth removed during construction.

3) It has been assumed that there were six horizontal stringers per structure, three to stabilize the wall poles and three to secure the thatching. An average circumference for the stringers is derived by averaging the floor area circumference with the circumference of a circle equal in area to the roof area as measured or estimated (see below). This figure is then multiplied by six to estimate the total length of stringers for each structure.

4) It has been assumed that the area of the roof is equal to the measured polygons defined by the interior support posts. In cases where no roof support pattern could be discerned or where no roof supports are present, the mean of all four-post roof areas has been used (.2731 x floor area).

5) The amount of thatching needed was approximately equal to the surface area of a hemisphere having the circumference of the floor area, minus the roof area.

6) The total length of pieces needed for the primary roof elements was equal to the roof area divided by 1 cm. This is converted into the number of 1.5 m long saplings needed to achieve this length by dividing the total length by 1.5 m.

Equations used to estimate perishable materials and employing these assumptions are presented in Table A.8, and the results of these manipulations are presented in Table A.9.

Based on these estimates, and assuming a five-post interior support system, the average structure would have required the following: 38 willow or cottonwood saplings approximately 2 m long (wall poles); five posts of mesquite approximately 1.7 m long (interior support posts); five poles of mesquite or other woods approximately 1.2 m long (rafters); 23 more cottonwood or willow saplings approximately 2 m long (stringers); 117 saplings or shoots of cottonwood, willow or other wood approximately 1.5 m long (primary roof elements); sufficient brush to cover an area approximately 2.7 m² with the desired thickness (secondary roof elements); and sufficient grass to cover approximately 13 m² of area to the desired thickness (thatching). Thus, even the smallest structures required a considerable amount of material for their construction, and the largest structure exceeds the averages by nearly 50 percent in most categories.

Use of Earth in Construction

The earth excavated during initial stages of construction was used to fill in postholes once the posts were in place, to fill the space left between the pit wall and the wall of the structure, and to create an earthen embankment around the base of the structure. Estimates of the volume of earth excavated for each structure derived above also provide a basis for estimating how much surplus earth remained after construction or, alternatively, how much additional material had to be procured elsewhere for completion of the structure.

As with perishable materials, a number of assumptions have been made in estimating the amounts of earth used in construction:

1) It has been assumed that the amount of space between the pit wall and the wall of the structure was equal to the area of the structure pit, minus the floor area of the structure, multiplied by the depth of the pit.

2) It has been assumed that the surrounding embankments had a 45-degree angle of repose, and thus would have extended out from the base of the structure to a distance equal to their height on the wall. Heights of 50, 60, and 70 cm have been assumed for purposes of estimation. The volume of embankments for individual structures is thus obtained by adding 50, 60, or 70 cm to the radius of the floor area, calculating the area of the new circle, subtracting the within-the-walls floor area from the result, and multiplying that area times .125 (50 cm), .18 (60 cm), or .245 (70 cm). The latter figures represent the areas of the cross sections of the three embankments of differing estimated heights.

3) It has been assumed that a layer of earth 10 cm thick was used to complete the roof. Thus, the volume of earth used in the roof is obtained by multiplying the roof area (see above) by .1.

4) It has been assumed that the amount of earth used to fill in wall postholes was equal to that excavated to create them.

Any of these parameters could be modeled with different values, but those used here provide a reasonable baseline for consideration of the amount of material used in any particular case. Perhaps the variable most subject to question is the thickness of the layer of earth on the roof. Equations used in these calculations are presented in Table A.10, and Table A.11 presents the results of these manipulations.

Figure 2.34 presents histograms representing the results for the 50 (a), 60 (b), and 70 (c) cm embankments for the five post alternative. This figure shows that if the desired outcome was to have enough earth to complete construction with a minimum remaining, the 60 cm embankment provides perhaps the best fit. It should be noted that no attempt was made to take into account the volumetric expansion that results during excavation of natural deposits; this factor probably increased the actual amount of earth available for construction in all cases.

Discussion

Taken as a whole, the estimates presented above indicate that a substantial amount of labor and material was invested in construction of even the smallest structures at Los Pozos. Given these estimates, the probable construction sequence discussed earlier, and the sheer kinetics of construction, it is almost certain that construction was a group undertaking rather than

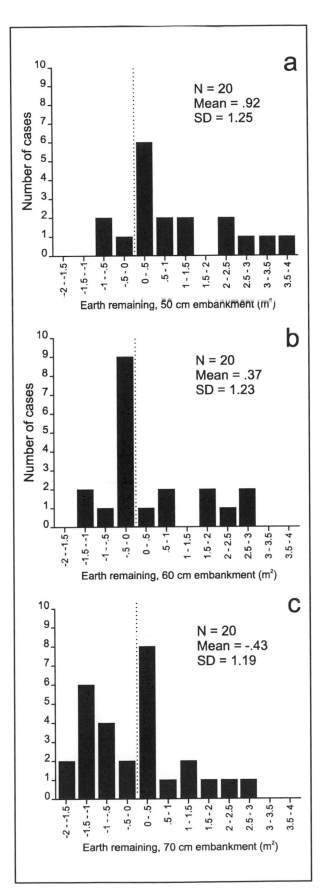

Figure 2.34. Plots of estimates of earth used in construction for 50-, 60-, and 70-cm embankments.

one performed by single individuals. Even the small storage structures (for which no estimates of labor and materials were attempted) were likely the result of a group enterprise. The proportionally much greater amounts of labor and materials required to build the large Feature 337(3) provide additional support for the proposition that this feature was somehow special and involved activities that included more than one social unit.

One aspect of labor investment may have involved a sexual division of labor. Although we have no basis for inferences regarding the gender of the individuals involved in construction of these features, it is worth noting that construction was a gender-specific activity among some aboriginal groups, including the Gila River Yumans as described by Spier:

> Housebuilding was man's work alone, whether a dwelling, storehouse, or meeting house: the women did not assist. A man was helped by his male friends and relatives in the construction of his dwelling. In building a meeting house [a larger version of the typical dwelling], all the men of the village were engaged and *built it in a day* (1933:83; emphasis added).

Parenthetically, it is unclear whether the one day construction time given by Spier includes the time necessary to collect all the materials necessary and bring them to the construction site.

Without detailed ethnographic data or ethnoarchaeological studies, it is difficult to estimate the amount of time required to collect perishable materials and prepare them. Given the derived estimates, a substantial amount of time and energy must have been devoted to this aspect of construction, an amount that would have increased with distance traveled to procure the various materials. Depending upon the number of structures present and their average use-life, this also raises the question of possible depletion of resources in the immediate vicinity of the settlement.

Given the regular use of mesquite for firewood as well as for some construction elements (see Chapter 9), it may be supposed that the local supply of dead and down wood, driftwood, and easily acquired lower mesquite branches would have been depleted fairly quickly. Similarly, recovered specimens of cottonwood or willow indicate that the trees used were at least several years old, and older in some cases. If the average structure required 150 6-ft saplings of various diameters, at least short-term depletion of this resource is a possibility as well. Only the grasses used in thatching and perhaps the shrubs used as secondary roof elements would have been naturally replenished on an annual basis.

The shift to true pithouses in the following Agua Caliente phase would have significantly reduced the amounts of perishable materials required for construction, despite a significant increase in the average size of structures. In particular, the number of willow or cottonwood saplings used would have been far fewer. Thus, a reasonable working hypothesis for the future is that this shift in construction techniques may have been related to the amounts of perishable materials required, possibly due to depletion of resources during earlier intervals or simply as a matter of greater efficiency in construction. We shall have occasion to return to this issue in Chapter 12.

ABANDONMENT AND POSTABANDONMENT PROCESSES

An important question relating to a number of issues concerning the nature, duration, and intensity of the occupation at Los Pozos is: how long did these constructions last? Given the construction techniques and materials described above, it may be inferred that some structural elements would have begun to deteriorate rather rapidly. The small wall poles, stringers, and roof elements would have become brittle as they dried out, and the unmudded thatch would have dried and begun to shed. In addition, the thatch would have provided a habitat for vermin including insects and small rodents, and it is probable that termites soon found and attacked the buried portions of wall poles and roof support posts. The soft cottonwood or willow elements would have been particularly susceptible to these creatures. As the woody elements of the roof dried and shrunk, the earth covering would have begun to loosen and filter between the spaces and into the structure.

Refurbishing of structures involving replacement of roof elements and thatching would leave no trace, and it is possible that the life of structures may have been extended by such efforts. Instances of more substantial remodeling and superposition cited above may represent cases where deterioration of the principal structural elements required greater efforts or dictated abandonment of the structures altogether. The sheer number and density of structures at Los Pozos and other Cienega phase sites may provide evidence of a relatively short use-life for the features, although a number of other factors could be responsible for this pattern (see Chapter 12). Taking all available evidence into account, it is estimated that none of these structures lasted more than two or three years, and most may have served for only a year (or season?).

Roughly one-fourth (10 of 42) of the structures at Los Pozos were ultimately destroyed by fire. Given the nature of the construction materials and the frequent presence of hearths, it is reasonable to infer that accidental fires probably occurred with some frequency. However, it is also possible that structures were intentionally burned when they became too vermin-infested or dilapidated to function or perhaps when an occupant died. It is impossible to be certain about intentional versus accidental conflagrations in each and every case. Several burned structures have what appear to be de facto floor assemblages (e.g., Features 333, 836, and 825) as does one large intramural pit (Feature 861), and perhaps in these instances a case can be made for an accidental fire. A similar argument may be made for those burned structures with complete bone tools and other materials apparently stored in their interior walls and ceilings.

However, other apparently unburned structures (e.g., Feature 416) and associated pits (e.g., in Feature 342) have floor assemblages that were clearly left in place within structures that were abandoned for some reason other than fire. It is also probable that some structures simply outlived their utility and were abandoned for the same reasons cited above as rationales for intentional burning of them. Some may have been scavenged for still useable building materials, or simply allowed to collapse and disintegrate.

When structures were finally abandoned for whatever reasons, they left shallow depressions, sometimes punctuated with a deeper area in cases where intramural pits were open when the structure was abandoned. These features would have been readily apparent to current and subsequent inhabitants of the settlement, and the data from Los Pozos indicate that they were almost always used as convenient receptacles for the discard of unwanted residues of everyday activities.

The make-up and density of these deposits and the rapidity with which they accumulated are important issues relating to the intensity, duration, and continuity of occupation. We shall have occasion in Chapter 12 to examine these materials in greater detail and in a comparative context. For the moment, they represent the final episodes in the use-life of structures which began with excavation of the pits in which they were constructed. Indirectly, these deposits inform on continuing activities involving the structures still in use at any given time.

The composition of these deposits and the densities of artifacts and other cultural residues represented provide the principal evidence that domestic trash is represented. Structure fills and intramural pit fills are essentially similar and, a few special cases aside, may be argued to represent the same general category of deposits.

Figure 2.35 illustrates variation in overall density of items in the deposits (see Tables A.12 and A.13). In order of their relative proportion of all items in a given deposit, the principal components of refuse are fragments of animal bone, flaked stone artifacts (primarily shell), and pieces of fire-cracked rock. With few

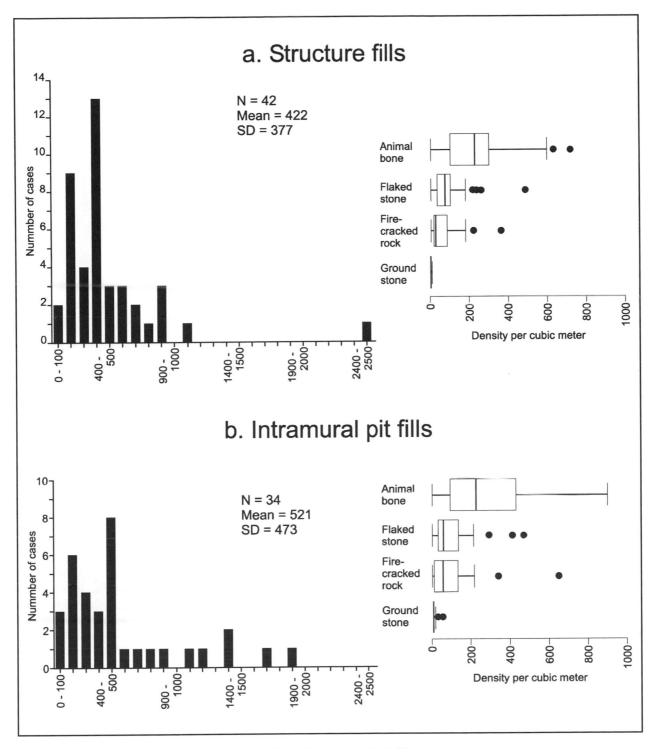

Figure 2.35. Densities of artifacts in: a) structure fills; and b) intramural pit fills.

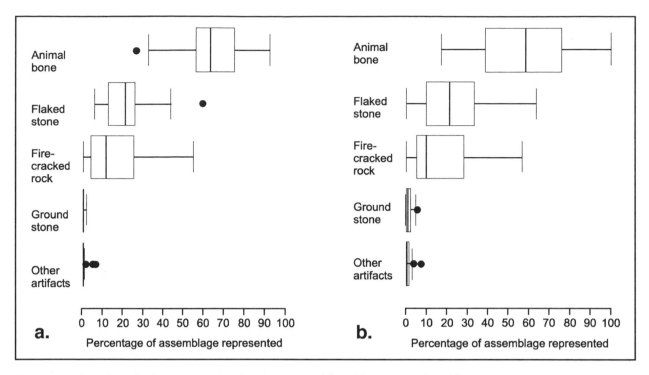

Figure 2.36. Box plots of refuse composition for: a) structure fill; and b) intramural pit fill.

exceptions, these three materials make up over 90 percent of all items contained within such deposits. Materials that occur in much lower frequencies or only occasionally include ground stone artifacts, shell, and other miscellaneous artifacts. The volumetric bulk of all deposits is composed of soil or sediment containing variable amounts of charcoal (including charred seeds; see Chapter 9), ash, fragments of burned earth, and sometimes tiny caliche flecks or nodules. Eolian and water-lain deposits probably contributed variably to the matrix, and soil may have been added intentionally by the inhabitants. Figure 2.36 illustrates variation in composition of deposits from these two contexts (see Tables A.14 and A15).

Based on the contents of excavated extramural pits (see Chapter 3), some refuse clearly resulted from the clean-out of these features. Much of the fire-cracked rock and charcoal and some ash probably originated in these contexts. As noted above, mesquite was used sparingly in construction, with most structural elements being cottonwood or willow. However, mesquite overwhelmingly dominates charcoal fragments recovered from flotation samples, indicating that it was the preferred firewood (see Chapter 9). Thus, there can be little doubt that much of this charcoal originated from extramural pits. Given the presence of hearths in many structures and the character of documented floor assemblages, it is also reasonable to infer that floor sweepings contributed to the refuse deposits. It is also possible that the remains of burned structures were cleaned out of their pits and the pits reused, with the charred structural remains being discarded as trash.

Most importantly, the process of discard appears to have contributed to the fill of nearly every investigated structure, and most appear to have filled relatively quickly in this way. Although some examples of refuse deposits separated by substantial natural water-lain sediments have been cited above, these are apparent in only a minority of the stratigraphic cross sections. Features 305 and 416 are the only two structures having purely natural water-lain sediments as the last units deposited, and thus, are the only two good candidates for structures which filled after the settlement was abandoned. However, radiocarbon dates from the two features (2120 ± 60 and 2240 ± 60, respectively) indicate otherwise. The early date from Feature 416 is an outlier to the other 18 dates, and perhaps indicates an earlier occupation followed by a hiatus. The date from Feature 305 falls in the middle of the tightly clustered dates from other features, and the two youngest dates from the site (1940 ± 60 and 1980 ± 60) come from structures that were filled with refuse.

Perhaps the best evidence for discontinuity in the occupation of the site comes from the sequence of deposits in Feature 890, where the fill of the intramural pit and structure indicates a period of refuse deposition, followed by accumulation of sterile water-lain deposits, followed by another episode of trash deposition, followed by a period of mixed water-lain and some trash, and finally by trash again. A similar but not as complex sequence may be seen in Feature 812. One intramural pit (Feature 342.01) remained open for a considerable period of time while it filled up with sterile water-lain deposits, and relatively thick lenses of similar character were observed in two other intramural pits (Features 355.09 and 324.01). Taken together with these other features which indicate some hiatus in the deposition of refuse, Features 305 and 416 provide perhaps the best evidence that the occupation of Los Pozos was at least sometimes intermittent on a short-term basis (seasons, years?), but was likely continuous on a larger time scale (decades, centuries?). Once again, much additional data are necessary to clarify this issue.

CHAPTER 3

EXTRAMURAL FEATURES

David A. Gregory

Excavated extramural features at Los Pozos (AZ AA:12:91 [ASM]) fall into one of three categories: pits of various shapes and sizes (25), wells (3), and inhumations (3). In addition, two canal exposures are described and discussed. Descriptions of individual features and associated deposits may be found elsewhere (Gregory 2001b).

Before proceeding, a word of caution is warranted concerning the morphology of extramural features and measurements of feature depths in particular. As with the structures discussed in Chapter 2, all extramural features had been truncated to an unknown degree by the plowzone, and perhaps some of what remained after plowing was removed in the process of machine stripping of the plowzone. Because of their smaller size, it may be assumed that a greater proportion of extramural features was probably destroyed by one or both of these processes than was the case with structures.

Direct evidence for such effects comes from the two inhumations interred in extramural pits: skeletal materials were visible at the tops of these features after machine stripping, and both skeletons were incomplete (Features 304 and 421; see Gregory 2001b and below). If it is assumed that the prehistoric inhabitants would have buried these individuals at least deep enough for their remains to be completely covered, then a significant portion of these features may have been removed. Some of the smaller extramural pits in particular appear to have been affected more than others by plowing and possibly stripping (see below). Allowing for variation in the portion of individual features destroyed by these agents, all would have been deeper, and differences between them greater or lesser than is apparent from recorded measurements.

As a result, any quantification and comparison involving feature depths (including shape and volume) must be approached with some caution. Acceptance of such measurements as accurate representations of the features requires at a minimum the assumptions that 1) all pits were originally excavated from approximately the same surface, and 2) all have been more or less equally truncated by the plowzone and by the process of machine stripping. Although the first is likely, the second is almost certainly not true, and neither assumption is strongly supported by empirical data. This caveat applies as well to extramural features from the Santa Cruz Bend, Stone Pipe, and Square Hearth sites, although it is not fully acknowledged in

a study of extramural features documented at those sites (Wöcherl 1998).

PITS

Eighty-eight extramural pits were identified as a result of machine stripping of the plowzone. A scatterplot of length against width for both excavated and unexcavated features (Figure 3.1) shows what is apparent from the site maps presented in Chapter 1: most of the stains exposed by stripping were roughly circular to oval in plan view. Twenty-five of these features were wholly or partially excavated, or approximately 28 percent of all those identified. This total includes two pits which contained inhumations but which appear to have been originally created for other purposes (Features 304 and 421), and seven features explored in conjunction with excavation of structures (see Gregory 2001a). Table 3.1 summarizes metric data for excavated pits, including pit type as discussed below. Figure 3.2 compares the surface area of all exposed pits (Figure 3.2a) to the surface areas of excavated pits (Figure 3.2b), and reflects the fact that size was the principal criterion applied in selecting extramural features for excavation (Gregory 1995).

Morphology and Function

With appropriate attention to the cautions offered above with respect to the effects of plowing and machine stripping of the plowzone, the physical attributes of extramural pits have been used to isolate three types of pits. Figure 3.3 is a scatterplot of pit volume against the diameter-to-depth ratios of the pits; in all cases, the average diameter and the maximum recorded depth of the features has been used. The three sets of features identified in this plot are designated as heuristic types and are described and discussed below. Truncation of the pits by modern agents would have reduced the measured volume in all cases. The diameter-to-depth ratio could have been either reduced—in the case of straight-sided pits or those with belled or undercut sides—or increased, in the case of outward sloping pit walls. These potential effects are noted below as appropriate. Not considered in this sample is a large, irregular feature of Hohokam age (Feature 422), cut into the fill of Feature 333, a pit structure (see Gregory 2001a:Figure 1.13).

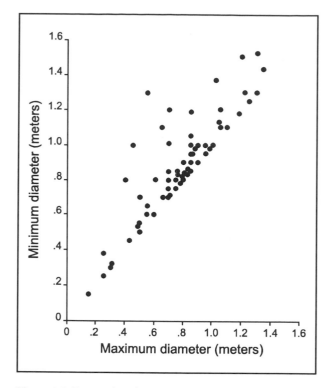

Figure 3.1. Scatterplot of minimum and maximum diameters for all extramural pits exposed by stripping.

Type 1 Pits

The three Type 1 pits (Figure 3.4) represent the largest of the excavated extramural pits, all having volumes greater than .4 m³ and diameter-to-depth ratios less than 2.5:1. Based on the shapes of the remaining portions of the features, truncation by modern agents would have reduced the diameter-to-depth ratios in all cases.

Feature 373 is unique in the sample of pits. This feature was originally dug in stepped tiers from south to north, creating three distinct levels within it (see Figure 3.4). The walls of the uppermost tier varied from straight-sided to slightly belled, and the lowest tier showed a similar configuration, with the belling being more pronounced. The central section was relatively straight-sided. Feature 373 is similar to several cache pits described for late prehistoric Arikara sites in Nebraska (Lehmer and Jones 1968). One of the pits described and illustrated by these authors is virtually identical to the feature at Los Pozos, although considerably larger. These authors refer to the tiers as secondary pits and note that:

> While secondary pits of this sort would have provided additional storage capacity, their most important function was probably concealment. Anyone looting the contents of the upper cache might well have overlooked the lower pit and its contents (Lehmer and Jones 1968:18).

Table 3.1. Characteristics of extramural pits.

Feature	Type	Length	Width	Avg Diam	Depth	W/D Ratio	Area	Volume
300	3	.65	.55	.60	.22	2.73	.28	.060
304	2	.85	.76	.80	.19	4.21	.50	.100
311	3	.43	.45	.44	.05	8.80	.15	.006
329	1	0	0	.95	.48	1.98	.71	.392
330	3	.95	.86	.91	.11	8.27	.65	.070
346	2	0	0	.98	.39	2.51	.75	.269
348	3	.80	.61	.70	.09	7.78	.38	.032
357	3	.84	.81	.83	.08	10.38	.54	.033
359	3	.85	1.19	1.02	.13	7.85	.82	.105
373	1	1.43	1.34	1.38	1.30	1.06	1.50	1.950
399	2	.60	.60	.60	.14	4.29	.28	.036
400	2	0	0	.83	.20	4.15	.54	.104
403	3	.83	.86	.85	.13	6.54	.57	.070
406	2	0	0	.78	.22	3.55	.48	.106
408	1	1.52	1.30	1.41	.55	2.56	1.56	.890
411	2	1.30	1.22	1.26	.31	4.06	1.25	.390
420	2	.95	.85	.88	.33	2.67	.61	.200
421	2	.98	.88	.93	.30	3.10	.68	.200
422	2	1.37	1.02	1.20	.37	3.24	1.13	.420
423	2	.71	.71	.71	.29	2.45	.40	.120
424	2	1.18	0	1.18	.30	3.93	1.09	.330
426	2	.53	.49	.51	.33	1.55	.20	.066
427	2	0	0	1.10	.32	3.44	.95	.300
431	2	.79	.82	.81	.22	3.68	.52	.110
872	3	.85	.60	.72	.07	10.29	.41	.029
874	2	.76	.83	.80	.21	3.81	.50	.079

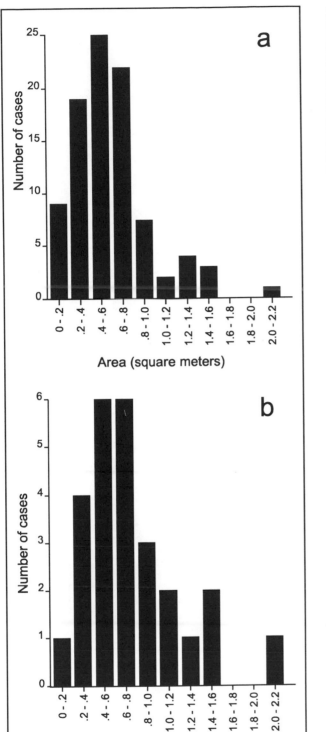

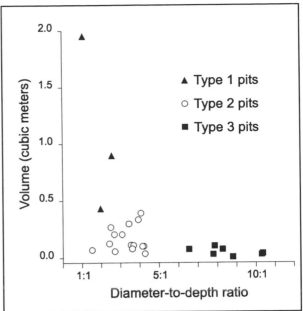

Figure 3.3. Scatterplot of pit volume against diameter-to-depth ratios.

Figure 3.2. Histograms of surface areas of extramural pits: a) all pits exposed by stripping; b) excavated pits.

Features 329 and 408 also stand out by virtue of size and shape (see Figure 3.4). Both were roughly round in plan, and were relatively large; one was markedly undercut (Feature 408) and the other had slightly belled sides (Feature 329). These two features more closely resemble intramural pits documented at the site than any of the other excavated extramural pits. Feature 408 was relatively isolated with respect to other extramural pits, and was in an area that was disturbed not only by the plowzone but by a modern irrigation ditch. The possibility that this feature represents an intramural pit for a completely destroyed structure was suggested by the excavator and must be considered. In size and cross section, Feature 408 resembles several pits discovered within structures at the Santa Cruz Bend and Stone Pipe sites (Mabry and Archer 1997:Figures 2.18, 2.27, 2.55, 2.79; Swartz and Lindeman 1997:Figure 4.48). Feature 329 is distinguished from most other extramural pits not only by its size, but with respect to its markedly belled walls. Feature 329 was located within a small cluster of pits (see below).

There was no evidence that the contents of the pit fills were related to their function. Relatively low densities of artifacts, animal bone, and fire-cracked rock suggest that Features 373 and 408 were filled primarily by natural agents with perhaps some addition of domestic refuse (see Table 3.2). High densities of these materials in Feature 329 suggest that it may have been intentionally filled with domestic refuse. Based on their size, morphology, and similarities with intramural pits

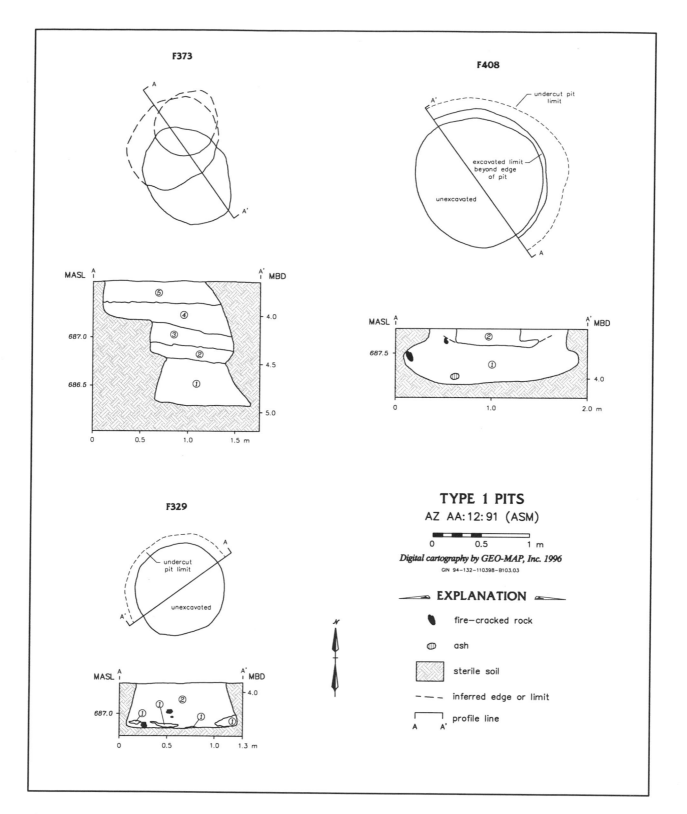

Figure 3.4. Type 1 pits.

Table 3.2. Extramural pits, artifact, and animal bone counts and densities.

Feature	n					Densities				
	Flaked Stone	Ground Stone	Animal Bone	Fire-cracked Rock	Total	Flaked Stone	Ground Stone	Animal Bone	Fire-cracked Rock	Overall Density
300	0	0	0	0	0	0	0	0	0	0
304	4	1	0	16	21	39.3	9.8	0	157.2	206.3
311	0	0	0	1	1	0	0	0	166.7	166.7
329	77	0	103	24	204	387.5	0	518.4	120.8	1,026.7
330	35	2	115	8	160	489.5	28.0	1,608.4	111.9	2,237.8
346	33	0	188	43	264	222.7	0	1,268.6	290.2	1,781.4
348	0	0	0	2	2	0	0	0	158.7	158.7
357	0	2	18	54	74	0	60.1	540.5	1,621.6	2,222.2
359	3	0	5	1	9	51.3	0	85.5	17.1	153.8
373	12	1	8	65	86	16.0	1.3	10.6	86.6	114.5
399	3	2	3	3	11	194.8	129.9	194.8	194.8	714.3
400	21	0	50	2	73	176.8	0	420.9	16.8	614.5
403	0	0	0	4	4	0	0	0	108.4	108.4
406	4	0	3	0	7	75.8	0	56.8	0	132.6
408	14	0	3	15	32	31.2	0	6.7	33.4	71.2
411	18	3	43	25	89	77.6	12.9	185.4	107.8	383.8
420	0	0	0	0	0	0	0	0	0	0
421	8	15	100	238	361	36.9	69.1	460.8	1,096.8	1,663.6
422	146	0	155	13	314	348.9	0	370.4	31.1	750.3
423	1	0	0	0	1	29.1	0	0	0	29.1
424	10	4	281	160	455	18.8	7.5	526.9	300.0	853.2
426	2	0	9	2	13	30.3	0	136.4	30.3	197.0
427	0	0	0	51	51	0	0	0	3,400.0	3,400.0
431	19	1	35	13	68	167.6	8.8	308.6	114.6	599.6
872	0	0	0	3	3	0	0	0	97.4	97.4
874	3	4	0	221	228	38.2	51.0	0	2,815.3	2,904.5

at the site, the three Type 1 pits are inferred to have served as storage facilities.

Type 2 Pits

Fifteen features are classified as Type 2 pits. These features have volumes less that .4 m³, with most examples having volumes less than .2 m³. Diameter-to-depth ratios range between 1.5:1 and 4.2:1, with all but two features having ratios greater than 2.5:1 and most having ratios greater than 3:1 (see Figure 3.3). Two basic shapes are represented.

Two of the pits have the shape of shallow to moderately deep basins with outsloping walls; one of these (Feature 424) had a deeper, secondary basin at the bottom (Figure 3.5). The remaining 13 Type 2 pits have straight to slightly undercut or belled walls; two (Features 411 and 874) had shallow, basin-shaped bottoms, while all others had relatively flat bottoms (Figure 3.6). Two of these pits (Features 304 and 421)

had burials placed in them after they were filled and abandoned (see below). Based on the shapes of the remaining portions of the features, truncation by modern agents would have reduced the diameter-to-depth ratios in all but the two pits with outsloping sides. In these two cases, the ratios may have originally been somewhat greater.

The two features with outsloping walls contained abundant amounts of charcoal and fire-cracked rock and few artifacts, and Feature 424 also produced abundant animal bone (see Table 3.2). Both pits appear to have been used as facilities for cooking, possibly of meat.

Contents of the remaining Type 2 pits varied considerably (see Table 3.2). Feature 874 contained abundant fire-cracked rock and charcoal, and trivets were present as well (Figure 3.7). Since ceramic containers of an appropriate size were not part of the material culture inventory of the inhabitants (see Chapter 8), we may infer that the trivets supported

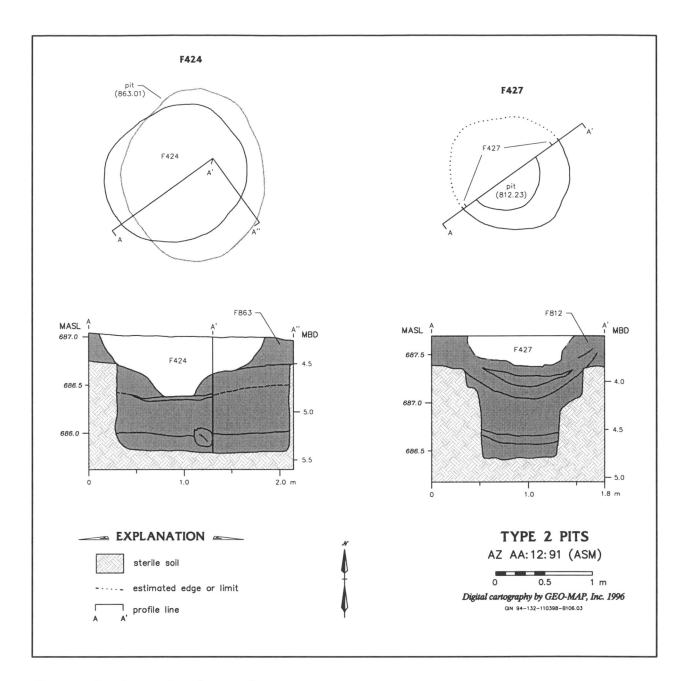

Figure 3.5. Type 2 pits with outsloping walls.

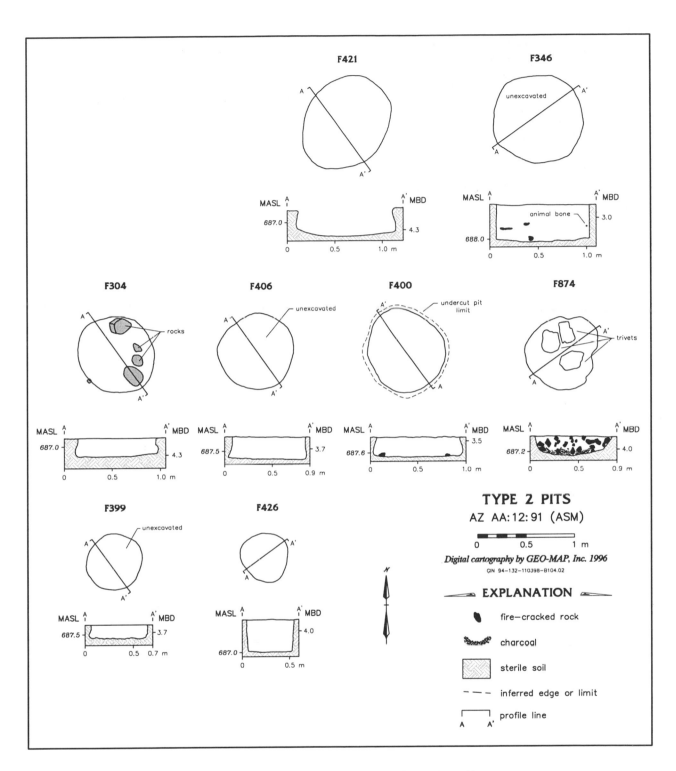

Figure 3.6. Type 2 pits with straight to slightly undercut walls and flat to basin-shaped bottoms.

Figure 3.7. Photograph of Feature 874 showing trivets.

baskets used in stone boiling. Several large metate fragments lying below the burial in Feature 304 (see below) could also have served as trivets; however, these fragments were present only in the half of the pit where the inhumation had been placed and their association is uncertain. Moderate amounts of fire-cracked rock were present in the portion of Feature 304 not disturbed by the burial. The portion of Feature 421 not disturbed by another intrusive burial (see below) contained abundant fire-cracked rock and animal bone, and may also have originally been a roasting pit. Four pits appear to have been filled with domestic refuse (Features 346, 400, 403, and 411), while six other Type 2 pits contained very few artifacts, pieces of animal bone, and fire-cracked rock (Features 399, 406, 423, and 426) or none at all (Features 300 and 420).

Type 3 Pits

Despite the fact that Type 3 pits cluster together in terms of their dimensions, this appears to represent a residual category created by modern effects. As shown in Figure 3.8, all Type 3 pits were quite shallow, and all may have been substantially modified by plowing and/or stripping. All have volumes of .1 m³ or less and all have diameter-to-depth ratios greater than 6:1.

Based on the shapes of the portions remaining, Features 330, 357, and 403 appear to represent truncated Type 2 pits. In all three cases, an increased depth would push them toward the cluster of Type 2 pits shown in Figure 3.3. This inference is further supported by the presence of abundant fire-cracked rock in Features 357 and 403, and possible trivets in Feature 403. Whatever its original configuration, Feature 330 appears to have been filled with domestic refuse.

The four remaining features contained either no artifacts, animal bone, or fire-cracked rock or very low numbers of these materials. This may be in large part due to the minimal portions of the features that remained. In addition, three other features (348, 359, and 872) are more oval in shape than most other pits. Once again, the degree to which truncation by the modern plowzone has affected these shapes cannot be determined.

Spatial Distribution

Two clusters of pits may be discerned in the exposed portion of the site. A small, tight cluster of seven pits is present between north coordinates 1670 and 1680 and between east coordinate 300 and the margin of the right-of-way (Figure 3.9). This cluster is surrounded on the north, west, and south by excavated and unexcavated structures, the former including Features 389, 390, 425, 812, and 813, and the latter Features 393, 394, 814, 395, 879, and 880. It is probable that additional pits belonging to this cluster were present outside the right-of-way to the east. Two of these pits were excavated (Features 399 and 400).

A larger, more dispersed cluster of pits with possible subdivisions is present between north coordinates 1740 and 1780, where 30 pits were discovered (Figure 3.10). Within this overall distribution, two separate clusters may be discerned, one between north 1750 and 1760 (13 pits), and another between north 1765 and 1780 (13 pits). Six pits in the former cluster were excavated, and three in the latter. The first cluster lies immediately south of a dense distribution of 13 pit structures, and one of the pits (Feature 430) intrudes one of the structures (Feature 840); interestingly, a possible entry for this structure faces onto the area where the other pits are clustered. The second cluster falls within this same distribution of structures, and two of the pits in this cluster (Features 420 and 423) intrude two of the structures (Features 342 and 824, respectively). Possible entries in Features 354 and 318 face onto the area where the pits are clustered.

It may be inferred that these clusters represent extramural work areas used consistently over some period of time. In the case of the larger cluster of pits and its two subdivisions, the extramural work area appears to have been maintained over a period during which nearby structures were constructed, used, abandoned, and replaced by other structures. Although some shift in the focus of activity seems to be represented by the two clusters, the combination of extramural work areas and a relatively high density of structures indicates that this portion of the site was continuously or intermittently used over a relatively long period of time.

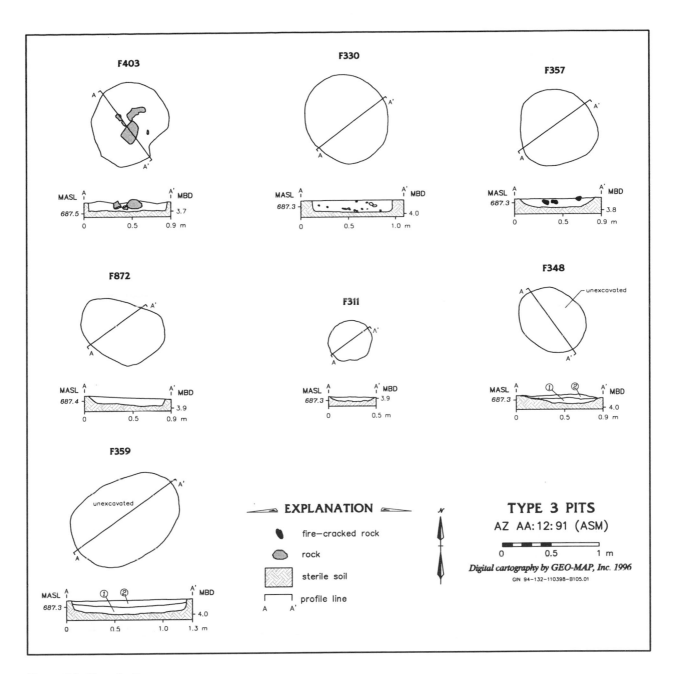

Figure 3.8. Type 3 pits.

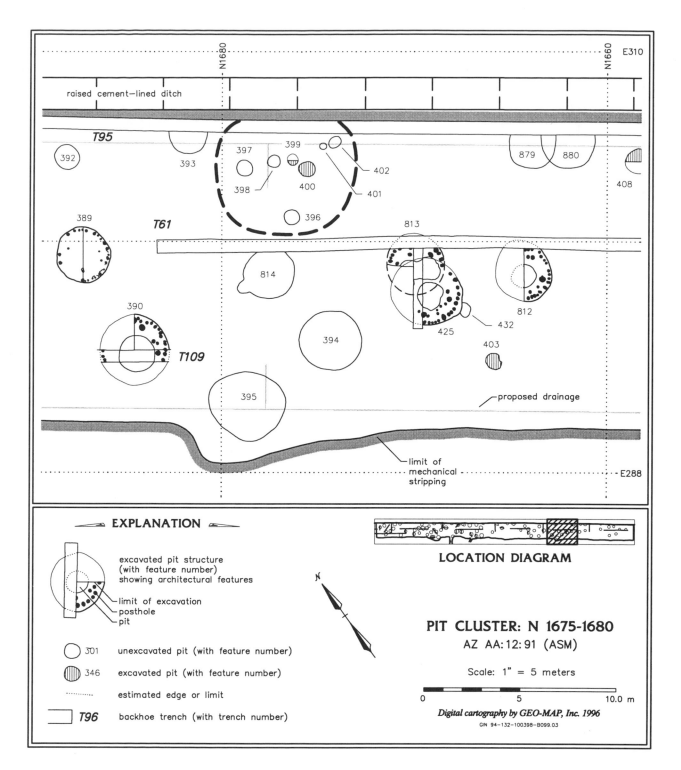

Figure 3.9. Pit cluster: N1675-1680.

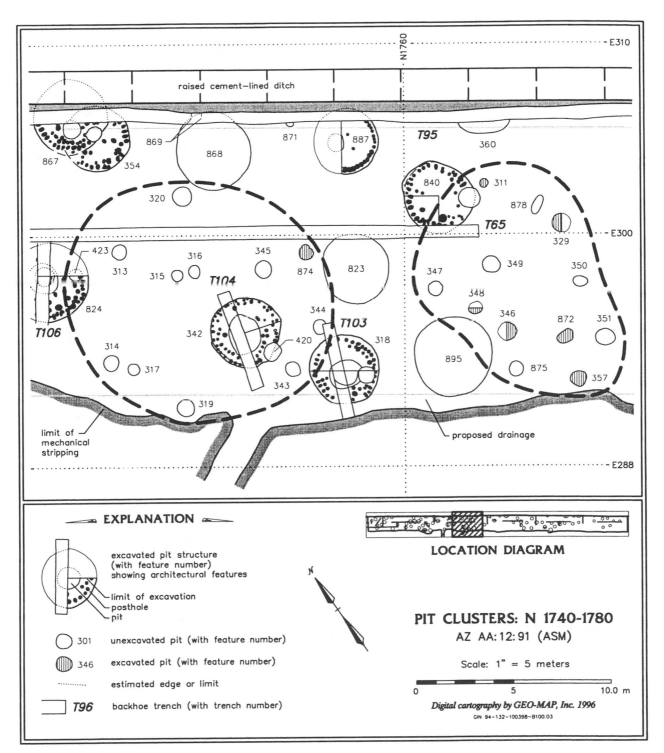

Figure 3.10. Pit cluster and possible subdivisions: N1740-1780.

Similar clusters of extramural pits have been described for the approximately contemporaneous Santa Cruz Bend and Stone Pipe sites (Mabry et al. 1997), and for the San Pedro phase Milagro site (Huckell 1990).

WELLS

Four features discovered at the site have been classified as wells, excavated to tap into subsurface deposits that would produce an accumulation of water in them. Two of these (Features 365 and 378) were partially excavated, while two others (Features 27 and 435) were documented only in trench exposures. Identification of the features as wells is based on: 1) their distinctive morphology, by comparison with other excavated features at the site and with prehistoric features previously identified as wells in southern Arizona and elsewhere; and 2) their relationship to natural strata that might have been the source for the water. Figure 3.11 provides a synoptic view of documented wells.

None of the wells was directly dated. Several red ware ceramics recovered from the fill of Feature 365 (see Chapter 8) indicate that the feature may have been at least partially filled during the Tortolita phase, several centuries after the occupation represented by the majority of investigated features. Feature 378 cut through a pit structure (Feature 379) and thus postdates it. The fact that both excavated wells were in an area of the site where there were few other features (see below), perhaps provides indirect evidence that the wells were associated with the period of occupation represented by the majority of features.

Morphology

Haury's (1976) description of the two forms of wells documented at the Hohokam site of Snaketown serves well as a starting point for discussion of the morphology of the features at Los Pozos. The wells at Snaketown were:

> (1) tubelike penetrations to the water table, not unlike our hand-dug wells, and (2) pits with wide mouths and sloping sides, resembling an inverted cone. Access to water in these was by walking into them, whereas in the former type a rope lift appears to have been needed, unless the water table was higher than seems to have been the case (Haury 1976:152).

As may be seen in Figure 3.11, at least one and possibly both of the two unexcavated features correspond to his "tubelike" features. Although Feature 27 was not excavated, the plowzone was stripped away above it, revealing a roughly circular outline corresponding to the maximum diameter at the top of the feature as represented in cross section. Similar removal of the plowzone from above the unexcavated Feature 435 produced less definitive results: the outline was not entirely clear, and it is possible that this feature was wider at the top than is indicated by the drawn section. The two excavated features (Features 365 and 378; Figures 3.12 and 3.13) are clearly in the shape of inverted cones, narrowing sharply to the tube-like lower portions of the features.

Feature 365 had what appeared to be a stepping or kneeling point in its upper portions, perhaps excavated to provide easier access to the water that accumulated in its bottom. In the case of Feature 378, multiple individual wells are represented and a partial sequence of use may be discerned from the exposures obtained.

As may be seen in Figure 3.11, it appears that the backdirt from the excavation of the individual wells designated 378b and/or 378c filled the hole initially made in the excavation of 378a. The relatively thick, parabolic lens of silt seen in the middle portions of 378a represents material dug out of the natural silt unit into which b and c (and previously, a) were excavated. There is little stratigraphic evidence to indicate whether 378b and 378c were used sequentially or simultaneously. The only possible clue comes from the different depths to which the features were dug: while 378c was approximately the same depth as 378a, 378b was dug over half a meter deeper. Since 378a was clearly dug and abandoned before b and c, it is suggested that the order of excavation and use was as follows: a, c, and b. Possibly, it was necessary or desirable for the prehistoric inhabitants to excavate deeper when 378b was constructed than they had for the previous two wells. Alternatively, both b and c could have been used simultaneously, with b deepened simply to provide a deeper pool of water from which to draw.

Feature 380 was also cut into the pit structure Feature 379 and was also a conical excavation. However, its maximum depth was less than half that of the features described above. This feature may represent an attempt to dig yet another well in this area that was aborted for unknown reasons. As Haury notes:

> The fouling and filling of wells of this kind by wind and human action and by the surface water run-off must have been an ongoing process. New wells were doubtless dug frequently, and in the process the old holes were obliterated by dumping freshly excavated earth and trash into them (Haury 1976:153).

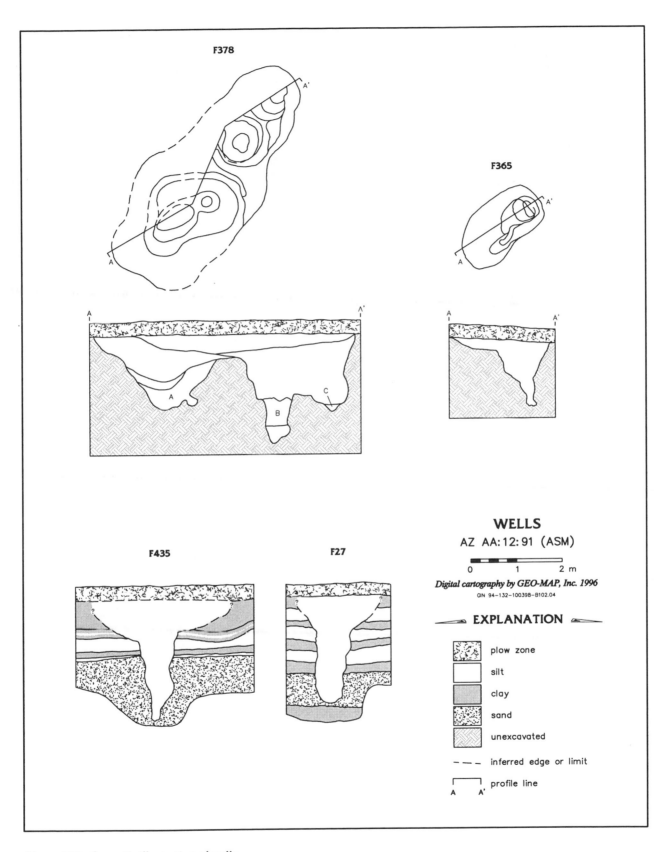

Figure 3.11. Synoptic illustration of wells.

Figure 3.12. Photograph of Feature 365.

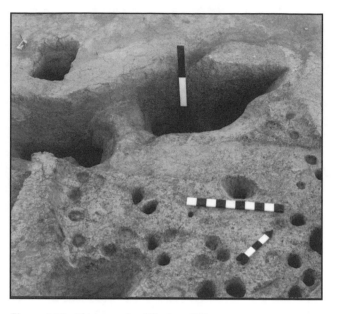

Figure 3.13. Photograph of Feature 378.

Relationship to Natural Stratigraphy

It is unlikely that the actual water table was being tapped by these relatively shallow features, and no staining of the sort to be expected if this were the case was observed in association with any of the Los Pozos features. Rather, all of the features penetrated to a point near the top of the natural unit which contained the Middle Archaic cultural deposits discovered at the site (Unit 510; see Gregory and Baar 1999). This unit is predominantly clay, and represents a relatively impermeable unit as compared to those overlying it. In all cases, the unit reached by the wells lies immediately above Unit 510 and consists of highly permeable coarse sands. Thus, Unit 510 may have served to create a perched water table and thus a situation in which wells could be used to tap the water.

The character of the immediately overlying unit (Unit 509) is variable across the site area, but is always composed of coarser materials than Unit 510 beneath. The overlying units into which the features penetrated were either a relatively porous, massive, sandy silt (Features 365 and 378), or a medium-to-coarse sand that appears to represent overflow channel deposits (Features 27 and 435).

Once again, Haury's (1976) description of the manner in which the Snaketown wells functioned provides an apt comparison:

To the northeast of Snaketown, Queen Creek debauches from the mountains onto the open flat in a myriad of rivulets before it reaches the bed of the Gila River. Much of this water goes underground where, given the proper aquifer, it may remain fairly close to the surface as it slowly seeps southward toward the river. In effect, this produced underground drainages, marked today by lines of heavier desert vegetation and thicker stands of mesquite (1976:152).

At Snaketown, a "massive caliche stratum" lying below a sandy layer (Haury 1976:152) formed the impermeable unit that kept water perched above and thus accessible via wells. If the interpretation offered here is correct, Unit 510 created similar effects at Los Pozos, and a similar knowledge and use of subsurface hydrology by the inhabitants is represented. In the case of the Los Pozos wells, water would have originated on the T3 terrace to the east, or perhaps as south-to-north underflow associated with the Santa Cruz channel.

Spatial Distribution

The two wells were both located between north coordinates 1710 and 1730, and in an area with a low density of structures and a relatively low density of other extramural features (Figure 3.14). The elongate shape of unexcavated Features 367 and 361, located nearby, suggests that they could represent additional wells present in this general area. No particular characteristics of the natural stratigraphy were noted that might make this a more desirable area in which to place these features.

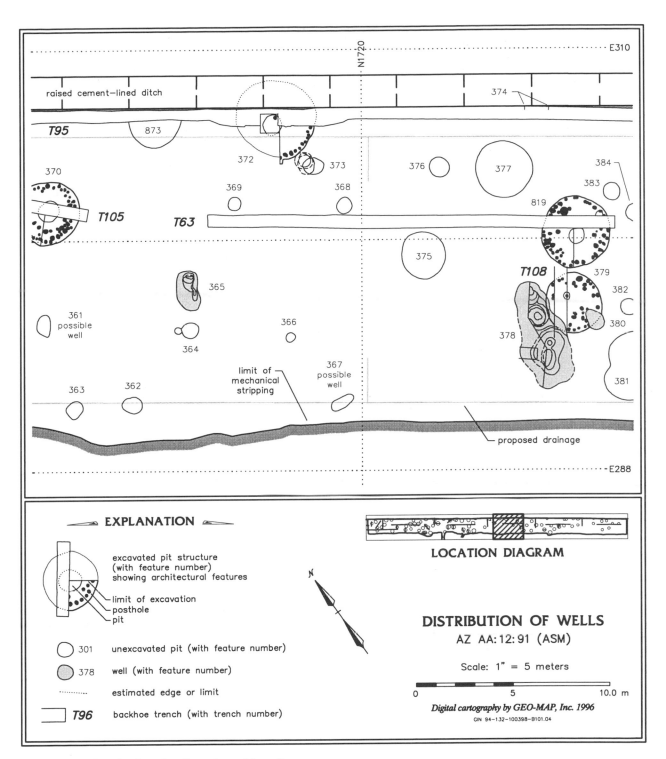

Figure 3.14. Distribution of wells and possible wells.

The two wells revealed only in trench exposures. Both appeared to be at the margins of the overall distribution of structures at the site (see Gregory 1995), and thus may have been located at the margins of the settlement at the time of their excavation and use. Both of these features penetrated into a coarse-to-medium sand unit. In the case of Feature 27, this unit was immediately above Unit 510 as described above. In the case of Feature 435, the sand was much deeper, and Unit 510 was not encountered in this particular exposure. This sand may represent deposits contained within an actual channel. This channel may have manifested itself on the surface by virtue of denser vegetation, which would have, in turn, signaled its presence to the prehistoric inhabitants. Thus, it is possible that the location for one or both of these features was chosen on the basis of observable surface phenomena.

INHUMATIONS

Three inhumations were discovered and excavated (Table 3.3), all located toward the northern end of the exposed site area (see below). As noted above, two of these were placed in pits originally excavated to serve other functions (Features 304 and 421). The third inhumation was placed in a pit dug specifically for the interment and cut into the fill of an abandoned structure and associated intramural pit (Feature 353, cut into Features 820 and 820.01; see Gregory 2001a:Figure 1.47). Detailed descriptions of recovered skeletal materials are presented in Appendix C.

Both of the two tightly flexed burials appear to have been placed to one side of the pits in which they were found (Figures 3.15 and 3.16), indicating that the previously filled pits may have been only partially dug out to accommodate the remains. In addition, both were only approximately 50 percent complete. Although some of the remains may have been disturbed by plowing, the incomplete character of the remains, their tightly flexed positions, and the relatively small size of the pits in which they were placed suggest the possibility that they may have been secondary rather than primary interments. Feature 353 was clearly a primary interment (Figure 3.17). Only Feature 304 contained possible grave goods, consisting of several metate fragments; these fragments appear to have been beneath the skeletal materials, perhaps providing additional support for the interpretation that a secondary interment is represented.

Table 3.3. Summary data for inhumations.

Feature	Type	Gender	Age	Head Orientation	Percent Preserved	Grave Goods
304	Tightly flexed (secondary?)	F	35-40	SE	50	Metate fragments (?)
308	Tightly flexed (secondary?)	F	25-35	SE (?)	45	None
353	Semi-flexed	M	40-50	NE	60	None

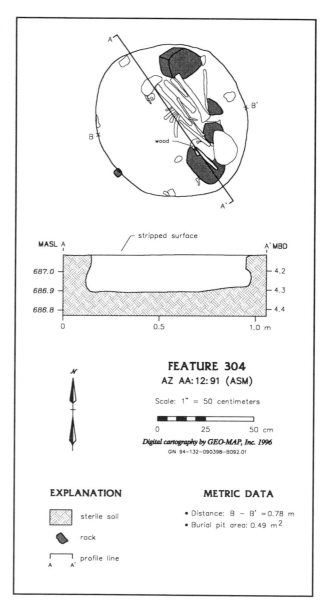

Figure 3.15. Feature 304 (inhumation).

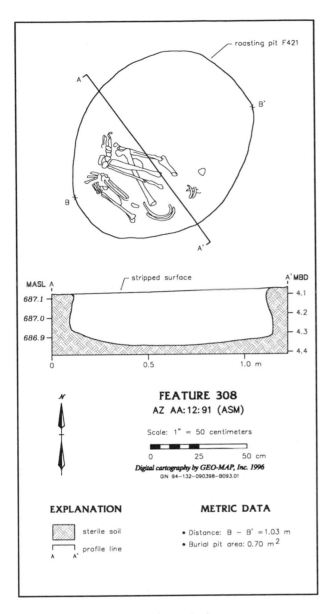

Figure 3.16. Feature 308 (inhumation).

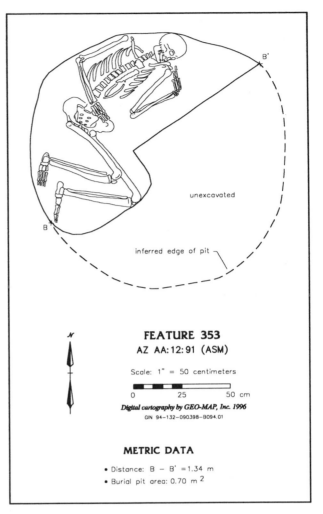

Figure 3.17. Feature 353 (inhumation).

Spatial Distribution

All three inhumations were found between north coordinates 1815 and 1833 (Figure 3.18), forming a relatively concentrated distribution within the overall site area. The distribution of non-burial human skeletal remains is more scattered, and does not reify this weak pattern (see Appendix C). Although human burials are known from a number of Cienega phase sites (e.g., see Eddy 1958; Hemmings et al. 1968; B. Huckell 1995), strong evidence for discrete cemetery areas within sites

of this interval comes only from the recently excavated Wetlands site (Mabry 1998) and from a site near the base of A-Mountain (Huckell 1988:65; Smiley et al. 1953).

It is of some interest that no such discrete areas have been found in direct association with the large and dense distributions of structures dating to this interval at Santa Cruz Bend, Stone Pipe, and now Los Pozos. This absence could still represent a sampling bias in these large sites, but it would appear that Cienega phase populations did not routinely bury their dead in close proximity to residential areas occupied during any particular interval. The fact that all of the Los Pozos burials are intrusive into features that had been abandoned and filled well before the interments were made would tend to support this conclusion.

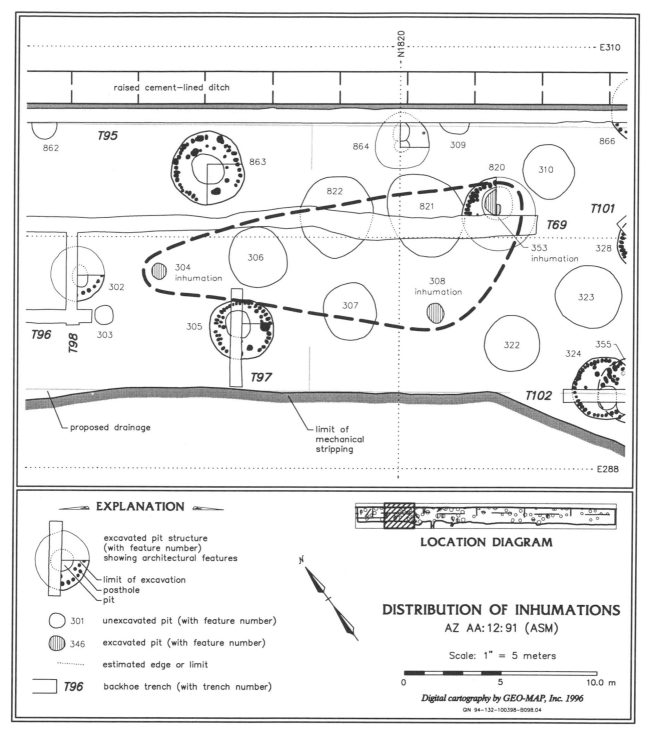

Figure 3.18. Distribution of inhumations.

POSSIBLE PREHISTORIC CANAL SEGMENTS IN THE PROJECT AREA

Two canal segments were discovered during the excavations at Los Pozos. Originally designated as Features 853 and 920, these segments were given new and separate site numbers, AZ AA:12:789 (ASM) and AZ AA:12:790 (ASM), respectively, in accordance with Arizona State Museum guidelines. Each is described, illustrated, and discussed below.

AZ AA:12:789 (ASM)

The feature now designated as AZ AA:12:789 was discovered in conjunction with excavations in the Middle Archaic component at Los Pozos (Gregory and Baar 1999:Figure 2.15). The top of the feature was at the interface between a zone of modern disturbance and underlying undisturbed deposits, and the feature was partially truncated by the disturbance. The canal was cut in several places at an oblique angle and was traced over a distance of approximately 20 m. These exposures showed that it had a trajectory running approximately 65 degrees west of north (Gregory and Baar 1999:Figure 2.3). This feature may be the same canal recorded within the site designated AZ AA:12:16 (ASM) and located approximately one-half km south of the more recent exposure (Adams and Macnider 1992a:Figure 10; Gregory 1993:Figure 9; see below).

The remaining portion of this canal was 52 cm deep and had an estimated width of approximately 70 cm; it was parabolic in cross section. The fill of the feature consisted of two strata: 1) a coarse sandy silt with some bedding, and 2) a compact clay that probably represents postabandonment deposition. No iron or manganese oxide staining was observed.

AZ AA:12:790 (ASM)

The canal segment designated AZ AA:12:790 was discovered during the testing phase of the project in Trench 94, located at the far eastern end of the project right-of-way (see Gregory et al. 1999:Figure A.5). The top of the feature was at the interface between the modern plowzone and underlying undisturbed deposits, and it had been partially truncated by the plowzone. Several trenches were excavated in the former field south of Trench 94 in an attempt to further trace the course of this canal. These efforts were largely unsuccessful, possibly due to the fact that the land surface in this area had been leveled for purposes of irrigation. The very bottom of the feature *may* have been present in two of these trenches. If the same feature is represented, it had a trajectory just slightly west of north (see below).

The canal appears to have been cut at an angle approximately perpendicular to its course. In the recorded section, it measured 70-cm wide by 42-cm deep and was parabolic in profile. The fill of the feature included four separate strata: 1) moderate-to-coarse sands showing some bedding; 2) a thin, compact clay band; 3) another unit of moderately coarse sand showing some bedding; and 4) a clayey-to-sandy silt containing occasional charcoal flecks. The first two strata probably represent materials deposited while the feature was in use, while the latter two probably represent postabandonment deposition. The origin of the charcoal flecks (cultural or natural) is unknown. Moderate iron and manganese oxide staining was present in a 3- to 4-cm zone below and roughly one-third of the way up the outer margins of the feature. This canal is cut into relatively coarse-grained sediments, and water loss due to infiltration probably would have been relatively high.

DISCUSSION

No materials suitable for dating were recovered from either of these features, and we cannot be absolutely certain about their respective ages. No records have been found of historic-period canals in these locations. Numerous Hohokam sherds were present on the surface in the vicinity of AZ AA:12:790, and a possible Hohokam pithouse (Feature 855) was recorded in the same stratigraphic position some 40 m to the east. In the absence of other data, it is reasonable to assume that both features represent Hohokam canals.

The two features are quite similar in size and configuration, and both probably represent main canals that took water directly off of the river. Both are somewhat smaller than probable Rincon phase main canals documented at the Canal site (Mabry and Holmlund 1998), but this could be a function of relative distance from the former heads.

The likely area of the former intake for AZ AA:12:789 was at the top of an eastward bend of the river approximately 3.2 km south of the point of exposure. As discussed elsewhere, it appears that this feature followed for at least some distance along a much older, buried braid of the river that continued to have effects on surface topography (Gregory and Baar 1999). Like a number of other documented Hohokam canals along the river (Mabry and Holmlund 1998), this feature essentially followed along the base of the T3 or Jaynes terrace (McKittrick 1988). As noted above, it is possible, if not probable, that this feature represents the same canal documented during an earlier project associated with gasoline pipeline construction along the west side of the Southern Pacific railroad tracks in this area (Adams and Macnider 1992a:Figure 10; Gregory 1993: Figure 9). The location of this previously documented feature would be consistent with the trajectory of the canal as projected upstream on the basis of the exposure at Los Pozos. The former intake area for AZ AA:12:790 (ASM) would have been somewhere along the top of the westward bend in the river that forms the lobe of the T2 terrace upon which Los Pozos was situated. This places the documented exposure roughly one-half to two-thirds of a kilometer from the head, and suggests that the canal was following a rather steep course away from the river.

CHAPTER 4

FLAKED STONE ARTIFACTS

R. Jane Sliva

This chapter reports on the analysis of 3,340 flaked stone artifacts from the Early Agricultural period occupation of Los Pozos (AZ AA:12:91 [ASM[). The analytical methods are the same as those employed for the Middle Archaic component (Gregory, ed. 1999). The assemblages from pithouse floors and floor pits were completely analyzed, but time constraints prevented pithouse fills from being completely sampled. At least one bag from each fill stratum was completely analyzed, except when the bags contained more than 200 artifacts; in those cases, the bag contents were scanned rather than coded. The assemblages from randomly selected extramural pits were completely analyzed. This strategy resulted in a sample being drawn from 37 of the 42 pithouses and seven of the 23 extramural pits, representing 55 percent of the recovered flaked stone artifacts. For the moment, the artifacts from the shrine in pithouse Feature 819 have been excluded from the analysis of the site assemblage. This leaves a total assemblage of 3,328 artifacts.

Local raw materials, most of which were available in the Santa Cruz River bedload and lag gravels, as well as the foothills of the nearby Tucson Mountains, dominated the assemblage. The most notable exotic materials were cherts from the Tonto Basin and an obsidian pendant from an unknown source (Shackley 1996a). Rhyolites and quartzites were the most prevalent raw materials, followed by unspecified porphyritic and aphanitic volcanic rock (Table 4.1). A wide variety of rhyolites is represented at Los Pozos, although these do not appear to have been selected by its occupants with any great regard for either the flaking or aesthetic qualities of the rock beyond a preference for medium- to fine-grained materials (Table 4.2). The most frequently occurring chert variety, which varies from grayish green to brown in color, was derived from a local, but as-yet unidentified, source. Cherts from the Santa Cruz bedload and Buff's Quarry (AZ AA:16:187 [ASM]) occurred in similar lesser quantities (Table 4.3). Only 10 of the 59 retouched implements recovered at the site were made of chert, in contrast to 17 made from rhyolite (Tables 4.4 and 4.5); other materials included fine-grained quartzite (10) and metasediment and silicified limestone (7).

Debitage accounted for 94 percent of the assemblage, which is typical for the Late Archaic. Several of the debitage attributes fall outside the range of variability expected for Late Archaic farming villages (Table 4.6), but the significance of this is debatable given the current limited scope of the database. The assemblage exceeds the Late Archaic average on attributes such as percentage of complete flakes, percentage of flakes with lipped platforms, percentage of flakes with cortical platforms, and average debitage size. The percentages of projected retouch flakes and noncortical flakes fall below the average. The large average flake size and relatively high percentage of cortical flakes and platforms are likely related to the small number of potential retouch flakes, since these flakes are both small and overwhelmingly noncortical. Similar patterns are apparent in the debitage assemblage at the Clearwater site (AZ BB:13:6 [ASM]), which also contained a low percentage of retouch flakes (Sliva 1997).

Three percent of the assemblage consisted of cores. This artifact class also bore a strong similarity to those at Clearwater, in that 39 percent of them were fragmentary (Table 4.7). Aside from the high number of fragments, the distribution of core types fit well with the average patterns in Late Archaic farming villages. Multiple platform cores were the most common type at Los Pozos, followed by single platform and bifacial cores. These represent a variety of reduction strategies, and the relatively large average size indicates the cores were not intensively reduced before being discarded. Not surprisingly, the exceptions to this are the five cores of cryptocrystalline materials, which averaged 56.39 mm in dmax at the time of discard, compared to the average dmax of 70.48 mm for the remaining cores.

Also recovered were 16 core hammers, 16 cobble hammers, and three core tools. The core tools included two choppers and a very large denticulate. The core and cobble hammers were dominated by medium- and coarse-grained materials, as expected, and the core hammers were quite large, averaging almost 25 mm more in dmax than the average for the cores at the site.

The flake implements at Los Pozos included both retouched artifacts and utilized unretouched flakes. Inferences of utilization were made very cautiously and limited to wear traces that could be observed macroscopically; the reasons for this have been discussed elsewhere (Sliva 1998a; Young and Bamforth 1990). Two of the 11 identified utilized flakes had wear traces on more than one edge, resulting in a total of 13 utilized edges (Table 4.8). The majority (nine) of these were convex or straight in plan view, and the most frequently observed wear pattern was extreme

Table 4.1. Raw material distributions.

General Material Class	Freq	Specific Material Type	Freq
Obsidian	< .01	Unknown source	< .01
		Cow Canyon	< .01
		Sauceda Mountains	< .01
		Superior	< .01
Basalt	.04	Fine-grained	.04
Rhyolite	.26	Unspecified (see Table 4.3)	< .01
		Fine-grained	.11
		Medium-grained	.15
		Coarse-grained	< .01
Unspecified porphyritic volcanic	.18	Fine-grained	.06
		Medium-grained	.12
		Coarse-grained	.01
Dacite	< .01	Fine-grained, lavender to white	< .01
Andesite	< .01	Medium-grained	< .01
Basaltic andesite	< .01	A-Mountain basalt	< .01
Unspecified aphanitic volcanic	.13	Fine-grained	.03
		Medium-grained	.11
		Coarse-grained	< .01
Unspecified volcanic or sedimentary	< .01	Extremely fine-grained	< .01
Unspecified sedimentary	.01	Fine-grained	.01
Chert	.02	Unspecified (see Table 4.2)	.02
Chalcedony	< .01	Unspecified	< .01
Jasper	< .01	Unspecified	< .01
Agate	< .01	Unspecified	< .01
Unspecified cryptocrystalline	< .01	Unspecified	< .01
Quartz	.02	Unspecified	.02
Metasediment	.06	Fine-grained	.06
		Medium-grained	< .01
Silicified limestone	.02	Fine-grained	.02
Unspecified metamorphic	.02	Fine-grained	.01
		Medium-grained	.01
Quartzite	.21	Fine-grained	.15
		Medium-grained	.06
		Coarse-grained	< .01
Schist	< .01	Unspecified	< .01
Unidentified	.01	Unknown	.01
	.01	Burned	.01

Note: Total n = 3,326.

Table 4.2. Distributions of specific rhyolite varieties.

Rhyolite Description	Freq
Medium-grained brown groundmass/white phenocrysts (Tucson Mountains)	.23
Fine-grained gray groundmass/black and white phenocrysts (Santa Cruz River)	.14
Medium-grained gray groundmass/black and white phenocrysts (Santa Cruz River)	.11
Fine-grained black groundmass/white phenocrysts (Santa Cruz River)	.08
Fine-grained black groundmass/black and white phenocrysts	.06
Fine-grained ashy gray groundmass/black and white phenocrysts (Santa Cruz River)	.05
Medium-grained black groundmass/white phenocrysts (Santa Cruz River)	.05
Medium-grained gray groundmass/white phenocrysts	.04
Medium-grained light gray-brown groundmass (Tucson Mountains)	.04
Medium-grained brown groundmass/black and white phenocrysts (Santa Cruz River)	.04
Fine-grained brown groundmass, with or without phenocrysts (Tucson Mountains)	.03
Fine-grained brown groundmass/black and white phenocrysts (Santa Cruz River)	.03
Medium-grained black groundmass/black and white phenocrysts (Santa Cruz River)	.02
Fine-grained black groundmass/white and red phenocrysts	.02
Medium-grained red groundmass/black and white phenocrysts (Santa Cruz River)	.02
Medium-grained pink groundmass/black and white phenocrysts	.02
Fine-grained red groundmass/white phenocrysts	.01
Coarse-grained brown groundmass/white phenocrysts (Tucson Mountains)	< .01
Fine-grained pink groundmass/black and white phenocrysts	< .01
Medium-grained red groundmass/white phenocrysts (Santa Cruz River)	< .01
Fine-grained red groundmass/black and white phenocrysts	< .01
Medium-grained pink-gray groundmass (Tucson Mountains)	< .01
Coarse pink groundmass/black and white phenocrysts	< .01
Fine-grained pink-gray groundmass (Tucson Mountains)	< .01
Coarse-grained pink groundmass/white phenocrysts (Tucson Mountains)	< .01
Other rhyolite	.01

Note: Total n = 857.

Table 4.3. Distributions of specific chert varieties.

Chert Description	Freq
Gray-green/brown variegated, dark green flecks (Tucson Basin)	.42
Buff's chert, from quarry site AZ AA:16:187 (ASM)	.13
Santa Cruz River bedload varieties	.09
Unspecified variety	.09
Windy Hill (Tonto Basin)	.03
White/cream/very light gray, single or variegated	.05
Similar to Buff's chert, but with a cream groundmass, some orange and brown	.04
Medium gray/light gray variegated	.04
Light gray	.01
Dark gray/brown variegated	.01
Semitranslucent cream/light gray variegated	.01

Note: Total n = 79.

Table 4.4. Frequencies of cherts among artifact classes.

	n	Santa Cruz River Bedload	Quarry Site AZ AA:16:187	Windy Hill	Unknown Source
Debitage	64	.55	.16	–	.30
Cores	3	1.00	–	–	–
Unifaces	5	.40	–	.20	.40
Bifaces	5	–	–	.20	.80
Projectile points[a]	4	–	–	.25	.75
All artifacts	79	.52	.13	.03	.33

[a]Projectile points are a subset of bifaces.

Table 4.5. Frequencies of rhyolites among artifact classes.

	n	Santa Cruz River Bedload	Tucson Mountains	Unknown Source
Debitage	801	.55	.31	.14
Cores	32	.53	.37	.09
Unifaces	11	.18	.55	.27
Bifaces	6	.50	.50	–
Projectile points[a]	3	.33	.67	–
All artifacts	857	.53	.30	.16

[a]Projectile points are a subset of bifaces.

smoothing and rounding of a lateral edge. Striations oriented parallel to the edge were visible under low magnification (< 40x), and occasionally were macroscopically visible as well. The wear on most of these extended down from the edge onto both aspects of the flake, and the edges themselves were frequently rounded or flattened. These flakes were probably used with a longitudinal (sawing/scoring) motion on very hard or abrasive materials such as stone, dried bone, antler, or shell (Jenny Adams, personal communication 1996). Two of the remaining flakes had unifacial microflaking and abrasion on the utilized edges, which may be indicative of use with a scraping motion. Even at this general level, uses were not inferred for four of the remaining edges whose wear traces were equivocal at best.

The retouched flake implements were fairly typical of Late Archaic farming villages, although more notches and projectile points were present than average, and fewer general bifaces. Unifaces accounted for 60 percent of the tool assemblage. These included notches, scrapers, denticulates, perforators, and composite tools, along with expedient unifaces and untypable fragments (Table 4.9; see Sliva 2001). Notches were the most common tool type and had a wide spatial distribution within the site. Scrapers were also prevalent, and included sidescraper, composite, and spurred varieties. The spurred forms may represent specialized tools; functional inferences will be tenuous at best in the absence of microwear analysis, but the shape of the retouched edge on these implements would make them ideally suited to bone awl manufacture. Only one of the spurred scrapers was recovered from a context that implied caching rather than secondary refuse (in a floor pit in Feature 867). Consequently, there is no direct evidence for where such manufacturing activities might have taken place. Occurring in lesser quantities were denticulates, perforators, and expedient unifaces. No patterns were observed in the spatial distributions of these implements.

Only five of the 26 bifaces recovered were not projectile points; these included a nonextensively retouched biface, a general biface, a short-bit drill, and two bifacial flake choppers. A wide range of projectile point types were recovered. The most common point type was represented by four small, corner-notched points, three of which are illustrated in Figure 4.1a-c. Their narrow necks and low neck-to-base width ratios are more suggestive of the Basketmaker Corner-notched style (Tagg 1994:101, Figure 37a-e) than the San Pedro style widespread in southern Arizona during this time period. The three complete specimens were

Table 4.6. Comparative debitage attributes (relative frequencies) for selected sites in southern Arizona.

Site (ASM)/Phase	Season/Function	n	Flake Type			Platform Type					Mean dmax, Complete Flakes (mm)	Mean dmax, All Debitage (mm)	Flake Mass Index	Reference
			Complete	Retouch[a]	Noncortical	Cortical	Plain	Faceted	Crushed	Platform Lipping				
AA:12:91/Chiricahua	Short-term/hunting	2,775	.38	.48	.86	.24	.53	.12	.12	.13	21.81	20.53	.088	Sliva 1999
BB:13:6/Chiricahua?	Short-term/hunting	1,565	.33	.48	.75	.26	.59	.05	.09	.09	25.24	22.80	.110	Sliva 1997
EE:2:102/Chiricahua	Winter-spring/hunting	692	.18	-	-	.23	.29	.05	.43	.33	-	-	-	Huckell 1984
EE:2:62/Chiricahua	Winter-spring/hunting, hide processing	1,615	.12	-	-	.08	.47	.10	.35	.55	-	-	-	Huckell 1984
All Middle Archaic period animal resource procurement camps		6,507	.29	.48	.82	.21	.50	.09	.19	.23	22.93	21.38	.096	
BB:9:127/Chiricahua	Summer-fall/general foraging	477	.35	-	.47	-	-	.13	-	.23	-	-	-	Dart 1986
EE:2:82/Chiricahua	Summer-fall/general foraging	1,385	.10	-	-	.10	.38	.05	.46	.44	-	-	-	Huckell 1984
EE:2:87/Chiricahua	Summer-fall/general foraging	312	.20	-	-	.21	.46	.05	.28	.28	-	-	-	Huckell 1984
All Middle Archaic period base camps (broad spectrum subsistence focus)		2,174	.18	-	-	.12	.40	.09	.42	.40	-	-	-	
EE:2:81/Late Archaic	Summer-fall/general foraging	17	.29	-	-	.27	.36	.36	-	.09	-	-	-	Huckell 1984
EE:2:103/Late Archaic	Summer-fall/general foraging	2,090	.20	-	-	.25	.47	.05	.22	.22	-	-	-	Huckell 1984
EE:2:86/Late Archaic	Summer-fall/general foraging	400	.21	-	-	.26	.47	.03	.24	.27	-	-	-	Huckell 1984
EE:2:128/Late Archaic	Summer-fall/general foraging	68	.13	-	-	.29	.43	.06	.22	.31	-	-	-	Huckell 1984
All Late Archaic generalized procurement camps		2,575	.20	-	-	.21	.38	.04	.18	.19	-	-	-	
AA:12:746/Cienega	Spring-fall/mixed agriculture and foraging	6,299	.34	.51	.78	.21	.61	.02	.15	.11	28.04	23.91	.364	Sliva 1998a
BB:13:425/Cienega	Spring-fall/mixed agriculture and foraging	1,608	.36	.53	.77	.22	.66	.03	.10	.08	28.79	24.48	.254	Sliva 1998a
AA:12:91/Cienega	Spring-fall/mixed agriculture and foraging	3,112	.40	.38	.73	.26	.54	.06	.12	.13	31.05	27.20	.233	Sliva 1997
BB:13:6/Cienega	Spring-fall/agriculture, limited foraging	2,329	.32	.31	.75	.25	.62	.04	.09	.10	26.25	23.96	.128	Sliva 1997
All Late Archaic period farming villages		13,348	.35	.45	.76	.23	.61	.03	.13	.11	28.64	24.75	.279	

[a] Estimated retouch flake population, calculated by totaling all bifacial thinning flakes and all flakes no more than one standard deviation greater than the average size attributes of the bifacial thinning flakes. The figure from AA:12:91 (Middle Archaic) also includes all debitage from flotation sample heavy fractions.

Table 4.7. Comparative core attributes (relative frequencies) from selected Middle and Late Archaic sites in southern Arizona.

Site (ASM)/Period	Season/Function	n	Single Platform	Opposed Platform	Bidirectional	Multiple Platform	Bifacial	Flake Core	Bipolar	Fragment	Tested Piece	Prepared	Mean dmax (mm)	Mean Weight (gm)	Reference
AA:12:91/Middle Archaic	Short-term/gearing-up	33	.09	.06	–	.06	.03	.03	–	.70	–	.06	49.47	49.09	Shackley 1986
AA:3:16/Middle Archaic	Short-term/plant procurement	14	.29	.07	NA	.50	–	–	.14	–	–	NA	NA	86.90	Sliva 1997
BB:13:6/Middle Archaic?	?/gearing up?	25	.12	–	–	.08	.04	.04	.12	.60	–	.04	47.23	56.52	
All Middle Archaic specialized resource procurement camps		72	.14	.04	–	.15	.03	.03	.07	.53	–	.04	48.50	52.29	
EE:2:103/Late Archaic	Summer-fall/general foraging	77	.14	.01	.04	.38	–	–	–	.34	.05	NA	NA	NA	Huckell 1984
AA:12:746/Late Archaic	Spring-fall/mixed agriculture and foraging	207	.27	.08	.05	.41	.08	.11	–	–	<.01	–	64.87	159.87	Sliva 1998a
BB:13:425/Late Archaic	Spring-fall/mixed agriculture and foraging	60	.25	.03	.07	.33	.17	.13	–	–	.02	–	70.80	198.87	Sliva 1998a
AA:12:91/Late Archaic	Spring-fall/mixed agriculture and foraging	113	.15	.03	.03	.22	.13	.03	.01	.39	.02	.02	69.85	203.92	Sliva 1997
BB:13:6/Late Archaic	Spring-fall/agriculture, limited foraging	18	.17	–	.06	.17	.06	.06	.06	.39	.06	.06	58.54	102.29	Sliva 1997
All Late Archaic farming villages		398	.23	.05	.05	.33	.11	.09	<.01	.43	.01	.01	66.89	175.65	

Table 4.8. Utilized flakes.

Feature	Raw Material	Dmax (mm)	Length of Utilized Edge (mm)	Utilized Edge Morphology				Inferred Function or Direction of Use		
				Concave	Straight	Convex	Concave-convex	Uncertain	Incising/ Longitudinal	Scraping/ Transverse
324.00	Medium-grained quartzite	49.53	40.82	-	-	+	-	-	+	-
416.00[a]	Metasediment	46.93	18.19	+	-	-	-	+	-	-
416.00[a]	Metasediment	46.93	33.83	-	-	-	+	+	-	-
813.00	Unspecified medium-grained aphanitic volcanic	69.45	40.65	-	+	-	-	-	-	+
817.00	Unspecified medium-grained aphanitic volcanic	70.58	26.46	-	-	+	-	-	+	-
827.01	Medium-grained quartzite	45.32	37.56	-	+	-	-	-	+	-
861.00	Unspecified medium-grained aphanitic volcanic	66.30	38.95	+	-	-	-	+	-	-
861.00[a]	Medium-grained rhyolite	64.72	67.62	-	-	+	-	-	+	-
861.00[a]	Medium-grained rhyolite	64.72	46.32	-	-	-	+	-	+	-
866.00	Medium-grained quartzite	53.56	14.24	-	+	-	-	+	-	-
867.00	Medium-grained quartzite	62.80	44.06	-	-	+	-	-	-	+
867.00	Fine-grained porphyritic volcanic	63.61	39.75	-	+	-	-	-	+	-
870.00	Medium-grained quartzite	43.56	26.70	-	-	+	-	-	+	-
Average or total		57.85	36.55	2	4	5	2	4	7	2

[a]Indicates single artifact with multiple utilized edges.

made of cherts that appear to have been acquired from sources in the Tonto Basin, including one from the Windy Hill source. The other was manufactured from Cow Canyon obsidian. The obsidian point was steeply reworked along the lateral edges, while the Windy Hill point (Figure 4.1a) had a crudely reworked tip. One large point, made of locally available silicified limestone (Figure 4.1d), has affinities to both San Pedro and wide, side-notched Basketmaker styles (Tagg 1994:101, Figure 37f). This specimen bears wear traces in the form of edge rounding along most of its edges, particularly near the distal tip. This indicates it saw heavy use as a cutting tool.

Three complete and three fragmentary Cienega points were recovered. The three complete or nearly complete specimens were identified as belonging to the Cienega Flared subtype (Figure 4.1e-g; see discussion below). One of the distal fragments may also be Cienega Flared. The other two fragments were not diagnostic of any particular subtype. All the Cienega examples were manufactured from fine-grained materials, although only one was made from chert. Another point is a fragmentary Elko Eared (Figure 4.1h). This specimen is a basal fragment, reworked with scraper retouch along the transverse snap across its blade. Two others are San Pedro (Figure 4.1i-j). One of these (Figure 4.1j) has an impact fracture at its tip and what appear to be wear traces along one blade edge. The final illustrated point is fragmentary and has a deeply serrated blade (Figure 4.1k); this is likely a variant of the San Pedro style. Additional artifacts included the medial fragment of what probably is an Early Archaic point, a Pinto base, and the distal fragment of a large, unidentifiable Archaic point.

Table 4.9. Retouched flake implements (excluding Feature 819.17).

Implement Type	Freq
Sidescrapers	.04
Composite scrapers	.03
Spurred scrapers	.06
Denticulates	.03
Triangular perforators	.03
Large flake perforators	.01
Notches	.16
Composite tools	.04
Expediently retouched unifaces	.09
Untypable uniface fragments	.10
Nonextensively retouched biface	.01
General bifaces	.01
Bifacial flake choppers	.03
Short-bit drills	.01
Projectile point preforms	.01
Untypable Archaic point fragments	.06
Untypable Early Archaic point fragments	.01
Pinto points	.01
Probable San Pedro point	.01
San Pedro or Basketmaker points	.07
San Pedro point	.03
Untypable Cienega point fragments	.03
Unspecified Cienega points	.01
Cienega Flared points	.04
Elko Eared point fragment	.01

Note: Total n = 69.

A shrine on the floor of pithouse feature 819, discussed in detail in Appendix B, contained 17 flaked stone artifacts, 13 of which were projectile points. The non-point artifacts included two unaltered flakes, one utilized flake, one Apache tear, and one curious side-notched biface with heavy use wear traces on each end. Five of the points were Cienega Long styles of varying sizes, ranging from 23.71 to 68.8 mm in length. Three were San Pedro; the blade of one of which appears to have been extensively reworked. One was an Elko Corner-notched. The identification of the remaining three very large points, none of which were manufactured from locally available materials, is more equivocal. One is reminiscent of two Archaic styles from Texas: Andice points, which date to the Early and Middle Archaic in east-central Texas (Turner and Hester 1987:64-67), and Shumla, which date to the Late Archaic in the lower Pecos and Big Bend region (Turner and Hester 1987:151). Shumla may be a more accurate identification, as it is noted in Turner and Hester that such points are usually made from chert that has been heat treated. This results in the artifacts having a pinkish cast and a vitreous sheen–attributes possessed by the point from the shrine. Another point has affinities to the San Pedro and Basketmaker corner-notched styles although, at 97.94 mm in length, it far exceeds the range of metrical variability associated with these points (Tagg 1994:Tables 7 and 8). The remaining point is extremely large (130.36 mm in length), with a triangular blade, deep corner notches, and an expanding, convex-based stem. It also appears to have been manufactured from heat-treated chert.

DISCUSSION

Settlement Type and Occupation Length

Long-term occupations of residential bases, encompassing a wide range of procurement and processing activities, are expected to produce assemblages with the following characteristics: 1) evidence of primary artifact manufacture (core reduction flakes, shatter, high proportion of utilized flake tools); 2) high proportions of exhausted cores and tools; and 3) high raw material diversity. Fabricating tools such as hammers and flakers are more likely to be discarded at this type of site than at others. Additionally, longer occupations are associated with a greater representation of wood, bone, and antler tools; the flaked stone implements used to fabricate these tools include gravers, drills, concave scrapers, and very sharp cutting tools (Shackley 1986:154). The Los Pozos flaked stone assemblage meets these three criteria, and the high number of notches and spurred scrapers may represent specialized tools for the manufacture of these other classes of artifacts.

Analysis of the assemblages from Desert Archaeology's excavations at the Early Agricultural Santa Cruz Bend and Stone Pipe sites revealed that a more complex lithic technology was in place than has traditionally been assumed for post-Archaic populations. Contrary to the usual expectations for an increasing reliance on expedient technology with increasing sedentism and reliance on agriculture (Allen 1985; Greenwald 1988a; Huckell 1981; Lancaster 1993:234; Parry and Kelly 1986), it was demonstrated that: 1) no direct relationship existed between subsistence/mobility and the proportions of expedient tools present at sites in the Tucson Basin; 2) the Santa Cruz Bend and Stone Pipe populations both manufactured high numbers of formal tools and incorporated lithic curation and reclamation behaviors into their technological repertoire; and 3) these reclamation behaviors are reflected in artifact size, which in turn can be used as the basis for inferring the nature of floor and pit deposits as de facto or secondary refuse (Sliva 1995, 1998a).

The Los Pozos assemblage reflects different abandonment behaviors than were present at the Santa Cruz

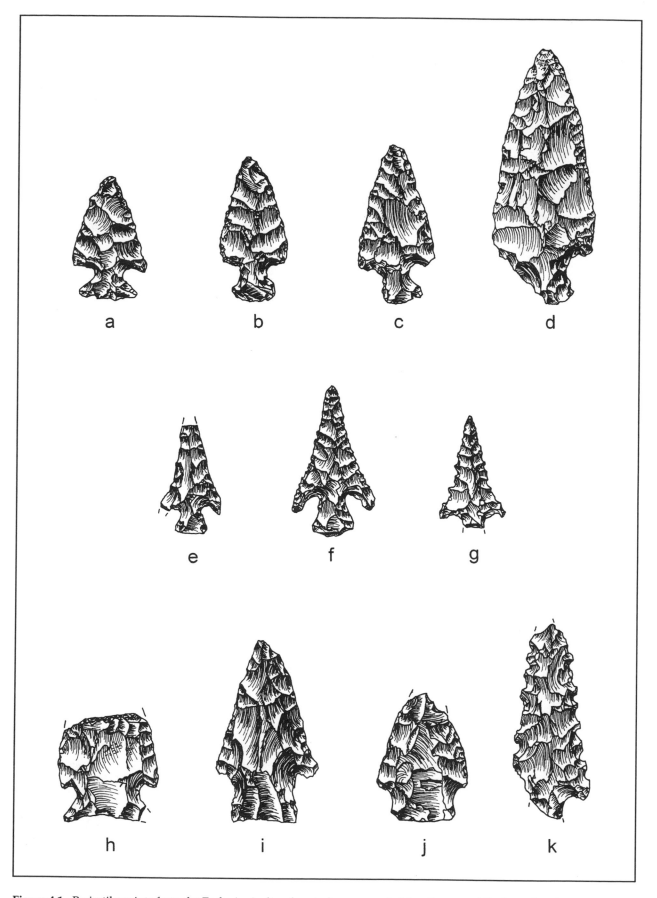

Figure 4.1. Projectile points from the Early Agricultural period component at Los Pozos: a-c) Basketmaker Corner-notched; d) San Pedro; e-g) Cienega Flared; h) Elko Eared; i-j) San Pedro; k) probable San Pedro.

Table 4.10. Average artifact dmax (mm) according to context in structures with possible de facto floor or floor pit assemblages. (Non-de facto floor pits not included.)

Feature	House Fill		Structural Collapse		Floor Contact		Floor Pit		Total
	No	Mean dmax	No	Mean dmax	No	Mean dmax	No	Mean dmax	No
324	79	31.74	–	–	1	97.33	54	27.50	134
354	126	26.76	–	–	4	65.54	23	40.75	153
355	73	31.40	–	–	3	47.28	3	56.90	79
416	–	–	61	34.05	8	59.87	–	–	69
866	93	27.31	–	–	1	101.16	1	48.21	95
867	75	38.15	–	–	1	63.61	56	36.70	132

Bend and Stone Pipe sites, where roughly one-third of the pithouses were inferred to contain de facto floor deposits. Floor assemblages at Los Pozos were rare, and those that were encountered had very small sample sizes. As a result, only one structure–Feature 416–was considered to have a de facto floor assemblage. Four others (Features 324, 354, 355, and 866) had large artifacts on their floors and in floor pits, but did not meet the sample size required by the model used here for inferring de facto deposits (Table 4.10; Sliva 1995). A floor pit within Feature 867 may have contained cached materials; its assemblage was composed of a sidescraper, a spurred scraper, the large San Pedro point that had been used as a knife, three cores, and a hammerstone, along with several small pieces of debitage.

These five floor pits are the only ones at Los Pozos to exhibit any evidence of caching behavior, which is a further departure from the patterns at Santa Cruz Bend and Stone Pipe. At those sites, cores were stored on floors and in floor pits, and occurred with the greatest frequency in these two contexts as well. Evidence from Los Pozos is more equivocal, partly due to the lack of robust floor assemblages. Here, cores were recovered in the greatest quantities from house fill, but floor pits were a close second. The pits, and particularly the pit bottoms, contained the largest cores. Extramural pits contained the second largest cores, but had an insufficient sample for making inferences about caching. Cores recovered from floors fell in the middle of the size distributions. Core hammer distributions mimicked those of the cores, with the greatest quantity and largest artifacts located on floors and, especially, in floor pits. Floor pits yielded the greatest quantities of cobble hammers as well. Because of the limited samples from floors and extramural pits, inferences should be limited to the probable use of floor pits for the caching of these large artifacts.

A possible relationship is indicated between Features 389 and 390, located adjacent to one another in the southern half of the site, by the presence of similar Basketmaker Corner-notched points–one on the floor of

Feature 389 and one in a floor pit within Feature 390. Both points were made of probable Tonto Basin cherts, one of which appears to be from the Windy Point source. The other Windy Point artifact, a composite scraper, was recovered from the fill of Feature 819, located three houses to the north of Feature 389. Feature 354, in the northern half of the site, contained the other two probable Basketmaker Corner-notched points, one on the floor and one in a pit. Feature 867, which intrudes/is intruded by Feature 354, contained the other possible Basketmaker point–the large, wide, side-notched specimen with heavy wear traces–in a floor pit.

Flaked Stone Technology and the Archaic Period: The View from Los Pozos

The presence of two temporal components at Los Pozos provides ample data for Middle Archaic-Late Archaic comparisons. This has proven valuable in increasing our understanding of the latter part of the Archaic period and how changes in lithic technology mirrored changes in time, economy, and perhaps, ethnicity. Available comparative data from Middle and Late Archaic sites in southern Arizona are presented for various artifact and assemblage attributes in Tables 4.6-4.7 and 4.11-4.12. In each, sites are grouped according to time period and subsistence economy. While more data need to be collected, the preliminary conclusions drawn here indicate that, despite the presence of temporally related artifact attributes, subsistence economy is the strongest predictor of flaked stone assemblage composition.

Differences in raw material distributions between the two time periods at Los Pozos were primarily limited to the sources of high-quality stone. The four most prevalent raw materials account for 61 percent of the assemblage in the Middle Archaic, and 78 percent in the Late Archaic. The same four general raw material categories (rhyolites, quartzites, unspecified porphyritic volcanics, and unspecified aphanitic volcanic) are

Table 4.11. Comparative distributions (relative frequencies) of retouched flake implements from Middle Archaic through Early Ceramic period sites in southern Arizona.

Site (ASM)/Phase	Season/Function	n Unifaces, Bifaces[b]	Expedient Unifaces	Scrapers	Denticulates	Perforators	Notches	Composite Tools	Uniface Fragments	General Bifaces	Other Bifaces	Drills	Projectile Point Preforms	Projectile Points	Reference
AA:12:91/Chiricahua	Short-term/hunting or gearing-up	25/34[c]	.12	.08	-	.05	.05	.03	.06	.22	.05	-	-	.31	Sliva 1997
BB:13:6/Chiricahua	Short-term/gearing up	9/13	.09	.23	-	.05	.05	-	-	.27	.32	-	-	-	
EE:2:102/Chiricahua	Winter-spring/hunting	55/93	.12	.14	.01	.01	-	.03	.04	.15	.08	.01	.16	.24	Huckell 1984
EE:2:62/Chiricahua	Winter-spring/hunting, hide processing	146/90	.06	.37	<.01	.04	.02	<.01	.12	.10	.03	.01	.05	.19	Huckell 1984
All Middle Archaic period hunting camps (specialized resource procurement)		228/237	.09	.25	<.01	.03	.02	.02	.08	.14	.06	.01	.08	.21	
AA:8:194/Chiricahua	Summer-fall/general foraging	45/46	.16	.23	-	-	.10	NA	NA	.35	NA	-	NA	.15	Shackley 1986
EE:2:82/Chiricahua	Summer-fall/general foraging	99/74	.14	.26	.03	.05	.01	.01	.06	.07	.04	-	.17	.15	Huckell 1984
EE:2:87/Chiricahua	Summer-fall/general foraging	23/13	.14	.31	.03	.08	.03	NA	.08	.03	.03	-	.06	.25	Huckell 1984
BB:9:127/Chiricahua	Summer-fall/general foraging	59/18	.19	.30	.22	.01	.04	NA	NA	.10	.06	-	NA	.06	Dart 1986
All Middle Archaic period base camps (generalized resource procurement)		211/166	.16	.27	.06	.03	.04	NA	NA	.14	.03	-	NA	.14	
U:3:286/Cienega	Short-term/hunting/gearing up	38/51	.09	.13	.05	.03	.03	.01	.08	.13	.02	.02	.15	.24	Sliva 2000
EE:2:81/Cienega	Short-term/task-specific	10/11	.10	.29	-	.05	.05	NA	-	.14	.05	-	.14	.19	Huckell 1984
AA:6:19/Cienega	Spring-summer/plant resource processing	0/27	-	-	-	-	-	-	-	.52	-	-	-	.48	Lancaster 1993
BB:9:127/Cienega/Agua Caliente	Spring-fall/plant procurement	92/17	.12	.38	.27	.01	.06	NA	NA	.05	.10	-	NA	.02	Dart 1986
All Late Archaic period specialized resource procurement camps		139/139	.08	.22	.12	.02	.04	<.01	.03	.14	.05	.01	.06	.24	
AA:8:133/Late Archaic	Summer-fall/general foraging	26/10	.22	.28	-	.11	.11	NA	NA	.14	NA	-	NA	.14	Roth 1995b
AA:8:166/Late Archaic	Summer-fall/general foraging	28/12	.12	.15	-	-	.02	NA	NA	.45	NA	-	NA	.25	Roth 1995b
AA:12:84/Late Archaic	Spring-fall/general foraging	52/32	.35	.24	-	.02	.01	NA	NA	.23	NA	-	NA	.15	Roth 1995a
EE:2:86/Late Archaic	Summer-fall/general foraging	37/11	.08	.44	.08	-	.06	.02	.08	.08	.04	-	.04	.06	Huckell 1984
EE:2:103/Late Archaic	Summer-fall/general foraging	114/49	.18	.35	.01	.02	.08	NA	.07	.09	.06	-	.06	.09	Huckell 1984
EE:2:128/Late Archaic	Summer-fall/general foraging	11/8	.26	.21	-	.05	-	NA	.05	.11	.05	-	.11	.16	Huckell 1984
All Late Archaic period generalized procurement camps		253/136	.21	.30	.01	.03	.06	NA	.07	.16	.06	-	.06	.13	

Table 4.11. Continued.

Site (ASM)/Phase	Season/Function	n Unifaces, Bifaces[b]	Expedient Unifaces	Scrapers	Denticulates	Perforators	Notches	Composite Tools	Uniface Fragments	General Bifaces	Other Bifaces	Drills	Projectile Point Preforms	Projectile Points	Reference
BB:10:46/San Pedro	All year?/mixed agriculture and foraging	10/23	.12	.18	-	-	-	-	-	.45	-	-	-	.24	Huckell et al. 1995
AA:12:746/Cienega	Spring-fall/mixed agriculture and foraging	88/42	.19	.22	.04	.03	.04	.07	.09	.03	.13	-	.01	.13	Sliva 1998a
BB:13:425[a]/Cienega	Spring-fall/mixed agriculture and foraging	23/15	.11	.29	.03	.03	-	-	.16	.05	-	-	.03	.32	Sliva 1998a[a]
AA:12:91/Cienega	Spring-fall/mixed agriculture and foraging	42/27	.09	.13	.05	.05	.16	.05	.10	.02	.05	.02	.02	.30	
AA:12:90, L 2/Cienega	Spring-fall/mixed agriculture and foraging	18/32[d]	.08	.06	-	.06	.12	.02	-	.24	.04	-	-	.36	Sliva 1998b
BB:13:6/Cienega	Spring-fall/agriculture, limited foraging	10/23[c]	.06	.09	.03	.06	-	-	.03	.15	-	-	-	.55	Sliva 1997
EE:2:30/Cienega	All year?/mixed agriculture and foraging	117/126	.08	.17	.03	.06	.06	NA	.08	.18	.14	<.01	-	.19	Huckell 1995
EE:2:137/Cienega	All year?/mixed agriculture and foraging	20/17	.05	.27	-	.05	.11	NA	.05	.24	.08	-	-	.14	Huckell 1995
All Late Archaic period farming villages		308/320	.11	.18	.03	.04	.06	.02	.08	.15	.10	<.01	<.01	.23	
AA:12:745/Agua Caliente	All year/mixed agriculture and foraging	9/4	.38	.07	.08	.07	-	-	.08	-	-	-	.15	.07	Sliva 1998a
BB:13:398/Agua Caliente	All year/mixed agriculture and foraging	77/42	.24	.29	-	.03	.08	NA	NA	.11	.12	-	-	NA	Huckell 1996a
BB:13:425/Agua Caliente	All year/mixed agriculture and foraging	6/2	.25	.37	-	-	-	-	.13	.12	.13	-	-	-	Sliva 1998a
All Early Ceramic period farming villages		99/41	.25	.28	.01	.03	.06	-	.01	.10	.11	-	.01	.01	

[a] At least one projectile point from this site was used as a drill.
[b] NA = Unreported data.
[c] Includes one backed flake and one bifacial microdenticulate (each .02 of flake tool assemblage).
[d] Includes one acutely, invasively retouched uniface (chopper/knife?).
[e] Includes two backed flakes (.04 of flake tool assemblage).

Table 4.12. Relative frequencies of expedient unifaces, formal unifaces, and bifaces from selected pre-Hohokam sites in southern Arizona (nondiagnostic fragmentary unifaces not included).

Site (ASM)	Phase	Season/Function	n	Expedient Unifaces	Formal Unifaces	Bifaces	Reference
AA:12:91	Chiricahua	Short-term/hunting?	56	.12	.27	.61	
BB:13:6	Possible Chiricahua	Short-term/hunting?	22	.09	.32	.59	Sliva 1997
EE:2:102	Chiricahua	Winter-spring/hunting	139	.15	.19	.65	Huckell 1984
EE:2:62	Chiricahua	Winter-spring/hunting, hide processing	206	.07	.50	.44	Huckell 1984
All Middle Archaic period hunting camps (specialized resource procurement)			423	.10	.36	.54	
AA:8:194	Chiricahua	Summer-fall/general foraging	91	.16	.33	.50	
EE:2:82	Chiricahua	Summer-fall/general foraging	157	.15	.37	.48	Huckell 1984
EE:2:87	Chiricahua	Summer-fall/general foraging	32	.16	.44	.41	Huckell 1984
BB:9:127	Chiricahua	Summer-fall/general foraging	77	.19	.57	.23	Dart 1986
All Middle Archaic period base camps (generalized resource procurement)			357	.17	.41	.43	
U:3:286	Cienega	Short-term/hunting/gearing up?	82	.10	.28	.62	Sliva 2000
EE:2:81	?	Short-term/task-specific	21	.10	.38	.52	Huckell 1984
AA:6:18	Cienega?	Spring-fall/?	32	–	.03	.97	Lancaster 1993
AA:6:19	Cienega?	Biseasonal/plant procurement	27	–	–	1.00	Lancaster 1993
BB:9:127	Cienega/Agua Caliente	Spring-fall/plant procurement	109	.12	.72	.16	Dart 1986
All Late Archaic period specialized procurement camps			271	.08	.41	.51	
EE:2:86	?	Summer-fall/general foraging	44	.09	.66	.25	Huckell 1984
EE:2:103	?	Summer-fall/general foraging	150	.19	.48	.33	Huckell 1984
EE:2:128	?	Summer-fall/general foraging	18	.28	.28	.44	Huckell 1984
AA:8:133	?	Summer-fall/general foraging	36	.22	.50	.28	Roth 1995b
AA:8:166	San Pedro (?)	Summer-fall/general foraging	40	.12	.18	.70	Roth 1995b
AA:12:84	Cienega (?)	Spring-fall/general foraging	84	.35	.27	.38	Roth 1995a
All Late Archaic period generalized procurement camps			373	.21	.42	.37	
BB:10:46	San Pedro	All year?/mixed agriculture, foraging	33	.12	.16	.89	Huckell et al. 1995
AA:12:746	Cienega	Spring-fall/mixed agriculture, foraging	118	.21	.44	.35	Sliva 1998a
BB:13:425	Cienega	Spring-fall/mixed agriculture, foraging	32	.12	.41	.47	Sliva 1998a
AA:12:91	Cienega	Spring-fall/mixed agriculture, foraging?	62	.10	.42	.44	
AA:12:90, L 2	Cienega	Spring-fall/mixed agriculture, foraging?	50	.08	.28	.64	Sliva 1998b
BB:13:6	Cienega	Spring-fall/agriculture, limited foraging	32	.06	.22	.72	Sliva 1997
EE:2:30	Cienega	All year?/mixed agriculture, foraging	223	.09	.35	.57	Huckell 1995
EE:2:137	Cienega	All year?/mixed agriculture, foraging	35	.06	.46	.49	Huckell 1995
All Late Archaic period farming villages			590	.11	.36	.52	
AA:12:745	Agua Caliente	All year/mixed agriculture, foraging	12	.42	.25	.33	Sliva 1998a
BB:13:398	Agua Caliente	All year/mixed agriculture, foraging	117	.24	.40	.36	Huckell 1996a
BB:13:425	Agua Caliente	All year/mixed agriculture, foraging	7	.29	.43	.29	Sliva 1998a
All Early Ceramic period farming villages			136	.26	.39	.35	

involved, but in different proportions. The greatest difference is that rhyolites and quartzites combine for 47 percent of the assemblage in the Late Archaic, but only 23 percent in the Middle Archaic. Among the rhyolites, the distributions of specific types are quite similar between the two time periods–both in terms of sources and the four most prevalent specific types– although differences do exist in the distributions of the less-frequently occurring types. The chert type distributions were quite different. In the Middle Archaic, only 18 percent of the chert was identified as having come from local sources, in contrast to 65 percent in the Late Archaic. This is in accordance with expectations that more exotic materials will be represented in Middle Archaic than Late Archaic assemblages.

Comparative debitage data from selected Middle and Late Archaic sites in southern Arizona are presented in Table 4.6, with sites grouped according to inferred subsistence function. The overall debitage data exhibit little variation between the Middle and Late Archaic, suggesting that few substantive technological differences existed between the two time periods. The most noticeable dichotomy appears in projected retouch flakes in the Late Archaic. More than half the debitage from the Santa Cruz Bend and Stone Pipe sites falls within the metrical range of retouch flakes. This strongly contrasts with the A-Mountain and Los Pozos sites, where roughly one-third of the debitage appears to have been produced during tool manufacture. The greatest difference between Middle and Late Archaic debitage is that Late Archaic debitage tends to have a slightly higher average dmax.

Unfortunately, there are no directly comparable size data from several non-Desert Archaeology Middle Archaic and non-agricultural Late Archaic assemblages, although the general pattern of smaller debitage in the earlier time period is reflected at the Rosemont sites as well (Huckell 1984). This is seen in the differences between core assemblages from the two time periods. Cores are substantially smaller in the Middle than Late Archaic, and they are dominated by fragments. Aside from the fragments, single platform cores dominate the Middle Archaic assemblages, while multiple platform cores are more prevalent in the Late Archaic. Bipolar cores are more strongly associated with the Middle than Late Archaic, and bidirectional cores occur exclusively in the Late Archaic. This means that cores were reduced more intensively, with more planned reduction episodes in the Middle Archaic. These are likely functions of overall higher raw material quality in that time period.

Very low numbers of utilized flakes were identified at each component, representing .2 percent of the Middle Archaic assemblage and .3 percent of the Late Archaic. Compared to the numbers of retouched flake implements, they occurred at rates of 10 percent of the number of Middle Archaic tools and 19 percent of the number of Late Archaic tools. The utilized flakes are interesting for a couple of reasons. First, they provide examples of the morphological attributes that were considered desirable by the prehistoric tool user, which in turn can be used for the de facto model. Second, they provide insight into a possible craft specialization, which has implications for the whole notion of "expedient" tools. The relatively greater number of Late Archaic utilized flakes may be due to a Late Archaic activity that was either not practiced or not emphasized in the Middle Archaic. An example would be working very hard or abrasive materials with a longitudinal motion (scoring stone, bone, antler, or shell, possibly for jewelry manufacture). This task would best be accomplished with an unretouched flake with a long, straight (as opposed to sinuous) edge.

This corresponds with the most common edge morphology and use-wear patterns of identified utilized flakes in the Los Pozos Late Archaic assemblage. That these flakes may have functioned as specialized tools is supported by the presence of flakes that appear to have resulted from resharpening flakes with extremely abraded and rounded edges. These retouch flakes are morphologically very similar to bifacial thinning flakes, but their platforms and much of their proximal edges are heavily worn and rounded, indicating they were struck from the edges of these utilized flakes. This indicates that curation/reclamation behaviors were aimed at implements that otherwise represent the most expedient level of lithic technology.

Implement curation must be addressed from a different angle than at the Santa Cruz Bend and Stone Pipe sites due to the absence of floor assemblages at Los Pozos. While the few unifaces from floor or pit contexts were large (average dmax = 45.31 mm), those from fill contexts were even larger on average (55.78 mm). However, the small sample size of the tool assemblage from non-fill contexts precludes meaningful inferences about tool curation behaviors based on relative artifact size. Still, evidence of tool curation behaviors is present in the form the flakes produced when the utilized flakes were retouched. At least two projectile points were reclaimed for other functions, including the large San Pedro, used as a knife, and the Elko Eared fragment, retouched and used as a scraper.

Ultimately, the only substantive differences between Middle and Late Archaic flaked stone technologies are related to raw material choices and reductive intensity. The lack of gross differences in debitage assemblages from the two time periods indicates that the basic reductive technologies employed changed very little, if at all, from the earlier time period to the later. In the Middle Archaic, higher quality raw materials predominated. These tended to be reduced more intensively than the lower grade raw materials that

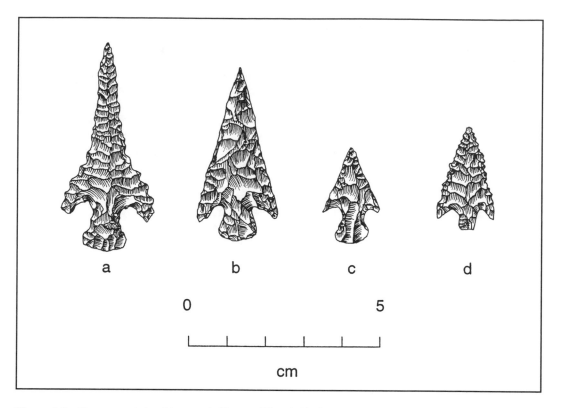

Figure 4.2. Cienega point subtypes: a) Cienega Flared; b) Cienega Long; c) Cienega Short; d) Cienega Stemmed.

formed the bulk of the Late Archaic assemblages. This resulted in the production of smaller flake blanks, and thus, smaller tools. The slightly higher incidence of pressure flaking in the Middle Archaic is again likely related to raw material factors. The relatively coarser materials used by Late Archaic knappers would not have responded well enough to pressure flaking to make the technique an efficient reduction strategy.

Throughout the Middle and Late Archaic, tool assemblage composition seems to be directly related to subsistence focus, rather than to temporal variability (Table 4.11). Specialized resource procurement camps–particularly hunting camps–are marked by low proportions of expedient unifaces and high proportions of bifaces, with the most common tool types being projectile points and scrapers. Generalized resource procurement camps produced higher proportions of expedient unifaces and more even distributions of formal unifaces and bifaces. Scrapers are the most common tool type in these assemblages; expedient unifaces are the second most common. Curiously, the assemblages from farming villages of the Late Archaic and Early Ceramic periods differ greatly from one another along the lines of this dichotomy, with the Late Archaic farming assemblages very similar to those produced by the specialized camps. The Early Ceramic assemblages are more anomalous, rather than fitting

neatly into this differentiation, but are the most similar to those of the generalized procurement camps. The proportions of expedient unifaces, formal unifaces, and bifaces in the Late Archaic tool assemblage at Los Pozos generally correspond to the pattern expected for Late Archaic farming villages, although more formal unifaces and fewer bifaces than average are represented (Table 4.12). The assemblage is distinguished from others in the region by the high number of notches and low number of non-projectile point bifaces. However, the distributions of other tools, particularly scrapers and projectile points, are typical of Late Archaic farming villages.

The projectile points in the assemblage suggest that Los Pozos should be placed chronologically in the middle of the Cienega phase. Three, and possibly four, distinctive subtypes are encompassed by the general definition of Cienega points as those with triangular blades, corner notching, and expanding, convex based stems (Figure 4.2). Cienega Flared points have concave, often serrated, blade margins that taper towards the tip (Figure 4.2a). While points of this style are typically quite large, with lengths that may exceed 60 mm, it is edge shape rather than size that is the primary criterion for inclusion in the subtype. Cienega Long points have straight blade margins, with long tangs and a relatively short expanding base (Figure 4.2b). Cienega Short

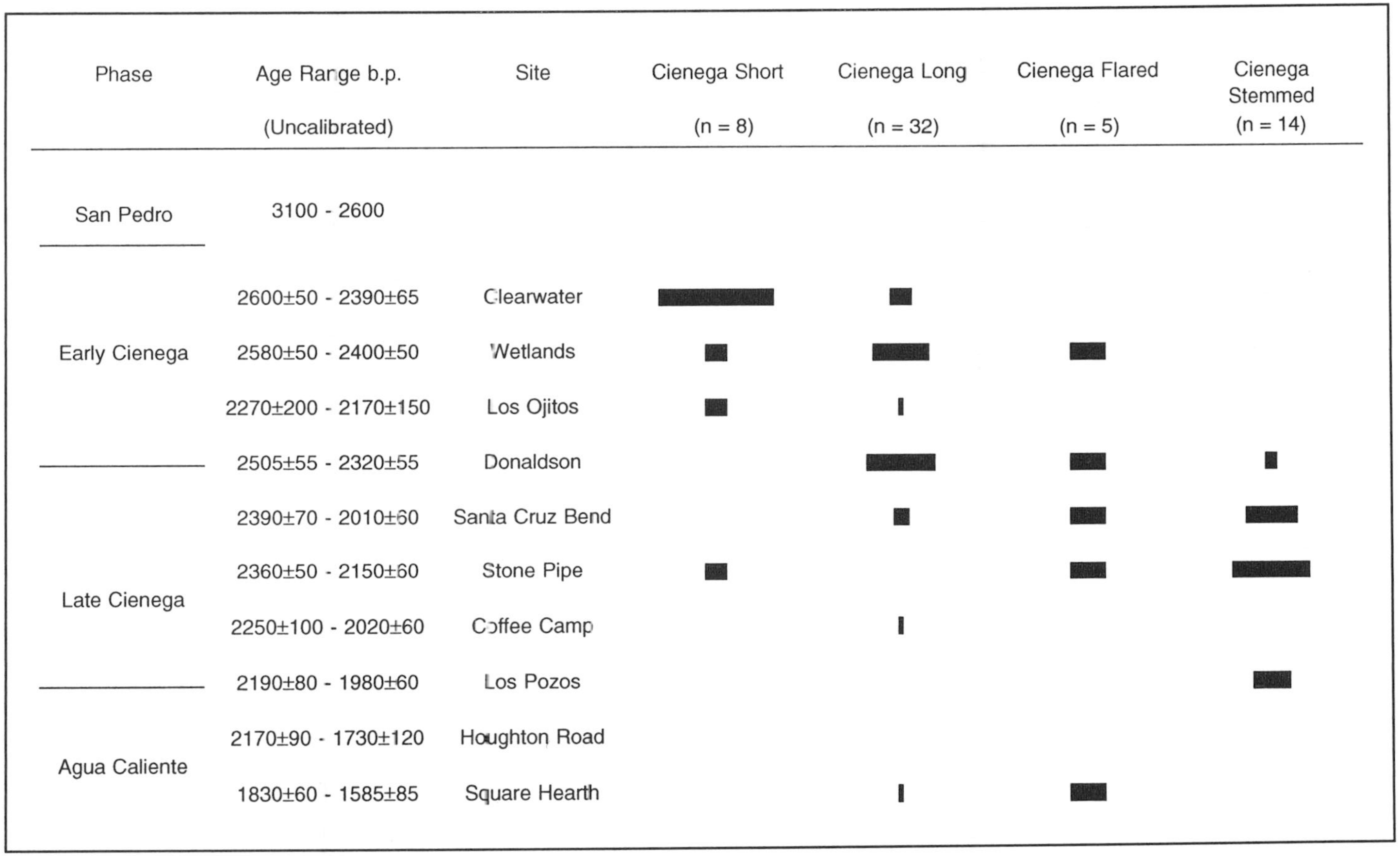

Figure 4.3. Temporal distribution of Cienega point subtypes from dated contexts in southern Arizona.

includes those points with short, straight-edged blades, short tangs, and relatively long expanding bases (Figure 4.2c). A fourth subtype, Cienega Stemmed, is differentiated from the others by its straight or contracting stem (Figure 4.2d). The distributions of the different Cienega styles at Late Archaic sites in southern Arizona (Figure 4.3) strongly suggest the Cienega Flared style is associated with the earlier portion of the Cienega phase (800-400 B.C.) and the Cienega Short style with the latter portion (400 B.C.-A.D. 150). Cienega Long is present throughout the Cienega phase, but tends to decrease in size over time. While the three Cienega points at Los Pozos are all of the Cienega Flared style, they are relatively small. This, in combination with the absence of Cienega Short points, places the site chronologically between Santa Cruz Bend/ Stone Pipe and the Wetlands (Freeman 1998) and A-Mountain sites, or on the cusp of the proposed division between the early and late Cienega phases (see Chapter 11, this volume).

The non-Cienega points at Los Pozos distinguish the site from other Late Archaic sites in the Tucson Basin, with the small number of Elko and, more interestingly, the large number of points that appear to be Basketmaker in origin. Additionally, the three small, corner-notched points appear to have been made of cherts from east-central Arizona; one from the fill of Feature 389 is Windy Hill chert, and the other two strongly resemble other varieties from the Tonto Basin. While Elko points occur frequently in Archaic sites in southern Arizona (e.g., Haury 1950; Huckell 1984; Shackley 1996a), the three from Los Pozos are a relatively rare occurrence in the Tucson Basin.

This has proven valuable in expanding the understanding of the latter part of the Archaic Period and how changes in lithic technology mirrored changes in time, economy, and perhaps ethnicity. Perhaps the most important lesson to be drawn from this is that, traditional expectations to the contrary, settled agriculture and expediency do not always go hand in hand.

CHAPTER 5

THE GROUND
STONE ASSEMBLAGE

Jenny L. Adams

INTRODUCTION

With the assemblage of ground stone artifacts from the site of Los Pozos (AZ AA:12:91 [ASM]), there is the opportunity to expand our understanding of grinding technology during an important timespan. The Early Agricultural to Early Ceramic time period along the Middle Santa Cruz River valley has become well-known through excavations at the Santa Cruz Bend (AZ AA:12:746 [ASM]), Square Hearth (AZ AA:12:745 [ASM]), and Stone Pipe sites (AZ BB:13:425 [ASM]) (collectively referred to as the other Santa Cruz settlements) (Mabry, ed. 1998). Los Pozos is 2.4-4.8 km north of these sites and has proveniences that date between about 1800 and 2300 B.P. Generally, this is later than the Cienega features at the Santa Cruz Bend and Stone Pipe sites and earlier than the Agua Caliente features at the Stone Pipe and Square Hearth sites.

The questions asked of the ground stone assemblage from Los Pozos are derived from the analysis of the assemblages from the other Santa Cruz settlements (Adams 1998). Do the food and pigment processing strategies recognized during the Cienega occupation at the Santa Cruz Bend site also occur at Los Pozos? Is there less of an emphasis on pigment processing, as during the Agua Caliente occupation at Stone Pipe and Square Hearth? Is there any difference in the design of manos and metates, or are they the same as at the other Santa Cruz settlements? Are there more metates recovered, or does the abandonment strategy recognized at the other Santa Cruz settlements also occur at Los Pozos? Are interior pits used to store ground stone artifacts in the same way at Los Pozos? Is grinding technology, in general, used differently at Los Pozos? Is there more or less secondary use of artifacts? All of these questions will be assessed through a technological analysis of the recovered ground stone artifacts from Los Pozos.

The technological approach used in this analysis, and in that of the other Santa Cruz assemblages, incorporates not only typological description, but also an analysis of how an artifact was used, reused, redesigned, or recycled, and its archaeological context. Through such an analysis, it is possible to track the "life history" of an artifact (J. Adams 1994, 1995b; Schiffer 1987; Schlanger 1990). The life history concept as a framework for ground stone analysis (J. Adams 1994,

1995b) makes it possible to discuss the technological aspects of artifact variation without confusing morphological attributes resulting from artifact design with those resulting from artifact use. The ways in which tools were manufactured and used leave distinctive morphological attributes that, when viewed macroscopically, reflect motor habits (Adams 1993b; Bartlett 1933; Morris 1990) and, when viewed microscopically, reflect the damage created by use wear (J. Adams 1988, 1989a, 1989b, 1993a; Flenniken and Ozbun 1988; Mills 1993).

Questions asked within the life history framework explore the possibility of tools having morphological differences because they are the same tool type, at different stages in their respective life histories. Alternatively is the possibility that differences are related to specific design requirements. Once life history factors are accounted for, it is possible to discuss technological traditions as being specific to cultural groups. The term "technology" encompasses not only the tools, but also the knowledge and behaviors associated with their manufacture and use (J. Adams 1993b, 1994, 1995a; Kingery 1989; Lemonnier 1986; Schiffer 1992; Schiffer and Skibo 1987). In this broad sense, ground stone morphology can be linked to technological traditions associated with specific patterns of social and economic organization (J. Adams 1994). For example, in the literature about the Southwestern Archaic, a distinction is commonly made between metate configurations, variously called slab, block, flat, shallow basin, or deep basin, which have been used to infer chronological or evolutionary developments, cultural or ethnic differences, or differences in the resources processed. However, as was discovered at the Santa Cruz Bend site, these inferences are weak if based on morphology alone, if assessed without concern for the context in which they were found, and/or if the manos are not analyzed in reference to the metates (J. Adams 1998, 1999).

The analysis of food-processing tools from the Santa Cruz Bend, Stone Pipe, and Square Hearth sites placed emphasis on the relationship between manos and metates. Two types of metates were found–flat/concave and basin. Flat/concave metates began with a flat surface, but a slight concavity became worn through constant use with a mano shorter than the width of the metate. (These have been classified in the past as slab, flat, or block metates.) With enough use in both circular and reciprocal strokes, the mano could have worn the concavity deep enough to be considered a basin. In contrast, a basin metate was specifically designed with borders that served to confine the meal. The mano used in a basin metate is smaller and more convex than the one used with a flat/concave metate. While there were many manos recovered from the Santa Cruz Bend, Stone Pipe, and Square Hearth sites–and most had been used against flat/concave metates–the few metates found are basin. Thus, the mano and metate data seem to indicate conflicting conclusions about which design was the most common at these Santa Cruz Bend sites. The final interpretation was that what remained of the food-processing metates was not indicative of the most common tool design used by the inhabitants of these settlements. The question becomes, why were there so few flat/concave metates left at these sites? The answer may be that they were removed by either abandonment or post-occupation scavenging.

Further, the analysis of the ground stone assemblages from the Santa Cruz Bend, Stone Pipe, and Square Hearth sites confronted the standard interpretation of food-grinding tool morphology as a reflection of the nature of the processed resources. The basin and flat/concave metates recovered from all time periods represented at the Santa Cruz Bend, Stone Pipe, and Square Hearth sites are typical of those previously considered to have been associated with the processing of wild resources. However, the ubiquity of maize suggested that domesticated resources were an important part of the diet by 600 B.C., centuries before the trough metates usually associated with maize agriculture appear in the archaeological record (Adams 1998, 1999). Thus, it was suggested that there needs to be a rethinking of what tool morphology implies about food production.

It was proposed that the prehistoric occupants of the Santa Cruz Bend, Stone Pipe, and Square Hearth sites continued to use the same technology to grind maize as they had developed to grind wild resources. This included two metate types. One was carefully designed, with a basin to confine a variety of seeds, nuts, pods, and other resources that were crushed with a small, spherical mano, easily held in one hand. The metate rested flat on the ground and the grinder knelt over it using both reciprocal and circular strokes to grind the meal. The other metate type had no specific design as any flat-surfaced rock would have sufficed. The manos used on these flat/concave metates were slightly larger, with flatter grinding surfaces than basin manos. The metates rested flat on the ground and the larger manos could have been used with either one or two hands in both circular and reciprocal strokes across the surface. Experiments have shown that oily seeds, such as sunflower seeds, or seeds that had been soaked prior to grinding, are most easily processed on the

flatter, more open, flat/concave metate surface (Adams 1989a). Hard seeds are difficult to confine on the flat surface.

Thus, it was proposed that when maize was introduced, there was no major change in the design of the tools used to grind it. If the kernels were dried before grinding, the basin configuration was quite adequate. If the kernels were soaked prior to processing, the flat/concave metate was perhaps preferable. Later design changes to a trough mano and metate were the result of requirements for more efficient flour processing tools (Adams 1993b, 1998, 1999). Mortars and pestles might have been used at certain times or during certain stages of processing some foods, but the evidence for them is minimal (Adams 1998).

The analysis of the contexts in which ground stone tools were found at the Santa Cruz Bend, Stone Pipe, and Square Hearth sites also indicated some differences in the location of stored tools and the amount of secondary use they received (Adams 1998). For example, it was found that, more than any other artifact, manos were more often stored in interior pits than on floors or in exterior pits. Further, those manos stored in interior pits were more likely to have been used only for food-processing activities while manos found on floors or in other contexts were more often secondarily used. These findings may have implications for understanding the nature of site occupation.

Several hypotheses are presented for consideration with the accumulation of more data. It is proposed that when people lived at a site for a long time, or returned repeatedly, existing artifacts were more likely to have been scavenged and used secondarily by people who were not the original tool users and who did not care to maintain the tool's original use. Evidence for this behavior exists as tools that are no longer usable in the activities for which they were originally designed; termed here *sequential secondary use* (see next section for definition of use categories). In contrast, it is proposed that during short-term occupations, tools were used only as they were originally designed; termed *primary use*. By extension, a third hypothesis is proposed that tools designed for a particular activity, but redesigned with attributes needed for use in a second activity without impeding use in the first activity, is a behavior of convenience and is termed here *concomitant secondary use*. A tool usable in more than one activity saves raw material–something that might be important to sedentary populations who have limited access to sources. Additionally, it lowers the number of tools that need to be stored and accounted for.

Another hypothesis proposes that artifacts may have been stored in pits to remove them from view and protect them from scavenging and secondary use activities. A tool placed in a pit and covered with dirt is less visible and susceptible to appropriation than a tool left outside or on a structure floor. Such storage may have been important to people who periodically left their possessions while they attended to business away from their homes. Thus, the amount and type of secondary tool use and the use of interior pits for tool storage may provide evidence for periodicity or duration of settlement occupation. Assemblages with higher percentages of sequential secondary use artifacts may be indicative of a site occupied for a long time with abandoned parts of the site serving as a source for tools to be redesigned. Alternatively, higher percentages of sequential secondary use tools may have been from seasonally occupied settlements whose returning occupants scavenged existing tools for redesign and use in new activities. These hypotheses about food-processing tools were formulated not to suggest that the mere presence or absence of secondarily used artifacts indicates one settlement strategy or another, but to add another line of evidence to others for recognizing different strategies.

It was further learned from the Santa Cruz Bend, Stone Pipe, and Square Hearth assemblages that pigment processing was perhaps a more common activity among the Cienega inhabitants than it was among the Agua Caliente inhabitants. Early in the occupation of the Santa Cruz settlements, there are lapstones and handstones exclusively used for pigment preparation, as well as reused and multiple use manos with pigment on them. Chunks of pigment in various stages of preparation were also found (Miksa and Tompkins 1998). During the later Agua Caliente occupation, there is less evidence of pigment, either as chunks or found on tools, and there are fewer varieties of pigment processing tools. The Los Pozos assemblage will be assessed for evidence of pigment processing. The research strategy used to assess all artifacts is presented in the next section.

RESEARCH STRATEGY

Questions about grinding technology at Los Pozos will be answered by considering artifact design, primary and secondary use, and whether an artifact was used to process food or nonfood resources, used in multiple activities, or was of ambiguous use. Artifact design is assessed in terms of complexity (J. Adams 1994, 1995a). If the natural shape of the rock was altered only through use, the artifact was considered of *expedient design*. Modifications that made the tool easier to hold, or to achieve a specific shape, indicate that it was of *strategic design*. An analysis of artifact design allows us to answer questions about whether strategically designed tools were treated differently than those of expedient design. Were they stored in more protective interior pits; were they subjected to more or less secondary use than tools of expedient design?

Primary and secondary use are categorized as single, reuse, redesign, multiple, and recycled (J. Adams 1994, 1995a). *Single-use* artifacts were employed only in the task for which they were designed. *Reused* artifacts were designed for a specific primary task, but employed in a second without altering the artifact design–such as a food-grinding mano reused to grind pigment. *Multiple-use* tools were designed for one task, but have another area or surface employed in a second task. Use in one would not inhibit use in the other task, even if tool configuration was slightly altered. For example, the non-working surface of a food-grinding mano may have been used as a lapstone to shape stone or shell ornaments. Such reused and multiple-use tools are considered to have been of *concomitant secondary use* (J. Adams 1994:41, 1998). The purpose of concomitantly used tools may have been to broaden the range of accomplishable activities without increasing the number of tools, or perhaps to conserve raw material or maintain low numbers of stored objects. The original designer and user were likely to have been the same person who reused or multiply used the tool and did not want to destroy its original function.

Redesigned tools were designed for a primary task and either remanufactured or altered through use in a second task to the extent that the tool could no longer function in the first. Such redesign might involve placing a groove across the working surface of a mano. *Recycled* tools were designed and used in one task, but were ultimately employed in a completely different context that may or may not have physically altered the tool (Adams 1995a:46; 1996a). Manos and metates used as building stones or as roasting rocks are examples of recycled tools. Such redesigned and recycled tools are considered to have been of *sequential secondary use* (J. Adams 1994:41-42, 1996a). The user of the redesigned or recycled tools may not have been the same person as the original designer and user, who did not care to maintain original tool function.

The task for which a tool was used can be determined through a combination of macroscopic and microscopic techniques (Adams 1993a, 1995a:45). Each artifact was examined under magnification using an Olympus stereoscope capable of scrolling from 18 to 110 power. Use-wear patterns were identified by comparing them to a baseline of experimentally created use-wear patterns (J. Adams 1988, 1989a, 1989b, 1993a). Macroscopically, design may indicate the intended function of a tool. By combining an assessment of design with microscopic use-wear analysis, artifacts can be categorized by how the artifact was actually used.

For example, manos and metates and some mortars and pestles were designed for use in food-processing activities. A food-grinding mano that has remnants of pigment was used in multiple activities, both food and nonfood processing. Nonfood-processing tools were used to shape or alter the surfaces of other artifacts, or were used to process nonfood substances (J. Adams 1994:44-46, 1995a:45, 1998). Polishing stones, abraders, and lapstones are examples of nonfood-processing tools. Some tools are generic enough (usually of expedient design) to have been used for processing either food or nonfood resources; their use is ambiguous. There are also ground stone artifacts that were not used for processing or making things, but rather are accoutrements, gaming pieces, or had symbolic meaning. These are categorized as *not for processing*.

In addition to being assessed for design, primary and secondary uses, and processing activity, each artifact was categorized by amount of wear. Some items have no evidence of use after they were manufactured. If the item was a tool but had no evidence of use wear, it was considered *unused*. If the item was *not for processing*, then wear categorization was *not applicable*. If the use wear was barely visible, it was categorized *lightly used*. *Moderate use* was identified by easily visible use wear that did not alter the original tool shape. If the tool surface was worn enough to alter the original shape, it was considered *heavily used*. A few tools, especially manos, can be recognized as being *nearly worn out* if their edges are too thin for comfortable holding. Wear amount may be impossible to estimate on broken artifacts and, as such, are *indeterminable*.

In combination, the information from the assessment of design, primary and secondary use, and amount of wear begins to provide an interesting picture of an artifact's life history: how it was made, how and how much it was used. All that is needed is an understanding of the relationships between artifact location and any human behavior (storage, discard, abandonment, etc.) that may have caused the artifact to be in a particular context when it was found.

The archaeological contexts in which the Los Pozos ground stone artifacts were found include *pit structure fill, pit structure floor, interior pits, post holes, exterior pits, burials, roasting pits, trash, well, disturbed,* and *unprovenienced*. Excavation notes, artifact condition (*whole* or *fragmentary, burned* or *unburned*), and information on primary and secondary use will help determine if artifacts were found where they were left by the site's occupants in either use or storage contexts, termed "de facto deposits" (sensu Schiffer 1987:89-97).

The next section describes the Los Pozos assemblage. Artifact type descriptions emphasize the technological attributes of design, primary and secondary use, and processing activities as presented in this introduction. A synthesis of archaeological context and interpretations of prehistoric behavior at Los Pozos will be presented in the conclusions section. All of the measurements, observations, and interpretations for each artifact have been recorded in a computerized database available from the Arizona State Museum (ASM),

Table 5.1. Ground stone artifact types.

Artifact	Number
Abraders	2
Balls	4
Disks	1
Geometrics	9
Handstones	50
Lapstones	17
Manos	26
Metates	3
Mortars	9
Natural	3
Netherstones	27
Ornaments	1
Pecking stones	2
Pestles	10
Polishing stones	7
Pulping stones	1
Roasting rocks	87
Shaped	1
Unidentified	24
Total	284

where the artifacts and written records are permanently stored.

THE LOS POZOS ASSEMBLAGE

The ground stone assemblage from Los Pozos includes 284 whole and fragmentary items. Most of the assemblage (n = 236) was recovered from 39 pit structures. The rest came from exterior pits, roasting pits, burials, and wells. The artifacts were sorted into 18 types (Table 5.1). A large percentage (39 percent) are unidentifiable by type, primarily because they were recycled as roasting rocks. Another 31 identifiable artifacts were also recycled at roasting rocks. Roasting rocks are discussed as a separate artifact type. The primary focus of this analysis will be on the 173 whole and fragmentary artifacts that can be identified and have good provenience information. Summary data tables for the Los Pozos assemblage may be found elsewhere (Adams 2001).

Artifact Descriptions

Abraders

Abraders are handstones with an asperite surface useful for shaping the surfaces of other items. The texture of the abrader determines the extent and type of damage done to the opposing surface, so that a finer texture may begin to polish more than abrade.

Two whole, flat abraders were recovered from the same pit structure (354). One was on the floor and the

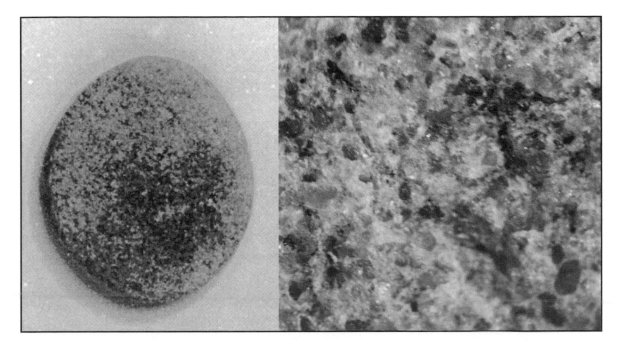

Figure 5.1. Abrader used against a stone surface (354/280.02); photomicrograph (40x) of artifact surface at right. (Actual size of artifact is 4.7 cm long x 4.1 cm wide x .9 cm thick.)

other in a posthole. Both are of expedient design and had been used moderately on two opposing surfaces. One abrader recovered from the pit is the smallest, and was used against a pliable, perhaps wooden surface. The larger abrader, from the floor, was probably used against another stone surface. Use-wear damage included flattened grains and a few abrasive scratches (Figure 5.1). The only other ground stone artifact on the floor of pit structure 354 was a lapstone. These tools were used to make or process nonfood items. Abraders were similarly scarce at the Cienega component at the Santa Cruz Bend site, with only seven found at this much larger site. All are flat and were probably used against wooden surfaces (Adams 1998).

Balls

Balls are roughly spherical pieces of stone that have been ground all over to shape. Through ethnographic studies of the Pueblo, O'odham, and other native people, stone balls are most commonly identified as gaming pieces, club heads, noise-making stones, or racing stones (Adams 1979:90; Culin 1975:340; Russell 1908:172-173, 179; Stephen 1936:271-280; Underhill 1939:146-150; Woodbury 1954:173).

Four whole balls were recovered from Los Pozos, all from the floor of the same pit structure (819) (see Appendix B). Three were located within a grouping of other artifacts on the floor (collectively called an array) that may have had some ritual significance. This array

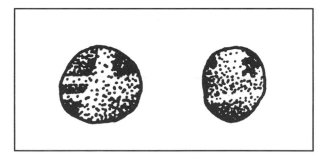

Figure 5.2. Small balls with evidence of wrapping (819.17/525.18, 819/540.03) (actual size).

is discussed in Appendix B. All of the balls had been either ground or polished. Two of the balls within the array, and one from elsewhere on the floor, have evidence that they were wrapped with a cordage or sinew (Figure 5.2). Such a wrapping could have been to haft a handle; to secure something such as a feather to the ball; or as a means of suspension, perhaps as decoration or as a counterweight. These balls are small, ranging from 1.6 to 3.4 cm in diameter. They were probably not used in processing activities, but rather may have had some ritual or gaming use. The two balls recovered from the Cienega component at the Stone Pipe site were larger (5.3 to 8 cm in diameter) and have no evidence useful for interpreting their use.

Disks

Only one perforated disk was recovered; it was found in a pit within pit structure 813 (Figure 5.3). This type of disk is also known as a "doughnut stone" and there is much speculation about its actual use (Di Peso et al. 1974:32, 307). Suggestions include a digging stick weight, a corn sheller, and a chunky stone rolled in a hoop-and-pole game (Haury 1976:290). I have suggested that some doughnut stones, especially those found at some of the Point of Pines sites, may have served as a type of abrader or shaftsmoother, based on use-wear damage in the holes (J. Adams 1994, 1998). Nothing similar is identified in any historic assemblage in the American Southwest.

The use-wear damage patterns on the Los Pozos doughnut stone are of little help in identifying its use. The hole was drilled from both sides, leaving a ridge in the middle of the hole (referred to as a biconical hole), where there is some rounding from contact with a pliable surface. Such damage could have been created by the passage of a wooden stick through the hole, which is 1.7 cm in diameter at its narrowest. One flattish side has been ground smoother than the other, which still has impact fractures from the manufacturing process. Perhaps this piece was never finished and eventually the entire surface was to have been smoothed.

Similar "doughnut stones" were found in Cienega contexts at the Santa Cruz Bend and Stone Pipe sites. One has red pigment on one side, perhaps from a processing activity that had nothing to do with the holes. The holes are too small (1.2 cm and 1.7 cm in diameter) for use with digging sticks, which are generally larger than 3 cm in diameter. Neither of these doughnut stones had evidence of use wear in the holes. Consequently, like the Los Pozos' disk, their use remains enigmatic.

Geometrics

Nine stones were carefully manufactured to specific shapes. Three are cruciform, four are essentially cylindrical, one is egg-shaped, and one is football-shaped.

Two cruciforms were found within pit structure 318, each in a different pit. One was carefully ground and polished to shape, with only one tine chipped. Another tine has a tiny groove just below the flattened end, on one narrow edge. The groove, barely visible without magnification, is not deep enough, nor is there use wear to indicate it was used for suspension, for shaping, or for anything else. The second cruciform was also carefully shaped, but not as nicely ground and polished as the first. Chipping scars are still visible, even though much of the piece has been polished. The

Figure 5.3. Perforated disk "doughnut stone" with biconical hole (813.01/524.04). (Actual size is 7.7 cm diameter x 3 cm thick.)

end of one tine is broken, but tiny chips along the break indicate either that the break occurred during manufacture, or it was repaired. A lapstone found in the same pit as the cruciforms has use wear similar to both cruciforms. Perhaps this lapstone was used in their manufacture.

The third cruciform was found in the fill of pit structure 337. It also was carefully ground and polished, but it is broken so that only two tines remain. Facets from grinding are still visible with some abrasive scratches and sheen from polishing.

Three cylindrical pieces were found in pit structure 819; one in the fill and two on the floor. One roughly cylindrical piece, found on the floor, is primarily a naturally shaped stone. It was polished all over, except for a long abraded area on one side. There is evidence that the piece was wrapped with string or cordage, perhaps to attach it to another object. The abraded area may have facilitated this hafting. The evidence is obvious due to a black residue that covers most of the stone but is absent in an encircling area toward one end and on the abraded side. Similar wrapping patterns are visible on other balls and geometric pieces found in this pit structure. The second cylindrical piece from the floor was associated with a concentration of other shaped items in an array that may have had some ritual significance. This naturally shaped cylinder was slightly enhanced by abrasion and heavily polished with both something hard and something soft. There is no evidence that this piece was wrapped.

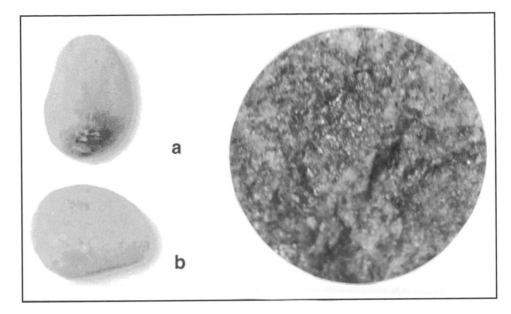

Figure 5.4. Handstones: a-b) handstones with two shades of red pigment (318.03/360.01, 352.01/366.04); photomicrograph (40x) of a) at right.

The cylindrical piece found in the fill of pit structure 819 has abundant abrasive scratches from being worked against something rough. It is unclear if this was strictly from shaping, or if it was being ground to a powder. The material is a soft, red sedimentary rock that may have been a useful pigment. A lapstone found on the floor of pit structure 819 has use-wear patterns consistent with the working of a similarly soft material and remnants of pigment are the same red shade (10R5/8) as the geometric.

The fourth cylindrical piece was found on the floor of pit structure 867. It was ground all over to shape, but has no other evidence of use. There were no other ground stone artifacts on the floor of this pit structure.

Two geometrics were found on the floor of pit structure 819 in association with the previously mentioned array. One is football-shaped and is made from an unusual jasper-like stone (see Appendix B). Tiny abrasive scratches visible under magnification indicate it was shaped with a reciprocal stroke against a smooth stone. A soft surface, perhaps a piece of leather, was used to induce a sheen or polish. The other geometric found in the array is egg-shaped (see Appendix B). It was probably selected for its natural shape and enhanced through grinding and polishing. There is no evidence of wrapping as on two other balls and a cylindrical geometric in the array.

Fewer geometrics were found at the other Santa Cruz settlements, with only one broken cruciform recovered from the fill of a Cienega pit structure at the Santa Cruz Bend site (Ferg 1998b).

Handstones

The category of handstones is reserved for those tools without specific attributes that allow them to be considered manos, polishing stones, pestles, or other artifacts. The use of handstones is more ambiguous. The term handstone also has meaning at a generic level to subsume the more specifically defined tool types (Adams 1996a).

Fifty handstones were recovered from Los Pozos. Most were found either in interior pits (46 percent) or on pit structure floors (24 percent). For the most part, they are whole (68 percent) and not burned (56 percent). Little effort was expended in making them, with 80 percent of expedient design, being pebbles or cobbles with no further modification. They were primarily used in only one activity (54 percent), but some were also used as hammerstones (n = 1), pecking stones (n = 2), pestles (n = 7), polishing stones (n = 1), or were recycled as roasting stones (n = 8). Half (50 percent) were used in nonfood-processing activities; 34 percent to process pigment and 4 percent perhaps to process caliche.

One of the handstones with pigment was recovered from an interior pit within pit structure 318. It had been used to process at least two shades of red pigment (Munsell 10R4/6 and 10R4/4). Use-wear patterns indicate it was worked against a smooth, stone surface (Figure 5.4). Another interior pit within the same pit structure contained a netherstone with which this handstone could have been used (Figure 5.5). Red

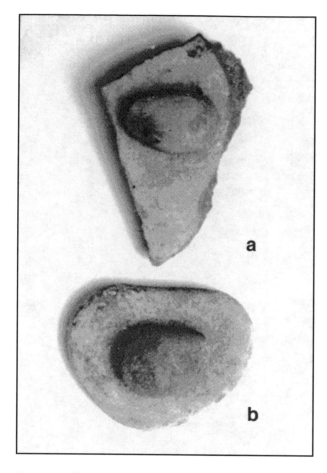

Figure 5.5. Handstones and lapstones as they may have been used together. (Actual size of handstone a) is 18.2 cm long x 14.7 cm wide x 4.3 cm thick.)

pigment is present on the netherstone as well, but with a slightly different shade of red (10R5/8). A clean spot in the center of the pigment-stained, netherstone surface makes it seem less plausible that the handstone and netherstone were used together. However, it was noted previously that this netherstone could have been used to shape the cruciforms found in pit structure 318. There were no ground stone artifacts found on the floor of this pit structure. The use of interior pits and floors for storage is discussed in the conclusion section.

A set including a compatible handstone and a lapstone were recovered from an interior pit within pit structure 352 (Figure 5.5). The handstone is covered with two shades of red pigment (10R4/6 above lesser amounts of 2.5YR5/8) and is so completely covered that the pigment was probably in solution when processed (Figure 5.6c). This handstone was sequentially used as a pestle with impact fractures on both ends that removed the pigment. The lapstone is a large flat cobble with two opposing surfaces, each used to process two shades of red pigment (10R5/6 and 10R4/6). Only one of the shades of pigment is the same

as is on the handstone; it does not appear as if the pigment was in solution on the lapstone. While these two stones could have been used together, the handstone might also have been used in a different pigment-related task, with its final use as a pestle in an unrelated task.

A handstone found in an interior pit in pit structure 370 is compatible with a lapstone found on the floor. The handstone is a pebble with one flat surface. The lapstone is a flat cobble with two opposite surfaces. The handstone and one of the lapstone surfaces have similar use-wear patterns, and the two fit well together. The opposite lapstone surface is more heavily worn than the first, with red pigment (10R4/8) in the interstices and wear concentrated in the center. Perhaps the lapstone had been used with more than one handstone, and the one used to process pigment was not stored in the pit structure.

Two handstones might have been involved in processing caliche for use as plaster or some other purpose. One from the fill of pit structure 337 (Figure 5.6a), the other from the fill of pit structure 425, have a mixture of caliche and sand visible in the interstices of the stone. Such a mixture is not consistent with the naturally deposited caliche found on some other stones (Beth Miksa, personal communication 1997). Magnified, the use-wear damage included abrasive scratches and impact fractures (Figure 5.6a).

A handstone recovered from an interior pit within pit structure 337 was perhaps used to work red pigment (10R5/8) into a hide (Figure 5.6b). Use-wear damage to the surface is most similar to an experimental stone used to work a deer hide. The pigment, visible at 40x magnification, is deep in the interstices between the grains of the stone (Figure 5.6). The opposite surface is very convex, and the roundest part has been used against a smooth hard surface, perhaps to process a slightly darker red pigment (10R4/6) against a smooth netherstone. Damage to the surface is visible at 40x magnification as flattened grains with abrasive scratches (Figure 5.6). Both ends are also battered with impact fractures from use as a pestle. Some of the lighter red pigment is on one end. Perhaps this end was also used in the hide working as it has rounded impact fractures as if used against a soft surface.

Two other handstones were probably also used to work pigment into hides. One was found on the floor of pit structure 836 and the other in an interior pit within pit structure 861. Both stones had red pigment; the one in the interior pit had a slightly lighter shade of red (10R6/6) than the one on the floor (10R5/6).

The handstones recovered from the other Middle Santa Cruz settlements were used similarly to the Los Pozos handstones. Slightly more than half (54 percent at Los Pozos and 54.2 percent at the other Santa Cruz settlements) were used in only one activity. A higher

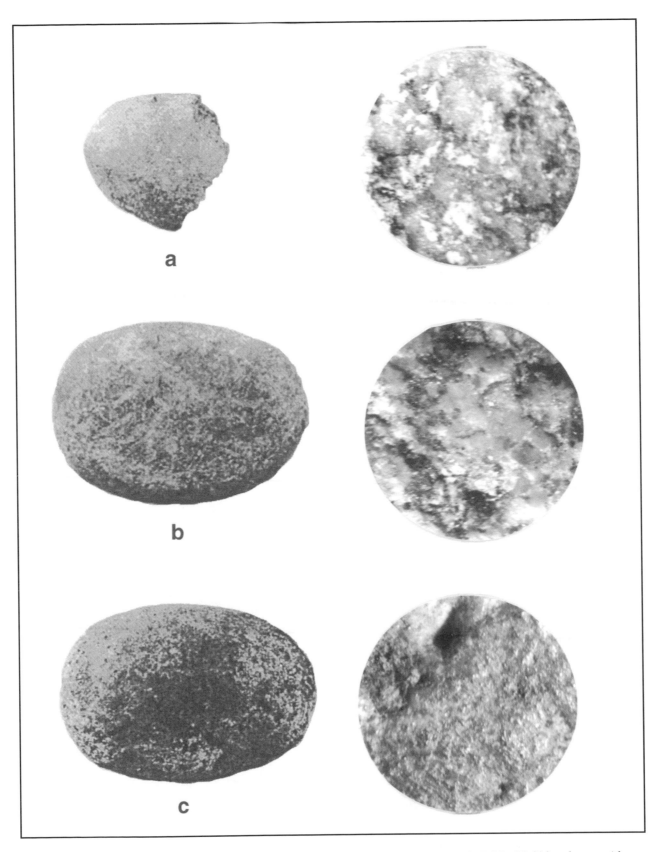

Figure 5.6. Multiple use handstones: a) handstone with caliche, perhaps from processing (337/251.07); b) handstone with one side used to work red pigment, possibly into a hide (337.14/277.08); c) opposite surface used to process pigment against a smooth netherstone; photomicrographs (40x) of surfaces at right. (Actual size of b) is 15 cm long x 10.7 cm wide x 7.8 cm thick.)

percentage (20.6 percent) were recycled into roasting or heating stones at the other settlements than at Los Pozos (16 percent), but a higher percentage (20 percent) were used in multiple activities at Los Pozos than at the other settlements (15 percent). The Los Pozos handstones were more commonly (50 percent) used in nonfood-processing activities than those from the other Santa Cruz settlements (33.6 percent), primarily in pigment-processing activities (34 percent at Los Pozos and 28 percent at the other settlements). Five handstones from the other Santa Cruz settlements were perhaps used to process hides. Thus, in general, handstones were used in the same range of activities at all the Middle Santa Cruz settlements.

Lapstones

Lapstones are small, hand-held netherstones (Adams 1996a, 1998). Most have areas on one or more surfaces where something was worked. Use-wear damage patterns include abrasive scratches and sometimes sheen, depending on the texture of the opposing surface. Stones too large to be hand held are categorized more generically as netherstones. Lapstones that have been used to process pigment are distinguished from palettes by their simple design–palettes have formal borders while lapstones do not. Past descriptions have used the term "palette" or "proto palette" for anything used to process pigment. However, this creates confusion with the palettes found in later Hohokam deposits (which may not have been pigment-processing tools), and leaves unclassified tools of the same, simple configuration but lacking pigment (Adams 1996a, 1998).

Seventeen lapstones were recovered from Los Pozos. Most (52.9 percent) were found on pit structure floors or in interior pits (23.5 percent). Almost all (94.1 percent) lapstones are whole, and most (88.2 percent) are not burned. There was no effort expended in manufacturing these tools to a specific shape–all are of expedient design. Most (76.5 percent) were used only in nonfood-processing activities; 65.2 percent to process pigment. Three lapstones may have been compatible with other artifacts. Two are described in the handstone section as compatible with specific handstones. The third was perhaps used to process a cylindrical piece classified as a geometric because of its shape but probably ground to that shape in the process of reducing it for pigment.

A few lapstones are described here in detail as typical of the others. The first was found in an interior pit, in pit structure 302. It is a flattish cobble with a surface on each opposing side. One surface has two shades of red pigment (7.5R5/6 and 10R5/6), but ultimately, a hard smooth stone was worked in the center, creating a pigment-free area. The opposite surface has the same shades of red pigment all over.

Another, found in an interior pit in pit structure 327, was used secondarily as both a handstone and a hammerstone. The flattest surface was used as a lapstone to process red pigment (10R5/8). The opposite surface was used as a handstone against a smooth, stone surface long enough to create a sheen in a small area. Both surfaces have impact fractures from use as a hammerstone.

A much larger assemblage of lapstones was recovered from the other Santa Cruz settlements (n = 61). However, they seem to be nearly identical in design and use to those found at Los Pozos: 67.2 percent were used to process pigment, with a few (26.2 percent) used in more than one task. It is rare to find a lapstone that has been manufactured to a specific shape; 72.1 percent of those from the other Santa Cruz settlements, and all from Los Pozos, of expedient design. Cobbles of the appropriate flatness must not have been difficult to find along the Santa Cruz River.

Manos

Manos and metates are two components of food-processing equipment; one does not work without the other. The metate is the stationary netherstone. The mano is the smaller, hand-held component, whose movement across the metate reduces any intermediate substances to a finer consistency. Because manos and metates were used together, the use wear on the surface of one tool reflects the use wear on the surface of the other tool. This concomitant wearing of surfaces makes it possible to identify manos and metates that have compatible surface configurations and could have been used together (Adams 1995a, 1996a, 1998). The fact that no whole metates were recovered from Los Pozos makes it impossible to identify possibly compatible mano/metate sets.

Twenty-six manos were recovered. Two (7.7 percent) were used against basin metates, but most (80.8 percent) were used against flat/concave metates (Figure 5.7). A basin mano has a convex surface and is worked within the basin of the metate in a combination of circular and reciprocal strokes, whereas a flat/concave mano has a flat to slightly convex surface and is moved against the metate primarily with reciprocal or elongated circular strokes (Adams 1996a, 1998). The metate surface changes from flat to concave as wear progresses, and the mano surface changes from flat to convex in response. In general, flat/concave manos are larger than basin manos (the issue of mano size is discussed further below). The distinction between metate types is discussed below. On all manos, use wear is visible as abrasive

Figure 5.7. Basin and flat/concave manos: a) one of only two basin manos recovered from Los Pozos (836.01/563.08); b) mano with two opposite surfaces used against a flat/concave metate (898.01/122.03); c) mano with one surface used against a flat/concave metate (861.01/457.03); photomicrograph (40x) of c) at bottom right. (Actual size of b) is 11 cm long x 9.1 cm wide x 4.9 cm thick.)

scratches and impact fractures (Figure 5.7, photomicrograph) (Adams 1993a).

The technological classification of manos used in this analysis differs from those that type manos either as one-hand or two-hand (Martin et al. 1957:42-49; Plog 1974:140; Woodbury 1954:67) or by assemblage specific categories of Type I, Type II, etc. (Di Peso et al. 1974; Haury 1976:281-282; Lancaster 1984:247-248). These classification techniques use size and shape as defining characteristics, which obfuscate technologically important characteristics. Manos used in each of the various metate configurations (basin, flat/concave, trough, flat) develop distinctive attributes that cross cut size. The

result is that size-based classifications can place manos used in basin metates in the same category as those used in flat/concave metates or small trough metates.

These technologically confused categories have been used by some to demonstrate that differences in subsistence strategies are reflected in mano sizes, proposing that larger manos (Diehl [1996b:109] > 128 cm^2; Lancaster [1984:Figure 17.2] > 15 x 10 cm; Mauldin [1993:325] > 75 cm^2; Plog [1974:140] average 20 x 10 cm) were used to process agriculturally grown maize while smaller manos were used to process wild or gathered foods. The assumption is that smaller manos (called handstones by some [Haury 1976:281]) were worked in basin metates or less formal slab metates (these would be called flat/concave in this technological analysis), and the larger manos were used in more formal trough or flat metates (true flat metates were used with manos as long as the metate surface is wide) (Guernsey and Kidder 1921:93; Lancaster 1984:247; Martin et al. 1949:134).

The open trough metate, specifically, is seen by Haury (1976:352) as one of several "traits," along with maize agriculture, brought into southern Arizona by immigrants from the south and introduced to the indigenous populations who used basin and slab metates to grind their gathered food resources. Trough metates, in general, are seen as indicative of maize agriculture throughout the American Southwest. It is true that most manos used in trough metates are larger than those used in basin or against flat/concave metates. Thus, it is easy to make the interpretation that larger manos reflect a greater reliance on maize agriculture (Diehl 1996b:113; Gilman 1988:412; Hard 1990; Hunter-Anderson 1986:48; Mauldin 1993; Schlanger 1990:103). Hard (1990:147) suggests that mano length can be used to construct "a relative index of the use of agricultural (maize) dependence." The arguments based on mano size alone, however, confuse design differences. The trough mano/metate design increases the relative area of contact between the mano and metate and requires a completely different motor habit (Adams 1993b:336-340) than the basin or flat/concave metate designs. The above arguments are also slightly tautological in that they assume that maize agriculture is not established until trough manos and metates are used. Data from the Santa Cruz settlements, as well as from other Late Archaic sites (L. Huckell 1995a:97; 1995b:40) forces us to reconsider the relationship between metate design and maize processing, because maize is plentiful centuries before trough metates are found in the archaeological record.

The combination of macrobotanical studies and a technological analysis of the manos from the Santa Cruz settlements sheds a different light on the subject of mano size and morphology and their relationships to subsistence. Macrobotanical studies at the Santa Cruz Bend, Stone Pipe, and Square Hearth sites found a high ubiquity of maize remains, indicating a reliance on agriculture (L. Huckell 1998). However, 80.4 percent of all manos are smaller than 15 x 10 cm; 45.1 percent are smaller than 123 cm^2. Using the size restrictions of Diehl (1996b:109), Lancaster (1984:Figure 17.2), and Plog (1974:140), these manos would not be considered as used to process maize, and using the typological restrictions of Haury (1976:352), Lancaster (1984:247), and Martin and others (1949:134), none would have been used to process maize because none were used in trough metates, nor were any trough metates recovered from these sites.

A technological analysis of the manos from Santa Cruz Bend, Stone Pipe, and Square Hearth sites identified most (78.9 percent) as having been used on flat/concave metates, with only a few (7 percent) used with basin metates. It was proposed that developments in mano/metate design reflect differing requirements for the production of flour (Adams 1998, 1999). Recognizing that larger tools are more efficient than smaller tools (Adams 1993b:338; Hard 1990:137; Mauldin 1993:319; Plog 1974:137), designs that increased surface area would be more desirable as flour production became more important. The results of design changes might have been either fewer grinders producing the same amount of flour, or the same number of grinders producing more flour. More flour would have either fed more people, or increased the amount of flour-based recipes in the diet of the same number of people (Adams 1993b:334, 1998, 1999).

The manos recovered from Los Pozos follow the same pattern with 36.4 percent smaller than 123 cm^2, and 76.2 percent smaller than 15 x 10 cm. Most (80.8 percent) were used with flat/concave metates and a few (7.7 percent), with basin metates. Macrobotanical analyses from Los Pozos indicate that maize ubiquity at Los Pozos was as high, if not higher, than at the other Santa Cruz settlements (see Chapter 9, this report). Thus, it is proposed that at all the Santa Cruz settlements there was a basic reliance on maize as an important part of the diet. Initially, maize was probably processed with the same basin mano/metate design developed to process wild resources; however, it is proposed that once flour production became important, design changes were enacted that increased grinding efficiency created by the larger grinding surface areas.

Several experiments were conducted to clarify the thinking on how different mano and metate designs work. The experiments demonstrated how certain mano/metate designs were more or less useful for processing different types of seeds. Amaranth, sunflower seed, blue pop corn, dried dent corn, and soaked white kernels were chosen for grinding. It quickly became obvious that everything is easily ground with the basin mano and metate. The same was not true with flat/concave manos and metates. Dried seeds (everything except sunflower seeds and the soaked kernels) are more difficult to grind, requiring additional time and effort to keep them on the flat/concave metate surface. Soaked kernels and sunflower seeds are easily ground, or mashed, with the broader, flatter grinding surface and slightly larger mano because they adhere to the metate surface. From these experiments, it is possible to suggest that design developments were perhaps related to differences in processing wet (or oily) and dry kernels or seeds, and to a desire for increased efficiency in the production of flour or dough. New designs were not motivated by the change from grinding wild to cultivated foods as both are easily ground with the tools developed to grind wild resources before maize was available.

It is interesting that the manos from the other Santa Cruz settlements were more commonly strategically designed (78.9 percent) than those from Los Pozos (53.8 percent). Strategically designed manos were manufactured to a specific shape (Figure 5.8a-b), some with finger grips or otherwise altered to make them more comfortable to hold. The implication is that strategically designed manos were intended for many hours of use, while those of expedient design (Figure 5.8c) were selected for convenience without concern for comfort. Considering that all these settlements used similar river cobbles to manufacture their manos, access to different material sources should not govern design. Perhaps the grinders at the other Santa Cruz settlements were more concerned than the Los Pozos grinders about mano comfort because they either spent more hours grinding or intended to use their manos for a longer period of time.

No matter what the intention, the manos from Los Pozos were used heavily more often (42.3 percent) than those from the other Santa Cruz settlements (19.7 percent). The Los Pozos manos were also more apt to have been used only for food processing (57.7 percent) than those from the other Santa Cruz settlements (43.7 percent). A sizeable percentage of manos from both Los Pozos (19.2 percent) and the other Santa Cruz settlements (16.9 percent) were reused to grind pigment (Figure 5.8d-e). Coupled with certain other handstones and lapstones, there is considerable evidence that pigment processing was an important activity.

In summation, while the manos from the other Santa Cruz settlements were more strategically designed, they did not receive as much use and were more likely to have been secondarily used than those from Los Pozos. The manos from all the Santa Cruz settlements reveal significantly more about the food-processing activities than the metates. There were a few whole metates recovered from the Santa Cruz Bend and Stone Pipe sites, so it was possible to find some compatible manos and metates of both basin and flat/concave design. One compatible, flat/concave set was found, probably left in storage, in a exterior pit at the Santa Cruz Bend site (Adams 1998).

Metates

Metates have been variously typed by archaeologists, sometimes according to overall shape (block, slab) and sometimes according to surface configuration (basin, trough, flat). However, the lack of attention to life history and use wear makes classification problematic. Metates are subtyped as basin if the surface has an intentionally manufactured, elliptical shape worn deeper by circular and reciprocal mano strokes. Manos worked in basin metates have convex surfaces and can develop use-wear facets on the edges and ends. Some metates started out with flat or unshaped surfaces and remained flat only if the mano was the same length as the width of the metate surface. If the mano was shorter than the width of the metate, eventually a concave surface was worn on the metate, and a convex surface on the mano, so the tools are typed as flat/concave. A new flat/concave metate is easily distinguished from a well-used basin, but may be easily confused with a new basin. The damage patterns remaining from the manufacture of a new basin may be the only way to distinguish the two.

The evidence for metates from Los Pozos is very sparse. Only three metate fragments were recovered. Only one of the fragments was large enough to determine design, and it was flat/concave. A shallow depression was worn from use, but it is not possible to determine the nature of the stroke. The other two fragments are too small to determine anything about the whole tools. The fact that there are few metates does not mean that food was not ground at Los Pozos; the mano evidence is substantial (see mano section). None of the metate fragments are burned or heat-cracked, so they were not recycled as roasting stones. One was found in the fill of a burial, but it is unclear if it was included as an offering or merely as the fill that covered the body.

The metate information from the other Santa Cruz settlements is only slightly better with the recovery of three whole metates. One basin and one flat/concave metate were recovered from exterior pits, probably in use during the Cienega occupation of the Santa Cruz Bend site. The third whole metate is a basin and was found anchored in place within an Agua Caliente pit structure at the Stone Pipe site. This is the only evidence from any of the Middle Santa Cruz settlements for the location of grinding activities. While the largest percentage of the metates and metate fragments recovered from the other Santa Cruz settlements were basins (35.6 percent), most of the manos were used with flat/concave metates (78.9 percent). Thus, the pattern from all the Middle Santa Cruz settlements seems to be that what remains of the metates is less of a reflection of the nature of food-processing activities than the manos.

Mortars

A mortar has a basin to confine the substance being crushed and ground. A downward stroke brings the pestle forcefully into contact with the mortar, crushing any intermediate substance, and creating impact fractures on the surfaces where the mortar and pestle come into contact. Circular or reciprocal movements of

Figure 5.8. Strategically and expediently designed manos: a) strategically designed mano with finger grips (815.05/415.01); b) mano strategically designed to a disk shape (342/275.01); c) mano of expedient design with no attempt to change the natural shape of the stone (861.01/457.02); d-e) manos from the floor of the same pit structure reused to process red pigment (389/582.03, 582.04); photomicrograph (40x) of d) at bottom right. (Actual size of a) is 18.3 cm long x 12.7 cm wide x 7.6 cm thick.)

the pestle in the mortar basin grind the intermediate substances and cause abrasive damage to the surfaces of the mortar and pestle. The pestles need not be of stone, and some use-wear patterns in the basins suggest the working of wooden pestles.

Food-processing mortars are identified by Hopi as used to pound dried meat to soften it for those who have no teeth (Adams 1979:25). They have been used by the Walapai, Maricopa, Pima, and other non-pueblo groups to crush the pods of mesquite beans (Castetter and Bell 1937; Doelle 1976; Euler and Dobyns 1983:259; Spier 1933:51). Once the pods were broken apart with mortars and pestles, they may have been processed further with a mano and metate (Spier 1933:51).

Research at the historic Hopi village of Walpi (Adams 1979:25-26) helped identify attributes of mortars used in food-processing activities and those of mortar-like tools employed in other activities. Some artifacts typed by archaeologists as mortars were identified by Hopi as eagle watering bowls. The distinctive attributes of a watering bowl are a flat bottom, a square rim, and a broad, deep basin damaged only through manufacture techniques (impact fractures and only minor abrasive scratches). Mortars used in food processing have rounded bottoms, variously shaped rims, and deep, conical basins with both impact fractures and numerous abrasive scratches caused by the pestle. Additional descriptions of food-processing mortars can be found in Euler and Dobyns (1983:259-262).

At Los Pozos, nine mortars were recovered from pit structure floors (22.2 percent), interior pits (22.2 percent), and pit structure fill (55.5 percent). That most were found in fill deposits is not surprising because most (88.9 percent) are fragmentary. Forty-four percent are heat-cracked, probably from being recycled as roasting stones.

Only one whole mortar was recovered, found on the floor of pit structure 333. It is a carefully shaped, rectangular mortar with a broad basin (Figure 5.9a). It was used moderately with a pestle no rougher than the basin surface. Use wear is primarily abrasive scratches from working a pestle with both reciprocal and circular strokes. One pestle recovered from pit structure 867 and another from an interior pit in pit structure 327 each fit in the basin and have similar use wear. The mortar was also used as an abrader (Figure 5.9a). The base is flat enough to rest fairly stable and it is this part that was used as an abrader. The use-wear patterns include slightly rounded grains and a sheen that looks most like wood wear created on experimental tools (Adams 1989a, 1989b, 1993a).

One broken mortar was partially reconstructible from several fragments of vesicular basalt found

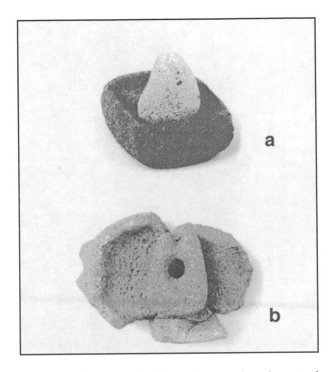

Figure 5.9. Mortars and pestles as they may have been used together. (Actual size of mortar a) is 13 cm long x 10.3 cm wide x 5.2 cm thick; mortar b) is 21.8 cm long x 13.3 cm wide and 5.6 cm thick.)

scattered across several proveniences on the floor of pit structure 416. The mortar (Figure 5.9b) was carefully shaped with nubs on both ends and a shallow channel on the base connecting the nubs. The basin bottom was worked with a pestle of similar texture so that the vesicles are worn level with few abrasive scratches and no impact fractures. A pestle recovered from an interior pit within pit structure 430 is compatible with this mortar in that its surface curvature fits the basin, and the use-wear patterns on both are similar (Figure 5.9b). This pestle also fits in the small, whole mortar, but is too big to have been worked within the basin. A second pestle (from an interior pit in pit structure 327) is compatible with both this broken mortar and the small whole mortar. While it is not possible to know if these tools were used together, their compatibility indicates the nature of companion mortars and pestles.

The mortar assemblages from Los Pozos (n = 9) and the other Middle Santa Cruz settlements (n = 8) are about the same size; however, that from the other settlements has a higher percentage of whole mortars (87.5 percent) than Los Pozos (11.1 percent). There is evidence that two mortars (25.5 percent) from the other settlements were used to process pigment, while none of the Los Pozos mortars were so used. These pigment processing mortars are called "disk mortars" and look

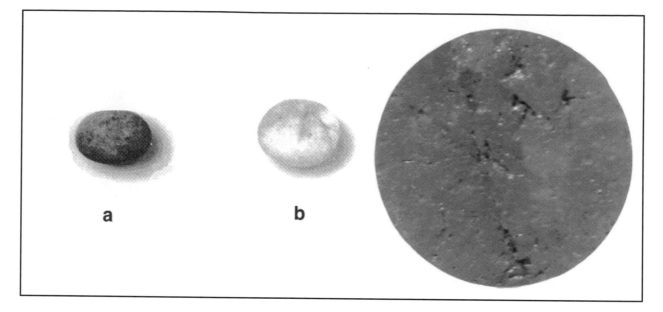

Figure 5.10. Natural stones with damage from possible use together as lightning stones (861.01/455.03; 861/114.02); photomicrograph (40x) of a) at right. (Actual size of b) is 2.9 cm long x 2.4 cm wide x 2 cm thick.)

like "doughnut stones" with incomplete holes. Nothing similar was recovered from Los Pozos. One fragment of what was called a vessel was recovered from an interior pit of a Cienega pit structure at the Stone Pipe site. Not enough of the piece was recovered to determine if the basin was used, and thus would have been a mortar. It is similar in both material and configuration to the broken, nubbed mortar described above.

Natural

Three stones, probably collected for their interesting or useful natural shapes, were found within two pit structures. One, found in a pit within pit structure 867, is a concretion that was enhanced by polishing. The sheen is spotty and may have been unintentionally created through contact with a soft surface, such as being carried in a leather pouch.

Two other natural stones were found within pit structure 861 (Figure 5.10). One was in a pit and the other in fill. These stones are nearly identical quartzite pebbles. On each stone there is an identical, small area of damage that may have resulted from the use of these stones together as lightning stones. When quartzitic pebbles are struck, or rubbed together they can create sparks. The use of more formally shaped lightning stones has been noted at Rio Grande pueblos (Kidder 1932:94-94). Nothing similar was recovered from the other Santa Cruz settlements.

Netherstones

Netherstones are bottom stones against which something was worked. Included in this category are items that do not have specific attributes to classify them as other types of netherstones. The term is also used in a generic sense to incorporate all tools that provided the bottom surface upon which an activity occurred. In this sense, lapstones, metates, mortars, anvils, and other similar items are all netherstones. Thus, netherstones were important in a variety of both food and nonfood-processing activities. Ladd (1979: 495) illustrates a Zuni man shaping a string of beads against a flat netherstone.

Most of the netherstones from Los Pozos are placed in this category because they are too fragmentary to categorize more precisely. Of the 27 netherstones recovered from Los Pozos, only 4 (14.8 percent) are whole. Most (85.2 percent) are broken, with 63 percent, heat-cracked from being recycled as roasting stones.

One of the whole netherstones was found in an interior pit within pit structure 318 (Figure 5.11). It is an irregular slab with one surface used to work red pigment (10R5/8). The center of the surface has been worn more and is cleaner than the edges, perhaps because something was worked after the pigment was processed. This lapstone was discussed in the hand-stone section and with the cruciforms. These artifacts were found in the same pit structure, have similar use

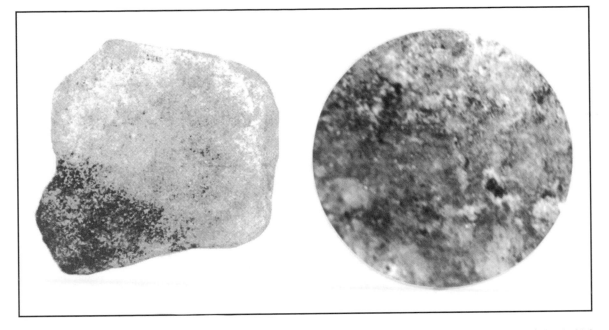

Figure 5.11. Netherstone used to grind red pigment; photomicrograph (40x) of surface at right. (Actual size is 20.8 cm long x 17 cm wide x 3.8 cm thick.)

wear and, if they were not used together, are at least good examples of the types of tools that could have been.

Another whole netherstone was found in an interior pit within pit structure 342. It is a slab that has been used lightly on two opposing surfaces to grind two shades of red pigment (10R4/8 and 7.5YR6/8) on one side and a third shade of red (10R5/8) on the other. This netherstone is made of fine-grain material. It may have been used to powder an existing cake of pigment as the use wear does not look like that created by stone-against-stone contact (Adams 1989a, 1989b, 1993a).

A third netherstone was found in an interior pit, this one within pit structure 342. It is a large slab that has been chipped, pecked, and perhaps ground, to shape the bottom and edges, but not much was done to create a surface. Even though there was a fair amount of attention to shaping this netherstone, it was not used.

Two fragments to the same netherstone were found in separate interior pits within pit structure 407. However, even rejoined, the two fragments are not large enough to tell much about how the netherstone was used. There are impact fractures, but whether this is from use or manufacture is indeterminable.

A smaller percentage (14.8 percent) of the Los Pozos netherstone assemblage is whole than that from the other Middle Santa Cruz settlements (36.8 percent). Only 21.1 percent of the assemblage from the other settlements is heat-cracked. More (23.7 percent) of the netherstones from the other Santa Cruz settlements

were used to process pigments than those from the Los Pozos site (11.1 percent).

Ornament

One broken piece may have been originally designed as an ornament, such as a bead or pendant, but after it broke, it was ground for use as something else. The piece is thin and broad with a biconical hole. It was found in the fill of pit structure 389. Information on the stone ornaments from the other Middle Santa Cruz settlements and more from Los Pozos can be found in Ferg (1998b) and in Vokes (1998a).

Pecking Stones

Pecking stones are handstones that have been used to alter other items with forceful, striking blows that create impact fractures on the item being shaped and on the pecking stone surface. Such stones could have been used in the initial shaping of manos, metates, and other large objects, or in renovating their grinding surfaces.

Two pecking stones were recovered from Los Pozos pit structures 389 and 817. Both pecking stones are of expedient design, having been pebbles altered only through use. One is spherical and has one edge covered with impact fractures (Figure 5.12). The other is a long, narrow cobble, with one end damaged by impact fractures and chips.

Figure 5.12. Pecking and pulping stones and pestles: a) pecking stone with one edge damaged by impact fractures (389/460.05); b) pulping stone with several edges used against a pliable surface (861/115.03); c) pestle end used to crush pigment (342.01/329.05); d) pestle used in a stone mortar and found in an array with other artifacts on the floor of pit structure 819 (819.17/525.24); photomicrographs (40x) of a) (top) and b) (bottom) at right. (Actual size of c) is 10.3 cm long x 5 cm wide x 2.4 cm thick.)

Pestles

Pestles are handstones used to crush or to crush and grind. Some pestles were worked in the basins of stone or wooden mortars to crush food or nonfood substances (Doelle 1976:53-68; Euler and Dobyns 1983:259-260). Others were worked against flat surfaces such as a netherstone or the ground. Sayles and Sayles (1948:28) illustrate a Maricopa woman using a large stone pestle to crush clay chunks on the blanket-covered ground. Thus, unlike manos, some pestles were damaged through use without a lower counter-part, and it may be this that distinguishes some nonfood-processing pestles from those involved in food processing.

Use-wear damage patterns include varying amounts of impact fractures, abrasion, and rounding, depending upon the force and direction of the stroke and the nature of the contact surface. Damage location helps identify whether the pestle was used in a mortar or against a flat surface. The nature of the damage helps identify whether the damage was created through use in a wood or stone mortar. A pestle used in a mortar has damage on the end and some distance up the side, depending somewhat on mortar basin depth. A forceful stroke against a stone mortar creates impact fractures and abrasive scratches. A similar stroke in a wood mortar creates impact fractures and abrasive scratches, but the suppleness of the wood smooths the angularity of the grains and impact fractures, creating a sheen. Use on the ground concentrates use-wear damage on the distal end of the tool, creating impact fractures, chips, and abrasion, depending on the hardness of the intermediate substances and the hardness of the contact surface.

Ten pestles were recovered from Los Pozos. Four (40 percent) are fragmentary; two are too small to determine the nature of their use and will not be described further. Both were found in fill contexts; one had been recycled as a roasting or heating stone and was found within a pit in pit structure 898. The other was found in the fill of pit structure 813.

An unusual pestle (locally referred to as a "tooth pestle") was recovered from exterior pit 430. The broken end of a similar pestle was found in the fill of an interior pit in pit structure 327. The whole pestle has a bifurcate distal end with a groove that connects the bifurcate end to a biconical hole located near the center of the tool (Figure 5.9b). The bifurcate end and the groove have been pecked and ground to shape, but there is no use-wear damage. Only the ridge inside the hole is worn from contact with something pliable, probably a wooden shaft. The hole is not perfectly round. The pestle surface has been worn almost flat. The configurations and use-wear patterns are compatible with an unusually shaped, but broken, mortar found in pit structure 416. A similar pestle and potentially compatible mortar were recovered from undated proveniences at the Santa Cruz Bend site (Adams 1998). Both pestles are shaped from vesicular basalt and the damage to the pestle surfaces is from mixing more than crushing. The pestles differ in that the one from Santa Cruz Bend has use-wear damage in the notch that creates the bifurcated end, in the groove, and more extensively, in the hole. It was used in multiple activities and may have been used to smooth and straighten wooden shafts as well as work as a pestle in a mortar. While the pestle from Los Pozos may have been designed for use in multiple activities, there is no evidence it was used as anything other than a pestle. Ferg

(1998b) describes the distribution of other pestles of this type throughout the greater Southwest.

A whole pestle, from an interior pit in pit structure 327, is a small, carefully shaped, ovoid piece of vesicular basalt. The pestle surface is worn so smooth that the margins of the vesicles are flat, and there is a sheen on the level areas between the vesicles. There are no impact fractures to indicate that the pestle was used to crush granular material. Therefore, it is proposed that this pestle was used more to mix a powdery or doughy substance. Similar use-wear patterns are on a small, triangular pestle recovered from the fill of pit structure 867 (see Figure 5.9a). The curvature of both pestle surfaces and the use-wear patterns are compatible with a small vesicular basalt mortar from Feature 333 and an unusually shaped, but broken, mortar from Feature 416. Whether these tools were actually used together is impossible to determine.

A pestle recovered from a pit in pit structure 342 (Figure 5.12c) had more than one use. Both ends were used to crush red pigment (Munsell 2.5YR5/6), and both broad surfs were used to abrade a pliable, perhaps wooden surface. These broad surfaces are also covered with the same shade of red pigment as covers the ends. The different uses of this tool might have been to process pigment and apply it with the broad surfaces to wooden items.

The largest pestles were recovered from pit structures 302, 819, and 890. Those from 302 and 819 were manufactured to conical shapes. The pestle from 819 was found on the floor as part of an array that might have had ritual significance (see Appendix B). Wear on the surface is mostly abrasive scratches with no impact fractures and only extends a little way up the side of the pestle–indicative of its use in a stone mortar with a grinding rather than a crushing stroke. The pestle from 890 was in a disturbed context in pit structure 890 and had been used in multiple activities. The pestle surface has two corners broken off from being used forcefully against a stone mortar. The opposite end is more pointed and was used to chop something pliable against a hard surface. Two broad sides of the pestle each have a depression from use as a netherstone where something hard and smooth was processed. The one from 302 has a finger grip on one edge. Several large chips have been removed to create an edge on the distal end that is covered with impact fractures from being used to chop or pound a substance against a flat stone surface.

Collectively, the pestles from Los Pozos were designed for a variety of activities. Most (70 percent) are of strategic design, pecked and ground to specific shapes or to create special features either for holding or for accomplishing more than one task. Use-wear damage patterns indicate that motor habits included strokes for mixing, crushing, and chopping. Three could have been used concomitantly in other activities. One was also an abrader, one a netherstone, and one a pestle used in a different context. One pestle was sequentially recycled as a roasting stone. There is little evidence to suggest what was being processed with the pestles, except for the red pigment remaining on one.

Polishing Stones

Polishing stones are defined here as handstones of smooth surface texture involved in the final stages of the manufacture or production of other items. The texture of polishing stones alter the surfaces of other objects by creating a smooth and frequently shiny surface (Adams 1993a). Polishing stones have been associated with the manufacture of pottery, wood, or bone items, as well as the application of plaster to walls and floors (Adams 1979:51; Woodbury 1954:93).

Seven polishing stones were recovered from Los Pozos. Six have use-wear patterns consistent with use against another stone surface. Four of these are flattish pebbles with both edges and flat surfaces used to polish another smooth stone surface (Figure 5.13a-b). There are no abrasive scratches on the surface but there is a sheen on the highest elevations of the stone. This is consistent with experimental polishing stones used to polish other stone surfaces. The polishing stones from Los Pozos would have been useful for shaping other small stone items, such as the cruciforms and geometrics. Another polishing stone has a broader surface (Figure 5.13c), also used until a sheen was created, perhaps on a stone item.

The sixth polishing stone is "mushroom" shaped and was collected because of its unusual shape (Figure 5.13d). It is not a typical polishing stone shape, and the use wear is not obvious. However, the edge of the "cap" has been used to polish and would have been a useful tool for shaping small stone items, such as the cruciforms or other geometrics. It was recovered from the fill of pit structure 355.

The seventh polishing stone has use-wear patterns most similar to those created by polishing pottery. However, the only pieces of polished pottery are fragments from small figurines (see Chapter 8). The stone is covered with a black residue that makes it difficult to see some of the use-wear patterns. It was recovered from an interior pit in pit structure 327.

All of the polishing stones are of expedient design, and most have been used moderately, with one used heavily. None had been used in more than one activity. Four were made from a material of fine-grain texture that might have been too abrasive for polishing when

the tool was new, but the surfaces had been worn smooth and continued in use to polish.

Six flattish pebbles were recovered from the other Middle Santa Cruz settlements that are similar to the four found at Los Pozos and thought to have been useful for shaping other small stone items. Small stone items such as a nose plug and a cruciform were also found at the other settlements. It may be more than just fortuitous that small disk polishing stones occur at both sites as do small stone items. One polishing stone with use-wear patterns similar to pottery polishing was found in an Agua Caliente deposit at the Square Hearth site.

Pulping Stones

Only one tool recovered from Los Pozos might have been used as a pulping stone. It was found on the floor of pit structure 861. The flattish cobble has several edges that were used to pound something pliable (Figure 5.12b). One edge has a few flakes removed that make the edge sharper. It is unclear whether flake detachment was intentional or the result of use. The use-wear damage covers the flake scars indicating that use continued after the flakes were detached. Such a stone might have been use to smash vegetal foods into pulp or to smash agave leaves in the production of fiber. Bernard-Shaw (1990b:188) describes using a "friable hammer" to pound agave leaves to help separate the pulp and fibers. The distinction between pulping stones and pecking stones is made at the microscopic level. Pecking stones have sharp margins to the impact fractures created by direct contact with a stone surface. The margins of impact fractures and any protruding grains become rounded by the pliable substance that cushions the pulping stone as it is struck against a hard surface (compare photomicrographs of Figures 5.12a-b).

Roasting Stones

Roasting stones are pieces of ground stone artifacts that have been heat-cracked because they were recycled in cooking or heating activities. Similarly damaged stones that were not originally ground stone items are called fire-cracked rock. In total, 5,524 roasting stones and fire-cracked rock were recovered from 71 features, including formal roasting pits, other exterior pits, pit structures and their interior pits, and from unprovenienced contexts. A small percentage (2.1 percent) of the fire-cracked rocks were ground stone artifacts; an even smaller percentage (.6 percent) were identifiable; the remainder were too broken to identify artifact type.

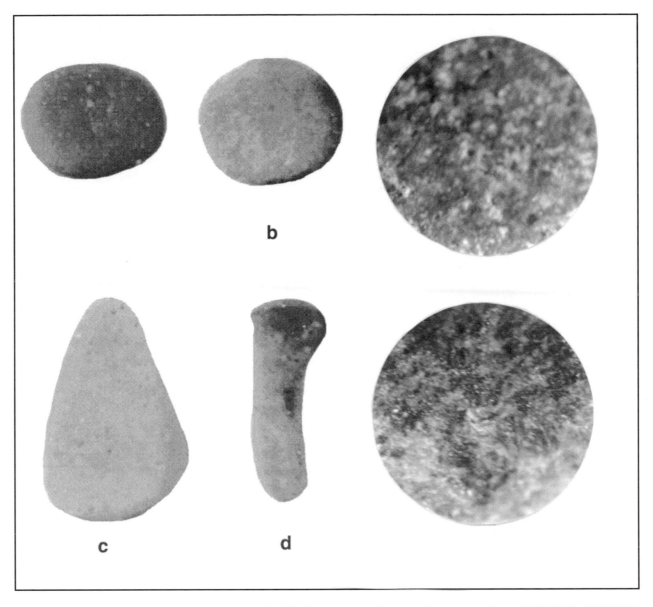

Figure 5.13. Polishing stones: a-c) flat pebbles used as polishing stones, perhaps against stone surfaces (416/492.02, 425/507.02, 820.01/177.08); d) mushroom-shaped polishing stone (355/332.04); photomicrographs (40x) of a) (top) and d) (bottom) at right. (Actual size of d) is 9.8 cm long x 6.1 cm wide x 1.8 cm thick.)

Shaped

One shaped piece was found in a pit within pit structure 327. This piece is thin, and tabular, ground on all edges and slightly onp one flat side. It has been burned on one side, and if it were larger and had smoother surfaces, it could be considered a griddle. Perhaps it was used as the lid to a small pot and the burning was not related to its use.

Unidentified

Twenty-four artifacts are not classifiable; 87.5 percent because they are too fragmentary. The rest have been ground for some reason, but it is unclear if the grinding was the result of manufacturing or use.

SUMMARY

Now that the artifacts have been assigned to types and described, it is possible to summarize what the assemblage consists of, where it was found, and the nature and condition of the artifacts. Eighteen artifacts types were identified and described (Table 5.2). Only 33.5 percent of the artifacts were used in the single activity for which they were designed. Most artifacts (59.9 percent) are fragments and fire-damaged, either burned (12.3 percent) or heat-cracked (44 percent). These figures are a result of a large percentage (42.6 percent) recycled into cooking or heating activities. In addition to roasting stones, the 57.1 percent of the assemblage used secondarily includes a mortar also used as an abrader, and manos used as pestles or to process pigment. A large percentage (43.3 percent) were of sequential secondary use so they were no longer usable in the activity for which they were originally designed.

How the artifacts were designed is determinable only on 46.1 percent of the artifacts. Of those, 67.2 percent are of expedient design where no effort was expended in creating a specific shape or in making tools comfortable to hold. The rest (32.8 percent) are of strategic design. Design effort was highest for three artifact types: manos (32.6 percent), geometrics (18.6 percent), and pestles (16.3 percent) (Table 5.3). Special note should be made of the geometrics and balls because they were all part of an arrangement of artifacts on the floor of pit structure 819 that may have had some ritual significance (see Appendix B). These ground stone artifacts were either ground to create specific shapes or polished to enhance their natural shapes. Several have evidence of some type of cordage or sinew wrapping.

Very few (6.3 percent) of the recovered ground stone artifacts were designed for food processing. However, as explained in the description of manos and metates, this fact should not be interpreted as a lack of food-processing activities at Los Pozos. There were many more manos (n = 26) than metates (n = 3), and all the metates were fragments. The whole metates used at Los Pozos were probably taken upon abandonment or scavenged sometime thereafter.

Evidence of pigment processing was found on 13 percent of the artifacts. Most common were handstones (n = 17), lapstones (n = 11), and manos reused to grind pigment (n = 5). A pestle and three metate fragments also had evidence of pigment processing. Several shades of red were created, ranging from red (10R5/6) to weak red (10R4/4) to reddish-yellow (7.5YR6/8).

The Los Pozos ground stone artifacts were recovered from nine contexts (Table 5.2). The largest percentages were found in interior pits (31.7 percent), in pit structure fill (29.9 percent), and on pit structure floors (17.7 percent). Considering the high percentage of fire-cracked ground stone, it is surprising that so few were actually recovered from roasting pits (6.7 percent). The contents of roasting pits were most likely cleaned out periodically and the fire-cracked rocks dumped as trash to fill abandoned pits and pit structures. The small percentage found in roasting pits does not adequately reflect roasting or heating activities as some 5,524 pieces of fire-cracked rock were counted from thermal pits.

These descriptive summaries of the ground stone artifacts do little to explore prehistoric behavior. The following section will explore in more depth the behaviors that helped create the archaeological record through an evaluation of archaeological context and comparisons with the assemblages from the other Middle Santa Cruz settlements.

CONCLUSIONS

At the beginning of this chapter, there were several questions formulated for comparing the Los Pozos ground stone assemblage with those from the other Santa Cruz settlements. These questions concern pigment processing, mano and metate design, the scarcity of metates, the use of interior pits, and the secondary use of artifacts. Comparisons between assemblages are made using percentages and the Brainerd-Robinson value which is computed to assess assemblage similarities (following Cowgill 1990:512-521). There is no guideline for deciding when assemblages are more or less similar. I have chosen 75 percent as the break between similar and dissimilar assemblages. Sample sizes are too small for significance tests, but some interesting patterns are visible in the data that may eventually be testable with the accumulation of more data from other sites.

The assemblages from the other Middle Santa Cruz settlements are divisible into Cienega (600 B.C. to A.D. 1) and Agua Caliente (A.D. 1 to 550) components, and there are some interesting differences in grinding technology between the two (Adams 1998). Los Pozos dates to about 400 B.C. to A.D. 100–a time encompassing part of both time periods. The Middle Archaic component at Los Pozos is discussed elsewhere (Gregory, ed. 1999). The question is: to which time period is the Los Pozos assemblage most similar?

As a start toward answering this question, the types of artifacts recovered were compared. The similarity values between the Los Pozos and Cienega assemblages (78.3 percent) and the Los Pozos and Agua Caliente assemblages (78 percent) are nearly identical (Table 5.4). There are slightly lower percentages of

Table 5.2. Summary data on all ground stone artifacts.

Variable	Number
Context	
Burial	3
Disturbed	5
Exterior pit	22
Interior pit	90
Pit structure fill	85
Pit structure floor	50
Roasting pit	19
Posthole	6
Well	4
Condition	
Fragments	171
Whole	113
Burned	
Heat cracked	125
Indeterminate	10
No	114
Yes	35
Design	
Expedient	88
Indeterminate	153
Strategic	43
Use	
Indeterminate	40
Multiple	18
Recycled	121
Redesign	2
Reused	6
Single	95
Unused	2
Second type	
Abraders	2
Hammerstones	1
Handstones	7
Netherstones	1
Offering	3
Pecking stones	3
Pestles	10
Polishing stones	1

Variable	Number
Second type	
Roasting rocks	118
Unidentified	1
Sequence	
Concomitant	24
Not applicable	137
Sequential	123
Processing type	
Ambiguous	19
Food	18
Indeterminate	36
Multiple	132
Nonfood	56
Non-processing	19
Uncertain	4
Texture	
Coarse	1
Fine	200
Medium/fine	6
Smooth	42
Vesicular	35
Material	
Basalt	15
Chert	2
Granite	5
Igneous	29
Jasper	2
Limestone	1
Metamorphic	6
Mudstone	1
Quartz	2
Quartzite	3
Rhyolite/andesite	57
Schist/gneiss	9
Sedimentary	106
Unknown	9
Vesicular basalt	36
Welded tuff	1
Total n	284

manos (15 percent) and lapstones (9.8 percent) in the Los Pozos assemblage than in either the Cienega (manos, 18.1 percent; lapstones, 18.5 percent) or the Agua Caliente assemblages (manos, 23.1 percent; lapstones, 15.4 percent). However, there are higher percentages of mortars (5.2 percent) than in the Cienega (3.9 percent) or the Agua Caliente assemblages (0 percent). Additionally, there is an arrangement of possible ritually associated geometrics on the floor of a Los Pozos pit structure that does not occur in any of the Cienega or Agua Caliente structures. Otherwise, the assemblages have the same types of artifacts, in roughly the same percentages. However, the Agua Caliente assemblage is somewhat smaller, with fewer artifact types.

Table 5.3. Strategically designed artifacts.

Artifact	Number
Ball	3
Disk	1
Geometric	8
Mono	14
Metate	2
Mortar	4
Netherstone	1
Ornament	1
Pestle	7
Pulping stone	1
Shaped	1
Total	43

Table 5.4. Comparison of identified artifact types.

Artifact	Los Pozos		Cienega		Agua Caliente	
	Number	Percent	Number	Percent	Number	Percent
Abraders	2	1.2	7	3.3	0	–
Balls	4	2.3	2	.8	0	–
Geometrics	9	5.2	0	–	0	–
Grinding slabs	0	–	4	1.7	0	–
Handstones	50	28.9	70	30.2	17	32.7
Lapstones	17	9.8	43	18.5	8	15.4
Manos	26	15.0	42	18.1	12	23.1
Metates	3	1.7	6	2.6	1	1.9
Mortars	9	5.2	3	1.3	0	–
Natural	3	1.7	0	–	0	–
Netherstones	27	15.6	19	8.2	9	17.3
Ornaments	1	.5	0	–	0	–
Pecking stones	2	1.2	1	.4	0	–
Perforated disks	1	.6	3	1.3	1	1.9
Pestles	10	5.9	16	6.9	1	1.9
Polishing stones	7	4.0	12	5.2	2	3.8
Pulping stones	1	.6	1	.4	1	1.9
Shaped	1	.6	0	–	0	–
Slabs	0	–	1	.4	0	–
Tabular tools	0	–	1	.4	0	–
Vessels	0	–	1	.4	0	–
Total	173	–	232	–	52	–

Note: Brainerd/Robinson value comparing Los Pozos with Cienega = 156.6/78% similar.
Brainerd/Robinson value comparing Los Pozos with Agua Caliente = 155.9/78% similar.

Table 5.5. Comparison of identifiable manos and metates.

Artifact	Los Pozos		Cienega		Agua Caliente	
	Number	Percent	Number	Percent	Number	Percent
Metate						
Basin	0	–	3	60.0	1	100.0
Flat/concave	1	100.0	2	40.0	0	–
Total	1		5		1	
Mano						
Basin	2	8.7	3	7.9	0	–
Flat/concave	21	91.3	34	89.5	10	100.0
Total	23		37		10	

One of the questions posed in the introduction dealt with the differing design of manos and metates. It was noted at the other Middle Santa Cruz settlements that most of the identifiable Cienega metates (60 percent) are basin, and the remainder are flat/concave. The only metate recovered from the Agua Caliente component is basin. No whole metates were recovered from Los Pozos, and the only identifiable fragment was from a flat/concave metate. The pattern of recovered manos provides a different picture. Almost all of the manos were used on flat/concave metates (Table 5.5). As has been noted, the presence of so many flat/concave manos and so few flat/concave metates is perhaps explained by either abandonment strategies of removing useful metates, or by post-abandonment scavenging. Based on the experiments described in the mano section, and the high percentage of flat/concave manos and metates at all the Middle Santa Cruz settlements, it is proposed that the inhabitants built upon their technological knowledge derived from using basin manos and metates, by expanding into a flat/concave design to more efficiently process soaked kernels and other wet or oily seeds. However, mano design strategies were not the same. The mano manufacturers at the other Middle Santa Cruz settlements created specific features to make the manos more comfortable to hold

Table 5.6. Comparison of artifacts with pigment.

Artifact	Los Pozos		Cienega		Agua Caliente	
	Number	Percent	Number	Percent	Number	Percent
Abrader	0	–	1	1.3	0	–
Grinding slab	0	–	2	2.6	0	–
Handstone	17	44.7	20	26.3	4	44.4
Lapstone	11	28.9	32	42.1	2	22.2
Mano	5	13.2	11	14.5	1	11.1
Metate	0	–	1	1.3	0	–
Mortar	0	–	2	2.6	0	–
Netherstone	3	7.9	7	9.2	2	22.2
Pestle	1	2.6	0	–	0	–
Polishing stone	1	2.6	0	–	0	–
Total	38		76		9	
Percent of assemblage		22.0		32.2		16.3

Note: Brainerd/Robinson value comparing Los Pozos with Cienega = 174.4/87% similar.
Brainerd/Robinson value comparing Los Pozos with Agua Caliente = 175.4/88% similar.

than the Los Pozos mano manufacturers. Perhaps the food grinders at the other settlements intended their manos to be used longer or during more intense grinding sessions.

The question about pigment processing can be evaluated by looking at what artifacts from each assemblage have been so used. The Cienega assemblage has the largest percentage (32.2 percent), with 16.3 percent of the Agua Caliente, and 22 percent of the Los Pozos assemblage having evidence of pigment processing tools (Table 5.6). Handstones, lapstones, and reused manos are the most common. The similarity values are nearly identical between the Los Pozos and Cienega assemblages (87.2 percent) and the Los Pozos and Agua Caliente assemblages (87.7 percent). The biggest differences are that higher percentages of lapstones (42.1 percent) and lower percentages of handstones (23.6 percent) were used during the Cienega component than at Los Pozos (lapstones, 28.9 percent; handstones, 44.7 percent) or during the Agua Caliente component (lapstones, 22.2 percent; handstones, 44.4 percent). Of the tools used in pigment processing, reused manos are nearly equally frequent within the Los Pozos (13.2 percent), Cienega (14.4 percent), and Agua Caliente (11.1 percent) assemblages. In general, however, there appear to be fewer artifacts (n = 9) and types of artifacts (n = 4) used in pigment processing in the Agua Caliente assemblage than in either the Los Pozos (n = 38; types = 6) or the Cienega (n = 76; types = 8) assemblages. The significance of this pattern cannot be statistically tested however, due to small sample sizes.

Another question was asked about archaeological context. In general, artifact context was more similar between Los Pozos and Cienega assemblages (86.3 percent) than between Los Pozos and Agua Caliente (66.1 percent) (Table 5.7). The strongest similarity is between the use of interior pits where ground stones are more commonly found than in any other archaeological context, except at the Agua Caliente component where there are few interior pits and even fewer ground stone artifacts in them. A lower percentage of the ground stone assemblage was found on floors at Los Pozos (17.6 percent) than at the Cienega components (30.2 percent) or at the Agua Caliente components (36.4 percent). A slightly higher percentage was found in roasting pits at Los Pozos (6.7 percent) than at the Cienega component (3.6 percent) or at the Agua Caliente component (1.8 percent). However, when totals are compared, it is clear that the recycling of ground stone items into roasting or heating activities is greater at Los Pozos (44 percent) than at the Cienega component (10.6 percent) or at the Agua Caliente component (21.8 percent). Recycled ground stone fragments at Los Pozos were found more often in pit structure fill and trash deposits.

In order to understand how these context distributions relate to prehistoric behavior such as artifact use, storage, discard, and abandonment, it is necessary to evaluate depositional types. For this study, two depositional types are compared: de facto and trash deposits. De facto deposits were defined by Schiffer (1987:89) as "... tools ... that although still useable (or reuseable), are left behind when an activity area is abandoned." The determination of whether a deposit is de facto or trash was made during excavation and requires an evaluation of stratigraphy and artifact associations. De facto deposits were identified in interior pits and on pit structure floors, and these are compared with all other trash deposits (Table 5.8). At Los Pozos, ground stone

Table 5.7. Comparison of archaeological contexts.

Context	Los Pozos		Cienega		Agua Caliente	
	Number	Percent	Number	Percent	Number	Percent
Disturbed	5	1.8	2	1.0	2	3.6
Exterior pit	22	7.7	22	8.9	8	14.5
Interior pit	90	31.7	71	28.6	3	5.5
Pit structure fill	85	29.9	64	25.8	20	36.4
Pit structure floor	50	17.6	75	30.2	20	36.4
Roasting pit	19	6.7	9	3.6	1	1.8
Other[a]	13	4.6	5	2.0	1	1.8
Total	284		248		55	

Note: Brainerd/Robinson value comparing Los Pozos with Cienega = 172.5/86% similar.
Brainerd/Robinson value comparing Los Pozos with Agua Caliente = 132.2/66% similar.
[a]Other includes burials, wells, postholes.

was most abundant in interior pits (31.7 percent), but only 21.3 percent of the artifacts found in interior pits were considered by the excavators to be de facto deposits. All the whole ground stone artifacts found on pit structure floors were thought to be de facto deposits by the excavators. In general, balls, geometrics, and lapstones are more abundant in de facto deposits, while handstones and polishing stones were more abundant in trash. The balls and geometrics, primarily from the floor of one particular pit structure (Feature 819), were among an array of artifacts in a possible ritualistic arrangement (see Appendix B).

Forty-eight whole artifacts were thought to have been in de facto deposits either on pit structure floors or in interior pits. Most interesting is the finding that no floor assemblages included food-processing metates and few manos. Perhaps food-processing activities occurred outside. Pigment processing was the most common activity represented, especially in pit structures 389 and 861 where more than one artifact found on the floor had been so used. Pit structures 815, 333, 416, 870, and 819 have a single floor artifact, each used in processing pigment. Pit structures 324, 342, and 861 have no floor assemblages, but do have pigment processing tools among those found in interior pits.

A similar analysis was completed for the assemblages from the other Middle Santa Cruz settlements that also had de facto deposits on floors and in interior pits. At the other settlements, it was found that most of the 17 whole and fragmentary metates were found in disturbed deposits with only three in de facto deposits: one in a fixed grinding position on the floor of an Agua Caliente component pit structure and the other two in separate Cienega exterior pits. Handstones were nearly equally represented on floors, in interior pits, and in trash fill deposits. The manos and lapstones recovered from de facto deposits, however, had more interesting patterns. Lapstones were found in higher percentages

Table 5.8. Comparison of de facto and trash deposits.

Artifact	De Facto		Trash	
	Number	Percent	Number	Percent
Abraders	1	2.1	1	1.7
Balls	4	8.3	0	–
Disks	0	–	1	1.7
Geometrics	5	10.4	3	5.1
Handstones	10	20.8	22	37.3
Lapstones	9	18.8	6	10.2
Manos	11	22.9	10	16.9
Mortars	1	2.1	0	–
Natural	1	2.1	2	3.4
Netherstones	3	6.3	1	1.7
Pecking stones	0	–	2	3.4
Pestles	2	4.2	4	6.8
Polishing stones	0	–	6	10.2
Pulping stones	1	2.1	0	–
Shaped	0	–	1	1.7
Total	48		59	

on pit structure floors than in interior pits, while manos were found in higher percentages in interior pits than on pit structure floors.

Patterns recognized at other Middle Santa Cruz settlements suggest that the manos found in interior pits were more likely to have been used only in food-processing activities than those found on floors. Sixteen and seven-tenths percent of manos on pit structure floors (n = 6) and 60 percent (n = 10) of those in interior pits were used only for food processing. Those used secondarily were most often used in pigment processing activities. The sample of de facto manos (n = 11) from Los Pozos is slightly smaller. Half (50 percent) of the four manos found in de facto deposits on pit structure floors were used only for food processing. Of the seven found in interior pits, five (71.4 percent) were

Table 5.9. Comparison of tool use.

	Los Pozos		Cienega		Agua Caliente	
	Number	Percent	Number	Percent	Number	Percent
Use						
Single	95	38.9	142	13.5	30	17.6
Multiple	18	7.4	29	11.2	9	21.6
Recycled	121	49.6	24	0.9	11	0
Redesigned	2	0.8	2	7.9	0	2.0
Reused	6	2.5	17	66.0	1	58.8
Unused	2	0.8	1	0.5	0	0
Secondary use						
Concomitant	24	16.3	33	46.5	3	18.8
Sequential	123	83.7	38	53.5	13	81.3

Note: Brainerd/Robinson value comparing Los Pozos with Cienega = 122.6/61% similar.
Brainerd/Robinson value comparing Los Pozos with Agua Caliente = 139.8/70% similar.
Brainerd/Robinson value comparing Los Pozos with Cienega secondary = 139.2/70% similar.
Brainerd/Robinson value comparing Los Pozos with Agua Caliente secondary = 195.1/98% similar.

used only for food processing; two (28.6 percent) were reused in pigment processing. Thus, the pattern first recognized at the other settlements seems to also occur at Los Pozos in that manos stored in interior pits were less likely to have been used in secondary, nonfood-processing activities than those found on pit structure floors.

There are other patterns recognizable with the secondary use of artifacts. When compared for secondary use, the Los Pozos and Agua Caliente assemblages are nearly identical (97.6 percent), with 83.7 percent of the Los Pozos assemblage and 81.3 percent of the Agua Caliente assemblage having sequential secondary use (Table 5.9). A higher percent of the Cienega assemblage had concomitant secondary use (46.5 percent), more often reused or used in multiple activities then either the Los Pozos (16.3 percent) or Agua Caliente (18.8 percent) assemblages. If the hypothesis outlined in the introduction is correct, this should reflect differences in settlement strategies. It is suggested that the occupants of the Cienega settlements were relatively more permanent, needing either to conserve raw material by making certain tools operable in more than one activity or were limiting the number of tools needing storage. They also more frequently strategically designed tools, especially manos, perhaps with the intent of using them longer. The occupants of Los Pozos and the Agua Caliente settlements were more likely to use tools of expedient design and to recycle or redesign existing tools into activities other than those for which they were originally intended. It is proposed that this behavior is more common to people who were not the original tool designers and users and may reflect the use of abandoned, discarded, or scavenged tools. Such behavior may have been common to people who were either reoccupying (either temporarily or permanently) abandoned settlements, or were scavenging tools from

abandoned portions of settlements. Secondary tool use alone is not enough to assess settlement strategy, but it does provide a line of evidence that, in combination with other evidence, can create an argument for a particular strategy.

In conclusion, this analysis of ground stone artifacts from Los Pozos has attempted to answer several questions about prehistoric behavior and its development through time. The evidence available for answering these questions is strong in some areas and weak in others. For example, the evidence for discussing food-processing activities is weakened by the lack of metates. However, comparisons of mano types suggest that most processing was done with flat/concave manos and metates beginning with the Cienega component and continuing through the Agua Caliente component. The Los Pozos assemblage is well within this continuum. Similarly, pigment processing appears to have been an important activity beginning with the Cienega component and continuing through the Agua Caliente component. Based on the fewer number of artifacts and smaller variety of types used in Agua Caliente pigment processing, however, there may have been a decline in this activity. The use of interior pits for storing artifacts, especially food-processing manos, also seems to decline to the point where there are very few interior pits and fewer ground stone artifacts in them, in the Agua Caliente component. At Los Pozos, the use of interior pits is more similar to the Cienega component than the Agua Caliente component. In general, the strategies employed for storing ground stone tools and using them in pigment processing are more similar to the Cienega component than the Agua Caliente component. At the same time, the secondary use of artifacts is more similar to the Agua Caliente component (which has more sequential secondary tool use) than the Cienega component (which has more concomitant

Cienega component (which has more concomitant secondary tool use). For these reasons, it is suggested that the Los Pozos inhabitants were most similar to nearby Cienega people in their application of grinding technology than to the later Agua Caliente inhabitants; however, they may have employed a slightly different settlement strategy than the Cienega occupants at the nearby Santa Cruz Bend settlement (the largest Cienega occupation in the Middle Santa Cruz Valley). Either Los Pozos was not occupied for as many years as Santa Cruz Bend, or Los Pozos was more repeatedly abandoned and reoccupied than Santa Cruz Bend. We know that the occupation time span was longer, perhaps by centuries, at Santa Cruz Bend (Mabry et al. 1997:6-7; see Chapter 11 and Appendix F). The ground stone data alone are not enough to decide which strategy was used, but perhaps in conjunction with other evidence, the answer will be clearer.

CHAPTER 6

SHELL ARTIFACTS

Arthur W. Vokes

The Early Agricultural component at Los Pozos (AZ AA:12:91 [ASM]) produced a shell assemblage of 166 pieces, representing an estimated 145 individual artifacts that include finished artifacts, fragmentary materials, and whole valves. This chapter provides a descriptive summary of the artifact forms present and the genera represented, as well as a comparison with contemporaneous and later assemblages from southern Arizona and northern Sonora. This comparative information is then used to interpret regional patterns related to the Early Agricultural period occupation and that of the ensuing Early Ceramic period and the subsequent development of the Hohokam.

METHODOLOGY

The assemblage was subjected to detailed analysis involving creation of a descriptive record–often including a scale drawing–along with a set of linear measurements made with a digital vernier caliper. Notes on condition, shape, decorative motifs, and technological aspects were recorded. Fragments that could be refitted were considered to be single occurrences, with the number of pieces recorded. In instances where fragments could not be refitted, but the evidence indicated a high probability they were from the same artifact, the pieces were also recorded as a single occurrence, with a count of the fragments included on the specimen's detail sheet. Specimens were generally considered to be complete if a full set of linear measurements could be obtained. The artifact taxonomy employed is largely based upon that developed by Haury (1945, 1965c, 1976) for the shell assemblages from the Hohokam sites of Snaketown and Los Muertos. Biological identification and nomenclature were made primarily in accordance with Keen (1971), with Abbott (1974) and Rehder (1981) as additional sources.

GENERA AND SPECIES REPRESENTED AND AREAS OF ORIGIN

There were two general sources of shell available to the prehistoric inhabitants of the region: marine shell from either the Pacific coast or the Gulf of California and local freshwater and terrestrial mollusks. With respect to identification of prehistoric sources of marine shell, archaeologists working in the American Southwest benefit from a natural division of oceanic environments off the western coast of the Baja Peninsula. Two different currents–the Panamic from the south and the Californian from the north–converge, and turn seaward in the area of Magdalena Bay. Consequently, many species of mollusca occur in only one of the two zones, or have a limited distribution and frequency in one zone relative to the other. While both biotic communities contributed to the shell material available to the prehistoric inhabitants of the southern Southwest, the principal source appears to have been the Gulf of California. Shell genera and species from Los Pozos are summarized in Table 6.1 and discussed below.

Pelecypods

As may be seen in Table 6.1, the number of pelecypod genera is relatively small by comparison with the gastropods represented. Only three pelecypods are present in the sample: *Laevicardium*, *Spondylus*, and either *Pteria* or *Pinctada*. The biological range of *Laevicardium elatum* extends north along the California coast into the area near San Pedro, California (Abbott 1974:486). However, it does not appear to be as common in these colder waters as it is in the Panamic province. Additionally, there is no clear evidence for its extensive use by the native populations of southern California (Gifford 1947). Therefore, it would seem likely that most, if not all, of the *Laevicardium* recovered at Los Pozos originated in the Gulf of California.

Spondylus species present off the western coasts of the Americas are restricted to the warmer Panamic waters, and three species are endemic to portions of the Gulf of California. The mottled orange and red coloration of the single *Spondylus* bead recovered during the current excavations suggests it was probably made from the shell of *Spondylus princeps*.

Pteria sterna and *Pinctada mazatlanica* are closely related species of the family Pteriidae. The shells of these species are characterized by a bluish white nacreous interior and a dark brown exterior cortex. Of the two, *Pinctada* has the heavier shell and a thicker nacreous mantle. Both species are restricted to the Panamic province, and prior to extensive pearl fishing in the past century, were quite common in the shallow waters of the gulf.

Table 6.1. Genera and species recovered at Los Pozos.

Genus or Species	NISP[a]	MNI[b]	Province[c]
Marine			
Pelecypods (bivalves)			
Laevicardium elatum	3	3	B
Spondylus sp.	2	2	P
Pteria or *Pinctada*	1	1	P
Unidentified	3	3	–
Gastropods (univalves)			
Olivella			
Olivella dama	5	5	P
Olivella sp.	58	58	–
Conus sp.	3	3	P
Columbella	2	2	P
(cf. *C. aureomexicana*)			
Trivia solandri	5	5	P
Vermetidae	1	1	B
Haliotis			
Haliotis cracherodii	3	1	C
Haliotis sp.	5	5	C
Unidentified nacreous shell	73	54	–
Unidentified shell	2	2	–
Freshwater and terrestrial			
Pelecypods (bivalves)			
Anodonta californiensis	20	3	–
Gastropods (univalves)			
Helisoma sp.	5	5	–
Succinea sp.	4	4	–

[a]NISP = Number of identified specimens per taxon.
[b]MNI = Minimum number of individuals.
[c]P = Panamic; C = California; B = Both Panamic and California.

Gastropods

The diversity of gastropods is largely due to the high frequency and diversity of whole shell beads in the assemblage. The genus *Olivella* is well represented in both biotic communities, but individual species are well segregated from each other. Silsbee (1958) suggests that one method of distinguishing the species occurring off the California coast from those of the gulf is in the shape of the callus. This permits a relatively simple method for identifying the general geographic source of the shell, even if the species cannot be determined. Residual coloration indicated that five of the specimens were the species *Olivella dama*, commonly occurring in the tidal pools in the gulf region. Fifty-five other specimens exhibited the extended callus characteristic of gulf species. Many of these are similar to *Olivella dama*, but lacked diagnostic features that would allow assignment to this species. No specimens having

characteristics indicating a coastal California origin were recovered.

Other univalves were also recovered, but these were not found in the same frequencies as that characterized for *Olivella*. Five specimens of *Trivia solandri* were recovered. The biotic range of this coffee bean cowrie extends as far north as the area around Palos Verdes, in southern California (Abbott 1974:148), but the species is more numerous in the Gulf of California waters. There is only one species of *Conus* that ranges into the colder waters off the coast of California; however, its size and form indicate it is not the species employed to make the artifacts recovered from Los Pozos. All of the species that are likely candidates for use in creating Los Pozos' artifacts are restricted to the gulf region. *Columbella* is a genus restricted to the Gulf of California. The specimens recovered appear to be the species *Columbella aureomexicana*, which is found throughout the gulf and south along the western coast of Mexico.

The most notable exception to this emphasis on the Panamic province of the gulf in the current assemblage is *Haliotis*. In North America, this genus occurs only in the colder waters off the Pacific coast. *Haliotis* was used extensively by native populations along the California coast, and was commonly exchanged with groups in the interior. Beads and ornaments made of abalone have been reported from numerous Archaic period sites in the Great Basin region (Bennyhoff and Hughes 1987) and at Basketmaker sites in northern Arizona and southern Utah (Lindsay et al. 1968). Recently, quantities of *Haliotis* have been reported from several Late Archaic/Early Agricultural sites in southern Arizona (Vokes 1998a).

A single segment of worm gastropod shell was recovered from the site surface prior to excavation. These animals form tubular shells that are initially coiled, but fairly quickly become extended. It is virtually impossible to distinguish the different genera and species on the basis of the segments. The term Vermetidae is used here to identify any of the tube-producing gastropods. Tubular shell-producing gastropods occur in both provinces, although they are more common in the warmer waters of the gulf region.

Three genera available to prehistoric populations of the southern deserts of the American Southwest are characterized by a heavy nacreous mantle. These are the various species of *Haliotis*, *Pteria sterna*, and *Pinctada mazatlanica*. The high frequency of artifacts manufactured from unidentified nacreous shell indicates the iridescent qualities of these genera were highly valued. Thickness and coloration suggest that many of these specimens were made of abalone; however, some *Pteria* and/or *Pinctada* is also likely to have been present.

Anodonta

The freshwater rivers and streams of southern Arizona provided an alternative source for nacreous shell. The Santa Cruz River–flowing just to the west of Los Pozos–would have provided a convenient source of freshwater shellfish for the inhabitants. *Anodonta californiensis* is a moderately large, very gracile nacreous bivalve, endemic to most of the permanent water courses in Arizona prior to the impoundment of the rivers earlier in this century (Bequaert and Miller 1973:220-223). It is commonly recovered in considerable quantities in prehistoric sites along the Salt and other Arizona rivers, leading to the suggestion that some prehistoric populations may have exploited this shellfish as a food (Haury 1976:308; Howard 1987:77; Vokes 1988:373). Additionally, it is known to have been employed as a raw material by local artisans. However, *Anodonta* is comparatively rare in the current assemblage, with an estimated three valves represented. This meager representation is also characteristic of other Early Agricultural period and Hohokam assemblages within the Tucson Basin. The reasons for its apparent under-utilization are unknown at present, but may reflect local ecological conditions in the river system.

THE ARTIFACT ASSEMBLAGE

The artifact assemblage is summarized in Table 6.2. In addition to finished artifacts, the assemblage includes some complete, unmodified valves and fragmentary items that are either worked in some manner or are unmodified.

Worked Shell Artifacts

A number of artifact forms were present in the assemblage. These included beads of several different types, and a number of cut shell, geometric pendants.

Beads

A total of 117 shell beads was recovered from the excavations. The majority were simple forms of whole shell beads, with disk beads being the second most common type.

Whole Shell Forms. Sixty-six beads were created simply by perforation of the valve. In general, these were not modified beyond what was required to suspend the shell from a cord. Four genera and two different methods of suspension are represented.

The simple spire-lopped bead form is the dominant type in the assemblage (65 specimens). Spire-lopped forms are known from other Late Archaic sites and

were present throughout the prehistoric sequence. In the current assemblage, nearly all were *Olivella* valves in which the apex of the spire was removed and the internal columellar structure broken away to permit the passage of a cord through the top of the spire and out the natural aperture.

Two methods were employed to remove the spire. One involved grinding down the apex until a hole of sufficient size for passage of a cord was achieved (Figure 6.1a). This generally required removal of only the apex, but a small portion of the middle whorl of the spire was also sometimes removed. The second method involved removal of the spire by percussion (Figure 6.1b). This method appears to have involved indirect percussion, with a punch placed against the side of the spire and struck with a hammer–usually along the lower suture of the penultimate whorl. The result was the removal of most, if not all, of the spire, along with the associated internal columellar structure. The remaining edge would have been somewhat irregular, although often roughly following the suture line. The point of impact may be marked by the presence of a notch with a crushed edge; in some instances, the resulting edge was subsequently ground smooth.

Approximately 80 percent (n = 49) of *Olivella* beads in the assemblage were perforated by grinding away the apex of the spire. However, 46 of these were recovered from Feature 836, suggesting that they may represent a single strand of beads and are perhaps best considered as a single occurrence. When considered by occurrence, 31 percent of the beads were formed by grinding away the apex, with 69 percent of the total created by breaking away the spire. This pattern is similar to that reported for the Santa Cruz Bend (AZ AA:12:746 [ASM]) assemblage (Vokes 1998a).

Olivella beads from Los Pozos ranged in size from 9.09 mm to 18.30 mm (mean = 12.96 mm). Intuitively, it might be expected that shorter specimens would have been made by the percussion method, as percussion tended to remove more of the spire than did grinding. This expected pattern does not hold however. Although the smallest bead was produced by percussion, the mean length for beads produced in this manner (13.03 mm) is greater than the mean for all *Olivella* beads. This may reflect selection for larger valves when this technique was employed. This inference is supported by the fact that the widths of valves modified by percussion–a dimension which would not be affected by manufacturing technique–also indicate a preference for larger valves. Specimens with the spire broken away averaged 7.19 mm in width, compared to 6.45 mm for beads with ground perforations.

Spire-lopped beads were also made from *Conus* valves (Figure 6.1c–d) and *Columbella* (Figure 6.1e), with each genus represented by two specimens. In all four cases, the valves were perforated by grinding

Table 6.2. Summary of the Los Pozos shell assemblage.

		Beads			Artifact Form						
Genus	Whole Shell	Cylindrical	Disk	Rectangular Disk	Cut Pendants	Cut Shell	Whole Shell	Reworked Shell	Worked Fragment	Unworked Fragment	Total
Marine											
Pelecypods											
Laevicardium	–	–	–	–	1	–	–	1	–	1	3
Spondylus	–	–	1(1)[a]	–	1	–	–	–	–	–	2
Pteria/Pinctada	–	–	1(1)	–	–	–	–	–	–	–	1
Unidentified	–	–	–	–	1	–	–	–	–	2	3
Gastropods											
Olivella	61(11)	–	–	–	–	–	–	–	–	2	63
Conus	2(1)	–	–	–	–	–	–	–	–	1	3
Columbella	2(2)	–	–	–	–	–	–	–	–	–	2
Trivia	1(1)	–	–	–	–	–	4	–	–	–	5
Vermetidae	–	1(1)	–	–	–	–	–	–	–	–	1
Haliotis	–	–	2(1)	–	2	1	–	–	1	–	6
Unidentified nacreous	–	–	44(6)	1(1)	5	–	–	–	4	–	54
Unidentified shell	–	–	1(1)	–	1	–	–	–	–	–	2
Freshwater/land											
Pelecypods											
Anodonta	–	–	–	–	2	–	–	–	–	1	3
Gastropods											
Helisoma	–	–	–	–	–	–	2	–	–	3	5
Succinea	–	–	–	–	–	–	3	–	–	1	4
Total	66(13)	1(1)	49(8)	1(1)	13	1	9	1	5	11	157

[a] #(#) = Frequency of beads (number of occurrences).

away the apex of the spire. Both *Conus* beads were recovered from the same deposit as the concentration of spire-lopped *Olivella* beads, in Structure 836. On one of these (Figure 6.1c), the entire spire and shoulder area of the shell had been ground to form a rounded dome. Only the apex was ground on the other *Conus* specimen (Figure 6.1d), which is heavily pitted from beach weathering.

A second form of whole shell bead is represented by a single *Trivia* valve (Figure 6.1f). In this instance, the shell was perforated by punching two holes through opposite ends of the dorsum, near the anal and siphonal canals. Thus the cord could pass through the body cavity without employing the natural aperture.

Cylindrical Beads. A single example of a cylindrical, or tubular, bead cut from "worm tube" segment from the family Vermetidae (Figure 6.1g) was recovered from the surface of the site prior to excavation. The

segment is 45.34 mm in length, with a maximum diameter of 8.68 mm–an unusually large specimen. Both ends have been cut and ground smooth.

Disk Beads. Forty-nine discoidal beads were recovered from eight different features. Forty-seven were made from nacreous marine shell, but most were devoid of cortex or other identifying features (Figure 6.1h). Two retained enough cortex to indicate they were manufactured from the shell of *Haliotis cracherodii* (Figure 6.1i and j), and a third appears to have been carved from either *Pteria* or *Pinctada*.

The average diameter of disk beads ranged from a minimum of 6.57 mm to a maximum of 12.35 mm. The smallest specimen was the only white marine shell disk bead in the present sample (Figure 6.1k). It was recovered from Feature 433, an extramural pit. The two largest specimens were the two *Haliotis* beads (Figure 6.1i–j), found together in a floor pit in Structure 337.

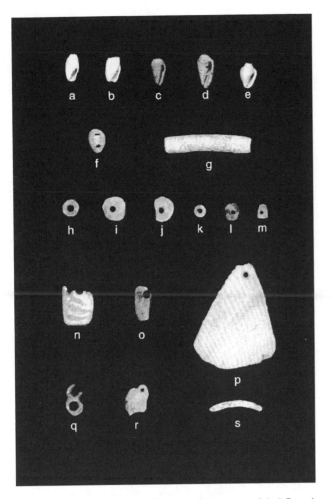

Figure 6.1. Shell artifacts. (Length of specimen a) is 1.5 cm.)

Other Cut Bead Forms. A cut shell bead related in form to the disk beads was recovered from the floor of Structure 836. It is a quadrilateral bead made of a whitish, nacreous marine shell of unidentified genus (Figure 6.1m) and represents a roughly trapezoidal form (7.51 mm x 5.67 mm) with a slightly off-center perforation. This perforation was predominantly uni-conical, with only a limited amount of counter drilling.

In the Tucson Basin, this form is known from the Santa Cruz Bend site, where one specimen was recovered (Vokes 1998a), and from the Milagro site where such two beads were found (Huckell and Huckell 1984:27; B. Huckell et al. 1995:237). The Los Pozos specimen is also comparable in size and shape to quadrilateral beads reported from a cremation at the Late Archaic Coffee Camp site (Halbirt and Henderson 1993). In the American Southwest generally, this form appears to be restricted to the Early Agricultural/Late Archaic interval. However, it has a much longer legacy among the cultures of coastal California and groups in the Great Basin (Bennyhoff and Hughes 1987).

Pendants

Thirteen cut shell pendants were recovered. In all cases where shape could be positively identified or generally assessed, the pendants appeared to have been geometric in form. No life forms appear to be present. This pattern duplicates that observed in the shell assemblages from Santa Cruz Bend and Stone Pipe (AZ BB:13:425 [ASM]) (Vokes 1998a).

The most common shape (three examples) is a rectangular form. The largest of these is a broad pendant carved from a *Haliotis* shell (Figure 6.1n) and was recovered from a floor pit in Feature 302. The specimen is missing the top segment, but the remaining portion measures 20.03 mm in length, 16.59 mm in width, and 3.73 mm in thickness. There are two perforations visible along the broken upper edge. One is centered between the sides, while the other is off to one side. A reasonable inference is that these were sequential perforations, with the off-center hole drilled after the centered perforation was rendered unusable, possibly due to breakage. Suspension from the second hole would have resulted in the pendant hanging tilted on its axis.

A second rectangular pendant is represented by a smaller, nearly complete specimen (Figure 6.1o) recovered from the fill of Feature 819. A non-nacreous marine shell is clearly represented, but the genus could not be determined. The pendant has a decided twist, suggesting that it was cut from near the umbo of a relatively thick-walled bivalve. Burning of the specimen eradicated all traces of its original coloration. The edges are well shaped, being rounded and quite

Most of the remaining beads were recovered from two concentrations of disk beads, one recovered from the fill of Structure 324 (n = 23) and the other from the fill of Structure 836 (n = 15).

The specimens from Feature 324 were made from a white nacreous shell with a slight purplish cast. One appears to have retained a portion of a muscle scar, suggesting it was cut from a bivalve, possibly *Pinctada* or *Pteria*. These beads range from 8.46 mm to 9.53 mm in diameter (mean = 8.81 mm). By comparison with the specimens in Feature 324, the beads recovered from Feature 836 are noticeably larger, ranging from 9.02 mm to 11.47 mm in diameter (mean = 9.96 mm). Unfortunately, this material was discolored by burning, and little can be said about the original color of the shell.

The only other non-nacreous disk bead is a some-what irregular specimen made from a *Spondylus* valve (Figure 6.1l). It retained its mottled orange/red color-ation and was recovered from a posthole in Feature 867.

smooth. The perforation is somewhat off-center, and largely drilled from one face. Owing to the thickness of the specimen (4.64 mm), the cone of the perforation is quite wide and deep. This probably weakened the edge and ultimately resulted in rupture at the narrowest point of the perforation perimeter. While one face is relatively smooth and flat, the other shows a number of broad grinding facets.

The third rectangular pendant was recovered from a floor pit in Feature 390 and is quite fragmentary. The former shape of this specimen is inferred on the basis of similarities with several specimens recorded by the author during the excavation of Feature 1541 at the nearby Wetlands site (Vokes 1998b). The current specimen is made of nacreous marine shell and is broken at both ends. Portions of three perforations are evenly spaced along its length. Two of the perforations are visible along the breaks, one at each end, with the third centered between these in the remaining strip. The segment is 10.93 mm in width; the central perforation is just over 4.0 mm in diameter.

Two triangular pendants were recovered, one from a floor pit in Feature 863, the other from the fill of Feature 352. The former is a large specimen cut from the lower back of a *Laevicardium* valve (Figure 6.1p) and measures just over 51.7 mm in length and 43.37 mm in width. The natural margin of the valve forms one edge, while the other two edges were roughly shaped by having been chipped and snapped to form and then smoothed by limited grinding. The perforation is biconical, although drilling was conducted primarily from the exterior surface. The second triangular pendant was made from a nacreous marine shell of unknown genus and represents a broad form with a rounded point. The upper portion has broken away, with the break passing through two perforations. In contrast to the rectangular pendant, these perforations are spaced roughly equidistant from the edges and may represent a set designed for a cord to loop through.

Another pendant recovered from a large floor pit in Feature 390 is shaped in the form of a figure "8" (Figure 6.1q). A portion of one of the loops has broken out. The outer perimeter is somewhat irregular, with small facets, but the edge is well ground. The specimen was carved from a nacreous shell, and its thickness indicates a marine origin. However, the specimen was burned to a dark gray color is devoid of cortex making more specific identification is impossible.

A complete pendant of somewhat irregular shape (Figure 6.1r) was recovered from the fill of an extramural pit, Feature 422. The specimen was cut from a white marine bivalve. The form was dictated in large part by the natural shape of the shell. One surface has an even convex curve, while the opposite face is relatively flat around part of the perimeter; the center portion has a sharply defined depressed channel that appears to be the interior cavity formed by the beak of the shell. Along one of the edges are indistinct shadows that may represent taxodontic teeth, suggesting the shell represented is either *Glycymeris* or *Chama*. A biconical perforation is present along one edge. Near this perforation is the depression of a second perforation in the ground edge of the pendant, indicating the current form represents reuse of a larger specimen. In its current form, this pendant measures 17.69 mm in length and 12.07 mm in width.

Five other pendant fragments were recovered from five different features, all too fragmentary to permit detailed description of their original form. However, the form of worked edges and perforations indicate that these specimens were probably geometric rather than zoomorphic in outline. In one case, a fragmentary piece of *Spondylus* recovered from the fill of a floor pit in Feature 318 had portions of two perforations visible on the surface along different broken edges. One of these was unfinished, not having completely penetrated the shell wall. This suggests the original pendant had broken, with the break passing through the finished perforation, and that an effort was made to redrill the remaining portion, only for the specimen to fragment before the process was completed. Two other pendant fragments were made from the local freshwater bivalve, *Anodonta californiensis*. In both instances, the forms appeared to be curvilinear, but the pieces' fragments were too small to support definitive assessment of specific form.

The final cut pendant in the collection was too fragmentary to permit any determination of original form. It is represented by five layer fragments of nacreous shell. There is evidence of grinding in several places along the edges, but the fragments cannot be reassembled to form a coherent shape.

Other Cut Shell

A reconstructible carved segment of *Haliotis cracherodii* was recovered from the fill of Feature 372 (Figure 6.1s). This specimen is a thin curved strip of shell 35.1 mm in length, 3.56 mm in width, and 1.38 mm in thickness. The sides are slightly beveled inward towards the exterior surface of the shell, and the ends are rounded. The intended function of this piece is not apparent. There is no evidence of perforation for purposes of suspension, although cordage could have been wrapped around the shaft. It is also possible it was mounted onto some larger object with an adhesive. The thin, fragile character of the specimen suggests it was not used without some form of support.

FRAGMENTARY MATERIALS

A number of fragments were recovered that are worked but lack diagnostic features to enable identification of form or are unmodified. Most of these fragments were probably derived from finished artifacts that were broken. However, it is possible that some were the product of local manufacturing activities or from breakage of whole valves.

Worked Fragments of Unknown Form

Eight fragments representing five specimens exhibit evidence of purposeful modification but cannot be identified as to the form of artifact represented. These pieces generally show one or more worked facets or edges, often well finished, suggesting they were pieces of finished artifacts. Four represent unidentified nacreous marine shell while the fifth is a fragment of *Haliotis*.

Unworked Fragments

Seven fragments of unworked shell were also identified. These include parts of two *Olivella* valves and a segment of a *Conus* shell. Both of these genera are represented by whole shell beads, and it is likely that these seven specimens represent fragments of whole beads or valves broken during the manufacturing process. The action of breaking away the spire of an *Olivella* valve is likely to produce failure at times, and the waste would be very difficult to identify.

The remaining fragmentary material included three pieces of marine bivalves and a small fragment of *Anodonta*. One of the marine specimens is a segment from the lower back of a *Laevicardium* valve. A second specimen may be a section from the side margin of a *Laevicardium* valve, but the fragment is quite small and the identification uncertain. A groove along one edge of this specimen is somewhat irregular and appears to be natural. The third specimen may be a piece of a *Chione* valve. If this identification is correct, it would be the only occurrence of this genus in the collection.

MANUFACTURING EVIDENCE

There is limited evidence indicating that local craftspeople were involved in the production of some shell artifacts. This evidence is mainly in the form of whole, unmodified valves. In addition, there is one fragment of shell that may represent an effort to refashion a fragment of a finished artifact.

Whole Valves

Four whole valves of the marine species *Trivia solandri* were recovered from deposits in Feature 390 at Los Pozos, two from the fill of the structure and two from different floor pits. This species is also represented in the assemblage by a single whole shell bead, and it is logical that these unmodified valves were also intended for such use. This evidence indicates that local artisans were attempting to supply at least a portion of the demand for these products; however, the effort seems to be limited in scale and scope.

Reworked Fragment

A long triangular fragment of the back of a *Laevicardium* valve was recovered from the fill of an extramural pit, Feature 428. One of the long side edges is well ground and polished to form a smooth, curved shape. The opposite edge has limited high point grinding present along a small portion of the edge, with the remaining portions being roughly broken. The narrow end is also a rough, unmodified break. This likely represents a fragment of a finished artifact in the process of being reworked, possibly into a pendant.

SUMMARY AND DISCUSSION

The assemblage of shell artifacts recovered from Los Pozos is dominated by relatively simple forms, being composed primarily of whole shell beads, various forms of carved beads, and pendants. The whole shell bead forms represented were created with minimal modification of the natural valve form through grinding or breaking away of the apex of the spire, punching a hole through the back of the shell, or sectioning a naturally occurring tubular segment. Cut shell artifacts would have required greater effort to create, but the forms represented are relatively simple geometrics, and no complex geometric or zoomorphic forms have been identified.

Whole shell beads were made from genera commonly present along the beaches and intertidal zones of the Gulf of California coastline. Much of the nacreous shell favored for artifacts produced by greater degrees of modification cannot be identified as to the genera represented, owing to extensive modification of the shell surface during the manufacturing process and to post-manufacture burning. When sufficient diagnostic features remain, the genus most often represented is the Pacific coast genus *Haliotis*. However, the evidence indicates that nacreous marine species from the Gulf of California, as well as the nacreous freshwater genus *Anodonta*, were being used as well.

Intrasite Distribution

Shell artifacts were widely distributed across the excavated portion of the site, with a few prominent concentrations (see Table 6.3). Most of the shell material was recovered from within pit structures, and 28 of the 42 wholly or partially excavated structures produced shell material, usually one or two specimens. Three pit structures (Features 324, 390, and 836) produced significantly higher numbers of shell artifacts. Feature 324 contained 23 nacreous disk beads and a fragmentary cut pendant made from *Haliotis*. While it is possible these were part of a single set of material (a necklace?), the pendant was recovered from the large floor pit and the beads were recovered from the fill of the structure, suggesting separate depositional episodes. The deposits associated with Feature 390 are somewhat more complex. All four of the whole unmodified *Trivia* valves were recovered from this structure, along with two cut pendants and two worked fragments of nacreous shell. The *Trivia* valves were recovered from the fill of the structure, from the fill of the large floor pit, and from a posthole (Feature 390.15). Both pendants and one of the worked fragments were recovered from the large floor pit. Along with the fact that only one-quarter of the structure was excavated, this distribution of shell within the feature is difficult to assess.

The single greatest concentration of shell artifacts was within Feature 836, a pit structure located near the north end of the corridor. A total of 66 artifacts was recovered from the excavated portion of the structure. Included within this total are 49 whole shell beads made primarily from *Olivella* but with some *Conus* also present; 15 disk beads of nacreous shell; one rectangular bead; and an unmodified fragment of an unidentified marine bivalve. This material was recovered from the fill of the structure, from the floor, from the fill of the large floor pit, and from two postholes. The structure had burned and collapsed and most of the shell artifacts recovered were burned to some degree, suggesting that all of the artifacts may have been deposited at the same time. The distribution of the artifacts within the structure suggests they could have been resting on the roof or (perhaps more likely) suspended from the interior framework and scattered when the structure burned and collapsed.

Intersite Comparisons

Until recently, the aggregate assemblage of shell from Early Agricultural period contexts was small and thus, our understanding of the acquisition and use of shell by Early Agricultural period populations was quite limited. Excavations at Milagro (Huckell 1990; Huckell and Huckell 1984), the Pantano Wash site, and La Paloma (Dart 1986) produced a handful of shell artifacts which provided only a tantalizing glimpse into the variability and composition of the shell materials in use. The largest assemblage was recovered from Ventana Cave (Haury 1950), but because of several problems relating to temporal assignment and interpretation of the deposits, this material must be viewed with care and is not used here. The shell artifact assemblage recovered from the excavations at Santa Cruz Bend and the Stone Pipe site (Vokes 1998a) substantially increased the sample for this interval and thus, a much clearer understanding of the nature of shell acquisition and use during this period of changing adaptations. The Los Pozos assemblage and those recovered from the Clearwater (Diehl 1997a) and Wetlands sites (Freeman 1998) further enlarge the available sample and provide a basis for a reassessment of previously recognized patterns. In addition, these more recent investigations have made possible a more refined temporal ordering of the respective assemblages (see Chapter 12). Table 6.4 summarizes the shell assemblages from all of the Late Archaic/Early Agricultural settlements investigated to date in the Tucson Basin, with the sites listed in the temporal order suggested in Chapter 12.

The earliest shell assemblage in this sequence is from the San Pedro phase Milagro site (B. Huckell 1990:236-237; Huckell and Huckell 1984:27; Huckell et al. 1995:63; L. Huckell 1993:313), which includes six artifacts recovered during several sequential excavations at the site. Two of these specimens–one square bead and a fragment of *Laevicardium*–have yet to be described in the published literature but are noted in a discussion of the material from the Coffee Camp site (L. Huckell 1993:Table 13.4).

Assemblages from the early Cienega phase Clearwater (Diehl 1997a) and Wetlands (Vokes 1998b) sites represent the next most recent assemblages. Clearwater failed to produce any marine shell artifacts, nor was *Anodonta* recovered in any form. Some terrestrial shell was recovered, but none of the specimens showed any evidence of having been modified. The absence of shell at Clearwater may be the result of a relatively small excavated sample, but evidence from the contemporaneous Wetlands site suggests that shell may not have been as common as it is in later assemblages. With one remarkable exception, the Wetlands assemblage is quite limited in the number and variety of shell artifacts represented. A total of four artifacts was recovered from two features, a pit structure and an extramural pit. The exception is a very unusual mortuary deposit (Feature 1541) which contained the partial remains of several individuals and a large quantity of shell artifacts–mostly beads and pendants.

Table 6.3. Shell artifacts by provenience.

Feature	Recovery Context	North	East	Stratum	Level	Artifact Type	Species	Cond[a]	NISP	MNI
0.00	Site surface	-	-	-	-	Cylindrical/barrel bead	*Vermetus* sp.	U	1	1
302.01	Intramural pit	1836.20	297.40	30	1	Whole shell bead	*Olivella* sp.	U	1	1
302.01	Intramural pit	1836.20	297.40	30	1	Cut pendant, rectangular	*Haliotis* sp.	U	1	1
318.02	Intramural pit	1761.60	292.35	30	1	Cut pendant, geometric	*Spondylus* sp.	U	1	1
324.00	Structure fill	1807.81	292.15	10	1	Disk bead	Unidentified marine, nacreous	U	23	23
324.00	Structure fill	1807.79	290.63	10	1	Unworked fragment	*Anodonta californiensis*	U	1	1
324.14	Intramural pit	1808.54	291.04	30	1	Cut pendant, geometric	*Haliotis* sp.	U	1	1
324.14	Intramural pit	1808.54	291.04	30	1	Whole valve	*Succinea* sp.	U	1	1
327.01	Intramural pit	1804.40	296.55	30	1	Unworked fragment	*Helisoma* sp.	U	1	1
328.00	Floor fill	1805.70	298.60	19R	1	Whole shell bead	*Olivella dama*	U	1	1
333.00	Structure fill	1792.60	301.87	10	1	Disk bead	Unidentified marine, nacreous	U	1	1
333.00	Structure fill	1794.00	301.87	10	1	Unworked fragment	*Conus* sp.	U	1	1
333.00	Floor contact	1796.02	303.14	20	1	Whole shell bead	*Olivella* sp.	U	1	1
337.08	Posthole	1781.66	297.02	30	1	Disk bead	Unidentified marine, nacreous	U	1	1
337.14	Intramural pit	1782.70	297.80	30	2	Disk bead	*Haliotis* sp.	U	1	1
337.14	Intramural pit	1782.70	297.80	30	2	Disk bead	*Haliotis* sp.	U	1	1
346.00	Extramural pit	1754.21	294.48	50	1	Whole shell bead	*Olivella* sp.	U	1	1
346.00	Extramural pit	1754.21	294.48	50	1	Cut pendant, unknown	Unidentified marine, nacreous	U	5	1
352.00	Structure fill	1744.87	295.86	10	1	Cut pendant, triangular	Unidentified marine, nacreous	U	1	1
354.00	Structure fill	1774.28	303.40	10	1	Worked fragment, unknown	*Haliotis* sp.	Ch	1	1
355.09	Intramural pit	1807.96	291.96	31	1	Whole shell bead	*Olivella* sp.	B	1	1

Table 6.3. Continued.

Feature	Recovery Context	North	East	Stratum	Level	Artifact Type	Species	Cond[a]	NISP	MNI
355.46	Intramural pit	1807.70	290.93	30	1	Whole shell bead	*Olivella dama*	U	1	1
370.00	Structure fill	1734.76	299.81	10	1	Whole shell bead	*Olivella* sp.	U	1	1
372.00	Structure fill	1722.48	303.98	10	1	Whole shell bead	*Olivella dama*	U	1	1
372.00	Structure fill	1724.30	305.60	10	1	Whole shell bead	*Columbella aureomexicana*	U	1	1
372.00	Structure fill	1722.48	303.98	10	1	Cut shell, unknown	*Haliotis cracherodii*	U	3	1
372.01	Intramural pit	1724.18	305.60	30	1	Cut pendant, geometric	*Anodonta californiensis*	U	1	1
390.00	Structure fill	1682.76	294.36	10	1	Whole valve	*Trivia solandri*	U	2	2
390.00	Structure fill	1682.76	294.36	10	1	Worked fragment, unknown	Unidentified marine, nacreous	U	1	1
390.15	Intramural pit	1684.60	295.90	30	1	Whole valve	*Trivia solandri*	U	1	1
390.16	Intramural pit	1683.55	293.74	30	1	Cut pendant, rectangular	Unidentified marine, nacreous	B	1	1
390.16	Intramural pit	1683.55	293.74	30	1	Cut pendant, other geometric	Unidentified marine, nacreous	B	2	1
390.16	Intramural pit	1683.55	293.74	30	1	Whole valve	*Trivia solandri*	U	1	1
390.16	Intramural pit	1683.55	293.74	30	1	Worked fragment, unknown	Unidentified marine, nacreous	U	2	1
399.00	Extramural pit	1676.08	304.00	50	1	Unworked fragment	*Olivella* sp.	U	1	1
417.00	Structure fill	1616.43	294.53	10	1	Whole valve	*Succinea* sp.	U	1	1
422.00	Extramural pit	1795.21	302.10	50	1	Whole shell bead	*Trivia solandri*	U	1	1
422.00	Extramural pit	1795.21	302.10	50	1	Cut pendant, irregular	Unidentified marine, bivalve	U	1	1
425.00	Structure fill	1667.52	295.68	10	1	Whole shell bead	*Olivella* sp.	U	1	1
425.00	Structure fill	1667.52	295.68	10	1	Whole shell bead	*Olivella dama*	U	1	1
425.00	Structure fill	1667.52	295.68	10	1	Whole shell bead	*Olivella dama*	U	1	1
425.01	Intramural pit	1669.16	296.43	30	1	Whole shell bead	*Columbella aureomexicana*	U	1	1
425.11	Posthole	1668.40	295.95	30	1	Whole shell bead	*Olivella* sp.	U	1	1
428.00	Extramural pit	1684.60	294.37	50	1	Fragment being reworked	*Laevicardium elatum*	U	1	1

Table 6.3. Continued.

Feature	Recovery Context	North	East	Stratum	Level	Artifact Type	Species	Cond[a]	NISP	MNI
433.00	Extramural pit	1683.68	293.74	50	1	Disk bead	Unidentified marine shell	Ch	1	1
812.23	Intramural pit	1663.65	297.62	30	1	Unworked fragment	*Olivella* sp.	B	1	1
813.01	Intramural pit	1668.13	298.02	30	1	Cut pendant geometric	*Anodonta californiensis*	U	18	1
815.00	Structure fill	1691.15	299.00	10	1	Whole shell bead	*Olivella* sp.	U	1	1
819.00	Structure fill	1707.28	301.13	10	1	Cut pendant, rectangular	Unidentified marine shell	B	1	1
819.00	Structure fill	1709.00	298.45	10	1	Unworked fragment	Unidentified marine bivalve	U	1	1
825.00	Structure fill	1852.23	298.00	10	1	Whole shell bead	*Olivella* sp.	U	1	1
836.00	Structure fill	1848.15	299.07	10	1	Whole shell bead	*Olivella* sp.	U	7	7
836.00	Structure fill	1848.15	299.07	10	1	Whole shell bead	*Olivella* sp.	B	22	22
836.00	Structure fill	1848.15	299.07	10	1	Whole shell bead	*Olivella* sp.	B	1	1
836.00	Structure fill	1848.15	299.07	10	1	Whole shell bead	*Olivella* sp.	B	1	1
836.00	Structure fill	1848.15	299.07	10	1	Whole shell bead	*Olivella* sp.	Ch	1	1
836.00	Structure fill	1848.15	299.07	10	1	Whole shell bead	*Olivella* sp.	Ch	1	1
836.00	Structure fill	1848.15	299.07	10	1	Whole shell bead	*Conus* sp.	B	1	1
836.00	Structure fill	1848.15	299.07	10	1	Whole shell bead	*Conus* sp.	B	1	1
836.00	Structure fill	1848.15	299.07	10	1	Disk bead	Unidentified marine, nacreous	B	15	14
836.00	Structure fill	1848.15	299.07	10	1	Whole valve	*Helisoma* sp.	U	1	1
836.00	Structure fill	1848.15	299.07	10	1	Unworked fragment	*Helisoma* sp.	U	1	1
836.00	Structure fill	1848.15	299.07	10	1	Unworked fragment	*Succinea* sp.	U	1	1
836.00	Floor contact	1848.50	300.40	20	1	Squared-disk bead	Unidentified marine, nacreous	U	1	1
836.01	Intramural pit	1849.47	299.98	30	1	Whole shell bead	*Olivella* sp.	U	1	1
836.01	Intramural pit	1849.47	299.98	30	1	Whole shell bead	*Olivella* sp.	B	1	1
836.01	Intramural pit	1849.47	299.98	30	1	Whole shell bead	*Olivella* sp.	B	1	1
836.01	Intramural pit	1849.47	299.98	30	1	Whole shell bead	*Olivella* sp.	B	1	1

Table 6.3. Continued.

Feature	Recovery Context	North	East	Stratum	Level	Artifact Type	Species	Cond[a]	NISP	MNI
836.01	Intramural pit	1849.47	299.98	30	1	Whole shell bead	*Olivella* sp.	B	1	1
836.01	Intramural pit	1849.47	299.98	30	1	Whole shell bead	*Olivella* sp.	B	4	4
836.01	Intramural pit	1849.47	299.98	30	1	Whole shell bead	*Olivella* sp.	B	1	1
836.01	Intramural pit	1849.47	299.98	30	1	Whole shell bead	*Olivella* sp.	B	1	1
836.01	Intramural pit	1849.47	299.98	30	1	Whole shell bead	*Olivella* sp.	Ch	2	2
836.01	Intramural pit	1849.47	299.98	30	1	Disk bead	Unidentified marine, nacreous	B	1	1
836.01	Intramural pit	1849.47	299.98	30	1	Whole valve	*Succinea* sp.	U	1	1
836.09	Posthole	1848.80	299.63	30	1	Unworked fragment	Unidentified marine bivalve	U	1	1
836.25	Posthole	1850.83	299.60	30	1	Whole shell bead	*Olivella* sp.	B	1	1
863.02	Intramural pit	1829.50	302.22	30	1	Cut pendant, triangular	*Laevicardium elatum*	U	1	1
864.00	Structure fill	1818.50	304.70	10	1	Disk bead	*Pteria/Pinctada*	U	1	1
866.00	Structure fill	1805.10	304.60	10	1	Disk bead	Unidentified marine, nacreous	U	1	1
866.00	Structure fill	1805.10	304.60	10	1	Disk bead	Unidentified marine, nacreous	B	1	1
867.00	Structure fill	1776.75	304.47	10	1	Disk bead	Unidentified marine, nacreous	U	2	1
867.00	Structure fill	1776.75	304.47	10	1	Disk bead	Unidentified marine, nacreous	U	1	1
867.00	Structure fill	1776.75	304.47	10	1	Worked fragment, unknown	Unidentified marine, nacreous	U	3	1
867.01	Intramural pit	1776.80	305.10	30	1	Worked fragment, unknown	Unidentified marine, nacreous	U	1	1
867.04	Posthole	1778.83	305.69	30	1	Disk bead	*Spondylus* sp.	U	1	1
870.00	Structure fill	1787.08	304.82	10	1	Whole valve	*Helisoma* sp.	U	1	1
882.00	Structure fill	1648.27	304.15	10	1	Unworked fragment	*Helisoma* sp.	U	1	1
890.00	Structure fill	1862.15	300.55	10	1	Cut pendant, geometric	Unidentified marine, nacreous	U	10	1

[a]U = Unburned; B = Burned; Ch = Charred.

Table 6.4. Shell material from other Late Archaic/Early Agricultural period sites within the Tucson Basin.

Site	Genera	Artifact Form	Count	Reference
La Paloma	*Laevicardium*	Unworked fragments	2	Dart 1986:147
	Glycymeris	Bracelet	1	
	Anodonta	Unworked fragment	1	
Pantano Wash	Vermetidae	Cylindrical bead	1	ASM Catalog A-24632
Valencia Road	*Haliotis*	Worked fragment	1	Mayro 1985:216
Milagro	*Pinctada*	Square bead	3	B. Huckell 1990:236-237; Huckell and Huckell 1984:27
	Olivella	Bead	2	L. Huckell 1993:313
	Laevicardium	Unworked fragment	1	Huckell et al. 1995:63
Santa Cruz Bend	*Glycymeris*	Cut shell pendant	2	Vokes 1998a
		Bracelet fragment reworked	1	
	Laevicardium	Pendants in process	2	
		Worked fragment, unknown	2	
	Spondylus/Chama	Irregular bead, pendant	1	
	Pteria/Pinctada	Disk bead	1	
	Unidentified marine bivalve	Disk bead	1	
		Cut shell pendant	1	
	Olivella	Whole shell bead	47(19)[a]	
		Complete valves	2	
		Worked fragment, unknown	1	
		Unworked fragment	4	
	Conus	Whole shell bead	4(4)	
	Columbella	Whole shell bead	3(3)	
	Trivia	Whole shell bead	9(7)	
		Complete valves	2	
		Unworked fragment	1	
	Agaronia	Whole shell bead	1	
	Mitrinae	Whole shell bead	2(1)	
	Acamea	Whole shell pendant	1	
		Unworked fragment	3	
	Vermetidae	Cylindrical bead	2(2)	
	Haliotis	Cut shell pendant	4	
		Pendant in process	1	
		Worked fragment, unknown	2	
	Unidentified marine univalve	Worked fragment, unknown	1	
		Unworked fragment	3	
	Unidentified marine nacreous shell	Disk bead	2(2)	
		Square bead	1	
		Cut shell pendant	1	
		Pendant in process	1	
		Worked fragment, unknown	5	
		Unworked fragment	2	
	Unidentified marine shell	Disk bead	1	
	Anodonta	Unworked fragment	2	
	Unidentified nacreous shell	Cut shell pendant	1	
	Unidentified shell	Cut shell pendant	1	

Table 6.4. Continued.

Site	Genera	Artifact Form	Count	Reference
Stone Pipe[b]	*Glycymeris*	Bracelet	1	Vokes 1998a
	Olivella	Whole shell bead	8(4)	
		Unworked fragment	1	
	Haliotis	Worked fragment, unknown	2	
		Saucer-shaped bead	1	
		Unworked fragment	1	
	Unidentified marine	Disk bead	1	
	nacreous shell	Worked fragment, unknown	1	
	Anodonta	Unworked fragment	1	
Wetlands[c]	Unidentified marine	Disk bead	3	Vokes 1998b
	nacreous shell	Cut pendant	2	
	Anodonta	Worked fragment, unknown	1	

[a]#(#) = Number of beads (number of occurrences).
[b]"Good contexts" only.
[c]Does not include assemblages from burial (Feature 1541).

This feature was not directly dated, but is thought to belong to the early Cienega phase (Freeman 1998). It is interesting that all of the artifacts from Wetlands deposits are made from nacreous shell (Figure 6.2), although in most cases the genus represented cannot be identified due to extensive modification of the bead and pendant surfaces. However, in all but one of those instances where an assignment is possible, the genus *Haliotis* is represented; the exception is a fragment of the nacreous freshwater genus *Anodonta*.

The assemblages from the Santa Cruz Bend and Stone Pipe sites represent the third temporal set of materials. Both sites probably witnessed early and late Cienega occupation or use, and there is some evidence that the later interval is most strongly represented (see Chapter 12). After eliminating deposits that may have been mixed with later Hohokam material, these sites had a combined assemblage of 141 specimens (Vokes 1998a). In this combined assemblage, there is a dramatic increase in both the number of shell artifacts and in the diversity of forms represented. Whole shell beads, carved beads, various cut shell pendants, whole shell pendants, and a few possible bracelets are present. For the first time, there is evidence to suggest local production of some artifacts (Vokes 1998a). The increase in diversity of forms is paralleled by a dramatic increase in the number of non-nacreous shell artifacts (Figure 6.2), largely resulting from the apparently enthusiastic adoption of whole shell beads. The wide variety of genera employed to make these beads (Table 6.3) perhaps suggests a period of experimentation with this simple artifact form. However, nacreous shell still accounts for over 20 percent of the assemblage, a proportion not duplicated in later Hohokam assemblages.

Los Pozos represents the next most recent assemblage in the sequence, as the excavated portion of the site represents a single component late Cienega phase manifestation. Not surprisingly, the Los Pozos assemblage is similar in many respects to the combined assemblage from Santa Cruz Bend and Stone Pipe sites discussed above (Vokes 1998a). Both sets of material stress a diversity of bead and cut pendant forms. However, the smaller assemblage from Santa Cruz Bend and Stone Pipe contains a number of genera and artifact forms not represented in the Los Pozos material. Although these genera and forms were present in relatively low frequencies, their absence may reflect an increasing standardization of accepted forms, particularly with respect to whole shell beads. *Olivella* accounts for nearly 75 percent of the whole shell beads from the combined Santa Cruz Bend and Stone Pipe assemblages, while over 92 percent of whole shell beads from Los Pozos were made from this genus. These possible developments may also help to explain the relative resurgence in forms employing nacreous shell material at this time (Figure 6.2). Another factor that helps to explain the persistence of nacreous material is that it was a desirable and perhaps favored medium for several different artifact forms. Of the features at Los Pozos with shell artifacts, half included some form of nacreous shell.

During the following Agua Caliente phase of the Early Ceramic period, a major shift in shell use occurs in southern Arizona with the widespread adoption of bracelets as the dominant artifact form. It is this development that sets the standard that is followed throughout the ensuing Hohokam era. The decline of nacreous materials in the assemblage seen in Figure 6.2 is largely a reflection of this pattern. Sixty percent of

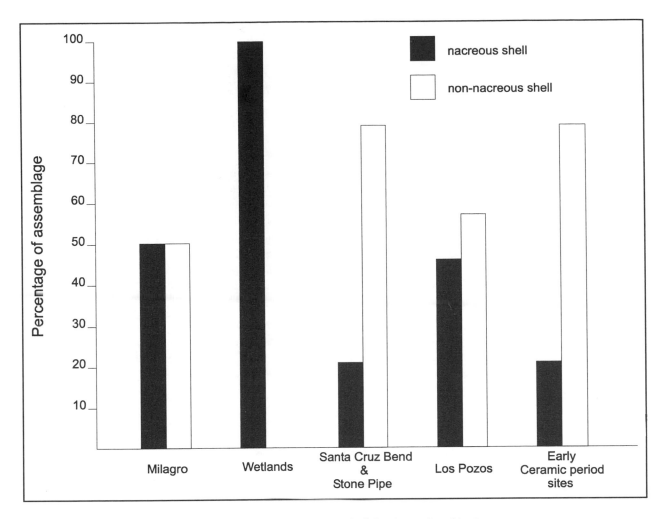

Figure 6.2. Relative frequency of nacreous versus non-nacreous shell for sites ordered in time.

the non-nacreous shell artifacts from securely dated Early Ceramic contexts at the Stone Pipe and Square Hearth were either bracelets or artifacts made from reworked bracelet segments. This shift would have been even more dramatic were it not for the presence of some freshwater nacreous material in the sample.

Virtually all of the artifact forms recovered from Los Pozos and other Early Agricultural period sites within the Tucson Basin have been reported from other sites outside of the basin (Table 6.5). However, the frequencies and the relative diversity of this material varies considerably. A single disk bead, made from a nacreous shell, was reported from the Coffee Camp assemblage (Huckell 1993:307-308), while the fill above a Late Archaic cremation at this site produced the remains of a necklace composed of 870 square and rectangular beads (Huckell 1993:308-309). In Sonora, similar specimens have been reported from the La Playa site (Johnson 1960:171), which has recently been shown to

have a substantial Late Archaic component. It should also be noted that this artifact form is widely distributed in California and Great Basin Late Archaic sites (Bennyhoff and Hughes 1987). No examples have been reported from Early Ceramic period contexts or from the following Hohokam interval, and this form appears to be restricted to the Early Agricultural/Late Archaic interval.

A striking difference is apparent in the frequency of whole shell beads when assemblages from the large Tucson Basin floodplain sites are compared with those from contemporaneous southern Arizona sites outside the basin. Two examples of this form are reported from the Donaldson site (L. Huckell 1993:313, B. Huckell 1995:68), but there were no examples represented in the material from either Ventana Cave (Haury 1950:361-374) or the Coffee Camp site (L. Huckell 1993:305-316). Another feature common to all of these Early Agricultural period assemblages is the rarity of bracelets. No

Table 6.5. Shell material from other Late Archaic/Early Agricultural period sites in southern Arizona outside of the Tucson Basin.

Site	Location	Period	Genera	Artifact Form	Count	Reference
Ventana Cave[a]	Papaguería	(Middle)-Late Archaic	*Sonorella*	Whole shell bead	1	Haury 1950:361-374; Vokes (n.d.b)
			Acmaea (Scurria Haury)	Whole shell pendant	1	
			Glycymeris	Bracelet	1	
			Glycymeris	Bracelet in process	2	
			Laevicardium	Worked fragment, unknown	4	
			Trachycardium	Worked fragment, unknown	2	
			Laevicardium	Unworked fragment	17	
			Glycymeris	Unworked fragment	1	
			Trachycardium	Unworked fragment	1	
			Dosinia	Unworked fragment	1	
			Sonorella	Unworked fragment	1	
			Unidentified marine shell	Unworked fragment	1	
Coffee Camp	Santa Cruz Flats	Late Archaic- (Post Archaic)	*Haliotis*/unidentified marine nacreous shell	Square beads	885 (1)[b]	Huckell 1993:13; Vokes (n.d.a)
			Unidentified marine nacreous shell	Disc bead	1	
			Laevicardium	Rectangular pendant	1	
			Haliotis	Artifact being reworked	1	
			Unidentified marine nacreous shell	Shaped piece	3	
			Unidentified marine shell	Shaped piece	1	
			Laevicardium	Worked fragment, unknown	1	
			Unidentified marine nacreous shell	Unworked fragment	1	
Donaldson	Cienega Creek	Late Archaic	*Laevicardium*	Ornament	1	Huckell 1993:313
			Olivella	Bead	2	
			Glycymeris	Bracelet	1	
			Anodonta	Unworked fragment	1	
AZ EE:4:1(ASM)	San Pedro River	Late Archaic	*Glycymeris*	Bracelet	1	Huckell 1993:313

[a]Levels 4-5 of the Upper Cave only (see discussion below).
[b]#(#) = Number of beads (number of occurrences).

bracelets were found at Los Pozos. One bracelet was recovered from Santa Cruz Bend (Vokes 1998a), but it is very small (external diameter = 32.96 mm) and may have been worn as a pendant. A bracelet recovered from the upper fill of Structure 189 at the Stone Pipe site exhibits the total eradication of the umbo that is a characteristic feature of Early Ceramic period bracelets from the site, suggesting that this artifact may have been intrusive from the later occupation. Haury reported several bracelets from the Archaic levels at Ventana Cave, but, as noted above, temporal assignment of these artifacts is problematic. Huckell (1995:68) reports a bracelet from the Donaldson site, but the specimen was found in a backdirt pile and its association with the Early Agricultural period component is questionable. This pattern clearly indicates that bracelets were not a significant aspect of Early Agricultural period material culture. Haury's (1950:368) conclusion that shell bracelets are a trait associated with pottery-making populations in southern Arizona appears to hold true.

Trade

Marine shell recovered from the Early Agricultural period settlements in southern Arizona was obtained from either the Gulf of California, or from the coastal waters off the state of California. As previously discussed, there are sufficient differences between these biotic communities to permit identification of species and some genera that are endemic to one or the other region. In the Los Pozos assemblage, 52 percent of the marine shell could be identified as originating from the gulf region, while only 4 percent was attributable to the colder waters off California. However, this observation is tempered by the fact that the assemblage includes 59 unidentified specimens (41 percent), most of which (54) represent nacreous material. Although unequivocal identification was not possible, this material generally exhibits luster and color more consistent with *Haliotis* than with *Pteria* or *Pinctada*. If most of this material is indeed *Haliotis*, then the ratio of California material to that from the gulf is far more evenly balanced.

It is likely that shell originating in the gulf was obtained through exchange with populations living along the river systems of northern Sonora, or those inhabiting the Papaguería region of southwestern Arizona. While it is possible that some of the material may have been directly acquired by journey to the gulf, as was the case with historic Tohono O'odham and Piman groups (Russell 1975:94; Underhill 1946:232-235), it seems more likely that Early Agricultural period populations in the Tucson Basin acquired most of their

shell by participation in exchange systems. This is most certainly the case with the material originating from the California coastal sources. It has been shown that an active exchange system existed between coastal California populations and the Great Basin region during this interval, and that considerable quantities of artifacts made of *Haliotis*-including beads and pendants-were being traded into the Great Basin and northern Arizona (Bennyhoff and Hughes 1987; Lindsay et al. 1968). The populations in southern Arizona may have obtained a share of this material either through a southern extension of the Great Basin trade system, or through more direct contact with the inhabitants of the desert regions of southern California. The Indian Hill Rockshelter (McDonald 1992; Wilke et al. 1986) is located in the Anza-Borrego Desert, approximately half-way between the California coast and the gulf. Excavations at this site show that the inhabitants were obtaining shell in some quantities from both sources. By extension, this acquisition system could have provided a link between the California coast and groups in southern Arizona.

Figure 6.3 illustrates the relative proportion of marine shell from both California coast and Gulf of California sources as well as the amount of the freshwater *Anodonta* for each of the Tucson Basin sites discussed above. Strictly on the basis of materials whose source could be definitively determined, and with minor exceptions, the Gulf of California appears to have been the major source of shell throughout the Early Agricultural period. None of the shell from Milagro was attributed to the California coast, but the *Olivella* was not identified to the species level. Even if these were from the gulf, it hardly seems unusual that such a small sample, which may represent the incipient stages of exchange system development, would emphasize the closer source. The Wetlands site material is exclusively nacreous, and while many artifacts were not specifically identified, most specimens appear to have greater affinities to *Haliotis* rather than to *Pteria* or *Pinctada*. Thus, it is quite possible that all of the shell from this site was from the California coast, but the fact that most of the items were recovered from an unusual mortuary deposit raises the issue of how representative the assemblage actually is.

For later assemblages considered here, California coastal material is probably underrepresented due to the bias of artifact forms and degree of associated modification. The cut beads and pendants associated with nacreous shell like *Haliotis* require far greater modification and reduction of the shell material than that associated with the whole shell beads and pendants. If one assumes that a large portion of the indeterminate nacreous shell is likely to be *Haliotis*, then the

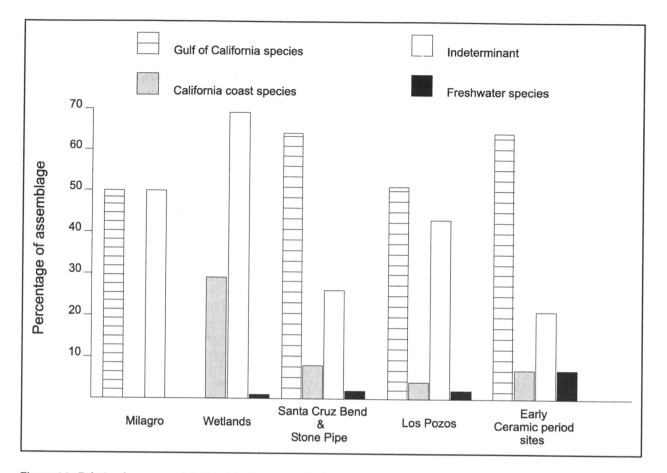

Figure 6.3. Relative frequency of shell by biotic community for sites ordered in time.

California source becomes substantially more important in the exchange system. This pattern changes significantly in the Early Ceramic period materials, with only one very small fragment included in the indeterminate nacreous category, and even this specimen may be freshwater rather than marine in origin. Thus, it appears that the coastal California source of marine shell may have declined in favor of Gulf of California sources at this time. The low but consistent occurrence of *Haliotis* in later Hohokam assemblages (Vokes 1984:470-472) indicates the connection was never entirely broken. Indeed, at the time of Spanish contact, there existed a well-established exchange system between the populations of southern Arizona and the California coast, as demonstrated by the presence of *Haliotis* among the Piman-speaking inhabitants encountered by Father Kino (Di Peso 1956:46-47).

CHAPTER 7

BONE ARTIFACTS

David A. Gregory and Jennifer A. Waters

The importance of bone and antler as raw materials for manufacture of a variety of artifacts is well attested by the Los Pozos (AZ AA:12:91 [ASM]) assemblage. These include tools, items of personal adornment, and artifacts of unknown function.

TOOLS

The bone and antler tool assemblage includes awls, beaming tools, chisel-like tools, needles, flakers, billets, and sockets or handles.

Awls

Artifacts classified as awls and awl fragments are the most common bone tools recovered. In terms of the portions of skeletal elements used, at least two distinct awl forms are represented: those in which the distal epiphysis was retained, presumably forming a part of the handle (Type 1), and those in which the epiphysis was purposefully removed and the top of the shaft ground or smoothed in the course of manufacture or by subsequent use (Type 2). This is a simple morphological typology and functional implications are not implied; tools assigned to different types may have served the same function. A number of other fragments clearly represent awls but the articular end is broken off, and therefore they cannot be assigned to one of these two heuristic types.

Type 1 Awls

Seven of the whole or reconstructible Type 1 awls in the assemblage are *notched awls* (Figure 7.1), a name derived from the overall shape resulting from the technique used to reduce the thickness of the bone shaft (Haury 1936:110). This technique involved scoring one side of the shaft horizontally, roughly a hand's width above the distal epiphysis, and then longitudinally from the horizontal scoring upward. This scoring provided a break line for removal of approximately half the width of the upper portion of the shaft, probably by directed percussion. This left a handle at the top of the shaft, including the epiphysis, while the thinned upper portion was subsequently ground to the desired

point. This process resulted in a characteristic notch approximately one-fifth to one-quarter of the way up the shaft of the completed artifact, and remnants of the telltale scoring marks often remain in the area of the notch. Four of the Los Pozos examples retain evidence of scoring, while the others have only the notch.

The resulting tool was long, with a thin working end; with complete specimens average over 20 cm in length. There is no indication that the notch served as a stop or guard during use, as polish, probably resulting from use, may be seen extending over the notch in several Los Pozos specimens. This feature also indicates the full length of the working end was used. Six of the seven examples were manufactured from artiodactyl metatarsals, with the seventh being identified as a metapodial. Thus, the rear leg bones of deer and perhaps bighorn sheep were preferred for making these distinctive tools.

The specific function of these artifacts is unknown. Given the length of the working end, it would seem that these awls would have been awkward to use in making baskets or perforating hides in preparation for sewing, and they are much longer and more gracile than ethnographically documented awls used for these purposes. In addition, the narrowness of the awl shaft would have made it relatively brittle, even when the bone was still green. Thus, a use motion involving any degree of torque would seem unlikely; a straight in-and-out movement seems probable and is consistent with the polish present on several specimens. A number of previously reported examples suggest that broken artifacts were resharpened for further use (e.g., Martin et al. 1952:Figure 62j; Thiel 1998:Figure 11.1e), but if the thinness and length of the tools were significant attributes in their original intended use, it does not seem likely that the same kinds of activities could have been accomplished with the resharpened specimens.

One similar artifact was recovered at the Santa Cruz Bend site (Thiel 1998:Figure 11.1e). This specimen is quite short, with tip being only approximately 2.5 cm from the notch, and it was likely broken and reworked. Similar artifacts appear to be represented in several levels at Ventana Cave (Haury 1950:375-378, Figure 86a-c). The 1935-1936 excavations at Snaketown produced a single example from a Sacaton phase context (Haury 1965a:Plate CXXVb), while the 1964-1965 work there resulted in three additional examples of the form, one from a Santa Cruz phase context, one from an Estrella phase context, and one unplaced specimen (Haury 1976:303, Figure 15.3e-f).

Awls manufactured by this technique are common in early Mogollon sites (e.g., see Haury 1936:335, 388-

389, Figure 13.33a-c; Martin 1939:Figure 32, 1943:Figure 84a, 1946:Figure 121; Martin et al. 1952:185, Figure 62i-k; Nesbitt 1938:107), and were in fact long ago recognized as a distinctive Mogollon trait. In his 1936 discussion of Mogollon culture, Haury noted the following about Mogollon bone tools:

> The chief item of interest is the notched awl which carries through from the San Francisco to the Mimbres phase. The notch, cut into the awl a few centimeters from the head, was probably only a means for assisting in the removal of surplus bone from the shaft, but it is so unique a feature and occurs in so limited an area that some cultural significance may be assigned to it. Large collections of bone tools from late sites, as Hawikuh (Hodge 1920) and Pecos (Kidder 1932), do not contain specimens of this sort, nor can they be traced in either early or late sites of the San Juan. That they should occur in the pit house horizon at Kiatuthlanna (Roberts 1931:Plate 25a) is not surprising, since a number of other Mogollon traits have already been noted from there. They reach their greatest density in the Mimbres proper, then die out again going south into Chihuahua. It is certainly one of the distinctive features of the Mogollon culture, being common in all phases except Georgetown, from which there is no information (1936:110-111; see also Nesbitt 1938:107, 130).

Writing nearly two decades later, Wheat documents the occurrence of notched awls in the Mimbres, Pine Lawn, and Black River Mogollon branches during Mogollon 1 and indicates that they appear later in all five Mogollon branches reviewed by him (Wheat 1955:Table 13, Figure 10d-e). At that time, he was still able to assert that these artifacts were characteristic of the "central Mogollon area" (1955:227), but occurred rarely in Anasazi sites on the Colorado Plateau. He cites the previously mentioned example from Kiatuthlanna as well as a single specimen from Shabik'eshchee Village (Roberts 1929:Plate 12) and one from the Ackmen-Lowry area (Martin 1939:426) as geographic outliers to the core of the distribution in the Mogollon area. Except for the three examples from Snaketown and the more recent recovery of the artifacts in Early Agricultural period contexts at Los Pozos and Santa Cruz Bend, the geographic distribution of notched awls as described by these earlier researchers has not been changed significantly by several additional decades of research. At present, the Los Pozos specimens represent the earliest well-dated occurrence of this distinctive form.

Several other specimens retained the epiphyses and are thus classified as Type 1 awls, but showed no evidence of notches. One long, relatively thin specimen and one short and stubby example are illustrated in Figure 7.1.

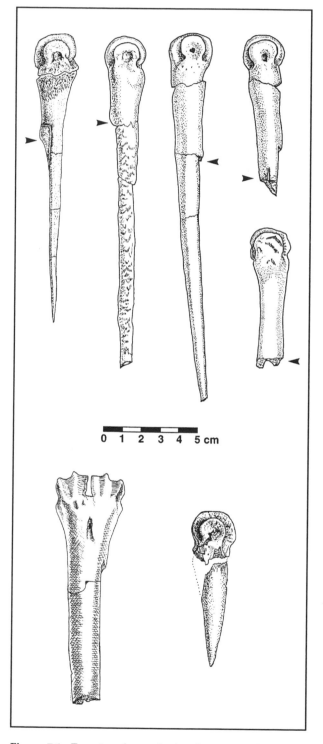

Figure 7.1. Type 1 awls; notched awls at top with notches indicated by arrows.

Type 2 Awls

Manufacture of Type 2 awls involved removal of the epiphysis by cutting or sawing and subsequent smoothing of the handle end of the shaft. Reduction of the shaft itself was also probably by sawing or splintering. While reduction of the shaft could have been by the technique described above for notched awls, no evidence of this was observed on any of the Type 2 awls (Figure 7.2). The Los Pozos specimens are variable in size, but are generally stouter and more gradually tapered than the Type 1 awls.

Most Type 2 awls were manufactured from the long bone shafts of artiodactyls, with metapodials, and specifically metatarsals, represented in those specimens where the element could be identified. Two smaller specimens were made from ulnae, one from an artiodactyl and the other from a bobcat. The bobcat ulna specimen is nearly identical in form to an awl from Santa Cruz Bend made from a canid ulna (Thiel 1998: Figure 11.1d).

Awls of this general type are common over a large geographic area and time range (e.g., see Haury 1936:335, Figure 13.33e, 1950:Figure 86f; Martin 1939: Figure 32, 1943:Figure 84b, Figure 85, 1947:Figure 121; Wheat 1955:Figure 10f-g).

Untyped Fragments

A number of fragments were recovered that undoubtedly came from awls but were not sufficiently complete to be assigned to one of the two morphological types. These include tips and medial fragments.

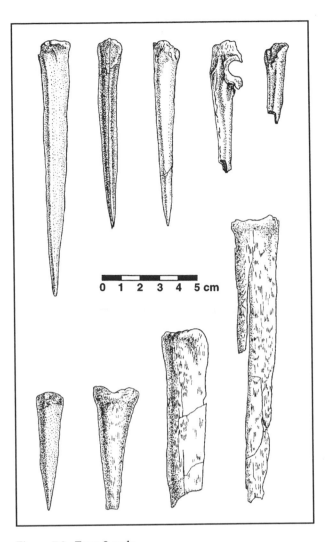

Figure 7.2. Type 2 awls.

Beaming Tools

Two artifacts are classified here as beaming tools (Figure 7.3), following some previous usages (e.g., Guernsey 1931:84). The name refers to artifacts inferred to have been used in the tanning of hides, perhaps to work tanning agents such as boiled brain matter into a stretched hide and to subsequently work the hide smooth and dry.

Both the Los Pozos specimens were fashioned from the tibiae of bighorn sheep. In both, the distal epiphyses were retained to form part of the handle and approximately the upper third of the shafts were reduced by sawing out a scoop-shaped wedge at the proximal end (Figure 7.3). This produced a stout, sturdy tool with a broad, rounded, and blunt tip.

Two specimens with a similar morphology were recovered from Santa Cruz Bend and called spatulas. Thiel (1998:Figure 11.2a-b) suggests that these artifacts "were probably used for stirring or spreading substances such as food or pigments." This interpretation seems unlikely, given the overall morphology and robust character of the tools and the heavy wear present on the working ends. Fragments of two possibly similar artifacts from Ventana Cave are illustrated by Haury (1950:Figure 88f-g) and are classified as scrapers. The two Los Pozos specimens are similar to an artifact from Cave 1 in Tsegi Canyon (Basketmaker III) illustrated by Guernsey and called a beaming tool (1931:84, Plate 56i). The only difference is the Basketmaker example had the epiphyses removed during manufacture.

Chisel-like Tools

Five artifacts have a chisel-like form (Figure 7.3). All but one are made from artiodactyl metatarsals, with the shaft of the bone left intact along most of the length and the working end reduced by sawing to create a beveled cross section and the chisel-like ends (Figure 7.3). All specimens are broken at the handle end of the tool, but two of the artifacts from Feature 379 show cancellous bone at the break, suggesting that the epiphysis may have been left attached. Further support

epiphysis may have been left attached. Further support for this interpretation is provided by the fact that two sets of distal epiphyses were recovered from the same provenience but could not be refit onto the tools.

The parallel diagonal striations at the working ends of the tools appear to be characteristic of this form and were probably produced during manufacture; it is difficult to envision how any use motion would have resulted in these features. The function of these artifacts remains uncertain. The ends do not show wear consistent with their use as flakers, and their use in some kind of scraping or gouging action seems more likely. However, the working edge is quite small and no obvious functional interpretations suggest themselves.

Similar artifacts have been documented from a number of sites, and various functional interpretations have been applied to them. Two specimens–one from Harris Village illustrated by Haury (1936:361, Figure 13.62i) and one from Tularosa Cave (Martin et al. 1952:188, Figure 63h)–are virtually identical to the Los Pozos specimens. The former was classified as a spatulate implement and the latter as an end scraper. One, and possibly two, similar artifacts from Ventana Cave are illustrated by Haury (Haury 1950:Figure 88d-e) and called flakers. The diagonal striations on the distal end that characterize the Los Pozos specimens may be seen on all these specimens. Preliminarily, the geographic distribution of these chisel-like tools appears to parallel that of the notched awls discussed above; early Mogollon sites have produced several examples, but none have been noted from Colorado Plateau sites. Once again, the specimens from Los Pozos represent the earliest well-dated examples of this form.

Other Bone Tools

A number of other bone tools were recovered, including a single artifact classified as a needle and a specimen of unknown function (Figure 7.4).

The single needle is fragmentary, including only the medial portion and the tip. The assumed eye is lacking, and the classification is based largely on size. Three artifacts of similar size and configuration were recovered from the Santa Cruz Bend site and classified as needles (Thiel 1998:Figure 11.2e); all of these specimens lack the diagnostic eye as well. It is also quite possible that these artifacts represent the working ends of composite awls having socket handles (see below).

Another artifact is unique in the assemblage. Manufactured from the long bone shaft of a large mammal, the specimen measures 11.46 cm in length and has a maximum width of 1.78 cm. It has an awl-like shape, but is flat and extremely thin; thickness is uniform along the entire length. The entire specimen is highly polished. A large hole was drilled in the wide

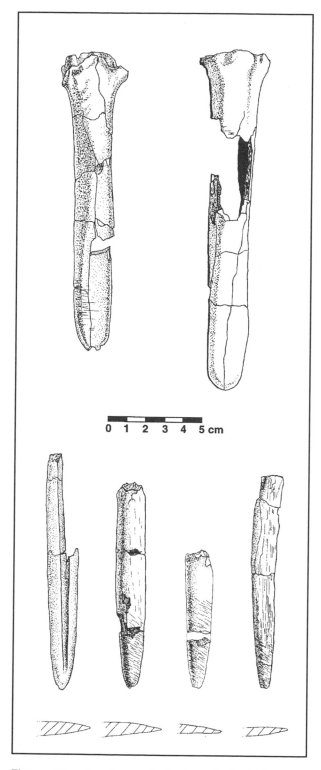

0 1 2 3 4 5 cm

Figure 7.3. Beaming tools (top) and chisel-like tools (bottom).

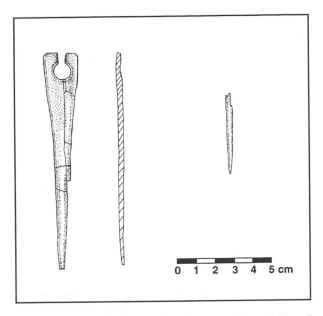

Figure 7.4. Tool of unknown function, two views (left) and needle (right).

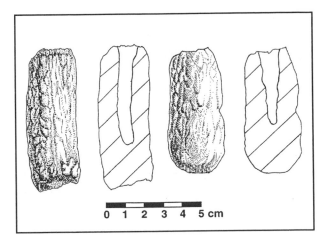

Figure 7.5. Antler sockets.

proximal end of the tool. A search of the literature revealed no similar specimens.

The function of this specimen is unknown. Given its thinness, it would have been relatively fragile even when the bone was green. Such an artifact might have served quite well as a large "needle" used to pass lashings of vegetal material back and forth through the walls of structures in the process of attaching thatch to the framework. The high degree of polish present would be consistent with such an interpretation. However, this is purely speculative and, if correct, we might expect to see more of these artifacts in the assemblage. The hole could have as easily served to provide for suspension by an attached string or cord.

Antler Tools: Flakers, Billets, and Sockets

Specimens recovered from Los Pozos show that deer antlers were used to create billets and flakers used in flaked stone tool manufacture, as well as sockets or handles in which stone or bone elements were mounted (Figure 7.5).

Flakers

One complete antler flaker and four fragments of probable flakers were recovered; all the fragments are quite small and probably represent portions of broken and discarded artifacts. The single complete specimen is simply the tine of an antler cut to a length conveniently held in the hand (15.5 cm) and retains some cut marks toward the base. No flakers were recovered from

Santa Cruz Bend or Stone Pipe, but similar artifacts have a wide temporal and geographic distribution. Haury reports numerous antler flakers from Ventana Cave (1950:387, Figure 90a-c), and they are common in early Mogollon sites and elsewhere (e.g., see Haury 1940:Figure 41m; Martin 1939:Figure 33; Wheat 1955:144-145).

Billets

Two antler billets were recovered, presumably used in soft hammer percussion. Both are poorly preserved and fragmentary. In both cases, the basal portion of the antler is represented, with the only observed modification being grinding to smooth the base. No billets were found at Santa Cruz Bend or Stone Pipe, but Haury reports similar artifacts from Ventana Cave (Haury 1950:384-387, Figure 90f-g).

Sockets

Two antler sockets were recovered, both fashioned from the basal portions of deer antlers cut to the desired length (Figure 7.5). In both specimens, the base has been smoothed and a hole drilled in the distal end; the margins of the drilled holes have a slight inward bevel.

These artifacts undoubtedly functioned as handles for composite tools, with stone or bone elements inserted in the hole and secured with some sort of resin or pitch, bound in place, or both. Examples of similar artifacts have been recovered from Colorado Plateau and Great Basin cave sites, some with stone and bone artifacts still hafted (e.g., see Aikens 1970:Figure 58a-b; Guernsey 1931:84, Plate 31b; Jennings 1957:Figure 184a), and there is little question about their general function as handles. No residues of pitch or resin were observed on the Los Pozos specimens. Two sockets were recovered from Santa Cruz Bend (Thiel 1998: Figure 11.2h-i). Four specimens are reported from Ventana Cave and referred to as awl handles (Haury 1950:384, Figure 90d-e).

NONUTILITARIAN ARTIFACTS

In addition to forming bone into a variety of utilitarian artifacts, the former inhabitants of Los Pozos at least occasionally employed bone to manufacture items of personal adornment, such as pendants and beads, and to fashion artifacts of unknown and possibly esoteric function such as bone tubes and objects made from artiodactyl femur heads.

Pendants

Two pendants were recovered, one manufactured from a mud turtle carapace and the other from the canine tooth of a canid. The specimen manufactured from a turtle carapace is incomplete and its former shape could not be determined (possibly rectangular?). Similar canine pendants are known from Great Basin Archaic sites (Aikens 1970:Figure 59b; Jennings 1957: Figure 180a).

Bead

A single fragmentary artifact is classified as a bead. Approximately one-quarter of the artifact is represented. This specimen is flat and circular with a hole removed from its apparent center.

Tubes

Four bone tubes were recovered. Three are whole or reconstructible, and one is fragmentary. Two are larger and two are smaller, and the smaller specimens could represent beads. However, there is no explicit basis for distinguishing tubular beads, and all are treated here as tubes.

Artifacts similar to the larger tubes from Los Pozos were recovered at Santa Cruz Bend and Stone Pipe (Thiel 1998:Figure 11.2c-d), and Haury documents numerous examples from Ventana Cave (Haury 1950:381, Figure 89a-d). Bone tubes of various sizes are a nearly ubiquitous low frequency item in early Mogollon assemblages, occurring in both plain and incised forms (e.g., see Haury 1940:Figure 41a, 1936:335, Figure 13.33h-j; Martin 1939:Figure 31, 1946:Figure 124; Wheat 1955:Figure 10r-t). They have a widespread temporal and spatial distribution across the American Southwest and the Great Basin.

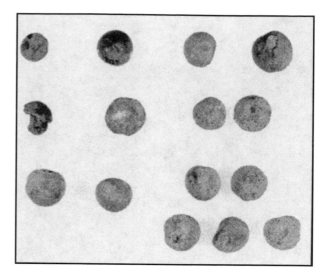

Figure 7.6. Photograph of artiodactyl femur heads. (Specimen at lower left is 2.61 cm in diameter.)

Artiodactyl Femur Heads

As discussed in Chapter 2, 16 bone artifacts were recovered which represent an artifact type previously unknown from sites of any age in southern Arizona. These artifacts are the heads of artiodactyl femurs that have been severed from the shaft, with the cut end and the edge between the two surfaces then variably ground (Figure 7.6). Removal of the head from the femur and subsequent grinding produced, in some cases, a rounded or slightly conical shape to the base, and a more flattened shape in others. The articular surfaces of the artifacts are variably polished, and three had a notch or divot cut into this end and polished over.

Also noted in Chapter 2 is the fact that six of these artifacts were recovered from postholes in structures, suggesting the possibility they were placed as votive or dedicatory deposits. Three of the five artifacts recovered from a posthole in Feature 318, and the one recovered from a posthole in Feature 337, retained evidence of having been coated or embedded with red ochre, perhaps providing further evidence for a votive function. Of the remaining 10 specimens, five were recovered from intramural pits. The possibility that these and other artifacts found in such pits might also represent votive or dedicatory deposits made when the pits were filled or abandoned was also raised in Chapter 2. One specimen from an intramural pit (Feature 342.01) was also embedded with ochre. Of the remaining four specimens, one was resting on the floor of a structure, two were recovered from the fills of structures, and one was found in an extramural pit.

None of these artifacts have been recovered from Tucson Basin sites, and a search of the literature revealed only one occurrence of similar items. Three "roughly spherical" artifacts classified as bone balls were recovered from Hogup Cave in central Utah (Aikens 1970:90). They are identical to the Los Pozos specimens in all respects save one: the Hogup Cave examples were manufactured from bison femurs and are consequently somewhat larger. Unfortunately, the exact provenience of these artifacts, and therefore their age, is unknown. Jennings (1957:Figure 175) illustrates the proximal end of a large mammal femur from Danger Cave that could represent a similar item in the process of manufacture.

TAXA AND SKELETAL ELEMENTS USED

Figure 7.7 illustrates artiodactyl skeletal elements used to make various kinds of bone artifacts. It is clear from this illustration that the leg bones and antlers of species belonging to the order Artiodactyla were the elements most commonly selected for manufacture of bone tools. In every case where more specific identifications could be made, deer, mule deer, or bighorn sheep are represented. There is some indication that the rear leg bones were most often used, perhaps suggesting some selectivity in the portions of the carcass brought back to the site (but see Chapter 10). The ulnae of small- to medium-sized animals, such as bobcat and canids, were also occasionally used to make small awls.

DISCUSSION

Bone tools or tool fragments were recovered from 26 of the 42 investigated structures, either from the fill of the structures or from intramural pits. Only two bone artifacts were recovered from extramural pits. Most of the complete or largely complete artifacts were recovered from within the collapsed structural debris of burned structures. This strongly suggests they were routinely stored in the thatch walls or ceilings of the structures, either by simply being stuck into the thatch, or possibly suspended by means of some attached string or cord.

Some patterns in the co-occurrence of specific tool types may be tentatively noted. Figure 7.8 illustrates the combinations of artifacts which occurred in the several burned structures. In all cases but one, awls are represented; and in seven cases, at least one long narrow awl and one shorter, more blunt awl were present. Combined with the storage of these tools in the walls or ceilings of structures, these patterns suggest that bone tools were consistently occurring items in personal tool kits, possibly those of women who engaged in basketmaking and the sewing of clothing. The tools from Feature 379 appear to represent a functionally specialized assemblage, with two beaming tools, four chisel-like tools, and at least two other tools of unknown form. This assemblage suggests the possibility that some individuals may have specialized in activities such as the tanning of hides.

Also of interest is the fact that most of the whole or reconstructible bone tools, all but one of the notched awls, both of the beaming tools, and all but one of the chisel-like tools were recovered from structures in the southern end of the stripped portion of the site. While the distribution of investigated structures is not sufficiently continuous to confirm or deny the reality of this pattern, the relative distribution of such artifacts warrants attention in future research. Cultural differences between groups of people occupying the site could be represented.

In general, the Late Cienega phase bone tool assemblages from the Tucson Basin are duplicated in almost every respect in later assemblages from early Mogollon sites, while there appear to be some significant differences between them and Basketmaker II and III assemblages from the Colorado Plateau. The geographic distributions of notched awls and possibly chisel-like tools have been noted as specific examples in this regard. Thus, cultural connections between Early Agricultural period populations in the Tucson Basin and later Mogollon populations may be indicated.

Finally, bone tools may provide an important source of inferences concerning the activities carried out at Early Agricultural period sites. Based on general ethnographic analogy, it may be inferred that bone tools were used in basketmaking, tanning of hides, sewing, flaked stone tool manufacture, and possibly woodworking. Microwear studies are needed to explore the possibility of discriminating at least general categories of use for these tools.

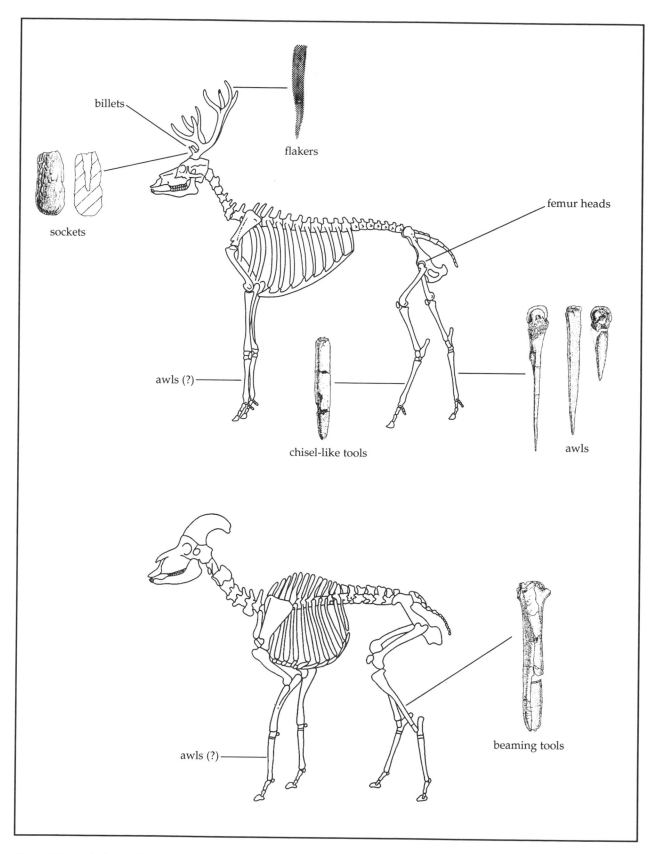

Figure 7.7. Artiodactyl skeletal elements used for bone tools.

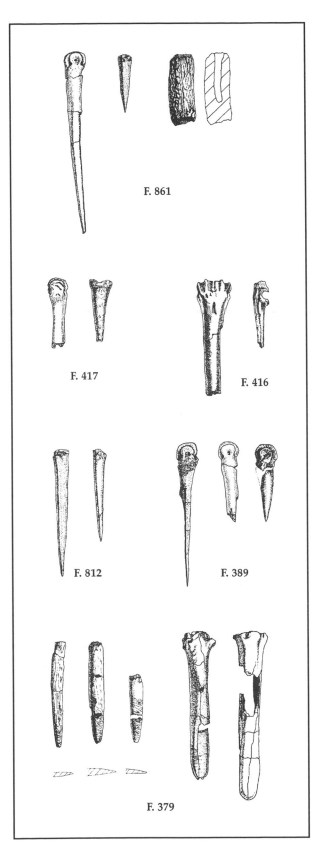

Figure 7.8. Selected bone tool assemblages from burned pit structures.

CHAPTER 8

CERAMIC CONTAINERS AND OTHER ARTIFACTS OF CLAY

James M. Heidke and Alan Ferg

Although the Cienega phase is currently identified as a preceramic interval, evidence from Los Pozos (AZ AA:12:91 [ASM]) and other sites dating to this phase suggests that the development of a ceramic container technology occurred over a relatively long period of time that extends back into "preceramic" intervals. Evidence for that development from Los Pozos and other sites is discussed, and interpretations of relevant materials are offered. Other artifacts of clay are also described and discussed below, including beads, figurine fragments, and miscellaneous fired and unfired clay items.

CERAMIC CONTAINERS

The pottery discussed in this chapter relates to the inception of the craft in the middle and lower Santa Cruz River Valley. These ceramics have been recovered from contexts that are securely dated circa 800 B.C.-A.D. 150 (the Early Agricultural period's early and late Cienega phases). Figure 8.1 summarizes the distribution of calibrated radiocarbon dates from features that have yielded pottery (see Chapter 12 for additional discussion of independent dates). As of now, these are the earliest well-dated ceramics from the North American Southwest. Much of the discussion is structured in terms of the operational tasks involved in the production sequence of handmade pottery (Rye 1981). In addition to that technological data, ideas regarding the social and cultural context of this technological innovation are presented, and previous explanations for the emergence of pottery are evaluated with respect to the southeastern Arizona case. Finally, the changing role of early pottery in the Sonoran Desert is briefly discussed.

Until quite recently, Archaic period sites in the North American Southwest have been defined by the lack of pottery and the presence of specific projectile point styles (Bayham 1986:6; Schroeder 1982:7). In the Hohokam area, the relationship between sedentism, agriculture, and ceramics remained undefined (Fish 1989:25). We now know that the occupation of settlements with multiple pit structures, large storage pits, thick trash middens, burials, and other types of features generally thought to represent some degree of sedentism correlates with the introduction of agriculture in the Southwest (Mabry 1998b).

Hill (1996) presents linguistic evidence that the diffusion of maize into the Southwest occurred during a period of coherence among southern Uto-Aztecan languages, but that the appearance of pottery occurred at a time when linguistic boundaries were starting to emerge. In southeastern Arizona, the first ceramic containers occurred in the context of agricultural settlements, but they were preceded by ceramic figurine production. The earliest maize and ceramic figurines in the Tucson Basin have been recovered from San Pedro phase contexts, circa 1200-800 B.C. (B. Huckell 1990; B. Huckell and L. Huckell 1984; B. Huckell et al. 1995), whereas ceramic containers were not produced until the early Cienega phase (circa 800-400 B.C.).

In the Tucson Basin, many Cienega phase sites are located on lowland alluvial landforms suitable for floodwater farming during the summer monsoons (B. Huckell 1998). Macrobotanical data indicate that some of these sites were occupied during the late summer (Diehl 1998), while others were occupied from at least early spring through late fall (L. Huckell 1998). One of the most striking aspects of Cienega phase pit structures is the large number and volume of floor pits found inside them. L. Huckell (1998) has suggested that, although there are no winter-indicator plant resources in the Sonoran Desert, the presence of maize remains in these storage pits can be considered a possible indicator for winter occupation.

The establishment of agricultural settlements would have affected the annual schedules of interaction with other groups that occurred before a settled lifeway was adopted and transformed the structure of communication within and among local groups (Wilcox 1986:141). The establishment of "Big Houses" at some Cienega phase sites may, in part, have been a response to that transformation. The term "Big House" has been applied to structures that are two to four times larger than other structures at a site (Mabry 1998a). However, the "Big House" at one site may be considerably smaller than the "Big House" at another site. For example, the "Big House" at Coffee Camp (AZ AA:6:19 [ASM])

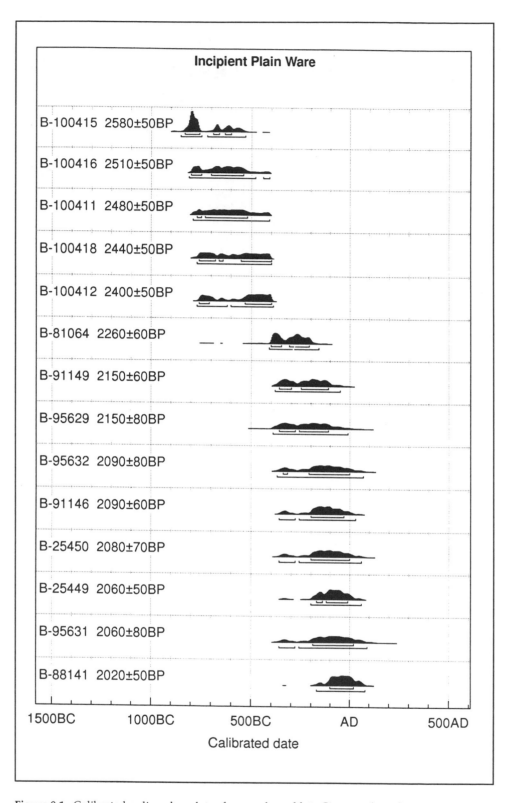

Figure 8.1. Calibrated radiocarbon dates from early and late Cienega phase features containing ceramics.

measures 4.5 m in diameter, whereas the largest "Big House" at Santa Cruz Bend (AZ AA:12:746 [ASM]) has a diameter of 8.3 m. This scalar variability may reflect functional differentiation much like that present among the Huichol Indians of north-central Mexico (a point made repeatedly by Mabry [1998a, 1998b], though he does not make reference to the Huichol case).

> The Huichols erect two types of religious buildings—the small oratories, *xíriki*, (local or family god houses) and the *tuki* (community temple). The *xíriki* resembles an ordinary Huichol house, and there may be one or more on each rancho. Here offerings are made and the souls of deceased relatives who have returned as rock crystals are kept; here one finds the gourds of sacred water, offerings, deer horns and tails, musical instruments, staffs of civil officials, and the like.... The *tuki* is constructed along the same lines as the *xíriki* but is generally much larger, typically thirty to forty feet in diameter.... On top of the *tuki* and *xíriki* are deer horns of Kauyumari (Sacred Deer Person). The mara'akame (shaman-priest) chanting inside the structure communicates with the deities by means of these horns (Myerhoff 1974:108-110).

The artifact assemblage recovered from Coffee Camp Feature 315, the site's "Big House," bears an uncanny similarity to the inventory reported by Myerhoff. Two complete deer antler racks were recovered atop several charred beams and roof fall (Halbirt et al. 1993:87), while the floor contained a phyllite baton/wand, four pieces of worked shell, a bone tube, a piece of malachite, and a figurine fragment in addition to a sherd, a mano, a handstone, and seven pieces of flaked stone (Halbirt et al. 1993:87, 90).

Cienega phase pottery was first described in Kisselburg's (1993) analysis of ceramics recovered from the Coffee Camp site. Heidke and others (1998) have described another small collection recovered from late Cienega phase deposits at the Santa Cruz Bend site, and early Cienega phase pottery recovered from the Wetlands site (AZ AA:12:90 [ASM]) (Heidke 1998) and Clearwater (AZ BB:13:6 [ASM]) (Heidke and Ferg 1997). Other Cienega phase sites, such as the Donaldson site (AZ EE:2:30 [ASM]) (B. Huckell 1995) and Stone Pipe (AZ BB:13:425 [ASM]), have not produced ceramics. The ceramic container fragments recovered from Clearwater, Coffee Camp, Los Pozos, Santa Cruz Bend, and Wetlands are portions of true pots; they do not resemble the unfired clay vessels recovered from Basketmaker sites in the San Juan area (Morris 1927:131-158), Danger Cave (Jennings 1957:208-209), and Hogup Cave (Aikens 1970:32).

To date, only plain wares have been recovered from typologically unmixed, Cienega phase contexts, even though significant quantities of processed iron oxides (i.e., "ochre") have been recovered from some of the pottery-bearing sites (Miksa and Tompkins 1998).

Figure 8.2. Coiled variety of incipient plain ware: a-c) recovered from Wetlands; d-e) recovered from Clearwater. (Maximum width of a) is 4.8 cm.)

Given the position that these pots hold at the beginning of the regional ceramic sequence and the fact that they do not resemble later, Tucson Basin Hohokam plain wares (Kelly 1978), we propose that the term "incipient plain ware" be used to refer to them. Four distinct varieties of incipient plain ware are indicated, based on differences in primary forming technique and surface treatment. We refer to these varieties as coiled (Figure 8.2), bumpy (Figure 8.3), incised (Figure 8.4), and impressed (Figure 8.5).

The first portion of this chapter reviews evidence regarding the manufacture and use of early plain ware ceramics recovered from Los Pozos. This ceramic collection represents some of the earliest, well-dated ceramics in the North American Southwest. The discussion is structured by an attribute-based approach to the ceramic production sequence. That presentation is followed by a comprehensive review of early and late Cienega phase pottery manufacture in the middle and lower Santa Cruz River Valley and the ceramic evidence for a late Cienega phase occupation at Snaketown. Other artifacts manufactured from fired clay are discussed in the second portion of the chapter.

Research Methods

The analysis was structured in terms of the operational tasks involved in the production sequence of handmade pottery (Rye 1981). Material correlates of multiple production steps were recorded: raw material procurement attributes; forming, finishing, and decorative attributes; and firing and postfiring attributes. Provenience, contextual, and typological attributes were recorded in addition to the production step attributes. Attributes recorded during the analysis are fully defined in Heidke (2001:Table 5.1).

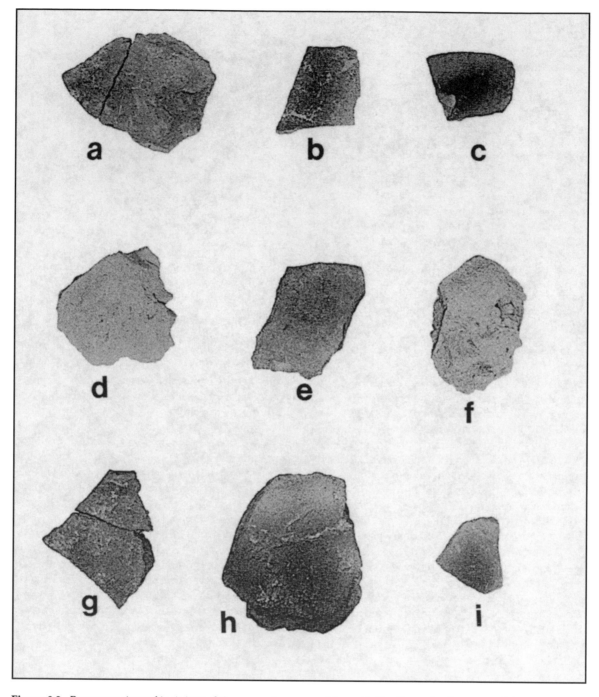

Figure 8.3. Bumpy variety of incipient plain ware: a) recovered from Coffee Camp; b-d) recovered from Wetlands; e-f) recovered from Los Pozos; g-h) recovered from Santa Cruz Bend; i) recovered from Clearwater. (Maximum width of a) is 3.7 cm.)

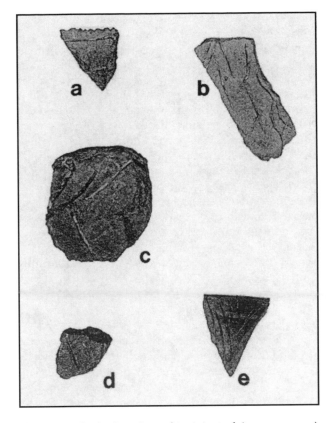

Figure 8.4. Incised variety of incipient plain ware: a-c, e) recovered from Los Pozos; d) recovered from Coffee Camp. (Maximum width of a) is 1.5 cm.)

Provenience, Contextual, and Typological Attributes

All sherds from a feature were laid out at one time in the order of the excavated strata and levels, along with any subfeatures, such as hearths and postholes, present. In some cases, a number of sherds within a given bag or from different strata, levels, or bags within a feature conjoined (i.e., the pieces literally refit together). In other cases, aspects of the sherd's morphology were similar enough to consider multiple sherds "matching" portions of a single vessel. When conjoins or matches were observed, the vessel was recorded in the provenience containing the largest portion of the pot. Because all diagnostic sherds recovered from a given feature were laid out at one time, it was possible to assess quickly whether the feature was temporally mixed (i.e., containing types of pottery inferred to have non-overlapping date ranges), as well as whether pieces of the same pot were recovered from more than one vertical or horizontal excavation unit. In so doing, we were able to obtain a more accurate estimate of the minimum number of vessels present in each deposit.

A total of 43 sherds, representing portions of 31 vessels, was recovered from the Los Pozos excavation. Twenty of those sherds (17 vessels) are typologically

Figure 8.5. Impressed variety of incipient plain ware: a-b) recovered from Coffee Camp. (Maximum width of a) is 3.1 cm.)

late Cienega phase, incipient plain wares. Nineteen of the remaining sherds (11 vessels) are Hohokam plain wares. Two of the remaining sherds (1 vessel) are portions of an unidentified red ware type, one of the remaining sherds is a portion of a Tanque Verde Red-on-brown bowl, while the final sherd could not be identified as to ware or type. Figure 8.6 plots the number of sherds and vessels recovered from each feature. Of special importance to this study is the fact that only Feature 422, a pit that intrudes into pithouse Feature 333, shows typological mixing of late Cienega phase incipient plain wares and later Hohokam plain wares.

Raw Material Procurement Attributes

The manufacture of pottery begins with the collection of raw materials, primarily water, clay, temper (if added), and fuel (Crown and Wills 1995:247; Rye 1981:29). Material procurement attributes recorded in this study were limited to aspects of the temper, which provide evidence regarding production technology and resource provenance. Temper attributes were recorded after examining the sherds at 10- to 15-power magnification, using a Unitron ZSM binocular microscope fitted with a Stocker and Yale Lite Mite Series 9 circular illuminator. The modal size of nonplastic grains was recorded after comparing the sand grains in a vessel's body against reference samples mounted on a W. F. McCollough "Sand-gauge."

Forming, Finishing, and Decorative Attributes

Rye (1981:62) distinguishes three main stages of vessel forming: primary forming, secondary forming, and surface modification. During primary forming, the

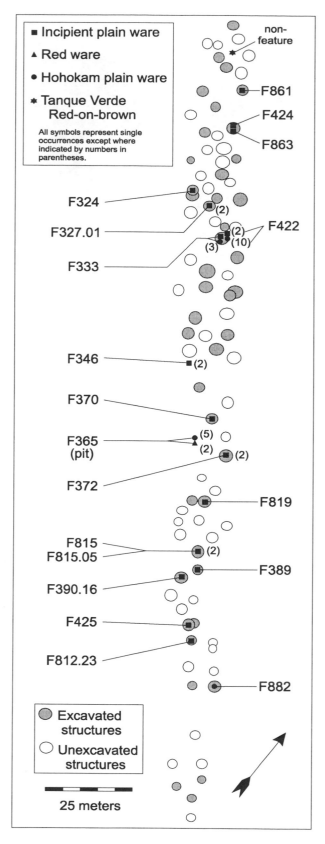

Figure 8.6. Distribution of ceramic types recovered from Los Pozos.

prepared clay body is manipulated into a form resembling the finished vessel (Rye 1981:62); the vessel shape attribute qualitatively characterizes a pot's primary form. During secondary forming, the shape of the vessel is further refined and the final, relative proportions of the pot are established (Rye 1981:62). In our study, the vessel form attribute qualitatively characterizes a pot's final proportions, whereas the vessel wall thickness, orifice diameter, and aperture diameter measurements provide quantitative data on those proportions. The final shape of a vessel's lip is qualitatively characterized by the rim shape attribute. Surface modifications considered part of the forming sequence include polishing, scraping, smoothing, incising, impressing, and carving (Rye 1981:62). Interior and exterior surface treatment attributes were used to qualitatively characterize this aspect of vessel forming and decoration.

Firing and Postfiring Attributes

The purpose of firing is to subject the formed vessel to sufficient heat for a sufficient time to insure the complete destruction of the clay mineral crystals, and insure the vessel exhibits the required hardness, porosity, and thermal shock resistance characteristics required of it (Rye 1981:96). Core color and fire clouding were recorded in this study; they are qualitative measures of the firing atmosphere and temperature (Rice 1987:343-345, 476; Rye 1981:114-118).

**Late Cienega Phase Incipient
Plain Wares from Los Pozos**

Attribute data recorded from the Clearwater, Coffee Camp, Los Pozos, Santa Cruz Bend, and Wetlands ceramics are discussed further below (see "Cienega Phase Pottery"). In this section, we focus solely on the material recovered from Los Pozos. Table 8.1 lists the recovery contexts of the incipient plain wares. Each row represents an individual vessel. The quantity of conjoining and/or matching sherds recovered from each vessel is reported in the "Number of Sherds" column; only three vessels were represented by more than one sherd. Most of the incipient plain ware sherds recovered from Los Pozos are quite small (i.e., less than 5 cm²), and none are larger than 16 cm². The collection contains portions of 10 vessels represented by body sherds, 6 vessels represented by rim sherds, and 1 vessel represented by an indeterminate vessel part. Four of the vessels display incised decoration; the remaining 13 vessels are the bumpy variety.

Table 8.1. Incipient plain ware recovery contexts at Los Pozos.

Feature Number	Stratum	Level	Number of Sherds	Sherd Size	Vessel Part	Incising Present?
324.00	10	1	1	< 5 cm²	Body sherd	No
327.01	30	1	2	5-16 cm²	Body sherd	No
346.00	50	1	2	< 5 cm²	Rim sherd	No
370.01	30	1	1	< 5 cm²	Body sherd	No
372.00	10	1	2	5-16 cm²	Body sherd	No
389.00	10	1	1	5-16 cm²	Body sherd	Yes
390.16	30	1	1	5-16 cm²	Rim sherd	No
422.00	50	1	1	5-16 cm²	Rim sherd	Yes
422.00	50	1	1	< 5 cm²	Body sherd	No
424.00	50	1	1	< 5 cm²	Body sherd	No
425.00	10	1	1	5-16 cm²	Body sherd	No
812.23	30	1	1	< 5 cm²	Indeterminate vessel part	No
815.00	10	1	1	< 5 cm²	Rim sherd	Yes
815.05	30	1	1	< 5 cm²	Rim sherd	No
819.00	10	1	1	< 5 cm²	Body sherd	No
861.00	10	1	1	< 5 cm²	Rim sherd	Yes
863.00	10	2	1	< 5 cm²	Body sherd	No

Materials Procurement

Six raw material procurement attributes were recorded. Three of those attributes (temper type, generic temper source, and specific temper source) provided little information, because all of the incipient plain wares recovered from Los Pozos appear to have been made from untempered clay (Table 8.2). These sherds exhibit a homogenous paste with sand-sized nonplastics making up less than 10 percent of the volume, based on comparison with visual estimation charts reproduced in Matthew and others (1991:240). Modal nonplastic grain size ranges from silt (< 1/16 mm) to fine sand (⅛-¼ mm). Grain shape ranged from subangular to rounded. Quartz and biotite are the two nonplastic grains observed most commonly.

Based on the binocular microscopic examination, it appears that natural nonplastics were present in the clay body, rather than added. Clay deposits located along the Santa Cruz River could have provided the raw material (see B. Huckell 1998). The late Cienega phase ceramic figurine fragments and beads recovered from Los Pozos were also examined. Nearly all of those artifacts were made of the same alluvial clay observed in the sherds. Thus, the ceramic technology used in late Cienega phase figurine, bead, and pottery manufacture seems to have been the same in most cases.

Kisselburg (1993:287-288) noted the presence of "deep holes of small diameter that may be the result of organic material burning out" and "charcoal flecks" in some of the late Cienega phase pottery recovered from Coffee Camp. About 25 percent of the Los Pozos sherds displayed one of these characteristics and, importantly, casts from burned-out organic material and charcoal flecks did not co-occur. Thus, it appears that about half of the incipient plain wares contained minor amounts of plant parts in their paste. Like the other nonplastics discussed above, we feel that this organic material was a natural component of the clay body and was not added by the potter.

Forming, Finishing, and Decorative Techniques

No attributes characterizing primary forming technique, such as coiling, pinching, preparation and joining of slabs, throwing, or molding (Rye 1981:62), or secondary forming technique, such as coiling, joining, beating, scraping, trimming, turning, or throwing (Rye 1981:62), were explicitly recorded in this study, although scraping marks were documented on interior and exterior surfaces. As noted by Rye (1981:58), attributes characteristic of techniques used early in the forming process may be obliterated by those used in a later stage. Therefore, the surface treatment attributes used in this study characterize the final, fired appearance of the pot, and may reflect textural and aesthetic modifications of the surface, such as scraping, smoothing, polishing, or burnishing (Rye 1981:62), that occurred after primary and secondary forming were completed. The judgements reflected in the surface

Table 8.2. Los Pozos incipient plain ware production sequence attribute data.

Attribute	Bumpy Quantity	Bumpy Percent	Incised Quantity	Incised Percent
Body composition				
Untempered clay	13	100.0	4	100.0
Modal nonplastic grain size				
Silt	8	61.5	1	25.0
Very fine sand	4	30.8	3	75.0
Fine sand	1	7.7	0	–
Organic temper casts visible				
Indeterminate	1	–	0	–
Absent	9	75.0	3	75.0
Present	3	25.0	1	25.0
Charcoal fragments in paste				
Absent	10	76.9	3	75.0
Present	3	23.1	1	25.0
Vessel form				
Indeterminate	10	–	2	–
Indeterminate bowl	1	–	0	–
Incurved bowl	1	50.0	1	50.0
Plate/platter	1	50.0	0	–
Outcurved bowl	0	–	1	50.0
Bowl orifice diameter				
Number of cases	1	–	2	–
Range	N/A	–	7.0-9.0 cm	–
Mean	8.0 cm	–	8.0 cm	–
Standard deviation	N/A	–	1.4 cm	–
Rim shape				
Rounded	3	100.0	2	66.7
Squared	0	–	1	33.3
Average vessel wall thickness				
Number of cases	11	–	4	–
Range	3.5-10.1 mm	–	5.0-8.5 mm	–
Mean	5.9 mm	–	6.9 mm	–
Standard deviation	2.0 mm	–	1.5 mm	–
Minimum vessel wall thickness				
Number of cases	13	–	4	–
Range	3.0-10.1 mm	–	5.0-6.5 mm	–
Mean	5.3 mm	–	5.9 mm	–
Standard deviation	2.2 mm	–	.6 mm	–
Maximum vessel wall thickness				
Number of cases	13	–	4	–
Range	4.5-11.0 mm	–	6.0-8.5 mm	–
Mean	6.9 mm	–	7.4 mm	–
Standard deviation	2.1 mm	–	1.3 mm	–
Difference between minimum and maximum vessel wall thickness				
Number of cases	13	–	4	–
Range	.0-3.5 mm	–	.0-2.5 mm	–
Mean	1.5 mm	–	1.5 mm	–
Standard deviation	.9 mm	–	1.2 mm	–

Table 8.2. Continued.

Attribute	Bumpy Quantity	Bumpy Percent	Incised Quantity	Incised Percent
Interior surface treatment				
Indeterminate	5	–	0	–
Polished/burnished	0	–	1	25.0
Scraped	3	37.5	2	50.0
Hand-smoothed	5	62.5	1	25.0
Exterior surface treatment				
Indeterminate	3	–	1	–
Polished/burnished	0	–	1	33.3
Scraped	3	30.0	1	33.3
Hand-smoothed	7	70.0	1	33.3
Incised decoration				
Interior	N/A	–	1	25.0
Interior and rim	N/A	–	1	25.0
Interior and exterior	N/A	–	1	25.0
Exterior	N/A	–	1	25.0
Carbon core				
Indeterminate	2	–	1	–
Absent	11	100.0	3	100.0
Fire cloud				
Indeterminate	2	–	1	–
Absent	10	90.9	3	100.0
Exterior	1	9.1	0	–

treatment attribute frequencies are the most subjective assessments recorded in this study. Pinching (Rye 1981:70) may be the primary forming technique used to create these bumpy and incised incipient plain wares; fingerprints were observed on many of the sherds.

Vessel Shape and Form, Orifice Diameter, and Rim Shape

The vessel form of most incipient plain wares recovered from Los Pozos could not be determined because they were body sherds. Among those sherds that could be determined, all were bowls. Three bowl vessel forms were documented: the incurved bowl, the shallow plate/platter, and the outcurved bowl. Only three of the six rim sherds were large enough to provide an orifice diameter measurement. The orifice diameter of these pots ranged from 7-9 cm, with an average orifice diameter of 8 cm. Two rim shapes were observed. Although the sample size is small, the rounded rim shape outnumbers the squared rim shape five-to-one.

Vessel Wall Thickness

Analysis of the incipient plain wares recovered from the Santa Cruz Bend site showed that the vessel wall thickness of individual pots was highly variable (Heidke et al. 1998). For that reason, four measurements of vessel wall thickness are reported in Table 8.2. The average, minimum, maximum, and difference between minimum and maximum vessel wall thickness measurements are reported. The overall range of the bumpy variety (3-11 mm) is greater than that of the incised variety (5-8.5 mm), although the mean difference between the minimum and maximum thickness of individual pots is the same in both varieties (1.5 mm). The mean "average thickness" of the incised variety (6.9 mm) is thicker than the bumpy variety (5.9 mm). However, a t-test comparing the "average thickness" of the two varieties shows that we cannot reject the null hypothesis that a difference this large could occur by chance ($t = -.912$; $df = 13$; $p = .378$).

Interior and Exterior Surface Treatments

All of the incipient plain wares had interior and exterior surfaces that either displayed dull hand-smoothed surfaces (Rye 1981:89-90), scrape marks (Rye 1981:86), or polishing/burnishing (Rye 1981:90). Exterior surfaces are usually somewhat bumpy, whereas interior surfaces are less so and are usually uniformly curved.

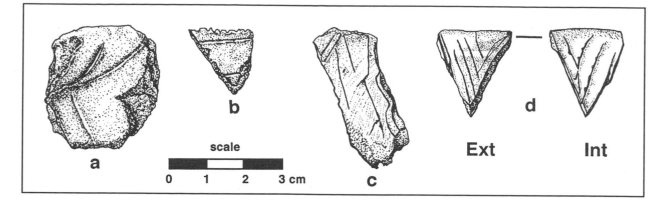

Figure 8.7. Incised incipient plain ware from Los Pozos.

Incising

Incising is a decorative forming technique produced by cutting into the pot's surface (Rye 1981:66, 90). Four of the incipient plain wares recovered from Los Pozos display incised decoration. The design field of each one of these vessels is different. One has an incised design on the interior surface (Figure 8.7a), one on the interior and rim (Figure 8.7b), one on the interior and exterior surfaces (Figure 8.7d), and one on the exterior surface (Figure 8.7c). Design elements include straight, curved, wavy, and parallel lines. These design elements are also common in the contemporary western Archaic rock art tradition (Wallace and Holmlund 1986:Figure D-3).

The stage of drying each vessel was in when incised was determined through an examination of the incised surface(s). One of the sherds displays ridges along both sides of the incised lines indicating that the design was cut into the clay when it was in a soft, plastic condition, whereas the other three sherds display clean lines indicating a leather-hard condition (Rye 1981:Figure 47). None of the four incised sherds displayed the chipped edges diagnostic of incising that has taken place after the vessel has dried hard. In cross section, the incision made while the clay was still soft is "U-shaped" and measures .5-mm wide and .8-mm deep. The incisions made when the clay was leather-hard are "V-shaped" and range from .1- to .8-mm wide and .7- to 1.1-mm deep.

Firing Technique

Carbon cores are black-to-gray areas observable in the interior cross section of a vessel wall and are associated with the incomplete removal of carbonaceous matter from the clay during firing (Rice 1987: 474). Carbon cores were absent from all specimens, indicating that the vessels were likely fired in an oxidizing atmosphere (Rye 1981:115-116). Fire clouds are darkened areas on a vessel's surface and are characteristic of firing conditions in which the fuel is in contact with the vessel (Rice 1987:476). Nearly all of the incipient plain wares lack fire clouds, indicating that, in general, fuel was not in contact with the pots when they were fired.

Hohokam Plain Wares and Other Pottery from Los Pozos

Hohokam Plain Wares

Portions of 11 Hohokam plain ware vessels were recovered from Los Pozos. Table 8.3 lists their recovery contexts. Each row represents an individual vessel. The quantity of conjoining and/or matching sherds recovered from each vessel is reported in the "Number of Sherds" column; only two vessels were represented by more than one sherd. Most of the Hohokam plain ware sherds recovered from Los Pozos are larger than the late Cienega phase incipient plain ware sherds (i.e., greater than 5 cm²), but none are larger than 49 cm². All 11 vessels are represented by body sherds.

The Hohokam plain wares recovered from Los Pozos differ from the late Cienega phase incipient plain wares in three notable respects. First, as mentioned above, the size distribution of sherds assigned to each group differs. A Fisher's exact test confirms that the two size distributions are significantly different (p = .024). Second, the Hohokam plain wares contain abundant gneiss/schist (1 case) or sand (10 cases) temper. The low percentage of gneiss/schist temper suggests that these sherds have a greater likelihood of having been produced during the time span from the Agua Caliente phase through the Snaketown phase (circa A.D. 150-750) or the time span from the Late

Table 8.3. Hohokam plain ware recovery contexts at Los Pozos.

Feature Number	Stratum	Level	Number of Sherds	Sherd Size	Vessel Part
333	10	1	1	5-16 cm^2	Body sherd
333	10	1	1	5-16 cm^2	Body sherd
333	10	1	1	< 5 cm^2	Body sherd
365	50	1	1	16-49 cm^2	Body sherd
365	50	1	2	16-49 cm^2	Body sherd
365	50	1	1	5-16 cm^2	Body sherd
365	50	1	1	5-16 cm^2	Body sherd
422	50	1	8	16-49 cm^2	Body sherd
422	50	1	1	5-16 cm^2	Body sherd
422	50	1	1	5-16 cm^2	Body sherd
882	10	1	1	< 5 cm^2	Body sherd

Table 8.4. Other ceramic recovery contexts at Los Pozos.

Feature Number	Stratum	Level	Number of Sherds	Sherd Size	Vessel Part	Ceramic Ware	Ceramic Type
0	4	1	1	5-16 cm^2	Rim sherd	Red-on-brown	Tanque Verde
333	10	1	1	5-16 cm^2	Indeterminate	Indeterminate	Indeterminate
365	50	1	2	5-16 cm^2	Body sherd	Red ware	Unknown red ware type

Rincon phase through the Tucson phase (circa A.D. 1100-1450), than they do from the intervening span (Cañada del Oro through Middle Rincon 3, circa A.D. 750-1100) when micaceous tempers were often used to produce plain wares (Wallace et al. 1995:Figure 6). Third, the modal temper grain size of the Hohokam plain wares is larger than that of the incipient plain wares. In eight of the Hohokam plain wares the modal temper grain size is medium sand (¼-½ mm), in two it is coarse sand (.5-1 mm), and in one it is very coarse sand (1-2 mm).

Other Pottery

Portions of three additional vessels were recovered from Los Pozos (Table 8.4). One is a Tanque Verde Red-on-brown bowl rim sherd recovered from a nonfeature context. Another is an indeterminate piece of fired clay that may not be pottery at all, but rather a piece of clay construction material that burned. The third vessel is an unknown red ware type. It was recovered from the upper-most level of fill in well Feature 365; portions of three Hohokam plain ware vessels were recovered from the same level (Table 8.3). The red ware vessel was slipped on its interior and exterior surfaces. It is unusual in two respects. First, it is tempered with a mixture of volcanic sand, crushed sherd, and a small amount of schist. Second, it is thin. The average vessel wall thickness of the vessel is 3.5 mm.

Cienega Phase Pottery: The Inception of a Ritual Ceramic Container Technology

Before exploring specific issues regarding the origin, iconography, and possible function of Cienega phase pottery, we summarize the extant production sequence data for all four varieties of incipient plain ware and their place in the Tucson Basin's developmental sequence of ceramic container technology. Comparisons are made with data recorded from 10 later sites' ceramic collections. Only data collected from rim sherds and reconstructible vessels recovered from well-dated contexts are used in the comparisons. Table 8.5 summarizes the dating and sample size of ceramic collections used in the comparisons that follow.

Review of Early and Late Cienega Phase Pottery Technology

So far, portions of 84 incipient plain ware vessels have been recovered from two early Cienega phase and three late Cienega phase sites (Table 8.6). The bumpy variety has been recovered from all five sites. The coiled variety was only recovered from the two early Cienega phase sites, whereas the impressed and the incised varieties were only recovered from late Cienega phase sites (Figure 8.8). Most of the 84 vessels are represented by body sherds, rather than rim sherds, a fact that limits our understanding of vessel forms and sizes.

Table 8.5. Data sets used in temporal studies.

Phase/Period	Site Name	ASM Site Number	Plain Ware	Red Ware	Red-on-brown	Polychrome	Other Ceramic Wares	Citation
Agua Caliente phase	Square Hearth	AA:12:745	46	0	0	0	0	Heidke et al. 1998
Agua Caliente phase	Stone Pipe	BB:13:425	59	0	0	0	0	Heidke et al. 1998
Tortolita phase	Hodges Ruin	AA:12:18	30	7	0	0	2	Heidke et al. 1996
Tortolita phase	Lonetree	AA:12:120	101	68	0	0	0	Heidke 1990
Tortolita phase	Romero Ruin	BB:9:1	31	21	0	0	0	Heidke 1991
Tortolita phase	Valencia	BB:13:15	109	16	0	0	4	Heidke 1993
Colonial period	Los Morteros	AA:12:57	25	0	4	0	0	Heidke 1995
Colonial period	Redtail	AA:12:149	156	0	24	0	0	Heidke 1989
Sedentary period	Los Morteros	AA:12:57	436	13	314	4	3	Heidke 1995
Sedentary period	Lonetree	AA:12:120	56	0	17	0	0	Heidke 1990
Classic period	Los Morteros	AA:12:57	103	2	75	1	1	Heidke 1995
Classic period	Bid Kih Ruin	AA:15:79	53	1	70	0	0	Heidke et al. 1994
Classic period	TaDai Ruin	AA:15:97	298	4	640	0	25	Heidke et al. 1994

Table 8.6. Production sequence attribute data recorded from Clearwater, Coffee Camp, Los Pozos, Santa Cruz Bend, and Wetlands incipient plain ware collections.

Attribute	Early Cienega Phase				Late Cienega Phase					
	Bumpy Quantity	Bumpy Percent	Coiled Quantity	Coiled Percent	Bumpy Quantity	Bumpy Percent	Impressed Quantity	Impressed Percent	Incised Quantity	Incised Percent
Site										
Coffee Camp (AZ AA:6:19)	0	–	0	–	4	17.4	6	100.0	1	20.0
Wetlands (AZ AA:12:90)	15	88.2	29	87.9	0	–	0	–	0	–
Los Pozos (AZ AA:12:91)	0	–	0	–	13	56.5	0	–	4	80.0
Santa Cruz Bend (AZ AA:12:746)	0	–	0	–	6	26.1	0	–	0	–
Clearwater (AZ BB:13:6)	2	11.8	4	12.1	0	–	0	–	0	–
Vessel part										
Indeterminate	3	–	5	–	2	–	0	–	0	–
Body sherd	9	64.3	25	89.3	16	76.2	6	100.0	2	40.0
Rim sherd	4	28.6	3	10.7	5	23.8	0	–	3	60.0
Whole vessel	1	7.1	0	–	0	–	0	–	0	–
Body composition										
Untempered clay	17	100.0	33	100.0	23	100.0	6	100.0	5	100.0
Modal nonplastic grain size										
Silt	5	29.4	13	39.4	10	43.5	0	–	1	20.0
Very fine sand	6	35.3	6	18.2	5	21.7	2	33.3	3	60.0
Fine sand	6	35.3	12	36.4	7	30.4	4	66.7	0	–
Medium sand	0	–	1	3.0	1	4.3	0	–	1	20.0
Coarse sand	0	–	1	3.0	0	–	0	–	0	–
Organic temper casts visible										
Indeterminate	0	–	0	–	2	–	1	–	0	–
Absent	13	76.5	28	84.8	13	61.9	3	60.0	4	80.0
Present	4	23.5	5	15.2	8	38.1	2	40.0	1	20.0
Charcoal fragments in paste										
Absent	17	100.0	30	90.9	18	78.3	4	66.7	4	80.0
Present	0	–	3	9.1	5	21.7	2	33.3	1	20.0
Coil width										
Number of cases	0	–	30	–	0	–	0	–	0	–

Table 8.6. Continued.

Attribute	Early Cienega Phase				Late Cienega Phase					
	Bumpy Quantity	Bumpy Percent	Coiled Quantity	Coiled Percent	Bumpy Quantity	Bumpy Percent	Impressed Quantity	Impressed Percent	Incised Quantity	Incised Percent
Range	N/A	–	3.7-8.6 mm	–	N/A	–	N/A	–	N/A	–
Mean	N/A	–	5.5 mm	–	N/A	–	N/A	–	N/A	–
Standard deviation	N/A	–	1.2 mm	–	N/A	–	N/A	–	N/A	–
Vessel form										
Indeterminate	13	–	30	–	19	–	6	–	2	–
Indeterminate bowl	2	–	2	–	1	–	0	–	1	–
Outcurved bowl	1	50.0	1	100.0	0	–	0	–	1	50.0
Incurved bowl	0	–	0	–	1	33.3	0	–	1	50.0
Plate	0	–	0	–	1	33.3	0	–	0	–
Seed jar	1	50.0	0	–	1	33.3	0	–	0	–
Bowl orifice diameter										
Number of cases	2	–	1	–	1	–	0	–	2	–
Range	1.5-6.0 cm	–	N/A	–	N/A	–	N/A	–	7.0-9.0 cm	–
Mean	3.7 cm	–	13.0 cm	–	8.0 cm	–	N/A	–	8.0 cm	–
Standard deviation	3.2 cm	–	N/A	–	N/A	–	N/A	–	1.4 cm	–
Jar aperture diameter										
Number of cases	1	–	0	–	1	–	0	–	0	–
Range	N/A	–	N/A	–	N/A	–	N/A	–	N/A	–
Mean	4.0 cm	–	N/A	–	2.0 cm	–	N/A	–	N/A	–
Standard deviation	N/A	–	N/A	–	N/A	–	N/A	–	N/A	–
Rim shape										
Indeterminate	2	–	1	–	0	–	0	–	0	–
Rounded	3	100.0	2	100.0	4	80.0	0	–	2	66.7
Tapered	0	–	0	–	1	20.0	0	–	0	–
Squared	0	–	0	–	0	–	0	–	1	33.3
Average vessel wall thickness										
Number of cases	16	–	31	–	17	–	6	–	5	–
Range	3.8-9.0 mm	–	3.0-5.3 mm	–	3.5-10.1 mm	–	4.8-10.2 mm	–	5.0-8.0 mm	–
Mean	5.8 mm	–	3.7 mm	–	5.9 mm	–	6.9 mm	–	6.8 mm	–
Standard deviation	1.4 mm	–	.6 mm	–	1.6 mm	–	1.9 mm	–	1.3 mm	–

Table 8.6. Continued.

Attribute	Early Cienega Phase				Late Cienega Phase					
	Bumpy Quantity	Bumpy Percent	Coiled Quantity	Coiled Percent	Bumpy Quantity	Bumpy Percent	Impressed Quantity	Impressed Percent	Incised Quantity	Incised Percent
Difference between minimum and maximum vessel wall thickness										
Number of cases	17	–	32	–	23	–	6	–	5	–
Range	.0-2.7 mm	–	0-3.3 mm	–	.0-3.5 mm	–	.2-3.6 mm	–	.0-2.5 mm	–
Mean	1.5 mm	–	.7 mm	–	1.4 mm	–	2.6 mm	–	1.3 mm	–
Standard deviation	.9 mm	–	.7 mm	–	1.1 mm	–	1.4 mm	–	1.1 mm	–
Interior surface treatment										
Indeterminate	5	–	29	–	10	–	0	–	1	–
Hand-smoothed	11	91.7	3	75.0	7	53.8	0	–	1	25.0
Scraped	1	8.3	0	–	6	46.2	0	–	2	50.0
Plant fiber or animal fur impressed	0	–	0	–	0	–	6	100.0	0	–
Polished/burnished	0	–	1	25.0	0	–	0	–	1	25.0
Exterior surface treatment										
Indeterminate	3	–	28	–	6	–	1	–	1	–
Hand-smoothed	14	100.0	4	80.0	12	70.6	5	100.0	2	50.0
Scraped	0	–	0	–	5	29.4	0	–	1	25.0
Polished/burnished	0	–	1	20.0	0	–	0	–	1	25.0
Incised										
Indeterminate	1	–	0	–	0	–	0	–	0	–
Absent	16	100.0	33	100.0	23	100.0	0	–	0	–
Interior	0	–	0	–	0	–	0	–	2	40.0
Interior and rim	0	–	0	–	0	–	0	–	1	20.0
Interior and exterior	0	–	0	–	0	–	0	–	1	20.0
Exterior	0	–	0	–	0	–	0	–	1	20.0
Carbon core										
Indeterminate	4	–	9	–	5	–	0	–	1	–
Absent	12	92.3	19	79.2	16	88.9	3	50.0	4	100.0
Present	1	7.7	5	20.8	2	11.1	3	50.0	0	–
Fire cloud										
Indeterminate	5	–	9	–	7	–	0	–	1	–
Absent	12	100.0	23	95.8	14	87.5	6	100.0	4	100.0
Exterior present	0	–	1	4.2	2	12.5	0	–	0	–

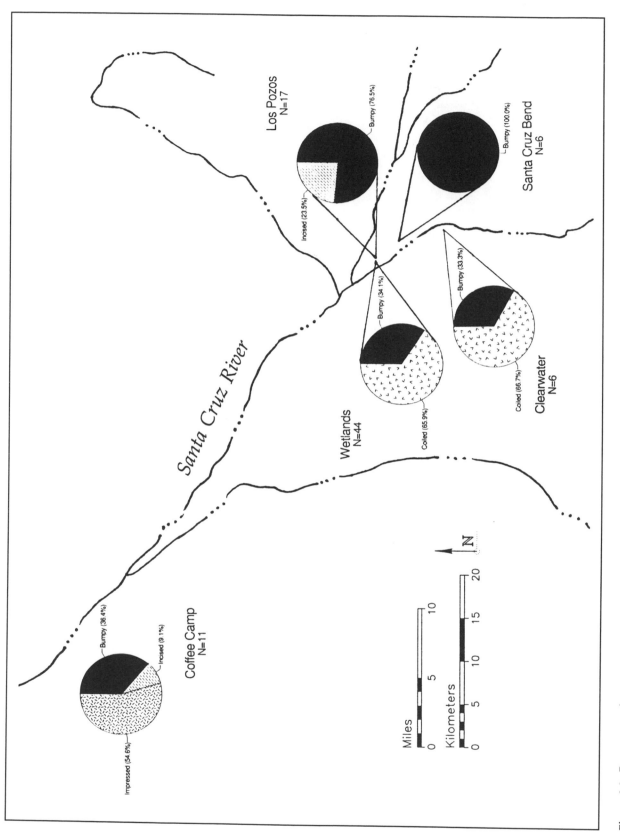

Figure 8.8. Percentage of incipient plain ware varieties recovered from five early and late Cienega phase sites.

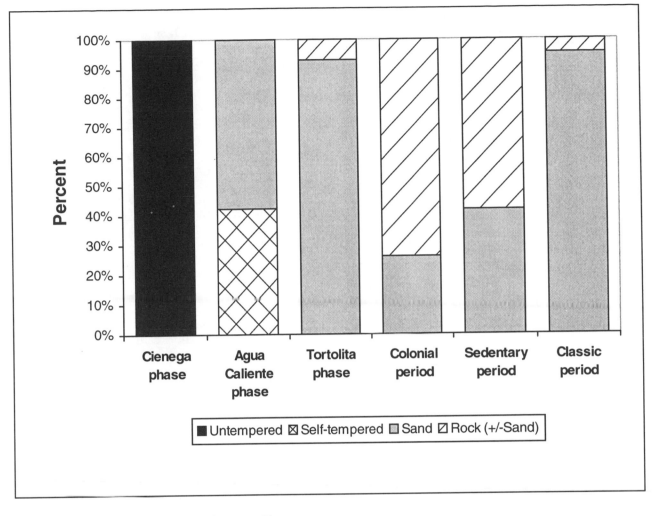

Figure 8.9. Temporal trends in ceramic composition.

All of the incipient plain wares appear to have been produced from clays that contain low percentages of naturally occurring geologic and organic nonplastics. Most of the rock and mineral grains observed in all four varieties range in size from silt to fine sand, although a few cases of medium and coarse sand were recorded. One of the bumpy variety from the Wetlands site incorporated a *Helisoma* sp. shell in its body. *Helisoma* is a genus of terrestrial snail that likes grassy or muddy areas near watercourses. It, too, was probably a natural component of the clay.

Casts from burnt-out organic material in the clay are present in all four varieties, as are flecks of charcoal. This organic material was likely a natural component of the clay body and not added by the potter. Similar small diameter holes and charcoal flecks are often present in later, Hohokam pottery produced in the Tucson Basin. This fact leads us to disagree with Kisselburg's (1993:294) assertion that the Coffee Camp

vessels were "fiber tempered" (a view which has already become embedded in the secondary literature, e.g., Reid and Whittlesey 1997:66).

The low percentage and small size of the nonplastics observed in the incipient plain wares suggests that Cienega phase potters consciously selected "untempered" clays. Manufacture of pottery from "untempered" clay is one of the diagnostic traits of incipient plain wares. As Figure 8.9 clearly shows, production of pottery from "untempered" clay is restricted to the Cienega phase. It is interesting to note, however, that "self-tempered" alluvial clays were used in the subsequent Agua Caliente phase (Heidke et al. 1998) but not thereafter. Throughout the rest of the prehistoric sequence, potters in the Sonoran Desert added sand or crushed micaceous rock tempers to clay. Taken together, the Cienega and Agua Caliente phase data suggest that it took potters many generations to gain familiarity with the various resources available in the region, and to develop mixtures of plastic and non-plastic materials that would produce workable clay bodies.

Two methods of primary forming were utilized: coiling and pinching. The coiled variety was, as its label implies, built up from coils. The average coil width is 5.5 mm. Superficially, coiled incipient plain ware sherds resemble corrugated pottery. However, unlike corrugated wares, the coil junctures are clearly visible on both the interior and exterior surfaces. Coils were pressed together, and many examples display finger marks (especially on their exterior surface). The coils overlap, and in cross section, some of the overlapping coils produce a "clapboard" appearance while others produce a "shiplap" appearance. The rim of one vessel displays a tapered point at the end of its terminal coil; this aspect makes the rim look like nothing so much as a basket made of clay. A few flat coils of small radius were recovered from the Wetlands site; these are interpreted as basal portions of spiral coiled vessels.

Vessels formed by pinching have either bumpy, hand-smoothed surfaces or incised surfaces. Vessels exhibiting fiber impressions may also have been formed by pinching, or the impressions may have resulted from molding the clay body over another object. The similarity of vessel wall thickness in the bumpy, incised, and fiber-impressed pots suggests that all three varieties were likely produced by a single method–pinching–and that the impressions resulted from fibrous materials being pressed into the clay after the vessel was formed.

The vessel shape represented by most sherds could not be determined, but we can offer inferences based on 13 rim sherds. Eleven of them, or approximately 85 percent, are bowls, and two (15 percent) are jars. The most common vessel form is the outcurved bowl (Figure 8.10b-d), followed by the incurved bowl (Figure 8.10e), the seed jar (Figure 8.10f-g), and the shallow plate/platter form (Figure 8.10a).

Among all incipient plain ware varieties, the bowl forms are small. Bowl orifice diameter ranges from 1.5-13.0 cm, and the average size is 7.4 cm. These are unusually small vessels relative to those produced throughout the rest of the Tucson Basin's prehistory (Figure 8.11).

As mentioned above, a low percentage of jars have also been documented in the incipient plain wares. Like the bowls, these are unusually small vessels (Figure 8.12), with an average aperture diameter of 3 cm. A single jar vessel form has been documented–the neckless "seed jar." That vessel form dominates the potters' output in the subsequent Agua Caliente phase (Figure 8.13). However, Agua Caliente phase seed jars are much larger (Heidke et al. 1998), and their average aperture diameter is 14.3 cm.

The most common rim shape observed in all varieties and vessel forms is rounded, although tapered and squared rim shapes were also documented.

The average vessel wall thickness varies by variety (Figure 8.14), though the bumpy, impressed, and incised varieties (all of which may have been formed by pinching) are similar to each other and are thicker than the coiled variety (which was clearly formed by another technique). The difference between the minimum and maximum vessel wall thickness measurements also varies by variety, with the bumpy, impressed, and incised varieties showing a greater range than the coiled variety.

Interior surface finish also varies by variety. A dull, hand-smoothed interior surface is common on the bumpy variety. The interior surface treatment of most coiled specimens is also dull, although only a few examples look hand-smoothed. All of the impressed variety exhibited plant fiber or animal fur impressions on their interior surface (Kisselburg 1993). The small sample of incised sherds shows the greatest variability in surface finish, with examples of hand-smoothing, scraping, and polishing/burnishing present. Exterior surfaces show more consistency than interior surfaces. Most specimens of all varieties display a hand-smoothed exterior.

The design field of the incised variety is highly variable. Two specimens display incising on their interior surface and nowhere else, one is incised on the interior and rim, one on the interior and exterior, and one on the exterior and nowhere else. Two of the sherds display ridges along both sides of the incised lines, indicating that the design was cut into the clay when it was in a soft, plastic condition. In cross section, these incisions are "U-shaped" and range from .5- to 1-mm wide and .8- to .9-mm deep. Three of the sherds display clean lines, indicating a leather-hard condition. In cross section, these incisions are "V-shaped" and range from .1- to .8-mm wide and .7- to 1.1-mm deep.

The general absence of carbon cores indicates that incipient plain wares were usually fired in an oxidizing atmosphere. The Munsell color of the interior surface, exterior surface, and core of a large sample of the incipient plain wares, those illustrated in Figures 8.2-8.5, was recorded (Table 8.7). Most surface and core colors are some shade of brown or gray. Those colors indicate firing conditions that ranged from incompletely oxidizing to relatively well oxidizing (Rice 1987:Table 11.3). The general absence of fire clouds indicates that fuel was rarely in contact with the vessels during firing.

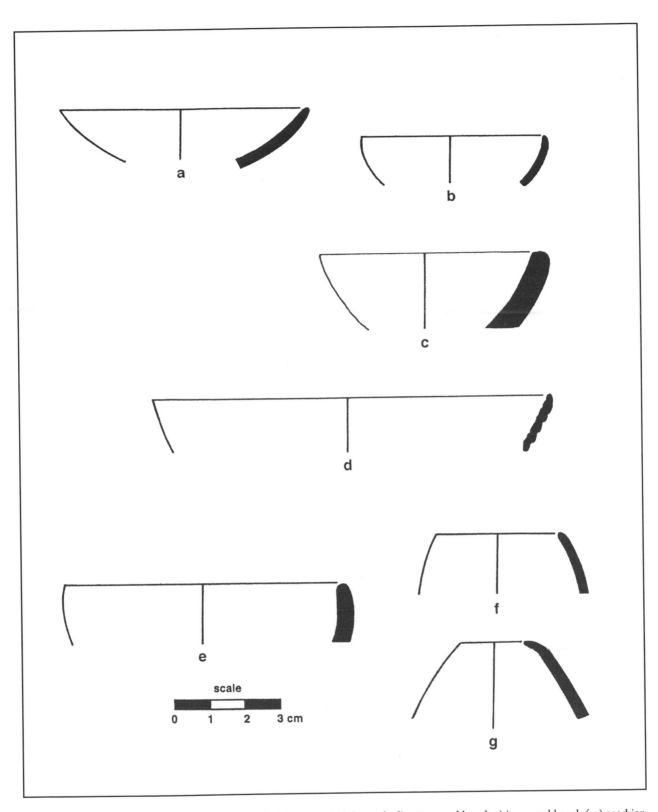

Figure 8.10. Incipient plain ware vessel forms: a) shallow plate/platter; b-d) outcurved bowl; e) incurved bowl; f-g) seed jar.

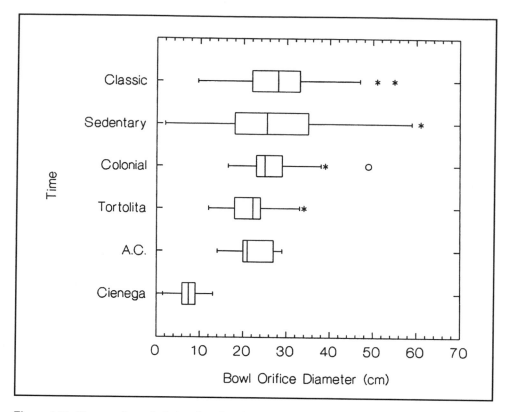

Figure 8.11. Temporal trends in bowl orifice diameter.

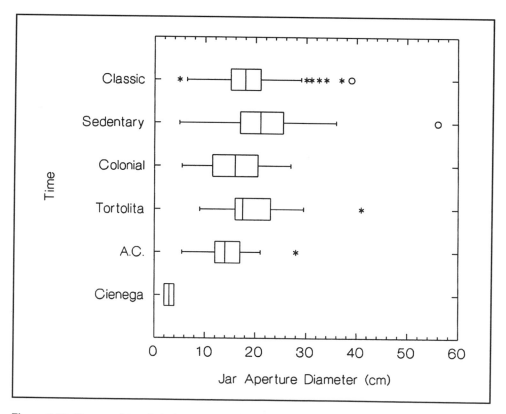

Figure 8.12. Temporal trends in jar aperture diameter.

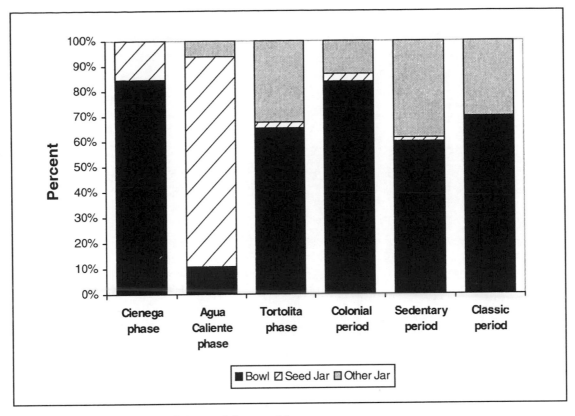

Figure 8.13. Temporal trends in vessel shape and form.

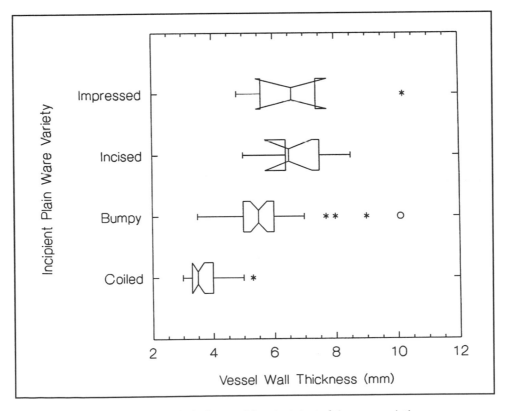

Figure 8.14. Trends in vessel wall thickness of four incipient plain ware varieties.

Table 8.7. Munsell colors of incipient plain wares illustrated in Figures 8.2-8.5. (The color of the sherd illustrated in Figure 8.3h was indeterminate; therefore, it is not listed.)

Interior Color	Munsell Color	Exterior Color	Munsell Color	Core Color	Munsell Color	Figure Number
Gray	10YR 5/1	Gray	10YR 5/1	Gray	10YR 5/1	8.3c
Gray	10YR 5/1	Light brown	7.5YR 6/4	Reddish-yellow	7.5YR 6/6	8.5b
Grayish-brown	10YR 5/2	Gray	10YR 5/1	Dark gray	7.5YR 4/0	8.3g
Grayish-brown	10YR 5/2	Grayish-brown	10YR 5/2	Light brown	7.5YR 6/4	8.4c
Light brownish-gray	10YR 6/2	Light brownish-gray	10YR 6/2	Light brownish-gray	10YR 6/2	8.3b
Light brown	7.5YR 6/4	Pink	7.5YR 7/3	Strong brown	7.5YR 5/6	8.3f
Light brown	7.5YR 6/4	Light brown	7.5YR 6/3	Dark gray	7.5YR 4/0	8.2b
Light brown	7.5YR 6/3	Light brown	7.5YR 6/3	Light brown	7.5YR 6/3	8.4a
Light brown	7.5YR 6/4	Light brown	7.5YR 6/4	Light brown	7.5YR 6/4	8.4b
Light gray to gray	5YR 6/1	Gray	5YR 5/1	Gray	7.5YR 5/0	8.3e
Light gray to gray	10YR 6/1	Gray	10YR 5/1	Dark gray	7.5YR 4/0	8.2a
Light reddish-brown	5YR 6/4	Light reddish-brown	5YR 6/4	Light reddish-brown	5YR 6/4	8.3d
Pale brown	10YR 6/3	Grayish-brown	10YR 5/2	Reddish-yellow	5YR 6/6	8.3a
Pale brown	10YR 6/3	Pale brown	10YR 6/3	Pale brown	10YR 6/3	8.4e
Pink	7.5YR 7/4	Pink	7.5YR 7/4	Reddish-yellow	7.5YR 7/6	8.2c
Pinkish-gray	7.5YR 6/2	Pinkish-gray	7.5YR 6/2	Pinkish-gray	7.5YR 6/2	8.3i
Pinkish-gray	7.5YR 6/2	Pinkish-gray	7.5YR 6/2	Pinkish-gray	7.5YR 6/2	8.2e
Pinkish-gray	7.5YR 7/2	Pinkish-gray	7.5YR 7/2	Dark gray	7.5YR 4/0	8.3d
Reddish-brown	5YR 5/4	Reddish-brown	5YR 4/4	Reddish-brown	5YR 4/4	8.4d
Reddish-yellow	5YR 6/6	Light brown	7.5YR 6/3	Reddish-yellow	5YR 6/6	8.5a

*The Origin, Iconography, and Function
of Cienega Phase Pottery*

If we believe Braun's (1983:107) now famous dictum that pots are "tools," we must search for the functions these early ceramic containers served. One hypothesis is that pottery was invented in order to detoxify foods and make them more palatable. Another set of hypotheses proposes that early pottery functioned as a prestige good used in ritual displays, particularly in the context of competitive feasting (Hoopes and Barnett 1995:3). Orifice diameter measurements reviewed above have shown that the incipient plain wares are very small vessels; many, in fact, would be considered miniature vessels. It seems unlikely that these small vessels would have been of much use in food processing or competitive feasting. However, the possibility that they may have been a "prestige" good used in ritual displays cannot be discounted. Before addressing the function of incipient plain wares further, we review possible antecedents of this early pottery and the iconographic tradition it was a part of.

Origins. Childe (1951:79, cited in Hoopes and Barnett 1995:2-3) has suggested that the earliest pots were imitations of containers made from natural materials, such as gourds, bladders, skins, baskets, and even human skulls, and that early forms of decoration helped to reinforce the connection between ceramic vessels and earlier materials. Similarly, Clark and Gosser (1995:219) have argued that the earliest Mesoamerican ceramic containers copied the forms of some perishable vessels already in use. We feel that the replacement of a perishable container technology–basketry–with a ceramic technology is a particularly satisfying explanation for the coiled variety of incipient plain wares that look like nothing so much as "clay baskets." The other incipient plain ware varieties are more problematic. However, we think that a case can be made that the bumpy and incised varieties replaced another type of perishable container–those made of gourds–given their size and type of decoration.

In southern Arizona, cucurbit remains (either squash or wild gourd) have been recovered from two late Cienega phase sites (Los Pozos and Los Ojitos [L. Huckell 1995b]). Therefore, we know that cucurbits were used by early occupants of the Tucson Basin. Three species of wild gourds occur in Arizona, the most common and widely distributed of which are the buffalo gourd (*Cucurbita foetidissima* H.B.K.) and fingerleaf gourd (*C. digitata* Gray). These species produce round, baseball-sized fruits (L. Huckell 1998). The average orifice diameter of the bumpy and incised bowls is 6.3 cm, slightly smaller than the diameter of a baseball. Finally, the thin rinds of buffalo gourds could be used as containers, but do not lend themselves to use as tools because they are easily broken (L. Huckell

1998). A ceramic container would, therefore, have made a less fragile substitute.

Iconography. Cross-culturally, burnishing and incising are two common techniques used to decorate gourds (Lathrap 1977, cited in Clark and Gosser 1995:216), and the presence of incising was the criterion used to define one of the incipient plain ware varieties. A review of data in Barnett and Hoopes (1995) suggests that incising may be the most common decorative technique used by early potters throughout the world (Table 8.8). Therefore, it is not surprising to find that some of the early ceramics made in southeastern Arizona were incised. The straight, curved, wavy, and parallel line incised motifs present on incipient plain wares are shared with the Western Archaic rock art tradition (Wallace and Holmlund 1986:Figure D-3). This iconographic tradition started about 8000 B.C. and continued until approximately A.D. 800 (Wallace 1995:34). These design elements were also used on ground stone artifacts and clay figurines and may also have been used to decorate less durable media (such as gourds).

Henry Wallace (personal communication 1995) first brought the similarity of incised incipient plain ware designs and elements of the western Archaic rock art tradition to the senior author's attention. He has previously pointed out that the earliest Hohokam decorated types–Estrella and Sweetwater red-on-gray and Snaketown and early Gila Butte red-on-buff–also utilized Western Archaic rock art elements in their design repertoire, and that these simple design motifs are shared with many other early, painted Southwestern ceramic types, such as Anchondo, Cascabel, and Mogollon red-on-brown (Wallace 1995; Wallace et al. 1995). Thus, it is not surprising to find that western Archaic design elements were used to embellish the surface of some incipient plain wares, nor would we be surprised if a similar usage was documented in those areas where the later red-on-brown types listed above were produced.

Function. Behavioral inferences regarding the function of incipient plain wares are hampered by two factors: most vessels are incomplete, and most have been recovered from secondary refuse deposits. Therefore, the archaeological record has placed something of a limit on our ability to ascertain the function that these containers played when they were in systemic context. We note, however, that a portion of one vessel was recovered from the burned floor of Coffee Camp Feature 315, the site's "Big House," in association with the phyllite wand, bone tube, and other unusual artifacts described earlier. Halbirt and others (1993:90) conclude that Feature 315 may well have served a special ceremonial or ritual purpose. Similarly, an incipient plain ware sherd was recovered from the near-floor fill of the "Big House" at the Santa Cruz Bend

Table 8.8. Types of decoration used on early pottery types throughout the world (x = present; from Barnett and Hoopes 1995).

Region	Incised	Impressed	Slipped or Painted	Burnished	Punctated	Applique	Grooved	Modeled	Stamped	Coated	Fluted	Gouged	Pinched	Scraped	Citation
Brazil (Lower Amazon)	x	–	x	–	x	–	–	–	–	–	–	–	–	–	Roosevelt 1995:126-127
Colombia	x	x	x	–	–	x	–	x	–	–	–	–	–	–	Oyuela-Caycedo 1995:139; Rodriguez 1995:148, 152
Panama	x	–	x	–	x	–	–	–	–	–	–	–	–	–	Cooke 1995:173
Costa Rica and Nicaragua	x	–	x	–	x	–	–	x	x	–	–	x	–	x	Hoopes 1995:187-188
El Salvador	x	x	x	x	–	–	x	–	x	–	–	–	–	–	Arroyo 1995:202-204
Mexico (Chiapas)	x	–	x	x	x	–	x	–	–	–	x	–	–	–	Clark and Gosser 1995:212-213
Japan	x	x	–	–	–	–	–	–	–	–	–	–	x	–	Aikens 1995:13
North Africa	x	x	–	–	–	–	–	–	–	–	–	–	–	–	Close 1995:26
West Asia	x	x	x	x	–	x	–	–	–	–	–	–	–	–	Moore 1995:40, 42-43
Greece	–	x	–	x	–	–	–	–	–	–	–	–	–	–	Vitelli 1995:59
Central Balkans	x	x	–	x	–	x	–	–	–	x	–	–	–	–	Manson 1995:66-67
Central Europe	x	x	–	–	–	–	–	–	–	–	–	–	–	–	Bogucki 1995:91
Southern Scandinavia	–	–	–	–	–	–	–	–	–	–	–	–	–	–	Gebauer 1995:101
Total number of cases	11	8	7	5	4	3	2	2	2	1	1	1	1	1	

site (Feature 310), while two were recovered from the near-floor fill of the "possible Big House" at the Wetlands site (Feature 200) and another three from post-holes in that feature's floor. Although all of these vessels are represented by sherds and only the fragment from Coffee Camp was recovered from a secure de facto refuse assemblage, an association between incipient plain wares and special purpose features is suggested. This relationship needs to be evaluated further as more Cienega phase sites are excavated and more incipient plain wares are recovered.

Incipient plain wares represented a durable (and perhaps more labor-efficient) alternative to perishable containers; they also shared elements with the contemporary rock art style. Given their small size, their iconography, and the recovery of a portion of at least one vessel from a non-domestic context, we suggest two ritual functions–rather than secular–this early pottery may have served. The small bowls comprising the majority of incipient plain ware vessels are well suited to the task of serving individual portions of a liquid or holding offerings. Their low numbers and small size make it appear unlikely they were used in competitive feasting, as has been argued for many other early pottery traditions (Hayden 1995). However, ritual uses of small containers are reported in ethnographic descriptions of Sonoran peoples and groups living in northern Mesoamerica.

The Tohono O'odham of the Sonoran Desert (Underhill 1938:21-41) used gourd cups in their saguaro wine ceremony (which marked the onset of the summer rainy season and the beginning of the agricultural cycle). Saguaro fruit ripens in June just at the end of the dry season. Mixed with water, the juice ferments in two days to a thick, dark-crimson, musty-tasting cider (Underhill 1938:22, 35).

Saguaro wine was first served at the community's "rain house" (Underhill 1938:24) from "great watertight willow baskets" (Underhill 1938:35). Afterward, each household returned home to its own jar of wine left buried to ferment in the even warmth of the earth (Underhill 1938:39). As each household's wine reached the peak of fermentation it was shared with the village. "The host holds in his hand a gourd cup. He dips it into the brownish-red liquor and hands it to a guest. 'Friend, be beautifully drunk'" (Underhill 1938:39). Once consumed, the cup was "covered" with a song that combined the sacred words "cloud," "rain," and "corn" (Underhill 1938:39).

Not only do we see the introduction of ceramic container technology during the Cienega phase, we also see an increased reliance on maize agriculture. Larger mano sizes were developed and the grinding surface area of metates was increased, making them more efficient for dry-grinding meal or flour than earlier manos and metates had been (Adams 1998).

Thus, the Mesoamerican sacred linkage of clouds, rain, and corn and its Sonoran Desert manifestation could have been forged at this early time, and the roots of a saguaro wine ceremony established. Indeed, saguaro wine rituals may have been particularly important at this time, since Cienega phase people relied on rainfall, rather than irrigation canals, to water their crops (Bahr et al. 1994:124).

Saguaro fruit was clearly important to the Cienega phase occupants of the middle and lower Santa Cruz River Valley–saguaro seeds were recovered from all five of the sites that have produced incipient plain wares (Diehl and Waters 1997; L. Huckell 1998; Hutira 1993:337-339)–and saguaro pulp and seeds are themselves important byproducts of wine making (Underhill 1938:23). Therefore, the small incipient plain ware bowls may have served a function similar to the gourd cups used in the Tohono O'odham saguaro wine ceremony.

An alternative function is suggested by the Huichol Indians' use of small gourd bowls to hold offerings to various deities (P. Liffman, personal communication 1996; Negrín 1975:19-20). Such bowls are kept in the local or family god house. In terms of their size and material culture, Huichol god houses and community temples (Myerhoff 1974:108-110) show a remarkable resemblance to the late Cienega phase "Big House" at Coffee Camp (Halbirt et al. 1993:87, 90). Based on those similarities, we suggest that incipient plain wares may have been used like Huichol prayer-bowls as a medium to convey prayers to the spirit world of ancestors and gods.

As with many sets of alternative hypotheses, we note that these two hypothesized functions of incipient plain wares need not be mutually exclusive. In fact, the "Big House" at Coffee Camp–the only burned "Big House" (Halbirt et al. 1993:90) to have been excavated so far, and the one containing an artifact assemblage that most resembles the Huichol family god house–also contained saguaro seeds (Hutira 1993:337). Regardless of whether or not either of the hypothesized functions prove to be correct, the low diversity in vessel shape and size documented here implies that these plain ware bowls served one or more highly specialized uses. Their untempered paste, small size, and rarity in the archaeological record suggest that they were not used for domestic tasks such as cooking or storage. Ethnographic data summarized by Varien and Mills (1997:Table II) indicate that the use lives of ritual vessels are generally much longer than those of utilitarian vessels. That observation provides another line of evidence in support of the ritual function(s) hypothesized here. The rarity of incipient plain wares in the archaeological record may reflect the relatively long time that each of these vessels was in use.

Ceramic Evidence for an Early Agricultural Period Occupation at Snaketown

Haury (1965b:Plate CCXIII n-q; 1976:Figure 13.24d-g, i) illustrates a number of sherds exhibiting incised decoration. He believed that these pots were produced during the Pioneer period, based on associated ceramic types (Haury 1976:268). However, he was disturbed by the fact that the incised patterns did not resemble the painted designs present on pottery of equivalent age (Haury 1976:268). Like the Cienega phase plain wares discussed above, the incised sherds recovered from Snaketown were produced from a fine clay similar to that used in figurine production (Haury 1976:268). The technological and iconographic resemblance of these sherds to those we have documented in Cienega phase contexts led us to re-examine the material from Snaketown, including a number of incised sherds that were not illustrated in either report (see Heidke 2001:Table 5.2).

Examination of the incised pottery from Snaketown revealed that it is, essentially, identical to the material recovered from late Cienega phase contexts. The incised vessels were produced from "untempered" alluvial clays containing low percentages of naturally occurring nonplastics; they were likely formed by pinching (an inference based on the variability observed in each sherd's vessel wall thickness), and all identifiable specimens were small bowls (average orifice diameter 4.9 cm). The presence of these incised sherds in Pioneer contexts is compatible with at least two hypotheses: either the sherds are related to an Early Agricultural period occupation of the site, and the contexts they were recovered from are typologically mixed; or, they document a continuity in ceramic technology and iconography from the Archaic period into the Pioneer period at Snaketown that is absent in the middle and lower Santa Cruz River Valley (i.e., no incised sherds have been recovered from Agua Caliente or Tortolita phase contexts).

In addition to the incised sherds, Haury (1976: Figure 13.25g-j) illustrated a number of coiled vessels that were also recovered from Pioneer period contexts. These four sherds were also examined. They resemble the incipient plain wares in that they were usually produced from "untempered" clay. However, their vessel wall thickness and coil width are much greater than that observed in the coiled variety of incipient plain ware recovered from early Cienega phase sites in the middle Santa Cruz River Valley. The average vessel wall thickness of the four coiled pots from Snaketown is 8.6 mm and their average coil width is 14.5 mm, whereas the average vessel wall thickness of the coiled incipient plain ware is 3.7 mm and their average coil width is 5.5 mm. The vessel form (and size?) of the coiled vessels from Snaketown also differs from that documented in the middle Santa Cruz River sample. As noted by Haury (1976:269), these vessels were formed by attaching up to three superimposed coils onto a flat, circular bottom disc. Therefore, unlike the incised sherds, the coiled vessels from Snaketown do not provide any ceramic evidence to support arguments regarding an Early Agricultural period occupation of the site.

Discussion

Arnold (1985:19, 225) has suggested that, in every culture, pottery making almost certainly originated as a result of innovation within the culture or diffusion from another culture. Recently, Kelley (1992, in Clark and Gosser 1995:209) has suggested a third process: "dependent invention." Dependent invention refers to the acceptance of ideas and technical knowledge by a borrowing group, and the technology's rapid application and modification in ways foreign to its use by the donor group (Clark and Gosser 1995:209).

At least three pottery complexes are known to have been present in Mexico by 1600 B.C. (Clark and Gosser 1995). They are the Barra complex of coastal Chiapas, the Purron-Espiridión complex of the Tehuacán Valley and Oaxaca, and the Chajil complex of northern Veracruz. Other pottery-producing societies were present in West Mexico by 1200-400 B.C. (Pollard 1997). Thus, the Cienega phase pottery recovered from sites in the middle and lower Santa Cruz River Valley may be a result of the diffusion of ceramic manufacturing technologies from the south, or a dependent invention that is contingent upon those technologies. As Woodbury and Zubrow (1979:52) note, "The explanation for the initial appearance of pottery in the Southwest that requires fewest unproved assumptions is that it spread northward from Mesoamerica, where it has far greater antiquity."

Unfortunately, there is so little archaeological data available from Early Agricultural period sites in Sonora and Chihuahua, Mexico (B. Huckell 1996:345, 357) that we cannot evaluate those hypotheses properly. Accordingly, we cannot yet rule out the possibility that pottery making in the Sonoran Desert is an independent innovation that arose during the early Cienega phase, or an invention that is dependent upon previous knowledge gained from making anthropomorphic fired clay figurines, such as those recovered from the San Pedro phase Milagro site (AZ BB:10:46 [ASM]) (B. Huckell 1990:239-240; B. Huckell and L. Huckell 1984).

The possibility that pottery making is an innovation, or an invention dependent upon local knowledge, is strengthened when we consider that the coiled variety has only been recovered from early Cienega phase sites. The replacement of a perishable container technology (basketry) with a ceramic substitute is a particularly satisfying explanation for this early variety, which looks like nothing so much as a "clay basket." The antecedents of the other incipient plain ware varieties are more problematic, but the bumpy and incised varieties may have replaced another type of perishable container–those made of gourds–given their size and type of decoration. The bumpy variety of incipient plain ware has been recovered from early Cienega phase sites too. Therefore, the two varieties of incipient plain wares recovered from early Cienega phase sites may have replicated in clay, earlier basketry and gourd container forms. Ceramic production continued on into the late Cienega phase (circa 400 B.C. to A.D. 150), when incised and impressed varieties were introduced.

Most of the plain ware vessels produced throughout the Cienega phase were small bowls. They were made from a raw material, untempered alluvial clay, that potters were already familiar with. The lack of temper in these vessels is likely related to their small size.

Raw material selection, primary forming technique, vessel form, and function all show dramatic changes by the Agua Caliente phase (circa A.D. 150-550). Heidke and others (1998) estimate that the replacement rate for a household's ceramic assemblage at this time would have been quite low, probably no more than one vessel each year. Agua Caliente phase potters practiced an expedient manufacturing technology. The untempered alluvial clay body preferred by Cienega phase potters was replaced with self-tempered alluvial clay that, in turn, was replaced by sand and clay mixtures. Incised and impressed decorative techniques ceased to be utilized. In this phase, vessels were produced by coiling, pinching, hand smoothing, smearing, scraping, and polishing. Agua Caliente phase pottery vessel walls are thin, although variability related to production source has been noted: plain wares produced from self-tempered clay have thinner vessel walls than those produced from clay and sand mixtures (Heidke et al. 1998). Vessel forms focused on jars with simple contours, especially the neckless "seed jar" form, and multiple lines of evidence indicate that these vessels were used principally for storage (Heidke et al. 1998; Heidke and Stark 1996). Hayden (1995:262) notes that even where communities lack the kind of competitive feasting structure that would make the diffusion of a prestige technology adaptive, such as our Sonoran Desert example, the diffusion of a practical, cost-effective derivative can easily occur. The change in "seed jar" frequency, from 15 percent in the Cienega phase to 83 percent in the Agua Caliente phase, appears to reflect just such a transition.

Potters began to produce red wares as well as plain wares by the Tortolita phase (circa A.D. 550-650).

Adams (1996b) has suggested that the introduction of the floury Maiz de Ocho at about this time stimulated design changes that led to the development of the trough metate and longer manos, both of which were specialized for efficient flour production. The increased diversity of ceramic vessel forms that also occurs at this time, indicates that pottery containers finally began to fulfill the range of food preparation, cooking, serving, and storage functions usually associated with the prehistoric Southwest (Heidke 1990, 1991, 1993; Heidke et al. 1996). Therefore, the model of economic intensification, and its effect on women's labor, proposed by Crown and Wills (1995), fits the Tortolita phase data nicely, but it does not explain the *origins* of Southwestern ceramic technology as they propose. The evidence from southeastern Arizona suggests that the origins may lie in ritual, and shows that it took somewhere between 1,000-1,500 years of ceramic production before Southwestern peoples became dependent on pottery for a wide range of daily activities.

OTHER ARTIFACTS OF CLAY

Fourteen pieces of fired clay artifacts and two samples of raw clay were recovered from 14 proveniences at Los Pozos site. The artifacts include three beads, one probable human figurine fragment, four more probable figurine fragments, and six fired clay fragments (Table 8.9).

All but one of these artifacts are Early Agricultural period in age. Probably all 13 of these are Cienega phase in age, although only seven are associated with directly dated Cienega phase features. These features are all pit structures with radiocarbon dates between 2020 and 2090 b.p. The remaining specimen is probably Hohokam in age, coming from a pit which contains Hohokam sherds and is intrusive into an earlier pit structure.

All of the Los Pozos fired clay artifacts were made of fine-paste clays containing little or no non-plastic material. What little did occur appeared to be fine sand that was a natural component of the clay. The source(s) for clay for all of these artifacts is probably the alluvial deposits exposed along the banks of the Santa Cruz River in the vicinity of Los Pozos.

Beads

One complete and two partial, fired, modeled clay beads were recovered from three different pit structures (Table 8.10). All three were smoothed but not polished. Two of the pit structures were radiocarbon dated to the Cienega phase, and the third is considered to be Early Agricultural period in age.

Table 8.9. Modeled ceramic artifacts from Los Pozos. (Measurements are in cm. Numbers in parentheses following artifact type indicate multiple pieces which either fit together or are so similar in appearance that they are clearly part of the same artifact.)

Artifact	Feature Number	Provenience Bag	Provenience	Length	Width/ Diameter	Thickness	Age
Bead, plain	324.18	292.01	Pit structure, posthole fill	N/A	2.2[a]	1.0	Early Agricultural period
Bead, plain	417.00	503.01	Pit structure, fill	N/A	1.9	1.0	Cienega phase (2140 ± 50 b.p.)
Bead, plain	861.00	114.05	Pit structure, floor fill	N/A	1.5	.7	Cienega phase (2090 ± 80 b.p.)
Figurine, human	0.00	110.01	Stripping	2.5	2.6	1.1	Probably Cienega phase
Figurine fragment?	327.01	299.15	Pit structure, floor pit fill	1.5	1.4	1.1	Cienega phase (2020 ± 50 b.p.)
Figurine leg?	408.00	618.90	Large extramural pit, fill	2.1	1.2	N/A	Early Agricultural period
Figurine fragment?	422.00	398.90	Fill of pit intrusive into Feature 333 pit structure	2.2	1.2	.9	Hohokam
Figurine leg	819.00	377.06	Pit structure, fill	3.7	1.1	1.0	Cienega phase (2150 ± 80 b.p.)
Fired clay fragment	400.00	474.90	Extramural pit, fill	2.4	1.0	.8	Early Agricultural period
Fired clay fragment	425.01	510.91	Pit structure, floor pit fill	1.5	1.3	.6	Early Agricultural period
Fired clay fragment	861.00	114.90	Pit structure, fill	1.2	.8	.6	Cienega phase (2090 ± 80 b.p.)
Fired clay fragment	836.00	561.09	Pit structure, fill	1.7	.8	.7	Early Agricultural period
Fired clay fragment	836.00	561.90	Pit structure, fill	1.9	1.7	1.1	Early Agricultural period
Fired clay fragment	815.05	414.90	Pit structure, floor pit fill	1.3	1.2	.8	Early Agricultural period
Unfired clay (5)	352.01	366.90	Pit structure, floor pit fill	1.9[b]	1.1[b]	.9[b]	Cienega phase (2190 ± 80 b.p.)
Unfired clay	898.01	121.90	Pit structure, floor pit fill	1.1	.7	.4	Cienega phase (2140 ± 60 b.p.)

Note: N/A = Not applicable.

[a]Estimate.

[b]Dimension of largest fragment, if the pieces do not all fit together.

Table 8.10. Sizes and weights of clay beads from Los Pozos. (Measurements are in mm and gm.)

Artifact	Feature Number	Provenience Bag	Body Diameter	Body Thickness	Hole Diameter	Weight	Figure Number
Bead, plain	324.18	292.01	22.0[a]	10.0	2.7	–	8.15c
Bead, plain	417.00	503.01	18.5	9.5	2.7[a]	–	8.15b
Bead, plain	861.00	114.05	14.7	7.1	3.7	1.3	8.15a

[a]Estimate.

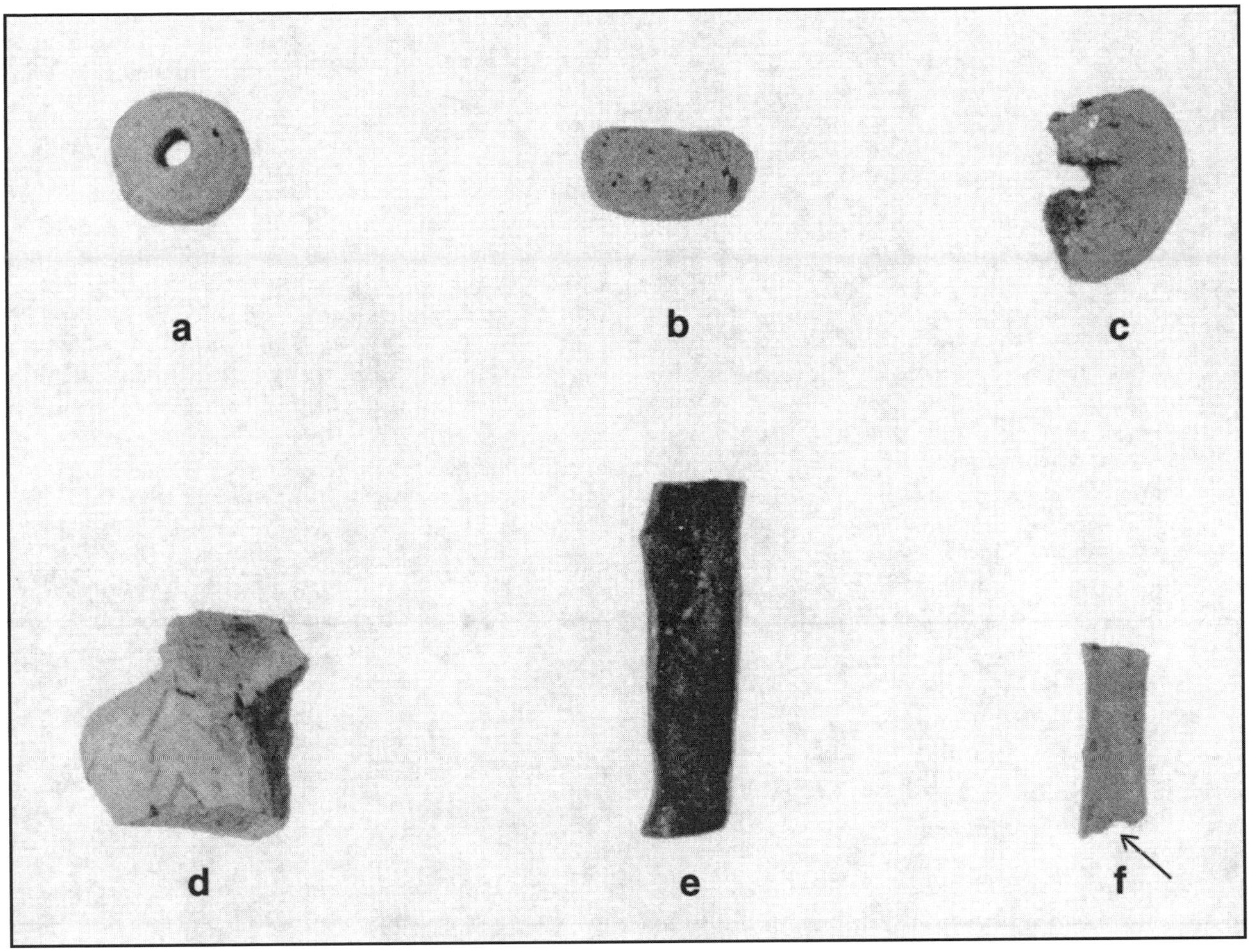

Figure 8.15. Other artifacts of clay. (Diameter of a) is 14.7 mm.)

The largest of the three beads (Figure 8.15c) is slightly convex on both faces with a rounded edge. The perforation is irregular in shape and is not at a right angle to the equator of the bead. The two definite Cienega phase beads (Figure 8.15a and b) are alike in having one distinctly flat face, as if each was formed by pressing a ball of clay against a flat surface. The other side of one bead is convex (visible to the viewer in Figure 8.15a). The other side of the second bead (Figure 8.15b) is concave. Both were then apparently perforated by pressing a stick through from the non-flat to the flat side. In both beads, the hole is slightly off-center, and not at a right angle to the equator of the bead. Those attributes, along with being small and lightweight, are the same traits which led to the conclusion at the Santa Cruz Bend site that these artifacts were in fact beads rather than early spindle whorls (Ferg 1998b). In fact, the whole bead from Los Pozos (Figure 8.15a) is the lightest in weight (1.3 gm) of the 23 clay beads recovered from the Cortaro Fan, Santa Cruz Bend, Los Pozos,

Wetlands, and Clearwater sites (Ferg 1998a, 1998b; Heidke and Ferg 1997). However, in body diameter, thickness, and hole diameter, the three beads from Los Pozos fit easily within the range of variation seen in the 23-bead sample (see Ferg 1998a:Table 14.3).

With only three specimens, there is little to be said about any pattern in the horizontal, intra-site distribution of clay beads, other than that they do not obviously cluster in any one area.

Human Figurine

What appears to be the right half of the torso of a human figurine (Figure 8.15d) was recovered during stripping, midway between Features 836 and 897, at the north end of the site, on the north side of Trench 70. Although this specimen does not come from a contained feature, it is presumed to be Early Agricultural period in age and, given the ages of surrounding features, it is quite probably Cienega phase in origin.

This specimen is currently unique among early figurines from southern Arizona in having a relatively elaborate incised design on its chest. Short, narrow, incised lines form a herringbone pattern, or four chevrons, nested, with their points up. Incised lines, possibly also chevrons, are on the edge of the right "shoulder stub" and at the base of the right side of the neck. Part of an incised line is also preserved on the small portion that remains of the left side of the neck. There appears to be a vertical line next to the broken midline of this fragment. The general arrangement of these various lines suggests that the incised decorations may have been arranged symmetrically on this figurine, with nested chevrons on the right and left breast, right and left "shoulders," and both sides of the neck. These incised designs may simply be decorative devices, as they appear to be on the small incised variety of incipient plain ware bowls from this site, or they could conceivably be depictions of body painting or tattooing. Unfortunately, this fragment is just that, and we can say nothing further about the treatment of the head, face, lower body, and legs, if it had any.

No other figurines from Early Agricultural or Early Ceramic period sites in the southern Southwest have this type of decoration (see Ferg 1998b:Figure 14.21). The only vaguely similar treatment that is at all close in time and space is the rounded bottom of a Pine Lawn phase figurine from the SU site (Martin 1943:Figure 87), which has both incised lines and punctate dot decorations. Both of the Los Pozos and SU site figurines are, in turn, reminiscent of Basketmaker III figurines from northeastern Arizona (see Morss 1954:Figure 19) and the potentially Early Archaic age "Horseshoe Shouldered" figurines from southeastern Utah (Coulam and Schroedl 1996). Although we do not know the shape of the bottom of the Los Pozos figurine, the SU site,

Basketmaker III, and Horseshoe Shouldered figurines all have rounded bottoms. The Basketmaker III and Horseshoe Shouldered figurines have rather amorphous heads, sometimes lacking features. And finally, the Los Pozos, Basketmaker III, and Horseshoe Shouldered figurines all have "shoulder stubs" with no depiction of arms per se.

The SU site and Horseshoe Shouldered figurines exhibit both incised and punctate decorations. However, the Los Pozos figurine, insofar as we can tell, differs from the Basketmaker III figurines in emphasizing incised over punctate designs. In that regard it is more similar to "Seri" figurines from coastal Sonora with their emphasis on paired incised line decorations which often include chevron-like motifs arranged symmetrically on the body (see Dockstader 1961: Figures 2, 4; Manson 1961:Figure 1; Moser and White 1968:Figure 4a, c, f; Owen 1956:Figure 2o, r, u). The bases of what are inferred to be the earliest of "Seri" figurines can have either a long pointed base, or a base split into two pointed legs (Dockstader 1961:Figures 2, 4; Moser and White 1968: Figure 2f, j). Unfortunately, the absolute ages and typological sequence of these figurines have yet to be determined because virtually all have been surface finds. Some are certainly of historic Seri origin, however many, including the earlier forms referenced above, are undoubtedly prehistoric in age. How truly old they may be will have to await excavations of stratified sites.

For the Early Agricultural period in southern Arizona, Gregory (personal communication, 1996) has suggested there may be at least two contemporaneous "traditions" of modeled, fired clay human figurines. The first is represented by figurines distinguished by usually having legs depicted, some indication on the head of eyes and mouth, and occasional decoration with fingernail indentations. Examples would include the two San Pedro phase figurines from Milagro, the Cienega phase seated figurine from Coffee Camp, and one or both of the Agua Caliente phase figurines from the Square Hearth site (see Ferg 1998b:Figure 14.21). It can be hypothesized that this "tradition" was indigenous to southern Arizona. The second "tradition" would include figurines with rounded bases, "shoulder stubs," and incised or punctate decoration; this "tradition" would be typified by the Basketmaker III figurines from northeastern Arizona. That this second "tradition" might have originated on the Colorado Plateau is suggested by the Horseshoe Shouldered figurines from southeastern Utah which may date as early as the Early Archaic. That such figurines are intrusive into areas south of the Plateau may be indicated by their scarcity (one base at SU site, one shoulder at Los Pozos), and by the discovery at Los Pozos of the unusual floor array in Feature 819 mentioned above, with its apparent northern symbolism/iconography (see Appendix B).

If, for the sake of argument and future testing, one accepts this hypothesis, one could argue that the northern "tradition" did not gain a foothold in southern Arizona, and predict that few such figurines will be found in southern Arizona and northern Sonora. This scenario would continue with the indigenous tradition of legged figurines with simple eyes and mouth ultimately being usurped by a more dominant figurine tradition seen in the rectangular- or trapezoidal-outline heads, flat faces, pinched noses, and occasionally appliquéd arms of Pioneer period Hohokam figurines. It is interesting to note that mixed in with these distinctively Hohokam figurines at Snaketown are a small number with much more amorphous heads and faces (Gladwin et al. 1937:Plates CCIIa-b, CCIIIb; Haury 1976:Figures 13.3a-b, 13.5a-b, g, o, 13.7b-c, 13.11a). While these may simply be less well executed figurines in the Hohokam tradition, it is possible that they are stylistic holdovers from the aforementioned earlier, indigenous, southern Arizona "tradition" of the Early Agricultural and Early Ceramic periods. The intra-site proveniences of these more amorphous figurines from Snaketown correspond with the distribution of the fine clay miniature vessels (Haury 1976: 268, Figure 13.24d-i) that are so similar in construction, size, and incised decorations to the incipient plain ware sherds from the Los Pozos, Coffee Camp, and Santa Cruz Bend sites (see above).

An unknown variable at this time is the place and time of origin of "coffee-bean" eyes on human figurines. A unique (for the time being) Cienega phase figurine was recovered from the Wetlands site (Ferg 1998a). Like the Los Pozos fragment, arms were not depicted except in the form of "shoulder stubs." A nearly spherical head was apparently pressed on to the top of the torso. It has a small point on top, and appliquéd straight strands of hair at the back. The nose was pinched up from the head, while the coffee-bean-shaped eyes were appliquéd. There is an appliquéd necklace around the neck, and a single appliquéd bump centered on the torso just above the break. Whether this bump was meant to represent a navel, or genitalia is unknown. This sophisticated figurine has no known close counterparts, and it appears to be the earliest figurine in the Southwest with coffee-bean eyes. The next appearance of this trait is a much more casual rendition on two Agua-Caliente-phase-equivalent figurines from the Bluff site (Haury and Sayles 1947:63, Figure 25) and a very similar-looking, slightly more recent figurine from a San Francisco or Three Circle phase pithouse at Turkey Foot Ridge site (Martin and Rinaldo 1950:Figure 134a; but see Morss 1954: Figure 13b for a much clearer photograph). After "skipping over" several cultural phases and hundreds of years, coffee-bean eyes serve as the hallmark of Santa Cruz phase Hohokam figurines (Gladwin et al. 1937:241). It should be recalled, however, that Haury

(1976:265) noted that dented appliqued pellets were present in the form of chin ornaments on figurines as early as the Vahki phase, and he felt that their use as eyes represented "only a minor shift." In Mexico, Huatabampo figurines exhibit coffee-bean eyes (Alvarez Palma 1982:Photos 12-15; Ekholm 1939:10), but in all likelihood they are contemporaneous with Santa Cruz figurines. Suffice it to say that this Cienega phase figurine now raises several questions regarding the age and origin of the use of appliquéd necklaces, hair, and coffee-bean eyes on Hohokam figurines. Although there are no incised designs on the body of the Wetlands figurine, its general similarity in shape to the Los Pozos shoulder fragment leaves us again wondering about what the head on the Los Pozos figurine may have looked like, and whether our discussion of figurine "traditions" during the Cienega phase in southern Arizona needs to address a possible third tradition.

Figurine Fragments

There are four more modeled fired clay fragments from Los Pozos which are apparently part of figurines of some kind. It is probable that they, like the specimen described above, are in fact parts of human or anthropomorphic figurines, since no figurines of animals or plants have been recognized from either Early Agricultural or Early Ceramic period sites in the southern Southwest.

Two are midsections of objects shaped like partially flattened cylinders, oval in transverse cross-section, with both ends of each broken away. They may be segments of human figurine torsos. One (Provenience Bag Number 299.15) has what appears to be a single fingernail indentation. Fingernail indentations used as (presumably) decorative elements have been observed on one figurine from the San Pedro phase Milagro site (B. Huckell 1990:Figure 5.11b), from the Cienega phase Wetlands site (Ferg 1998a:Figure 14.2d), and one from the Agua Caliente phase Square Hearth site (Ferg 1998b:Figure 14.20a).

The second probable torso segment (Provenience Bag Number 398.90) is the one specimen thought to be Hohokam in age. It does not, however, differ appreciably in color, or the appearance of its paste and temper, from the Early Agricultural period specimens. And it is too fragmentary to say anything further about its form. Had it not come from a Hohokam provenience, it would not have been segregated from the other fired clay artifacts being discussed here.

The other two figurine fragments are thought to be parts of legs. Legs rather than arms, in that some of the Early Agricultural and Early Ceramic period figurines from southern Arizona do have legs, but none recovered so far have separated arms. The first fragment is an essentially complete right leg; the inner aspect is shown in profile in Figure 8.15e. Visible at the top is a roughened area where this leg joined the left; if genitalia were modeled, they have been broken away. At the bottom is a petite foot with a flat sole and no depiction of toes. The outer sides of this leg were well smoothed, and may even have been lightly stone-polished, although this is not certain.

The second presumed leg fragment is a roughly cylindrical midsection, flared slightly at both top and bottom indicated by the arrow in Figure 8.15f. It is decorated with a 2-mm-deep dimple. Although we cannot be absolutely certain of the original orientation of this fragment (it could conceivably be upside down in Figure 8.15f), this dimple may well have been intended to indicate the knee. A tapering cylindrical figurine fragment from the Wetlands site (Ferg 1998a: Figure 14.2h) has a pair of similar dimples midway up it. It, too, is presumed to be a leg, and the location of its dimples supports their identification as depicting a knee.

Fired Clay Fragments

Six specimens from five proveniences across the site are similar only in that all are irregular in shape and cannot be positively identified as anything more specific than fired clay fragments (Table 8.9). Most or all appear to be the result of absent-minded manipulation of small pieces of clay which then got fired, perhaps intentionally, but it seems equally possible that it was by accident. Alternatively, they may be bits of excess clay pinched off some other object during the latter's manufacture, such as a figurine, a modeled clay bead, a small Cienega phase vessel or some other unknown object. One piece in particular (Provenience Bag Number 561.90) bears partial fingerprints from being handled while relatively moist.

Unfired Clay

Two samples of tan or light orange-colored, unfired clay were found, one each in the fill of the large central floor pits of the Feature 352 and 898 pit structures. They may be residues of unfired architectural daub. They are not classified here as raw clay in that both appear to have been handled and molded to a limited extent. The sample from Feature 352.01 preserves impressions of what look like bits of grass or rootlets and may have been formed into a vaguely cylindrical mass. The sample from Feature 898.01 preserves a smooth, curved impression of something cylindrical that it was pressed against, perhaps a twig or piece of cane (*Phragmites* sp.) about the diameter of a pencil (approximately 7-8 mm).

CHAPTER 9

MACROBOTANICAL REMAINS AND LAND USE: SUBSISTENCE AND STRATEGIES FOR FOOD ACQUISITION

Michael W. Diehl

In the fall of 1995, Desert Archaeology excavated the Los Pozos site (AZ AA:12:91 [ASM]), a spatially extensive cluster of shallow architectural features and extramural pits located west of the present-day channel of the Santa Cruz River. Prior research during exploratory testing indicated that the site was occupied during the Early Agricultural period (1500 B.C.-A.D. 150), during the San Pedro and Cienega phases. Since preservation was exceptionally good, an opportunity existed for a detailed investigation of Early Agricultural period resource use–a subject that has been of great interest among area archaeologists for the last decade. Accordingly, a program of extensive flotation and palynological sample collection was initiated, with the goal of obtaining a sample of features, contexts, and species that adequately represent the greater population of features at the site. In the interest of avoiding tedium and distracting digressions, the methods of handling, processing, and identification of macrobotanical specimens, as well as raw frequency counts of the taxa in each sample, are reported elsewhere (see Diehl 2001).

The paleobotanical research reported here was designed to address several questions of interest to area archaeologists. These questions included the following: 1) What plant resources were economically important to the occupants of the site? 2) What constraints did the use of these resources impose on the organization of subsistence? 3) Are there consistencies between Early Agricultural period sites that constitute a common pattern of resource use or the organization of subsistence? 4) What are the implications of regional macroplant assemblages for assessing extant models of Early Agricultural period land use?

This chapter is divided into five sections. The first section is a brief technical discussion of the definition of taxonomic "ubiquity" and limits on the use of ubiquity for comparing the distributions of different taxa. Based on attributes of seed size, growing locality, likely processing methods, and requisite technology, it is suggested that plants can be divided into five analytical groups. The ubiquities of seeds within each group are used to rank seeds in their general order of the inten-sity of their use and their importance to prehistoric people. In the second section, the potential yields and energetic costs of economically important plants are assessed. Resources are ranked in order of their net energetic returns. In the third section, limits on human mobility imposed by the energetic constraints associated with the use of different resources are discussed. In the fourth section, the ubiquities of plant remains from Los Pozos and other Tucson Basin sites are examined for common patterns of land use. It is shown that the suite of plants used by Early Agricultural period forager-horticulturists was similar at most sites that were occupied during this period. In the final section, the implications of Tucson Basin macrobotanical assemblages for extant models of Early Agricultural period land use and subsistence are discussed. It is suggested that the extant macroplant assemblages are consistent with most regional models of land use in the Tucson Basin. Implications for models that infer residential mobility beyond the Tucson Basin are discussed. Energetic constraints on the movement of maize indicate that, logistically organized long-distance hunting forays would have been energetically inefficient and an unlikely strategy for the procurement of large game by occupants of the Tucson Basin.

ESTABLISHING ANALYTICAL COMPARABILITY AMONG SEED TAXA

Analysts of macrobotanical remains encounter a problem that limits the analytical comparability of different species of seeds. Simply stated, it may be inappropriate to compare raw or transformed data about the distributions of *different* seed taxa in an effort to assess their relative importance to prehistoric people. This issue has been extensively discussed elsewhere (e.g., Miksicek 1987; Minnis 1981; Pearsall 1989; Popper 1988), and is briefly recapitulated here.

It is generally inappropriate to compare the seeds of different taxa since their histories of human use may have been quite different. Seeds and other macrobotanical remains arrive in archaeological sites through a wide range of cultural formation processes. For example, seeds may be deposited as an indirect consequence of the consumption of the fruits that contain them, or directly as a consequence of their consumption. Seeds may be handled in different ways; some may be boiled, others parched, or still others ground into flour. Differences in the ways that seeds (or the fruits that contain them) were harvested, processed, and prepared can lead to differences in the rates that they are deposited in archaeological sites. As a general rule, seeds survive centuries of exposure to the decay processes of archaeological soils only if they are carbonized as a result of their accidental exposure to fire. Obviously, seeds that are commonly exposed to heat (for example, as a result of parching) tend to be preserved more frequently than those that are boiled or consumed raw. Consequent differences in seed use and preservation promote differences in the frequencies of different seed taxa in archaeological deposits. Hence, differences in the observed frequencies of different seed taxa may not be strongly related to their relative importance.

Limitations on the Use of "Ubiquity" as a Measure of Taxonomic Importance

As a rule, archaeologists use an index called "ubiquity" to compare the importance of any given taxon at different archaeological sites (or at different components of a single site). The ubiquity of any taxon is the proportion of all analytical units containing at least one specimen of that taxon. In many instances, the analytical unit is the flotation sample. For example, if 10 flotation samples were analyzed and five of them contained *at least one* juniper seed, then it is said that the ubiquity of juniper is 50 percent. In this study, as in most recent studies of Early Agricultural period flotation samples (for example, Diehl 1998), the analytical unit is the feature.

One advantage of using ubiquity as a measure of seed importance is that it diminishes the effects of samples that contain exceptionally large quantities of seeds. Consider a particularly disastrous cooking accident, as might occur when a clumsy person drops a basket of parched seeds into a firepit full of hot coals; the result would be hundreds or even thousands of charred seeds that would likely be recovered (centuries later) in a single flotation sample by an archaeologist. The ubiquity index gives equal weight to samples that contain such cooking accidents, and other samples that contain only a few seeds that were deposited under circumstances that are more representative of their general use. In effect, the ubiquity index provides one

kind of analytical smoothing that reduces the importance of statistical outliers.

A major disadvantage of the use of the ubiquity index is the widely accepted caution against comparing seeds of different taxa. Different ubiquity scores of a single species such as amaranth might be used to compare the importance of plants from different sites; however, differences in the ubiquity of amaranth and maize may have no interpretive significance at all. All other things being equal, the ubiquities of different species are not usually compared, since archaeologists are generally unable to account for differences in the processing, use, and preservation characteristics of different kinds of seeds.

A Method for Making Ubiquity More Useful for Intertaxonomic Comparisons

It should be apparent from the preceding discussion that the chief concern among paleobotanists is that differential use and preservation may lead to disproportionate representation of different plants. It follows that seeds of different taxa are comparable to the extent that their methods of collection, processing, cooking, and consumption are similar, and to the extent that the seeds themselves are similar in size and density. It is suggested here that the ubiquities of seeds of different taxa may be directly compared when it can be established that the seeds are comparable in size and that they were probably handled in the same way.

The various taxonomic groups listed in Table 9.1 may be compared with respect to seed size, phenology, and likely processing techniques (see Diehl 2001). When these factors are taken into consideration, five categories of plants may be identified. The groups, and the bases for their creation and use in this report, are discussed below.

Internally Homogeneous (Analytically Comparable) Groups of Plants

Forty-eight taxa were identified in the west-side flotation samples. These may be inductively divided into groups on the basis of seed size, growth habits, and processing techniques. Differences exist in the plant phenology and processing methods associated with each group, such that one may assume that each group represents a different kind of resource with unique considerations for their use by prehistoric people. The identified groups include: Group 1–small starchy seeds (commonly less than 1 mm in diameter) that grow well in disturbed, floodplain soils; Group 2–mesquite pods; Group 3–analytically obscure plants

Table 9.1. Identified plant taxa and the attributes of their seeds and their use.

Scientific Name	Seed Size	Attributes	Associated Tools	Analytical Group
Agavaceae/*Yucca* sp.	Large	Soft	Baskets for fruit	3
Agrostis/*Muhlenbergia* sp.	Small	Hard/dense	Baskets, knives, mano, metate	1
Artemisia sp.	Small	Hard/dense	Baskets, knives, mano, metate	1
Astragalus sp.	Small	Hard/dense	Baskets, knives, mano, metate	1
Bouteloua sp.	Small	Hard/dense	Baskets, knives, mano, metate	1
Bromus sp.	Small	Hard/dense	Baskets, tongs, for fruit	4
Cactaceae	Small	Hard/dense	Baskets, knives, mano, metate	1
Carex sp.	Small	Hard/dense	Baskets, knives, mano, metate, poles, tongs	4
Carnegiea gigantea	Small	Hard/dense	Baskets, knives, mano, metate	1
Chenopodium/ *Amaranthus* sp.	Small	Hard/dense	Baskets, knives, mano, metate	1
Cleome sp.	Small	Hard/dense	Baskets, knives, mano, metate	1
Compositae	Small	Hard/dense	Baskets, knives, mano, metate	1
Cruciferae	Small	Hard/dense	Baskets, knives, mano, metate	1
Cucurbita sp.	Large	Soft	Baskets, knives	3
Descurainia sp.	Small	Hard/dense	Baskets, tongs, for fruit	4
Echinocereus sp.	Small	Hard/dense	Baskets, knives, mano, metate	1
Eleocharis sp.	Small	Hard/dense	Baskets, knives, mano, metate	1
Eragrostis sp.	Small	Hard/dense	Baskets, other unknown	3
Euphorbiaceae	Vary	Hard	Baskets, other unknown	3
Euphorbia sp.	Small	Hard	Baskets, knives, mano, metate	1
Eschscholtzia sp.	Small	Hard/dense	Baskets, knives, mano, metate	1
Gramineae	Small	Hard/dense	Baskets, knives, mano, metate	1
Helianthus sp.	Medium	Hard/dense	Baskets, for fruit, unknown others	3
Juniperus sp.	Large	Hard	Baskets, knives, mano, metate	1
Kallstroemia sp.	Small	Hard/dense	Baskets, other unknown	3
Labiatae	Vary	Hard	Baskets, other unknown	3
Leguminosae	Large	Dependent on use	Baskets, knives, mano, metate	1
Malvaceae	Small	Hard/dense	Baskets, knives, mano, metate	4
Mammilaria sp.	Small	Hard/dense	Baskets, tongs, for fruit	4
Opuntia sp. var. "platyopuntia"	Medium	Hard/dense	Baskets, knives, mano, metate	1
Panicum sp.	Small	Hard/dense	Baskets, knives, mano, metate	1
Polanisia sp.	Small	Hard/dense	Baskets, knives, mano, metate	1
Prosopis sp.	Large	Hard/dense	Baskets, mortars, pestles, manos, metates	2
Phragmites sp.	Small	Hard/dense	Baskets, knives, mano, metate	1
Portulaca sp.	Small	Hard/dense	Baskets, knives, mano, metate	1
Salvia sp.	Small	Hard/dense	Baskets, knives, mano, metate	1
Solanaceae	Medium	Porous/fragile	Baskets	3
Solanum/*Physalis* type	Medium	Porous/fragile	Baskets	3
Sporobolus sp.	Small	Hard/dense	Baskets, knives, mano, metate	1
Suaeda sp.	Small	Hard/dense	Baskets, knives, mano, metate	1
Trianthema sp.	Small	Hard/dense	Baskets, knives, mano, metate	1
Zea mays	Large	Hard/dense	Baskets, mano, metate; possibly also mortars, pestles	5

such as juniper, gourds, *Solanum/Physalis* types, and other plants with poor or unknown preservation characteristics; Group 4–cactus fruit and their seeds; and Group 5–maize.

Group 1 plants include those with relatively low yields, moderate to high harvesting costs, and moderate processing costs. In creating this analytical group, several observations were noted. First, the yields (kg/ha) of nondomesticated cheno-ams,

Descurainia, grasses, and other herbaceous, small-seeded plants, are low to moderate in floodplains and similar in most contexts (see Diehl 2001). Second, the seeds are small and generally similar in size and density. Third, none of these plants were domesticated, and it is reasonable to assume that all generated similar concerns about monitoring productive patches in order to minimize losses to interplant variation in ripening and dispersal habits, and to competition from birds and rodents. Finally, it is noted that these sites were probably harvested and processed using a single suite of tools and a common set of processing steps. Ethnographic descriptions of the use of these plants consistently note that their young shoots and leaves may have been consumed as potherbs, and that seeds were generally gathered into a container, parched, ground into a flour, and consumed (for example, see Adams 1988; Minnis 1991). Tools required would likely include baskets or sacks for collecting seed heads, knives (possibly) for cutting seed heads from stems, baskets for parching and winnowing remnant vegetative tissue from seeds, and basin metates and small manos for grinding the seeds.

It is suggested that commonality in seed size and in processing methods probably promoted similar overall preservation rates and postdepositional resistance to deterioration. Paleobotanists are on reasonably safe ground when comparing the ubiquities or overall frequencies of different taxa within this group. Seeds that have been assigned to analytical Group 1 include the taxa listed in Table 9.1.

Group 2 plants include mesquite (*Prosopis* cf. *velutina*). This plant can occur in very great densities in highly productive patches (see Diehl 2001) and requires extensive processing effort in order to render it edible for humans. Minimally, mesquite pods must be dried, extensively pounded (to crush the inedible exocarp and separate the seeds), winnowed (to remove pod chaff), sifted (to separate the starchy mesocarp flour from the remaining seeds), and possibly ground a second time (to reduce the mesocarp to a fine flour). Mesquite seeds could also be consumed, but required additional pounding, grinding, and light winnowing. Harvesting tools probably included baskets for collection; mortars and pestles for pounding the dried pods and for crushing the seeds; and shallow, dish-shaped baskets for winnowing the mixed mesocarp and seeds from the inedible pod tissue and for separating seeds from the starchy mesocarp flour. Since the processing pathway for this plant was probably unique, it is probably not safe to compare its ubiquity with that of other taxa.

Group 3 plants include other plants that cannot be easily compared with those of other groups or with each other since they are generally incomparable in size and density and since their associated processing requirements are not well known. Processing steps probably varied from plant to plant. One juniper seed was found, and its presence in the west-side samples may be indicative of long-distance forays into the surrounding montane uplands. However, it would be inappropriate to make any interpretive leaps of faith based on the observation of a single seed. Also included in this category are Agavaceae (agave/*Yucca* family), Euphorbiaceae (spurge–a plant that may have

been toxic and whose use as food is questionable), Labiatae (Mint family), unidentified Leguminosae (Legume family), *Solanum/Physalis* type (nightshade/chokecherry) seeds, whose fruits may have been consumed but whose seeds are exceptionally fragile and porous, and "Unknowns" (whose potential uses cannot be assessed).

Group 4 plants are cacti. The seeds may have been consumed after the fashion of other small, starchy seeds, and similar tools would have been required to parch, winnow, and grind them. However, the large fruits were undoubtedly consumed, and these may have been the principal focus of the harvesting strategy that resulted in the preservation of their seeds. Harvesting costs would have been moderately high, owing principally to transportation costs incurred in gathering these plants where they grow–in the bajadas. Tools would have included long poles for knocking down saguaro fruit, tongs for harvesting the fruit of shorter cacti, and baskets for carrying the fruit. In the absence of ceramic vessels, it seems unlikely that the fruits would have been reduced to a syrup after the fashion of ethnographically documented Papago use (Castetter and Bell 1937). It is possible they were de-spined (singed, perhaps) and dried before transportation. Drying would have been a low-cost processing strategy and would have permitted the transportation of large quantities of fruit.

Group 5 plants include only maize (*Zea mays*). The most common maize remnants in archaeological sites are cupules–rachis segments that are the locus of attachment of pairs of kernels to a maize cob. The preservation of maize cupules is generally attributed to their use as fuel, or to burning as a means of trash reduction. In this study, cupules and kernels are treated as analytical equivalents, and their occurrences are combined for the purpose of calculating maize ubiquity in this study. Maize is processed with manos and metates; however, mortars and pestles may also have been used. Maize is cultivated, which involves planting and monitoring, and the attributes of maize growth are so unique that the harvesting tactics associated with its use are unique. Hence, the ubiquity of maize is not deemed directly comparable to the ubiquity of any other plant.

The Importance of Different Species of Plants

Assuming that the derived groups of plants described in Table 9.1 and the preceding paragraphs are internally comparable, the ubiquities of different plants within each group may be compared in order to rank them in their order of economic importance. Table 9.2 ranks the identified taxa relative to other members of

Table 9.2. The occurrence of seeds from flotation samples ranked within their analytical groups in order of ubiquity.

Analytical Group	Scientific Name	Rank	Ubiquity (%)
Group 1: Plants with small starchy seeds	*Chenopodium/Amaranthus* sp.	1	81
	Descurainia sp.	2	63
	Gramineae	3	46
	Sporobolus sp.	3	43
	Agrostis/Muhlenbergia sp.	4	22
	Trianthema sp.	5	14
	Compositae	5 or 6	13
	Panicum sp.	5 or 6	11
	Astragalus sp.	5 or 6	11
	Cruciferae	5 or 6	11
	Portulaca sp.	5 or 6	8
	Eragrostis sp.	6 or 7	7
	Artemisia sp.	6 or 7	6
	Bouteloua sp.	7	4
	Helianthus sp.	7	3
	Suaeda sp.	7	3
	Cleome sp	7	1
	Kallstroemia sp.	7	1
	Phragmites sp.	7	1
	Bromus sp.	7	1
	Eschscholtzia sp.	7	1
	Malvaceae	7	1
	Eleocharis sp.	7	1
	Polanisia sp.	7	1
	Carex sp.	7	1
	Salvia sp.	7	1
Group 2: Mesquite	*Prosopis* cf. *velutina*	1	40
Group 3: Analytically obscure plants	cf. Labiatae	1	15
	Unidentified	1	14
	Euphorbiaceae	2	6
	Leguminosae	2	4
	Solanaceae	2	3
	Chenopodiaceae	2	3
	Agavaceae	2	1
	Juniperus sp.	2	1
	Solanum/Physalis type	2	1
Group 4: Cacti	*Carnegiea gigantea*	1	58
	Echinocereus sp.	2	29
	Opuntia sp. "platyopuntia"	3	10
	Mammillaria sp.	3	7
	Cactaceae	3	6
Group 5: Maize	*Zea mays*	1	88

their analytical group, in order of highest to lowest ubiquity. In these samples, the unit of analysis for the ubiquity score is the depositional context defined as follows: all samples from a single house and all of its subfeatures (intramural pits) are combined into a single observation, and all samples from a single extramural pit are combined into a single observation. Samples that were obtained from trench profiles are omitted since their depositional contexts are not certain. Samples from burials are omitted entirely since they are manifestly different depositional contexts from intramural and extramural pit fill. Features that did not contain charred seeds were omitted entirely.

Discussion

Group 1 plants are interesting because several plants have outstandingly high ubiquity scores. Cheno-ams, *Descurainia*, *Sporobolus*, and Gramineae have scores exceeding 40 percent. It is noted that of the top three ranks, cheno-ams and *Sporobolus*, are taxa that may occasionally grow in very dense stands in floodplain contexts in the Sonoran Desert (see Diehl 2001). Moreover, although information on the wild densities of *Descurainia* were not available for the Tucson Basin, Jones and Madsen (1989) noted that *Descurainia* grows in dense stands in the central Great Basin, and they have identified it as a high-return resource.

The Gramineae are a family whose high ubiquity score indicates that grass seeds, generally, were important components of the diet. It should be noted that of the low-ubiquity plants, grass seeds are the predominant type. Were these other grass seeds combined with the Gramineae, the ubiquity of grass seeds at the Los Pozos site would exceed 50 percent, making it comparable to other sites in the Tucson Basin.

Groups 2 and 5 were also dietarily important plants. As discussed later in this chapter (see also Diehl 2001), mesquite is a plant that offers potentially very high yields, and that is known to have been used by Native American groups throughout the southwestern United States during Protohistoric and Historic times. The timing and location of the availability of ripening plants would have been well known. Maize yields and locations would have been controlled by those who planted it. Mesquite is a phreatophytic plant that provides good harvests, even in relatively dry years. It is noteworthy that both plants would have been located in or near the Santa Cruz River floodplain, and it may be presumed that these would have been obtained at short distances (within a few kilometers) of floodplain villages. It is assumed that both maize and mesquite made very important contributions to the diets of the occupants of the Los Pozos site.

Group 4 includes cacti, and it is observed that saguaro had the greatest ubiquity. It is suggested that saguaro was an important resource. Saguaro and prickly pear fruits have high sugar contents and correspondingly high energetic yields (see Diehl 2001). These attributes are probably characteristic of cactus fruits in general. As discussed in Diehl (2001), saguaro grow densest and most reliably on south-facing bajada slopes. The timing and locations of the availability of saguaro fruit were therefore quite predictable, except after very cold winters. The other cacti in the samples have wider ranges of distribution than saguaro, and they are more homogeneously distributed throughout the basin. It is suggested that prickly pear, pincushion, hedgehog, and other cacti were potentially important resources that were opportunistically used when encountered.

RESOURCE-SPECIFIC LIMITS ON MOBILITY

So far, the analysis presented here has considered only the kinds of plants that were used, and their relative importance. It has been shown that although a wide range of plants were used, the most frequently recovered specimens appear to be those that grew in dense stands, or whose spatial and temporal availability was predictable. Based on these observations, it has been suggested that the most important plants were probably monitored and intensively harvested as they became available, and that the less frequently observed plants may have been exploited opportunistically.

By examining the potential yields and the energetic costs associated with the use of different plants, it is also possible to determine the practical limits on mobility associated with the use of different plants. One can consider the question, "For any given resource, what is the maximum distance that one may have traveled to obtain the resource?"

Comparability between estimates is difficult to evaluate, because some researchers report only the "net" energetic returns provided by different resources, and it is not clear which of the associated energetic costs (searching, harvesting, transporting, or processing) were taken into consideration. Moreover, as is noted by Jones and Madsen (1989), the energetic costs associated with different activities or the use of different plants is, under the best circumstances, usually based on a single experimental observation. In the discussion that follows, the costs and returns associated with different taxa are based on a combination of judgmentive estimates and reported actualistic research. They are admittedly crude estimates of energetic returns provided by different taxa, and it is hoped that future researchers will obtain better information in an effort to validate or revise the figures that are presented here.

Information from four arenas of interest are compiled in the tables that follow. These arenas include: 1) limited archaeological studies of the use of resources located in the Tucson Basin (Doelle 1976, 1978); 2) limited archaeological studies on the energetic costs and returns of small starchy seeds (Jones and Madsen 1989; Wright 1994); 3) general considerations of resource use by foragers (e.g., Kelly 1995); and 4) botanical (and related) scientific studies of plant densities and phenology of wild and domesticated plants (see Diehl 2001).

Table 9.3. Energetic returns from three Sonoran Desert resources.

Resource	Harvest Rate (kg/hr)	Gross Energy Returns	
		Yield (kcal/kg)	Rate (kcal/hr)
Mesquite	.9	3,400	3,060
Saguaro fruit	2.2 (fresh)	1,100	2,200
Cholla buds	.5	3,500	1,750

Table 9.4. Energetic return rates for selected Great Basin resources observed in the flotation samples.

Resource	Harvest Rate (kg/hr)	Energy Returns	
		Yield (kcal/kg)	Rate (kcal/hr)
Bouteloua	.14	3,340	455
Carex	.08	2,590	202
Descurainia	.36	3,600	1,307
Grasses	.13	2,942	383
Helianthus	.13	3,650	486

Note: Energy return rates are from Jones and Madsen (1989), averaging their estimates for foxtail barley, Great Basin wild rye, Indian ricegrass, and peppergrass.

Studies of Sonoran Desert Resource Use

As part of the Conoco-Florence archaeological study, Doelle (1976:65-67) engaged in the collection and processing of mesquite pods, cholla buds, and saguaro, and observed the same activities conducted by Native American Papago. Table 9.3 combines the results of three episodes of research conducted by Doelle (1976, 1978, 1980) and the raw energetic yields of resources as documented in Diehl 2001. Based on information of energy costs of light duty activities among African agriculturists, Doelle (1976:67) estimated that walking costs 3.1 kcal/min (3.4 kcal/min when carrying a load), picking costs 2.5 kcal/min, and processing (mesquite) costs 5.8 kcal/min.

Although Doelle's estimates account for the harvesting rate, no experimental information on the processing cost is provided. As discussed below, the amount of energy required to grind seeds into flour was probably an important limiting factor on energetic rates of return. Hence, the energetic return rates are expected to have been substantially lower than those estimated by Doelle.

Studies of the Use of Small, Starchy Seeds in Arid Environments

Jones and Madsen (1989) determined the energetic return rates from selected resources that were available to occupants of the central Great Basin (Nevada and Utah), based on original estimates in Simms (1987) (the latter was not available for this study). Their research may be combined with estimates of processing costs, and the results are summarized in Table 9.4.

As is noted by Wright (1994), the net rates of energetic returns from seed harvesting may be quite high, but when the entire food acquisition and processing system is examined, grinding seeds into flour is calorically and temporally expensive. Wright (1994: 245) reported net energetic returns from small-seed harvesting among ethnographically studied foragers. Using African grinding tools, grass seeds and "chenopods" required 5-6 hrs of grinding per kg of seed, and

netted 200-500 kcal/hr. It is noted that these numbers accord well with those observed by Jones and Madsen (1989).

Energetic Returns from Early Agricultural Period Maize

The estimation of the energetic returns from Early Agricultural maize requires a structure of informed guesswork and assumptions, with which all may not agree. In Appendix D it was argued that the maize grown by the occupants of the Los Pozos site yielded 25-36 percent per hectare of the amounts provided by modern Native American varieties, and that actual yields of Early Agricultural period maize were probably 100-300 kg/ha. For this study, I will assume seed yields of 200 kg/ha, and that ripe maize could be harvested at a rate of 5 kg/hr. It is assumed that harvesting required 100 kcal/hour. Accordingly, the initial yield of maize would have been reduced from 3,600 to 3,580 kcal/kg, after harvesting costs are included.

The energetic return rates from maize are affected by other processing costs as well. In an experimental study of archaeological manos and metates from northern Arizona pueblos, Wright (1993:350-351) was able to process roughly .6-.8 kg/hr of modern maize, using trough metates with large manos, and roughly 3 percent of the meal was lost to spillage and other causes. It is a well-known fact that the grinding technology available to Early Agricultural period farmers included basin metates with smaller manos that may have been less efficient for grinding maize than trough metates (see Diehl 1996b; Mauldin 1993). Moreover, the onset of fatigue experienced by grinders, and the amount of pressure that may be brought to bear on grinding surfaces varies with metate form (Adams

Table 9.5. Travel distances limited by net yield per unit of weight and by rate of energetic return.

Resources	Distance Limited by Net Yield			Distance Limited by Rate of Return		
	Net Yield (kcal/kg)	Capacity (kcal/Load)	Distance per Load (km)	Energy Return (kcal/hr)	Movement Supported by 1 hr Work	Travel Distance (km) Supported by 1 hr Work
Descurainia, cheno-ams[a]	2,700	54,000	432	11,501	3.0	9.0
Other Group 1 seeds[b]	2,700	54,000	432	575	1.8	5.4
Group 2: Mesquite[c]	1,960	39,200	314	544	1.5	4.5
Group 4: Cactus fruit[d]	1,100	22,000	176	2,530	6.7	20.1
Cactus Fruit seeds[e]	4,380	87,600	700	3,265	8.7	26.1
Group 5: Maize	3,000	60,000	480	1,200	3.2	9.6

[a]Maximum returns for *Descurainia* obtained by Jones and Madsen (1989) and assigned a processing tax of 150 kcal/hr, 900 kcal/kg.
[b]Maximum rate of return from grasses including processing costs is 575 kcal/hr (Wright 1994:245) and are assigned a processing tax of 900 kcal/kg.
[c]Maximum returns for mesquite obtained from Doelle (1978:253) and assigned a processing tax of 240 kcal/hr, 1,440 kcal/kg.
[d]Cactus fruit collection rates from Doelle (1980:65), with energetic yields of 1,100 kcal/kg as discussed in Diehl 1999.
[e]Collection rates for seeds from Doelle (1980:65) are assigned a processing tax of 150 kcal/hr and 900 kcal/kg.

1993a). For this study, it is assumed that maize could be ground at a rate of .4 kg/hr. Wright (1994:245) apparently estimated that small-seed grinding required 165 kcal/hr using similar ground stone tools from the Middle East. Since maize kernels are large, I will assume that their grinding cost exceeded that of small seeds. However, maize probably required less energy than the 240 kcal/hr required to process mesquite. Hence, it is assumed that maize grinding required 200 kcal/hr, or 500 kcal/kg. Net return rates from maize would have been 3,080 kcal/kg and 1,232 kcal/hr (assuming that the real limit on maize return rates was the time required to grind it).

Practical Limits on Mobility

Given the systemic costs for processing different plant foods, what were the practical limits on the distances that different resources could be transported, while still providing an energy surplus? The question is an important one, because these distances are the *absolute* limits on the distances that might have been traveled to obtain food, or the distances that food might have been moved to promote the use of other resources.

There are many ways that the maximum transport distances of different resources can be calculated. Jones and Madsen (1989:529-531) suggested that the limitations on transport distance may be affected by the amount of food that can be stowed in a basket. Where variation in food density is great, variation in transport distances is correspondingly large. Others may prefer to determine the maximum transport distance based on

the net energetic yields per kilogram of food. This study calculates the maximum transport distance using two methods. The first method assumes that the rate of energy return is the limiting factor on transport distance. The second method assumes that the net yield per kilogram of food is the limiting factor on transport distance. Since most foods that are compared must be processed into flour before consumption, it is assumed that the densities of foods are roughly equivalent. It is also assumed that a 20-kg load is a reasonable cargo for a single human. Following Jones and Madsen (1989:531) and Kelly (1995:133), it is assumed that the cost of transporting 20 kg for a distance of 1 km is 125 kcal. It is also assumed that a reasonable overland travel speed with a load was 3 km/hr.

Discussion

The travel distances and energetic returns of different plant groups discussed in Table 9.5 are interesting in light of the ubiquity scores of these different resources described in Table 9.2. The resources with the highest ubiquities within their plant groups are the resources that provide the highest energetic yields. Moreover, although it may be inappropriate to compare the ubiquity values of plants in different groups, it is nevertheless quite interesting that the plants with highest return rates and yields per unit of weight all have ubiquities greater than 40 percent. Accordingly, it is suggested that Early Agricultural period forager-horticulturists selected plant resources that provided the highest energetic returns per unit of weight, or the highest energetic returns per unit of time.

What are the implications of the observation that energetic returns were probably maximized? Kelly (1995:53-54) reviewed some of the conditions under which humans may be expected to "forage optimally;" that is, to maximize energetic rates of return. When behavioral ecologists assume that natural selection favors (in reproductive or cultural success) individuals who maximize energetic returns, then it follows that such maximization improves their selective fitness in terms of reproductive or cultural success when time constraints are of concern, when certain key nutrients are in short supply, or when food-gathering exposes individuals to risk (Kelly 1995:54). It is suggested that one or more of these conditions affected resource selection among Early Agricultural period forager-horticulturists of the Tucson Basin.

In this study, I have only considered energetic returns, and have not discussed the other nutritional characteristics of various plants. Although it may be said that Early Agricultural period forager-horticulturists were clearly concerned with obtaining energy, one cannot stipulate that other nutrients were not a matter of prehistoric concern. If energetic returns were the only consideration, the low-ubiquity plants should have been completely ignored, and they should not have occurred in the flotation samples. Instead, it is suggested that the mere presence of low-energy plants such as Solanaceae, *Solanum/Physalis* types, low-ubiquity cacti, and *Cucurbita* was a consequence of the consumption of herbs, flowers, or fruit. As is noted in Diehl (2001), each of these plants offers high quantities of vitamins A, B-series, or C, or calcium, and *Trianthema* is a plant with unusually high quantities of protein.

EARLY AGRICULTURAL PERIOD RESOURCE USE IN THE GREATER TUCSON BASIN

It has been suggested that the occupants of the Los Pozos site maximized energy returns from plants by relying heavily on several key resources, including cheno-ams, tansy mustard, Gramineae (generally), mesquite, maize, and saguaro fruit. To what extent were the resources represented in the flotation samples consistent with the resources consumed by the occupants of other Early Agricultural period sites? The excavation of numerous sites of similar age provides an abundance of comparative data.

In the following discussion, the ubiquity scores have been calculated using data obtained from other Early Agricultural period sites. These include: the Clearwater site (AZ BB:13:6 [ASM]; Diehl 1996a), the Coffee Camp site (AZ AA:6:19 [ASM]; Hutira 1993), the Donaldson site (AZ EE:2:30 [ASM]; B. Huckell 1995), the Milagro site (AZ BB:10:46 [ASM]; Huckell et al. 1995; L. Huckell 1995b), AZ AA:12:105 [ASM] (Mabry 1990), the Santa Cruz Bend site (AZ BB:12:746 [ASM];

L. Huckell 1998), and the Stone Pipe site (AZ BB:13:425 [ASM]; L. Huckell 1998). Ubiquity scores were calculated using the published raw data and following these rules: 1) only seeds and *Zea mays* cupules were counted, 2) all samples from the same feature were combined into a single observation, 3) features that did not contain charred seeds were not included in the total number of analytical observations. The ubiquities of plants from Early Agricultural period sites are listed in Table 9.6.

Discussion

It is noteworthy that most sites have consistent maize ubiquities. With the exception of Coffee Camp (at which no maize was recovered), maize ubiquities exceed 80 percent. As is noted by B. Huckell (1995:120), ubiquities of 80 percent are considered high in comparison with maize ubiquities in Hohokam assemblages that were excavated during the early 1980s. It is apparent that maize was an important component in the diet of Early Agricultural forager-horticulturists. It is assumed that the plant was grown locally, within a few kilometers of floodplain villages.

Cactus fruit consumption was important at all sites. Saguaro was apparently the most important resource. Saguaro ubiquities are higher at Los Pozos and the Brickyard site than at other sites, and only Coffee Camp and Donaldson had low saguaro ubiquity scores. Coffee Camp's low ubiquity score for saguaro is complemented by an unusually high ubiquity for hedgehog (*Echinocereus*). In general, high proportions of saguaro indicate that the occupants of the floodplain villages made extensive use of resources located in the surrounding bajadas.

Mesquite beans were strongly represented at most sites, albeit somewhat weakly at the Brickyard and Milagro sites. Since mesquite is a phreatophytic plant, the consumption of mesquite at most sites is consistent with B. Huckell's (1995) characterization of Early Agricultural period occupants of the Tucson Basin as people who made intensive use of floodplain and cienega resources. Mesquite also occurs in the floodplains, and its use would have (minimally) entailed local harvesting forays.

Every site had a high ubiquity score for at least one taxonomic group of plants that bear small, starchy seeds. Among the Group 1 plants, cheno-ams were strongly represented at all sites, and tansy mustard (*Descurainia*) was strongly represented at all but the Donaldson site. The grasses (Gramineae) had high ubiquity scores at most sites and were absent only from Coffee Camp. These plants grow best in floodplain areas where competition for light by mesquite and other shrubs is not great. In contrast, most of the low-energy return, small-seeded plants had low

Table 9.6. Ubiquities (by feature) of plant taxa from Early Agricultural period sites in the greater Tucson Basin.

Taxon	Plant Group	Brickyard (BB:13:6 [ASM]) n = 15	Coffee Camp n = 27	Donaldson n = 9	Los Pozos n = 72	Milagro n = 15	Santa Cruz Bend n = 41	Stone Pipe n = 45	AA:12:105 n = 1
Agrostis / Muhlenbergia	1	0	0	0	22	0	0	0	0
Artemisia	1	0	0	0	6	0	0	0	0
Astragalus	1	7	0	0	11	0	0	0	0
Bouteloua	1	0	0	0	4	0	0	0	0
Bromus	1	0	0	0	1	0	0	0	0
Carex	1	0	0	0	1	0	0	0	0
Chenopodiaceae	1	0	0	0	3	0	0	2	0
Chenopodium / Amaranthus	1	73	59	100	81	80	49	49	0
Cleome	1	0	0	0	1	0	0	0	0
Compositae	1	20	0	0	13	0	0	2	0
Cruciferae	1	7	0	0	11	0	0	0	0
Cyperaceae	1	0	0	89	0	0	0	0	0
Descurainia	1	60	19	0	63	53	56	38	0
Eleocharis	1	0	0	0	1	0	0	0	0
Eragrostis	1	0	0	0	7	0	0	0	0
Eschscholtzia	1	0	0	0	1	0	0	0	0
Gramineae	1	27	0	50	46	13	44	62	0
Helianthus	1	0	0	0	3	0	0	0	0
Juncus	1	0	0	27	0	0	0	4	0
Kallstroemia	1	0	4	0	1	0	0	0	0
Malvaceae	1	0	0	27	1	0	0	0	0
Mentzelia	1	0	0	0	0	20	2	0	0
Panicum	1	0	0	0	11	0	0	0	0
Phragmites	1	0	0	0	1	0	0	0	0
Polanisia	1	0	0	0	1	0	0	0	0
Portulaca	1	7	0	50	8	0	10	0	0
Rumex	1	20	0	22	0	0	0	0	0
Salvia	1	0	4	0	1	20	5	2	0
Scirpus	1	13	0	0	0	0	0	0	0
Sporobolus	1	7	7	0	43	0	0	13	0
Suaeda	1	0	0	0	3	0	5	2	0
Trianthema	1	7	56	56	14	87	29	22	0
Prosopis	2	13	22	33	40	13	29	36	0
Agavaceae	3	0	0	0	1	7	0	0	0
Atriplex	3	27	4	0	0	13	10	2	0
Celtis	3	0	0	0	0	0	0	2	0
cf. Labiatae	3	0	0	0	15	0	0	0	0
Euphorbiaceae	3	0	0	11	6	0	0	13	0
Juniperus	3	0	0	0	1	7	0	0	0
Leguminosae	3	0	27	33	4	0	2	25	0
Nicotiana	3	0	0	0	0	0	0	7	0
Quercus	3	0	0	0	0	7	0	0	0
Solanaceae	3	0	0	0	3	7	0	2	0
Solanum/Physalis type	3	7	0	0	1	0	2	0	0
Yucca	3	0	0	11	0	0	0	0	0
Cactaceae	4	0	0	0	6	0	2	0	0
Carnegiea	4	53	7	11	58	27	34	42	0
Echinocereus	4	40	7	0	29	7	34	2	0
Mammillaria	4	0	7	0	7	7	0	0	0
Opuntia sp. "platyopuntia"	4	7	0	11	10	7	5	0	0
Zea mays	5	87	0	100	88	0	83	84	100

ubiquity values. Only *Trianthema* was strongly represented at most sites. The high representation of this plant is possibly attributable to its unusually high protein content (32.9 percent; see Carr et al. 1985:510).

The use of plants by Early Agricultural period foragers was generally consistent between sites. It is suggested that resource acquisition combined strategies of targeting specific, high-yield resources with a more generalized (and less intensive) secondary strategy of harvesting the small seeds of less productive plants. High yield resources were the focus of intensive acquisition strategies. Their occurrence and growth were probably carefully monitored. As a domesticated plant, maize was planted close to settlements and protected from predation and competition from weeds. The locations of dense stands of cheno-ams, unusually dense stands of grasses, *Descurainia,* and saguaro fruits were noted, and their progress toward ripening was monitored. On ripening, these plants were probably the target of intensive harvesting efforts. Given the potentially high energy returns from these plants, it is likely that upon ripening, proportionally large numbers of villagers engaged in their acquisition. The use of more distant resources, particularly saguaro, probably entailed the wholesale abandonment of floodplain villages for an interval of days to weeks.

The remaining small starchy seeds, and the analytically problematic Group 3 plants, occurred in low frequencies. Generally, these are plants that provide low energy returns, and it is suggested these were harvested as part of a generalized foraging strategy that made use of locally available plants within a limited radius around sites. The use of low-density grasses and other floodplain weeds was made possible by their proximity to floodplain villages. Their use may have been limited to individuals whose mobility was restricted. Alternatively, their use may have been "embedded" in other activities such as the acquisition of flaked stone raw material. In such instances, they were probably opportunistically acquired only when they were encountered in exceptionally dense stands.

IMPLICATIONS FOR EXTANT MODELS OF EARLY AGRICULTURAL PERIOD RESOURCE USE

Recent research at Early Agricultural period sites has generated a number of models of subsistence. Being new, these models have not been critically evaluated or adequately tested. They are easily summarized in a few short paragraphs.

Early Agricultural Villagers as Classically Sedentary Farmers

Some suggest that the Early Agricultural period occupants of the Tucson Basin were sedentary farmers in the most familiar and common sense. Farmers were highly entrenched people predominantly dependent on crops and possibly a few species of important seed plants such as amaranth. This basic set of staples was supplemented by the addition of a few intensively harvested foods such as cactus fruit and animals. The floodplain villages in which these sedentary farmers lived were occupied year-round for numerous years. This is essentially the pattern of crop-dependent subsistence observed in subsequent Hohokam and historic-period occupations in southeast Arizona. In other contexts (Diehl 1996b), I have referred to this model as the "classically sedentary" model, and I will continue to use that shorthand description here.

B. Huckell (1995; Huckell et al. 1995) is an advocate of this model, and it is best conveyed using his own words: "Domestic structures, agricultural products, storage pits, a thick and culturally rich midden deposit, and plants representing multiple seasons all suggest that late preceramic people were in residence at the Donaldson site and probably Los Ojitos for a major portion of the year, if not the entire year . . . . In my opinion, *they may be considered villages inhabited both intensively during the course of a year and for periods of time best measured in decades, if not centuries*" (B. Huckell 1995:131). Also, "In fact, the pattern of mixed farming and foraging established during the Late Archaic persisted *with few changes* until the arrival of the Spanish" (Huckell et al. 1995:3; emphasis added).

It should be noted that preliminary interpretations of the use of the Santa Cruz Bend site (Mabry and Archer 1997:2-132) and the Stone Pipe site (Swartz and Lindeman 1997:4-96) concur. Moreover, Huckell's (1995) characterization is generally consistent with the results of some area surveys. Downum and others (1986) surveyed and conducted limited test excavations in the Avra Valley, about 12 km west of Tucson. They identified sites that included dense surface scatters and possible pithouses. These sites are said to be linked to the floodplain settlements as a component of a land use strategy that includes "permanent" floodplain settlements, and dune sites that are either "permanent base camps" or temporary "camps" (Downum et al. 1986: 196). In other words, large floodplain sites such as Santa Cruz Bend are, from their point of view, unquestionably villages occupied year-round. The nature of the use of secondary camps in dune fields remains to be assessed.

Alternatives to Classically Sedentary Models

Other scholars have suggested that the degree of residential and logistical mobility remains to be assessed, and that observed differences between artifacts found at different sites allow for the possibility of greater variation. Based on intensive survey data and some limited site excavations, Roth (1988:212, 1992:311-312) recognized two alternative models of Early Agricultural period land use and subsistence.

One model holds that the floodplain and bajada sites may be the material consequences of the existence of two groups of people engaged in fundamentally different settlement-subsistence strategies (Roth 1992 cites Fish et al. 1990). In this model, floodplain groups were wholly entrenched farmers who were relatively immobile in every sense of the word, and bajada groups were more transitory, engaging in a thoroughly mixed hunting-gathering with possibly a supplemental farming strategy.

Roth's preferred second model holds that the most intensively occupied sites were located on the floodplains due to the constraints and demands required to bring crops to fruition. Despite the mandates imposed by maize cultivation, these farmers are said to have made intensive use of some bajada sites by means of short-duration logistical forays to harvest cactus fruit and game (Roth 1995a). This model is consistent with Huckell's, but differs to the extent that it does not require year-round occupation of floodplain sites.

Early Agricultural Villagers as Long-distance Hunters

A fourth model compares the land use strategies of the occupants of the Southern Basin and Range (in effect, Sonoran Desertscrub) biotic province with those of "cool temperate climates" (in effect, the Mogollon Highlands and the Colorado Plateau). Building on a model proposed by Bayham (1982), Wills (1995:238-240) suggested that long-distance hunting by occupants of the low desert (he cites sites from the Tucson Basin) gave them a capacity to acquire large game during the autumn. Transportation of agricultural surplus to montane camps allowed low-desert farmers to compete with the occupants of the Colorado Plateau. The latter are said to have used the Mogollon Rim in a manner consistent with high residential mobility and "foraging" land-use strategies (see Binford 1980; Kelly 1983, 1992). According to Wills, the strategy pursued by the low-desert farmers displaced that of the Colorado Plateau dwellers during the earliest centuries of farming in the Southwest.

Discussion

Unfortunately, macrobotanical data cannot be used to resolve differences in the interpretation of resource use when such use is said to be restricted to the Tucson Basin, the surrounding bajadas, and the closest montane uplands (e.g., Downum et al. 1986; B. Huckell 1995; Huckell et al. 1995; Roth 1988, 1992). B. Huckell (1995) and proponents of the classically sedentary model argue that the mere presence of maize in combination with large storage pits, "middens," and observable architectural remnants provides a compelling circumstantial case for year-round sedentism. In such circumstances, one would expect the presence of a "logistically organized" resource acquisition strategy in which small groups of individuals leave the village to obtain specific resources, acquire them, and return with said resources to the village. The macrobotanical evidence that has been reviewed here certainly confirms that saguaro moved a modest distance, and the occasional juniper seed hints at the use of distant montane zones. It may be said that the macrobotanical evidence is generally "consistent" with the classically sedentary model because longer range movement of wild resources is at least circumstantially supported by the macrobotanical evidence.

However, one could argue that the presence of dense lithic scatters in the saguaro zones of the bajadas, the presence of special purpose sites such as Coffee Camp, and hints of residential use of montane environments point to a land-use strategy that entailed a high degree of wholesale, seasonal residential movement (for example, Roth 1992:311-312). A "residentially organized" land-use strategy could combine the movement of agricultural surpluses into local montane areas, with fall and winter hunting (Dart 1986:180). Movement from montane areas could have occurred around the time that cactus fruit ripened, or when early grasses became available (incorporating sites like Coffee Camp). The harvested fruit and any leftover gathered grass seeds could have been transported to familiar, summer-only agricultural villages.

Plenty of circumstantial support exists for a model that characterizes floodplain villages such as Los Pozos as seasonal agricultural encampments incorporated into a much larger land use area. The transportation of maize to upper bajada and lower montane areas is supported by the observation of maize pollen at one upper bajada site (Dart 1986). Moreover, area surveys of bajadas have identified numerous, very dense artifact and flaked stone debris scatters in upper bajada zones (Dart 1989; Roth 1988; Simpson and Wells 1983; Wellman 1994). Small architectural sites have been noted in the ecotone between dune fields and floodplains (Czaplicki and Dart 1984:36-60; Halbirt and Henderson 1993), and these may have been good locations for harvesting certain varieties of small seeds or mesquite pods. In general, the macrobotanical analyses of samples from floodplain villages are consistent with this overall characterization as long as one assumes that food moved between seasonally occupied locations.

Fortunately, evidence considered in the analyses of macrobotanical assemblages from floodplain settlements may be used to consider the model of Early Agricultural villagers as long-distance hunters. Wills (1995) proposed that inhabitants of the Sonoran Desert displaced hunters from the Colorado Plateau in an area where their resource strategies competed–the Mogollon Rim. The evidence from Early Agricultural period sites indicates that, *if* Tucson Basin forager-horticulturists were concerned with maximizing energy returns, *then* Wills' (1995) model is unlikely.

For the sake of argument, the "Mogollon Rim" is defined as the nearest boundary of the Great Basin Conifer Woodland biological province (Brown 1995) (more commonly dubbed the "Pinyon-Juniper Zone"), on the south face of the Mogollon Rim geographic province. Defined as such, the Mogollon Rim is roughly 150 to 200 km from Tucson (see Brown and Lowe 1995). Between Tucson and the Mogollon Rim, there are several mountain ranges, and we may assume that hunters skirted the base of these rather than crossing them directly. The total distance traveled would have been roughly 200 km, from Tucson to the Natanes Mountains.

The energetic costs of transporting food have been discussed earlier in this report. The maximum transport distance for a 20-kg load of maize would have been roughly 492 km, and 9.9 km of motion could be supported by 1 hr of maize grinding. If one only considers the gross energetic yields of maize, then it is apparent that the occupants of the Tucson Basin could have used maize to support logistical forays into the Mogollon Rim. Assuming that hunters traveled for 12 hrs each day, a one-way trip would have required 8.5 days (at 3 km/hr), and such a trip would have required roughly 43,000 kcal (assuming 50 kcal/hr were used during the other 12 hours each day). Each kg of maize provides a gross yield of 3,600 kcal, so a 20-kg basket has an effective capacity of 72,000 kcal. Subtracting the two numbers, it is apparent that 26,650 kcal would remain in the basket. Disencumbered, the hunter may be presumed to pay an average energetic cost of 100 kcal/hr (2,400 kcal/day is a reasonable estimate for a moderately active human of average stature). On arrival, the hunter could count on 11 days of food to support hunting (if he is confident of success), or 3 days of food to support hunting and 8.5 days of food to support the return trip (if he is not confident of success). To prepare for this foray, a person would have to grind maize for approximately 50 hrs.

So far in this discussion, the energy provided by maize has been considered only in terms of its gross energetic yields. As discussed earlier, if one considers the systemic cost of growing and harvesting maize, then the net yield for each kg of maize is 3,080 kcal. A 20-kg load would have provided 61,600 kcal, of which 18,600 would have remained in the basket on arrival in the Mogollon Rim. A hunter would have to be confident of success, because insufficient calories would remain in the basket to support a return trip. The confident hunter could hunt for 7¾ days before depleting his rations.

This systemic perspective is important. From the perspective of behavioral ecology, a strategy is only viable if it achieves a very high energetic return rate in comparison with other strategies. If Wills is correct in asserting that Early Agricultural period farmers from the Tucson Basin hunted in the Mogollon Rim, then several facts are apparent.

First, if Early Agricultural period foragers were maximizing their energy returns, then archaeologists and zoosteologists should be able to identify a faunal resource whose net energetic return (after paying the 86,000-kcal cost of a round-trip to the Mogollon Rim, plus all associated search, pursuit, and processing costs) exceeds the energetic returns of other available strategies. For the purpose of this discussion, the baseline "other strategy" is defined as "stay at home and grow maize" at gross and net return rates of 3,600 or 1,200 kcal/kg. Another alternative would be to hunt closer to the Tucson Basin, for example, in the nearby Santa Catalina Mountains.

Second, let us assume that Early Agricultural period hunters were minimizing their energy costs in pursuit of non-energy resources such as meat (protein). This assumption allows for the recognition that the pursuit of game may have been motivated by desires not directly associated with simple energetic returns. Early Agricultural period foragers may have been willing to accept net energy deficits in order to increase protein consumption. If so, then archaeologists and zoosteologists should be able to identify a meat resource in the Mogollon Rim that returned greater quantities of protein per unit of energy expended than other meat resources located closer to the Tucson Basin.

Finally, if the resource strategy pursued by the logistically organized occupants of the Tucson Basin was so successful that it displaced the residentially organized acquisition strategies of the occupants of the Colorado Plateau, then we must assume that the Tucson Basin farmers' strategy was more energetically efficient (either in terms of net energy returns or in rates of protein return per unit of energy expended) than that of the Colorado Plateau people. To assume otherwise would be inconsistent with the principles of the behavioral ecology paradigm that underlies Wills' (1995) model. This potential finding remains a possibility, especially if contemporary occupants of the Colorado Plateau lacked maize agriculture and had to rely heavily on the less-productive starchy seeds. On the other hand, if Colorado Plateau hunters were even moderately successful at meeting their energetic requirements through the consumption of marrow, meat fat, or pinyon nuts, then the Tucson Basin farmers probably could not have competed with them.

The macrobotanical analyses of samples from Tucson Basin sites are very useful for generating criteria by which Wills' (1995) model of Early Agricultural period subsistence may be tested. On the whole, long-distance forays into the Mogollon Rim from the Tucson Basin were possible. However, based on the energetic returns associated with different plants, a long-distance hunting strategy of this sort would be, energetically speaking, very expensive and inefficient.

CONCLUSION

The analysis of macroplant remains from the Los Pozos site was useful in identifying five categories of internally comparable plants. These included small, starchy seeds, mesquite, analytically obscure plants (such as *Solanum/Physalis* types), cactus fruit, and maize. It was shown that the ubiquities of certain key seeds, particularly cheno-ams, tansy mustard, and various grasses were very high. It was suggested that their high ubiquities, as well as the ubiquity scores of maize, mesquite, and saguaro seeds, are consistent with a land-use strategy that specifically targeted resources with demonstrably high energetic returns. Seeds with lower energy yields were used less frequently and may have been harvested opportunistically or only within a limited radius around villages.

Overall, the types of seeds observed in Los Pozos site flotation samples were consistent with those observed in macroplant assemblages observed in most other Early Agricultural period sites from the greater Tucson Basin. With reference to models of prehistoric subsistence that are limited to resources within and around the Tucson Basin, the observed plant frequencies are consistent with most area characterizations of land use, even though these models differ markedly in character. However, the macrobotanical data are very useful for deriving predictions for models of long-distance hunting by Tucson Basin farmers. On the whole, Wills' (1995) suggestion that Sonoran Desert farmers transported maize into the Mogollon Highlands to support hunting activities is implausible since such a strategy would have been energetically costly.

CHAPTER 10

FAUNAL REMAINS

Helga Wöcherl

Data tables of faunal remains can be found in Waters and Wöcherl (2001).

Prior to the excavation of the Santa Cruz Bend (AZ AA:12:746 [ASM]) and Stone Pipe (AZ BB:13:425 [ASM]) sites along I-10, little was known about Early Agricultural (Late Archaic) period settlements in floodplain settings. Although artifacts indicative of hunting, such as projectile points, and of processing, such as ground stone, were present, Early Agricultural faunal assemblages from Tucson Basin floodplain sites, such as San Xavier Bridge (AZ BB:13:14 [ASM]; Gillespie 1987), or from the Santa Cruz Flats (Tator Hills site (AZ AA:6:18 [ASM]; James 1993) were either not well dated, or were too small to allow interpretations of subsistence systems (e.g., Tator Hills: n = 219; San Xavier Bridge: n = 9, Stratum 90-100; Donaldson (AZ EE:2:30 [ASM]): n = 108 (B. Huckell 1995); Clearwater (AZ BB:13:6 [ASM]): n = 407). In addition, and in contrast to such sites as Ventana Cave (AZ Z:12:5 [ASM]; Haury 1950), faunal preservation at open air sites is usually poor. Thus, the recovery of large samples of well-preserved faunal remains from Santa Cruz Bend and Stone Pipe provided unique opportunities to investigate the relationships of human and animal populations on a larger scale. The co-occurrence of hunting and processing artifacts with artiodactyl remains at large village sites along the middle Santa Cruz indicated that deer and other ungulates were actively hunted and brought back to the site for further processing and consumption. Large numbers of lagomorph remains showed that small mammals formed an important part of the diet.

Although both Santa Cruz Bend and Stone Pipe (see Thiel 1998) produced large faunal assemblages, it was not until the excavation of Los Pozos (AA:12:91 [ASM]) that another Tucson Basin floodplain site matched the over 8,000 analyzed fragments from Santa Cruz Bend, a large Cienega phase settlement. Over 17,000 fragments of animal bone from Los Pozos were recovered from well-defined contexts, many of which were artifact rich and radiocarbon dated. Almost 8,400 fragments (49 percent) were analyzed. Natural preservation at Los Pozos is also excellent, and recovery damage is comparatively low (J. Waters, personal communication 1996; see also Table 10.3). Only 1.1 percent of the faunal fragments could not be identified at all (see Table 10.1). Recovery contexts include 20 completely excavated and 21 sampled pit structures and their interior pits, and over 20 extramural pits. Thus, the faunal assemblage from Los Pozos provides an excellent opportunity to augment and supplement existing data and to evaluate current interpretations of subsistence economies of early floodplain villages in the Santa Cruz Valley.

To accurately describe the assemblage, this chapter will investigate the composition and characteristics of the assemblage, such as fragmentation, body part representation, and burning. Intra-site variation is examined to characterize the spatial distribution of faunal remains and its interpretation. Comparisons with other Early Agricultural sites in southern Arizona will address patterns of resource exploitation to place interpretations of Los Pozos' subsistence economy in a larger context. Ethnographic data are presented throughout these sections.

METHODOLOGICAL AND THEORETICAL ISSUES

The main unit of analysis used in this chapter is NISP (number of identified specimens per taxon). While bone fragment counts are available for all I-10 sites, including Los Pozos, other reports (e.g., James 1993) often do not list numbers of fragments by species. With small assemblages, this practice is justified, and their comparison is best done based on NISP (e.g., Grayson 1984). As not all faunal assemblages examined in this chapter are as large as that from Los Pozos, NISP represents the most applicable analytical unit, particularly for inter-site comparisons. In addition, not all bone fragmentation is original. Recovery from hard or clayey matrices often leads to fresh breaks, which are distinguishable, but which do increase fragment counts. NISP, in conjunction with descriptions of fragmentation based on old breaks (Table 10.3), is a better measure of species and elements represented.

Traditional zooarchaeological literature defines NISP as "the number of identified specimens per taxon" where taxon "can be a subspecies, species, genus, family, or higher taxonomic category" (Lyman 1994:100). Thus, taxon customarily refers to an observational unit that can be expressed in biological nomenclature at various levels of specificity. Although not identifiable in a traditional taxonomic sense, mammal remains can often be classified by size.

Table 10.1. Summary of faunal taxa from the Early Agricultural component at Los Pozos.

Taxon	Number of Fragments	Percent of Fragments	NISP	Percent of NISP
Bony fishes (Osteichthyes)	8		8	
Total fishes	**8**	**.01**	**8**	**.20**
Frogs/toads (Salientia)	12		11	
Toads (*Bufo* sp.)	51		50	
Total amphibians	**63**	**.80**	**61**	**1.50**
Indeterminate turtles (Testudinata)	66		11	
Mud turtles (*Kinosternon* sp.)	21		11	
Sonoran mud turtle (*Kinosternon sonoriense*)	8		3	
cf. Desert tortoise (cf. *Gopherus agassizi*)	354		22	
Desert tortoise (*Gopherus agassizi*)	99		8	
Lizards (Sauria)	1		1	
Indeterminate lizard (Iguanidae)	5		4	
Nonpoisonous snakes (Colubridae)	1		1	
Total reptiles	**555**	**7.20**	**61**	**1.50**
Kites/hawks/eagles/Old World vultures (Accipitridae)-medium hawk	1		1	
Large hawks (*Buteo* sp.)	7		2	
Sharp-shinned hawk (*Accipiter striatus*)	2		2	
Quail (*Callipepla* sp.)	19		19	
Blackbirds/orioles/allies (Icteridae)	1		1	
Ravens/crows (Corvidae)	1		1	
Roadrunner (*Geococcyx californianus*)	10		6	
Goatsuckers (Caprimulgidae)	2		2	
Ducks (Anatidae)	1		1	
Perching birds (Passeriformes)	10		9	
Total birds	**54**	**.60**	**44**	**1.00**
Rodents (Rodentia)	1		1	
Squirrels/ground squirrels (*Spermophilus/Ammospermophilus*)	4		4	
Harris' antelope squirrel (*Ammospermophilus harrisii*)	1		1	
Rock squirrel (*Spermophilus variegatus*)	1		1	
Cotton rat (*Sigmodon* sp.)	2		2	
Woodrat (*Neotoma* sp.)	12		10	
Kangaroo rat (*Dipodomys* sp.)	2		2	
Pocket gopher (*Thomomys* sp.)	2		2	
Pocket mouse (*Perognathus* sp.)	23		21	
Total rodents	**48**	**.60**	**44**	**1.00**
Lagomorphs	11	.13	11	.30
Cottontails (*Sylvilagus* sp.)	638	8.10	532	13.20
Jackrabbits (*Lepus* sp.)	1,556	18.60	1,066	26.50
Antelope jackrabbit (*Lepus alleni*)	251	3.00	134	3.30
Black-tailed jackrabbit (*Lepus californicus*)	461	5.50	290	7.20
Total lagomorphs	**2,917**	**35.30**	**2,033**	**50.60**

Table 10.1. Continued.

Taxon	Number of Fragments	Percent of Fragments	NISP	Percent of NISP
Dogs/coyotes/wolves/fox (Canidae)	1		1	
Dogs/coyotes/wolves (*Canis* sp.)	27		14	
Gray fox (*Urocyon cinereoargenteus*)	1		1	
Bobcat/mountain lion (*Felis* sp.)	1		1	
Bobcat (*Felis rufus*)	3		3	
Total carnivores	33	.40	20	.50
Artiodactyls (Artiodactyla)	901	11.40	202	5.00
Deer (*Odocoileus* sp.)	358	4.30	38	.90
Mule deer (*Odocoileus hemionus*)	2	.02	1	.02
Pronghorn (*Antilocapra americana*)	34	.40	5	.10
Bighorn sheep (*Ovis canadensis*)	183	2.20	16	.40
Total artiodactyls	1,478	18.30	262	6.50
Total identified taxa	5,156	63.20	2,533	62.80
Other birds and mammals				
Large bird	20	2.40	8	.20
Medium bird	4	.05	2	.05
Medium-small bird	1		1	.02
Large rodent	1		1	.02
Medium rodent	17	.20	17	.40
Small rodent	6	.07	6	.10
Large mammal	1,195	14.20	406	10.10
Large-medium mammal	17	.20	9	.20
Medium mammal	16	.20	13	.30
Medium-small mammal	18	.20	15	.40
Small mammal	1,614	19.30	1,007	25.00
Total other birds and mammals	1,905	35.50	1,485	37.00
Total identified taxa + other birds and mammals	8,061	96.20	4,018	100.00
Unidentified mammal	224	2.70		
Non-identifiable animal	94	1.10		
Total, all faunal remains	8,383	100.00		

Southwestern faunal analysis has long used the term "unidentified" to describe remains classified as mammals, and sometimes other classes, of various known size groups reflecting well-known Southwestern species. In this chapter, NISP includes categories like "large mammal" under such headings as "Other Birds and Mammals," but excludes mammals that cannot be identified to size class (here called "unidentified mammal") and animals that cannot be identified any further ("non-identifiable animal"). The inclusion of size-classed mammals has a number of analytic and descriptive advantages: it greatly reduces the number of non-identifiable remains and allows further description and quantification of the assemblage. Since, combined with artiodactyls and lagomorphs, large and small mammals make the greatest contributions to Early Agricultural

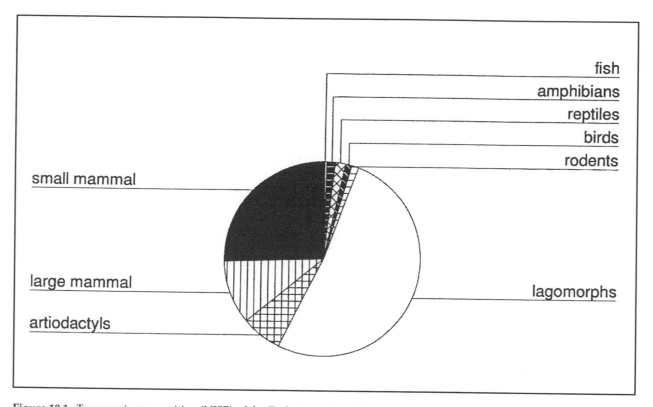

Figure 10.1. Taxonomic composition (NISP) of the Early Agricultural faunal assemblage at Los Pozos.

diets, this approach provides a more proportionate picture of faunal subsistence economies (see also Figure 10.1). In the following discussion, bone artifacts are included in NISP.

Although some researchers use MNI (minimum number of individuals) calculations in addition to NISP, not all faunal analyses report MNI. Since some reports consulted do not contain the appropriate data, it is not always possible to determine MNI counts in retrospect. Therefore, in this chapter, MNI is used comparatively only when other analyses reported MNI, and if that MNI was determined in the same fashion (following White 1953:397).

TAXONOMIC COMPOSITION OF THE LOS POZOS ASSEMBLAGE

Early Agricultural faunal remains from Los Pozos (NISP = 4,018) represent eight orders and 30 individual species (Table 10.1). The taxonomic groups include fishes, amphibians, reptiles, birds, rodents, lagomorphs, carnivores, and artiodactyls. In terms of size classes, large birds are hawk-sized and are most likely raptors smaller than eagles. Medium birds are duck-sized and likely represent Anatidae. Small birds are perching birds about the size of a sparrow. Large rodents may be as large as a rock squirrel or a muskrat. Medium rodents correspond to woodrats or ground squirrels. Small rodents are mouse-sized. The group of large mammals includes deer, antelope, and sheep. This group is treated as additional artiodactyls in the remainder of this chapter. Large to medium mammals may represent either a small ungulate or a large carnivore. Depending on the fragmentation or the amount of surface modification of the specimen, the body size of the animal may be difficult to determine. Since this size class can contain more than one taxa group, its numbers are generally not included with artiodactyl or carnivore counts. Medium mammals comprise smaller, and more common carnivores, such as bobcat, coyote, and wolf. While medium to small mammals may include jackrabbits, they also include small carnivores. Without clear assignments to one or the other order, counts in this category are not included in the description of leporids or carnivores. Rabbits and rodents form the group of small mammals. As rodents are clearly less frequent at Early Agricultural sites than rabbits, small mammals are interpreted as lagomorphs in most of this chapter. Unidentified mammals and non-identifiable animals are included in fragment counts, but not in NISP. When all classified specimens are considered, the taxonomic proportions for NISP in Figure 10.1 indicate that the faunal assemblage is dominated by lagomorph/small mammal, and artiodactyl/large mammal remains. The composition of each taxonomic group is summarized below.

Fishes

Eight fish (Osteichthyes) fragments (NISP = 8) were recovered from the interior pits of two pit structures. Three specimens are indeterminate bones, five are skull fragments. All are unburned, but show natural surface modification indicating their age. Finds of fish remains are rare at prehistoric Southwestern sites. Their paucity is generally assumed to be a result of sampling techniques (i.e., screen size or of food preferences). Szuter (1989), among others, suggests that fish was basically not consumed by the Hohokam, in spite of the proximity of some sites to aquatic resources.

Amphibians

Frogs and toads (Salientia) are represented by 63 fragments (NISP = 61). Since none of them are burned, and because they do not show any surface modification other than occasional signs of erosion, they are probably not of cultural origin. Although most prehistoric faunal assemblages from sites with riparian access contain some amphibians, signs of human consumption are rare to nonexistent. The burrowing habit of toads (*Bufo* sp.) in particular best explains their presence at archaeological sites.

Reptiles

Reptile remains occur in unusually large numbers at Los Pozos. While the large number of fragments (555) derives from badly broken carapaces of mud turtles (*Kinosternon* sp.), particularly desert tortoises (*Gopherus agassizi*), the total reptile NISP (61) is much higher than at other Early Agricultural sites in the vicinity (see Thiel 1998). Turtles and tortoises occur in about equal proportions. Castetter and Underhill (1953:43) stated that the Papago did not hunt tortoises, but "people seeing one would take it home and cook it for food." Ethnographically, the consumption of reptiles is well known, if disputed by the consumers (Russell 1975:83). However, the majority of reptile bones at Los Pozos are not burned, but carnivore gnawing is a frequent surface modification, especially on carapace fragments from pit structures. One piece of carapace is a pendant-like ornament. Another is fossilized and was perhaps collected by Los Pozos inhabitants. Both are from intramural pits.

Birds

Birds, including a duck fragment, are represented by 54 fragments (NISP = 44). They cover a wider range of genera than at other sites nearby (see Thiel 1998), and raptors are represented by at least two distinctive species of hawks (*Accipiter striatus* and *Buteo* sp.). Quail (*Callipepla* sp.), roadrunner (*Geococcyx californianus*), goatsuckers (Caprimulgidae), and perching birds (Passeriformes) are the most frequent bird taxa. Goatsuckers are migratory birds with species-specific habitats, and thus are excellent seasonal indicators. Unfortunately, the particular species of two Caprimulgidae at Los Pozos could not be determined.

Although only one bird bone is burned, some bird elements may represent food refuse. While birds, especially quail, are consumed ethnographically, Bayham (1982) suggests that quail bones at Ventana Cave be considered noncultural because they showed no signs of cultural modification. However, it is possible that prehistorically birds were also eaten without cooking, similar to the fresh meat consumption of small mammals among the Washoe (Downs 1966:27). Later ceremonial treatments of raptor bones suggest that they were not food animals (e.g., James 1994). Since no raptor damage was found on any non-bird remains, hawks, and possibly also other birds, were probably brought to the site by humans. Other bird element fragments (NISP = 11) were unidentifiable beyond class. Thus, the comparatively high diversity of birds, and of raptors in particular, suggests that birds were important to Los Pozos' inhabitants.

Rodents

Pocket mouse (*Perognathus* sp.) and woodrat (*Neotoma* sp.) bones are the most frequent rodent remains at Los Pozos. Most rodent remains are unburned, and mandibular fragments, with or without teeth, are the most frequent fragments. Although rodents are much better represented at Los Pozos than at the I-10 sites (see Thiel 1998), at 1 percent they are not as frequent as one would expect if they contributed significantly to the human diet as Szuter (1989) suggests. Since rodents often occur in pit structure fill, they may represent vermin infestation rather than food items. However, some rodent remains in intramural pits are burned, and rodent consumption is known ethnographically. Packrats (woodrats) were "a very common food" among the Papago (Castetter and Underhill 1935:42; see also Russell 1975:80-83). Again, unburned bones do not necessarily imply a noncultural origin.

Lagomorphs

Lagomorphs are represented by 2,917 fragments (NISP = 2,033). Only .3 percent could not be identified to genus. Jackrabbits, including antelope jackrabbit

(*Lepus alleni*) and black-tailed jackrabbit (*Lepus californicus*), form the bulk of identified lagomorphs with an NISP of almost 1,500. However, cottontail (*Sylvilagus* sp.), most likely desert cottontail (*S. audubonii*), is also well-represented. All lagomorphs combined constitute over 80 percent of the identifiable assemblage. Complete bones are phalanges, metatarsals, and metacarpals. The vast majority of fragments are unburned limb bones. For burned bone, lagomorph remains outnumber artiodactyl bones only in the category of "light brown," implying some (but not vigorous) cooking (Figure 10.3), including the roasting of whole animals. There are no significant differences between the species of jackrabbits and cottontails in terms of presence of burning (see Figure 10.3) or element representation. Fetal/newborn and young/juvenile individuals (2 percent of total lagomorphs) were recorded for both cottontails and jackrabbits. Carnivore gnawing was found on 3.3 percent of lagomorph bones. Red pigment (ocher) or staining was found on a very small number (.8 percent) of bones.

Carnivores

The vast majority of carnivore remains belong to dog/coyote/wolf (*Canis* sp.). All major regions of the body are represented in the remains, as are teeth. One canine tooth was perforated and perhaps used as a pendant. Both gray wolf (*Canis lupus*, mainly cf. *baileyi*) and coyote (*Canis latrans*) occur in the Sonoran Desert life zone, although wolves have become quite rare (Hoffmeister 1986:465). Dog (*Canis familiaris*) burials are known from a number of Early Agricultural sites, including Santa Cruz Bend (Thiel 1998) and the Donaldson site in the Cienega Creek Valley (Eddy and Cooley 1983), and from Early Ceramic sites, such as Houghton Road (Cairns and Ciolek-Torrello 1998).

Domesticated dogs may have been used for hunting, as among historic Papago (Szuter 1989:328). At Los Pozos, some mammal bones in the assemblage had been carnivore-digested. These may be examples of damage from dogs living at the site during its occupation. Gray fox (*Urocyon cinereoargenteus*) is a relatively common Sonoran Desert dweller and, similar to coyote, another likely scavenger near human settlements (Hoffmeister 1986:475). Bobcat (*Felis rufus*) is represented by three, possibly four, fragments from the appendicular skeleton, plus one canine tooth.

Presence of burning is not confined to one species, but occurs across all carnivores. Of the total faunal assemblage, only 180 specimens (4.5 percent) exhibited evidence of carnivore gnawing. While carnivores were definitely present at Los Pozos (percent NISP = 6), they probably did not represent an important food resource.

Artiodactyls

As the second most common order (percent NISP = 10.3), artiodactyls are represented by 1,478 fragments (NISP = 262). Most remains belong to deer (*Odocoileus* sp.), and probably to mule deer (*O. hemionus*). However, bighorn is also well-represented (NISP = 16, possibly 17). Rear feet and legs, but also ribcage elements, are the most frequent body parts (Figure 10.2). Complete bones are limited to phalanges and metatarsals. Fifteen specimens of antler/horn were recovered. Twelve of them are deer antler, four of which are potentially worked pieces. Since no proximal ends were recovered, it is not possible to determine whether the antler was shed or cut. While most artiodactyl remains are unburned, some are charred to various degrees. Carnivore gnawing was noted on 1.1 percent.

Other Birds and Mammals (NISP = 37)

Large Birds (NISP = 8)

Eight large bird remains belong to hawk-sized species. Compared with other Early Agricultural sites along the Santa Cruz River, large birds are unusually frequent at Los Pozos. Although all hawk remains are unburned, the fact that most of them were found in postholes may indicate cultural origin. Since postholes were also repositories for deer femur heads, in some cases intentional burial of certain animal parts may have been a custom. Other specimens came from interior pits. Additionally, hawk body part representation indicates it is most likely whole birds were brought to the site. Thus, their deposition is probably not from occasional carnivore discard.

Medium Birds (NISP = 2)

The medium bird category refers to duck-sized birds. With a riparian zone in close proximity to the site, it is quite possible that this remain represents another Anatid. Although unburned, the bones were found in an interior and an extramural pit, rather than pit structure fill. This context, and the high food value of waterfowl (e.g., Speth 1983:158), suggest that the remains are indeed of cultural origin.

Medium-Small Birds (NISP = 1)

Birds in this size class may also represent food animals. Quail-sized, these may indeed be *Callipepla* sp., which was eaten by the Pima and Papago (e.g., Russell 1975). They showed no cultural modifications, such as burning or butcher marks; however, they may

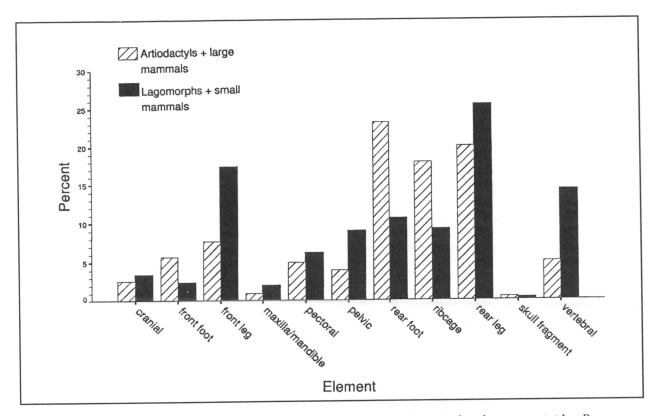

Figure 10.2. Body part representation for selected combined taxa from the Early Agricultural component at Los Pozos.

have been prepared by crushing their bones and consumed without cooking, much like small mammals elsewhere (Downs 1966:27). Quail could have been hunted and "collected" from traps as an embedded activity.

Large Rodents (NISP = 1)

Large rodents are the size of rock squirrels or muskrat. Since *Spermophilus variegatus* is identified from the site, this may well be another rock squirrel. However, muskrats (*Ondrata zibethicus*, likely *O. z. pallidus*) "lived in many of the larger [Arizona] streams in the past" (Hoffmeister 1986:447) and are known from Early Ceramic sites along the Santa Cruz River (Gillespie 1987). They may well be part of a subsistence system that includes riparian faunal resources.

Medium Rodents (NISP = 17)

Woodrats and ground squirrels are examples of this size class. Both have been identified in the assemblage; in fact, woodrats represent the second most common species among the identified rodents.

Small Rodents (NISP = 6)

Small rodents are of field mouse or pocket mouse size. Pocket mouse (*Perognathus* sp.) is the most common species among the identified rodents.

Large Mammals (NISP = 406)

Since large mammals are the size of deer, antelope, and sheep, they probably represent artiodactyls. At 10.1 percent of the assemblage, these remains constitute a significant food resource. While the majority of large mammal and artiodactyl bones is unburned, large mammal remains more often show signs of burning. Both large mammal and artiodactyl remains show the same general body part representation and are highly fragmented. However, the relationship between fragments preserved at one-half to less than one-quarter of the original element size is inverse between the two groups (Table 10.2). Essentially all large mammal fragments are less than one-quarter the original element size, while the majority (60 percent) of identified artiodactyl fragments are less than one-quarter. This may reflect their destruction for marrow extraction and

Table 10.2. Bone fragmentation (NISP) of selected taxa from Los Pozos (percent in parentheses).

Fragmentation	Artiodactyls		Large Mammals		Lagomorphs		Small Mammals	
Complete	29	(11.3)	0		145	(7.10)	0	
Complete except epiphysis	0		0		1	(.05)	0	
Nearly complete	10	(4.0)	0		73	(3.60)	0	
> ¾	6	(2.3)	0		69	(3.40)	1	(.1)
½ to ¾	11	(4.3)	0		171	(8.40)	0	
¼ to ½	63	(24.5)	2	(99.5)	619	(30.50)	6	(.6)
< ¼	138	(53.7)	401	(.5)	954	(47.40)	997	(99.3)
Total	257	(100.0)	403	(100.0)	2,032	(100.00)	1,004	(100.0)

Table 10.3. Bone fragmentation (NISP) from the Early Agricultural components at the Los Pozos, Santa Cruz Bend, Stone Pipe, and Wetlands sites (percent in parentheses).

Amount	Los Pozos		Santa Cruz Bend		Stone Pipe		Wetlands	
Complete	213	(5.00)	262	(5.0)	64	(5.0)	74	(6.7)
Complete except epiphysis	4	(.09)	12	(.2)	4	(.2)	2	(.2)
Nearly complete	122	(2.90)	18	(.4)	3	(.2)	23	(2.0)
> ¾	109	(2.60)	34	(.7)	10	(.7)	17	(1.5)
½ to ¾	216	(5.10)	150	(3.0)	27	(2.0)	35	(3.2)
¼ to ½	772	(18.20)	592	(12.0)	160	(11.0)	132	(12.0)
< ¼	2,804	(66.10)	3,799	(78.0)	1,130	(81.0)	817	(74.3)
Total	4,240		4,867		1,398		1,100	

bone grease production, practices that are known ethnographically (Castetter and Underhill 1935:40) and archaeologically (Speth 1983:158). Their greater frequency in trash-filled pit structures suggests disposal after final processing.

Large-Medium Mammals (NISP = 9)

Although this size class includes small ungulates, specimens identified to this group are not included in the large mammal count since they can not be separated from large carnivores, the other members of this class. Bobcats and mountain lions (*Felis concolor*) correspond to this size class, and *Felis rufus* has been identified in the assemblage. While mountain lion ranges throughout the state at elevations from 61-2,483 m, jaguar (*Felis onca*) has always been rare, even in the southern part of Arizona; ocelot (*Felis pardalis*) did occur in southeastern Arizona in the past, but no recent records exist (Lowe 1964:258). Probably not a frequent prey, carnivores were nevertheless eaten ethnographically (Steward 1938:255) and were prized for their pelts. Since possible carnivore remains are found burned in intra- and extramural pits at Los Pozos, they may represent food waste. One long bone from an interior feature was filled with gypsum.

Medium Mammals (NISP = 13)

Animals of this size class include felids and canids. Since both groups have been identified in the assemblage, and because most remains are very fragmentary, it is not clear which is represented here. However, some elements are more canid-like, including a complete caudal vertebra from a pit structure. Five elements are burned. The majority of specimens are ribs, suggesting that whole animals were brought to and consumed at the site.

Medium-Small Mammals (NISP = 15)

More carnivores may be included in this group; however, they would be either young animals or belong to different, smaller species than the above. Large jackrabbits, such as *Lepus alleni*, also fit the size criterion for this class. Since jackrabbits represent 30.7 percent of all faunal remains, they may well form the majority of this group. Out of five specimens from pit structure fill, only one is burned; it is identified as a possible muskrat. *Ondrata zibethicus* is a very likely riparian prey species with a high nutritional value. Since bones from most regions of the body are represented, the animals were probably brought to the site whole.

Small Mammals (NISP = 1,007)

Both rabbits and rodents belong to this size class, and both have been identified at Los Pozos. Lagomorphs constitute 50.6 percent of the assemblage; small mammals 25 percent. Small mammal bones are highly fragmented and generally either unburned or calcined (see below). They may well represent those osseous elements of lagomorphs that were more exposed during cooking, such as legs. The relationship between elements preserved at one-quarter to one-half the original element size is the reverse from that in large mammals. Most bones are fragmented almost beyond recognition. This may reflect processing practices such as those described ethnographically by Michelsen (1967). Baja California groups would pound cooked small mammal carcasses on hard, flat surfaces and eat the resulting paste, including the bone. Large mammal long bone processing for marrow and bone grease would leave larger fragments that could also not as easily find their way into the edible portions.

Unidentified Mammals

Of a total of 8,383 fragments, 224 (2.7 percent) could not be identified beyond class. This number compares favorably with other Early Agricultural sites, such as the Donaldson site (.5 percent), La Paloma (AZ BB:9:127 [ASM]) (8.9 percent), and Split Ridge (AZ EE:2:103 [ASM]) (58.3 percent) (Szuter and Bayham 1995:Table 4.1).

Non-identifiable Animals

Only 1.1 percent (94 fragments) of the Los Pozos assemblage could not be identified beyond the level of "animal." Other Early Agricultural sites along the Santa Cruz River show somewhat lower counts: Santa Cruz Bend (.09 percent) and Stone Pipe (.05 percent; includes Early Ceramic component) (Thiel 1998). Coffee Camp (AZ AA:6:19 [ASM]) (James 1993), on the other hand, produced a somewhat higher percentage of non-identifiable remains (1.7 percent). Within this rather small range of variation, Los Pozos again compares favorably.

CHARACTERISTICS OF THE ASSEMBLAGE

Taphonomy

Although buried in a floodplain with evidence of major flooding events, abrasion and erosion are not the most common form (11.6 percent) of surface alteration on the animal bone from Los Pozos; however, some fluvial action is indicated. The depositional age of the assemblage is suggested by the frequent presence of calcium carbonate (29 percent) and root etching (32.1 percent). Crystals adhering to the bone (7.1 percent) are also a good indication of the bones' age. Since no bleached bones were recorded, bone was probably deposited quickly and permanently. Although bone in pit structure fill is relatively protected from trampling, much of the upper fill at Los Pozos represents trash deposits, whose contents may have been exposed to some trampling during processing at the site before deposition. However, deep scratches (Lyman 1994:297) and multiple fine parallel striae, characteristic of trampled bone, particularly on sandy substrates (Behrensmeyer et al. 1986), are absent. Carnivore gnawing occurred on 180 specimens (4.5 percent); three were digested (.07 percent). Although raptors are represented in the assemblage, no raptor damage to bone was recorded. Only .9 percent showed cut or chop marks. Other cultural alterations include red pigment. However, since hematite and ocher were abundant at Los Pozos, it is not clear whether the applications were always intentional.

As Thiel (1998) pointed out, ¼-inch and ⅛-inch mesh screens produce comparable results in terms of faunal identifiability. Since the consistent use of ¼-inch mesh screens at Los Pozos produced fish bones and a multitude of small animal remains, and because no appreciable small animal remains were found in flotation heavy fractions, it is likely that few faunal remains were lost due to recovery techniques. The proportion of identified (62.8 percent NISP) versus size-classed remains (37 percent NISP) is another good indicator of preservation and of recovery damage.

Fragmentation

Five percent of the assemblage is complete skeletal elements (Table 10.3). Since bone that survives taphonomic processes intact is usually of a small, dense type (e.g., Lyman 1994), it is primarily foot bones that remained complete at Los Pozos. This is true for large and small mammals. Table 10.3 shows that, compared with other Santa Cruz floodplain sites, Los Pozos has a relatively lower fragmentation rate, which greatly increases identifiability. At Santa Cruz Bend, 70 percent are identified to size class; at Los Pozos it is 37 percent. About 63 percent of the assemblage was identified to the generic level, compared to about 30 percent at Santa Cruz Bend. However, the general patterns of fragmentation are the same as at Los Pozos and the other sites along the Santa Cruz (see Table 10.3).

At Los Pozos, almost half of all cases show a 1:1 ratio of fragments to NISP. For the majority of remains, the number of fragments ranges between one and four. This holds for most taxa and across most elements. However, for large mammals and small mammals fragment counts are often higher, and large mammal long bones are particularly fragmented. This pattern suggests special processing after butchering, such as for marrow extraction and bone grease production. Exceptionally high fragment counts also occur with antler and with turtle/tortoise carapaces. In contrast to large mammal bones, this destruction is largely due to the friability of the material and to recovery damage.

Body Part Representation

While some of the presence/absence of some body parts may be the result of carnivore activity, general element patterns reflect human behaviors. Figure 10.2 indicates that most artiodactyl/large mammal remains are rear foot and leg elements, suggesting that hind legs with foot "riders" were the most frequently transported artiodactyl part. However, since elements from all other regions of the body are also present, whole animals were probably also brought to the site. While antler/horn (included in "cranial") is present, maxillary/mandibular, and skull elements in particular, are underrepresented. Teeth are also rare. This suggests that antler found at the site was either collected shed antler, or was cut at the kill or butchering site away from Los Pozos. Whole lagomorphs and small mammals were probably brought back more frequently than large game due to lower transport costs and greater local abundance. Elements from all areas of the skeleton are present, and front legs and vertebral pieces feature much more prominently than in artiodactyls. Since ribs and vertebral elements are present, carnivores were, at least occasionally, brought to the site whole, or may represent site dogs.

Amphibian elements do occur in feature contexts; however, they probably represent few individuals. Over 80 percent of *Bufo* sp. remains were found in a single feature, an intramural pit (Feature 318.01); none of the elements occur twice. This skeletal representation suggests that the animal(s) is intrusive into the soft pit fill. Reptiles are represented mostly by pieces of carapace. Since even those show signs of carnivore damage, other turtle elements may have been completely destroyed by canids, either before or after human use of the reptiles.

The identified bird elements cover most regions of the body and thus, probably represent originally complete individuals at the site. Rodents are generally identified from leg bones, but most other body parts are present as well. Whole animals may have been processed and consumed, as was done ethnographically (e.g., Russell 1998). The fact that leg and foot elements of small mammals were burned supports this interpretation. Since fishes are represented by head elements as well as vertebral ones, they were probably brought to the site whole.

Burning

The degree of burning varies by skeletal element within taxa (Figure 10.3). While lagomorph legs are usually unburned, those of small mammals are usually calcined. This difference may indicate a differential treatment of some small mammals, or it may reflect the effect of fragmentation and burning on faunal analysis. Smaller scrap is harder to identify, especially if it is extensively burned. When the main taxa at Los Pozos are combined (Figure 10.4), over 60 percent are unburned. This is particularly true for lagomorphs plus small mammals, in comparison to artiodactyls plus large mammals. Large game was more often exposed to fire, and to more varied degrees. Presence and absence of burning vary by species. Smaller animals were more often unburned. Thus, they may have been consumed without cooking, or the preserved body parts are those that were not usually consumed. The latter interpretation is more likely. Other animals, such as amphibians, may be intrusive, particularly if the species is in the habit of burrowing in soft soil. Pit structure fill and interior features provide excellent burrowing media.

INTRA-SITE VARIABILITY

With a coverage of almost 50 percent of all identified pit structures (Locus B2), Los Pozos represents an unusually comprehensive sample of recorded intramural contexts (Tables 10.4 and 10.5). Figure 10.5 shows that the majority of faunal remains were recovered from interior features. The sample of non-intrusive extramural contexts is smaller (23 percent) and contained 10.9 percent of all faunal remains (Table 10.4). The following discussion examines the faunal remains in different contexts (Table 10.4), their distribution in intra- and extramural space, and their association with particular features and artifacts indicative of processing, storage, and disposal.

Pit Structure Fill and Floor

Out of 42 pit structures excavated or sampled, 38 contained faunal remains. Animal bones were found either in structure fill and near-floor/floor contexts (n = 26), or in intramural features (n = 12). Oxidized areas, interpreted as "hearths," were found on the floors

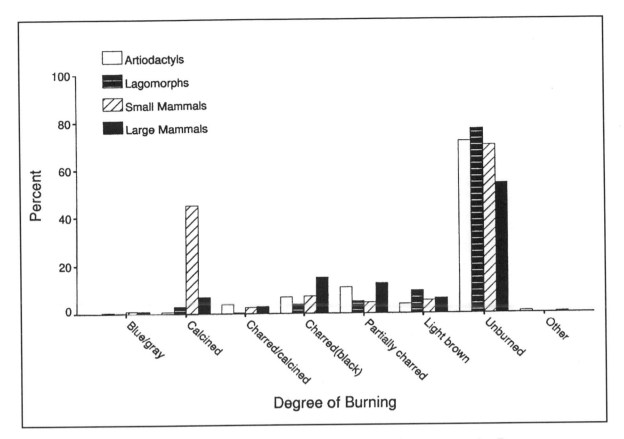

Figure 10.3. Degree of burning for selected taxa from the Early Agricultural component at Los Pozos.

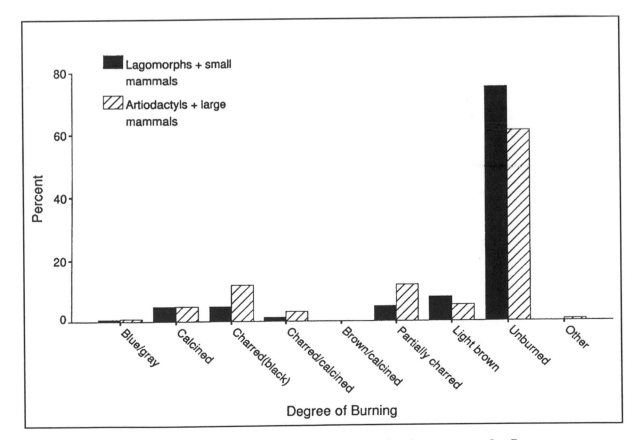

Figure 10.4. Degree of burning for combined taxa from the Early Agricultural component at Los Pozos.

Table 10.4. Faunal remains by feature context for the Early Agricultural component at Los Pozos.

Feature Context	Number of Fragments	Percent of Fragments	NISP	Percent of NISP
Pit structure fill				
Stratum 10	2,139	25.50	1,233	28.90
Stratum 11	5	.05	3	.07
Stratum 19	36	.40	26	.60
Stratum 19R	122	1.50	72	1.70
Stratum 40	17	.20	14	.30
Pit structure floor (Stratum 20)	658	7.80	89	2.10
Subtotal	2,977	35.50	1,437	33.70
Intramural features (includes postholes)	4,639	55.30	2,362	55.40
Total pit structure + intramural features	7,616	90.80	3,799	89.10
Extramural features	767	9.10	465	10.90
Total	8,383		4,265	

Table 10.5. Distribution of faunal remains (NISP) in excavation strata at Los Pozos (percent in parentheses).

Taxon	Stratum 10 (Fill)		Stratum 11/19/19R (Near-floor Fill, Including Roof/Wall Fall)		Stratum 20 (Floor)	
Amphibians	5	(.40)	0	–	0	–
Reptiles	11	(.80)	1	(1)	22	(21.0)
Birds	10	(.70)	1	(1)	0	–
Rodents	23	(2.00)	2	(2)	0	–
Lagomorphs	513	(38.00)	39	(39)	30	(29.0)
Carnivores	7	(.50)	2	(2)	0	–
Artiodactyls	98	(7.30)	2	(2)	20	(19.2)
Large bird	1	(.07)	0	–	0	–
Medium rodent	4	(.30)	1	(1)	0	–
Small rodent	1	(.07)	0	–	0	–
Large mammal	279	(20.70)	14	(14)	8	(8.0)
Large-medium mammal	1	(.07)	0	–	0	–
Medium mammal	6	(.40)	0	–	0	–
Medium-small mammal	5	(.30)	0	–	0	–
Small mammal	297	(22.00)	33	(33)	20	(19.2)
Mammal	65	(5.00)	3	(3)	2	(2.0)
Non-identifiable animal	23	(2.00)	0	–	2	(2.0)
Lagomorphs + small mammals	810	(60.00)	71	(71)	29	(27.0)
Artiodactyls + large mammals	377	(28.00)	15	(15)	51	(48.0)
Total	1,349		99		107	

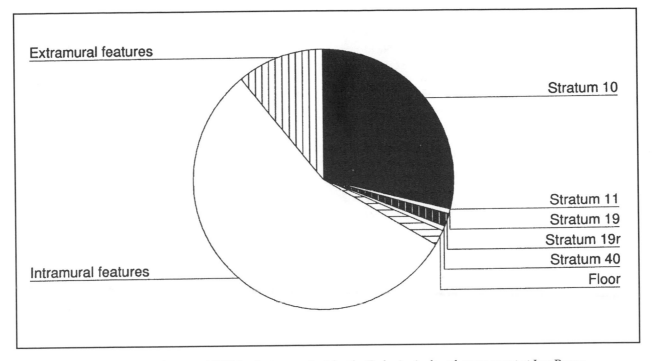

Figure 10.5. Faunal remains (percent NISP) by feature context for the Early Agricultural component at Los Pozos.

of 22 pit structures, 13 of which also contained faunal re-mains either on the floor or in interior pits. Almost all of the burned pit structures (n = 14) contained animal bone.

Stratum 10 (Fill)

Stratum 10 contains the highest number of species (seven) of all excavation strata. Although amphibians and reptiles are present, over 90 percent are unburned and may have burrowed into the softer fill after a structure was abandoned. Other faunal remains show frequent surface modification by calcium carbonate deposits, which attests to their age. Lagomorphs and small mammals represent 60 percent of the faunal remains, compared with 28 percent artiodactyls and large mammals. The two latter groups are represented exclusively by highly fragmented long bone shafts. The disposal of such exhaustively used faunal remains corresponds with the fact that Stratum 10 is largely trash fill. The fact that mammalian remains too fragmented to identify (5 percent) are relatively frequent in this stratum supports this conclusion.

Medium mammals are represented by six specimens, half of which are burned ribs. Since a number of carnivore remains across different contexts are burned felid ribs, these medium mammals are probably carnivores, and possibly bobcats, the most frequently identified felid. The general patterns of Stratum 10 faunal remains are the same whether or not pit structures show evidence of burning in lower strata and on the floor.

Stratum 11/19/19R (Near-floor Fill, Including Roof/Wall Fall)

Five pit structures contained an above-floor stratum that was clearly distinct from general fill. Only one structure (Feature 416) contained roof/wall fall without evidence of burning of the superstructure. In the others, the last 5 cm or more above the floor represented burned material collapsed into the structure. Faunal remains in these pit structures showed various stages of burning, some of which may have been due to the burning of the structure. However, since the general pattern follows that of bone in unburned strata, it probably reflects processing activities. Seventy percent of the faunal remains from near-floor context are small fragments of various limb and foot bones. This is true across the species of the five taxa groups identified, and only 3 percent were not identifiable above the level of "mammal." Frequent calcium carbonate encrustation (44 percent) indicates the age of the remains. Lagomorph and small mammal bones (71 percent) clearly outnumber those of artiodactyls and large mammals (15 percent) (Table 10.5). The presence of faunal remains in roof/wall fall may indicate that animal parts were stored on the roofs, hung from supports/walls, or leaned against posts or walls. Ethnographic sources (e.g., Underhill 1946:86) report that the Papago put artiodactyl bones where dogs could not get to them; roofs would have been a likely place. Szuter's (1989:332-333) compilation of ethnographic accounts also suggests that antler/horn and artiodactyl bones received special treatments. James (1993:363-364) analyzed mule deer racks from burned pit structures at Coffee Camp, but suggests that there was no special treatment beyond storage for later use in lithic manufacture.

At Los Pozos, no specimens of antler or horn were found in the roof/wall fall or near-floor fill. Artiodactyl bones from Strata 11, 19, 19R were in the same fragmented state as those from other contexts, and co-occurred with remains from other species. Thus, either processing activities occurred on the roofs, or animal remains on the floor became mixed into higher strata as roof and wall collapsed. Since the roofs of pit structures may have been too rounded and/or not solid enough to support roof activities, the latter explanation is more likely. The fact that artiodactyl elements from the near-floor in pit structure Feature 861 could be refitted with a metatarsal from Stratum 10 indicates that some mixing of deposits occurred, particularly at the contact. Another refitting of an element from Stratum 19 with artiodactyl bone from one of two intramural pits (Feature 825.01) in a very burned pit structure (Feature 825) provides additional support for the interpretation of some movement of faunal material.

Stratum 20 (Floor)

Compared to Stratum 10, few faunal remains were found in direct floor contact. The floors of nine pit structures produced a total of 104 faunal elements. Only three taxa groups are represented: artiodactyls plus large mammals, lagomorphs plus small mammals, and reptiles (see Table 10.5). Although the latter are very frequent (21.1 percent), they probably do not feature this prominently in the human diet. Since most of the reptile remains are very small pieces of carapace, the actual number of individual animals may be rather small. In addition, not all turtle/tortoise remains may be food waste, but may be the remains of more recent burrowing animals.

The proportion of large to small mammals reverses in this stratum (Table 10.5). Artiodactyls and large mammals (48 percent) are more frequent on pit structure floors than in other contexts. Lagomorphs and small mammals account for only 27 percent. Seven of the large mammal bones are artifacts, such as awls, a spatula, and a polished femur head. If we assume that faunal remains on pit structure floors are in situ, and thus representative of human behaviors relating to animal bone, artiodactyls are certainly prominent as the most important animal resource.

Artifacts Associated with Pit Structure Fill and Floors

Chipped Stone and Cobble Hammers. Only one projectile point was associated with faunal remains in a floor context. Feature 354 produced one artiodactyl fragment from Stratum 20. Although projectile points were recovered from near-floor contexts, none were associated with faunal remains. Not all features that produced projectile points also contained faunal remains. Projectile points from Stratum 10 are unidentified Archaic, Cienega, and San Pedro styles, and most are broken. They represent discard in most cases, as do the faunal remains from this stratum. Feature 379 produced the highest number of Archaic points (n = 3), from the upper fill and also contained a greater than average variety of animal remains (quail, small mammals, rodents, carnivores, general artiodactyls, bighorn, and several broken awls).

Debitage was found in all structures on the floor and in near-floor fill. However, while chipped stone flakes are highly efficient in the processing of game, those structures with the highest debitage counts (range = 1-165) did not also have the highest faunal NISP. This is true regardless of the dominant species in the respective structure. Two comparatively shallow pit structures (Features 416, 417) contained no flaked stone in Stratum 10, and the faunal counts in these structures are sometimes very low. If the low-volume trash in these shallow structures is representative of the total original fill, it probably did not come from contexts of lithic manufacture or animal processing. Cobble hammers and hammer fragments (n = 5) were rare. These artifacts may be used to process animal bone (as during marrow extraction, for instance). Only one hammer was found on a pit structure floor (Feature 866); it may have been used to break the carapace/plastron of a desert tortoise, the only faunal remain on that floor. In summary, since there is no correlation between the presence and frequency of flaked stone and faunal remains in near-floor and floor contexts, game was probably processed elsewhere, and the remains of processing, including some tools, were disposed of in pit structures that were not in use. In addition, some processing may have involved tools and methods that do not preserve archaeologically.

Ground Stone. Ground stone may also have been used to process animal bone. Long bone shafts can be broken on the edge of a metate, or a metate can be used as an anvil on which to crush bone. Small game may also be processed with ground stone. Ethnographic groups in Baja California pounded cooked rodents on metates and ate the product (Michelsen 1967). If animal bone was disposed of in or near the location of processing, associations of ground stone and faunal remains could be expected. At Los Pozos, however, no correlations appear between ground stone and animal bone. Ground stone is present in relatively small numbers in pit structure fill and on floors. Structures with large numbers of processed animal bone did not produce corresponding high counts of ground stone implements. A handstone used for hide processing was found on the floor of Feature 836. Since only one fragment of artiodactyl femur was associated with that context, butchering and other preliminary work probably took place elsewhere.

Fire-cracked Rock. In terms of pit structure fill and floors, there does not seem to be a relationship between the numbers of faunal remains with fire-cracked rocks. Pit structures with high faunal NISP do not contain the most fire-cracked rocks. In fact, the structures with the highest rock counts, particularly in the upper fill, contain no faunal remains at all. In other cases, fire-cracked rock may be found on a floor devoid of animal bone, while fewer rocks were recovered from an upper fill rich in faunal remains. Apparently, some unused pit structures served as disposal areas for cooking stones, but not for the waste from the cooked items. Other structures were filled with food waste, but not cooking stones.

Shell. The highest shell counts came from Stratum 10, which represents largely trash filling and does not allow direct conclusions on associations with faunal remains.

Intramural Features

Bell-shaped Pits

From their excavations at the Late Archaic Milagro site, Huckell and Huckell (1984:12) suggest that bell-shaped pits are storage facilities by definition. The small aperture-to-depth ratio makes bell-shaped pits poor candidates for frequent domestic activities. Six intramural pits (Features 324.14; 416.01; 815.05; 864.01; 864.02; 882.01) at Los Pozos have a smaller aperture than bottom diameters and support that interpretation. None of the features are burned. Two of the features occur within the same small pit structure (Feature 864), leaving little room on the floor for domestic activities. Faunal remains also indicate a probable storage function. Compared with other intramural pits, faunal counts are low in bell-shaped pits. While few artiodactyl bones were found, antler did occur (Feature 882.01). Most animal bone was identified as lagomorph and was unburned. Elements, such as vertebrae and teeth, indicate that whole animals may have been processed in these pit structures. If lagomorph meat attached to bone was stored inside the pits, it was probably short term and in preservable form. Szuter (1989:332) cites ethnographic sources describing the drying and storing of rabbit meat among the Papago. Roadrunner and one carnivore bone are the only uncommon species from these pits. The absence of rodent remains suggests that these pits were closed off well when not in use.

Large Pits

About half of the large pits (diameter > 1.5 m) are burned or show intermittent signs of burning in the form of oxidized patches. The higher faunal counts, the greater variety of animal species, the higher frequency of burned bones, and the presence of rodent remains indicate more domestic activity. A total of 904 faunal specimens was recovered from 12 pits. Although the vast majority is lagomorphs/small mammals, artiodactyls are present to about the same degree as in the total assemblage.

In general, pits that contained higher numbers of large mammal remains also produced "unusual" remains, such as birds. For instance, Feature 863.01 yielded the highest number (n = 35) of artiodactyl specimens, as well as quail and roadrunner. Two bighorn bones were found in intramural pits in Feature 836; two hawk elements came from pit Feature 836.01. Several of these pits produced fish and Salientia, but no turtles. Although none of them were burned, their elements indicate that they may represent complete animals that were processed at the site. Desert tortoise remains, on the other hand, were burned. Burned bones generally are much more frequent in large pits than in bell-shaped pits, but are largely restricted to small mammals. Unburned Feature 390.16 contained birds, as well as deer teeth and antler fragments. While some of the bird remains are burned, the antler may have been stored for later use. The bottom portion of this pit appears straight-sided. Hackbarth (1993) suggests that large, cylindrical pits were the most frequent type of storage pit at post-Archaic sites (see also Fritz 1974). The same is likely at the Santa Cruz Bend site 3.2 km southeast of Los Pozos (Wöcherl 1998).

Small Pits

Twenty small pits (diameter < 1.5 m) contained faunal remains (NISP = 1,244). Half of the pits were burned or partially burned. Rodents are much more frequent than in other pit types, and since some of their remains are burned, they may constitute food waste. Pits with overall high counts of animal bone also contain higher numbers of artiodactyls. Large mammals are present in about the same proportion as in the assemblage as a whole. Identified artiodactyl remains include two pronghorn antelope, two bighorn sheep, four deer, and one mule deer. Feature 825.01 contained the highest number of artiodactyl remains (n = 33) and, in addition to lagomorphs, also produced a great variety of other species, including Salientia, mud turtles, rodents, and a possible carnivore. Some carnivore remains are burned, and the elements present suggest they are food waste. Quail is the most frequent bird remain, but duck, hawk, Corvidae, goatsuckers, and passerine birds are also represented. Feature 318.02 is one of the few contexts containing burned aquatic animals, including fish. Since the other faunal remains in this feature are unburned, the fish, frogs/toads, and turtle may well have been cooked.

Postholes

Postholes (n = 20) also produced faunal remains. Forty-two specimens from postholes are distributed between one to seven pieces per feature. Most postholes contained animal bone belonging to the general spectrum seen in the assemblage and follow the same pattern of burning. However, some features contained remains unusual in number, species, or element. Feature 333.48 produced a bead made from artiodactyl bone. The element could not be determined. Feature 840.02 produced seven specimens of unburned hawk-sized bird, which may belong to the same individual. Bird burials in pits are known from later sites in the Tucson Basin (e.g., University Indian Ruin; Romero Ruin; San Xavier Bridge). According to James (1994:280), hawk burials are more common than eagle burials, but raptor burials in general increase over time at pre-Classic and Classic Hohokam and Salado sites. To my knowledge, there are no references to bird burials in postholes. Although somewhat irregular in outline, Feature 840.02 does align with other features around the interior perimeter of the pit structure. The posthole was cut by a backhoe trench; consequently, its complete dimensions are not known. Other unusual remains from postholes include a nearly complete *Canis* sp. scapula. Dog remains have been found at other Early Agricultural sites, such as Coffee Camp (James 1993), and dog burials are known from sites of the same time period at the Donaldson site (Huckell 1995) and at Santa Cruz Bend (Thiel 1998). However, these burials are not in postholes, but in extramural pits. Perhaps most unusual is the find of five complete artiodactyl femoral heads in Feature 318.03. One of the bones is worked. Feature 337.28, another posthole, contained a single, polished artiodactyl femur head with red pigment. Five others were found in intramural pits; one on the floor of a pit structure (Feature 324). This suggests that these elements were placed intentionally and that their placement carried special meaning. The presence of red pigment, often a mark of special objects or circumstances, in features that do not contain ochre otherwise supports this interpretation.

Artifacts Associated with Intramural Features

Flaked Stone and Cobble Hammers. Only four intramural features with faunal remains also contained projectile points. All are large pits. Three of these produced unusual faunal assemblages. They contained rare animals, such as birds and tortoise. Deer teeth and antler were found in Feature 390.16, which yielded a San Pedro point made from the same material as a point on the floor of Feature 354, about 90 m to the northeast. An intramural pit in this structure produced bird and artiodactyl remains. Feature 867.01, a large and partially burned pit, contained a San Pedro point that was used as a knife (see Chapter 4, this volume). The faunal assemblage from this pit is unusual in terms of variety and numbers. It contained burned and very fragmented tortoise and bird remains, a larger proportion of cottontails, and nine artiodactyl specimens. Two cobble hammers were also recovered from this pit. The fragmented state of the faunal remains and the associated artifacts, as well as the partial burning of the pit, indicate that this feature may have been used for game processing. Another cobble hammer was found in a large sealed pit. Feature 355.09 contained almost exclusively fragmented lagomorph remains, again linking small mammal processing with the presence of cobble hammers. Only two hammers were found, one each, in small intramural pits. Both features contain relatively high numbers of small mammals, and Feature 825.01 also produced fragmented large mammal long bones. Associated with these are comparatively high counts of debitage, suggesting that some butchering may also have taken place indoors. With one exception (Feature 324.14), debitage counts in bell-shaped pits are generally low (range = 0-43). Counts in other intramural pits range from zero to almost 100. In many cases (45 percent), high debitage counts are correlated with high lagomorph/small mammal NISP, indicating skinning and dressing tasks.

Although very artifact-rich in terms of retouched flaked stone, no faunal remains were associated with Feature 819.17. No projectile points were found in postholes. However, one posthole (Feature 840.13) produced 80 pieces of debitage; other postholes contained none, or only up to five pieces. The few faunal remains from Feature 840.13 do not support an alternative classification of the feature as a small intramural pit.

Ground Stone. While intramural pits with high counts of lagomorph and small mammal remains do contain ground stone implements, the same types of implements are also present in features without faunal remains. Bone fragmentation in pits with ground stone follows the same pattern as in contexts lacking ground stone. Burning and body part representation do not vary with the presence of ground stone. However, two ground stone tools from pits were analyzed as hide processing tools (see Chapter 5, this volume) and were found in pits with high lagomorph/small mammal counts. Thus, several uses of these small animals may have taken place in the same structure and in or near its pit. Uses would include skinning, other preparation for consumption, possibly consumption, and hide processing.

Fire-cracked Rock. In contrast to pit structure fill and floors, there is a clear correlation between fire-cracked rock and faunal remains in intramural pits. Features that contained high numbers of animal bone, most of which are lagomorphs and small mammals, also produced the highest counts of fire-cracked rocks. The vast majority of these pits also show signs of burning, suggesting that animal food may have been prepared in them. The Yavapai prepared rabbits by either cooking in ashes, boiling, or by "skinning, charring slightly, and hanging up" (Gifford 1936:266). The first two methods could have been used in many of the intramural pits described above, using sharp, non-retouched flakes for skinning. The third treatment is also likely to have been used at Los Pozos, since most lagomorph remains are charred slightly rather than completely. Additionally, the desert climate is ideal for drying and preserving dried meat.

Shell. With general counts per feature of one to two, Features 390.16 (n = 7) and 836.01 (n = 15) stand out. Both are large pits and contain unusual faunal remains. In Feature 390.16, the shell may be associated with the remains of birds, deer teeth, and antler, while Feature 836.01 contained hawk remains. Assuming that the presence of shell signals special circumstances, these two features are again marked as unusual.

Ceramics. Pottery sherds were found in five intramural pits, including Feature 390.16. With the exception of Feature 815.05, a bell-shaped pit, these features contain faunal remains other than small and large mammals. Less frequent remains include birds, carnivores, and identified bighorn sheep.

Extramural Space

No large trash deposits or middens were discovered within the right-of-way. Pit structures that were no longer in use may have served as trash dumps. The high frequency of charred, fragmented faunal remains in pit structure fill (Stratum 10) supports this interpretation.

No trash pits were identified. Other extramural pits containing faunal remains can be divided into five categories: bell-shaped pits (n = 6), large pits (n = 12), small pits (n = 20), roasting pits (n = 2), and wells (n = 1). Only one bell-shaped pit, containing three lagomorph elements, was found extramurally (Feature 408). The single large pit (Feature 346) produced mainly lagomorph legs, all unburned. Other faunal remains are from desert tortoise, unburned, but encrusted with calcium carbonate; four unburned artiodactyl elements; and the axis vertebra of a carnivore. This bone was burned, as well as encrusted, indicating its probable cultural modification at the time of Los Pozos' occupation.

Small pits (n = 6) also contained a number of different species, although the variation is not as great as for intramural pits. Birds (n = 3) are represented in two pits (Features 329, 330) by quail, hawk, and a possible duck fragment. Rodents are very rare. Most remains are lagomorphs, particularly jackrabbits. They are generally unburned, and some pits contain enough variable elements to suggest that whole animals were processed. Artiodactyls are also well represented. As with intramural pits, those features that contain species other than lagomorphs and artiodactyls also produce uncommon remains. For instance, in addition to lagomorph remains, a small pit (Feature 330) contained quail remains, bones of two possible carnivores, and 20 artiodactyl bones. Two of the latter were ocher-stained, as were two lagomorph bones and the scapula of a large-to-medium mammal, another possible carnivore. One of the stained artiodactyl bones may be worked.

Among the special use pits are roasting pits. Only two such pits were excavated, and only one produced the predicted burned faunal remains. Feature 421 contained mainly lagomorph elements, almost all lightly burned. It also contained an unburned fragment of a bobcat leg. The other roasting pit produced only three artiodactyl bones, highly fragmented, but unburned. Wells are another type of special use pit. One well contained some charred faunal remains, suggesting that household waste found its way into the well.

Artifacts Associated with Extramural Features

Flaked Stone and Cobble Hammers. No cobble hammers were found in extramural contexts. However, the correlation in intramural pits between debitage and lagomorph remains may exist outdoors as well. Two extramural pits contained debitage, and both had a high lagomorph NISP. Feature 421, a roasting pit, contained almost exclusively lagomorphs. Only one extramural feature contained a projectile point.

Feature 408 is the only exterior bell-shaped pit; it produced the tip of an Archaic point and few whole-body lagomorph remains.

Ground Stone. Twenty-six pieces of ground stone were recovered from 17 extramural pits. However, only six of these features contained faunal remains. No correlations were found between animal bone and ground stone artifacts. Specific uses relating to faunal processing were not determined.

Fire-cracked Rock. The same correlation between fire-cracked rock and faunal remains found in intramural pits applies to extramural features: pits with large numbers of lagomorph remains contain the highest rock counts. Feature 373, a well, is the exception. It contains only five animal bones, but produced the largest number of fire-cracked rocks. The well may have become unproductive and then used as a disposal for cooking stones.

Shell. A total of seven shell artifacts was recovered from five extramural features. Only one feature also contained faunal remains. Although among extramural pits Feature 346 produced by far the highest number of animal bone (NISP = 145), the remains themselves are not unusual. The vast majority are unburned lagomorph bones.

Intramural vs. Extramural Features

Postholes and wells were not included in the following comparison.

The main difference in faunal remains between the two types of features lies in faunal elements. Almost half of the elements in extramural pits are rear legs and feet, compared to about 20 percent in interior pits. This is true for both large and small mammals. Although sample size (see Table 10.4) may have an effect, human behavior may account for the differences in element distributions. In terms of artiodactyls, this difference suggests that more activities relating to meat removal after field-butchering took place outdoors. Szuter (1989:332) cites ethnographic sources that report formal meat distribution systems among the Tewa and Havasupai. Since rear feet and legs are the most frequent artiodactyl elements at Los Pozos, their processing in extramural space may relate to the communal sharing of successful hunts.

While skull fragments are absent in both types of pits, antler is present only in intramural contexts, suggesting it was a valuable item, kept in private space. Parts of the cranium proper, however, are somewhat more frequent in extramural pits as a result of whole lagomorph carcass processing. The lower incidence of fragmented long bone shafts in extramural contexts may indicate that final processing, such as marrow extraction, took place indoors after shares had been received. Indoor processing is not only spatially constrained, and thus likely to leave spatially contained remains, but it also has an effect on patterns of consumption and their visibility during the occupation of a site. The fact that associations of debitage with lagomorph remains and cobble hammers with fragmented small and large mammal remains are much stronger in intramural pits supports the interpretation of a functional differentiation of indoor-outdoor space with potential social ramifications.

RESOURCE SELECTION AND USE

All the species recovered at Los Pozos occur in the greater Tucson Basin today. The resource potential of the great variety of habitats within easy reach of Los Pozos is described in Chapter 9. All of these environments were exploited to some degree, and many species could have been hunted or collected during other activities away from the site. In the following discussion, faunal remains present at Los Pozos are compared with the actual resource potential to arrive at conclusions about prehistoric resource selections.

Resource Potential Exploited

Although represented only by small numbers, aquatic and riparian species were probably consumed. For example, it is unlikely that entire fish are intrusive in pit structures and intramural pits. Bird remains are comparatively frequent, and various species would have been attracted to river-edge trees, grassland, and desertscrub/mesquite bosques in the site vicinity. Raptors, present in relatively high proportions, would have found roosts in the intermittent gallery forest along the Santa Cruz. They would have had plenty of prey in the form of birds, rodents, and lagomorphs occupying the grassland and desertscrub areas. Cottontails and jackrabbits were available due to the probable presence of both open areas and ground cover. The proximity of the river and the preferred habitats attracted these species which breed prolifically and practically year-round. These characteristics make lagomorphs an attractive resource, both in terms of availability and ease of procurement, explaining their large proportions in the Los Pozos assemblage.

Rodents may also have been collected during activities outside of the village. Conversely, they may represent the remains of unwelcome visitors to pit structures and storage pits, and they may have been caught there. Rodents did not form a major part of the diet of Early Agricultural people as they did for the later Hohokam. Rodent remains are relatively infrequent at Los Pozos, and few are burned. Some rodents, such as pocket mice, prefer grassland habitats (Hoffmeister 1986), where they would have been carnivore prey.

Other grassland prey, for both carnivores and humans, would have been antelope. As is the case with most large game near human settlements, antelope was probably not often present on the grassland

Table 10.6. Faunal ratios for selected Early Agricultural sites in southern Arizona.

Site	Artiodactyls/ Artiodactyls + Lagomorphs	*Sylvilagus/Lepus*	Large/Small
Coffee Camp[a]	.03	.04	.13
Donaldson[a]	.16	.07	1.32
Fairchild (AZ FF:10:2)[a]	0	.11	.35
Los Pozos	.11	.26	.22
Santa Cruz Bend[a]	.16	.28	.39
Stone Pipe[a]	.04	.33	.15
Wetlands (AZ AA:12:90)	.12	.37	.35

[a]From Thiel (1996).

immediately around Los Pozos, but would have been procured further away. The low numbers of pronghorn reflect the greater procurement cost, possibly balanced when antelope was hunted in interior chaparral as an embedded activity of deer hunts. Most artiodactyl remains at Los Pozos are deer (*Odocoileus* sp.). Although the animals were surely attracted to the river for its water and the forest browse, many were probably procured in the mountain ranges east and west of the Santa Cruz Valley. Deer occur in both the Santa Catalina Mountains and the Tucson Mountains. Bighorn sheep were found in both mountain ranges historically (James R. Heffelfinger, personal communication 1996) and are present at Los Pozos.

In summary, a number of resources, including riparian resources, were exploited close to home. The emphasis, however, was on lagomorphs and artiodactyls. While both could be found near the site, some artiodactyls, such as white-tailed deer and bighorn sheep, had to be procured further away. Although most artiodactyls and large mammals–other than antelope and bighorn sheep–could not be identified to species, the homogeneous patterns of body part representation at Los Pozos suggests that one artiodactyl species was the hunting focus. Since mule deer are the most prolific, least habitat-specific, and occurs with the highest density, *Odocoileus hemionus* was likely the species hunted most often.

Body part representation indicates that hunters did not always bring back whole carcasses, but that they only took choice pieces. Rear feet and legs, the most frequent large mammal body parts at Los Pozos, fall into this category. They provide good meat, long-bone marrow, bone suited for bone tools, and tendons for hafting tasks. They also contain the most body fat during those times when the animal is nutritionally stressed, and they are easily transported. Ethnographic sources describe non-meat uses of artiodactyl body parts. Castetter and Underhill (1935:41) report that tendons were used, perhaps for hafting and other tasks that needed tying, brains were used for hide-tanning, and fat was used as a base for paints. The Havasupai

used spinal marrow for tanning; antlers were used as picks and as flakers, dewclaws were made into rattles, and sinew was strung on bows (Spier 1928). The fragmentation of artiodactyl long bones in particular, indicates that faunal resources were used intensively, extracting all useable portions. Burned pits and fire-cracked rock indicate that resources were cooked, and that bone grease may have been rendered. The high numbers of fire-cracked rocks disposed of in abandoned pit structures suggest that cooking with hot stones was an important method of resource preparation.

Dietary Contributions of Different Taxa

Fishes, amphibians, reptiles, birds, rodents, and carnivores comprise between .2 and 1.5 percent of NISP. Some of these animals may not have been consumed. In contrast, small mammals represent almost 80 percent of all faunal remains. By comparison, artiodactyls and large mammals account for nearly 17 percent (see Table 10.1), the second highest percentage. This focus on two taxa groups is known from other Early Agricultural sites (Thiel 1998). Table 10.6 compares the faunal ratios of seven Early Agricultural sites in southern Arizona. The ratio of large to small mammals (L/S) also reflects the emphasis on small game. Although artiodactyls at Los Pozos occur much less frequently than lagomorphs, the artiodactyl index (A/A+L) indicates that Los Pozos occupants obtained many artiodactyls. Comparisons of the ratio of cottontails (*Sylvilagus* sp.) to jackrabbits (two species of *Lepus*) have been used to reconstruct prehistoric environments. While cottontails prefer protective ground cover, jackrabbits thrive in open areas with intermittent clumps of vegetation (e.g., Bayham and Hatch 1984). At Los Pozos, the number of cottontails is higher than at a number of other Early Agricultural sites, suggesting that both types of vegetation existed in the vicinity. Ethnographic sources report that cottontails were preferred over jackrabbits, as food, by historic Papago

Table 10.7. Meat weight (kg) estimates for three Early Agricultural (Cienega phase) sites in the Middle Santa Cruz Valley (percent in parentheses).

Site	*Sylvilagus*	*Lepus*	Artiodactyl	Total Meat Weight
Los Pozos	3.16 kg (.8)	23.76 kg (6.0)	362.88 kg (93.0)	390.0
Santa Cruz Bend[a]	10.27 kg (3.0)	42.16 kg (13.0)	181.44 kg (84.0)	233.9
Stone Pipe[a]	7.9 kg (12.0)	13.60 kg (20.0)	45.36 kg (68.0)	66.9

[a]From Thiel (1996).

(Castetter and Bell 1942:66). Food preferences thus provide an alternative explanation of the relatively high proportion of cottontails at Los Pozos.

Cost-Yield Analysis

The pursuit of large game, especially far from home, carries costs that small game procurement does not incur. Since abundant small game and plant resources were available to Los Pozos occupants within a relatively small radius, the selection for artiodactyls must be explained. Bayham (1979:223) states that the natural availability of a prey species does not change its preference rank. Species are ranked by their food value and processing time. Since the simple calculation of contribution of protein oversimplifies the importance of a species (Bayham 1979), a number of aspects such as amount of meat, pursuit costs, transport, processing, and non-food byproducts, must be considered to determine a species' rank and thus, the probability of selection.

Protein and Fat

Meat weight estimates provide another perspective on the importance of species. Following White (1953), estimates of meat weight were established, using MNI calculations. As Grayson (1984) stated, MNI counts cannot control for sexual dimorphism or seasonal variations, and must be used with caution. With respect to meat weight, MNI counts can provide rough estimates of the minimum amount of meat available from the archaeofauna recovered (Cairns and Ciolek-Torrello 1998). Standards of "useable meat per individual" are based on average modern individuals of southern Arizona species (Cairns and Ciolek-Torrello 1998:Table 8.5). Based on these estimates, Table 10.7 shows that over 90 percent of all meat consumed at Los Pozos came from large mammals. In spite of their high NISP, small mammals simply do not provide much meat per individual animal. This is particularly true of cottontails as opposed to jackrabbits, and to antelope jackrabbits in particular. If meat and other animal products are a subsistence focus, the pursuit of large game, even far from home, is unavoidable.

The main effect of season on game are changes in the nutritional value of the meat. Late winter/early spring animals are particularly meager. Since a diet of lean meat leads to so-called "rabbit starvation," the Papago would not hunt deer in January or in February, "when they smelled bad" (Underhill 1946:86). Ethnographic evidence indicates that hunter-gatherers may shift to species that maintain higher fat levels during the winter, such as waterfowl and beaver (Speth 1983:158). Although duck, and possibly muskrat, are present at Los Pozos, they occur in very small numbers.

Early Agricultural people may have dealt with nutritional stress in other ways, while maintaining their focal resources. Fat, the lacking nutrient, is depleted last in an ungulate's lower legs and feet (Speth 1983). The needed nutrient could have been obtained by extracting marrow from the frequent foot and leg bones at sites like Los Pozos. Bone grease rendered from the abundant shaft fragments would have provided additional fat. This could have been accomplished in boiling water heated, with the now fire-cracked rock found in large numbers at Los Pozos. According to Castetter and Underhill (1935:40), the Papago processed fat in the winter. Thus, the use of large game was predictable for Los Pozos occupants in a number of ways. The Santa Cruz River and its effects on surrounding areas attracted game close to the site. Lacking seasonal migrations, even game further away was predictable in terms of location. Finally, periods of nutritional stress followed a seasonal pattern that could be safeguarded against through cultural behaviors.

Energy Yield

To arrive at the "net energy gain" of a species, Bayham (1979:219) suggests that the meat gained be compared to the energy expended in capture. An expanded assessment of costs and yields would also include time spent butchering in the field, transport, and processing in camp or in the village. Simms (1987:45) presents energy return rates for Great Basin animal species, many of which are the same as those at

Los Pozos. He includes "handling time" (pursuit + infield butchering for transport) in his calculations. Artiodactyls, deer, and bighorn sheep in particular, rank by far the highest with return rates of 15,725-31,450 calories per hour. Antelope has a lower return rate by comparison. At Los Pozos, the small number of antelope may also be explained by the species' unpredictability. Although common in the valleys of southern Arizona, antelope was not considered a dependable food source (Castetter and Bell 1942:65). The low return for antelope is followed closely by jackrabbits at 13,475-15,400 calories per hour. At lower caloric yield, pursuit and butchering time is about the same as for deer and bighorn. Cottontails clearly yield the least energy of those species common at Los Pozos (8,983-9,800 calories per hour). Perhaps taste preferences, as described earlier, or ease of "collection" as an embedded activity such as trapping, explains their comparatively high numbers at the site. However, the result of distance and weight, as well as transport costs, are difficult to calculate. Some transport cost can be estimated by comparing distances, energy expended in walking, and energy return from food.

According to Kelly (1995:133), a leisurely pace across three km burns about 300 calories. If the person is carrying food, the rate increases by 30 percent. Thus, a one-km walk, carrying food, requires 130 kilocalories from the walker. Using Simms' (1987:45) caloric values of animal species, an artiodactyl provides about 12.6 kilocalories per kg. A one-km walk, carrying food, would require 10.3 kg of venison to recuperate the energy expended. A Great Basin study determined a load of about 20 kg to be a reasonable weight to carry at a leisurely pace (Jones and Madsen 1989). The distance to the two upland sources of artiodactyls near Los Pozos, the Santa Catalina and the Tucson Mountains, is about 11 km and 8 km, respectively. Assuming that food was provided for travel to the mountain ranges, a trip to the Tucson Mountains requires four loads of 20 kg of venison simply to recuperate the energy expended on the trip back. A trip from the Catalina Mountains would require 5.7 loads. Thus, a party of four hunters in the Tucson Mountains would have been needed to cover transport cost. To make the venture worthwhile, hunters would either have to carry significantly heavier loads, or task group size would have to be increased.

Hunting and Biomass

Assuming that game does not occur in large herds, two factors argue in favor of small task groups: a) hunters can, and do, eat at the kill site, so their caloric requirements for the trip home are covered, or even exceeded, leaving the transported food to nourish the other villagers; and b) in spite of ethnographic reports

on the tradition of communal hunting (e.g. Szuter 1989), success rates for large game are higher for solitary hunters (Speth 1983). Average hunting success is another critical factor in determining the value of a food species. Ethnographic reports conflict in their accounts of yearly returns of deer (see Szuter 1989:330). For instance, a rate of 12 deer per year was considered good for the Papago (Underhill 1946:86), and each hunter supplied meat for 2-10 families (Underhill 1939:99). Seasonal variations of hunting success would add another limiting factor to game availability. However, since artiodactyls in southern Arizona do not have true seasonal migrations (Welch 1960), they are in relatively predictable locations year-round. Deer densities vary by location and life zone. Reported densities for deer in southern Arizona vary greatly, with estimates as high as 20 per mi^2 (Hanson 1954:16). An average density for the Tucson Basin is 12 deer per mi^2 (2.6 km^2) (James R. Heffelfinger, personal communication 1996). Thus, within a 50-km radius, the density is 231 deer; within a 100-km radius, 462 deer. According to many ethnographic sources compiled by Kelly (1995:133), hunter-gatherers will move camp when hunting failure within a 5-6 km radius becomes unacceptable. This radius corresponds to a 20-30 km daily round trip in a variety of environments. From Los Pozos, both upland source areas for deer and bighorn sheep can be reached; hunted, foraged, and gathered; and returned from, in a day trip. Due to the site's location on the river however, such trips may not have been necessary on a frequent basis. Based on an average density of 12 deer per mi^2, 24 deer could have been found within a 5-km radius around Los Pozos. Since game is generally frightened away from settlements, a 5-km radius may not have been productive. The density within a 10-km radius would be 48 deer, within a 20-km radius, 96 deer. Due to the permanence of pit structures, moving camp when resources become scarcer near home may not have been as much of an option as it is for extant hunter-gatherers, who often build no, or very temporary, shelters.

Co-variation with Plant Use

Similar to Bayham's (1979) conclusions on prey rank based on yield for animal species, the most ubiquitous plants at Los Pozos also provide the greatest energy returns (Chapter 9, this volume). Focal wild plant resources for Los Pozos occupants were cheno-ams, tansy mustard, Gramineae, mesquite, maize, and saguaro fruit (Chapter 9, this volume). Emphasis on annuals, maize in particular, indicates a planned harvest/collection strategy that could easily have been combined with trapping, snaring, and other embedded procurement techniques for lagomorphs. Gathering of key plant resources also lead gatherers to the various life zones within walking distance from the site, where supplemental animals could be procured.

Models of Early Agricultural land use fall into two main categories. Huckell (1995) suggests that floodplain villages were fully sedentary for most of the year, if not the entire year, and that their dependence on agricultural products was supplemented by wild plants and animals. Conversely, Roth (1989, 1992, 1995b) describes contemporary groups that focus on upper bajada resources, and have residential camps there, and lowland groups who live mainly, but not permanently on the floodplain, supplementing their diet with cactus fruit and game from bajada sites. Residentially mobile groups (Roth 1992) spend fall and winter at higher elevations, relying on transported surplus and hunting. They move to the floodplain in the summer, harvesting cactus fruit on the way.

At Los Pozos, faunal remains, in combination with plant identifications, indicate that forays into montane life zones did occur. Bighorn sheep and juniper seeds could only be obtained at higher elevations. Both types of remains are scant however, and no other elevationally sensitive, montane species were recovered. The presence of cactus fruit indicates upper bajada resources were also exploited. Further, all animal species in the assemblage can occur at elevations above the floodplain; 5,000 ft is the limit for many. Since all species represented inhabit the floodplain and adjacent habitats within a day's reach, further logistical forays may have been organized when particular resources were needed for nutritional or other reasons. Seasonal food stresses may represent such a reason.

Macrobotanical evidence of maize cultivation suggests at least a summer presence at Los Pozos. This would be consistent with models that propose a summer residential move to the floodplain. The strong emphasis on locally available, storable wild plant resources, in combination with stored maize, permanent housing, and a large faunal assemblage may suggest a presence at the site for more than the summer. The presence of saguaro fruit can be explained as one type of seasonal return from logistical task groups to the bajada(s). The majority of faunal remains at Los Pozos are inconclusive markers of seasonality. Deer, mule deer in particular, can be hunted year-round, and "there appears to be some breeding throughout the year." (McCulloch 1954:2) The cut or shed status of antler from Los Pozos could not be determined. With the exception of high elevation varieties of cottontail rabbits (cf. *Sylvilagus nuttalii*), southern Arizona lagomorphs breed year-round. Thus, for both artiodactyls and lagomorphs, the presence of juveniles and even of neonates does not indicate season of death. Only one species from Los Pozos is a seasonal marker. However, it must be kept in mind that the animal may not have

found its way into the assemblage at the time of its death, or that it may have been transported to the site from elsewhere. The sharp shinned hawk, *Accipiter striatus*, "winters commonly in southern and western Arizona, uncommonly on the Mogollon Plateau." (Lowe 1964:189) Two elements of the hawk were recovered from a large intramural pit (Feature 836.01), which also contained 14 artiodactyl and many jackrabbit remains. A winter visitor, the hawk may signal a cold season, and therefore year-round, occupation at Los Pozos.

INTER-SITE VARIATION

Before comparing Los Pozos to other Early Agricultural sites, the comparability of faunal assemblages must be established. Assuming that taphonomic factors in the floodplain are equal, assemblage fragmentation is a good indicator of comparability. Table 10.3 showed that Los Pozos, Santa Cruz Bend, Stone Pipe, and recently excavated Wetlands (Freeman 1998) have very similar fragmentation profiles. Most faunal specimens are present at less than 25 percent. The similar patterns also indicate that sample size (NISP) does not affect fragmentation, rather, bone breakage is a result of other factors. Similar recovery methods may result in similar fragmentation rates, but cannot be solely responsible. Although excavated with the same basic techniques, the I-10 sites for instance, presented with different primary matrices, different degrees of bioturbation, and varying extent of calcium carbonate encrustation of bone (see Mabry 1997; Thiel 1998), but with similar fragmentation profiles. Thus, prehistoric cultural factors are reflected in bone fragmentation from the sites under discussion, are similar across sites, and establish assemblage comparability for Early Agricultural sites along the Middle Santa Cruz. Comparisons with sites for which fragmentation profiles are unknown must be regarded with more caution.

Resource Selection

Bayham and Hatch (1985:421) suggest that the proportions of cottontails and jackrabbits in an assemblage are, "probably a good reflection of their local availability," and that, due to the clear habitat preferences of the species, the,"relative abundance of these two species in a faunal assemblage can be used as an index of the amount of prehistorically available cover." Cottontails will not be as numerous in the open, alluvial plains. Therefore, if the ratio of jackrabbits to cottontails is incongruent with other environmental indicators, alternative explanations of frequencies must be sought.

Table 10.8. Comparison of frequencies (NISP) and ratios of cottontails (*Sylvilagus*) and jackrabbits (*Lepus*) at five Early Agricultural sites (percentages in parentheses).

Species	Los Pozos	Santa Cruz Bend	Stone Pipe	Wetlands	Coffee Camp	Donaldson Eddy and Cooley (1983)	Huckell (1995)	Szuter and Bayham (1995)
Cottontail	532 (26.2)	392 (29.5)	153 (31.2)	123 (37.1)	29 (4.3)	2 (7.0)	18 (38.0)	15 (.7)
Jackrabbit	1,490 (73.3)	921 (70.2)	290 (59.0)	210 (63.0)	535 (78.4)	25 (93.0)	30 (62.5)	22 (10.5)
Cottontails + jackrabbits	2,022	1,313	443	333	564	27	48	37
Rabbits and hares	11 (.5)	17 (1.3)	48 (10.7)	2 (.6)	118 (17.3)	0	0	172 (82.3)
Total lagomorphs	2,033	1,330	491	335	682	27	48	209
Jackrabbits: cottontails	2.8	2.4	1.9	1.7	18.2	13.5	1.6	1.5

Table 10.8 compares the ratio of jackrabbits to cottontails at six Early Agricultural sites. Coffee Camp shows the most outstanding ratio of more than 18 jackrabbits to 1 cottontail. This ratio can be explained by environmental characteristics of the site. Coffee Camp lies in the Santa Cruz Flats, an expansive, open area of low elevation southwest of the Picacho Mountains. The main drainages are Greene Canal and the Santa Cruz River, which provided narrow riparian zones. The open desertscrub habitat is preferred by jackrabbits. The unusually high ratio of jackrabbits at Coffee Camp corresponds to other site characteristics that may also relate to the environmental setting. In contrast to other sites listed in Table 10.8, no maize was found at Coffee Camp. James (1993:365) suggests that intensive animal processing was a focal site activity, due to subsistence stress.

The Donaldson site has the second highest jack-rabbit:cottontail ratio of 13 to 1. However, as Table 10.8 indicates, the ratio is heavily dependent on the particular sample examined. In Eddy and Cooley's (1983) report on Eddy's 1958 findings, jackrabbits represent 93 percent of all lagomorphs recovered. Later reports by Huckell (1995) and Szuter and Bayham (1995) list different NISPs for lagomorph species, resulting in lagomorph ratios much closer to, and even lower than those at other sites. The lower rate reflects the site's environment, since the site lies in a drainage with significant riparian vegetation.

At comparable sample sizes, the I-10 sites along the Middle Santa Cruz River show ratios of about 1.5 to 3 jackrabbits to cottontail. If Bayham and Hatch (1984) are correct in assuming that lagomorph ratios reflect a site's environment, the similar ratios for the I-10 sites and Wetlands indicate that in these reaches of the Santa Cruz, both open areas and places with more ground cover could be found. Assuming that cottontails were preferred dietarily (Castetter and Bell 1942:66), higher jackrabbit counts in places where both species were present may indicate general availability and/or may be the result of human procurement techniques better adapted to the acquisition of jackrabbits.

Taxonomic Richness

The number of animal species and taxa groups present in an assemblage is an important indicator of the relationship between the environmental resource potential and the fauna actually exploited. Figure 10.6 compares the number of taxa groups (birds, rodents, and so on), with site NISP at five Early Agricultural sites. Four of these sites lie in close proximity along the Santa Cruz River, and presumably shared most environmental and faunal habitats, as well as approximate travel times to more distant resources. However, the sites do not group together. Table 10.9 lists faunal diversity ratios for seven Early Agricultural sites. The ratio is calculated by dividing the number of distinct species by NISP. Plotted graphically, it is evident that faunal diversity is at least partly dependent on sample size. Figure 10.7 clearly shows that sites do not group environmentally, but that sites with larger samples also have higher species diversity.

Both Los Pozos and Santa Cruz Bend are at the high end of species diversity and produced large samples. In the case of Coffee Camp, the low number of species from a large assemblage may be explained by the site's processing focus centering on lagomorphs and artiodactyls almost exclusively. A similar explanation may apply to Ventana Cave, Levels 4 and 5. Compared with Los Pozos and Santa Cruz Bend, cave strata dated to the Early Agricultural period produced small samples and few taxa. Bayham (1982) suggests that while the cave was often frequented in earlier times, it was used as a specialized and temporary camp for logistical task groups during the Early Agricultural. The higher number of species, compared to small sample sites at lower elevations may result from upland taxonomic diversity. It could also result from better preservation,

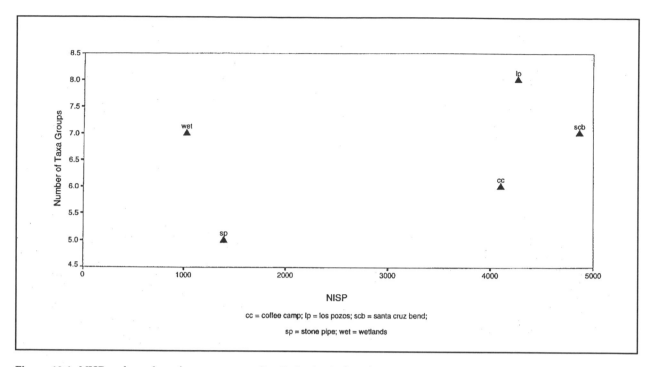

Figure 10.6. NISP and number of taxa groups at five Early Agricultural sites in southern Arizona.

Table 10.9. Faunal diversity ratios for selected Early Agricultural sites in southern Arizona.

Site Name or Number	Number of Species	NISP	Diversity Ratio
Coffee Camp[a]	13	4,103	.003
Donaldson[b]	11	1,058	.010
Los Pozos	29	4,018	.007
Santa Cruz Bend[a]	22	4,861	.004
Stone Pipe[a]	10	1,398	.007
Ventana Cave, Level 4[b]	15	604	.025
Ventana Cave, Level 5[b]	13	295	.044
Wetlands	16	1,049	.015

[a]From Thiel (1996).
[b]From Szuter and Bayham (1995).

and thus better identifiability, in a protected cave environment.

While the Wetlands, Stone Pipe, and Donaldson sites are located in areas with access to various habitats and rich faunal resources, their faunal diversity is comparatively low. Since the Wetlands and Stone pipe sites lie in the same general environment as Los Pozos, their smaller NISP may explain the diversity ratios. Thiel (1998) suggests that length of occupation and the presence and number of agricultural fields also affect diversity ratios. While Los Pozos certainly has a longer occupation span (Chapter 11, this volume) than Santa Cruz Bend or Stone Pipe, radiocarbon dates at Wetlands also span about 500 years or more (Freeman 1998). Because it is the earliest site among the Early

Agricultural sites along Interstate-10, Wetlands' faunal remains may not be as well preserved as those at other sites. Additionally, the clayey matrix in many Wetlands features may have increased recovery damage to the animal bone, thereby decreasing identifiability (Jenny Waters, personal communication 1996).

Dietary Contributions of Different Taxa

Table 10.6 presents faunal indices for seven Early Agricultural period sites. Artiodactyls appear in similar proportions at all sites, except Coffee Camp and the Stone Pipe sites. Small mammals are the focus at these sites. Large mammals feature predominantly at the

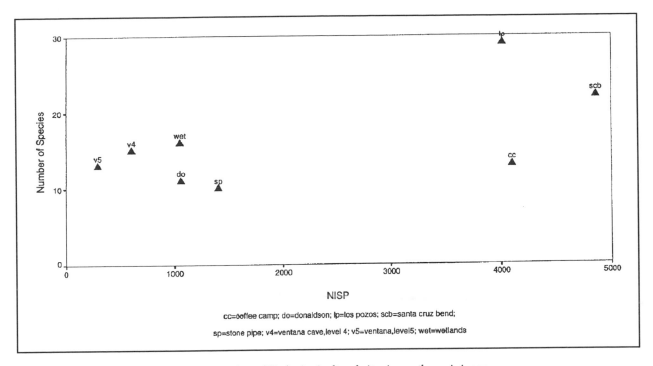

Figure 10.7. NISP and faunal diversity at selected Early Agricultural sites in southern Arizona.

Donaldson site. Situated in a comparatively smaller drainage with riparian environments and other life zones in very close proximity, artiodactyls and other large mammals may have been highly accessible, more so than at Los Pozos or other I-10 sites. Percentages of lagomorphs and artiodactyls at five of the above sites are plotted in Figures 10.8 and 10.9. Among the I-10 sites, Santa Cruz Bend has the highest percentage of artiodactyls, Stone Pipe the highest percentage of lagomorphs. Los Pozos appears mid-field with a slight preponderance of artiodactyls.

Comparing artiodactyl and lagomorph proportions simultaneously, Figure 10.10 indicates Stone Pipe and Coffee Camp are quite similar. The high lagomorph counts at Coffee Camp have been explained through environmental factors which strongly favored lagomorphs, jackrabbits in particular. The same environmental attributes cannot be invoked for Stone Pipe, which has a relatively high cottontail ratio (see Table 10.8). Wetlands, Santa Cruz Bend, and Los Pozos all have similar percentages of small and large mammals. Santa Cruz Bend shows the highest percentage of artiodactyls, possibly due to well-preserved intramural caches containing antler and horn. Large game certainly provided a higher percentage of dietary meat at Los Pozos (see Table 10.7).

Reptiles were recovered at Santa Cruz Bend, but not at Stone Pipe. Along with the presence of water duck, these species indicate that aquatic environments were exploited at some I-10 sites, but not at others. In terms of other bird remains, Santa Cruz Bend and Los Pozos are more similar to each other. Only two bird specimens were found at Stone Pipe, both of them probably quail. In spite of extensive rodent disturbances in the more silty matrix, rodent counts are lower at Santa Cruz Bend than at Los Pozos, and the most common species is pocket gopher (*Thomomys* sp.), as opposed to pocket mouse (*Perognathus* sp.). The former is a more likely food species due to its size, but both may have been consumed.

Storage and processing facilities, as well as projectile points and ground stone artifacts, were found at all the I-10 sites. Combined with similar fragmentation profiles, these patterns suggest animal resources were used intensively. However, estimates of total meat weight available (Table 10.7) indicate that inhabitants at sites dating to the later part of the Early Agricultural, such as Stone Pipe, acquired substantially less meat.

Co-variation with Plant Use

Wild plant resources at Early Agricultural sites in the Middle Santa Cruz Valley were collected from several biotic communities. Aside from riparian species, disturbance plants such as chenopods and amaranth, were also exploited. The latter grow in extensive stands providing large quantities of seeds in a circumscribed area (L. Huckell 1998). Since the seeds can be harvested by simple means, cheno-ams, tansy mustard,

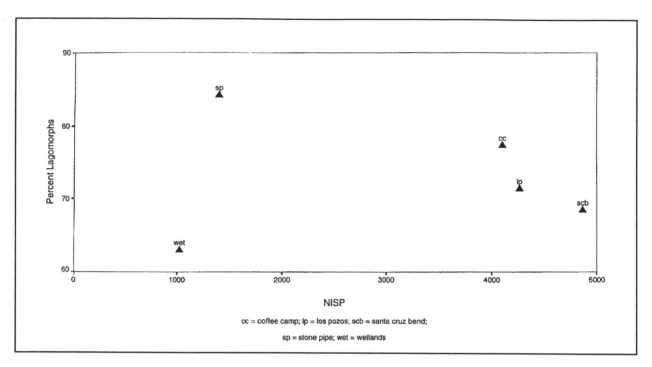

Figure 10.8. Percent of lagomorphs and NISP at five Early Agricultural sites in southern Arizona.

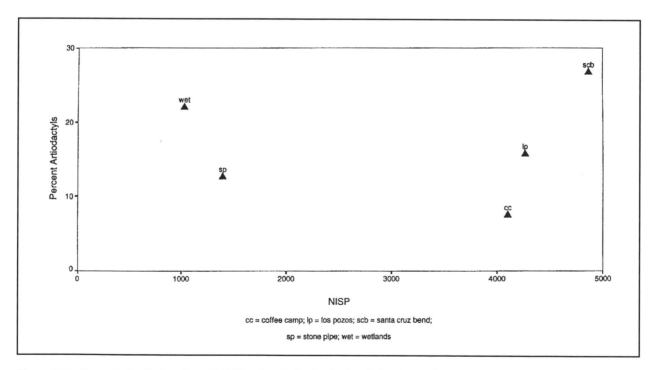

Figure 10.9. Percent of artiodactyls and NISP at five Early Agricultural sites in southern Arizona.

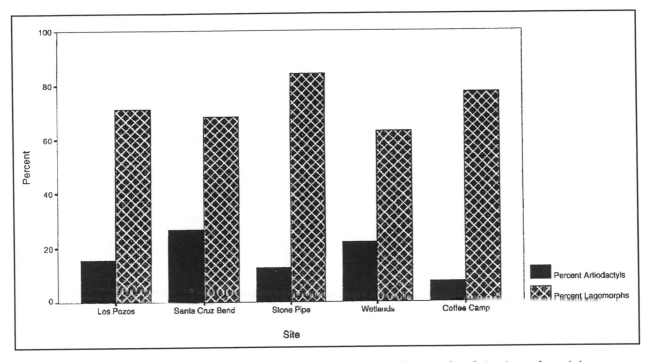

Figure 10.10. Comparison of percentages of artiodactyls and NISP at five Early Agricultural sites in southern Arizona.

and horse purslane may have been an important dietary element (L. Huckell 1998). Their pervasive presence supports this interpretation. Along with the collection of such wild plants and seeds, lagomorphs and other small mammals could have easily been procured as an embedded activity. Large, probably predictable stands, would have created set locations to be targeted and revisited. Ethnographic sources (cited in Szuter 1989:327-29) describe hunting with rocks or sticks, bow and arrow, trapping, and/or simply running the animal down. Wormington (1944:38) reports that Basketmaker people used snares made from human hair. Few such "weapons" preserve archaeologically, but small projectile points were found at the I-10 sites. Large task group gathering activities may have been complementary with communal hunts, which are reported ethnographically, particularly for lagomorphs (Spier 1928:121).

Higher elevation plants were also collected. Saguaro fruit remains in the form of seeds from Los Pozos demonstrate bajada use, as do prickly pear and cholla (*Opuntia* spp.) at the I-10 sites, however in modest amounts (L. Huckell 1998). Mule deer, found in comparatively high numbers at Santa Cruz Bend, would have been frequent in this environment. Upland plant remains other than agave were thought lacking at central basin sites (L. Huckell 1998), until the recovery of juniper at Los Pozos. Available in the nearby foothills and mountain ranges, the acquisition of higher

elevation species would have afforded gathering trips that could have incorporated artiodactyl procurement. White-tailed deer and bighorn sheep, found at the I-10 sites, Los Pozos, and Wetlands, as well as black bear recovered at Santa Cruz Bend, could have been hunted during such logistical trips.

Along the Santa Cruz River, wild plants supplemented the cultivation of maize, tepary beans, possibly squash or wild gourd, and tobacco (L. Huckell 1998). The presence of water brought large game close to the I-10 sites, and agricultural fields provided new habitats for animal species, such as jackrabbits that thrive in disturbance environments. Open areas, perhaps from field clearing, and the fields themselves, provided easy access to small mammal prey for raptors. Rodents would have found easy burrowing in pit structure fill and concentrated food in intra- and extramural storage facilities. While such large settlements scare away game in the immediate site vicinity, they also create new environments for other animal resources.

Vegetal seasonal indicators at the I-10 sites are maize, dropseed, tansy mustard, agave, chia, and stickleaf. These plants suggest an early spring through fall presence (L. Huckell 1998). Fall through winter presence at floodplain sites may be indicated by mule deer antler with attached frontal bone found at Santa Cruz Bend. Arizona deer gain full antler growth by September and shed their racks in February (Hoffmeister 1986:542). James (1993) suggests that unshed antler at Coffee Camp also may point to a year-round occupation.

SUMMARY AND CONCLUSIONS

Early Agricultural Period Sites

While lagomorphs dominate most assemblages and may have been a staple food, artiodactyls were critically important. Over half the meat consumed at the sites came from large game. This pattern corresponds with Bayham's (1979) model of prey size ranking. Large amounts of meat and nutrition in transportable packages will be pursued, even if distance costs are relatively high due to decreased local availability. However, riparian areas at the floodplain edge attracted large game in relatively close proximity to the sites, so logistical forays to upland locations may not have been very frequent. The modest number of upland plant species support this interpretation. With intersite variations in cottontail to jackrabbit ratios, the highest small mammal counts are of jackrabbits. This species is well-adapted to disturbed landscapes that offer more open areas than those favored by cottontails. When land is "cleared, . . ., the grasses may become more extensive, and black-tailed jackrabbits will become far more abundant." (Hoffmeister 1986:142)

Two sites stand out in this comparison. The Donaldson site, located in a comparatively smaller drainage, has an extraordinarily high artiodactyl index. Although maize was found at the site, agriculture may not have been as entrenched as at sites on expansive floodplains. The low artiodactyl count at the Stone Pipe site is difficult to explain without detailed knowledge of micro-environments. Stone Pipe may have been further away from the prehistoric river course than other I-10 sites. If so, grasslands were not present right at the site, and large game would have to be procured further away. The comparatively high ratio of cottontails indicates a less open environment. The absence of pocket mouse (*Perognathus* sp.), a grassland rodent, supports this interpretation. However, cultigens, as well as storage facilities and processing equipment, were found at Stone Pipe. With an occupation span of about 407-259 B.C. (Mabry 1997), followed by an early Ceramic period occupation, Stone Pipe dates to the later part of the Early Agricultural period. Later Hohokam settlements produce fewer artiodactyl remains than some Early Agricultural sites, and show a strong reliance on lagomorphs and even rodents (Szuter 1989). Thus, Stone Pipe may represent the beginning of a subsistence trend carried through the Early Ceramic period into Hohokam times.

Los Pozos

With a large faunal assemblage, Los Pozos provides evidence of the exploitation of a wide range of environments. The taxonomic richness at Los Pozos derives from the presence of species not found at other Early Agricultural period sites. The taxa groups of fishes, reptiles, and birds are particularly rich by comparison. Remains of these taxa are found in floor and near-floor contexts, as well as in intramural pits. They are also sometimes burned and often are calcium carbonate encrusted. These indicate the taxa are likely to have been exploited by Los Pozos' residents. Birds remains occur in specific contexts, potentially for ritual reasons. Reptiles, and the presence of waterfowl and possible muskrat, indicate that the aquatic micro-environments around Los Pozos were indeed exploited, including during the cold season.

Several factors suggest a non-residentially mobile, logistically organized subsistence model for Los Pozos. High energy return plant and animal resources were exploited near the settlement in the form of cultigens and large game presumably attracted to water. These resources were supplemented by plants and animals from locations further away and at higher elevations. Pocket mouse (*Perognathus* sp.) remains, for instance, indicate that the site was situated in a grassland environment near the river's edge. Jackrabbit counts also indicate that areas near the settlement were open. The presence of maize suggests that agricultural activities may have been responsible. While there are no winter indicator plants, faunal remains provide evidence of a potential winter presence at Los Pozos. The sharp-shinned hawk (*Accipiter striatus*) is a winter visitor in southern Arizona, and waterfowl and muskrat are species exploited during the cold months and early spring when traditional game is too lean. Large numbers of fragmented long bone shafts at Los Pozos suggest that marrow extraction and bone grease rendering occurred, a processing activity that, ethnographically, is reserved for winter (Castetter and Underhill 1935:40). Although not identified as shed or cut, deer antler from intramural pits provides indirect evidence of a fall/winter presence by analogy with similar Early Agricultural sites, such as Santa Cruz Bend, about 2 mi south. Thus, the faunal assemblage produced additional evidence of a year-round occupation at Los Pozos. While logistical subsistence forays away from the site did occur, full residential mobility is unlikely. Huckell's (1995:131) statement about the Cienega Creek sites applies to Los Pozos and to other Early Agricultural settlements, "they may be considered villages inhabited both intensively during the course of a year and for periods of time measured in decades, if not centuries."

CHAPTER 11

AN EVALUATION OF EARLY AGRICULTURAL PERIOD CHRONOLOGY IN THE TUCSON BASIN

David A. Gregory

In order to place the occupation of Los Pozos in broader chronological perspective and to provide a basis for temporal ordering of materials to be compared in the final chapter, the chronology of the Early Agricultural and Early Ceramic periods is considered here. Radiocarbon dating of currently recognized phases is first evaluated. Second, the effects of calibration on potential temporal resolution and date distributions are described and discussed. Finally, a more detailed consideration of the dating and proposed subdivisions of the Cienega phase are presented.

CHRONOLOGY AND SYSTEMATICS

Recognition of a long preceramic interval during which maize cultivation appeared and became a significant aspect of prehistoric subsistence, has in the last score of years, fundamentally altered previous conceptions of mid- to late-Holocene prehistory in the American Southwest (e.g., see B. Huckell 1995, 1996; Matson 1991; Wills 1988, 1995) and more specifically in the Tucson Basin (Altschul 1995; Deaver and Ciolek-Torrello 1995; B. Huckell 1995, 1996; Mabry 1997, 1998c; Wallace et al. 1995; Whittlesey 1995). The rapidity with which new data for the Tucson Basin and environs has accumulated is well illustrated by a yearly plot of the number of late-Holocene radiocarbon dates reported since 1980 (Figure 11.1).

As is to be expected when an interval of time once poorly known benefits from a rapid influx of new and challenging data, the period of concern here has been recently subdivided, characterized, and interpreted in alternative ways. As a result, there is considerable variation in the temporal, terminological, and conceptual frameworks now used to refer to the interval between approximately 1500 B.C. and A.D. 500. Four recently developed chronological schemes for the Tucson Basin are reviewed briefly below. Each emphasizes somewhat different criteria for discrimination and focuses on different portions of the larger interval, but all acknowledge development of maize cultivation and ceramic vessel technology as significant features, and all depend heavily upon radiocarbon dates for

establishing subdivisions at the phase level. Since the appearance of a fully developed ceramic container technology plays a significant role in defining the period of interest, the chronology of early ceramic manifestations must also be dealt with to some degree. Thus, two of the schemes reviewed below deal primarily with the ceramic rather than the preceramic interval.

As an aspect of a three-part scheme for the Archaic period in the American Southwest, B. Huckell (1995, 1996) has used the designation *Late Archaic/Early Agricultural period* to refer to the interval between the appearance of maize and the introduction of ceramic container technology. This semantically awkward term is designed to accommodate the possibility that maize cultivating populations (Early Agricultural) and hunting and gathering populations (Late Archaic) may have coexisted in the same area or region over extended periods of time (B. Huckell 1995:118, 1996:345). That is, it incorporates the plausible hypothesis that the arrival and incorporation of maize cultivation into subsistence strategies was a time-transgressive line across or within geographic areas or regions. For southern Arizona, B. Huckell's Early Agricultural period includes three intervals (1995:Figure 8.1, 1996:344-346). The earliest of these is unnamed and simply acknowledges the arrival of maize in the American Southwest sometime between approximately 1500 and 1000 B.C. Based on reassessment of the earlier work of Sayles (1941, 1945, 1983) and more recent excavations at several sites (B. Huckell 1990, 1995; B. Huckell and L. Huckell 1984; B. Huckell et al. 1995; Mabry et al. 1997; Mabry 1998), two phases following this unnamed interval are defined: San Pedro phase, dated between approximately 1000 and 500 B.C.; and Cienega phase, dated between 500 B.C. and the appearance of ceramic container technology, placed at approximately A.D. 200 (B. Huckell 1995: Figure 8.1).

Another recently offered framework employs the term *Formative* to denote the presence of "fully sedentary and agriculturally dependent village life" (Deaver and Ciolek-Torrello 1995:482-483). These authors argue that these criteria are not met until the appearance of a fully developed ceramic container technology. Thus, *Late Archaic* refers to:

a period of increasing dependence on maize agriculture and decreasing residential mobility, even though Late Archaic farmers were neither fully dependent on maize agriculture nor were they fully sedentary (Deaver and Ciolek-Torrello 1995:483)

and the Late Archaic is not further subdivided in this scheme. *Early Formative period* is used as a "generic" term to refer to the earliest ceramic period manifestations, and is subdivided into a sequence of *Plain Ware*, *Red Ware*, *Early Broadline*, and *Snaketown* horizons (Deaver and Ciolek-Torrello 1995:484-488). Only the first two are treated here and, for the Tucson Basin, these are equated with a newly defined Agua Caliente phase (Ciolek-Torrello 1995) and the previously defined Tortolita phase (Bernard-Shaw 1990a), respectively. The beginning of the Agua Caliente phase is placed at the B.C./A.D. boundary, while the end of the phase is dated at A.D. 400 (Ciolek-Torrello 1995:561) or A.D. 425 (Deaver and Ciolek-Torrello 1995:512, Figure 2). The Tortolita phase is dated between the end of the Agua Caliente phase and A.D. 650 (Deaver and Ciolek-Torrello 1995:512), essentially duplicating Bernard-Shaw's original dating of the phase (Bernard-Shaw 1990a:209).

In their consideration of Hohokam origins, Wallace and others (1995) employ B. Huckell's Late Archaic/Early Agricultural terminology, but designate the *Early Ceramic* horizon within this period (1995:Figure 2; see also Elson 1994:Table 1.2). Their Early Ceramic horizon marks the presence of a fully developed ceramic container technology, restricted to plain ware ceramics and essentially equivalent to Deaver and Ciolek-Torrello's (1995) Plain Ware horizon and the Agua Caliente phase in the Tucson Basin. The Early Ceramic horizon is dated between approximately 100 B.C. and A.D. 450 by these authors (Wallace et al. 1995:Figure 2). They also recognize the Tortolita phase without reference to a Red Ware horizon and, like Deaver and Ciolek-Torrello, they confirm Bernard-Shaw's original dating of the phase between A.D. 450 and 650. It should be noted that this framework appeared simultaneously with that of Deaver and Ciolek-Torrello (Altschul 1995:463).

Employing Huckell's *Late Archaic/Early Agricultural* distinction and the *Early Ceramic* designation of Wallace and others (1995), Mabry (1997:Table 1.3) has provided a framework that combines the first three schemes. In this formulation, however, the Early Ceramic horizon is given *period* status and is distinguished from the Late Archaic/Early Agricultural *period*, rather than having the Early Ceramic horizon within the Early Agricultural period as formulated by Wallace and others (1995:Figure 2). The Late Archaic/Early Agricultural period includes B. Huckell's San Pedro and Cienega phases, while the Early Ceramic

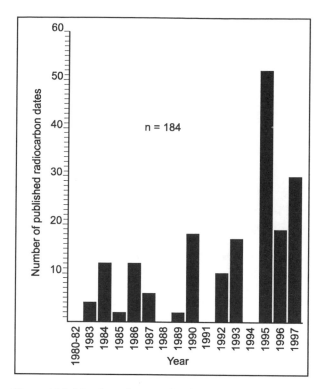

Figure 11.1. Number of reported radiocarbon dates per year, 1980-present.

period incorporates only the Agua Caliente and Tortolita phases. Thus, this scheme eschews use of not only the Formative referent but the Plain Ware, Red Ware, and Early Broadline horizon designations as well. Based on data from several sites investigated since presentation of the three earlier frameworks (including Los Pozos), dating of the periods and constituent phases is adjusted in Mabry's scheme, in some cases substantially. The unnamed interval included by B. Huckell to account for some period of time between the arrival of maize and recognizable San Pedro phase manifestations is not included, with everything before 1200 B.C. falling in the Middle Archaic Chiricahua phase (3000-1200 B.C.). The San Pedro phase is dated between 1200 and 800 B.C., and is thus pushed back in time and shortened somewhat. This backward shift of San Pedro results in a substantially longer Cienega phase, dated between 800 B.C. and A.D. 150. The start of the Early Ceramic period Agua Caliente phase is consequently shifted forward in time, as is its ending date, placed by Mabry at A.D. 550 (1997:Table 1.3). The end of the following Tortolita phase remains unchanged from earlier formulations (Bernard-Shaw 1990a; Deaver and Ciolek-Torrello 1995; Wallace et al. 1995), so that the phase is shortened by a century and dated between A.D. 550 and 650.

A number of issues relating to the several criteria for, and implications of, horizon, period, and phase definition are taken up in the final chapter. For the present, the Late Archaic/Early Agricultural and Early Ceramic period terminology is used to refer to the larger intervals, and attention is focused on dating of the four generally agreed upon phases: San Pedro, Cienega, Agua Caliente, and Tortolita.

RADIOCARBON DATING OF EARLY AGRICULTURAL PERIOD AND EARLY CERAMIC PERIOD PHASES

As noted above, a large set of radiocarbon dates relevant to current concerns has accumulated over the last decade. A recent compilation of many of these dates (Mabry 1998c:Table 1.3) serves as a baseline data set for selection and evaluation of dates considered below. This list is augmented with dates from Los Pozos, as well as those obtained during yet more recent investigations at the Wetlands site (Freeman 1998), the Rillito Fan site (Wallace 1996), and the Costello-King site (Ezzo and Deaver 1995). Following the method used by Eighmy and La Belle (1996) in their consideration of the dating of North American Plains phases and complexes, radiocarbon dating of the four phases discussed above is evaluated.

Calibrated Pooled Probability Age Ranges

Eighmy and LaBelle (1996:54) present the creation of calibrated pooled probability age ranges for a given phase or complex as a three-step process. First, all dates associated with materials characteristic of the phase or complex are calibrated to generate a calibrated age probability distribution corresponding to the Gaussian probability of the ^{14}C value (Stuiver and Reimer 1987, 1993). All calibrated age probabilities are then pooled and standardized by the number of radiocarbon determinations for each phase, according to the following formula:

$$P_t = 1/n \sum_{i=1}^{n} p, t = 1, ...j$$

where *p* equals the calibrated age probabilities for each date, and *n* is the number of dates for the interval.

Application of this formula results in a histogram representing the calibrated pooled probability distribution for the phase or complex (Eighmy and LaBelle 1996:54, Figure 1). The 1 sigma (PR68) and 2 sigma (PR95) age ranges for the phase include those intervals having pooled probabilities between .158 and .841 and between .025 and .975, respectively. Eighmy and

LaBelle suggest, on the basis of their study, that age ranges derived in this manner are not affected by sample size once the number of dates per interval is 10 or more (1996:65).

This method has a number of advantages. Since phases are not single events, the central tendencies or means of individual dates are less important than the age range represented by a set of dates (Eighmy and LaBelle 1966:54). Following a similar logic, the method may be extended to evaluation of sets of dates from individual sites to assess the overall length of site occupations. In addition, the method is relatively simple and, as Eighmy and LaBelle note:

> PR95s and PR68s are intuitively interpretable. Periods of highest probability for the age of a phase reflect (1) periods to which individual samples have a high probability of dating and (2) periods when many individual samples overlap. Distributions that are highly unimodal result from internal agreement of individual ^{14}C determinations. Distributions that are not unimodal, but strung out, result when sets of dates do not cluster . . . . the periods of highest probability indicate not only the number of overlapping samples, but also the periods of high dating probability for the individual samples (1996:54, 56).

Further, the method appropriately emphasizes the identity of radiocarbon determinations as probability distributions. The resulting graphic expressions are more precise and easily comprehensible than those provided by the segmented bar plots commonly used to represent the 1 and 2 sigma age ranges of individual calibrated dates and often combined graphically to evaluate and represent the age ranges of phases (Gregory 1996; Schott 1992).

For the present study, all conventional radiocarbon ages of dates from sites assigned to one of the four phases were calibrated using the CALIB 3.0.1 program (Stuiver and Reimer 1993), regardless of the type of date or type of material dated. The annual probability distributions contained in files created by the CALIB program for each date were then compiled into databases on a site-by-site basis, with a single field for the calibrated calendar year (B.C. or A.D.) and the probabilities for each year, the pooled probabilities, and the standardized probabilities included as separate fields.

Following evaluation of individual samples (see below), selected dates were recombined into separate databases for each phase. These data were then transferred to SPSS data-base files, where calculation of cumulative probabilities and 100-year running averages was accomplished. Graphic representations of the various distributions derived in this manner and presented below were generated using the SPSS program. In these graphic representations, a consistent range has been maintained for both the probability axis (0-.006) and the calendar year axis (1,400 years) to facilitate comparison.

Sample Selection

A number of general criteria were applied in the selection of dates used in analyses reported here, essentially resulting in a "best case" approach to dating of the phases (Dean 1991:69; Schiffer 1982). First, only dates from the Tucson Basin have been considered, since 1) areal and/or regional variation in the timing of events and processes may be later discerned, and 2) the overwhelming majority of dates from southern Arizona have resulted from investigations of sites within the Tucson Basin. Dates from sites outside the area are noted when relevant. Second, whenever possible, only AMS dates derived from annual plants and including measured rather than estimated $^{13}C/^{12}C$ ratios have been used.

For the San Pedro, Cienega, and Agua Caliente phases, recent work has provided a sufficiently large set of dates so that this criteria is easily met. For the Tortolita phase of the Early Ceramic period, this criteria was relaxed to provide a reasonable number of dates with which to generate the calibrated pooled age range (see below). Third, dates with measurement errors greater than ± 100 years were rejected. This is an arbitrary requirement, but takes into account the fact that calibrated ranges for dates having large measurement errors are too large to be of much use in chronology building. Typically, accelerator dates on annuals produce errors less than 100 years, and few dates were eliminated by this criterion.

Finally, only dates from well-documented contexts having associated material culture elements considered at present to be characteristic of the respective phases are used. No previously reported dates from unre-

ported investigations are used, since it is impossible at present to evaluate the overall context of such dates. Similarly, dates obtained from samples recovered from unexcavated features known only from stratigraphic exposures have not been not used, even though they may have been recovered from sites where more intensive excavations were carried out. Despite substantial material culture assemblages from a number of sites, there are, as yet, relatively few well-established material criteria that can be used to infer that particular features or sites belong in the constituent San Pedro and Cienega phases of the Early Agricultural period, independent of absolute dates. Thus, inclusion of particular dates and rejection of others on the basis of this criterion involves a measure of judgment, and every attempt has been made to err on the side of conservatism. The selection process is somewhat easier for the following Agua Caliente and Tortolita phases, with inclusion in the former requiring unmixed contexts containing only plain ware ceramics and, in the latter, an assemblage that includes both plain ware and red ware ceramics but no decorated pottery of any kind. Factors considered in selection of particular dates for each interval are discussed below as appropriate.

San Pedro Phase

Sample Selection

Eleven dates from three sites are used to evaluate the San Pedro phase (Table 11.1): 5 dates from Milagro (B. Huckell 1984; B. Huckell et al. 1995), 5 dates from the Costello-King site (Ezzo and Deaver 1998), and 1 date from the Wetlands site (Freeman 1998). Milagro is situated on a terrace immediately above Tanque Verde Wash, while the other two sites are located in the floodplain of the Santa Cruz River.

Table 11.1. Dates used in evaluation of the San Pedro phase.

Site Number (ASM)	Site Name	Sample Number	Feature Number	Material Dated	Radiocarbon Age	Error ±	Reference
AZ AA:12:503	Costello-King	B-89863	201.03	Maize	2620	60	Ezzo and Deaver 1998
		B-89862	178.00	Maize	2690	60	
		B-89859	19.00	Maize	2780	60	
		B-89860	19.00	Maize	2770	60	
		B-89861	23.00	Maize	2770	60	
AZ BB:10:46	Milagro	AA-12055	57.00	Maize	2930	45	Huckell and Huckell 1984; Huckell et al. 1995
		AA-12056	27.00	Maize	2915	45	
		AA-12053	53.00	Maize	2910	45	
		AA-01074	46.00	Maize	2780	90	
		AA-12054	42.00	Maize	2775	60	
AZ AA:12:90	Wetlands	B-100413	1300.01	Maize	2790	50	Freeman 1998

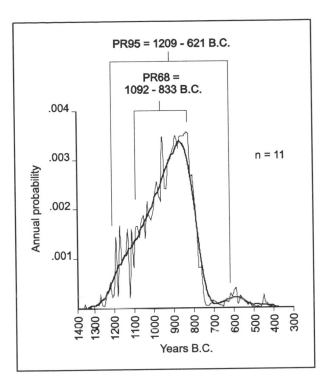

Figure 11.2. Calibrated pooled age range for the San Pedro phase.

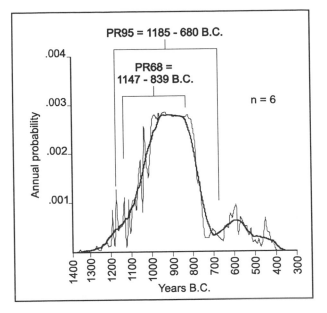

Figure 11.3. Calibrated pooled age range for early maize dates.

At present, Milagro is the most intensively investigated San Pedro phase site. The house form represented contrasts with later forms, only San Pedro style projectile points are represented, and the dates from the site are internally consistent (B. Huckell 1984; B. Huckell et al. 1995). The single excavated structure at the Costello-King site most closely resembles documented San Pedro phase forms, the only projectile point style represented is San Pedro, and the five dates from the site are internally consistent (Ezzo and Deaver 1995). The selected date from the Wetlands site comes from a house that appears to represent a San Pedro phase form (Freeman 1998). All 11 dates are on maize remains.

Results and Additional Observations

Figure 11.2 illustrates the calibrated pooled age range for the San Pedro phase sites, while Figure 11.3 presents the calibrated pooled age range for the phase. The resulting PR95 range is 1209 to 621 B.C. and the PR68 range is 1092 to 833 B.C.

As noted above, B. Huckell included an unnamed period preceding the San Pedro phase to accommodate the as yet undetermined timing of the arrival of maize in the southern Southwest. Thus, it is useful to consider several other early maize dates relative to the dates used here to evaluate the phase. These dates are of interest in that–along with maize dates from defini-

tively San Pedro phase sites–they constitute the current evidence for the earliest occurrences of maize in the region.

The first set of dates considered includes six direct determinations on maize older than the *youngest* date used above to evaluate the San Pedro phase (2620 rcybp; Table 11.2). All are from well-documented archaeological contexts, but none is associated with definitively San Pedro phase material culture. For purposes of this comparison, the geographic boundaries of the Tucson Basin are not observed, allowing three dates from the San Pedro drainage to be included. The six dates include: one date each from the Solar Well site (Mabry 1990), the Rillito Fan site (Wallace 1996), the Cortaro Fan site (Roth 1989, 1992), and the Fairbank site (B. Huckell 1990); and two dates from the West End site (B. Huckell 1990). The first four sites are located in the Tucson Basin, while the last two are located along the San Pedro River.

Comparison of Tables 11.1 and 11.2 shows that none of these six dates is earlier than the three earliest San Pedro dates from Milagro. Figure 11.3 presents the calibrated pooled probability age range for the set of early maize dates. The pooled probability age range of these dates is quite similar to that for the selected San Pedro phase dates described above, but defines a somewhat shorter interval on both the early and late ends of the distribution. Figure 11.4 combines the early maize dates with the San Pedro phase dates used above (total = 17 dates). Not surprisingly, this figure shows that if we assume the presence of a San Pedro phase component at these five sites, the PR68 and PR95 age ranges for San Pedro phase do not change appreciably.

Table 11.2. Other early dates on maize from southern Arizona.

Site Number (ASM)	Site Name	Sample Number	Radiocarbon Age	Error (±)	Reference
AZ AA:12:105	Solar Well	AA-6641	2835	85	Mabry 1990
AZ AA:12:788	Rillito Fan	B-90318	2860	40	Wallace 1996
AZ AA:12:486	Cortaro Fan	AA-2782	2790	60	Roth 1992
AZ EE:8:1	Fairbank	AA-4457	2815	80	B. Huckell 1990
AZ EE:8:5	West End	AA-4810	2735	75	B. Huckell 1990
AZ EE:8:5	West End	AA-4811	2675	80	B. Huckell 1990

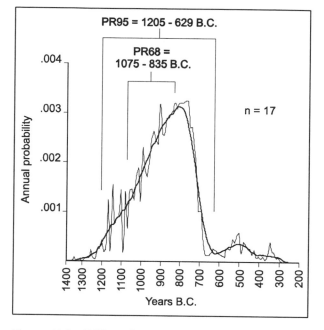

Figure 11.4. Calibrated pooled age range for San Pedro phase and early maize dates.

Cienega Phase

Sample Selection

By far, the greatest number of Early Agricultural period dates come from sites assigned to the Cienega phase, owing to several recent investigations at sites belonging to this interval, including Los Pozos (Diehl 1997; Freeman 1998; B. Huckell 1995, Mabry et al. 1997; Wallace 1996). Fifty-eight dates from five sites are used for evaluation of the Cienega phase (Table 11.3): 13 dates from the Clearwater site (Diehl 1997), 10 from the Wetlands site (Freeman 1998), 9 from the Santa Cruz Bend site (Mabry 1997), 3 from the Stone Pipe site (Mabry 1997), and 19 dates from Los Pozos (see Chapter 2). All five sites are located in the floodplain of the Santa Cruz River.

All dates from Los Pozos are from samples recovered from round pit structures (or intramural pits within such structures), now considered to be characteristic of the phase (B. Huckell 1995, 1996; Mabry 1998a). All except one of the dates from Santa Cruz Bend are from similar contexts–the single exception being a sample from a pit that intrudes a round structure (Feature 406, B-81063). Two of the dates from Stone Pipe, from Clearwater, and from Wetlands come from similar pit structures. All other dates from the latter three sites come from extramural pits that are not diagnostic of the phase on the basis of their morphological characteristics alone. However, based on their spatial association with diagnostic structures, the assemblages of projectile points and ground stone from the sites (B. Huckell 1995; Sliva 1997), and internal consistency of the respective sets of dates, samples from these pits have been included. It may be noted that rejection of the several dates from extramural pits would not significantly alter the results presented below.

Results and Additional Observations

Figure 11.5 illustrates the calibrated pooled age range for the Cienega phase. The resulting PR95 interval for the phase is 775 B.C. to A.D. 57, while the PR68 interval is 668 to 101 B.C.

Huckell's original definition of the Cienega phase was based, in part, on data from the Donaldson and Los Ojitos sites, located in the Cienega Creek drainage and thus, outside the Tucson Basin proper (B. Huckell 1995). Two dates from these sites meet all other criteria established for present concerns (2320 ± 55 and 2505 ± 55 b.p.; AA-13124 and AA-13125, respectively). These dates are essentially duplicated by determinations included for purposes of calculating the pooled age range for the phase, and the range would not change appreciably if they were included. Further consideration is given to the Cienega phase in a subsequent section.

Table 11.3. Dates used in evaluation of the Cienega phase.

Site Number (ASM)	Site Name	Sample Number	Feature Number	Material Dated	Radiocarbon Age	Error (±)	Reference
AZ BB:13:6	Clearwater	B-90227	1010.01	Mesquite bean	2600	50	Diehl 1997
		B-90228	1016.00	Maize	2390	50	
		B-90229	1029.00	Maize	2420	50	
		B-90232	1032.00	Maize	2250	50	
		B-90225	1006.02	Maize	2580	60	
		B-90231	1028.01	Mesquite bean	2500	50	
		B-90226	1006.03	Maize	2500	60	
		B-92617	1009.00	Mesquite bean	2390	70	
		B-92618	1022.00	Mesquite bean	2440	60	
		B-92619	370.00	Maize	2430	60	
		B-92620	1014.00	Mesquite bean	2510	50	
		B-92621	1020.00	Mesquite bean	2440	60	
		B-92622	371.00	Mesquite bean	2480	50	
AZ AA:12:91	Los Pozos	B-88140	866.26	Maize	1980	60	Chapter 1, this volume
		B-88142	407.00	Grass stems	2150	50	
		B-88139	825.00	Grass stems	1940	60	
		B-88141	327.01	Mesquite pod	2020	50	
		B-91140	898.00	Mesquite seed	2140	60	
		B-91141	305.01	Maize	2120	60	
		B-91143	318.01	Maize	2050	50	
		B-91142	337.14	Maize	2150	50	
		B-91144	355.10	Maize	2170	60	
		B-91145	333.01	Maize	2110	50	
		B-91146	389.0	Maize	2090	60	
		B-91147	416.01	Maize	2240	60	
		B-91148	417.00	Maize	2140	50	
		B-91149	812.23	Maize	2150	60	
		B-95628	352.01	Maize	2190	80	
		B-95629	819.00	Maize	2150	80	
		B-95630	840.00	Maize	2110	80	
		B-95631	815.00	Maize	2060	80	
		B-95632	861.01	Maize	2090	80	
AZ AA:12:746	Santa Cruz Bend	B-81062	85.01	Maize	2440	50	Mabry 1997
		B-67489	11.01	Maize	2390	70	
		B-81059	100.03	Maize	2290	60	
		B-81058	111.01	Maize	2290	60	
		B-81063	406.00	Maize	2260	60	
		B-81064	310.00	Maize	2260	60	
		B-67490	32.01	Maize	2200	60	
		B-81060	90.01	Maize	2180	60	
		B-81061	110.01	Maize	2010	60	
AZ BB:13:425	Stone Pipe	B-81066	100.00	Maize	2390	50	
		B-81069	364.00	Maize	2360	50	
		B-81067	84.00	Maize	2150	60	
AZ AA:12:90	Wetlands	B-100408	1001.00	Mesquite bean	2520	50	Freeman 1998
		B-100409	152.00	Maize	2510	50	
		B-100410	1015.00	Maize	2550	50	
		B-100411	148.01	Maize	2480	50	
		B-100412	200.00	Mesquite bean	2400	50	
		B-100414	1162.00	Mesquite bean	2400	50	
		B-100415	177.01	Maize	2580	50	
		B-100416	193.00	Mesquite bean	2510	50	
		B-100417	1397.00	Maize	2480	40	
		B-100418	1578.00	Maize	2440	50	

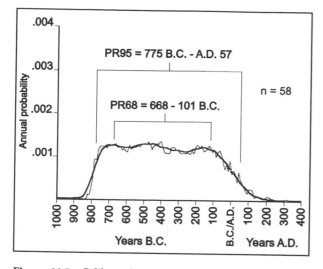

Figure 11.5. Calibrated pooled age range for the Cienega phase.

Agua Caliente Phase

Sample Selection

Thirteen dates from two sites are used for evaluation of the Agua Caliente phase (Table 11.4): 3 from Stone Pipe (Mabry 1997) and 10 from Square Hearth (Mabry 1997). Both sites are located in the floodplain of the Santa Cruz River. All selected dates are direct dates on annuals, and all are from features at the respective sites having unmixed ceramic assemblages consisting solely of plain wares. Eight of the 10 dates from Square Hearth have estimated rather than measured $^{13}C/^{12}C$ ratios (Mabry 1997:Table 1.3). Square Hearth had a late Rillito-early Rincon phase Hohokam component in addition to the Agua Caliente phase manifestations, while Stone Pipe witnessed an Early Agricultural period occupation as well (Mabry 1998c).

Ciolek-Torrello (1995) used data from the Houghton Road site as a basis for his definition and dating of the Agua Caliente phase, and four dates from this site were the only ones used by Deaver and Ciolek-Torrello (1995) to date this phase. Although Houghton Road is technically the type site for the Agua Caliente phase, none of the six reported dates from this site have been used here in evaluation of the phase (Deaver and Ciolek-Torrello 1995:Table 1). All six are from wood charcoal (albeit outer rings), and the full report that will allow further evaluation of the dates and their contexts has not yet been published (but see Ciolek-Torrello 1995:543-560). Two of the Houghton Road dates are rejected by Deaver and Ciolek-Torrello as being too old (1995:502; 2200 ± 80 and 2170 ± 90; TX-7063 and TX-7062, respectively), and the authors suggest laboratory error to explain the two early dates (1995:502). However, they also acknowledge the site is clearly multicomponent in character, spanning an interval from the Late Archaic through Colonial period Hohokam (1995:501). Thus potential mixing of earlier materials must be considered in evaluating these dates. It may be noted that the other four dates used by these authors to define the phase fall toward the early end of the Agua Caliente dates from Stone Pipe and Square Hearth with substantial overlap (Deaver and Ciolek-Torrello 1995:Tables 1, 4).

Results and Additional Observations

Figure 11.6 illustrates the calibrated pooled age range for the Agua Caliente phase. The resulting PR95 interval is 12 B.C. to A.D. 594, while the PR68 interval is A.D. 203 to 514.

Dates from Square Hearth fall into two overlapping groups. Four of these dates present interpretive problems in that they represent two pairs of dates from two separate features, a stone-lined pit (Feature 27), and a

Table 11.4. Dates used in evaluation of the Agua Caliente phase.

Site Number (ASM)	Site Name	Sample Number	Feature Number	Material Dated	Radiocarbon Age	Error ±	Reference
AA:12:745	Square Hearth	AA-13262	60.00	Mesquite bean	1675	55	Mabry 1997
		AA-13259	27.00	Maize	1765	55	
		AA-13256	27.00	Maize	1630	65	
		AA-13261	55.00	Maize	1645	60	
		AA-13264	69.00	Maize	1565	60	
		B-67491	35.03	Mesquite bean	1830	60	
		B-67492	44.00	Mesquite bean	1980	60	
		AA-13783	33.00	Mesquite bean	1810	60	
		AA-13782	33.00	Mesquite bean	1675	65	
		AA-13263	67.00	Mesquite bean	1585	55	
BB:13:425	Stone Pipe	B-81065	99.00	Maize	1720	60	Mabry 1997
		B-81071	392.00	Maize	1650	60	
		B-81068	337.00	Reed	1560	60	

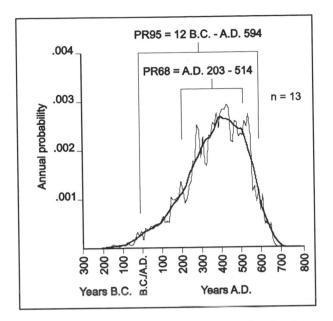

Figure 11.6. Calibrated pooled age range for the Agua Caliente phase.

east and coming from round houses, and the later group to the southwest and coming from extramural pits (see Wöcherl and Clark 1997:Figure 3.1). This suggests the possibility of two occupations and perhaps a change in site function or at least a change in the use of the excavated portion of the site.

If the younger of the two dates from the single rectangular structure at the site (Feature 33) is correct, a sequence of architectural form may be represented. Two dates from Stone Pipe come from subrectangular pit structures (Features 337 and 392) and are later than the dates from round structures at Square Hearth. Once again, if the later of the two dates from the rectangular structure at Square Hearth reflects the true age of this house, it would appear that the round to subrectangular/rectangular sequence of house form is supported. Given the length of the phase as currently defined and apparent variation in material culture, especially house form, it seems likely that subdivision of the Agua Caliente phase will be possible as additional data accumulate.

rectangular house (Feature 33). In each case, there is one date that falls into the early group and one into the later group. Of the remaining six dates, the two earlier determinations were obtained on samples taken from two round houses (Features 35 and 44), and four were from extramural pits containing early plain ware ceramics (Features 55, 60, 67, and 69). Feature 67 (a pit) intruded another round house (Feature 66) and thus, postdates it on the basis of stratigraphic superposition. There is a general spatial separation of the earlier and later dates, with the earlier group being to the north-

Tortolita Phase

Sample Selection

Ten dates from three sites are used for evaluation of the Tortolita phase (Table 11.5): 6 dates from Lonetree (Bernard-Shaw 1990a), one date from the Dairy site (Fish et al. 1992), and 3 dates from Rabid Ruin (Slawson 1990). The single Dairy site date is on maize. One of the six dates from Lonetree is on an annual (reeds), while the remaining five dates from Lonetree and the three

Table 11.5. Dates used in evaluation of the Tortolita phase.

Site Number (ASM)	Site Name	Sample Number	Feature Number	Material Dated	Radiocarbon Age	Error ±	Reference
AZ AA:12:46	Rabid Ruin	GX-14931	121.00	Wood charcoal	1480	75	Slawson 1990
		GX-14930	119.00	Wood charcoal	1420	75	
		GX-14932	122.01	Wood charcoal	1400	75	
AZ AA:12:120	Lonetree	B-22708	31.00	Wood charcoal	1510	60	Bernard-Shaw 1990a
		B-27710	149.00	Wood charcoal	1414	60	
		B-26782	41.00	Wood charcoal	1380	70	
		B-27711	24.00	Wood charcoal	1380	60	
		B-26785	149.00	Wood charcoal	1240	70	
		B-26784	139.00	Reed	1410	80	
AZ AA:12:85	Dairy	AA-2155		Maize	1470	55	Fish et al. 1992

dates from Rabid Ruin were all derived from wood charcoal. Thus, the criteria of dates on annuals used for the previous three phases is relaxed with respect to this phase. In addition, the Dairy site materials were excavated from the face of a long stratigraphic exposure (Fish et al. 1992:Figure 6.3), thereby violating another of the general criteria for date selection delineated above. Of four dates obtained from Rabid Ruin, Ciolek-Torrello and Deaver (1995) reject one because it was a composite sample and came from a possibly mixed context (GX-14933; Slawson 1990:57-61); this date is also rejected here. In their assessment of Tortolita phase dating, Wallace and others (1995:Table 3) reject all but one of the dates from Rabid Ruin because the species of wood represented is not reported. They also reject two of the six dates from Lonetree due to possible rodent disturbance of sample contexts, but they accept the single Dairy site date used here (Wallace et al. 1995:Table 2; see pp. 578-579 for a discussion of the selection criteria employed in that study).

Deaver and Ciolek-Torrello used dates from five sites in establishing dates for the Red Ware horizon of their late Formative period and the Tortolita phase in the Tucson Basin: the Dairy site (2 dates; Fish et al. 1992), El Arbolito (4 dates; B. Huckell 1987), Rabid Ruin (4 dates; Slawson 1990), Lonetree (6 dates; Bernard-Shaw 1990a), and Valencia North (4 dates; B. Huckell 1993). One of the two dates from the Dairy site is not used here because the sampled feature contained a sherd of Snaketown Red-on-buff (Fish et al. 1992:Table 6.3). Although four dates from El Arbolito were included by Deaver and Ciolek-Torrello (1995) for purposes of defining the Red Ware horizon, none are used here. Only 13 red ware sherds were recovered from the site, suggesting that an Agua Caliente phase occupation may also be present. Two of the four dates were derived from wood charcoal, and one of the dates on annuals has a measurement error of ± 150 years (mesquite seeds; AA-1883). The four dates from the Valencia Road North site are not used. All are from wood charcoal samples and at least a few red-on-gray sherds were recovered from the relevant deposits, suggesting that the site is not a pure Tortolita phase manifestation (B. Huckell 1987). Interestingly, all four Valencia Road dates are younger than those from any other Tortolita phase site.

Results and Additional Observations

Figure 11.7 illustrates the calibrated pooled age range for the Tortolita phase. The resulting PR95 interval is A.D. 435 to 864, while the PR68 interval is A.D. 523 to 721.

Relaxation of two principal criteria for date selection makes the assessment of Tortolita phase the most

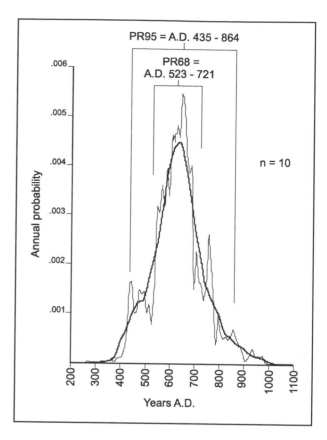

Figure 11.7. Calibrated pooled age range for the Tortolita phase.

tenuous of the four considered here. In addition, the phase is only 100 years long as currently defined, and this degree of resolution may not be expected with radiocarbon dates alone (see below). Given other available data (Bernard-Shaw 1990a; Deaver and Ciolek-Torrello 1995; Wallace et al. 1995), the late end of the PR95 range is clearly too late (see Wallace et al. 1995), while the PR68 range is relatively close to the A.D. 550 to 650 range given by Mabry (1997). Thus, the pooled average probabilities of radiocarbon dates are not terribly useful in evaluating the dating of the Tortolita phase. With respect to refinement of the dating of this phase, and to some degree that of the preceding Agua Caliente phase as well, seriation techniques will likely prove to be a necessary complement.

Differences between the pooled age distributions and current temporal frameworks for these two phases highlight an obvious fact: with the introduction of ceramics and the potential for temporal variation in the adoption of that plastic medium, temporal resolution afforded by radiocarbon dates will not be sufficient to accommodate the relatively rapid rates of change that appear to characterize various aspects of ceramic container technology almost from the time of its adoption. Thus, although additional high quality radiocarbon dates are needed for both phases, and in particular for the Agua Caliente phase, it is unlikely that such dates will provide adequate resolution for bracketing of the Tortolita phase and for the study of changing ceramic technology during the Early Ceramic period.

Summary and Discussion

Table 11.6 presents the age ranges for the phases defined in the four chronological frameworks reviewed above, as well as the calibrated PR68 and PR95 age ranges and intervals of overlap for the PR95 ranges derived from the analyses described above. Given the fact that Mabry's (1997) chronology is the most recent of the four reviewed above and thus benefits from a much larger database, it is not surprising that his scheme most closely approximates results of the analyses presented here.

Figure 11.8 illustrates the calibrated pooled age ranges for the four phases and highlights the intervals of PR95. As may be seen in Table 11.6 and Figure 11.8, the lengths of the respective phases as defined by the PR95 ranges are 588 years (San Pedro), 832 years (Cienega), 606 years (Agua Caliente), and 429 years (Tortolita). The lengths of the periods of overlap are 154 years for the San Pedro and Cienega phases (midpoint = 698 B.C.), 69 years for the Cienega and Agua Caliente phases (midpoint = A.D. 35), and 159 years for the Agua Caliente and Tortolita phases (midpoint = A.D. 514). None of the PR68 ranges for the respective phases overlap. Assuming a generational length of 25 years, the number of generations per phase may be estimated at 23 for San Pedro, 33 for Cienega, 24 for Agua Caliente, and 17 for Tortolita; the estimated number of generations in the periods of overlap are 6, 3, and 6 generations long, respectively.

Figure 11.8 also highlights the fact that the probability distributions for the San Pedro, Agua Caliente, and Tortolita phases are all strongly peaked, while the Cienega phase distribution is relatively flat. The reasons for the differing shapes of the respective distributions and related issues are explored in the following section.

THE EFFECTS OF CALIBRATION

A number of authors have noted the potential effects of calibration on temporal resolution (Aiken 1990; Eighmy and LaBelle 1996; Schott 1992) and, as will be shown below, these same factors can produce artificial clustering of dates as well.

The proximal cause of variation in calibrated age ranges is the shape of the calibration curve itself:

> The form of calibration curves over any time interval of interest may . . . complicate results or at least frustrate attempts to gain precise resolution (Aiken 1990:98-99; Asch and Brown 1990). If a curve is essentially horizontal over some interval, samples of different true ages can yield the same radiocarbon result. If a curve reverses slope, a younger sample can yield an older radiocarbon date than one of older true age. Steep slopes in sections of calibration curves exaggerate the dispersion of a series of dates by distributing them over a radiocarbon time range broader than the calendrical range they occupy (Schott 1992:203).

Variation in the shape of calibration curves results in turn from de Vries effects, or secular variations in the amount of atmospheric carbon which create the need to calibrate radiocarbon dates in the first place (Damon and Linnick 1986; Suess 1961, 1986; de Vries 1958). The ultimate cause of such variation involves a complex interaction of numerous factors, but the principal one appears to be fluctuations in solar activity (Damon et al. 1978; Grey and Damon 1970; Stuiver et al. 1991; Taylor 1987:Table 2.1).

Variation in the shape of the curve is particularly pronounced during the interval subsumed by the Early Agricultural period. Figure 11.9 shows the decadal calibration curve (Stuiver and Reimer 1993) superimposed over a plot of atmospheric carbon values for the period 1200 B.C. to A.D. 200 (radiocarbon ages between 3000 and 1500 b.p.). The earlier of two spikes in atmospheric carbon corresponds to a Spörer-type sunspot minimum lasting 220 years, between approximately 820 and 600 B.C.; the later spike corresponds to a Maunder-type sunspot minimum lasting 180 years, between approximately 460 and 280 B.C. (Stuiver and Brazunias 1988; Stuiver et al. 1991:14-15, Figure 13). The first corresponding sharp drop in the calibration curve includes approximately the first half of the first interval (820-750 B.C.), while the later drop includes the first half of the second (460-350 B.C.), with the curve being relatively flat between the two steep drops. Both before and after this period of pronounced variation, the curve has a relatively constant slope for extended periods of time.

Echoing Schott's observations cited above and expressed in terms of Taylor's (1987) metaphor that radiocarbon time is elastic relative to calendar time, Figure 11.9 illustrates the fact that this interval is characterized by:

1) a period during which very little real time passes while a long period of radiocarbon time is represented—that is, when radiocarbon time is "stretched"

Table 11.6. Comparison of existing chronological schemes with calibrated pooled age ranges derived from selected dates.

Period	Horizon	Phase	Huckell 1995, 1996	Deaver and Ciolek-Torrello 1995	Wallace et al. 1995	Mabry 1997	PR95 (Overlap with Succeeding Interval)	PR68
Early Agricultural/ Late Archaic	–	Unnamed	1500-1000 B.C.	–	–	–	–	–
	–	San Pedro	1000-500 B.C.	–	–	1200-800 B.C.	1209-621 B.C. (775-621 B.C.)	1092-833 B.C.
	–	Cienega	500 B.C.-A.D. 200	–	–	800 B.C.-A.D. 150	775 B.C.-A.D. 57 (12 B.C.-A.D. 57)	668-101 B.C.
Early Ceramic/ Formative	Plain ware	Agua Caliente	A.D. 200- (unspecified)	A.D./B.C.-A.D. 400	100 B.C.-A.D. 450	A.D. 150-550	12 B.C.-A.D. 594 (A.D. 435-594)	A.D. 203-514
	Red ware	Tortolita	–	A.D. 400/425-650	A.D. 450-650	A.D. 550-650	A.D. 435-864	A.D. 523-721

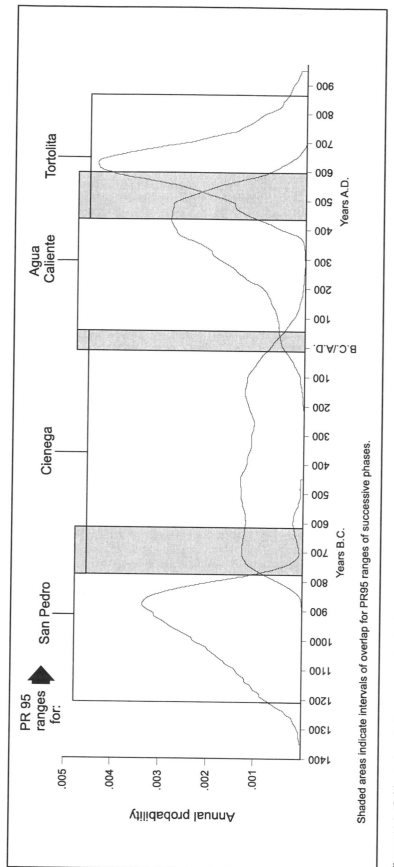

Shaded areas indicate intervals of overlap for PR95 ranges of successive phases.

Figure 11.8. Calibrated pooled age ranges for the four phases as currently defined.

relative to calendar time; followed by

2) a period during which a long interval of real time passes in contrast to a relatively short span of radiocarbon time–that is, when radiocarbon time is "compressed"; followed by

3) another period like the first, where little real time but much radiocarbon time elapses, with radiocarbon time once again being "stretched" relative to real time.

In order to further explore the effects of calibration, a recent study simulated dates from 7000 b.p. to the present and examined the results in various ways (Gregory 1996). Radiocarbon dates representing even 10-year intervals from the present to 7000 b.p. (e.g., 5000, 5010, 5020, 5030, etc.) and having measurement errors of ± 20, 50, 60, 70, and 100 years were assumed to exist. Each date was then calibrated using the decadal calibration set contained in the CALIB 3.0.1 program (Stuiver and Reimer 1993). The length of each calibrated age range at the 1 sigma (cal 1) and 2 sigma (cal 2) ranges was calculated, as were the means, standard deviations, and Z scores for the derived ranges within each simulation. Data from this study are used below to illustrate some specific effects of calibration during the Early Agricultural period.

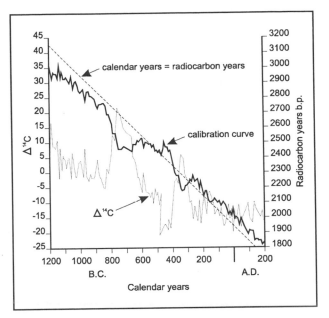

Figure 11.9. Calibration curve and atmospheric carbon values, 1200 B.C.-A.D. 200.

Variation in Resolution

Variation in temporal resolution represented in sets of calibrated dates may be defined by variation in the lengths of cal 2 age ranges. Figure 11.10 is a plot of the length of cal 2 age ranges for simulated radiocarbon dates between 3000 and 1800 b.p., using the ±50-year simulation (Gregory 1996:Table 2).

Clearly, there are substantial differences in the degree of temporal resolution afforded by calibrated dates over the span of the Early Agricultural period. Resolution is relatively poor during the first part of the San Pedro phase, but improves markedly over the latter half of the phase. A rapid shift to poor resolution marks the beginning of the Cienega phase, and this pattern lasts through roughly the first half of the phase. Resolution then improves rapidly at about 2350 b.p., deteriorates, and improves again during the latter half of the phase. It follows that the relative effects of calibration on resolution for any given interval will be the same, regardless of the measurement error of a particular date.

Figure 11.10 also illustrates what Eighmy and LaBelle (1996:54) refer to as the "false precision" that may result from calibration. Some dates falling between 2610 and 2720 b.p. produce cal 2 ranges *less* than twice the measurement error (±50) for the conventional date.

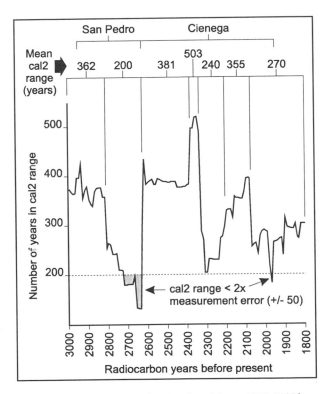

Figure 11.10. Cal 2 ranges for simulated dates, 3000-1800 b.p. (±50).

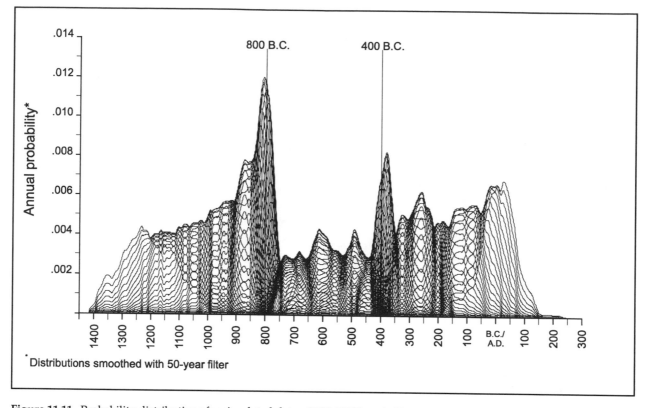

Figure 11.11. Probability distributions for simulated dates, 3000-2000 b.p. (±50 error assumed).

Another perspective on these variations is illustrated in Figure 11.11, a plot of the annual probability distributions for simulated, calibrated dates between 3000 and 1800 b.p. (±50), smoothed with a 50-year running mean (Gregory 1996). The two sharp spikes in the probability distributions correspond to the two sunspot-related spikes in the atmospheric carbon curve and the two steep drops in the calibration curve cited above. The interval of low annual probabilities between the two spikes corresponds to the flat portion of the calibration curve (see Figure 11.9).

Clustering of Dates

Figure 11.12 presents block plots of simulated radiocarbon dates between 3100 and 1700 b.p., using the ±50-year simulation. This figure shows that, beginning with conventional radiocarbon ages of approximately 2860 b.p., the younger ends of calibrated dates begin to stack up between 850 and 750 B.C. and the lengths of the cal 2 ranges shorten. At approximately 2620 b.p., the ranges flop to the other side of the line, and a cluster of dates falling between approximately 850 to 750 B.C. and 400 to 350 B.C. (2350-2620 b.p.) is apparent. There is little overlap between dates in this cluster and those immediately before and after it, and

dates toward the middle of this interval are characterized by 1 and 2 sigma ranges that are nearly equal. At approximately 2350 b.p., the dates flop to the younger side once again, and the older end of calibrated ranges for dates from this point to approximately 2120 b.p. tend to stack up between 400 and 350 B.C.

The two peaks in the probability distributions shown in Figure 11.11 represent the boundaries of the separate clusters seen in the block plots, between 850 and 750 B.C. and again between 400 and 350 B.C. These peaks are separated by an interval of relatively flat distributions with annual probabilities significantly lower than in the preceding and following intervals and corresponding to the cluster of dates between approximately 800 to 750 B.C. and 400 to 350 B.C. seen in the block plots. Eighmy and LaBelle (1996:54) acknowledge the influence of de Vries effects on the shape of probability histograms and suggest that use of 100-year running averages smooths and diminishes these effects when applied to calibrated pooled age ranges. However, as clearly shown in Figures 11.11 and 11.12, the effects resulting from major perturbations lasting several hundreds of years are not significantly reduced by such smoothing.

That these same effects manifest themselves in real-world situations where measurement errors are free to vary is illustrated in Figure 11.13, which includes block

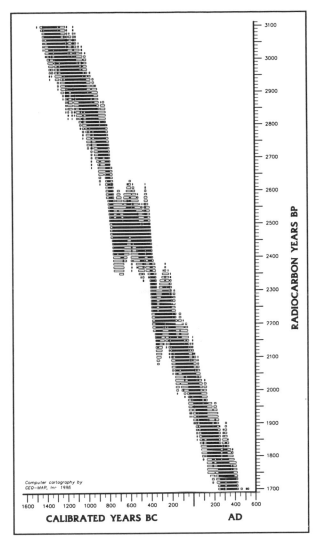

Figure 11.12. Block plots of simulated dates, 3100-1700 b.p.

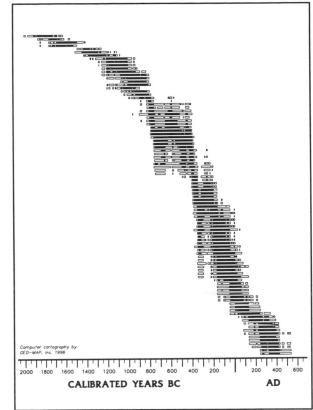

Figure 11.13. Block plots of 80 maize dates from the American Southwest.

plots of 80 maize dates from across the American Southwest. Assuming there was human occupation in any given area over this interval, and if radiocarbon dates are acquired from materials representing those occupations, sooner or later, *three clusters of dates will tend to accumulate*: one group will include dates for which the later end of the calibrated ranges fall between approximately 850 and 750 B.C., with the older end of the range being variable. A second cluster will include dates with calibrated ranges falling between approximately 850 to 750 B.C. and 400 to 350 B.C. A third cluster will include dates with the older end of calibrated ranges falling between approximately 400 and 350 B.C., with the younger end of the ranges being variable. Figures 11.12 and 11.13 also show clearly that there will be very little overlap between these clusters of dates.

Further Consideration of the Cienega Phase

From the above discussion, it should be clear that the current boundary between the San Pedro and Cienega phases (800 B.C.) is strongly influenced by the effects of the calibration curve. It should also be apparent that the length of the Cienega phase as currently defined masks the presence of two clusters of dates, and that the low, flat curve that represents the calibrated pooled age range for the phase is also a function of the calibration curve (see Figure 11.5).

Dates recently obtained from Clearwater, Wetlands, and Los Pozos in particular, have brought these patterns into much sharper focus, as the site-by-site plots of pooled probability distributions for Cienega phase sites show (Figure 11.14). The distributions for Clearwater and Wetlands are largely isomorphic, falling in the middle cluster created by the calibration curve. The pooled age ranges for these sites show little overlap with that for Los Pozos, which falls in the third cluster created by the curve. Both Stone Pipe and Santa Cruz Bend produced some dates falling in each of these clusters (see Table 11.3), and when grouped together by

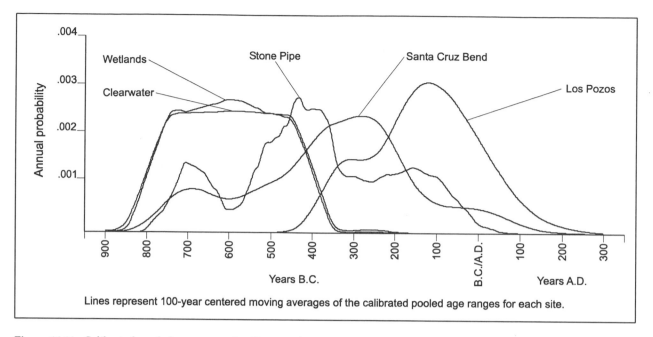

Figure 11.14. Calibrated pooled age ranges for Cienega phase sites.

site, these dates produce pooled probability distributions that span the entire phase as currently defined. However, when the dates from Stone Pipe and Santa Cruz Bend are separated into early (2 dates each) and late (1 date and 7 dates, respectively) sets, the two clusters are apparent (Figure 11.15).

A REVISED CHRONOLOGY

Based on the foregoing analysis and discussion, minor revisions of the existing Early Agricultural period chronology are indicated. A revised chronology is presented in Table 11.7 and discussed below. With

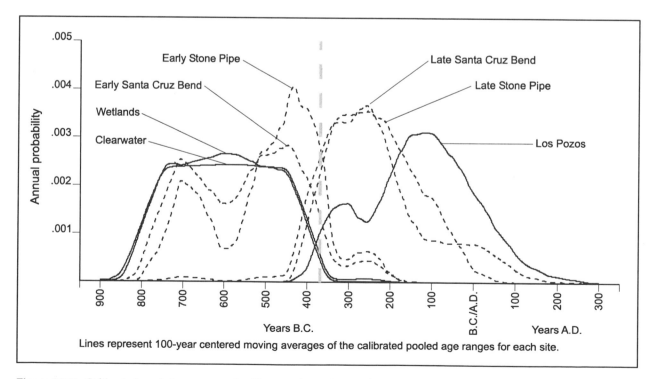

Figure 11.15. Calibrated pooled age ranges for Cienega phase sites, with Santa Cruz Bend and Stone Pipe dates grouped into early and late sets.

Table 11.7. Revised Early Agricultural period chronology.

Unnamed period	1500-1200 B.C.
San Pedro phase	1200-800 B.C.
Early Cienega phase	800-400 B.C.
Late Cienega phase	400 B.C.-A.D. 150
Agua Caliente phase	A.D. 150-450

Table 11.8. Temporally ordered sequence of previously investigated San Pedro, Early and Late Cienega, and Agua Caliente phase sites.

Phase	Site
San Pedro	Milagro
	Costello-King
	Wetlands (1 structure)
Early Cienega	Wetlands
	Clearwater
	Solar Well (?)
Mixed Early/	Santa Cruz Bend
Late Cienega	Stone Pipe
	Donaldson
	Los Ojitos (?)
Late Cienega	Los Pozos
	Coffee Camp
Agua Caliente	Square Hearth
	Stone Pipe
	Houghton Road

the exception of a two-part division of the Cienega phase, this scheme is quite similar to that presented by Mabry (1997) and described above. This framework also provides a basis for establishing an appropriate sequence of previously investigated sites for purposes of temporally ordered analyses of any data set (Table 11.8).

Given that: 1) the earliest documented San Pedro manifestations represent populations that had already fully incorporated maize cultivation into their subsistence base; and 2) somewhat earlier dates have been obtained on maize from elsewhere in the American Southwest (Gilpin 1994; Smiley 1994; Wills 1988), it seems prudent to retain B. Huckell's (1995) unnamed interval preceding the San Pedro phase to account for the arrival and adoption of the cultigen. If the definition of the Early Agricultural period is based on the presence of maize, regardless of its relative importance in subsistence, then an interval is needed to separate the better-documented San Pedro phase from the Middle Archaic.

The manner in which maize arrived in the various parts of the Southwest, the rate at which it was adopted by indigenous populations, and the timing of these events and processes are empirical questions that await new data. Similarly, it remains to be seen whether or not material culture associated with the earliest maize will be appropriately classified as San Pedro. For the moment, retention of B. Huckell's original 1500 B.C. date for the early end of this unnamed interval is appropriate, and Mabry's 1200 B.C. date for the start of the San Pedro phase is also retained. The calibrated pooled age range derived above for the San Pedro phase suggests the possibility that this beginning date may be ultimately moved forward in time.

With respect to the Cienega phase, a simple early and late division is proposed, one that acknowledges the immutability of the patterns created by the calibration curve. Thus, the *Early* Cienega phase is defined to include the interval between approximately 800 B.C. and 400 B.C., while the *Late* Cienega phase falls between 400 B.C. and A.D. 150. Greater chronological control within these intervals will depend upon careful evaluation of suites of dates from individual

occupations, and in particular, upon development of seriation techniques applied to various material classes. As discussed in Chapter 12 and Appendix F, this strictly temporal division of the phase has already proven useful in identifying material variation and changes that may have occurred over the nearly 1,000 years included in Mabry's (1997) definition of the phase.

Refinement of the Cienega/Agua Caliente phase boundary–which appears to fall beyond the influence of the 460-350 B.C. spike in the calibration curve–must await new data. The calibrated pooled age ranges suggest that the boundary could be pushed backward by perhaps 100 years, but this may change as additional data accumulate. One of the dates from Los Pozos is identical to the oldest date from the Agua Caliente component at Square Hearth (1980 b.p.), and one Los Pozos date is actually younger (1940 b.p.; see Tables 11.3 and 11.4). As discussed in Chapter 8, Incipient Plain Ware was being manufactured in very limited quantities for at least several centuries prior to adoption of the fully developed ceramic container technology that marks the beginnings of the Early Ceramic period and the Agua Caliente phase. A full understanding of the timing and processes involved in this important technological development will require much more data than are currently available. However, on strictly logical grounds and limited empirical evidence, it is plausible to suggest that, at some time during the first two centuries A.D., there may have been some populations that employed a full complement of ceramic technology and some that did not.

Thus, there seems little point in a revision at this time, and the A.D. 150 date included in Mabry's (1997) scheme is retained. As discussed above, subdivision of the Agua Caliente phase on the basis of architectural form and perhaps other material differences seems a likely prospect for the future, and additional radiocarbon dates from good contexts are needed. As also noted above, further refinement of the Tortolita phase will require chronometric techniques other than radiocarbon dates, and no revisions are proposed for this phase.

CHAPTER 12

VARIATION AND TREND
DURING THE
EARLY AGRICULTURAL PERIOD

David A. Gregory

The materials from Los Pozos add an important data set to a rapidly accumulating body of information concerning the Early Agricultural period. These materials and studies of associated radiocarbon dates have provided the impetus for discrimination of the Early and Late Cienega phases as described in Chapter 11. While it is possible—if not probable—that earlier and later components are present in the larger site area, the sample from the Central Cluster at Los Pozos represents the first pure Late Cienega phase occupation yet documented in the Tucson Basin. Furthermore, the occupation at Los Pozos occurred immediately prior to, or possibly overlapping with, the adoption of a fully developed ceramic container technology by some Tucson Basin populations (see Chapter 8). The Los Pozos data thus represent a new reference point falling toward the end of the millennium and a half now included in the Early Agricultural period, creating an enhanced opportunity to explore variation and general trends during this long and important interval.

Table 12.1 presents the phase sequence for the Early Agricultural period and lists Tucson Basin sites used in subsequent analyses in their appropriate temporal position. This table is partially based upon the analyses of radiocarbon dates presented in Chapter 11, while the division of materials from Santa Cruz Bend and Stone Pipe into Early Cienega and Late Cienega phase components is based on analyses presented in Appendix F. Sites of the Early Ceramic period Agua Caliente phase are included for purposes of further comparison and contrast.

Using this refined temporal ordering, variation and trend in several selected categories of phenomena are considered here: settlement composition and site structure, architecture, storage technologies and associated behaviors, the composition and density of domestic refuse and selected characteristics of some artifact assemblages. Consideration is given to potential sources of observed variation in each case, and these analyses also provide a context for addressing several of the research issues and questions that guided the investigations at Los Pozos. These comparisons also provide a basis for highlighting similarities and differences between materials dating to the Early and Late Cienega phases. As noted in Chapter 11, this distinction was made to acknowledge the unavoidable effects of the calibration curve, which dictates that these two temporal intervals will always emerge from a large number of radiocarbon dates falling within the Early Agricultural period. The time-ordered perspectives presented here allow assessment of whether or not significant material and other differences correlate with these two purely temporal constructs.

There are several strengths in the sample of sites considered here. Most of the sites listed in Table 12.1 were investigated by the same organization, and in some cases the same individuals participated in the excavations, resulting in overall consistency in the sampling strategies and data recovery techniques employed. Those techniques include volumetric control over excavated samples, so that density measures of artifacts and other materials may be derived for most of the sites. All sites but Milagro are located in the flood-plain of the Santa Cruz River, and all are similar in their riverine ecological setting. All of the sites except Clearwater proved to be spatially extensive and were composed of from dozens to hundreds of features and associated deposits. There is some evidence to suggest that the investigated portions of the Clearwater site also lie at the margins of a much more extensive distribution of features (Diehl 1997a, 1997b). Thus, despite substantial differences between some sites, all appear to have resulted from continued commitment to a particular place along a major drainage, whether by dint of frequently repeated short-term occupations, single or multiple occupations of longer duration, or some combination of these. In most cases, large numbers of features were excavated, large assemblages of artifacts and other materials were recovered, and large numbers of samples for specialized analyses were collected.

However, there are limitations inherent in this data set as well, and a number of caveats must be entered. The spatial sample of the sites available for investigation was limited in all cases. In the instances of Milagro, Stone Pipe, Santa Cruz Bend, and Los Pozos, intensive investigations were largely restricted to a relatively narrow, linear right-of-way. Other similar constraints

Table 12.1. Early Agricultural and Early Ceramic period phases and associated sites.

Period	Phase	Dates	Representative Sites or Components
Early Ceramic	Agua Caliente	A.D. 100-550	Stone Pipe
			Square Hearth
Early Agricultural	Late Cienega	400 B.C.-150 A.D.	Los Pozos
			Late Santa Cruz Bend
			Late Stone Pipe
	Early Cienega	800-400 B.C.	Early Santa Cruz Bend
			Early Stone Pipe
			Clearwater
			Wetlands
	San Pedro	1200-800 B.C.	Wetlands (one feature)
			Costello-King
			Milagro

affected the sample at the other sites. In no case was it possible to physically define the full extent of the remains and to sample that whole on the basis of purely archaeological considerations, with Wetlands probably coming closest to that ideal (Freeman 1997). Unless specifically indicated, the materials from all sites are assumed to be representative of the whole to some degree, but this assumption may be questioned to varying degrees for particular sites.

Another equally significant problem lies in the relatively crude temporal control over groups of features and associated assemblages of materials within sites and components. Even with the division of the Cienega phase presented in Chapter 11, the Early Agricultural period phases of concern here are 400 (San Pedro), 400 (Early Cienega), and 550 (Late Cienega) years long. With some limited exceptions, assignment of features and deposits to one of these phases is largely dependent upon direct radiocarbon dating or documented associations between undated features and directly dated ones. Combined with the apparent palimpsest character of the sites themselves (see below), such limited temporal control dictates that the analyses presented below often rely on only a limited number of features per site per phase and are all quite coarse-grained.

SETTLEMENT COMPOSITION AND FUNCTIONAL VARIATION

As noted above, large numbers of features have been excavated at several Early Agricultural sites. Identified physical elements of these settlements include the following: pit structures inferred to have been used for habitation, storage, food processing activities, or some combination of these; one extra-large pit structure inferred to have served some community function; a variety of extramural pits, including wells in the case of Los Pozos; canals or ditches; and inhumations. Elements of site structure identified on the basis of perceived or measured spatial relationships among features include: house groups representing the spatial domains of social groups, extramural work areas indicated by clusters of extramural pits, a possible plaza area, and cemetery areas. Most sites have been plowed or otherwise subjected to modern disturbance, so that extramural living surfaces and the remains of any less substantial features such as ramadas or above-ground storage features are lacking. Most of the sites considered here are spatially extensive, but current evidence suggests that only relatively small subsets of the features at any site may have been in use at the same time.

There appears to be at least one major dimension of contrast between sites with respect to composition of the settlements represented. In the case of the San Pedro phase Costello-King site and the San Pedro and Early Cienega phase Wetlands site, the ratio of extramural pits to structures is quite high–as great as five or six to one. While the Early and Late Cienega phase components at Santa Cruz Bend and Stone Pipe cannot be fully separated (see Appendix F), this ratio is at least somewhat lower, and probably substantially lower. At Los Pozos, the ratio of extramural pits to structures is approximately one to one.

These different combinations of elements suggest at least some differences in the manner in which the settlements functioned. Nor are these differences as entirely straightforward as they might seem initially. Wetlands had relatively few structures and numerous pits, but a relatively large number of inhumations were recovered from the site. By contrast, no burials were recovered at Costello-King. Despite a nearly equal number of structures and extramural pits, Los Pozos produced only three inhumations.

A principal difficulty in determining the import of these differences lies in the poor temporal control over features and deposits noted above. It is not possible in most cases to sort the sites into relatively contemporaneous groups of features within phases, and many features cannot even be confidently assigned to a particular phase. Even the identification of house groups, work areas, and possible plaza areas at Santa Cruz Bend (Mabry 1998a) does not account for most features at the site, and alternative interpretations of these elements have been suggested (see Appendix F). For the moment, it may be argued that all sites considered here represent palimpsests of features, only a relatively few of which were present at the same time. A challenge for future research lies in the development of alternative methods for accomplishing an effective temporal sorting of these features and deposits.

ARCHITECTURE

Figure 12.1 presents a synoptic illustration of Early Agricultural period architectural variability. Variation in architectural form and construction techniques has been summarized elsewhere (Gregory and Huckell 1998; Mabry 1998a) and previously identified general trends may be summarized as follows:

The shape of structures changes from roughly oval during the San Pedro phase to predominantly circular during both the Early and Late Cienega phases. Early Cienega phase structures are more variable in shape than Late Cienega phase structures, with some roughly oval and irregularly shaped examples represented. As compared to the present sample of San Pedro phase structures, both Early and Late Cienega phase structures are more variable in size and form, and functional differentiation of structures developed by the Late Cienega phase and probably before. Formal entries were not a feature of most Early Agricultural period structures. Two structures at the Wetlands site and possibly another at Santa Cruz Bend appear to represent exceptions to this generalization.

Also previously noted is a general increase in the floor area of structures over the span of the Early Agricultural period. Figure 12.2 illustrates variation in total floor area for structures of the San Pedro, Early Cienega, Late Cienega, and Agua Caliente phases. The so-called big houses at Santa Cruz Bend and Stone Pipe have not been included in the calculations. Given the amount of time represented, the change in floor area is relatively small.

However, as previously shown for the structures at Los Pozos (see Chapter 2), effective floor area varied over the life of individual structures by virtue of intramural pits being intentionally filled. Stratigraphic relationships between structures and intramural pits

are not available for other sites, so it is not possible to compare effective floor areas across this set of sites. It is possible that–were this kind of comparison possible–the differences between phases would be greater. For the present, the greatest differences lie 1) between San Pedro phase structures and those documented for later sites, and 2) differences between Early Ceramic period Agua Caliente phase structures and earlier ones.

STORAGE FACILITIES AND ASSOCIATED BEHAVIORS

Two aspects of Early Agricultural period storage facilities and associated behaviors are considered: 1) the locus of storage within settlements, and 2) storage volume and storage pit morphology.

The Locus of Storage Facilities

Based on ethnographic data from the American Southwest, some authors have argued that variation in the location of storage facilities is correlated with dependence upon agriculture as a subsistence strategy, residential mobility of groups, and occupational stability of settlements:

> Specifically, these data suggest off-site pits for highly mobile people with little dependence on cultivation; large, on-site, extramural storage pits for seasonally mobile groups that are still without major dependence on agriculture; and intramural storage rooms for sedentary pueblo societies that make heavy use of cultivated plants. The crucial factor is how long edibles must be kept. Storage pits are suitable for periods of a few months, Gilman (1983) argues, while indoor storage rooms can reserve crops for several years. In a word, Gilman's ethnographic data indicate that on-site storage pits are associated with occupations of intermediate stability (periods of a few months) . . . while they are not characteristic of permanent or sedentary occupations (Whalen 1994:132; see also Whalen and Gilman 1990).
>
> Seasonally mobile groups with some dependence on agriculture (e.g., the Yuma) store food in large pits outside of the houses, but on the winter residential sites. Small stocks of food for immediate use are kept inside houses in small storage pits or other containers. This is an effective food-keeping strategy, Gilman asserts, because Southwestern storage pits are in use during the dry winter months, when there is little groundwater (Whalen 1994:7).

As is often the case, the archaeological record presents a more difficult and complex picture than that generated using ethnographic data. A principal problem is that the ethnographic continuum does not include maize-cultivating peoples dwelling in pit structures, as is true for the entire Early Agricultural period. Both intramural and extramural storage pits are associated with pit structures in Early Agricultural period settlements of all phases. While the issue of absolute contemporaneity of intramural and extramural features at individual sites or components cannot be definitively resolved, it is likely that storage facilities in both locations were in use at the same time in most cases. Further, settlement pattern data are woefully incomplete, and we do not know if there were contemporaneous "off-site" pits (storage pits located at or near the locus of collection for particular resources, as opposed to within base camps or more permanent settlements).

There does appear to be some shift in emphasis with respect to storage pit location. Large extramural storage pits were the most commonly encountered feature type at the San Pedro phase Milagro site (Huckell and Huckell 1984; Huckell et al. 1995), and all excavated structures had interior storage pits as well. Large extramural pits were also common at the San Pedro phase Costello-King site, where only one structure was found; this single structure also had a large intramural pit (Ezzo and Deaver 1998).

Only five of the excavated extramural pits at Santa Cruz Bend were classified as storage pits, and only two of those at Stone Pipe (Wöcherl 1998:Table 7.2). As noted in Chapter 3, there are problems with the typology applied to the extramural pits, in that features classified as trash pits likely served some other function before becoming repositories for domestic refuse. In addition, some relatively small pits were assigned a storage function by virtue of containing cached artifacts. Thus, the number of extramural storage pits at these two sites may be somewhat higher than is indicated by this typology, and the pits cannot be effectively sorted into Early and Late Cienega phase groups. However, it is clear that intramural storage features were common at both sites during both the Early and Late Cienega phases (Mabry 1998a; Mabry and Archer 1997; also see Appendix F).

At Los Pozos, only three excavated extramural pits can be confidently inferred to have served storage functions (see Chapter 3), while numerous structures had associated intramural storage pits. Some of these intramural pits were filled in during the use-life of the structures in which they were found, and in a number of cases they were originally constructed as covered storage pits and were not present at all during the use-life of the overlying structures (see Chapter 2). However, a large number of intramural pits were definitely used with the associated structures for at least some period of time. A possible functional dichotomy of these large intramural pits has been suggested, based on relative size and associated artifact assemblages (see

(Chapter 2); the analogy of pantries versus grain bins has been used to indicate the nature of these different uses. Parenthetically, it may be noted that the covered storage pits referred to here would have been essentially similar in size and construction to Basketmaker storage cysts, except that they lack the sandstone slabs normally incorporated into the Colorado Plateau features.

Intramural storage pits were absent from Agua Caliente phase structures at the Square Hearth and Stone Pipe sites, and no Agua Caliente phase extramural storage pits were identified at either site (Swartz and Lindeman 1997; Wöcherl and Clark 1997).

Thus, with respect to the location of storage facilities within settlements, the Early Agricultural period sites considered here represent a general pattern intermediate between the extremes of large, on-site, extramural features on the one hand and intramural storage rooms on the other. Both intramural and extramural storage pits were present throughout the period, there appears to have been an increased emphasis on intramural storage through time, and specialized storage structures developed by Late Cienega phase and possibly before. The increased emphasis on intramural facilities is likely related to the increased ratio of structures to extramural features of all types discussed previously. The clearest change in the sequence comes with the virtual disappearance of storage pits in the Agua Caliente phase of the ensuing Early Ceramic period.

The variable patterns within the Early Agricultural period perhaps fit best with the winter residential sites of seasonally mobile groups with some dependence on agriculture cited above. However, paleobotanical remains from Los Pozos and other sites indicate occupation during every season *except* winter, and occupation during the winter season is notoriously difficult to demonstrate archaeologically. Further, these same data show that, in addition to maize, a wide range of wild plants were exploited and the products from them stored in large pits. Taken together, data from Early Agricultural Tucson Basin sites suggest that ethnographic data may be of limited utility in making inferences concerning relative dependence upon agriculture, residential mobility, and occupational stability of settlements, and that other approaches to these important issues must be developed.

Storage Volume and Storage Pit Morphology

Regardless of the locus of storage, another important aspect of storage behaviors is the amount of storage space created and used. The average amount of interior storage space through time may be quantified through comparison of the measured or estimated volumes of intramural pits (Figure 12.3).

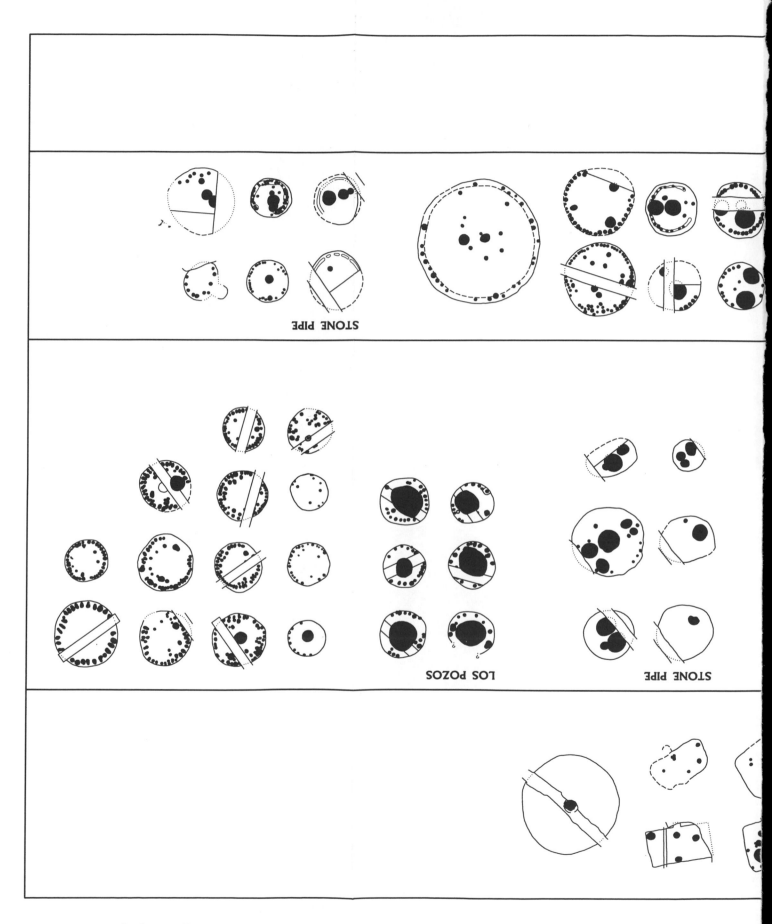

STONE PIPE

LOS POZOS

STONE PIPE

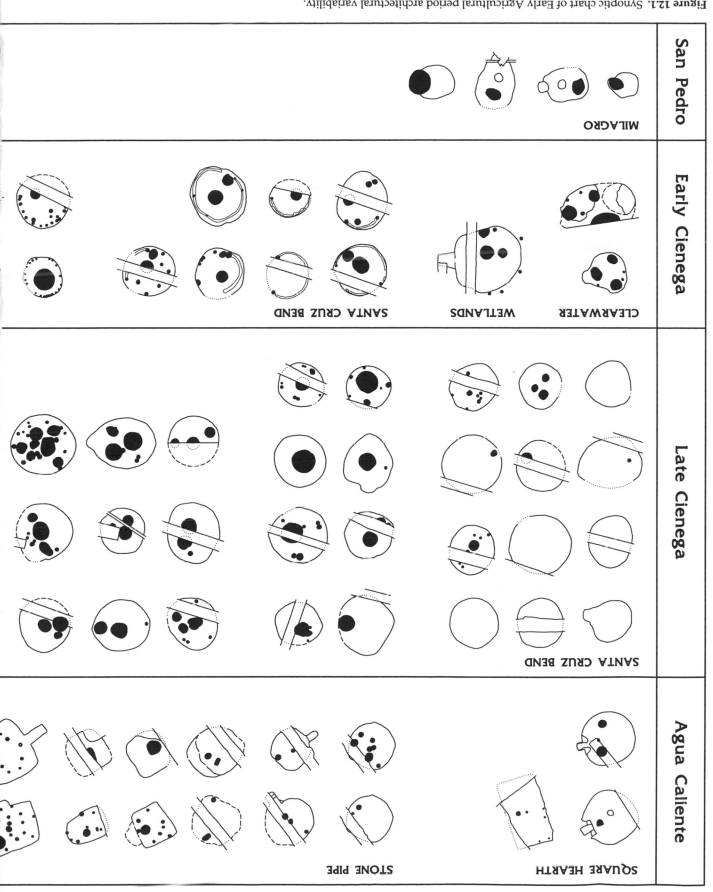

Figure 12.1. Synoptic chart of Early Agricultural period architectural variability.

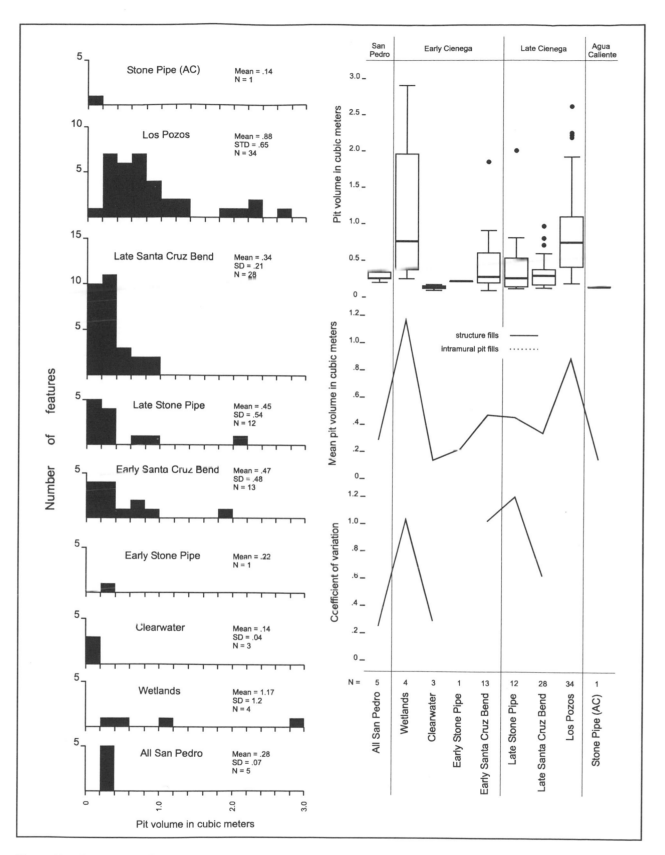

Figure 12.3. Storage pit volumes.

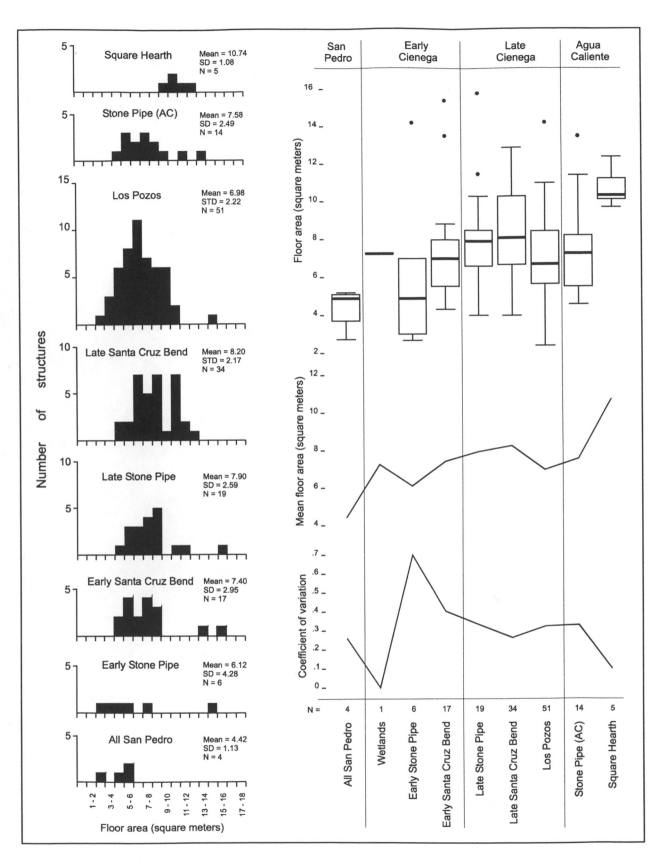

Figure 12.2. Structure floor areas.

Since storage pits have not been uniformly defined and identified for some sites, an arbitrary definition of cylindrical, bell-shaped, or otherwise undercut pits with volumes greater than .2 cubic meters has been used, thus excluding basin-shaped pits. This definition may include some pits with former functions other than storage and may also exclude some small storage pits. With the exception of Wetlands, there is a general trend toward increasing intramural storage pit volume through the Early Agricultural period, and the greatest contrast is between Los Pozos and other sites. Without single high volume outliers within the early Stone Pipe and late Santa Cruz Bend components, the temporal trend would be more marked and Los Pozos would stand out even more.

Along with increasing size of intramural storage pits, there appears to have been a general shift in pit morphology. While most San Pedro phase features are truly bell-shaped or significantly undercut, there are relatively few true bell-shaped or markedly undercut pits in Early and Late Cienega phase components. During these intervals, the largest pits tend to be only slightly belled or cylindrical in shape, and this is particularly true of the Late Cienega phase pits at Los Pozos (see Figure 2.11). In some cases, crumbling of the upper pit margins may also have been a factor in determining shape as revealed by excavation, but many are too regular for this hypothesis to provide a consistent explanation. The change in morphology may be related to the shift of pits to interior space, where the structure would have afforded protection from the elements and eliminated the need for a smaller aperture at the top of the pit. Cylindrical pits would have been easier to dig and would have provided for better air circulation as well. In addition, undercut pits located in structures used for other activities would have been in danger of collapsing under the weight of human traffic near the aperture margins.

Owing to the difficulty in dating extramural features within multicomponent sites and a lack of volumetric data in some cases, detailed temporal comparison of the volumes of extramural storage pits is not possible. For Milagro, the mean volume of extramural storage pits ranges between .38 and .87 m^3, with a mean of .57 (5 pits). For Stone Pipe and Santa Cruz Bend, only cylindrical and bell-shaped pits with volumes greater than .2 m^3 are considered here. For Santa Cruz Bend, the mean is .34 m^3 (range: .25-.41, 3 pits), and for Stone Pipe, the mean is .36 m^3 (range: .22-.48, 3 pits). The pits from these two sites date to either the Early Cienega or Late Cienega phases. Using the same criteria for the Los Pozos extramural pits, the mean is .62 (8 pits). This value is inflated by a single very large (1.95 m^3) and unusual pit with a false bottom (see Chapter 3). If this pit is removed from the sample, the

mean drops to .43 (range: .26-.89, 7 pits). For Los Pozos, we may assume that the extramural pits date to the Late Cienega phase.

While the sample is small and not systematic, several things may be noted. While their ranges overlap, extramural pits at Milagro are as large or larger than the intramural pits, and the total volume of extramural pits is much greater. For Santa Cruz Bend and Stone Pipe, the ranges once again overlap, but there are many intramural pits as large or larger than their extramural counterparts. The largest pits occur in intramural contexts at these two sites, and the total volume of intramural pits far exceeds that of extramural features. A similar pattern exists at Los Pozos. These data tend to support the proposition that there was increasing emphasis on intramural storage through time. The contrast between intramural and extramural storage facilities promises to be a fruitful avenue of inquiry and deserves attention in future studies of Early Agricultural period sites.

COMPOSITION AND DENSITY OF DOMESTIC REFUSE

For sites of all phases, it is clear that abandoned structures and extramural pits frequently served as convenient places for disposal of domestic refuse. Much of this material was probably routinely and sequentially deposited as a result of daily activities over a relatively limited period of time, as indicated by minor deposits of wind- and water-deposited materials within the fills. As noted in Chapter 2, large intramural pits at Los Pozos were sometimes intentionally filled with such refuse, presumably garnered in a single episode from existing deposits elsewhere in the settlement. While not proven, it is likely that this same process occurred at other sites as well.

It is probably also the case that most or all of the fill of individual features was occasionally deposited in a single episode related to specific activities. For example, structures containing extremely high densities of fire-cracked rock and animal bone may have been largely filled with debris from a one-time cleaning of large roasting pits. More specifically, features containing high densities of rabbit bone may represent the one-time residues of communal rabbit hunts and the processing of carcasses. Proximity of abandoned structures to extramural pits dedicated to these or similarly specific activities may also have been a factor in producing variation in the composition and density of feature fills. Future analyses should focus on the sorting of refuse deposits based on characteristics such as those suggested in these hypothetical examples. For present purposes, it is assumed that the fill of most structures and associated intramural pits was likely produced by the daily deposition of domestic refuse over relatively short periods of time.

Along with the sediment, ash, and bits of charcoal that make up the matrix of feature fills, several categories of items occur consistently: flaked stone artifacts, primarily broken flakes and shatter; animal bone; fragments of fire-cracked rock; and ground stone artifacts or fragments thereof. Temporal variation in the composition and density of these elements is explored here using density measures. Densities have been derived on the basis of measured volumes of excavated deposits within individual features. An arbitrary lower limit of .10 m^3 of excavated volume has been used to avoid inflation of densities resulting from small volumes. Two contexts have been examined for purposes of these analyses: intramural pit fills and structure fills.

For each material type or combination of them, a composite graphic is presented which provides visual comparison and contrast of the temporally ordered sites and components. In each case, these graphics include: histograms of measured values for individual features; box plots of the median values, quartiles, extremes, and outliers; line graphs of the overall mean value and mean values for structure fills and intramural pits; and a line graph of the coefficient of variation based on the mean for all features.

Densities Based on the Sums of Various Material Classes

Densities based on the sum of various material classes are presented in three ways. Because fire-cracked rock was not consistently recorded at the Stone Pipe site, it is not possible to include the three components represented there in comparisons that involve this category of items. Thus, comparisons of densities based on the sum of all items contained in a deposit–flaked stone, ground stone, animal bone, fire-cracked rock, and sherds in the case of Agua Caliente phase components–do not include Stone Pipe. Densities calculated on the basis of all materials except fire-cracked rock and those based on artifacts only (flaked stone, ground stone, and sherds) include all sites.

For densities based on the sum of all four categories of items (Figure 12.4), there is no overall temporal trend in the mean. In all Early Agricultural period sites, densities for extramural pits are somewhat higher than those for structure fills, and the ranges for all sites show considerable overlap. There is a marked increase in density from Early Cienega to Late Cienega Santa Cruz Bend features, and again from Late Cienega Santa Cruz Bend to Los Pozos, and then a marked drop to the

Agua Caliente phase features at Square Hearth, which lacks intramural pits.

For densities that exclude fire-cracked rock from the total (Figure 12.5), there is–with the exception of the Clearwater features–a clear trend. Mean densities increase throughout the period and then drop again, markedly in the Agua Caliente phase components at Square Hearth and Stone Pipe. Once again, densities for intramural pits are somewhat consistently higher than those for structure fills and the ranges for all Early Agricultural period sites show considerable overlap. The box plots show that the spike created by the Clearwater features is created by a single anomalous feature; if this feature were eliminated, the temporal trend would be further reified. For densities based on the sum of flaked stone and ground stone artifacts (Figure 12.6), a similar trend is apparent, with densities gradually increasing throughout the period and then dropping markedly during the Agua Caliente phase and intramural pit densities being somewhat higher than those for structure fills. Clearwater features once again create a spike due to a single anomalous feature, and the ranges for individual sites again show considerable overlap.

Flaked Stone, Ground Stone, Animal Bone, and Fire-cracked Rock Densities

The graph of flaked stone densities (Figure 12.7) is similar to that for the combined flaked stone and ground stone totals, including the spike created by the anomalous Clearwater feature and showing intramural pit densities generally higher than those of structure fills. However, the Early Cienega phase Stone Pipe features show the next highest intramural pit densities of flaked stone, also violating the general trend of increasing densities through time.

Ground stone artifacts are the least common of the four classes of items considered here (Figure 12.8), and the differences between intramural pits and structure fills show up markedly for this artifact class. The lower mean structure fill densities show a slight increase through time, while those for intramural pits are highly variable. Once again, the ranges of values for individual sites show considerable overlap.

Mean animal bone densities show a marked increase through time through the Early Agricultural period (Figure 12.9), with a precipitous drop in the Agua Caliente phase; intramural pits again have consistently higher densities than structure fills. Outliers to the Wetlands and Clearwater distributions raise the means for these sites, and without these outliers, the temporal pattern would be sharper.

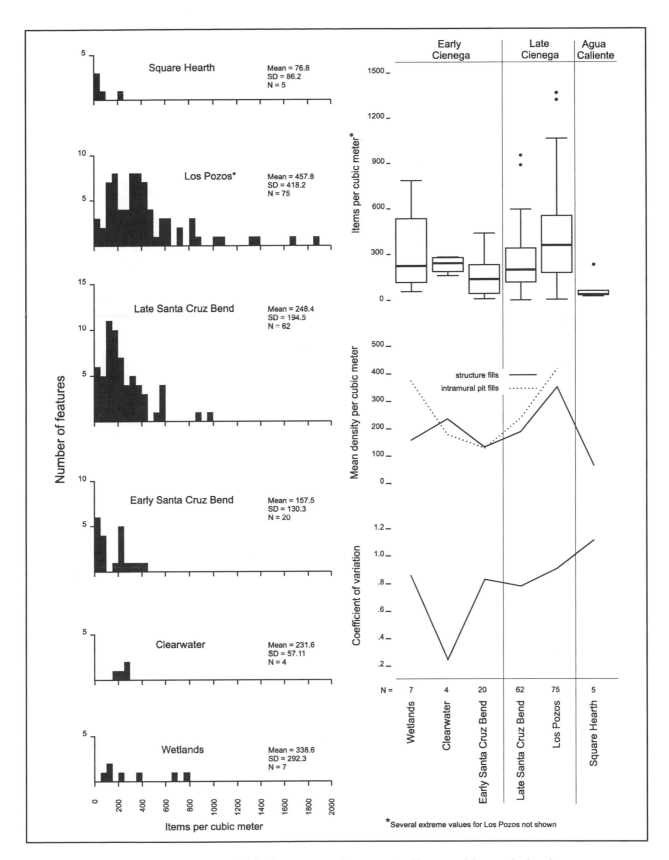

Figure 12.4. Densities based on the sum of flaked stone, ground stone, animal bone, and fire-cracked rock.

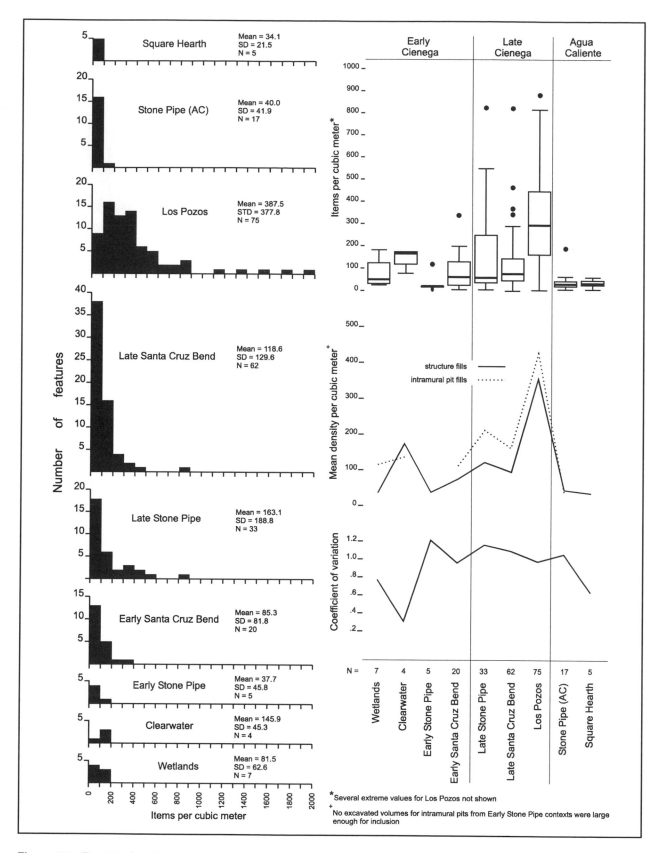

Figure 12.5. Densities based on the sum of flaked stone, ground stone, and animal bone.

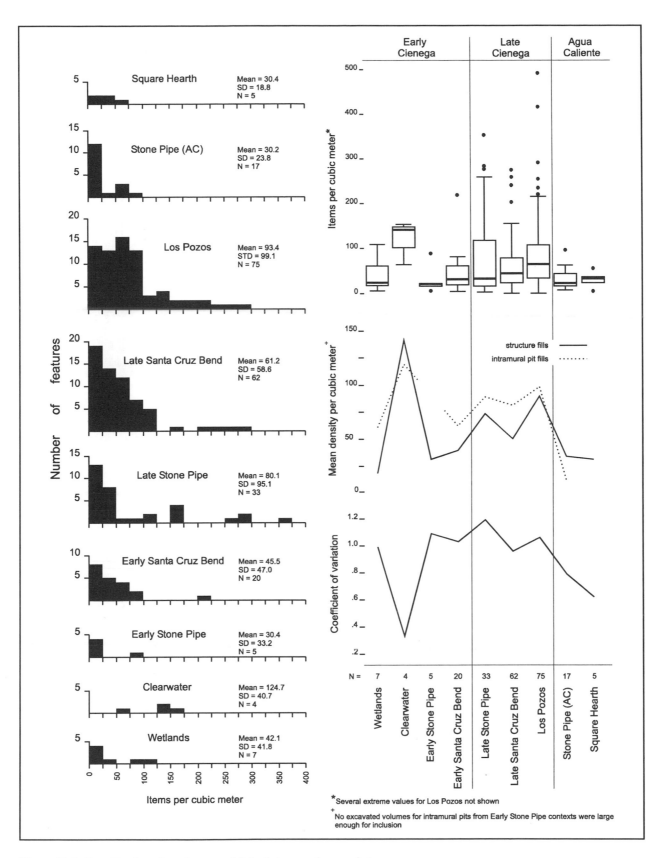

Figure 12.6. Densities based on the sum of flaked stone and ground stone.

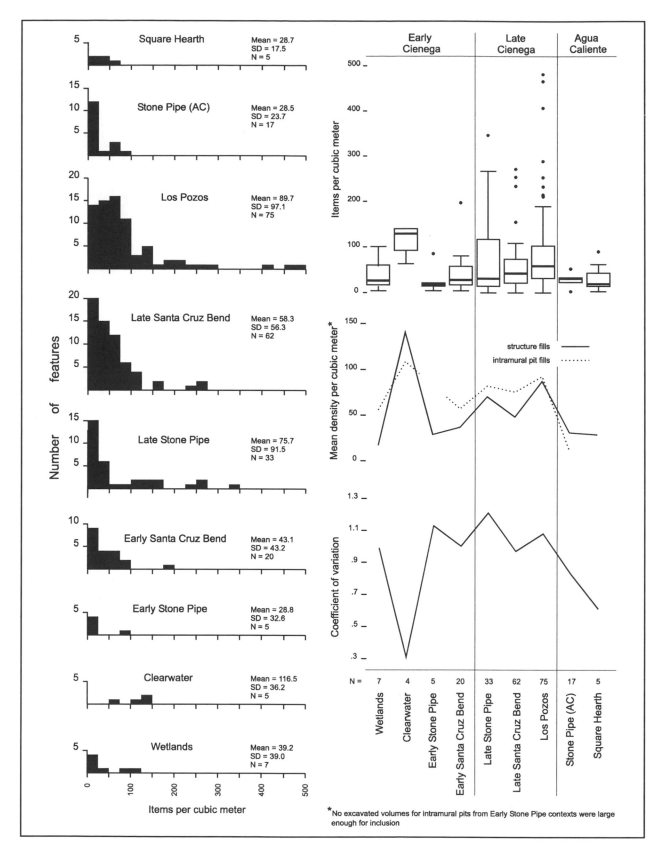

Figure 12.7. Flaked stone densities.

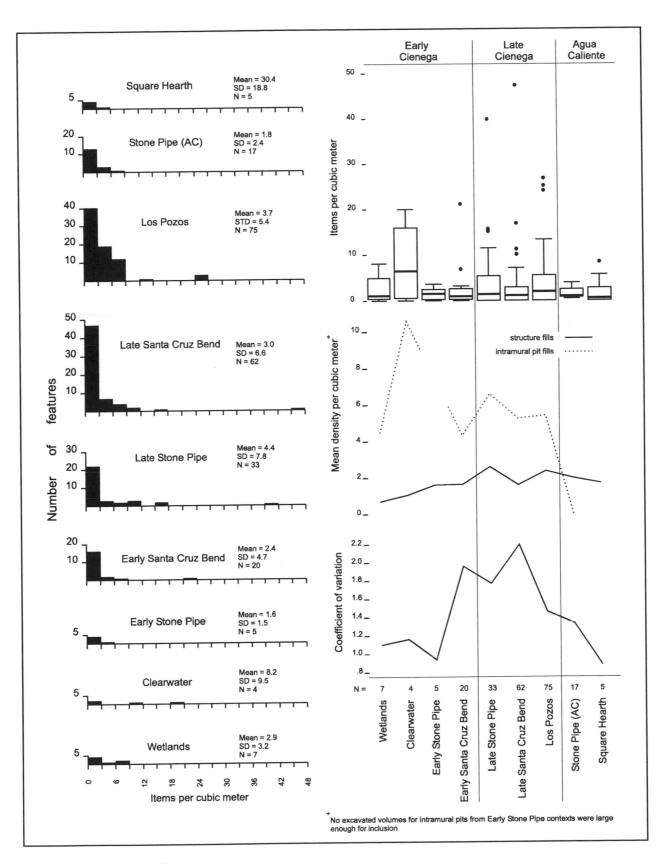

Figure 12.8. Ground stone densities.

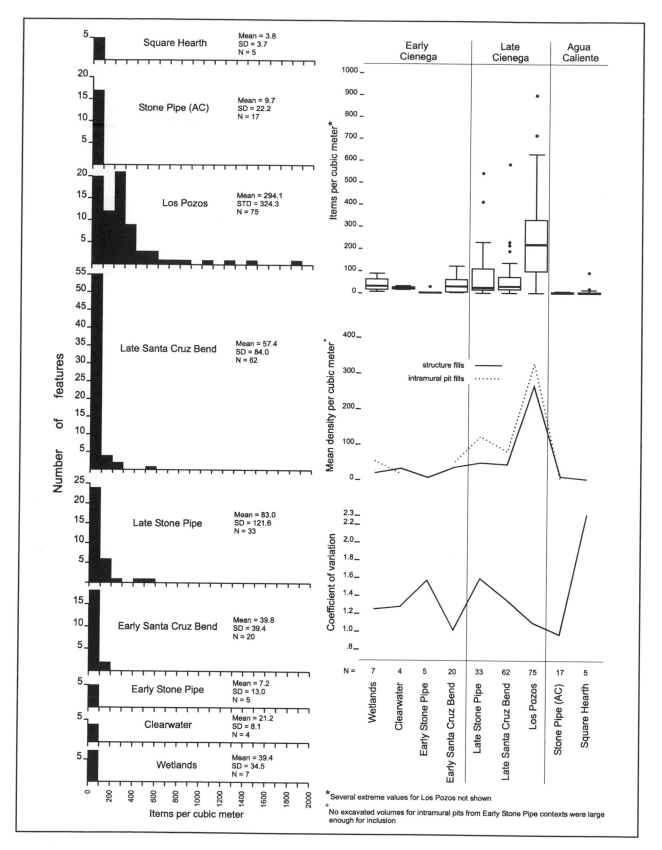

Figure 12.9. Animal bone densities.

While there is considerable overlap in the values for individual sites, Los Pozos stands out has having extremely high densities of animal bone.

Finally, the graph of mean fire-cracked rock densities is relatively flat for all sites save Wetlands (Figure 12.10), and the intramural pit versus structure fill dichotomy is less marked for this category of items. The ranges for all sites once again show considerable overlap.

Discussion

The density of materials in domestic refuse deposits may be inferred to represent the duration of occupation, the intensity of occupation, or both. The data presented above suggest a number of things about the various occupations represented and about possible temporal trends. First, it is possible that the identified trends represent a general increase in the intensity and/or duration of occupation through time. However, the ranges of density measures at individual sites overlap considerably for all material categories and combinations of them. Although some increase in other artifact classes is apparent, it is also clear that the substantially higher densities of animal bone at Los Pozos strengthen the temporal trends apparent in comparisons involving multiple material classes. Thus, any generalizations about increasing intensity and/or duration of occupation within the Early Agricultural period must be considered suspect.

The most marked contrast, and probably the most meaningful one, is found between the Early Agricultural period sites and the two Agua Caliente phase components. When the number and kinds of features present and the spatial extent of the sites are considered, a strong argument may be made that these two Early Ceramic components represent fundamentally different kinds of occupations. That is, they represent less total time and/or different sets of activities when compared to any of their Early Agricultural counterparts.

The considerable overlap in the range of densities for Early Agricultural period sites points up the need to develop methods by which the features and deposits within these sites can be temporally sorted. Even if every feature were radiocarbon dated, the temporal resolution afforded by this method is not sufficient to address issues of occupational duration and intensity. As previously noted, there are substantial differences in the ratio of extramural pits to structures among the several sites. In this regard, it is unfortunate that density measures could not be derived for the Costello-King site, which looks much more like Wetlands than it does Milagro or any of the later sites discussed here.

VARIATION IN SELECTED ARTIFACT CLASSES

Several classes of artifacts show apparent temporal trends during the Early Agricultural period and are discussed here. These include shell artifacts, rare or infrequently occurring artifacts of stone and clay, and obsidian artifacts.

Shell Artifacts

Two aspects of shell artifacts appear to show temporal trends: the genera and species used for shell artifacts and the proportion of whole shell artifacts to those subjected to more complex reduction and manufacturing techniques. Table 12.2 illustrates the genera and species of shell represented in the several assemblages, while Table 12.3 shows the artifact forms. Figure 12.11 illustrates the proportion of artifacts made on whole shells versus those artifacts subjected to more complex reduction and manufacturing techniques. There is a clear increase in the diversity of genera and species used, and a marked decrease in the proportion of shell artifacts made by minimal modifications of whole shells.

Infrequently Occurring Artifacts

Rare or infrequently occurring artifacts include stone and clay items of personal adornment, "eared" stone trays and perforated "pestles," figurines, and the like. Table 12.4 summarizes the occurrence of rare or infrequently occurring items of stone and clay by phase, and a general increase in the diversity of such artifact forms is apparent.

Obsidian Sources

Obsidian is relatively rare in Early Agricultural period and Early Ceramic period assemblages. No obsidian has yet been recovered from a San Pedro phase site. Only three pieces have been recovered from features assigned to the Early Cienega phase (one site), 12 from Late Cienega phase features (3 sites), and two from Agua Caliente phase contexts (1 site). All of these items have been sourced by means of X-ray fluorescence (Shackley 1998).

As shown in Table 12.5, all the Early Cienega examples are from the Cow Canyon or Mule Creek sources near the central Arizona/New Mexico border. Multiple sources reflecting a much wider geography are represented in the Late Cienega examples, including Cow Canyon, Superior, the Sauceda Mountains, and three unknown sources.

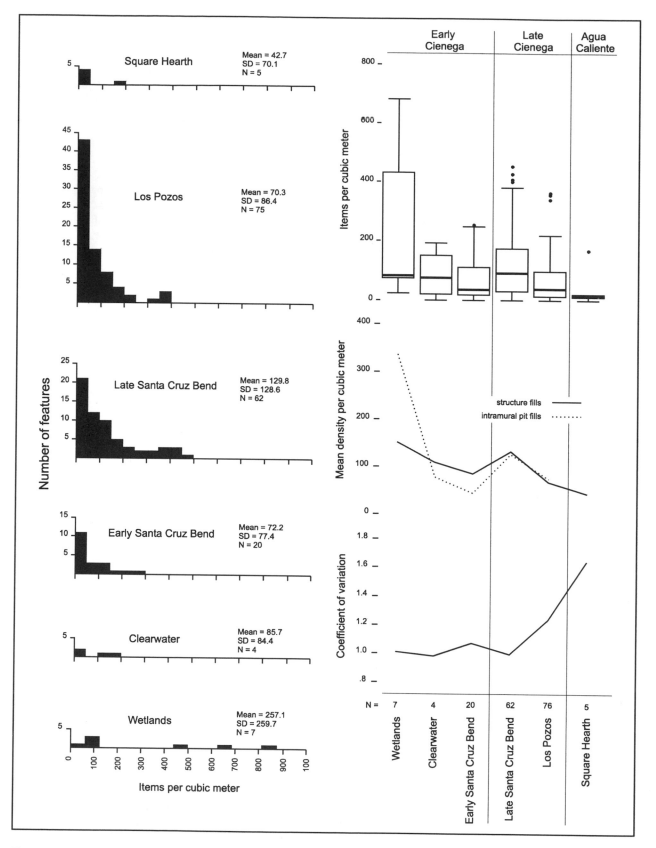

Figure 12.10. Fire-cracked rock densities.

Table 12.2. Shell genera and species.

Phase	San Pedro	Early Cienega			Late Cienega			Agua Caliente	
Site	Milagro	Wetlands	Early Stone Pipe	Early Santa Cruz Bend	Late Stone Pipe	Late Santa Cruz Bend	Los Pozos	Square Hearth	Stone Pipe
Unidentified marine nacreous		●		●	●	●	●		
Haliotis sp.		●			●	●	●		●
Haliotis corrugata									
Haliotis rufescens				●	●	●	●		
Haliotis cracherodii				●					
Haliotis fulgens									
Olivella sp.	●		●	●	●	●	●		
Olivella dama				●	●	●	●		
Olivella biplicata					●	●			
Trivia sp.				●		●	●		
Trivia solandri				●					
Laevicardium sp.	●					●	●		
Laevicardium elatum				●	●	●	●		
Conus sp.						●			
Conus regularis						●			
Columbella sp.						●			
Columbella fuscata									
Columbella (cf. aureomexicana)				●			●		
Glycymeris sp.						●		●	●
Glycymeris gigantea			●	●		●	●	●	●
Trachycardia sp.									
Pteria/Pinctada	●			●			●		
Spondylus/Chama				●					
Mitra sp.						●	●		
Vermetidae							●		●
Anodonta sp.		●			●		●		

Table 12.3. Shell artifact forms.

Phase	San Pedro	Early Cienega			Late Cienega			Agua Caliente	
Site	Milagro	Wetlands	Early Stone Pipe	Early Santa Cruz Bend	Late Stone Pipe	Late Santa Cruz Bend	Los Pozos	Square Hearth	Stone Pipe
Whole shell pendant		●							
Whole shell bead						●	●	●	
Whole valve			●	●	●	●	●		
Cut pendant, rectangular		●		●		●	●		
Cut pendant, geometric		●				●	●		
Cut pendant, triangular		●				●	●		
Cut pendant, solid disk						●	●		●
Cut pendant, washer					●	●			
Cut pendant, other				●		●	●		
Bead/pendant, irregular				●		●			●
Disk bead	●	●	●	●	●	●	●		
Disk bead, squared		●							
Disk bead, rectangular						●	●		
Cylindrical bead					●		●		
Saucer bead									
Cap bead									
Plain bracelet		●	●	●		●		●	●
Reworked bracelet segment									●
Plain perforated shell						●			

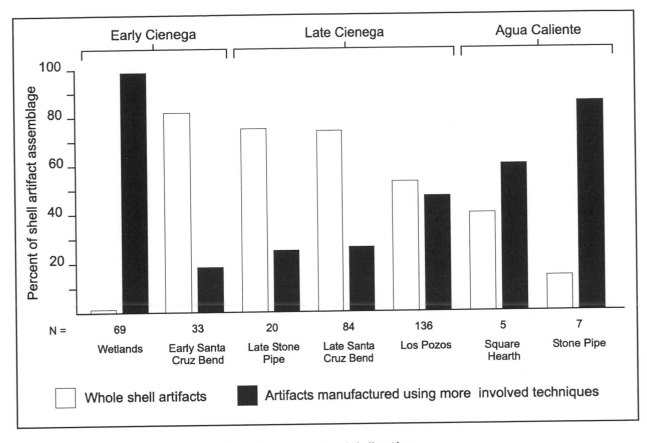

Figure 12.11. Relative proportions of whole shell to manufactured shell artifacts.

One of the unknown sources (Unknown X) is probably located somewhere in Chihuahua or Sonora and another in western Arizona (Unknown A), while the third is entirely unplaced (Appendix E; Shackley 1998). The single Late Cienega Cow Canyon specimen is a projectile point from the ritual floor array found in Feature 819 at Los Pozos (see Appendix B). This point is stylistically earlier and probably was not manufactured during occupation of the site. The two Agua Caliente phase Sauceda specimens are both from the same feature at Square Hearth (Feature 35).

While the sample is small, two patterns may be tentatively identified. First, there is a relative increase in the frequency of occurrence of obsidian artifacts. Second, there is an increase in the diversity of sources from the Early Cienega phase to the Late Cienega phase, with a marked drop-off in the Agua Caliente phase. The source areas are restricted to the northeast during Early Cienega phase, while Late Cienega phase specimens came from the northwest, west, and south. These patterns parallel those noted above for rare or infrequently occurring artifact forms.

THE ENVIRONMENTAL CONTEXT

Given the lengthy period involved, it is possible that environmental variation was a significant variable influencing subsistence strategies during the Early Agricultural period. Figure 12.12 shows correlation between the stratigraphic sequences of floodplain deposits at Santa Cruz Bend, Square Hearth, and Los Pozos (Gregory and Baar 1999; B. Huckell 1998) and inferred rates of deposition during various intervals. Radiocarbon dates from individual sites and components are presented elsewhere (Gregory and Mabry 1998:Figure 4). In addition, a more general perspective on the larger environmental context is provided by inclusion of graphs of solar activity, variation in temperature, and glacial fluctuations over the interval represented. A number of observations serve to summarize the relationships expressed in this graphic and to highlight future research needs and potentials. B. Huckell's (1998) sequence of depositional units is used to provide a consistent frame of reference.

Table 12.4. Rare or infrequently occurring artifacts.

Phase	San Pedro	Early Cienega			Late Cienega			Agua Caliente
Site	Milagro	Wetlands	Clearwater	Early Santa Cruz Bend	Late Stone Pipe	Late Santa Cruz Bend	Los Pozos	Square Hearth
Stone								
Ovoid/disk	●	●	-	-	●	-	-	-
Ball	-	●	-	-	●	●	●	-
Tray, plain	-	●	-	-	-	-	●	-
Bead	-	-	-	●	-	-	-	-
Nose plug	-	-	-	●	-	●	-	-
Pendant	-	-	-	-	-	●	-	-
Tray, knobbed	-	-	-	-	-	●	●	-
Notched pestle	-	-	-	-	-	●	●	-
Cruciform	-	-	-	-	-	●	●	-
Rod	-	-	-	-	●	-	-	-
Pipe	-	-	-	-	●	-	-	-
Clay								
Rod figurine	●	-	-	-	-	●	-	-
Figurine fragment	●	-	●	-	-	●	●	●
Bead, grooved	-	-	-	●	-	●	●	-
Bead, plain	-	-	-	●	-	●	-	-
"Doughnut"	-	-	-	-	-	●	-	-
Ball	-	-	-	-	-	-	-	●
Wide shouldered figurine	-	-	-	-	-	-	●	-
Other								
Artiodactyl femur head	-	-	-	-	-	-	●	-

Table 12.5. Obsidian sources.

Phase	Early Cienega	Late Cienega			Agua Caliente
Site	Early Santa Cruz Bend	Late Stone Pipe	Late Santa Cruz Bend	Los Pozos	Stone Pipe
n=	3	4	2	6	2
Source:					
Mule Creek	●	-	-	●	-
Cow Canyon	●	-	-	-	-
Unknown A (western Arizona?)	-	●	-	-	-
Unknown X (Chihuahua/Sonora?)	-	●	●	-	-
Sauceda	-	●	-	●	●
Superior	-	-	●	●	-
Unknown	-	-	-	●	-

The latter graphs duplicate portions of a figure presented by Bayham and Morris (1986, 1990) as a part of their interpretation of Archaic occupation and use of the Picacho Reservoir area. They argue that periods of high solar luminosity resulted in higher global temperatures and a northward shift in the high pressure zone that affects southern Arizona. These processes would have, in turn, resulted in greater amounts of summer rainfall, a greater availability of water overall, a higher water table, and increased surface retention of water (Bayham and Morris 1990:31-37, Figure 2.4). In the relatively marginal Picacho area, episodes of human occupation from the Middle Archaic to the Protohistoric were found to correlate with intervals of high solar luminosity. What would have been the effects in the Santa Cruz floodplain?

The marked downward trend in solar activity that began at approximately 1800 B.C. and the associated downward trend in temperatures that began somewhat earlier–at approximately 2200 B.C.– appear to correlate with a major shift in the depositional regime of the Santa Cruz. This shift resulted in a rapid accumulation of deep alluvium within the floodplain. All Early Agricultural period and later features documented thus far are intruded into Huckell's Unit 5, with the upper portions of the features and the unit truncated by a modern plowzone.

Deposition of Units 4 and 5 was largely complete prior to the Early Agricultural occupations now represented at numerous sites. Given the dating of these features, Units 4 and 5 appear to have been deposited rapidly, and the start of deposition of Unit 4 appears to signal a shift in the dominant geomorphic processes operating in the floodplain. Based on dates from the Middle Archaic occupation at Los Pozos (in Unit 3), the earliest possible date for the onset of Unit 4 deposition is approximately 2000 B.C.; given the dates from Early Agricultural features intruded through Unit 5, deposition of Units 4 and 5 was largely complete by at least 1000 B.C. and possibly somewhat earlier. Rapid deposition of these units is indicated, and no cultural features have yet been identified *within* them.

The current evidence demonstrates that maize was incorporated into the subsistence strategies of Tucson Basin populations sometime during the interval represented by Units 4 and 5 (Gregory 1999:117-119, Figure 8.33). With reference to the chronology of cultural manifestations, there is as yet little evidence for use or occupation of the floodplain during the San Pedro

phase: a single structure documented at the Wetlands site is the only definitively San Pedro feature yet discovered (Archer and Freeman 1998).

Of interest is the fact that the marked change in floodplain deposition represented by Unit 4 occurred during an interval of decreasing solar activity, decreasing temperatures, and glacial advances. While correlations do not imply causality, these apparent relationships provide a basis for generating hypotheses for future testing. It appears that the shift in deposition created a floodplain having deep alluvium and thus, probably more land suitable for cultivation than was true in the preceding interval. In addition, environmental changes may have increased the productivity of wild plants and thus provided a kind of buffer for populations adopting maize agriculture.

It may also be noted that the two largest Early Agricultural period settlements thus far identified– Santa Cruz Bend and Los Pozos–are both located on the east side of the river on lobes in the floodplain created by broad, westward bends in the river. The Early Cienega phase Wetlands site (Freeman 1997) is located still closer to the present channel and on the same lobe as Los Pozos. This suggests that the river channel has been in approximately the same position along this reach since approximately 1300 B.C., an inference supported by exposures of paleochannels at Los Pozos located far to the west of the zone of occupation.

Deposition of Unit 4 and much of Unit 5 altered the floodplain environment substantially and essentially created a new niche for exploitation by the prehistoric populations. The present evidence suggests that populations who had adopted maize agriculture immediately began to exploit that niche more intensively. Given its relatively restricted spatial extent, we may surmise that groups from a relatively wide geographic area would have been drawn to the area. Thus, the possibility that culturally different groups were present and interacting in the floodplain during the Early Agricultural period must be considered. The current evidence does not rule out such a circumstance and may even, in some cases, provide preliminary support for such an interpretation (see Appendix F).

These issues need further quantification and study. For the present, we can tentatively conclude that environmental conditions were not constant throughout the Early Agricultural period, and that environmental variation may have been an important factor influencing the structure of subsistence-settlement systems and residential mobility during the interval.

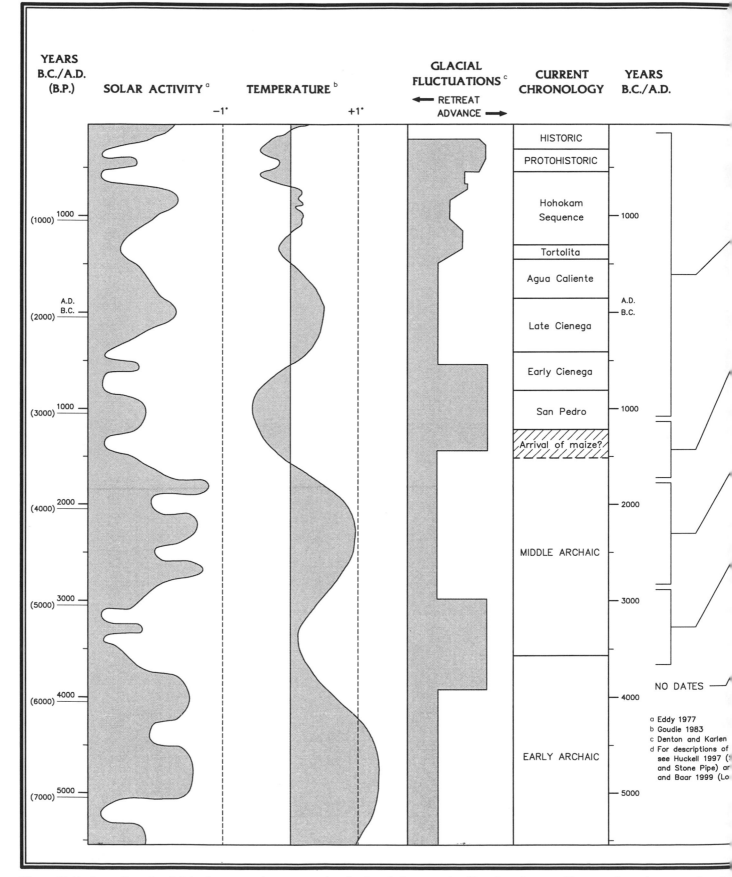

Figure 12.12. Santa Cruz floodplain depositional units, associated cultural phases and radiocarbon dates and large-scale environmental varia

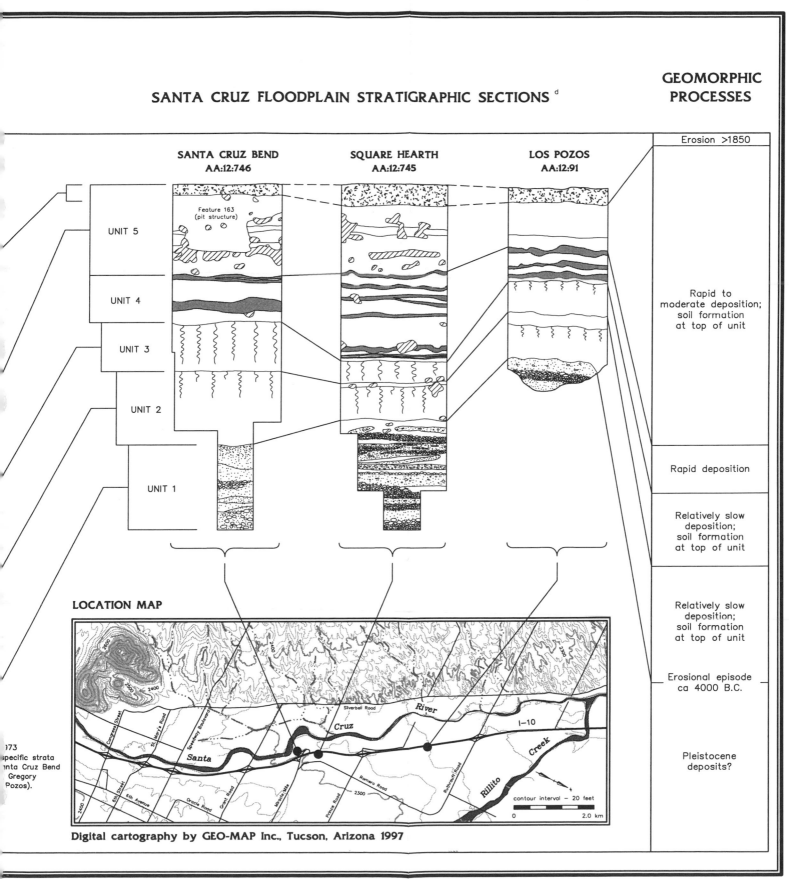

SANTA CRUZ FLOODPLAIN STRATIGRAPHIC SECTIONS [d]

GEOMORPHIC PROCESSES

SANTA CRUZ BEND
AA:12:746

SQUARE HEARTH
AA:12:745

LOS POZOS
AA:12:91

UNIT 5

UNIT 4

UNIT 3

UNIT 2

UNIT 1

Feature 163
(pit structure)

Erosion >1850

Rapid to moderate deposition; soil formation at top of unit

Rapid deposition

Relatively slow deposition; soil formation at top of unit

Relatively slow deposition; soil formation at top of unit

Erosional episode ca 4000 B.C.

Pleistocene deposits?

LOCATION MAP

Silverbell Road

River

Cruz

I-10

Santa

Rillito

Creek

contour interval - 20 feet

0   2.0 km

Digital cartography by GEO-MAP Inc., Tucson, Arizona 1997

973
specific strata
nta Cruz Bend
Gregory
Pozos).

ion.

ARCHITECTURAL DATA TABLES AND FORMULAS USED IN ANALYSIS

David A. Gregory

Table A.1. Comparative data for areas enclosed by different roof support systems.

Feature	Within-the-walls Floor Area	Roof Area: Five Post Option	Percent of Floor Area	Roof Area: Four Post Option	Percent of Floor Area
Best cases					
328[a]	5.98	1.91	31.90	1.31	21.90
389	5.81	1.81	31.20	1.70	29.30
407	4.08	1.20	34.30	1.27	31.10
840	9.10	2.89	31.40	2.35	25.60
Reconstructions					
305	6.97	2.47	35.40	1.85	26.50
327	8.45	2.99	35.40	2.36	27.90
337(1)[b]	6.60	2.75	41.70	2.16	32.70
352	5.81	1.93	33.20	1.61	27.70
355	8.45	2.71	32.10	1.99	23.60
370	7.16	2.83	39.50	2.36	33.00
379	6.42	2.79	38.50	1.97	30.70
819	9.51	2.80	29.40	1.76	18.50
342	10.18	3.12	30.60	2.18	21.40
815	9.08	2.85	31.30	1.83	20.20
318	8.55	3.74	43.70	3.39	39.60

Note: All measurements in m^3.

[a]The six post option produces an area of 1.91 m^2 and a floor percentage of 31.9.

[b]Number in parentheses indicates a sequence of two or more houses subsumed under the same feature number. The number indicates the chronological order from earliest (1) to latest.

Table A.2. Wall posthole data for completely exposed structures.

Feature	Estimated Number of Wall Postholes	Pit Circumference	Mean Distance between Postholes and Pit Margin	Mean Distance between Posthole Centers	Length	Width	Average Diameter	Average Depth
305.00	39	10.18	.13	.26	.18	.12	.15	.13
318.00	37	11.40	.17	.31	.15	.12	.14	.24
324.00	47	10.27	.07	.22	.19	.12	.12	.21
327.00	46	10.65	.06	.23	.17	.13	.15	.19
328.00	42	9.20	.09	.22	.18	.13	.16	.19
337(2)	37	14.01	.10	.38	.30	.20	.35	.25
342.00	41	11.44	.02	.28	.14	.11	.13	.18
352.00	37	8.95	.07	.24	.18	.13	.16	.30
355.00	39	10.81	.08	.28	.22	.15	.19	.31
370.00	42	10.46	.16	.25	.16	.12	.14	.21
379.00	27	9.39	.07	.35	.17	.13	.15	–
389.00	32	8.98	.07	.27	.10	.09	.10	.06
407.00	5	7.79	.10	.00	.06	.06	.06	.06
416.00	17	7.76	.02	.44	.12	.10	.11	.17
815.00	40	11.56	.14	.29	.20	.15	.18	.15
819.00	39	11.28	.06	.29	.17	.13	.15	.22
840.00	35	11.53	.13	.33	.21	.13	.17	.23
863.00	48	11.91	.14	.25	.20	.15	.18	.14
337(1)	42	11.47	.06	.27	.17	.13	.15	.19
355.95	39	10.05	.11	.26	.22	.19	.19	.31

Table A.3. Wall posthole data for partially excavated structures.

Feature	Estimated Number of Wall Postholes	Pit Circumference	Mean Distance between Postholes and Pit Margin	Mean Distance between Posthole Centers	Length	Width	Average Diameter	Average Depth
867.00	45	12.10	.17	.27	.24	.15	.20	.22
302.00	28	8.89	.23	.32	.13	.12	.13	.14
333(3)	45	12.57	.13	.28	.21	.16	.19	.25
354.00	34	10.81	.08	.32	.22	.14	.18	.30
372.00	54	12.97	.09	.24	.14	.12	.14	.21
390.00	47	11.34	.15	.24	.15	.12	.14	.08
425.00	42	11.34	.11	.27	.15	.12	.14	.17
812.00	40	9.49	.12	.24	.13	.10	.12	.10
813.00	39	9.77	.10	.25	.16	.12	.14	.22
817.00	28	7.38	.25	.26	.10	.07	.09	.10
820.00	50	11.97	.12	.24	.26	.16	.21	.22
824.00	53	12.63	.16	.24	.21	.15	.18	.23
825.00	26	9.71	.09	.37	.17	.13	.15	.23
827.00	29	7.54	.11	.26	.17	.13	.15	.17
836.00	44	10.46	.08	.24	.22	.16	.19	.00
861.00	41	10.24	.34	.25	.13	.10	.12	.20
866.00	44	12.79	.08	.29	.15	.12	.14	.13
870.00	47	12.28	.10	.26	.22	.17	.20	.29
882.00	39	11.56	.02	.30	.27	.15	.21	.19
887.00	51	10.71	.13	.21	.16	.14	.15	.18
890.00	30	9.17	.17	.31	.17	.15	.16	.16
898.00	28	11.15	.25	.40	.16	.14	.16	.17
333(2)	48	11.10	.13	.23	.17	.13	.15	.28
333(3)	36	9.39	.13	.26	.21	.16	.19	.27

Table A.4. Distances between wall postholes indicating possible entries.

Feature	Mean Distance between Wall Postholes	Entry Width		Orientation	
		1	2	1	2
389.00	.27	.44	.45	NW	E/NE
318.00	.31	.70	.60	SW	N/NW
370.00	.25	.39	–	E/NE	–
327.00	.23	.40	.42	N/NE	N/NE
342.00	.28	.45	–	E	–
815.00	.29	.51	.51	S/SE	E/SE
819.00[a]	.29	.56	.47	S/SW	NE
379.00	.35	.63	–	S/SE	–
305.00	.26	.97	–	S/SE	–
328.00	.22	.43	–	W	–
352.00	.24	.56	.41	N	S
812.00	.24	.42	–	SE	–
866.00	.29	.52	–	S/SW	–
898.00	.40	.64	–	S/SE	–
354.00	.32	.65	–	S/SE	–
863.00	.25	–	–	SW	–

[a]A third possible entry was present in this structure, 46 cm wide and oriented northeast.

Table A.5. Estimates of within-the-walls areas.

Feature	Pit Area	Mean Distance between Postholes and Pit Margin	Estimated within-the-walls Area
Completely exposed structures			
305.00	8.26	.13	6.97
318.00	10.35	.17	8.55
324.00	8.40	.07	7.74
327.00	9.00	.06	8.45
328.00	6.72	.09	5.98
337.00	15.80	.10	14.25
342.00	10.38	.02	10.18
352.00	6.40	.07	5.81
355.00	9.30	.08	8.45
370.00	8.70	.16	7.16
379.00	7.03	.07	6.42
389.00	6.43	.07	5.81
407.00	4.83	.10	4.08
416.00	4.80	.02	4.68
417.00	5.56	.00	5.56
815.00	10.64	.14	9.08
819.00	10.15	.06	9.51
840.00	10.60	.13	9.19
863.00	11.31	.14	9.73
337.95	10.46	.06	6.60
355.95	8.04	.11	6.97
318.95	10.35	.17	8.55
Partially excavated structures			
302.00	6.28	.23	4.45
333.00	12.58	.13	10.99
354.00	9.27	.08	8.45
372.00	13.41	.09	12.32
390.00	10.24	.15	8.66
425.00	10.22	.11	9.08
812.00	7.18	.12	6.07
813.00	7.59	.10	6.70
817.00	4.34	.25	2.72
820.00	11.40	.12	10.07
824.00	12.70	.16	10.75
825.00	7.51	.09	6.70
827.00	4.54	.11	3.73
836.00	8.70	.08	7.94
861.00	8.36	.34	5.23
864.00	6.50	.00	6.51
866.00	13.00	.08	12.07
867.00	11.65	.17	9.73
870.00	9.90	.10	8.76
882.00	10.61	.02	10.41
887.00	9.13	.13	7.84
890.00	6.70	.17	5.23
898.00	9.90	.25	7.35
333.95	8.30	.13	6.97
333.96	5.94	.13	4.83
864.95	6.50	.00	6.51

Table A.6. Metric data and other attributes for intramural pits.

Feature	Diameter/depth Ratio	Maximum Diameter	Average Width	Average Diameter	Area (m³)	Depth	Vol (m³)	Open When Structure Abandoned	Filled in During Use-life of Structure	Evidence of Refurbishing	Used as Hearth after Filling	Posthole Present	Sand Lining Present	Floor Assemblage Present
302.01	1.125	.90	.80	.85	.57	.80	.46	-	-	-	-	-	-	-
305.01	2.273	1.50	1.30	1.40	1.54	.66	1.02	+	-	-	-	-	-	-
318.01	2.759	1.60	1.40	1.50	1.77	.58	1.03	-	+	-	-	-	-	-
324.14	1.616	1.18	.95	1.07	.90	.73	.66	-	+	-	-	-	-	+
327.01	1.579	1.50	1.50	1.50	1.77	.95	1.68	-	+	-	-	-	+	-
337.14	1.154	1.05	1.03	1.04	.85	.91	1.40	-	+	-	-	-	-	+
342.01	2.412	2.05	1.62	1.84	2.66	.85	2.26	-	+	-	-	-	-	+
352.01	1.444	1.30	1.20	1.25	1.23	.90	1.11	-	+	-	+	-	-	-
354.01	1.444	.78	.70	.74	.43	.54	.23	?	?	-	-	-	-	-
355.09	1.084	1.03	.99	1.01	.96	.95	.72	-	+	-	-	+	-	-
355.10	1.186	.70	.67	.69	.37	.59	.22	-	+	-	+	-	-	+
370.01	1.130	1.13	1.00	1.07	.90	1.00	.90	-	-	+	-	-	+	-
372.01	3.382	1.15	.93	1.04	.85	.34	.27	-	-	-	-	+	-	-
390.16	3.268	1.83	1.83	1.83	2.63	.94	2.47	-	+	-	-	-	-	-
416.01	1.316	.75	.70	.73	.42	.57	.24	+	-	-	-	-	-	-
425.01	3.452	1.45	1.20	1.33	1.39	.42	.58	+	-	-	-	-	-	-
812.23	1.290	1.20	1.19	1.20	1.13	.93	1.05	+	-	+	-	-	-	+
815.05	2.750	1.32	1.20	1.26	1.25	.48	.60	-	+	-	+	-	+	-
817.01	2.727	.60	.50	.55	.24	.22	.05	+	-	-	-	-	-	-
819.02	1.118	.85	.77	.81	.52	.76	.40	-	-	-	-	-	-	-
820.01	1.596	1.74	1.74	1.74	2.38	1.09	2.59	-	-	+	+	+	+	-
824.02	1.867	1.40	1.10	1.25	1.23	.75	.92	-	+	+	-	-	-	-
825.01	2.643	1.11	1.11	1.11	.97	.42	.41	-	+	+	-	-	-	-
827.01	3.619	1.52	1.45	1.49	1.74	.42	.73	+	-	-	-	-	+	-
836.01	2.414	1.69	1.13	1.41	1.56	.70	1.09	-	+	-	-	-	+	+
861.01	2.200	1.10	1.07	1.09	.93	.50	.47	+	-	-	-	-	-	+
863.01	1.868	1.70	1.50	1.60	2.01	.91	1.83	-	+	+	-	-	-	-
864.02	1.638	.77	.65	.71	.40	.47	.19	-	+	-	-	-	-	-
864.01	1.852	1.00	.80	.90	.64	.54	.35	-	+	+(?)	-	-	-	+
867.01	1.614	.92	.92	.92	.66	.57	.38	?	?	-	-	-	-	-
882.01	1.154	1.20	1.20	1.20	1.13	1.04	1.18	-	+	-	-	-	+	-
890.01	1.613	1.21	1.16	1.19	1.11	.75	.83	-	-	-	-	-	-	-
898.01	1.688	1.08	1.00	1.04	.85	.64	.54	-	+	-	+	-	-	-

Table A.7. Equations for estimating volume of earth excavated during construction.

Total earth removed = structure pit volume + intramural pit volume (if any) + (number of estimated wall postholes × mean wall posthole volume) + (number of roof support posts × mean interior posthole volume)

Mean posthole volume = (.5 × average diameter)² × 3.1416

Table A.8. Equations used in estimating perishable materials used in construction.

Total length of wall posts = number of estimated posts × (2 dm + mean posthole depth)

Total length of roof support posts = (1.5 m + mean interior posthole depth) × number of support posts

Total length of rafters = sum of measured distance between roof support postholes OR mean value for all measured examples

Total length of pieces used in roof covering = $\frac{roof\ area}{.01}$

Total surface area of thatching = (area of a hemisphere with a base equal to the within-the-walls area) - (roof area)

Table A.10. Equations for estimating amounts of earth used in construction.

Posthole volume = number of estimated wall postholes × mean posthole volume

Volume of space between pit wall and wall of structure = area of structure pit - within-the-walls area

Embankment volume ={[(radius of floor area + 50, 60, or 70 cm)² × 3.1416] - within-the-walls area} × .125, .18, or .245

Roof volume = roof area × .10

Total used in construction = posthole volume + wedge volume + embankment volume + roof volume

Total earth remaining/additional earth needed = total earth removed - total used in construction

Table A.9. Estimates of perishable materials used in construction.

Feature	Floor Area[a]	Estimated No of Wall Posts	Total Wall Post Length	Total Roof Support Length	Total Rafter Length	Total Stringer Length	Total Roof Element Length	Area of Thatch[a]
305.00	6.97	39	83.07	6.64	6.11	44.86	164.67	11.47
318.00	8.55	37	82.88	6.88	–	49.19	194.67	14.18
324.00	7.74	47	103.87	6.64	–	46.93	176.67	12.83
327.00	8.45	46	100.74	6.84	7.19	49.18	199.33	13.91
328.00	5.98	42	91.98	7.00	5.29	40.71	127.33	10.05
337(2)	14.25	37	83.25	6.32	–	63.52	324.67	23.63
342.00	10.18	41	89.38	6.96	6.95	52.59	208.00	17.24
352.00	5.81	37	85.10	7.04	5.40	40.34	127.33	9.71
355.00	8.45	39	90.09	6.88	6.44	48.43	180.67	14.19
370.00	7.16	42	92.82	6.92	5.99	46.37	188.67	11.49
379.00	6.42	27	–	6.00	6.17	44.68	186.00	10.05
389.00	5.81	32	65.92	6.24	5.28	39.98	120.67	9.81
407.00	4.08	–	–	6.32	4.67	34.12	93.33	6.76
416.00	4.68	17	36.89	6.00	–	36.38	106.67	7.76
417.00	5.56	–	–	6.76	–	39.59	126.67	9.22
815.00	9.08	40	86.00	6.68	–	50.70	207.33	15.05
819.00	9.51	39	86.58	6.76	6.62	50.53	186.67	16.22
840.00	9.19	35	78.05	6.80	6.61	50.32	192.67	15.49
863.00	9.73	32	68.48	6.88	–	52.59	222.00	16.13
337(1)	6.61	42	91.98	6.60	–	45.06	183.33	10.47

[a]Measurements in m³; all others in linear meters.

Table A.11. Estimated earth used in construction: four post roof support system.

Feature	Volume of Earth Removed	Embankment Volume			Volume of Earth in Roof	Volume of Space between Structure Wall and Pit Wall	Volume of Earth Used in Construction			Amount of Earth Remaining		
		1	2	3			1	2	3	1	2	3
305.00	3.46	.68	1.98	1.22	.19	.32	1.19	1.73	2.49	2.27	1.73	.97
318.00	1.99	.75	2.16	1.32	.34	.67	1.76	2.33	3.17	.23	-.34	-1.20
324.00	2.51	.72	2.07	1.27	.21	.11	1.04	1.59	2.39	1.47	.92	.12
327.00	1.25	.74	2.14	1.32	.24	.08	1.06	1.64	2.46	.19	-.39	-1.20
328.00	2.04	.64	1.86	1.14	.13	.19	.96	1.46	2.18	1.08	.58	-.14
337.00	5.09	.94	2.67	1.65	.39	.43	1.76	2.47	3.49	3.33	2.62	1.60
342.00	1.40	.81	2.32	1.43	.22	.04	1.07	1.69	2.58	.33	-.29	-1.20
352.00	1.79	.63	1.84	1.13	.16	.13	.92	1.42	2.13	.87	.37	-.34
355.00	1.49	.74	2.14	1.32	.20	.14	1.08	1.66	2.48	.41	-.17	-.99
370.00	1.18	.69	2.00	1.23	.24	.28	1.21	1.75	2.52	-.03	-.57	-1.30
379.00	.41	.66	1.92	1.18	.20	.12	.98	1.50	2.24	-.57	-1.10	-1.80
389.00	1.21	.63	1.84	1.13	.17	.11	.91	1.41	2.12	.30	-.20	-.91
407.00	1.06	.55	1.61	.98	.13	.16	.84	1.27	1.90	.22	-.21	-.84
416.00	.75	.58	1.69	1.03	.13	.01	.72	1.17	1.83	.03	-.42	-1.10
417.00	.30	.62	1.81	1.11	.15	.25	1.02	1.51	2.21	-.72	-1.20	-1.90
815.00	5.32	.77	2.21	1.36	.18	.70	1.65	2.24	3.09	3.67	3.08	2.23
819.00	3.61	.78	2.25	1.38	.18	.17	1.13	1.73	2.60	2.48	1.88	1.01
840.00	1.62	.77	2.22	1.36	.24	.14	1.15	1.74	2.60	.47	-.12	-.98
863.00	2.15	.79	2.27	1.40	.26	.44	1.49	2.10	2.97	.66	.05	-.82
337.95	3.92	.67	1.94	1.19	.22	.25	1.14	1.66	2.41	2.78	2.26	1.51

Note: All measurements in m³.

Table A.12. Densities of materials in structure fill.

Feature	Excavated Volume (m³)	Flaked Stone	Ground Stone	Animal Bone	Fire-cracked Rock	Total	Densities (per m³)				
							Flaked Stone	Ground Stone	Animal Bone	Fire-cracked Rock	Overall Density
302.00	.4048	13	0	69	28	110	32.11	.00	170.45	69.17	271.74
305.00	.6386	25	2	63	11	101	39.15	3.13	98.65	17.23	158.16
318.00	.8246	49	0	88	5	142	59.42	.00	106.72	6.06	172.20
324.00	1.0725	81	0	263	11	355	75.52	.00	245.22	10.26	331.00
327.00	.2835	9	0	13	10	32	31.75	.00	45.86	35.27	112.87
328.00	.4550	61	0	828	162	1,051	134.07	.00	1,819.78	356.04	2,309.89
333.00	1.1592	157	6	293	22	478	135.44	5.18	252.76	18.98	412.35
337.00	1.1934	48	4	358	97	507	40.22	3.35	299.98	81.28	424.84
342.00	.5928	8	1	108	11	128	13.50	1.69	182.19	18.56	215.92
352.00	.7050	27	1	195	29	252	38.30	1.42	276.60	41.13	357.45
354.00	.7089	126	5	236	15	382	177.74	7.05	332.91	21.16	538.86
355.00	1.2008	74	8	294	22	398	61.63	6.66	244.84	18.32	331.45
370.00	.3768	33	3	108	82	226	87.58	7.96	286.62	217.62	599.79
372.00	1.6775	83	1	404	595	1,083	49.48	.60	240.83	354.69	645.60
379.00	.9916	72	1	228	4	305	72.61	1.01	229.93	4.03	307.58
389.00	1.1600	110	2	244	76	432	94.83	1.72	210.34	65.52	372.41
390.00	1.2288	312	1	774	151	1,238	253.91	.81	629.88	122.88	1,007.49
407.00	1.0100	80	0	95	9	184	79.21	.00	94.06	8.91	182.18
416.00	.4800	61	3	5	6	75	127.08	6.25	10.42	12.50	156.25
417.00	.2800	1	0	9	7	17	3.57	.00	32.14	25.00	60.71
425.00	1.7848	383	11	489	644	1,527	214.59	6.16	273.98	360.82	855.56
812.00	1.0665	95	0	177	111	383	89.08	.00	165.96	104.08	359.12
813.00	.6460	75	3	49	62	189	116.10	4.64	75.85	95.98	292.57
815.00	1.7244	31	2	283	105	421	17.98	1.16	164.12	60.89	244.14
817.00	.3458	2	2	0	4	8	5.78	5.78	0.00	11.57	23.13
819.00	1.5618	364	3	510	22	899	233.06	1.92	326.55	14.09	575.62
820.00	.8119	18	0	76	32	126	22.17	.00	93.61	39.41	155.19
824.00	1.1408	23	0	93	2	118	20.16	.00	81.52	1.75	103.44
825.00	1.2150	106	1	264	24	395	87.24	.82	217.28	19.75	325.10
827.00	.1960	5	0	2	16	23	25.51	.00	10.20	81.63	117.35
836.00	1.5312	252	0	571	121	944	164.58	.00	372.91	79.02	616.51
840.00	.2438	118	2	78	2	200	484.00	8.20	319.93	8.20	820.34
861.00	1.2030	96	0	465	0	561	79.80	.00	386.53	0.00	466.33
863.00	.9510	49	3	356	53	461	51.52	3.15	374.34	55.73	484.75
864.00	.4564	37	0	56	81	174	81.07	.00	122.70	177.48	381.24
866.00	1.3690	138	7	813	28	986	100.80	5.11	593.86	20.45	720.23
867.00	1.4079	151	9	329	42	531	107.25	6.39	233.68	29.83	377.16
870.00	.6480	14	2	184	0	200	21.60	3.09	283.95	0.00	308.64
882.00	.7208	72	0	517	14	603	99.89	.00	717.26	19.42	836.57
887.00	1.1613	61	7	240	128	436	52.53	6.03	206.66	110.22	375.44
890.00	.5950	42	0	130	12	184	70.59	.00	218.49	20.17	309.24
898.00	.7524	15	0	75	15	105	19.94	.00	99.68	19.94	139.55

Table A.13. Densities of materials in intramural pit fill.

Feature	Excavated Volume (m³)	Flaked Stone	Ground Stone	Animal Bone	Fire-cracked Rock	Total	Densities (per m³)				
							Flaked Stone	Ground Stone	Animal Bone	Fire-cracked Rock	Overall Density
305.01	.2646	9	1	6	2	18	34.01	3.78	22.68	7.56	68.03
318.01	.3074	90	0	50	0	140	292.78	.00	162.65	.00	455.43
318.02	.3600	31	1	0	0	32	86.11	2.78	.00	.00	88.89
324.14	.2886	40	0	124	0	164	138.60	.00	429.66	.00	568.26
327.01	1.4500	166	11	136	72	385	114.48	7.59	93.79	49.66	265.52
337.14	.5168	18	3	27	12	60	34.83	5.80	52.24	23.22	116.10
342.01	.5625	8	5	144	59	216	14.22	8.89	256.00	104.89	384.00
352.01	.4284	35	1	57	63	156	81.70	2.33	133.05	147.06	364.15
354.01	.2500	16	0	27	2	45	64.00	.00	108.00	8.00	180.00
355.09	.5244	6	3	203	18	230	11.44	5.72	387.11	34.32	438.60
355.10	.1541	5	0	20	0	25	32.45	.00	129.79	.00	162.23
370.01	.1660	10	4	35	23	72	60.24	24.10	210.84	138.55	433.73
372.01	.2610	7	2	70	44	123	26.82	7.66	268.20	168.58	471.26
390.16	.5764	214	2	283	24	523	371.27	3.47	490.98	41.64	907.36
416.01	.1248	9	0	10	0	19	72.12	.00	80.13	.00	152.24
425.01	.3318	47	1	193	112	353	141.65	3.01	581.68	337.55	1,063.89
812.23	.5170	30	2	123	51	206	58.03	3.87	237.91	98.65	398.45
813.01	.3276	14	1	6	14	35	42.74	3.05	18.32	42.74	106.84
815.05	.3360	1	0	71	6	78	2.98	.00	211.31	17.86	232.14
817.01	.0528	0	5	0	0	5	0.00	94.70	.00	.00	94.70
819.02	.3700	17	2	27	3	49	45.95	5.41	72.97	8.11	132.43
820.01	.9374	60	1	328	38	427	64.01	1.07	349.90	40.54	455.52
824.02	.2542	5	0	3	1	9	19.67	.00	11.80	3.93	35.41
825.01	.4410	84	0	203	39	326	190.48	.00	460.32	88.44	739.23
827.01	.1848	4	0	274	29	307	21.65	.00	1,482.68	156.93	1,661.26
836.01	.4389	93	2	239	25	359	211.89	4.56	544.54	56.96	817.95
861.01	.4200	1	2	62	70	135	2.38	4.76	147.62	166.67	321.43
863.01	.7488	42	10	335	68	455	56.09	13.35	447.38	90.81	607.64
864.01	.2146	17	1	31	46	95	79.22	4.66	144.45	214.35	442.68
864.02	.0836	14	4	23	54	95	167.46	47.85	275.12	645.93	1,136.36
867.01	.3560	47	9	368	46	470	132.02	25.28	1,033.71	129.21	1,320.22
882.01	.2700	7	0	70	0	77	25.93	.00	259.26	.00	285.19
890.01	.2100	11	1	64	8	84	52.38	4.76	304.76	38.10	400.00
898.01	.2496	102	2	224	14	342	408.65	8.01	897.44	56.09	1,370.19

Table A.14. Composition of deposits from structure fill.

Feature	Excavated Volume (m³)	Flaked Stone	Ground Stone	Animal Bone	Fire-cracked Rock	Total	Percent Flaked Stone	Ground Stone	Animal Bone	Fire-cracked Rock
305.00	.6386	25	2	63	11	101	24.75	1.98	62.38	10.89
318.00	.8246	49	0	88	5	142	34.51	.00	61.97	3.52
324.00	1.0725	81	0	263	11	355	22.82	.00	74.08	3.10
327.00	.2835	9	0	13	10	32	28.13	.00	40.63	31.25
328.00	.4550	61	0	828	162	1,051	5.80	.00	78.78	15.41
333.00	1.1592	157	6	293	22	478	32.85	1.26	61.30	4.60
337.00	1.1934	48	4	358	97	507	9.47	.79	70.61	19.13
342.00	.5928	8	1	108	11	128	6.25	.78	84.38	8.59
352.00	.7050	27	1	195	29	252	10.71	.40	77.38	11.51
354.00	.7089	126	5	236	15	382	32.98	1.31	61.78	3.93
355.00	1.2008	74	8	294	22	398	18.59	2.01	73.87	5.53
370.00	.3768	33	3	108	82	226	14.60	1.33	47.79	36.28
372.00	1.6775	83	1	404	595	1,083	7.66	.09	37.30	54.94
379.00	.9916	72	1	228	4	305	23.61	.33	74.75	1.31
389.00	1.1600	110	2	244	76	432	25.46	.46	56.48	17.59
390.00	1.2288	312	1	774	151	1,238	25.20	.08	62.52	12.20
407.00	1.0100	80	0	95	9	184	43.48	.00	51.63	4.89
416.00	.4800	61	3	5	6	75	81.33	4.00	6.67	8.00
417.00	.2800	1	0	9	7	17	5.88	.00	52.94	41.18
425.00	1.7848	383	11	489	644	1,527	25.08	.72	32.02	42.17
812.00	1.0665	95	0	177	111	383	24.80	.00	46.21	28.98
813.00	.6460	75	3	49	62	189	39.68	1.59	25.93	32.80
815.00	1.7244	31	2	283	105	421	7.36	.48	67.22	24.94
817.00	.3458	2	2	0	4	8	25.00	25.00	0.00	50.00
819.00	1.5618	364	3	510	22	899	40.49	.33	56.73	2.45
820.00	.8119	18	0	76	32	126	14.29	.00	60.32	25.40
824.00	1.1408	23	0	93	2	118	19.49	.00	78.81	1.69
825.00	1.2150	106	1	264	24	395	26.84	.25	66.84	6.08
827.00	.1960	5	0	2	16	23	21.74	.00	8.70	69.57
836.00	1.5312	252	0	571	121	944	26.69	.00	60.49	12.82
840.00	.2438	118	2	78	2	200	59.00	1.00	39.00	1.00
861.00	1.2030	96	0	465	0	561	17.11	.00	82.89	0.00
863.00	.9510	49	3	356	53	461	10.63	.65	77.22	11.50
864.00	.4564	37	0	56	81	174	21.26	.00	32.18	46.55
866.00	1.3690	138	7	813	28	986	14.00	.71	82.45	2.84
867.00	1.4079	151	9	329	42	531	28.44	1.69	61.96	7.91
870.00	.6480	14	2	184	0	200	7.00	1.00	92.00	0.00
882.00	.7208	72	0	517	14	603	11.94	.00	85.74	2.32
887.00	1.1613	61	7	240	128	436	13.99	1.61	55.05	29.36
890.00	.5950	42	0	130	12	184	22.83	.00	70.65	6.52
898.00	.7524	15	0	75	15	105	14.29	.00	71.43	14.29

Table A.15. Composition of deposits from intramural pit fill.

Feature	Excavated Volume (m³)	Flaked Stone	Ground Stone	Animal Bone	Fire-cracked Rock	Total	Percent Flaked Stone	Ground Stone	Animal Bone	Fire-cracked Rock
305.01	.2646	9	1	6	2	18	50.00	5.56	33.33	11.11
318.01	.3074	90	0	50	0	140	64.29	.00	35.71	.00
318.02	.3600	31	1	0	0	32	96.88	3.13	.00	.00
324.14	.2886	40	0	124	0	164	24.39	.00	75.61	.00
327.01	1.4500	166	11	136	72	385	43.12	2.86	35.32	18.70
337.14	.5168	18	3	27	12	60	30.00	5.00	45.00	20.00
342.01	.5625	8	5	144	59	216	3.70	2.31	66.67	27.31
352.01	.4284	35	1	57	63	156	22.44	.64	36.54	40.38
354.01	.2500	16	0	27	2	45	35.56	.00	60.00	4.44
355.09	.5244	6	3	203	18	230	2.61	1.30	88.26	7.83
355.10	.1541	5	0	20	0	25	20.00	.00	80.00	.00
370.01	.1660	10	4	35	23	72	13.89	5.56	48.61	31.94
372.01	.2610	7	2	70	44	123	5.69	1.63	56.91	35.77
390.16	.5764	214	2	283	24	523	40.92	.38	54.11	4.59
416.01	.1248	9	0	10	0	19	47.37	.00	52.63	.00
425.01	.3318	47	1	193	112	353	13.31	.28	54.67	31.73
812.23	.5170	30	2	123	51	206	14.56	.97	59.71	24.76
813.01	.3276	14	1	6	14	35	40.00	2.86	17.14	40.00
815.05	.3360	1	0	71	6	78	1.28	.00	91.03	7.69
817.01	.0528	0	5	0	0	5	.00	100.00	.00	.00
819.02	.3700	17	2	27	3	49	34.69	4.08	55.10	6.12
820.01	.9374	60	1	328	38	427	14.05	.23	76.81	8.90
824.02	.2542	5	0	3	1	9	55.56	.00	33.33	11.11
825.01	.4410	84	0	203	39	326	25.77	.00	62.27	11.96
827.01	.1848	4	0	274	29	307	1.30	.00	89.25	9.45
836.01	.4389	93	2	239	25	359	25.91	.56	66.57	6.96
861.01	.4200	1	2	62	70	135	.74	1.48	45.93	51.85
863.01	.7488	42	10	335	68	455	9.23	2.20	73.63	14.95
864.01	.2146	17	1	31	46	95	17.89	1.05	32.63	48.42
864.02	.0836	14	4	23	54	95	14.74	4.21	24.21	56.84
867.01	.3560	47	9	368	46	470	10.00	1.91	78.30	9.79
882.01	.2700	7	0	70	0	77	9.09	.00	90.91	.00
890.01	.2100	11	1	64	8	84	13.10	1.19	76.19	9.52
898.01	.2496	102	2	224	14	342	29.82	.58	65.50	4.09

A RITUAL ARRAY OF ARTIFACTS
FROM THE FLOOR OF FEATURE 819

David A. Gregory

One floor assemblage stands apart from all others. This remarkable array of artifacts was found on the floor of Feature 819 and provides an unprecedented glimpse into the ritual life and belief systems of Early Agricultural populations in southern Arizona. Positioned near the west wall of the structure, this array was composed of 33 objects, including both artifacts and unusual natural items, purposefully and specifically arranged. Figure B.1 illustrates the array, and its relationship to the floor of Feature 819, with each item numbered, while Figures B.2 and B.3 provide more detailed illustrations of the items included. Table B.1 provides a listing of the items corresponding to the numbers in Figure B.1.

The objects themselves attest to the special nature of this deposit: 13 projectile points (5-11, 14, 21, 26-27, 30, 33); two large pieces of basalt, one larger (1) and one smaller (4), both minimally shaped but apparently not designed for any other use; a fossil horse tooth (13) and an unfossilized mammoth or mastodon vertebra (12); a beautifully made football-shaped object of translucent red-orange chalcedony (?) (2); six round pebbles or stone balls (2-3, 16, 24, 31-32); a number of other unmodified natural rocks, including an Apache tear (28), a hematite (?) concretion (29), and three geode fragments (15, 17, 19).

Three other objects were recovered from the fill of the structure immediately above and around the floor array before its presence was discerned. These include a gastropod fossil that has the appearance of an animal head; a minimally worked, oblong piece of red siltstone/mudstone (an atlatl weight?); a large fragment of quartz crystal; and one of the unusual artiodactyl femur heads discussed previously as a possible votive deposit (see also Chapter 7). It is possible these items also belonged to the array and had been moved from their original location by rodent activity or other agents. A figurine fragment was also recovered from the floor of the structure approximately 1 m east of the array (see Chapter 8).

A number of the items in the array came from distant sources. X-ray fluorescence analyses of the two obsidian projectile points and the Apache tear reveal one of the points was made of material from Superior, Arizona, the other point of material from Cow Canyon in western New Mexico, and the Apache tear originated in the Sauceda Mountains of southwestern Arizona (see Appendix E). Another of the points (10) has been identified as an Andice point, an Archaic type common in west Texas (Shum and Jelks 1962), and the chert from which this point was made appears to be nonlocal (see Chapter 4). Thus, this point may well have been manufactured in Texas and carried to the Tucson Basin.

The manner in which these objects were arranged with respect to one another also attests to the special character of the array. Eight of the projectile points form a size-graded series, stacked upon one another in a formal arrangement. Although two of the points appear to have slipped somewhat from their original position, each level in the stack was originally oriented in the opposite direction of the underlying points. Four of the stone balls were positioned in two pairs of two, located opposite each other and on either side of the larger piece of basalt (2 and 3) and the deeply notched, broken lanceolate projectile point (31 and 32).

The interpretation of this array offered here springs from a somewhat unexpected source–rock art. It is argued that the content and structure of the Los Pozos floor array show similarities to the content and structure of petroglyphs and pictographs widely distributed across the American Southwest, many of them dated to approximately the same time period. These include: wide-shouldered anthropomorphic figures, often shown with a larger figure paired with or attached to a smaller one (Cole 1992:Figures 5-6; Davenport et al. 1992:Figures 2, 5; Warner 1994:Figures 4, 7, 13-14); round objects held by or attached at the ends of the arms of such figures, which have been interpreted as trophy heads or medicine pouches (Davenport et al. 1992:Figure 5; Schaafsma 1980; Warner 1994); atlatls held by figures or shown unattached but nearby (Heizer and Baumhoff 1962:34-35; Schaafsma 1980:55-56); and projectile points, which occur as separate elements or variably attached to the heads, shoulders, or hands of anthropomorphic figures (Grant et al. 1968:48-56; Heizer and Baumhoff 1962:37; Jackson 1938; Schaafsma 1980:55-56, 119, Figures 34-35; Sutherland and Steed 1974; Warner 1994:Figure 13).

Based on comparisons with these rock art elements and motifs, the Los Pozos array may be interpreted as a construction designed to represent two wide-shouldered anthropomorphic figures, a larger one in the form of the large piece of basalt (2) and a smaller one indicated by the lanceolate, deeply side-notched projectile point with the tip broken off (30). Each of the figures is flanked by two round objects (round pebbles/stone balls: 2 and 3, and 31 and 32), one on each side; these objects may have been attached directly to the figures by means of arms made of perishable material (see Chapter 5). The placement of these round pebbles shows formal asymmetry, with the larger of the two being to the left of the larger figure (3) and to the right of the smaller (31). The smaller figure may be interpreted as being upside down, since the wider end of the broken point is down. The other piece of basalt (25) appears to be an extension of the larger figure (1), and could represent an atlatl held by the figure, with

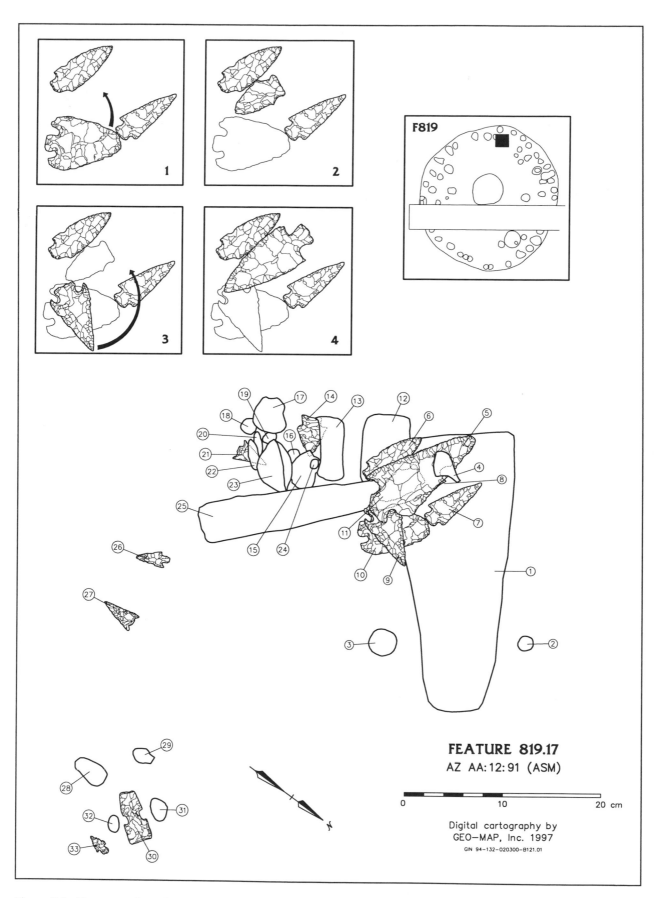

Figure B.1. Floor array from Feature 819.

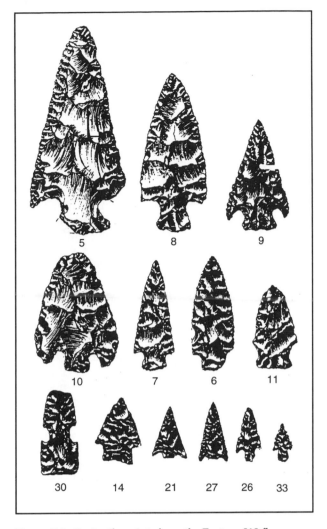

Figure B.2. Projectile points from the Feature 819 floor array (numbers correspond to Table B.1 and Figure B.1). (Length of point at top left is 13.5 cm).

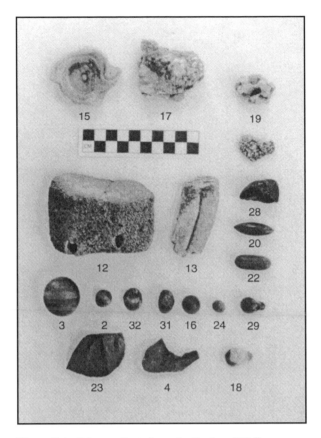

Figure B.3. Other artifacts from the Feature 819 floor array (numbers correspond to Table B.1 and Figure B.1; unnumbered geode fragment from fill above feature).

the stack of seven projectile points positioned at one end. Each of the two proposed figures has a cluster of items positioned above and to the left, in each case including projectile points and unusual natural items. Examples of rock art analogs for individual items represented in the array and their interrelationships are illustrated in Figure B.4, where the pieces of basalt, the notched projectile point, and the stone balls are also shown and shaded to highlight the elements of shape and composition which underlie the interpretation offered here.

As noted above, the rock art motifs referred to here are found widely across the American Southwest and into even California, Sonora, and Chihuahua, with illustrated examples being from the Big Bend area of Texas, the northern Rio Grande, the San Juan Basin, the Colorado Plateau, central Utah, and southern California. However, these same elements are largely or

completely lacking in the Archaic rock art of southern Arizona (Burton and Farrell 1990; Kolber 1992; Thiel 1995; Wallace and Holmlund 1986; Wallace et al. 1995).

The closest known rock art site with possibly related motifs is on the eastern side of the Chiricahua Mountains in southeastern Arizona and includes projectile points and possible atlatls but no wide-shouldered anthropomorphs (Henry Wallace, personal communication 1997). The projectile points represented in these panels are morphologically similar to the five largest points in the Los Pozos array. Why rock art motifs similar to those invoked here are largely absent from southern Arizona remains an interesting aspect of the interpretation offered here. This aspect of the problem is made even more interesting by Matson's hypothesis that the Western or San Juan variant of Basketmaker II represents a San Pedro Cochise migration onto the Colorado Plateau before A.D. 200 (Matson 1991, 1994). A number of the rock art elements and motifs cited above are from this general area.

It has been suggested that some of the rock art figures referred to here represent shamans with special powers associated with hunting, and some panels with projectile points, atlatls, and animal figures have been

Table B.1. Items in the array of artifacts from the floor of Feature 819.

1. Large piece of basalt
2. Stone ball (round pebble)
3. Stone ball (round pebble)
4. Flake
5. Projectile point
6. Projectile point
7. Projectile point
8. Projectile point
9. Projectile point
10. Projectile point
11. Projectile point
12. Mammoth/mastodon *(Mammuthus/Mammut)* vertebrae (unfossilized)
13. Horse tooth *(Equus* sp.) (fossilized)
14. Projectile point
15. Geode fragment
16. Stone ball (round pebble)
17. Geode fragment
18. Flake
19. Geode fragment
20. Worked oblong stone (quartzite?; atlatl weight?)
21. Projectile point
22. Translucent red rock, "football" shaped (chalcedony?; atlatl weight?)
23. Flake
24. Stone ball (round pebble)
25. Piece of basalt
26. Projectile point
27. Projectile point
28. Apache tear
29. Concretion
30. Projectile point (deeply side-notched, broken tip)
31. Stone ball (round pebble)
32. Stone ball (round pebble)
33. Projectile point

interpreted as hunting shrines (Furst 1974; Heizer and Baumhoff 1962; Schaafsma 1980:71; Warner 1994). Several of the items included in the Los Pozos array or recovered nearby clearly suggest hunting or animal imagery: the projectile points, the fossil horse tooth, the mammoth/mastodon vertebra, the gastropod fossil cast that has the appearance of an animal head; and possibly a representation of an atlatl attached to or included as an extension of the larger figure. Faunal remains from the site show that hunting, especially of deer and rabbits, remained an important subsistence pursuit for these early farmers (see Chapter 10). Similarly, the floor array suggests that rituals and beliefs associated with animals and hunting were still important aspects of their cosmology and world view. The paired large and small figures, often connected or closely adjacent to one another, hint at some concept of duality (Warner 1994) and were perhaps meant to symbolize perceived relationships between "real" and spirit worlds, wherein human beings have a Doppelgänger or spirit double.

We cannot say precisely how this array functioned after it was put in place, nor can we say whether it was a one-time, occasional, or permanent feature on the floor of this structure. Aside from the presence of the array itself, there is nothing distinctive about Feature 819, and a mano was found on the floor against the wall opposite the array. The structure clearly burned and collapsed directly upon the array, and perhaps the burning was an intentional event somehow related to the creation of the array itself. We do not know if it was created by and meant to be seen by only one person or by a group of people; the size of the structure would suggest that if multiple persons were involved, it must have been a relatively small number. Was it a kind of altar, created by and the responsibility of a single person, perhaps a shaman in his role as conduit to spirit worlds? Was it prepared in a ritual of sympathetic magic, to reinforce the luck and skill of a hunting party about to depart for the nearby mountains to hunt deer or mountain sheep? Was it created to commemorate the death of a shaman, whose residence was intentionally burned after the array was created? For the present, all of these are equally plausible hypotheses.

If the interpretation offered here is correct, the array combines elements or motifs that occur over an extremely large geographic area, suggesting a certain degree of continuity in cosmology and world view during the first millennium B.C. This general conclusion is perhaps supported by an approximately contemporaneous feature including large projectile points manufactured specifically for inclusion with a cremation-related deposit, reported from the site of La Playa in northern Sonora (J. Holmlund and J. Carpenter, personal communication 1996); these points are morphologically similar to those recovered from the Los Pozos array.

Whatever the specific purpose and meaning, it is clear that this array represents an intentionally constructed ritual composition, rich in symbolism. It demonstrates that interior space was sometimes devoted to esoteric purposes as well as the mundane.

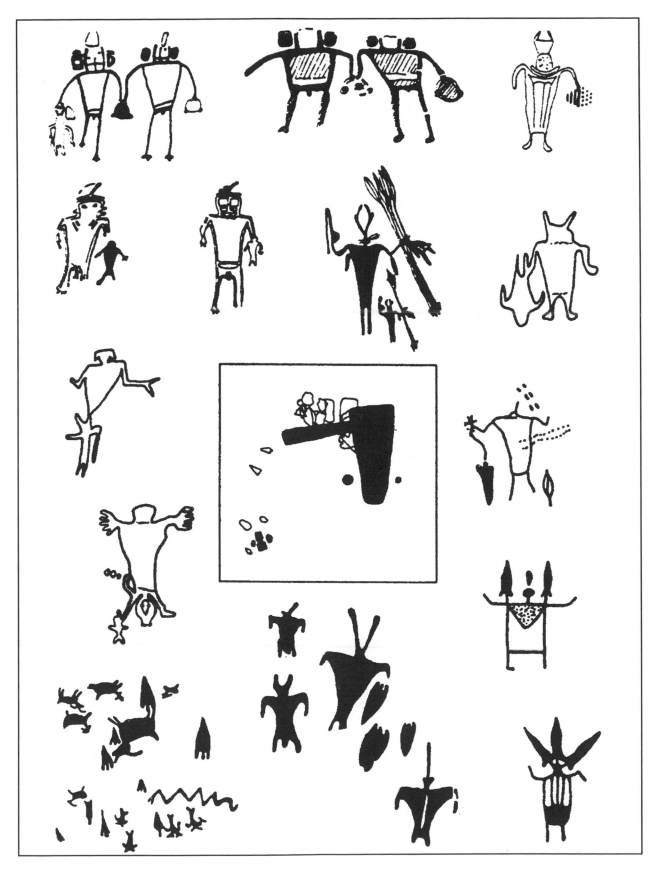

Figure B.4. Rock art figures used in interpretation of the Feature 819 floor array.

HUMAN OSTEOLOGICAL REMAINS

Penny Dufoe Minturn and Lorrie Lincoln-Babb

Human remains were recovered from three formal inhumations and five apparently non-burial contexts at Los Pozos (AZ AA:12:91 [ASM]). All bone was identified to element, sided if possible, examined for pathologies, and measurements were taken when the bone was well enough preserved. Teeth were examined for degree of wear and evidence of dental pathologies, including caries and enamel hypoplasias. When possible, the materials were aged and sexed using standard techniques from Bass (1987) and Buikstra and Ubelaker (1994).

FORMAL INHUMATIONS

Feature 304

Feature 304 contained the tightly flexed inhumation of an adult female, aged 35-40 years, with the skeleton approximately 50 percent preserved. Sex estimation is based on general gracility of the bone, a femur head measurement of 40 mm, and a mandibular angle of near 120 degrees. Age is based on dental wear, which is extreme, with some dentin exposure in all teeth and other teeth represented by only root nubs.

Nineteen teeth are present. Recovered maxillary dentition consists of the central and lateral incisors, both canines, and the four premolars. Recovered mandibular teeth include the central and lateral incisors, the first premolars, the right second premolar, and the first molars. Alveolar bone is limited to two small sections of the mandible, each with several teeth in position. Preservation is fair for both the teeth and bone.

Dental wear is extreme for nearly all the teeth. The occlusal surfaces of the crowns have been almost entirely replaced by deposits of secondary dentine and have angular wear planes or are cupped. Carious lesions are present on the upper canines, and a lingual abscess is present between the lower right second premolar and the first molar.

Feature 308

Feature 308 contained the tightly flexed inhumation of an adult female, aged 35-50 years, with the skeleton approximately 45 percent preserved. Sex estimation is based on a broad sciatic notch, substantial pre-auricular sulcus, and femur head measurements of 39.6 (left) and 39.9 (right). Age is based on the absence of evidence for arthritis on any articular surfaces and heavy dental wear.

The left first metatarsal and first proximal phalange exhibited a developmental congenital defect. The distal articular surface of the metatarsal has a slight depression which was mostly filled with an extra boney growth. The proximal articular surface of the first proximal phalange is excessively cupped. Neither element is arthritic. These features appear to represent a congenital abnormality that probably did not manifest itself in any outward manner.

Three very worn teeth are present, including the mandibular left first premolar, the maxillary left third molar, and an upper canine or central incisor. The latter tooth exhibits a greatly reduced crown and root and is best described as a tooth nub. Age estimation is based on root resorption of the tooth nub and extreme wear on the toothy nub and the premolar. In addition, the root of the molar exhibits hypercementosis, another feature related to advanced age. No alveolar bone is present. The only pathologies observed are calculus deposits, in varying amounts, on all three teeth.

Feature 353

Feature 353 contained the partially flexed inhumation of an adult male aged 40-50 years, with the skeleton approximately 60 percent preserved. Sex estimation is based on a square chin, narrow sciatic notch, flat auricular surface, and right femur head measurement of 43.3 mm. Age is based on dental wear and degree of arthritis, the latter especially prominent on the right pubic bone and right ribs.

This male exhibits marked "swelling" of the left humerus, extra boney growth on the left glenoid fossa of the scapula, extra boney growth and thickening of the proximal end of the left ulna, and thickening of the occipital, frontal, and parietal bones in the skull. The left ribs exhibit external lamellar bone (sclerotic) on the sternal ends. Both femurs show a slight abnormal anterior curve. This is possibly a case of Paget's disease, or osteitis deformans, a chronic bone disease that affects a single, several, or many bones in the skeleton but never all of them (Ortner and Putschar 1985). The cause of the disease is unknown, but it results in a rapid distortion of normal bone deposition and is most often seen in males over the age of 40. A strict diagnosis is not offered here, but Paget's disease is suggested on the basis of: 1) the distribution of abnormal bone, 2) the appearance of the abnormal bone, and 3) the curvature of the femurs. Also present is sacralization of the fifth lumbar vertebra (developmental) and auditory exostosis in the right ear canal (developmental).

Eighteen teeth are present. Maxillary teeth include the central and lateral incisors, both canines, the left first premolar, both second premolars, the right first molar, the left second molar, and both third molars. Mandibular teeth include the central incisors, the left canine, and the left first and second premolars. Preservation of the teeth and alveolar bone is fair.

Dental wear is extreme for the maxillary and mandibular teeth, with nearly all of the occlusal surface enamel worn away. The cusps of the maxillary molars have been worn smooth and exhibit little secondary dentine. The alveoli of the mandibular molars exhibit total resorption, indicating ante-mortem loss of these teeth. It is not possible to determine how long these teeth had been missing; however, extreme wear on the maxillary and mandibular anterior teeth and the lack of wear to the maxillary molars indicate masticatory dependence on the anterior dentition for an extended period of time. Three carious lesions were observed–on the maxillary left central incisor and canine–and the mandibular left canine. One abscess was observed at the labial root apex of the left upper canine. No evidence of periodontal disease was observed; however, given the condition of the alveolar bone, such evidence may have been obliterated. A minimal amount of calculus is present on some teeth, and no evidence of enamel hypoplasia was observed.

HUMAN REMAINS FROM NON-BURIAL CONTEXTS

Feature 372.01

Three human teeth and several post-cranial elements were recovered from Feature 372.01. These materials include one upper premolar, two upper central incisors, two cuneiforms, a navicular, four metatarsals, one metacarpal, two distal toe phalanges, six middle toe phalanges, seven middle hand phalanges, and six phalange epiphyses. These elements are probably all from the same individual.

Based on the teeth recovered, the individual was approximately 15-18 years old at time of death. The maxillary central incisors and the first left premolar are present, and the suggested age is consistent with the minimal wear observed on these teeth. There is no dentine exposure and the cusps are present. No alveolar bone was recovered, and no dental pathologies were observed.

Feature 342.01

Two human adult teeth were recovered from Feature 342.01, including an adult premolar (reduced by wear) and a single root.

Feature 420

One adult premolar, one rib fragment, and one metatarsal fragment were recovered from Feature 420.

Feature 422

A cremated distal hand phalange (completely calcined) was recovered from Feature 422.

Feature 872

Four left distal and two left middle hand phalanges, a hamate, and a navicular were recovered from Feature 872.

FLOTATION SAMPLES: METHODS, PROCEDURES, AND IDENTIFIED TAXA

Michael W. Diehl

One hundred forty-eight flotation samples were recovered from Early Agricultural period features in the Los Pozos site (AZ AA:12:91 [ASM]). This appendix describes the methods used to extract and identify the macrobotanical remains contained in the samples. General descriptive information about the samples is presented. The frequencies of charred seeds and woods of the different taxa observed in the flotation samples are listed in two tables (one for seeds and one for woods).

In the course of this research, substantial effort was invested in identifying the ethnographically known uses of these plants. Additional information on potential and actual yields of plants in Native American and modern industrial agricultural settings was also recorded, along with information on the nutritional components of seeds and other edible tissues. Information on the growth habits of the identified taxa was obtained from common botanical references. This information is distilled and summarized by taxon.

METHODS AND PROCEDURES

Flotation samples were collected from all features by excavating large quantities of soil and storing the samples in large paper bags. The volumes of the individual samples varied, but excavators were instructed to obtain samples that equaled or exceeded 6 liters wherever possible. In some cases, the volumes of small pits did not exceed that amount. In these instances, the feature fill was collected in its entirety.

Macrobotanical remains were separated from the flotation samples using a recirculating, pump-driven flotation machine similar to the Ankara-type machine described by Pearsall (1989:57). Differences included the installation of a submerged carburetor mesh settling platform between the water inlet pipe and the flotation chamber to catch heavy fractions and prevent cross-sample contamination. Poppy seed tests indicate that the apparatus used by Desert Archaeology recovered 75 to 95 percent of the seeds from samples that were obtained at this site. Light fractions were captured in nets made of pre-cut, fine nylon mesh, with a mesh size of less than .5 mm. The samples were tied shut and suspended from a line until dry. Processed light fractions are permanently stored in plastic zip-lock bags.

Laboratory Identification of Seeds and Wood

Light fractions were opened, weighed, and processed through a nested series of geological sieves in order to expedite the identification process. Samples were examined under a 17-144x stereoscopic zoom microscope equipped with a fiber-optic ring illuminator. The presence (and estimated quantity) of uncharred seeds, gastropod shells, and insect exoskeleton fragments was recorded. Following Minnis (1981) and Miksicek (1987), only the charred plant specimens were identified, since only the charred remains can reasonably be assumed to be the products of prehistoric human activities.

All charred seeds were identified by comparing the specimens in flotation samples against an extensive comparative collection of southwestern United States plant seeds and illustrations in several common references (Martin and Barkley 1961; Montgomery 1978; U.S. Department of Agriculture 1974). In addition, the presence or absence of charred "columnar celled seed coat" fragments was recorded. Plant taxonomists define species on the basis of differences in vegetative tissue, principally flower structures, rather than seed morphology. Seeds of different species within the same genus may be quite similar in size, shape, and surface texture. It is therefore inappropriate to identify plant seeds more precisely than the generic level of identification, except when local diversity within a particular genus is very low (one or two morphologically distinct species in an area) and a compelling case for a specific identification can be made. In this study, only *Zea mays* (maize) and *Carnegiea gigantea* (saguaro) were identified to the specific level of taxonomic precision.

Large charred seeds were often observed in fragmentary condition. To render the data comparable, a "minimum number of individuals" approach was taken. Mesquite seeds and maize cupules and large cupule fragments that were captured in the 2-mm and 1-mm mesh were counted. Smaller fragments (captured in mesh sizes less than 1 mm) were not counted.

Charred woods were treated in a manner identical to the methods employed for the study of charred seeds, with one exception. Since tiny flecks of wood were innumerable in flotation samples, only those fragments that were caught in the 2-mm and 1-mm geological sieves were examined. In general, only the first 20 charcoal fragments were identified. In some cases, fewer fragments were available. In a few instances, when a sample was found to be especially replete with wood charcoal, a larger number of pieces were identified. The latter tactic increased the confidence that the full range of wood taxa that occurred in each sample was observed.

GENERAL CHARACTERISTICS OF THE FLOTATION SAMPLES

Table D.1 presents descriptive data of the most general kind for each flotation sample. Information includes the feature number, provenience, volume of unfloated dirt (in liters), the weight of the light fraction (in grams), the number of prehistoric seeds counted, and the number of seed taxa identified. Three of the 148 samples contained no charred plant remains and are not considered further. Samples that completely lack charred plant remains are not included in calculations of ubiquity or plant taxon diversity presented in Chapter 9. These three may be identified in the table as samples that have the value zero in the columns "Number of Seeds" and "Number of Taxa."

For the purposes of statistical analysis it is important to identify outliers that, for reasons of exceptional preservation or unusually disastrous events during food preparation, produced samples with large quantities of charred seeds. The inclusion of such outliers in parametric analyses may contribute to the spurious production of statistically insignificant results by increasing the standard deviation of mean values, obscuring any central tendencies in the distribution. In the case of Los Pozos flotation samples, two produced unusually large quantities of seeds (proveniences 511.06 and 603.01). The mean number of seeds per sample was 81.7 seeds per sample (n = 145, standard deviation = 250.3, minimum = 1, maximum = 2,340). Outliers are defined as those samples with a total seed recovery that exceeds the mean plus two standard deviations (582 seeds).

CHARRED SEEDS: FREQUENCIES, ATTRIBUTES OF GROWTH, AND ETHNOGRAPHIC ACCOUNTS OF THEIR USE

Table D.2 lists the frequencies of seeds (in the case of maize, seeds, and cupules) from each taxon in each sample. In the discussion that follows, basic information on the new growth, flowering (pollen dispersal) and ripening periods for each plant is presented. A brief synopsis of the known ethnographic uses of plants is also presented. As discussed elsewhere, the potential yields of edible tissue per hectare is an important consideration for modeling prehistoric subsistence practices. To foreshorten that discussion, the documented and derived yields of different species are presented here.

Agavaceae sp. cf. *Yucca* (Yucca)

Yucca are widespread throughout Arizona, flowering May-July and fruiting July-August. Ethnographical and archaeological known uses of yucca include the use of leaf fibers for applying pigment to vessels and in the construction of footwear. Green fruit from the banana yucca (*Y. baccata*) are edible, and the hearts of other species have been used as "famine foods" (Minnis 1991:239). Yucca pods are most edible shortly after their formation, and they become less palatable as they desiccate during ripening. Yucca begin to bear fruit during their fifth or sixth year, bearing 75 to 200 flowers (also edible) per stalk; roughly 30 percent of the flowers bear fruit (USDA 1974:857). No other information is available on density, yields, or nutritional composition.

Trianthema sp. (Horse Purslane)

This is a common weed that thrives in alkaline soils throughout Arizona up to elevations of about 4,000 ft (Parker 1990:130), flowering May-November. *T. portulacastrum* is an unremarkable plant with respect to carbohydrate yields, but it is known to contain unusually large quantities (32.9 percent) of protein (Carr et al. 1985:510). No information on natural plant density or seed-yields was located during this study.

Cactaceae (Cactus Family)

Small seeds of an unidentified cactus were found in several flotation samples. Cactus fruit are generally rich in iron, vitamin C, and calcium, and have high sugar concentrations (Ensminger et al. 1994:892-893).

Carnegiea gigantea (Saguaro)

Saguaro is common in the Sonoran Desert, Arizona Upland Subdivision, and in and around the Tucson Basin (Turner and Brown 1994). Saguaro prefer rocky slopes at elevations up to 3,500 ft (Kearney and Peebles 1973), up to the limits of the temperature-moderating effects of thermal inversion (Steenbergh and Lowe 1983:xiv). Flowering occurs May-June, with fruit ripening in June-July (Kearney and Peebles 1973).

Saguaro are a well-known, economically important plant among ethnographically documented Pima and Papago and among present-day Tohono O'odham (Castetter and Bell 1937; Castetter and Underhill 1935; Crosswhite 1980). Saguaro fruit were annually harvested for immediate consumption, drying and storage, or fermentation. Rods made from saguaro ribs have been used to make fruit harvesting tools. In the recent past, saguaro seeds were consumed; more recently they have been used as chicken feed.

The yields of saguaros and the demographic stability of patches are affected by exposure to severe cold (Steenbergh and Lowe 1983). Almost all deaths occur as a direct or indirect consequence of freezing.

Table D.1. General characteristics of ICD flotation samples.

Feature	Provenience	Vol (liters)	Weight (g)	Number of Seeds	Number of Taxa
863.00	101.01	5.0	19.4	6	5
863.00	102.01	6.9	46.1	77	6
864.00	104.03	6.5	1.7	5	4
864.01	105.04	4.5	23.9	5	3
861.00	117.01	8.2	23.4	46	8
304.00	118.04	6.6	103.4	14	2
863.00	123.01	8.5	7.8	4	1
863.01	125.05	7.2	20.2	27	5
898.00	138.01	12.2	12.2	22	6
898.00	138.02	9.5	2.9	25	7
898.01	139.01	8.0	14.7	31	5
898.01	139.02	9.2	35.6	95	9
898.01	139.03	2.5	11.6	4	3
866.00	147.11	10.0	8.4	22	4
305.00	154.01	7.6	51.7	11	2
305.01	155.01	6.8	39.3	20	5
305.01	156.01	6.8	52.4	18	5
302.01	157.01	9.0	29.2	15	3
302.01	158.01	9.0	9.4	33	5
825.01	170.01	6.2	8.5	3	2
353.00	176.03	6.5	3.6	6	2
820.00	178.01	8.0	20.8	1	1
820.01	179.01	8.2	13.3	3	1
820.01	180.01	9.0	12.8	18	9
820.01	182.01	1.0	14.0	19	5
890.00	198.01	–	19.4	31	8
890.00	199.01	7.0	31.6	33	6
890.01	200.01	7.8	48.2	107	9
890.01	201.01	7.5	87.9	58	4
870.00	205.01	6.0	54.9	377	6
866.00	207.01	9.5	36.3	5	2
302.00	208.01	8.2	27.5	71	6
867.01	209.07	6.9	7.0	20	4
867.00	221.01	9.0	18.9	61	8
887.00	224.01	11.0	10.3	4	2
328.00	229.01	7.8	26.6	11	4
324.00	238.01	8.0	14.5	10	6
324.01	245.01	8.0	8.8	9	6
324.14	246.01	6.0	21.5	53	6
867.00	248.01	8.4	12.8	35	5
337.00	252.01	9.0	23.9	57	6
354.01	269.07	11.0	32.7	38	6
354.01	269.08	12.0	32.0	8	1
342.00	271.04	4.2	16.4	33	7
337.14	278.01	10.0	13.6	86	8
337.14	279.01	9.0	100.5	10	5
327.01	297.01	8.5	14.9	6	5
327.01	298.01	9.0	13.3	54	8
327.00	301.01	8.0	14.2	42	5
318.00	306.01	8.0	12.1	35	6

Table D.1. Continued.

Feature	Provenience	Vol (liters)	Weight (g)	Number of Seeds	Number of Taxa
417.00	313.02	6.0	31.6	343	4
370.00	319.01	8.0	35.9	14	3
370.01	320.01	9.0	30.5	31	7
342.01	326.02	8.0	13.0	12	2
342.01	328.05	8.5	57.3	80	9
355.00	330.07	7.0	27.2	58	7
420.00	344.04	10.0	36.5	27	5
318.01	345.01	5.8	17.6	168	8
355.09	350.11	6.0	7.4	11	3
355.46	351.01	7.0	3.0	5	2
355.46	352.01	6.2	3.3	24	5
318.02	353.01	7.4	21.1	816	11
318.01	354.01	6.2	5.4	19	9
355.10	355.05	7.0	9.3	15	3
355.10	356.01	6.0	6.8	33	7
352.00	364.01	9.0	33.7	25	6
352.01	368.01	9.0	58.0	30	7
352.01	369.01	9.0	26.2	26	4
300.00	376.01	10.0	5.7	0	0
819.00	377.05	10.0	12.2	91	11
819.02	381.01	8.5	11.2	32	9
840.01	384.02	6.0	40.7	2	2
840.00	394.01	10.0	20.0	38	4
422.00	398.10	6.0	5.4	46	4
372.00	400.01	9.0	36.6	6	2
372.00	401.01	10.2	18.2	9	3
372.01	402.01	9.0	16.3	17	4
372.01	403.01	7.5	43.5	17	6
333.00	405.06	5.0	26.9	124	7
357.00	410.03	11.0	23.5	8	2
815.00	417.06	9.0	34.0	14	5
824.01	424.01	13.0	.6	1	1
330.00	430.05	10.0	51.4	27	3
824.02	432.05	9.0	12.1	16	3
824.24	434.01	8.0	27.9	8	3
423.00	439.01	7.5	14.5	10	4
824.00	440.01	11.0	8.9	1	1
333.00	441.05	7.0	17.9	36	4
333.01	442.04	–	13.7	101	6
861.01	456.01	8.0	48.5	235	8
861.01	458.01	7.0	18.2	187	8
346.00	459.01	8.0	25.8	14	5
389.00	463.01	7.0	52.1	341	8
389.00	464.01	7.0	18.2	76	3
348.00	471.01	10.5	8.4	2	1
403.00	473.01	7.0	6.2	14	2
400.00	474.05	9.0	33.2	24	6
882.00	476.07	–	20.2	17	3
407.00	480.01	8.0	4.3	0	0

Table D.1. Continued.

Feature	Provenience	Vol (liters)	Weight (g)	Number of Seeds	Number of Taxa
407.00	481.01	–	42.5	53	7
882.01	482.08	3.0	2.7	24	3
882.01	483.01	–	14.9	16	5
431.00	485.01	11.0	15.1	29	4
373.00	486.01	10.0	12.4	58	4
416.01	490.01	7.0	60.3	101	6
416.00	491.02	7.1	7.3	12	4
429.00	495.03	7.5	8.7	3	3
428.00	496.09	7.5	37.9	7	3
365.00	497.01	6.0	1.3	2	2
365.00	498.01	5.0	.9	0	0
359.00	501.01	10.0	36.5	13	4
373.00	506.01	8.0	13.1	39	3
411.00	511.06	6.9	14.9	1,533	6
817.00	513.01	8.0	4.0	40	3
329.00	515.01	8.5	32.3	47	6
406.00	518.01	12.0	6.8	24	5
399.00	519.05	7.7	36.8	48	7
817.01	520.01	12.0	–	22	5
817.01	520.03	7.3	95.7	36	5
339.00	526.01	9.0	38.7	103	7
339.01	527.01	10.0	16.4	38	7
379.00	529.08	9.0	10.0	4	4
893.00	535.01	11.0	60.9	11	3
886.00	536.01	8.0	113.8	30	3
886.00	537.01	10.0	33.3	91	8
818.00	538.01	–	12.7	59	8
819.00	539.09	7.0	14.4	187	14
876.00	545.01	11.0	33.5	16	6
425.00	548.01	9.0	27.2	25	3
425.01	549.01	11.0	22.6	50	6
813.00	550.01	9.0	7.4	3	3
813.01	551.01	11.0	29.3	3	2
836.00	561.11	2.0	9.9	16	7
836.00	561.12	6.2	39.3	61	10
836.01	563.13	7.3	26.7	79	10
880.01	577.01	11.0	44.9	143	4
880.00	578.01	12.0	20.0	8	3
879.01	579.01	10.0	53.6	58	11
879.00	580.01	9.0	31.2	29	1
390.00	597.01	7.5	9.8	32	5
812.23	602.01	8.5	21.8	63	7
812.23	603.01	8.0	69.6	2,340	16
812.23	604.01	7.5	25.0	64	9
427.00	605.01	–	57.9	281	7
812.00	606.01	8.0	29.2	26	7
433.00	614.01	7.0	43.2	763	9
390.16	615.01	7.3	28.2	9	2
408.00	620.01	8.0	3.0	1	1

Table D.2. Frequencies of charred seeds of different taxa, by sample.

Provenience	Bag	Feature	cf. *Yucca* sp.	*Trianthema* sp.	Cactaceae	*Carnegiea gigantea*	*Echinocereus* sp.	*Mammillaria* sp.	*Opuntia* sp.	*Opuntia* sp. (Playtopuntia)	Chenopodiaceae	Cheno-am	*Chenopodium* sp.	*Suaeda* sp.
208	1	302.00	0	0	0	5	0	0	0	0	0	2	0	0
157	1	302.01	0	0	0	0	0	1	0	0	0	0	0	0
158	1	302.01	0	0	0	3	1	8	0	0	0	0	0	0
118	4	304.00	0	0	0	1	0	0	0	0	0	0	0	0
154	1	305.00	0	0	0	0	0	0	0	0	0	8	0	0
155	1	305.01	1	0	0	1	0	0	0	0	0	8	0	0
156	1	305.01	0	0	0	2	0	0	0	0	0	3	4	0
306	1	318.00	0	0	0	0	1	0	0	0	0	6	0	0
345	1	318.01	0	0	1	0	0	0	0	0	0	23	2	0
354	1	318.01	0	0	0	1	0	0	0	0	0	7	0	0
353	1	318.02	0	0	0	1	0	15	0	0	0	141	0	0
238	1	324.00	0	0	0	1	1	0	0	0	0	1	0	0
245	1	324.01	0	0	0	1	0	0	0	0	0	17	0	0
246	1	324.14	0	0	0	2	1	0	0	0	0	11	0	0
301	1	327.00	0	0	0	0	0	0	0	0	0	5	0	0
297	1	327.01	0	1	0	0	0	0	0	0	0	0	0	0
298	1	327.01	0	0	0	0	0	0	0	0	0	12	0	0
229	1	328.00	0	0	0	0	0	0	0	0	0	0	6	0
515	1	329.00	0	0	0	7	0	0	0	0	0	6	0	0
430	5	330.00	0	0	0	0	0	0	0	0	0	0	0	0
405	6	333.00	0	0	0	0	0	0	0	0	0	1	0	0
441	5	333.00	0	0	0	0	0	0	0	0	0	2	0	0
442	4	333.01	0	0	0	0	0	0	0	0	0	9	0	0
252	1	337.00	0	0	0	4	0	0	0	0	0	8	0	0
278	1	337.14	0	0	0	0	0	0	0	0	0	14	0	0
279	1	337.14	0	0	1	2	0	0	2	0	0	0	0	0
526	1	339.00	0	0	0	2	1	0	0	0	0	13	0	0
527	1	339.01	0	0	0	3	1	0	0	0	0	6	0	0
271	4	342.00	0	0	0	6	0	0	0	1	0	15	0	0
326	2	342.01	0	0	0	0	0	0	0	0	0	7	0	0
328	5	342.01	0	0	0	2	2	0	0	0	0	59	0	0
459	1	346.00	0	0	0	1	0	0	0	0	0	1	0	0
471	1	348.00	0	0	0	0	0	0	0	0	0	0	0	0
364	1	352.00	0	1	0	4	2	0	0	0	0	8	0	0
368	1	352.01	0	0	0	4	0	0	0	0	0	1	7	0
369	1	352.01	0	0	0	1	0	0	0	0	0	5	0	0
176	3	353.00	0	0	0	0	0	0	0	0	0	1	0	0
269	7	354.01	0	0	0	6	1	0	0	0	0	12	0	0
269	8	354.01	0	0	0	0	0	0	0	0	0	0	0	0
330	7	355.00	0	0	0	1	1	0	0	0	0	3	0	0
350	11	355.09	0	0	0	2	0	0	0	0	0	0	0	0
355	5	355.10	0	0	0	0	0	0	0	0	0	1	0	0
356	1	355.10	0	0	0	0	0	0	0	0	1	3	0	0
351	1	355.46	0	0	0	0	0	0	0	0	0	2	0	0
352	1	355.46	0	0	0	0	0	0	0	0	0	6	0	0
410	3	357.00	0	0	0	0	0	0	0	0	0	0	0	0
501	1	359.00	0	0	0	0	1	0	0	0	0	3	0	0
497	1	365.00	0	0	0	0	0	0	0	0	0	0	0	0

Cleome sp.	Polanisia sp.	Compositae	Artemisia sp.	Helianthus sp.	Viguiera sp.	Cruciferae	Descurainia sp.	Cucurbitaceae	Cucurbita sp. (wild)	Juniperus sp.	Cyperaceae	Carex sp.	Eleocharis sp.
0	0	0	0	0	0	0	0	0	0	1	0	0	0
0	0	0	0	0	0	0	10	0	0	0	0	0	0
0	0	0	0	0	0	0	4	0	0	0	0	0	0
0	0	0	0	0	0	0	0	0	0	0	0	0	0
0	0	0	0	0	0	0	0	0	0	0	0	0	0
0	0	0	0	0	0	1	0	0	0	0	0	0	0
0	0	0	0	0	0	0	0	0	0	0	0	0	0
0	0	0	0	0	0	0	14	0	0	0	0	0	0
0	0	0	0	0	0	4	44	0	0	0	0	0	0
0	0	0	0	0	0	0	2	0	0	0	0	0	0
0	2	0	0	0	0	0	0	0	0	0	0	0	0
0	0	0	0	0	0	0	4	0	0	0	0	0	0
0	0	0	0	0	0	0	12	1	0	0	0	0	0
0	0	0	0	0	0	0	30	0	0	0	0	0	0
0	0	0	0	0	0	0	1	0	0	0	0	0	0
0	0	0	0	0	0	1	0	0	0	0	0	0	0
0	0	3	0	0	0	0	12	0	0	0	0	0	0
0	0	0	0	0	0	0	0	0	1	0	0	0	0
0	0	0	0	0	0	2	6	0	0	0	0	0	0
0	0	0	0	0	0	0	0	0	0	0	0	0	0
0	0	0	0	0	0	0	22	0	0	0	0	0	0
0	0	0	0	0	0	0	2	0	0	0	0	0	0
0	0	0	0	0	0	0	35	0	0	0	0	0	0
0	1	0	0	0	0	0	12	0	0	0	0	0	0
0	2	0	2	0	0	0	0	0	0	0	0	0	0
0	0	0	0	0	0	0	0	0	0	0	0	0	0
0	0	0	0	0	0	0	61	0	0	0	0	0	0
0	0	0	0	0	0	0	1	0	0	0	0	0	0
0	0	0	0	0	0	0	3	0	0	0	0	0	0
0	0	0	0	0	0	0	0	0	0	0	0	0	0
0	0	0	0	0	0	0	10	0	0	0	0	0	0
0	0	1	0	0	0	0	0	0	0	0	0	0	0
0	2	0	0	0	0	0	0	0	0	0	0	0	0
0	0	0	0	0	0	0	0	0	0	0	0	0	0
0	0	0	0	0	0	0	0	0	0	0	0	0	0
0	0	0	0	0	0	0	13	0	0	0	0	0	0
0	0	0	0	0	0	0	5	0	0	0	0	0	0
0	0	0	0	0	0	0	0	0	0	0	0	0	0
0	0	0	0	0	0	0	0	0	0	0	0	0	0
0	0	0	0	0	0	0	22	0	0	0	0	0	0
0	0	0	0	0	0	0	0	0	0	0	0	0	0
0	0	0	0	0	0	0	7	0	0	0	0	0	0
0	0	0	0	0	0	0	8	0	0	0	0	0	0
0	0	0	0	0	0	0	0	0	0	0	0	0	0
0	0	0	0	0	0	0	7	0	0	0	0	0	0
0	0	0	0	0	0	0	0	0	0	0	0	0	0
0	0	0	0	0	0	0	0	0	0	0	0	0	0
0	0	0	0	0	0	0	1	0	0	0	0	0	0

Table D.2. Continued.

Provenience	Bag	Feature	cf. *Yucca* sp.	*Trianthema* sp.	Cactaceae	*Carnegiea gigantea*	*Echinocereus* sp.	*Mammillaria* sp.	*Opuntia* sp.	*Opuntia* sp. (Playtopuntia)	Chenopodiaceae	Cheno-am	*Chenopodium* sp.	*Suaeda* sp.
319	1	370.00	0	0	0	0	0	0	0	0	0	1	0	0
320	1	370.01	0	0	0	6	3	0	0	0	0	4	0	0
400	1	372.00	0	0	0	0	0	0	0	0	0	2	0	0
401	1	372.00	0	0	0	0	0	0	0	0	0	5	0	0
402	1	372.01	0	0	0	7	0	0	0	0	0	0	4	0
403	1	372.01	0	0	1	7	1	0	0	0	0	1	0	0
486	1	373.00	0	0	0	1	0	0	0	0	0	46	0	0
506	1	373.00	0	0	0	0	0	0	0	0	0	12	0	0
529	8	379.00	0	0	0	0	1	0	0	0	0	1	0	0
463	1	389.00	0	2	0	3	0	0	0	0	3	0	0	0
464	1	389.00	0	0	0	0	0	0	0	0	0	0	0	0
597	1	390.00	0	0	0	1	0	0	0	0	0	15	0	0
615	1	390.16	0	0	0	0	0	0	0	0	0	7	0	0
519	5	399.00	0	0	0	4	0	0	0	0	0	14	0	0
474	5	400.00	0	0	0	1	0	0	0	0	0	2	0	0
473	1	403.00	0	0	0	0	0	0	0	0	0	0	0	0
518	1	406.00	0	0	0	0	1	0	0	0	0	10	0	0
481	1	407.00	0	0	0	0	0	0	0	0	0	7	0	0
620	1	408.00	0	0	0	0	0	0	0	0	0	0	0	0
511	6	411.00	0	0	0	1	0	0	0	0	0	950	0	0
491	2	416.00	0	0	0	0	0	0	0	0	0	0	0	0
490	1	416.01	0	0	0	0	0	0	0	0	0	16	0	0
313	2	417.00	0	0	0	0	0	0	0	0	0	1	0	0
344	4	420.00	0	0	0	3	0	0	0	0	0	17	0	0
398	10	422.00	0	0	0	0	0	0	0	0	0	1	0	0
439	1	423.00	0	0	0	1	0	0	0	0	0	1	0	0
548	1	425.00	0	0	0	6	0	0	0	0	0	8	0	0
549	1	425.01	0	0	0	1	1	0	0	0	0	13	0	0
605	1	427.00	0	4	0	1	0	0	0	0	0	208	0	0
496	9	428.00	0	0	0	0	0	0	0	0	0	3	0	0
495	3	429.00	0	1	0	0	0	1	0	0	0	0	0	0
485	1	431.00	0	0	0	0	0	0	0	0	0	3	0	0
614	1	433.00	0	0	0	4	0	0	3	0	0	13	0	0
606	1	812.00	0	1	0	4	1	0	0	0	0	3	0	0
602	1	812.23	0	0	0	25	2	0	0	0	0	0	18	0
603	1	812.23	0	1	0	164	0	1,212	1	0	0	0	0	400
604	1	812.23	0	0	0	4	1	0	0	0	0	30	0	0
550	1	813.00	0	0	0	0	0	0	0	0	0	1	0	0
551	1	813.01	0	0	0	0	0	0	0	0	0	2	0	0
417	6	815.00	0	1	0	1	1	0	0	0	0	0	4	0
513	1	817.00	0	0	0	0	0	0	0	0	0	12	0	0
520	1	817.01	0	0	0	0	0	0	0	0	0	3	1	0
520	3	817.01	0	0	0	0	0	0	0	0	0	4	0	0
538	1	818.00	0	0	0	1	0	0	0	0	0	4	0	0
377	5	819.00	0	0	0	1	0	1	0	0	0	0	2	0
539	9	819.00	0	0	0	2	0	1	0	0	0	0	17	6
381	1	819.02	0	0	0	1	0	0	0	0	0	0	3	0
178	1	820.00	0	0	0	0	0	0	0	0	0	0	0	0

Cleome sp.	Polanisia sp.	Compositae	Artemisia sp.	Helianthus sp.	Viguiera sp.	Cruciferae	Descurainia sp.	Cucurbitaceae	Cucurbita sp. (wild)	Juniperus sp.	Cyperaceae	Carex sp.	Eleocharis sp.
0	0	0	0	0	0	0	0	0	0	0	0	0	0
0	0	0	0	0	0	0	0	0	0	0	0	0	0
0	0	0	0	0	0	0	0	0	0	0	0	0	0
0	0	0	0	0	0	3	1	0	0	0	0	0	0
0	0	0	0	0	0	0	0	0	0	0	0	0	0
0	0	0	0	0	0	0	5	0	0	0	0	0	0
0	0	0	0	0	0	0	0	0	0	0	0	0	0
0	0	0	0	0	0	0	4	0	0	0	0	0	0
0	0	0	0	0	0	0	1	0	0	0	0	0	0
0	0	0	0	0	0	0	319	0	0	0	0	0	0
0	0	0	0	0	0	0	62	0	0	0	0	0	0
0	0	0	0	0	0	0	0	0	0	0	0	0	0
0	0	0	0	0	0	0	2	0	0	0	0	0	0
0	0	0	0	0	0	0	11	0	0	0	0	0	0
0	0	0	0	0	0	0	7	0	0	0	0	0	0
0	0	0	0	0	0	0	2	0	0	0	0	0	0
0	0	0	0	0	0	0	6	0	0	0	0	0	0
0	0	0	0	0	0	0	31	0	0	0	1	0	0
0	0	0	0	0	0	0	0	0	0	0	0	0	0
0	0	0	0	0	0	0	575	0	0	0	0	0	0
0	0	0	0	0	0	0	3	0	0	0	0	0	0
0	1	0	0	0	0	0	46	0	0	0	0	0	0
0	0	0	0	0	0	0	102	0	0	0	0	0	0
0	0	0	0	0	0	0	0	0	0	0	0	0	0
0	0	0	0	0	0	0	41	0	0	0	0	0	0
0	0	0	0	0	0	0	0	0	0	0	0	0	0
0	0	0	0	0	0	0	0	0	0	0	0	0	0
0	0	0	0	0	0	0	0	0	0	0	0	0	0
0	2	0	0	0	0	0	40	0	0	0	0	0	0
0	0	0	0	0	0	0	1	0	0	0	0	0	0
0	0	0	0	0	0	0	0	0	0	0	0	0	0
0	0	0	0	0	0	0	0	0	0	0	0	0	0
0	0	0	0	0	0	0	246	0	0	0	0	0	0
0	0	0	0	0	0	0	0	0	0	0	0	0	0
0	0	8	0	0	0	0	1	0	0	0	0	0	0
0	0	0	300	0	0	1	50	0	1	0	0	0	0
0	0	6	0	0	0	0	3	0	0	0	0	0	0
0	0	0	0	0	0	0	0	0	0	0	0	0	0
0	0	0	0	0	0	0	0	0	0	0	0	0	0
0	0	0	0	0	0	0	18	0	0	0	0	0	0
0	0	0	0	0	0	0	0	1	0	0	0	0	0
0	0	0	0	0	0	0	25	0	0	0	0	0	0
0	0	0	0	0	0	0	0	0	0	0	0	0	0
0	0	1	0	0	0	0	35	0	0	0	0	0	0
0	0	1	2	0	0	0	23	0	0	0	0	0	0
0	0	1	0	0	0	0	0	0	0	0	0	0	0
0	0	0	0	0	0	0	0	0	0	0	0	0	0

Table D.2. Continued.

Provenience	Bag	Feature	cf. *Yucca* sp.	*Trianthema* sp.	Cactaceae	*Carnegiea gigantea*	*Echinocereus* sp.	*Mammillaria* sp.	*Opuntia* sp.	*Opuntia* sp. (Playtopuntia)	Chenopodiaceae	Cheno-am	*Chenopodium* sp.	*Suaeda* sp.
179	1	820.01	0	0	0	0	0	0	0	0	0	0	0	0
180	1	820.01	0	1	0	1	0	0	0	0	0	0	0	0
182	1	820.01	0	0	0	0	0	0	0	0	0	8	0	0
440	1	824.00	0	0	0	0	0	0	0	0	0	0	0	0
432	5	824.02	0	0	0	2	0	0	0	0	0	0	0	0
434	1	824.24	0	0	2	0	1	0	0	0	0	0	0	0
170	1	825.01	0	0	0	0	0	0	0	0	0	1	0	0
561	11	836.00	0	0	0	2	0	0	0	0	0	1	0	0
561	12	836.00	0	0	0	4	1	0	0	0	0	8	0	0
563	13	836.01	0	0	0	2	0	0	0	0	0	22	0	0
394	1	840.00	0	0	0	0	0	0	0	0	0	12	0	0
384	2	840.01	0	0	0	1	0	0	0	0	0	0	0	0
117	1	861.00	0	2	0	0	0	0	0	1	0	1	0	0
456	1	861.01	0	0	0	0	1	0	0	0	0	0	15	0
458	1	861.01	0	0	0	1	0	0	0	0	0	1	12	0
101	1	863.00	0	0	0	0	0	0	0	0	0	0	0	0
102	1	863.00	0	0	0	10	0	0	0	7	0	8	0	0
123	1	863.00	0	0	0	0	0	0	0	0	0	0	0	0
125	5	863.01	0	0	0	0	0	0	0	0	0	3	0	0
104	3	864.00	0	0	0	0	0	0	0	0	0	0	1	0
105	4	864.01	0	0	0	0	0	0	0	0	0	3	0	0
147	11	866.00	0	0	0	2	0	0	0	0	0	0	2	0
207	1	866.00	0	0	0	0	0	0	0	0	0	0	0	0
221	1	867.00	0	0	0	2	0	0	0	0	0	22	0	0
248	1	867.00	0	0	0	1	0	0	0	0	0	0	27	0
209	7	867.01	0	0	0	1	0	0	0	0	0	2	0	0
205	1	870.00	0	0	0	0	0	0	0	0	0	0	5	0
545	1	876.00	0	0	0	1	0	0	0	1	0	4	0	0
580	1	879.00	0	0	0	0	0	0	0	0	0	0	0	0
579	1	879.01	0	4	0	1	1	0	0	0	0	17	0	0
578	1	880.00	0	0	0	1	0	0	0	0	0	3	0	0
577	1	880.01	0	0	0	7	0	0	0	0	0	110	0	0
476	7	882.00	0	0	0	3	0	0	0	0	0	0	0	0
482	8	882.01	0	0	0	0	0	0	0	0	0	14	0	0
483	1	882.01	0	0	0	0	0	0	0	0	0	4	0	0
536	1	886.00	0	0	0	2	0	0	0	0	0	0	0	0
537	1	886.00	0	0	0	10	0	0	0	1	0	23	0	0
224	1	887.00	0	0	0	0	0	0	0	0	0	2	0	0
198	1	890.00	0	0	0	7	0	0	0	0	0	7	0	0
199	1	890.00	0	0	0	1	1	0	0	0	0	0	11	0
200	1	890.01	0	0	0	5	4	0	0	0	0	0	0	0
201	1	890.01	0	0	0	2	0	0	0	0	0	0	2	0
535	1	893.00	0	0	0	1	0	0	0	0	0	1	0	0
138	1	898.00	0	0	0	3	0	0	0	0	0	2	0	0
138	2	898.00	0	0	0	0	0	0	0	0	0	0	10	0
139	1	898.01	0	0	0	4	0	0	0	0	0	4	0	0
139	2	898.01	0	0	0	0	0	0	0	0	0	20	0	0
139	3	898.01	0	0	0	0	0	0	0	0	0	1	0	0

Cleome sp.	Polanisia sp.	Compositae	Artemisia sp.	Helianthus sp.	Viguiera sp.	Cruciferae	Descurainia sp.	Cucurbitaceae	Cucurbita sp. (wild)	Juniperus sp.	Cyperaceae	Carex sp.	Eleocharis sp.
0	0	0	0	0	0	0	0	0	0	0	0	0	0
0	0	0	0	0	0	0	3	0	0	0	0	0	0
0	0	2	0	0	0	0	5	0	0	0	0	0	0
0	0	0	0	0	0	0	0	0	0	0	0	0	0
0	0	0	0	0	0	0	0	0	0	0	0	0	0
0	0	0	0	0	0	0	0	0	0	0	0	0	0
0	0	0	0	0	0	0	0	0	0	0	0	0	0
0	0	0	0	0	0	0	0	0	0	0	0	0	0
0	0	1	0	0	0	0	0	1	0	0	0	0	0
0	1	0	3	0	0	0	5	0	0	0	0	0	0
0	0	0	0	0	0	0	0	0	0	0	0	0	0
0	0	0	0	0	0	0	1	0	0	0	0	0	0
0	0	0	0	0	0	0	3	0	0	0	0	0	0
0	0	0	0	0	0	0	160	0	0	0	0	0	0
0	1	0	0	0	0	0	139	0	0	0	0	0	0
0	0	1	0	0	0	0	2	0	0	0	0	0	0
0	3	0	0	0	0	0	7	0	0	0	0	0	0
0	0	0	0	0	0	0	0	0	0	0	0	0	0
1	0	0	0	0	0	0	4	0	0	0	0	0	0
0	0	0	0	0	0	0	2	0	0	0	0	0	0
0	0	0	0	0	0	0	0	0	0	0	0	0	0
0	0	0	0	0	0	0	3	0	0	0	0	0	0
0	0	0	0	0	0	0	0	0	0	0	0	0	0
0	0	0	0	0	0	3	11	0	0	0	0	0	0
0	0	0	0	0	0	0	4	0	0	0	0	0	0
0	0	0	0	0	0	0	0	0	0	0	0	0	0
0	0	10	0	0	0	0	300	0	0	0	0	0	0
0	0	0	0	0	0	0	0	0	0	0	0	0	0
0	0	0	0	0	0	0	29	0	0	0	0	0	0
0	0	0	0	0	0	0	0	0	0	0	0	0	0
0	0	0	0	0	0	0	0	0	0	0	0	0	0
0	0	0	0	0	0	0	0	0	0	0	0	0	0
0	0	0	0	0	0	0	0	0	0	0	0	0	2
0	0	0	0	0	0	0	2	0	0	0	0	0	0
0	0	0	0	0	0	0	0	0	0	0	0	0	0
0	0	0	0	0	0	0	15	0	0	0	0	0	0
0	0	0	0	0	0	0	0	0	0	0	0	0	0
0	0	0	0	0	0	0	2	0	0	0	0	4	0
0	0	0	0	0	0	0	9	0	0	0	0	0	0
0	0	0	0	1	0	0	22	0	0	0	0	0	0
0	0	0	0	0	0	0	48	0	0	0	0	0	0
0	0	0	0	0	0	0	0	0	0	0	0	0	0
0	0	0	0	1	0	0	4	0	0	0	0	0	0
0	0	1	0	1	0	0	6	0	0	0	1	0	0
0	0	0	0	0	0	0	5	0	0	0	0	0	0
0	0	0	0	0	10	0	20	0	0	0	0	0	0
0	0	0	0	0	0	0	0	0	0	0	0	0	0

Table D.2. Continued.

Provenience	Bag	Feature	Euphorbiaceae	Euphorbia sp.	Gramineae	Agrostis/Muhlenbergia type	Bouteloua sp.	Bromus sp.	Eragrostis sp.	Panicum sp.	Phragmites sp.	Sporobolus sp.	Zea mays
208	1	302.00	0	0	0	0	0	0	0	0	0	2	59
157	1	302.01	0	0	0	0	0	0	0	0	0	0	4
158	1	302.01	0	0	0	0	0	0	0	0	0	0	17
118	4	304.00	0	0	0	0	0	0	0	0	0	0	13
154	1	305.00	0	0	3	0	0	0	0	0	0	0	0
155	1	305.01	0	0	0	0	0	0	0	0	0	0	9
156	1	305.01	0	0	0	0	0	0	0	0	0	0	8
306	1	318.00	0	0	0	0	0	0	0	0	0	0	5
345	1	318.01	0	0	0	0	0	0	0	0	0	0	11
354	1	318.01	4	0	1	0	0	0	0	0	0	1	2
353	1	318.02	0	0	3	0	0	0	0	1	0	123	9
238	1	324.00	0	0	0	0	0	0	0	0	0	0	2
245	1	324.01	0	0	0	0	0	0	0	0	0	0	6
246	1	324.14	0	0	0	0	0	0	0	0	0	0	3
301	1	327.00	0	0	0	1	0	0	0	0	0	3	32
297	1	327.01	0	0	1	0	0	0	0	0	0	0	1
298	1	327.01	0	0	0	3	0	0	0	1	0	9	13
229	1	328.00	0	0	1	0	0	0	0	0	0	0	3
515	1	329.00	0	0	0	0	0	0	0	0	0	10	16
430	5	330.00	0	0	0	0	0	0	0	0	0	0	27
405	6	333.00	0	0	3	0	0	0	0	0	0	26	62
441	5	333.00	0	0	25	0	0	0	0	0	0	7	0
442	4	333.01	0	0	0	0	0	0	0	0	0	42	10
252	1	337.00	0	0	0	0	0	0	0	0	0	0	21
278	1	337.14	22	0	31	2	0	0	0	0	0	0	13
279	1	337.14	0	0	1	0	0	0	0	0	0	0	4
526	1	339.00	0	0	0	0	0	0	0	0	0	20	5
527	1	339.01	0	0	2	0	0	0	0	0	0	0	24
271	4	342.00	0	0	0	0	0	0	0	0	0	2	3
326	2	342.01	0	0	0	0	0	0	0	0	0	0	5
328	5	342.01	0	0	0	0	0	0	1	0	0	0	3
459	1	346.00	0	0	0	0	0	0	0	0	0	1	10
471	1	348.00	0	0	0	0	0	0	0	0	0	0	0
364	1	352.00	0	0	0	0	0	0	0	0	0	0	8
368	1	352.01	0	0	0	1	1	0	0	0	0	0	14
369	1	352.01	0	0	0	0	0	0	0	0	0	0	7
176	3	353.00	0	0	0	0	0	0	0	0	0	0	0
269	7	354.01	0	0	0	0	0	0	0	0	0	0	13
269	8	354.01	0	0	0	0	0	0	0	0	0	0	8
330	7	355.00	0	0	15	0	0	0	0	0	0	7	9
350	11	355.09	0	0	0	0	0	0	0	0	0	0	7
355	5	355.10	0	0	0	0	0	0	0	0	0	0	7
356	1	355.10	0	0	5	0	0	0	0	1	0	0	14
351	1	355.46	0	0	0	0	0	0	0	0	0	0	3
352	1	355.46	0	0	1	0	0	0	0	0	0	2	8
410	3	357.00	0	0	0	0	0	0	0	0	0	0	6
501	1	359.00	0	0	0	0	0	0	0	0	0	1	8
497	1	365.00	0	0	0	0	0	0	0	0	0	1	0

Labiatae	Salvia sp.	Leguminosae	Prosopis sp.	Malvaceae	Eschscholtzia sp.	Portulaca sp.	Solanaceae	Nicotiana sp.	Solanum/Physalis type	Kallstroemia sp.	Unidentified/unknown	Miscellaneous uncharred
0	0	0	0	0	0	0	0	0	0	0	2	0
0	0	0	0	0	0	0	0	0	0	0	0	0
0	0	0	0	0	0	0	0	0	0	0	0	0
0	0	0	0	0	0	0	0	0	0	0	0	0
0	0	0	0	0	0	0	0	0	0	0	0	0
0	0	0	0	0	0	0	0	0	0	0	0	0
0	0	0	0	1	0	0	0	0	0	0	0	0
0	0	0	0	0	0	0	0	0	0	0	9	0
79	0	4	0	0	0	0	0	0	0	0	0	0
0	0	0	0	0	0	0	0	1	0	0	0	0
0	0	0	1	0	0	0	0	0	0	0	520	0
0	0	0	1	0	0	0	0	0	0	0	0	0
0	0	0	2	0	0	0	0	0	0	0	0	50
6	0	0	0	0	0	0	0	0	0	0	0	0
0	0	0	0	0	0	0	0	0	0	0	0	0
0	0	0	2	0	0	0	0	0	0	0	0	0
0	0	0	1	0	0	0	0	0	0	0	0	0
0	0	0	0	0	0	0	0	0	0	0	0	50
0	0	0	0	0	0	0	0	0	0	0	0	0
0	0	0	0	0	0	0	0	0	0	0	0	0
1	0	0	0	0	0	0	0	0	0	0	9	0
0	0	0	0	0	0	0	0	0	0	0	0	0
0	0	0	3	0	0	0	0	0	0	0	2	0
11	0	0	0	0	0	0	0	0	0	0	0	0
0	0	0	0	0	0	0	0	0	0	0	0	0
0	0	0	0	0	0	0	0	0	0	0	0	0
0	0	0	1	0	0	0	0	0	0	0	0	0
0	0	0	1	0	0	0	0	0	0	0	0	0
3	0	0	0	0	0	0	0	0	0	0	0	0
0	0	0	0	0	0	0	0	0	0	0	0	0
2	0	0	1	0	0	0	0	0	0	0	0	0
0	0	0	0	0	0	0	0	0	0	0	0	0
0	0	0	0	0	0	0	0	0	0	0	0	0
0	0	0	2	0	0	0	0	0	0	0	0	0
0	0	0	2	0	0	0	0	0	0	0	0	0
0	0	0	0	0	0	0	0	0	0	0	0	0
0	0	0	0	0	0	0	0	0	0	0	0	0
4	0	0	0	0	0	2	0	0	0	0	0	0
0	0	0	0	0	0	0	0	0	0	0	0	0
0	0	0	0	0	0	0	0	0	0	0	0	0
0	0	0	2	0	0	0	0	0	0	0	0	0
0	0	0	0	0	0	0	0	0	0	0	0	0
0	0	1	0	0	0	0	0	0	0	0	0	0
0	0	0	0	0	0	0	0	0	0	0	0	0
0	0	0	0	0	0	0	0	0	0	0	0	0
2	0	0	0	0	0	0	0	0	0	0	0	0
0	0	0	0	0	0	0	0	0	0	0	0	0
0	0	0	0	0	0	0	0	0	0	0	0	0

Table D.2. Continued.

Provenience	Bag	Feature	Euphorbiaceae	Euphorbia sp.	Gramineae	Agrostis/Muhlenbergia type	Bouteloua sp.	Bromus sp.	Eragrostis sp.	Panicum sp.	Phragmites sp.	Sporobolus sp.	Zea mays
319	1	370.00	0	0	0	0	0	0	0	0	0	0	10
320	1	370.01	0	0	1	0	0	0	0	0	0	1	14
400	1	372.00	0	0	0	0	0	0	0	0	0	0	4
401	1	372.00	0	0	0	0	0	0	0	0	0	0	0
402	1	372.01	0	0	0	0	0	0	0	0	0	0	3
403	1	372.01	0	0	0	0	0	0	0	0	0	0	2
486	1	373.00	0	0	0	0	0	0	10	0	0	0	1
506	1	373.00	0	0	0	0	0	0	0	0	0	0	23
529	8	379.00	0	0	0	0	0	1	0	0	0	0	0
463	1	389.00	0	0	1	0	0	0	0	0	0	3	8
464	1	389.00	0	0	0	0	0	0	0	0	0	12	2
597	1	390.00	0	0	4	0	0	0	0	0	0	3	9
615	1	390.16	0	0	0	0	0	0	0	0	0	0	0
519	5	399.00	0	0	7	0	0	0	0	0	0	0	9
474	5	400.00	0	0	0	1	0	0	0	0	0	0	12
473	1	403.00	0	0	0	0	0	0	0	0	0	0	12
518	1	406.00	0	0	0	0	0	0	0	0	0	0	5
481	1	407.00	0	0	3	3	0	0	0	0	0	7	1
620	1	408.00	0	0	0	0	0	0	0	0	0	0	1
511	6	411.00	0	0	5	0	0	0	0	0	0	0	0
491	2	416.00	0	0	0	0	0	0	0	0	0	5	3
490	1	416.01	0	0	4	0	0	0	0	0	0	30	4
313	2	417.00	0	0	0	0	0	0	0	0	0	236	4
344	4	420.00	0	0	1	0	0	0	0	0	0	0	5
398	10	422.00	0	0	0	2	0	0	0	0	0	0	2
439	1	423.00	0	0	0	0	0	0	0	0	0	0	7
548	1	425.00	0	0	0	0	0	0	0	0	0	0	11
549	1	425.01	0	0	0	20	0	0	0	0	0	0	13
605	1	427.00	0	0	0	0	0	0	0	0	0	0	23
496	9	428.00	0	0	0	0	0	0	0	0	0	0	3
495	3	429.00	0	0	1	0	0	0	0	0	0	0	0
485	1	431.00	0	0	0	3	0	0	0	0	0	0	23
614	1	433.00	0	0	4	12	0	0	0	0	0	438	27
606	1	812.00	0	0	0	0	0	0	0	0	0	1	14
602	1	812.23	0	0	0	1	0	0	0	0	0	0	8
603	1	812.23	0	20	12	105	0	0	0	0	0	33	28
604	1	812.23	0	0	0	0	1	0	0	0	0	7	10
550	1	813.00	0	0	0	0	0	0	0	0	0	0	1
551	1	813.01	0	0	0	0	0	0	0	0	0	0	1
417	6	815.00	0	0	0	0	0	0	0	0	0	0	7
513	1	817.00	0	0	0	0	0	0	0	0	0	10	0
520	1	817.01	0	0	0	0	0	0	0	0	0	10	7
520	3	817.01	0	0	0	0	0	0	0	0	0	4	2
538	1	818.00	10	0	0	1	0	0	0	0	0	10	31
377	5	819.00	0	0	2	17	0	0	0	0	0	24	6
539	9	819.00	0	0	10	27	0	0	5	23	0	65	4
381	1	819.02	0	0	0	12	0	0	2	1	0	2	9
178	1	820.00	0	0	0	0	0	0	1	0	0	0	0

Labiatae	*Salvia* sp.	Leguminosae	*Prosopis* sp.	Malvaceae	*Eschscholtzia* sp.	*Portulaca* sp.	Solanaceae	*Nicotiana* sp.	*Solanum/Physalis* type	*Kallstroemia* sp.	Unidentified/unknown	Miscellaneous uncharred
0	0	0	3	0	0	0	0	0	0	0	0	0
0	0	0	2	0	0	0	0	0	0	0	0	0
0	0	0	0	0	0	0	0	0	0	0	0	0
0	0	0	0	0	0	0	0	0	0	0	0	0
0	3	0	0	0	0	0	0	0	0	0	0	0
0	0	0	0	0	0	0	0	0	0	0	0	0
0	0	0	0	0	0	0	0	0	0	0	0	0
0	0	0	0	0	0	0	0	0	0	0	0	0
0	0	0	2	0	0	0	0	0	0	0	0	0
0	0	0	0	0	0	0	0	0	0	0	0	0
0	0	0	0	0	0	0	0	0	0	0	0	0
0	0	0	0	0	0	0	0	0	0	0	0	0
0	0	0	2	0	0	0	1	0	0	0	0	0
0	0	0	1	0	0	0	0	0	0	0	0	0
0	0	0	0	0	0	0	0	0	0	0	0	0
0	0	0	0	0	0	2	0	0	0	0	0	0
0	0	0	0	0	0	0	0	0	0	0	0	0
0	0	0	0	0	0	0	0	0	0	0	0	0
0	0	0	1	0	0	0	1	0	0	0	0	0
0	0	0	0	0	0	0	0	0	0	0	1	0
0	0	0	0	0	0	0	0	0	0	0	0	0
0	0	0	0	0	0	0	0	0	0	0	0	0
1	0	0	0	0	0	0	0	0	0	0	0	0
0	0	0	0	0	0	0	0	0	0	0	0	0
0	0	0	0	0	0	0	0	0	0	0	0	0
0	0	0	0	0	0	0	0	0	0	0	0	0
0	0	0	2	0	0	0	0	0	0	0	0	0
0	0	0	3	0	0	0	0	0	0	0	0	0
0	0	0	0	0	0	0	0	0	0	0	0	0
0	0	0	0	0	0	0	0	0	0	0	0	0
0	0	0	0	0	0	0	0	0	0	0	0	0
0	0	0	0	0	0	0	0	0	0	0	16	0
2	0	0	0	0	0	0	0	0	0	0	0	0
0	0	0	0	0	0	0	0	0	0	0	0	0
0	0	0	7	0	0	0	0	0	5	0	0	0
0	0	0	2	0	0	0	0	0	0	0	0	0
0	0	0	1	0	0	0	0	0	0	0	0	0
0	0	0	0	0	0	0	0	0	0	0	0	0
0	0	0	0	0	0	0	0	0	0	0	0	0
0	0	0	0	0	0	0	0	0	0	0	0	0
0	0	0	1	0	0	0	0	0	0	0	0	0
0	0	0	1	0	0	0	0	0	0	0	1	0
1	0	0	0	0	1	0	0	0	0	0	0	0
0	0	0	1	0	0	0	0	0	0	0	0	0
0	0	0	0	0	0	0	0	0	0	1	0	0
0	0	0	0	0	0	0	0	0	0	0	0	0

Table D.2. Continued.

Provenience	Bag	Feature	Euphorbiaceae	Euphorbia sp.	Gramineae	Agrostis/Muhlenbergia type	Bouteloua sp.	Bromus sp.	Eragrostis sp.	Panicum sp.	Phragmites sp.	Sporobolus sp.	Zea mays
179	1	820.01	0	0	0	0	0	0	0	0	0	0	3
180	1	820.01	0	0	3	0	0	0	0	0	0	1	4
182	1	820.01	0	0	0	0	0	0	4	0	0	0	0
440	1	824.00	0	0	0	0	0	0	0	0	0	0	1
432	5	824.02	0	0	13	0	0	0	0	0	0	0	1
434	1	824.24	0	0	0	0	0	0	0	0	0	0	5
170	1	825.01	0	0	0	0	0	0	0	0	0	0	2
561	11	836.00	3	0	2	0	0	0	0	0	0	1	6
561	12	836.00	0	0	8	0	0	0	0	0	0	5	24
563	13	836.01	0	0	1	1	0	0	0	0	0	21	17
394	1	840.00	0	0	0	0	0	0	0	0	0	3	22
384	2	840.01	0	0	0	0	0	0	0	0	0	0	0
117	1	861.00	0	0	0	1	0	0	0	0	0	4	33
456	1	861.01	0	0	2	18	0	0	0	1	0	5	33
458	1	861.01	0	0	18	0	6	0	0	0	0	0	9
101	1	863.00	0	0	1	0	0	0	0	0	0	1	1
102	1	863.00	0	0	0	0	0	0	0	0	0	0	42
123	1	863.00	0	0	0	0	0	0	0	0	0	0	4
125	5	863.01	0	0	0	0	0	0	0	0	0	8	11
104	3	864.00	0	0	1	0	0	0	0	0	0	0	1
105	4	864.01	0	0	0	0	0	0	0	0	1	0	1
147	11	866.00	0	0	0	0	0	0	0	0	0	0	15
207	1	866.00	0	0	0	0	0	0	0	0	0	0	4
221	1	867.00	0	0	0	0	0	0	0	0	0	19	2
248	1	867.00	0	0	0	2	0	0	0	0	0	0	1
209	7	867.01	0	0	0	0	0	0	0	0	0	15	2
205	1	870.00	0	0	0	0	0	0	0	0	0	20	37
545	1	876.00	0	0	0	0	0	0	0	0	0	0	7
580	1	879.00	0	0	0	0	0	0	0	0	0	0	0
579	1	879.01	0	0	18	1	0	0	0	3	0	1	10
578	1	880.00	0	0	0	0	0	0	0	0	0	0	4
577	1	880.01	0	0	10	0	0	0	0	0	0	0	16
476	7	882.00	0	0	7	0	0	0	0	0	0	0	7
482	8	882.01	0	0	8	0	0	0	0	0	0	0	0
483	1	882.01	0	0	0	0	0	0	0	0	0	0	5
536	1	886.00	0	0	0	0	0	0	0	0	0	0	24
537	1	886.00	0	0	0	0	0	0	0	0	0	0	38
224	1	887.00	0	0	0	0	0	0	0	0	0	0	2
198	1	890.00	0	0	1	0	0	0	0	0	0	0	8
199	1	890.00	0	0	0	0	0	0	0	0	0	0	10
200	1	890.01	0	0	38	15	0	0	0	1	0	0	19
201	1	890.01	0	0	0	0	0	0	0	0	0	0	6
535	1	893.00	0	0	0	0	0	0	0	0	0	0	9
138	1	898.00	0	0	0	0	0	0	10	0	0	0	2
138	2	898.00	0	0	0	0	0	0	0	0	0	1	5
139	1	898.01	0	0	1	0	0	0	0	0	0	0	17
139	2	898.01	0	0	0	0	0	0	1	10	0	10	21
139	3	898.01	0	0	1	0	0	0	2	0	0	0	0

Labiatae	Salvia sp.	Leguminosae	Prosopis sp.	Malvaceae	Eschscholtzia sp.	Portulaca sp.	Solanaceae	Nicotiana sp.	Solanum/Physalis type	Kallstroemia sp.	Unidentified/unknown	Miscellaneous uncharred
0	0	0	0	0	0	0	0	0	0	0	0	0
0	0	0	2	0	0	0	0	0	0	0	1	0
0	0	0	0	0	0	0	0	0	0	0	0	0
0	0	0	0	0	0	0	0	0	0	0	0	0
0	0	0	0	0	0	0	0	0	0	0	0	0
0	0	0	0	0	0	0	0	0	0	0	0	0
0	0	0	0	0	0	0	0	0	0	0	0	0
0	0	0	1	0	0	0	0	0	0	0	0	0
0	0	0	6	0	0	3	0	0	0	0	0	0
0	0	0	6	0	0	0	0	0	0	0	0	0
0	0	0	1	0	0	0	0	0	0	0	0	0
0	0	0	0	0	0	0	0	0	0	0	0	0
1	0	0	0	0	0	0	0	0	0	0	0	0
0	0	0	0	0	0	0	0	0	0	0	0	0
0	0	0	0	0	0	0	0	0	0	0	0	0
0	0	0	0	0	0	0	0	0	0	0	0	0
0	0	0	0	0	0	0	0	0	0	0	0	0
0	0	0	0	0	0	0	0	0	0	0	0	0
0	0	0	0	0	0	0	0	0	0	0	0	0
0	0	0	0	0	0	0	0	0	0	0	0	0
0	0	0	0	0	0	0	0	0	0	0	0	0
0	0	0	1	0	0	0	0	0	0	0	0	0
0	0	0	1	0	0	1	0	0	0	0	0	0
0	0	0	0	0	0	0	0	0	0	0	0	0
0	0	0	0	0	0	0	0	0	0	0	0	0
0	0	0	0	0	0	0	0	0	0	0	5	0
0	0	0	2	0	0	0	0	0	0	0	1	0
0	0	0	0	0	0	0	0	0	0	0	0	0
0	0	0	0	0	0	1	0	0	0	0	1	0
0	0	0	0	0	0	0	0	0	0	0	0	0
0	0	0	0	0	0	0	0	0	0	0	0	0
0	0	0	0	0	0	0	0	0	0	0	0	0
0	0	0	0	0	0	0	0	0	0	0	0	0
0	0	0	3	0	0	0	0	0	0	0	0	0
0	0	0	4	0	0	0	0	0	0	0	0	0
1	0	0	2	0	0	1	0	0	0	0	0	0
0	0	0	0	0	0	0	0	0	0	0	0	0
0	0	0	0	0	0	1	0	0	0	0	1	0
0	0	0	1	0	0	0	0	0	0	0	0	0
0	0	0	2	0	0	0	0	0	0	0	0	0
0	0	0	0	0	0	0	0	0	0	0	0	0
0	0	0	0	0	0	0	0	0	0	0	0	0
0	0	0	0	0	0	0	0	0	0	0	0	0
0	0	0	0	0	0	0	0	0	0	0	0	0
0	0	0	0	0	0	0	0	0	0	0	0	0
0	0	0	1	0	0	0	0	0	0	0	0	0
0	0	0	0	0	0	0	0	0	0	0	0	0

For any patch of cacti, a severe winter frost can eliminate reproductive growth during the following summer by killing off older plants and forcing younger plants to invest energy in tissue repair rather than fruiting. Other factors that increase saguaro mortality include fire, which disproportionately affects younger plants, and animal predation during drought years.

It is suggested that one consequence of frost vulnerability is that there exist predictable differences in the long-term reliability of different saguaro patches. The most stable populations that reliably produce fruit crops occur on south-facing slopes (Steenbergh and Lowe 1983). In these locations, a healthy patch can achieve plant densities of 160 plants/ha, with 120 of these bearing fruit (Steenbergh and Lowe 1983:94). In contrast, patches located on north-facing slopes or in higher elevations have densities that average about 51 plants/ha, with fewer than 36 bearing fruit (Steenbergh and Lowe 1983:94). There is greater variation in plant density in marginal areas, with some extant colonies experiencing long-term decline. Since freezes occur more frequently on north-facing slopes and in marginal areas, years with low- or zero-fruit yields are more frequent.

Reproductive growth in saguaros begins sometime during the sixth through tenth years, and continues throughout their 200-year life (Steenbergh and Lowe 1983:19). Branching occurs after 40 to 50 years. In a healthy plant, each branch produces roughly the same amount of fruit as the original column (Steenbergh and Lowe 1983:49); hence, a cactus with the main column and one branch produces about twice the yield of a plant with no branches.

Despite the amount of information on plant density, it is difficult to estimate fruit yields for different locations. No information on the average number of branches per patch or the number of fruit per branch was located during this study. Crosswhite (1980:16-25) reviewed ethnographic accounts of fruit harvesting and estimated that in a typical family, two adults typically harvested (1650 kg/750 lb) of fresh fruit during a season. His model requires two trips per day by two people, each carrying 15-20 lb of fruit in a basket, with an average yield of 34 calories of energy (mostly carbohydrates from sugar) per fruit. Doelle (1978) observed Papago fruit harvesters to obtain 3-4.6 kg pulp (about four plants) per hour of work, and to achieve gross energetic returns of 6,000-9,000 kcal. Elsewhere, Doelle (1976) estimated energetic costs of 2.5-3.5 kcal/minute harvesting plants in the desert.

Echinocereus sp. (Hedgehog)

Echinocereus is common at 3,000-6,000 ft, flowering May-July and fruiting by the end of July (Kearney and Peebles 1973). Among the Papago, hedgehog fruit were consumed fresh or dried and stored for later consumption; seeds were parched and ground after the fashion of saguaro (Castetter and Underhill 1935). Ethnographies do not record the formation of task groups for the specific purpose of obtaining hedgehog, and harvesting and consumption may have been embedded in other foraging tasks. In a survey of the vegetation in the Tonto National Monument, hedgehog were observed growing at densities of 50-100 plants/ha (Jenkins et al. 1995:57-65). These densities are lower than the densities observed for saguaro and yields were probably lower.

Mammillaria sp. (Pincushion/Fishhook)

These comprise a diverse genus common at 1,200-3,000 ft in Pima County, flowering in July (Kearney and Peebles 1973). The tiny edible fruit were likely obtained and consumed in the same manner as hedgehog. *Mammillaria* sp. is commonly observed at densities of 100 plants/ha in the Tonto National Monument (Jenkins et al. 1995:57-65). No information on fruit yields or nutrition content was obtained during this study.

Opuntia sp. (Prickly Pear)

This is a diverse genus widely distributed throughout North and South America (Furlow and Mitchell 1990:51). In the Southwest, they flourish at elevations between 1,000 and 7,500 ft, flowering from April through June and fruiting in late June and July (Kearney and Peebles 1973).

Prickly pear fruit are a well-known contributor to the diets of many indigenous Southwestern North Americans, who consumed the fresh or dried fruit and young pads (Castetter and Underhill 1935; Minnis 1991:238-239). The buds of the related chollas (also *Opuntia* spp.) were consumed (Doelle 1976; Gasser 1982).

An experimental analysis of green Indian fig *(O. ficus indica)* pads (Teles 1977:144-145) revealed a nutrient content (per 100 g) comprised as follows: crude protein = .05 g, carbohydrate = 11.3-11.8 g, crude fiber = .7-1.6 g, water = 83-95 g. Fresh fruits provide about 67 kcal/100 g (Ensminger et al. 1994:892-893). From 1954 through 1959, an experimental farm in California annually yielded 237-328 U.S. tons (wet weight) per 60-acre parcel (about 8,626 kg/ha) in an area that receives 13.6-21.3 in of rain annually (Curtis 1977:176). Wild populations of this and other species are expected to produce substantially smaller yields. Doelle (1976) noted that cholla buds yield about 340 kcal/100 g, and could be harvested by Papago farmers at a rate of 2 to 5.2 kg/hour, depending on the density of plants and on the density of fruits on each plant. Li (1992:9) noted that pollens typically yield 5 kcal/g and has suggested that they may become an economically important food source.

Chenopodium/Amaranthus sp. (Goosefoot/Amaranth)

Plants of these families are not closely related, but their growth habits are similar and their seeds are similar in appearance. Both thrive in disturbed contexts (especially in floodplain contexts) from elevations through 9,000 ft (Kearney and Peebles 1973). *Amaranthus* flowers continuously from May-November, and *Chenopodium* May-October (Kearney and Peebles 1973). K. Adams' (1988:158) study of *Chenopodium* in southeastern Arizona riparian contexts at 5,700-6,000 ft indicated that it flowered in August, and the fruit remained available for another eight weeks.

Ethnographic references in an exhaustive list reviewed by K. Adams (1988:170-175) consistently noted that the leaves of young plants were consumed as a pot herb, and that seeds were dried or parched, ground into meal, and consumed. Cheno-ams are found in archaeological features and cooking pots in numerous Southwestern sites (K. Adams 1988:178-180), as well as paleofeces (Minnis 1989:549), and their consumption as food by prehistoric Southwesterners is obvious. Nabhan (1983:136) noted that in modern Papago fields, the growth of *Amaranthus palmeri* was tolerated by farmers until plant density increased to the point where it competed with maize (*Zea mays*) or until amaranths became infested with insects.

Nabhan (1983) indicated that amaranth yielded .23 kg/m^2 (fresh vegetable weight) although little of this was consumed by modern farmers. Fresh greens are high in vitamins A and C and offer about 36 kcal/100 g (Nabhan 1985:71). Seeds are slightly higher in protein (13.6 percent) than most small seeded pants (Reed 1988:16). Although amaranth seeds contain low quantities of saponins that slightly inhibit nutrient digestion, these are removed by cooking (Fleming and Galway 1995:29; Williams and Brenner 1995:153). Toasted amaranth seeds yield 350-389 kcal/100 g from semi-domesticates (Ensminger et al. 1994:830; Williams and Brenner 1995:168).

Yields vary considerably between species. For wild amaranths grown in industrial, irrigated conditions, optimum seed yields are achieved at 100,000 plants/ha in irrigated conditions (Williams and Brenner 1995:155-156) and yield about 25.5 g/plant (or 2,500 kg/ha). However, seed yields are commonly as low as 200-250 kg/ha and under typical industrial conditions, 1,500 kg/ha (5.8 x 10^6 kcal/ha) is considered "good" (Williams and Brenner 1995:155-156). Common dry land yields of amaranth fall between 450 and 700 kg/ha in industrial settings and using "the better cultivars"

(Stallknecht and Schulz-Schaeffer 1993:213). It is assumed that maximum seed yields for non-irrigated, wild amaranths did not exceed 50 kg/ha.

Suaeda sp. (Seep Weed)

Seep weed is found in moderately to highly saline soils and dry ground at elevations 3,000-5,000 ft (Kearney and Peebles 1973). No other information on seasonality, plant density, seed yields, nutritional characteristics, or ethnographically known uses was located during this study.

Cleome sp. (Spider Flower)

Cleome sp. is found primarily along streams at elevations of 2,000-6,000 ft, flowering May-September, varying by species (Kearney and Peebles 1973:355-356).

Compositae (Composites)

Seeds of unknown composites were identified in many of the samples in this study.

Artemisia sp. (Sage)

This diverse genus prefers dry slopes at elevations of 2,500-8,000 ft. A survey of ethnohistoric accounts of the medicinal uses of plants indicated that at least seven species of *Artemisia* were used by Eurasian colonists and eastern Native Americans. In all cases, the leaves were used in a tea to treat a variety of internal complaints, and in one case the crushed seeds were recommended as an oral vermifuge (Erichsen-Brown 1979:407-412). No information on stand densities, yields, or nutrition was obtained during this study.

Helianthus cf. annuus (Common Sunflower)

Wild sunflowers are ubiquitous in disturbed ground throughout the American West at elevations from 100 to 7,000 ft (Kearney and Peebles 1973). In Arizona, *H. annuus* (the most common variety) flowers from March-October (Parker 1990:298). In higher elevations in southeastern Arizona, K. Adams (1988:253) observed sunflowers flowering during September and bearing ripe seeds from October through early November.

An extensive list of ethnohistoric and ethnographic accounts of its use (K. Adams 1988:254-259) mentions the use of every part of this plant by Native Americans. Examples include the use of flowers to make dye, chewing gum, or decorations; the medicinal use of flower heads, leaves, roots, and stem fragments; and the consumption of leaves, stems, and seeds (prepared in a variety of ways) as food.

H. annuus was domesticated by Russian plant scientists in the early twentieth century, and the large-seeded plant is presently vital in many parts of the world. Domesticated varieties grown in industrial settings commonly yield 960-1,132 kg/ha of unshelled seed (Cobia 1978:390), with yields as high as 3,400 kg/ha occasionally obtained (Robinson 1978). Seeds of the domestic variety are consistently 4-20 mm longer and 3-12 mm wider than the wild variety (Cobia 1978). The seeds are nutritious, offering 339 kcal/100 g, iron, and B-vitamins (Ensminger et al. 1994:838). Information on the stand densities and yields of the wild plant was not available.

Descurainia sp. (Tansy Mustard)

Tansy mustard flowers from March-April at elevations of 100-7,000 ft (Kearney and Peebles 1973; Parker 1990:146-147). The minute seeds are dispersed in the two months that follow flowering (K. Adams 1988:205). Ethnographically described uses of the plant are numerous, with all parts consumed as food and used to make teas. Seeds were ground into a "mush" by some groups, or added to other foods, and the harvesting and processing techniques for the Kawaiisu (California) have been described (K. Adams 1988:205-211). No information on plant densities or yields was obtained during this study.

Cucurbita sp. (Squash/Gourd)

Wild gourds and domesticated squashes are frequently found in Southwestern archaeological sites. Domesticated plants grow where cultivated (typically in floodplain fields). Wild varieties thrive at elevations from 100-5,000 ft and flower for about one month from June through October (K. Adams 1988:190; Parker 1990:272), with fruit ripening two-three months after flowering (K. Adams 1988:190). The seeds identified in this study fell within the range of size variation for both domesticated and wild varieties, and there were no diagnostic morphological features.

Ethnographic and historic documentation of the use of wild and domesticated varieties (fruit tissue and seeds) as food by Native Americans is extensive (K. Adams 1988:191-194). In domesticated varieties, the fruit yields 20-40 kcal/100 g (Ensminger et al. 1994), and the seeds are high in carbohydrates. The large roots of *C. foetidissima* may contain up to 56 percent of their dry weight in starch, but require leaching to render them edible (Ng 1993:543). The roots may reach 50 kg after four growing seasons. Each fruit yields 200-300 seeds that are comprised of 30-40 percent edible oil and 30-35 percent protein (DeVeaux and Schultz 1985:454-455). Under modern agricultural conditions the fruit might yield 600 kg/ha of protein and 780 kg/ha of oil, and roots might yield 13,500 kg/ha of starch (DeVeaux and Schultz 1985:461-462). It is also noted that cucurbit pulp is generally high in vitamin A (Ensminger et al. 1994).

Juniperus sp. (Juniper)

Juniper is found throughout Arizona at elevations of 3,000-5,000 ft. *J. deppeana*, observed by K. Adams (1988:283-297), flowers March-May, with new ripe fruit available from September through the following May. Generally, the fruit of Arizona species ripen August-October of their second year, with *J. monosperma* ripening in the year they form (USDA 1974:462-469).

Documented uses include the consumption of the ripe fruit as food and as ornamentation, the needles in tea, the branches in ceremonies, the bark for making dye and as a "famine food" chew, and the wood for fuel, construction, and the manufacture of small tools and ceremonial objects (K. Adams 1988:285-290). No information on the plant densities, seed yields, or nutritional composition of bark or seeds was located during this study.

Carex sp. (Sedge)

Sedge rarely occurs in Arizona at elevations lower than 5,000 ft; it flowers May-August (Kearney and Peebles 1973:157-164). Any particular species flowers for about two months, and most prefer wet soil (K. Adams 1988:152-153). Ethnographic and ethnohistoric sources reviewed by K. Adams (1988:155) indicate that the seeds (ground and cooked), and stems and bases were consumed as food, and the plant was used in a tea and as a moccasin liner. No information on the density, yields, or nutritional characteristics was located during this study.

Eleocharis sp. (Spike Rush)

One variety of Spike Rush was observed by K. Adams (1988:215-216) to flourish in aquatic environments in uplands cienegas. It flowered from April through July and bore ripe fruit in September. Parts of this plant have been used medicinally by the Ramah Navajo as an emetic, and leaves have been used as weaving material. Seeds have been found in paleofeces (K. Adams 1988:216). No other information on the density, seed yield, or nutritional composition was located during this study.

cf. *Euphorbia* sp. (Spurge)

Varieties of spurge have been observed in Arizona at elevations 100-5,000 ft, flowering from February through October (Kearney and Peebles 1973). K. Adams

(1988:234-235) observed flowering spurges in upland, dry-soil contexts May-August, with ripe fruit available August-October. Spurges contain a milky sap that is toxic to humans when ingested and that may cause skin inflammation. Despite, or perhaps because of, their toxicity, ethnographic references exist regarding its medicinal use by Native Americans (K. Adams 1988:234-235). One species was observed at densities of 250-2,100 plants/ha in the Tonto National Monument (Jenkins et al. 1995:57-65). No information is available on yield or nutritional composition.

Agrostis/Muhlenbergia sp. (Bentgrass/Muhly)

This plant is found in Arizona at elevations up to 9,000 ft, flowering August-September and ripening in October (K. Adams 1988:329; Kearney and Peebles 1973). Muhly thrives in a wide range of conditions, including some submerged conditions, but generally prefers drier soil (K. Adams 1988:331). Bentgrasses prefer moister conditions (Hitchcock 1971:337-354). The use of muhly grains as food and stems in basket weaving, hair brushes, and brooms is documented among most Southwestern groups (K. Adams 1988:334-335). No information on the density, seed yield, or nutritional composition was located during this study.

Bouteloua sp. (Grama)

Members of this genus occur throughout Arizona. Two species discussed by K. Adams (1988:142-147) were used in the same fashion as bentgrass. They flowered August-September and offered ripe seeds October-November. This plant has been observed at densities of 50-6,400 plants/ha in the Tonto National Monument (Jenkins et al. 1995:57-65). No information on the density, seed yield, or nutritional composition was located during this study.

Bromus sp. (Brome)

This plant is widespread, and observed at elevations up to 11,000 ft in open woodlands and dry meadows, as well as in shade near the margins of riparian communities (K. Adams 1988:149-151; Hitchock 1971: 31-57). The species observed by K. Adams (1988:149) flowered July-August and carried ripe seeds through November. However, given its range of distribution and the diversity of habitats in which it thrives, generalization is not attempted here. K. Adams (1988:150-151) noted that it was used by various California groups in the same fashion as bentgrass. No information on the density, seed yield, or nutritional composition was located during this study.

Eragrostis sp. (Lovegrass)

Lovegrass is found in open ground and waste places above 2,000 ft, usually in well-drained soils but some in wet soils (Kearney and Peebles 1973:86-87). *E. intermedia* flowers July-September; seeds are available August-November (K. Adams 1988:229). Seeds consumed in Historic times by some lower Colorado Native Americans have been observed in some archaeological sites (K. Adams 1988:229-231). It has been observed to produce 183-239 lb/acre (79-262 kg/ha) of herbage in areas cleared of competing overstory plants (Williams 1976), and plant densities as high as 44,000 plants/ha have been observed in semi-desert grassland localities in the Tonto National Monument (Jenkins et al. 1995:57-65). No information was found on seed yields or nutrition.

Panicum sp. (Panicgrass)

This plant is found in open ground and waste places in dry or moist soils, at elevations from 1,000-7,000 ft (Kearney and Peebles 1973:135-137). Two species have been observed to flower August-September with seeds available October-November (K. Adams 1988:347). Seeds were consumed by prehistoric groups, and horticulture was practiced by some Paiute bands (K. Adams 1988:348-350). No information on density, yields, or nutrition was located during this study.

Phragmites sp. (Reed)

Reed is found worldwide in marshes or wet or submerged ground; in Arizona, growth occurs from July-October (Kearney and Peebles 1973:89). There are numerous ethnographic and archaeological reported uses for stems, including cigarettes, arrow shafts, and woven products. No information was found on density, yields, or nutrition.

Sporobolus sp. (Dropseed/Alkali Sacaton)

This plant occurs in Arizona from 1,000-7,000 ft in wet or dry soils (Kearney and Peebles 1973:112-114). *S. airoides* is very common in the Tucson Basin; at higher elevations it flowers July-August with seeds available in September (K. Adams 1988:535). Numerous ethnographic instances have been observed of seed consumption (ground, boiled as tea) after threshing, and stems used as brushes, prayer sticks, and in woven objects (K. Adams 1988:536-537). It forms "almost pure grasslands" in some Mexican riparian areas, and growth occurs "even in a dry year" (de Alba Avila 1983:2). No other information on density, yields, or nutrition was available.

Zea mays (Maize)

This plant is a familiar New World domesticate and dietary staple. Its growth interval varies depending on subspecies, generally requiring 120 frost-free days and 20 cm rainfall. Moderate moisture stress can cause 25-65 percent loss of yield, with highest losses if stress occurs during silking (third-fifth week of growth) (Fall 1991:13-22; Monasterio 1981:55-56). Yields vary with variety, planting density, and the use of irrigation. Industrial varieties grown with irrigation yield 6,000-10,000 kg/ha (e.g., Fall 1991) and provide highest grain yields of any domesticated grain. The Hopi "blue" variety grown without irrigation at a modern experimental farm near the Hopi reservation yielded 1,020-3,360 kg/ha (Johnson and Jha 1993:228). The figures given probably represent yields achieved near optimum plant density. In one experiment, Hopi varieties grown in dry conditions yielded an average of .46 kg/6 plants (Grove 1969).

Ethnographic accounts of Hopi farming have consistently failed to document plant density, resulting in a wide range of estimated yields. Bradfield (1971) observed modern Hopi farmers obtaining yields of 41.5 kg/ha (dry) and 90.3 kg/ha (irrigated). Hegmon (1988) used figures in Ford's (1968) and Wetterstrom's (1976) studies of New Mexico pueblos to infer yields of 667 kg/ha in "better watered" Hopi fields. Castetter and Bell (1942:54) observed that Pima farmers obtained yields of 10-12 bushels of shelled corn per acre (roughly 1,676 kg/ha). That this quantity is roughly half the yield obtained by the USDA using the same seed in the same environment. Doelle (1980) observed Pima floodwater farms that produced 523-951 kg/ha. The energy yield is 360 kcal/100 g, with 8-11 percent protein (Ensminger et al. 1994:486); however, protein content in Hopi blue was observed to be 30 percent greater than common dent grown in adjacent Arizona fields (Johnson and Jha 1993:228).

The determination of maize yields in prehistoric agricultural settings is complicated by the absence of any reliable means for estimating the plant density. It is further complicated by the fact that Early Agricultural period maize ears were substantially smaller than modern varieties (K. Adams 1994; Galinat 1988; Upham et al. 1987, 1988) and likely produced substantially lower yields (Ford 1981:11; Winter 1973). B. Huckell (1995:121) has objected to the contention that early maize provided low yields in comparison with modern varieties, on the grounds that botanists lack information about the phenology of the prehistoric plant, and his caution is noted. However, all other things being equal, kernel size and cob size are the primary determinants of seed yield in maize. Cupule size and cob length are the only data available for the estimation of prehistoric plant yields.

K. Adams (1994) noted that modern Puebloan and Pima-Papago varieties of maize average 18-24 and 20-25 cm in length, respectively, whereas modern chapalote average only 11 cm in length. B. Huckell (1995:120) estimated that Early Agricultural period maize measured around 8.2 cm in length and yielded 22 g/cob. However, if Huckell's size estimate is accurate, then in accordance with Doelle's (1980:72) regression equation, 16 g/cob is a more reasonable estimate of Early Agricultural maize yield. Combining the various estimates, it is expected that Early Agricultural period maize provided yields that were 64-75 percent lower than yields from modern varieties grown under similar circumstances. Accordingly, it is suggested that Early Agricultural period maize returned approximately 110-250 kg/ha.

Maize harvesting costs can be said to be moderate. The energetic costs of planting and occasional tending are unique to this group. However, the harvesting and transport costs would have been nominal since it was locally grown and since maize lacks effective seed dispersal mechanisms. Grinding costs would probably have been higher than for small starchy seeds, since the large kernels would have required more grinding to achieve comparable levels of refinement, but lower than the costs associated with mesquite. Since maize requires substantially less effort in harvesting, transporting, and processing than mesquite, it may be assumed that the processing costs were lower than 240 kcal/kg. Experimental studies using prehistoric manos and metates have indicated processing losses of 2-4 percent (Wright 1993:351).

Salvia sp. (Sage/Chia)

Salvia is found in dry soils on plains, slopes, and mesa tops at elevations up to 9,000 ft, but with ranges of about 2,000 ft for any given species (Kearney and Peebles 1973:740-743). *S. reflexa* was observed flowering and bearing ripe seeds from August-November (K. Adams 1988:510). Nutlets and leaves were used as a tea by Native Americans (K. Adams 1988:510-512). No information on plant density, yields, or nutritional composition was located during this study.

Prosopis sp. cf. *juliflora* (Honey Mesquite)

This plant is very common alongside streams or other areas with high water tables at elevations up to 6,000 ft in Arizona (Kearney and Peebles 1973:401). Water stress stimulates growth of pods at the expense of wood growth, leading to higher pod yields in drier years than in wet years (Felker et al. 1981:91-92). Pericarp and seeds were consumed by Southwest Native Americans (Minnis 1991:240). They flower

March-May, with fruit ripening August-September (USDA 1974:656-657).

Maximum pod yields in California experimental farms were achieved at tree intervals of 1.2 m, yielding 3,120 kg/ha, with yields as high as 50 kg/tree, but normal yields vary from 10.3-30.8 kg/tree (Felker et al. 1981:91). It usually grows in conditions that are "too saline for agricultural crops" (Felker et al. 1981:i). Some "unmanaged Arizona desert" localities have been observed to yield 2,000 kg/ha (Felker and Bandurski 1979:179).

Most of the carbohydrates are contained in the pericarp and are produced by 10 days after flowering (63.4 percent as opposed to only 79.9 percent after 75 days) (Harden and Zolfaghari 1988:522-526), which indicates that pods could be harvested and processed while green (i.e., as an early crop) without great loss of caloric yield. With seeds, uncooked pods yield 347 kcal/100 g, 15.4 g protein, and 7.3 g indigestible fiber (Ensminger et al. 1994:296). Figures on cooked nutritional composition were not available.

Mesquite would have been a very attractive plant for Archaic horticulturists in the Tucson Basin. With rare pod yields as high as 2,000 kg/ha, the maximum observable gross returns would have approached 6.8 million kcal/ha (3,400 kcal/kg). Doelle (1976) noted that roughly 70 percent of the pod is discarded as inedible tissue and seeds, and that 248 kcal are required to process one kilogram. It is assumed that mesquite yielded 500 kg/ha in healthy bosques.

Portulaca sp. (Purslane)

All varieties prefer dry soil and full sunlight, occurring mostly at elevations 1,500-5,500 ft, flowering August-November (K. Adams 1988:416-417; Kearney and Peebles 1973:290). The seeds, young stems, and greens were used by Native Americans in the same fashion as the amaranths (K. Adams 1988:417-419). No information was available on plant density, yields, or nutritional composition.

Solanaceae (Nightshade Family)

See *Solanum/Physalis* below.

Nicotiana sp. (Tobacco)

Five species grow throughout the state in or near sandy washes at elevations lower than 7,000 ft (Kearney and Peebles 1973:760-761). Only one small seed was found at AA:12:91, and a fragment of charred cigarette paper was found in the same sample; it is regarded as a contaminant and is not included in any of the analyses in these volumes.

Solanum/Physalis sp. (Nightshade/Ground Cherry)

Two seeds belonging to the nightshade family, probably *Solanum* sp. (Nightshade), but possibly *Physalis* sp. (Ground cherry), were found. Members of these genera occur at elevations from 100-7,000 ft (Kearney and Peebles 1973:753-759). *P. virginiana* was observed to flower July-September and ripen September-October (K. Adams 1988:361). Fruits were consumed by Native Americans, and the leaves were used medicinally in a tea (K. Adams 1988:362-363). Native Americans also consumed the fruits and tubers of some species of *Solanum* as a "famine food" (Minnis 1991:241-242). No information was available on plant density, yields, or nutritional composition.

Kallstroemia sp. (Caltrop/Arizona Poppy)

The Arizona poppy grows ubiquitously in Arizona from 100-5,000 ft, flowering from March through October but mostly in July and August (Kearney and Peebles 1973:491-492; Parker 1990:196-197). No information on plant density, yields, nutritional composition, or ethnographically known uses was available.

Eschscholtzia sp. (Gold Poppy)

The plant occurs throughout Arizona in plains and mesas at elevations lower than 4,500 ft, flowering February-May (Kearney and Peebles 1973:323). No information was available on plant density, yields, nutritional composition, or ethnographically known uses.

Unidentified

Unidentified seeds are those that, because of their condition, were not identifiable, or those for which no closely matching seed was observed in the comparative collection or in reference texts.

CHARRED WOODS: FREQUENCIES AND ATTRIBUTES OF GROWTH

The taxonomic suite of charred woods observed in the flotation samples consists entirely of species that flourish in the floodplain of the Santa Cruz River in the Tucson Basin. Table D.3 presents the frequency counts of the charred wood taxa in each flotation sample. In the discussion in Chapter 9, it is assumed that all charred wood specimens occurred in the samples as a consequence of their use as fuel, or as a consequence of the burning of structures made of wood.

Table D.3. Taxa represented by charred wood remains from flotation samples.

Provenience	Feature	Atriplex sp.	Quercus sp.	Gramineae	Phragmites sp.	Leguminosae	Cercidium sp.	Prosopis sp.	Populus/Salix sp.	Gymnosperm	Angiosperm
101.01	863.00	3	0	0	0	0	0	17	0	0	0
102.01	863.00	0	0	0	0	0	0	20	0	0	0
104.03	864.00	0	0	0	0	0	0	0	0	0	20
105.04	864.01	0	0	0	0	0	0	20	0	0	0
117.01	861.00	1	0	0	0	0	0	16	3	0	0
118.04	304.00	1	0	0	0	0	0	19	0	0	0
123.01	863.00	1	0	0	0	0	0	18	1	0	0
125.05	0.00	0	0	0	0	0	0	19	0	0	1
138.02	898.00	3	0	0	0	0	0	11	5	0	3
138.02	898.00	0	0	0	0	0	0	20	0	0	0
139.01	898.01	0	0	0	0	0	0	9	11	0	0
139.02	898.01	1	0	0	0	0	0	12	27	0	0
139.03	898.01	0	0	0	0	0	0	4	0	0	5
147.11	866.00	0	0	0	0	0	0	10	9	0	0
154.01	305.00	3	0	0	0	0	0	17	0	0	0
155.01	305.01	2	0	0	0	0	0	16	0	0	2
156.01	305.01	1	0	0	0	0	0	14	1	0	4
157.01	302.01	1	0	0	0	0	0	19	0	0	0
158.01	302.01	0	0	0	0	0	0	20	0	0	0
170.01	825.01	1	0	0	0	0	0	19	0	0	0
176.03	353.00	0	0	0	0	0	0	20	0	0	0
178.01	820.00	0	0	0	0	0	0	20	0	0	0
179.01	820.01	1	0	0	0	0	0	16	3	0	0
180.01	820.01	0	0	0	0	0	0	18	2	0	0
198.01	890.00	2	0	0	0	0	0	7	0	0	11
199.01	890.00	1	0	0	0	0	0	18	1	0	0
200.01	890.01	0	0	1	0	0	0	19	0	0	0
201.01	890.01	0	0	0	0	0	0	18	2	0	0
205.01	870.00	0	0	0	0	0	0	18	2	0	0
208.01	302.00	0	0	0	0	0	0	9	11	0	0
209.07	867.01	11	0	0	0	0	0	9	0	0	0
221.01	867.00	6	0	0	0	0	3	7	0	0	4
224.01	887.00	0	0	0	0	0	0	19	1	0	0
229.01	328.00	0	0	0	0	0	0	6	0	0	14
238.01	324.00	0	0	0	0	0	0	20	0	0	0
245.01	324.01	0	0	0	0	0	0	20	0	0	0
246.01	324.14	0	0	0	0	0	0	20	0	0	0
248.01	867.00	0	0	0	0	0	0	20	0	0	0
252.01	337.00	1	0	0	0	0	6	13	0	0	0
269.07	354.01	0	0	0	0	0	0	20	0	0	0
269.08	354.01	1	0	0	0	0	0	19	1	0	0
271.04	342.00	1	0	0	0	0	0	8	11	0	0
278.01	337.14	0	0	0	0	0	0	19	0	0	1
279.01	337.14	0	0	0	0	0	0	6	14	0	0
297.01	327.01	0	0	0	0	0	0	13	7	0	0
301.01	327.00	0	0	0	0	0	0	20	0	0	0
306.01	318.00	0	0	0	0	0	0	18	0	0	2
313.02	417.00	0	0	0	0	0	0	1	18	0	1
319.01	370.00	0	0	0	0	0	0	20	0	0	0
320.01	370.01	0	0	0	0	0	0	19	1	0	0
326.02	342.01	0	0	0	0	0	0	20	0	0	0

Table D.3. Continued.

Provenience	Feature	*Atriplex* sp.	*Quercus* sp.	Gramineae	*Phragmites* sp.	Leguminosae	*Cercidium* sp.	*Prosopis* sp.	*Populus/Salix* sp.	Gymnosperm	Angiosperm
328.05	342.01	1	0	0	0	0	0	17	2	0	0
330.07	355.00	0	0	1	0	0	0	19	0	0	0
344.04	420.00	0	0	0	0	0	0	20	0	0	0
345.01	318.01	5	0	0	0	0	0	15	0	0	0
350.11	355.09	0	0	0	0	0	0	20	0	0	0
351.01	355.46	0	0	0	0	0	0	20	0	0	0
352.01	355.46	0	0	0	0	0	0	20	0	0	0
353.01	318.02	3	0	0	0	0	0	15	0	0	2
354.01	318.01	0	0	0	1	0	0	18	1	0	0
355.05	355.10	0	0	0	0	0	0	20	0	0	0
356.01	355.10	0	0	0	10	0	0	19	1	0	0
364.01	352.00	0	0	0	0	0	0	20	0	0	0
368.01	352.01	0	0	0	0	0	0	20	0	0	0
369.01	352.01	0	0	0	0	0	0	20	0	0	0
377.05	819.00	0	0	0	0	0	0	20	0	0	0
381.01	819.02	2	0	0	0	0	0	18	0	0	0
384.02	840.01	1	0	0	0	0	0	18	0	0	1
394.01	840.00	3	0	0	0	0	0	17	0	0	0
398.10	422.00	0	0	0	0	0	0	20	0	0	0
400.01	372.00	0	0	0	0	0	0	20	0	0	0
401.01	372.00	0	0	0	0	0	0	20	0	0	0
402.01	372.01	0	0	0	0	0	0	20	0	0	0
403.01	372.01	0	0	0	0	0	0	13	0	0	0
405.06	333.00	0	0	0	0	0	0	12	8	0	0
410.03	357.00	0	0	0	0	0	0	19	1	0	0
417.06	815.00	0	0	0	0	0	0	20	0	0	0
430.05	330.00	0	0	0	0	0	0	20	0	0	0
439.01	423.00	0	0	0	0	20	0	0	0	0	0
441.05	333.00	1	0	0	0	0	0	19	0	0	0
442.04	333.01	0	0	0	0	0	0	12	8	0	0
456.01	861.01	0	0	0	0	0	0	12	8	0	0
458.01	861.01	1	0	0	0	0	0	15	4	0	0
459.01	346.00	0	0	0	0	0	0	20	0	0	0
463.01	389.00	0	0	0	0	0	0	20	0	0	0
464.01	389.00	0	0	0	0	0	0	15	5	0	0
471.01	348.00	0	0	0	0	0	0	20	0	0	0
473.01	403.00	0	0	0	0	0	0	20	0	0	0
474.05	400.00	0	0	0	0	0	0	20	0	0	0
480.01	407.00	0	0	0	0	0	0	0	20	0	0
481.01	407.00	0	0	0	0	0	0	8	12	0	0
485.01	431.00	4	0	0	0	0	0	16	0	0	0
486.01	373.00	5	0	0	0	0	0	15	0	0	0
490.01	416.01	0	0	0	0	0	0	1	39	0	0
491.02	416.00	0	0	1	0	0	0	6	13	0	0
495.03	429.00	1	0	0	0	0	0	19	0	0	0
496.09	428.00	0	1	0	0	0	0	17	2	0	0
497.01	365.00	0	0	0	0	0	0	9	0	0	0
498.01	365.00	0	0	0	0	0	0	2	0	0	0
501.01	359.00	0	0	0	0	0	0	20	0	0	0
506.01	373.00	3	0	0	0	0	0	17	0	0	0
511.06	411.00	0	0	0	0	0	0	15	0	0	1

Table D.3. Continued.

Provenience	Feature	*Atriplex* sp.	*Quercus* sp.	Gramineae	*Phragmites* sp.	Leguminosae	*Cercidium* sp.	*Prosopis* sp.	*Populus/Salix* sp.	Gymnosperm	Angiosperm
513.01	817.00	0	0	0	0	2	0	0	0	0	0
515.01	329.00	1	0	0	0	0	0	19	0	0	0
518.01	406.00	1	0	0	0	0	0	19	0	0	0
519.05	399.00	1	0	0	0	0	0	19	0	0	0
520.01	817.01	0	0	0	0	0	0	18	1	0	1
520.03	817.01	0	0	0	0	0	2	12	26	0	0
526.01	339.00	0	0	0	0	0	0	20	0	0	0
527.01	339.01	0	0	0	0	0	0	20	0	0	0
529.08	379.00	0	0	0	0	0	0	9	0	0	0
536.01	886.00	0	0	0	0	0	0	20	0	0	0
537.01	886.00	0	0	0	0	0	0	20	0	0	0
538.01	818.00	0	0	0	0	0	0	20	0	0	0
539.09	819.00	0	0	0	0	0	0	18	2	0	0
548.01	425.00	0	0	0	0	0	0	20	0	0	0
549.01	425.01	0	0	0	0	0	1	16	3	0	0
561.11	836.00	0	0	0	0	0	0	19	0	0	1
561.12	836.00	1	0	0	0	0	0	15	4	0	0
563.13	836.01	0	0	0	0	0	0	16	3	0	1
577.01	880.01	1	0	0	0	0	0	10	5	0	4
579.01	879.01	0	0	0	0	0	0	18	2	0	0
580.01	879.00	0	0	0	0	0	0	7	13	0	0
597.01	390.00	0	0	0	0	0	0	20	0	0	0
602.01	812.23	0	0	0	0	0	1	19	0	0	0
603.01	812.23	2	0	0	0	0	0	18	0	0	0
604.01	812.23	1	0	0	0	0	0	19	1	0	0
605.01	427.00	0	0	0	0	0	0	20	0	0	0
606.01	812.00	1	0	0	0	0	0	19	0	0	0
614.01	433.00	0	0	0	0	0	0	20	0	0	0
615.01	390.16	4	0	0	0	0	0	12	4	0	0
620.01	408.00	0	0	0	0	0	0	12	0	0	0
1013.02	916.00	0	0	0	0	0	0	0	0	0	5
1025.01	917.00	0	0	0	0	0	0	1	0	0	0
1037.01	0.00	0	0	0	0	0	0	5	0	0	0
1047.03	918.00	0	0	0	0	0	0	20	0	0	0
1057.01	0.00	0	0	0	0	0	0	3	0	1	0
1082.03	0.00	0	0	0	0	0	0	2	0	0	0
1083.02	0.00	0	0	0	0	0	0	1	0	0	0
1093.02	918.00	0	0	0	0	0	0	3	0	0	0
1116.02	0.00	0	0	0	0	0	0	1	0	0	0
1118.01	0.00	0	0	0	0	0	0	20	0	0	0
1119.02	0.00	0	0	0	0	0	0	1	0	0	0
1121.02	0.00	0	0	0	0	0	0	1	0	0	0
1140.01	0.00	0	0	0	0	0	0	1	0	0	0
1165.00	923.00	0	0	0	0	0	0	20	0	0	0
1182.02	924.00	0	0	0	0	0	0	1	0	0	0

AN ENERGY DISPERSIVE X-RAY FLUORESCENCE (EDXRF) ANALYSIS OF OBSIDIAN ARTIFACTS FROM AZ AA:12:91 (ASM), TUCSON, ARIZONA

M. Stephen Shackley

The following report documents the EDXRF analysis of six obsidian artifacts recovered from Early Agricultural contexts at Los Pozos (AZ AA:12:91 [ASM]) along the Santa Cruz River north of Tucson, Arizona. All artifacts were produced from obsidian procured from sources in Arizona with one sample that could not be assigned to a known source in the greater Southwest (Shackley 1995).

ANALYSIS AND INSTRUMENTATION

All samples were analyzed whole and were washed in distilled water before analysis. The results presented here are quantitative in that they are derived from "filtered" intensity values ratioed to the appropriate x-ray continuum regions through a least-squares fitting formula rather than plotting the proportions of the net intensities in a ternary system (McCarthy and Schamber 1981; Schamber 1977). More essentially, these data, through the analysis of international rock standards, allow for inter-instrument comparison with a predictable degree of certainty (Hampel 1984).

The trace element analyses were performed in the Department of Geology and Geophysics, University of California, Berkeley, using a Spectrace® 400 (United Scientific Corporation) energy dispersive x-ray fluorescence spectrometer. The spectrometer is equipped with an Rh x-ray tube, a 50 kV x-ray generator, with a Tracor x-ray (Spectrace®) TM 6100 x-ray analyzer using an IBM PC-based microprocessor and Tracor reduction software. The x-ray tube was operated at 30 kV, .20 mA, using a .127 mm Rh primary beam filter in a vacuum path at 250 seconds livetime to generate x-ray intensity Kα-line data for elements titanium (Ti), manganese (Mn), iron (as Fe^T), rubidium (Rb), strontium (Sr), yttrium (Y), zirconium (Zr), and niobium (Nb). Weight percent iron ($Fe_2O_3{}^T$) can be derived by multiplying ppm estimates by 1.4297^{10-4}. Trace element intensities were converted to concentration estimates by employing a least-squares calibration line established for each element from the analysis of international rock standards certified by the National Institute of Standards and Technology (NIST), the United States Geological Survey (USGS), the Canadian Centre for Mineral and Energy Technology, and the Centre de Recherches Pétrographiques et Géochimiques in France (Govindaraju 1989). Further details concerning the petrological choice of these elements in Southwest obsidians is available in Shackley (1988, 1990, 1992, 1995; also Hughes and Smith 1993 and Mahood and Stimac 1991). Specific standards for the best fit regression calibration for elements Ti through Nb include G-2 (basalt), AGV-1 (andesite), GSP-1 and SY-2 (syenite), BHVO-1 (hawaiite), STM-1 (syenite), QLM-1 (quartz latite), RGM-1 (obsidian), W-2 (diabase), BIR-1 (basalt),

SDC-1 (mica schist), TLM-1 (tonalite), SCO-1 (shale), all USGS standards, and BR-N (basalt) from the Centre de Recherches Pétrographiques et Géochimiques in France (Govindaraju 1989). In addition to the reported values here, Pb, Ni, Cu, Zn, Ga, and Th were measured, but these are rarely useful in discriminating glass sources and are not generally reported. These data are available on disk by request.

The data from the Tracor software were reported directly into Quattro Pro for Windows software for manipulation and into SPSS for Windows for statistical analyses. In order to evaluate these quantitative determinations, machine data were compared to measurements of known standards during each run. Table E.1 shows a comparison between values recommended for three international obsidian and rhyolite rock standards, RGM-1, NBS (SRM)-278, and JR-2. One of these standards is analyzed during each sample run to check machine calibration. The results shown in Table E.1 indicate that the machine accuracy is quite high, particularly for the mid-Z elements, and other instruments with comparable precision should yield comparable results. Further information on the laboratory instrumentation can be found on the World Wide Web at: http://obsidian.pahma.berkeley.edu/xrflab.htm.

Trace element data exhibited in Tables E.1 and E.2 are reported in parts per million (ppm), a quantitative measure by weight. Table E.2 and Figure E.1 exhibit the data for the archaeological samples.

DISCUSSION

The small sample indicates quite a diversity of procurement strategies regardless of whether or not the raw material was procured through direct procurement or exchange (Shackley 1996b). The sources are located in the Lower Sonoran (Sauceda Mountains and Superior) and Piñon-Juniper uplands (Cow Canyon) in three directions from the site (west, north, and northeast). Cow Canyon glass, however, is also available through secondary deposition as close as the San Simon Valley, so the distance is not necessarily that great (Shackley 1995). So little archaeological obsidian has been analyzed from this time period anywhere in the Southwest that definitive conclusions are impossible. It does suggest either an extensive procurement range and/or interaction with other Early Agricultural groups in a relatively large region.

One specimen that could not be assigned to source exhibits a chemistry not yet seen in any temporal context in Arizona. It is not from any known source or one detected in archaeological collections from Arizona, New Mexico, Chihuahua, or Sonora.

Table E.1. X-ray fluorescence concentrations for selected trace elements of three international rock standards.

Sample	Ti	Mn	Fe	Rb	Sr	Y	Zr	Nb	Ba
RGM-1 (Govindaraju 1989)	1,600	279	12,998	149	108	25	219	8.9	807
RGM-1 (Glascock and Anderson 1993)	1,079 ± 120	323 ± 7	863 ± 210	145 ± 3	120 ± 10	n.r.[a]	150 ± 7	n.r.	826 ± 31
RGM-1 (this study)	1,516 ± 58	259 ± 19	13,991 ± 143	152 ± 3	108 ± 2	24 ± 1	226 ± 4	10 ± 1	806 ± 12
SRM-278 (Govindaraju 1989)	1,469	402	14,256	127.5	63.5	41	295	n.r.	1,140[b]
SRM-278 (Glascock and Anderson 1993)	875 ± 162	428 ± 8	9,932 ± 210	128 ± 4	61 ± 15	n.r.	208 ± 20	n.r.	891 ± 39
SRM-278 (this study)	1,376 ± 96	372 ± 17	15,229 ± 399	129 ± 2	68 ± 2	42 ± 2	290 ± 3	17 ± 2	1,090 ± 38
JR-2 (Govindaraju 1989)[b]	540	852	6,015	297	8	51	98.5	19.2	39
JR-2 (this study)	343 ± 51	680 ± 17	7,358 ± 65	300 ± 5	10 ± 1	49 ± 3	94 ± 2	16 ± 2	34 ± 6

Note: ± values represent first standard deviation computations for the group of measurements. All values are in parts per million (ppm) as reported in Govindaraju (1989) and this study. RGM-1 is a USGS rhyolite standard, NBS (SRM)-278 is a National Institute of Standards and Technology obsidian standard, and JR-2 is a Geological Survey of Japan rhyolite standard. Fe^T can be converted to $Fe_2O_3^T$ with a multiplier of $1.4297^{(10-4)}$ (see also Glascock 1991).
[a]n.r. = No report.
[b]Values proposed not recommended.

Table E.2. X-ray fluorescence concentrations for the archaeological data. (All measurements in parts per million [ppm]).

Sample	Ti	Mn	Fe	Rb	Sr	Y	Zr	Nb	Source
283-2	935.16	570.72	8,795.62	136.49	106.38	23.15	131.97	21.84	Cow Canyon
600-3	619.96	388.03	9,100.11	153.47	5.27	45.31	149.49	53.69	Unknown
539-4	740.20	507.65	7,040.08	110.81	14.15	23.65	91.13	27.64	Superior
525-17	993.10	262.89	11,547.59	139.46	136.36	25.44	157.59	13.76	Cow Canyon
525-25	1,337.98	276.48	10,598.09	168.02	95.56	22.71	170.43	15.58	Sauceda Mts.
121-1	1,419.07	398.94	10,618.81	155.91	68.75	31.67	182.34	17.97	Sauceda Mts.

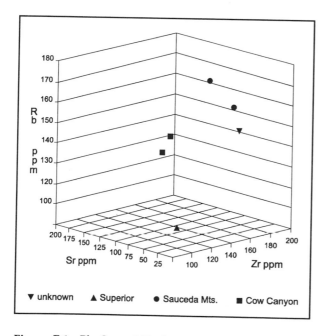

Figure E.1. Rb, Sr, and Zr three-dimensional plot of the archaeological samples.

A RECONSIDERATION OF CHRONOLOGY, ARCHITECTURAL VARIATION, AND SITE STRUCTURE AT SANTA CRUZ BEND AND STONE PIPE

David A. Gregory

As discussed in Chapter 11, radiocarbon dates from Santa Cruz Bend and Stone Pipe indicate that both sites were occupied during the 950-year interval formerly referred to as the Cienega phase and now subdivided into Early and Late Cienega phases. As a consequence, all features and deposits from these two sites not directly dated must be treated as potentially dating to either of these two intervals. Since the materials from these sites represent two of the largest Early Agricultural period data sets now available, the ability to sort them into two or more components would represent a significant advance in establishing a basis for temporal comparisons of various data classes. Evaluation and reanalysis of architectural data indicate that such sorting is indeed possible. The basis for segregation of features at the two sites into Early and Late Cienega phase groups is presented here and employed in the analyses presented in Chapter 12.

Data relevant to the current discussion are found in various chapters and associated figures and tables presented in two separate volumes (Mabry 1998; Mabry et al. 1997). The first contains primarily descriptive data, while the second presents syntheses and interpretations of those data. Mabry (1998a) describes the basis for classification of architectural features at Santa Cruz Bend as follows:

> The 63 completely or partially excavated Cienega phase pit structures at the Santa Cruz Bend site (Mabry and Archer 1997) can be divided into at least five classes based on a combination of size, effective floor area (the interior area minus the total area of intramural pits), number of pits, total intramural pit volume, varieties and characteristics of other intramural features such as postholes, and techniques of construction (Figure 6.1). *This variability is interpreted to be largely related to functional differences. Independent of architectural variability, artifact contents and locations relative to other pit structures also help identify their different functions* (Mabry 1998a:210; emphasis added).

The five classes referred to include one, two, five, five, and 50 structures (Classes I-V, respectively). Location relative to other pit structures refers to perceived rings of structures discussed in a subsequent section of the chapter (Mabry 1998a:231-233, Figure 6.16).

The 25 Cienega phase structures from Stone Pipe are grouped into three classes on the basis of "covariation" in the attributes of interior area, effective floor area, and total volume of intramural pits. The three classes include two, eight, and 15 structures (Classes I-III, respectively). Mabry notes that these three classes are defined for Stone Pipe only and do not necessarily correspond with those defined for Santa Cruz Bend (Mabry 1998a:212-214).

Several aspects of this approach to architectural variation at the two sites limit its utility. First, inclusion of location relative to perceived house rings at Santa Cruz Bend as a variable results in a classification skewed toward structures within such groups while excluding most of the structures not included in such rings. Only one complete ring of structures and two or three partial examples were identified on the basis of excavated structures, and membership of individual structures is not mutually exclusive between them (Mabry 1998a:232). As Mabry notes:

> It must also be acknowledged that most of the pit structures at the site are not located within any of these proposed house groups, implying that house groups were not the normative pattern of occupation at the settlement (1998a:232).

Given the narrow exposure achieved at Stone Pipe (see Swartz and Lindeman 1997) and the inability to recognize similar house rings there, use of this variable also precludes a typology that incorporates architectural variation at both sites. There are, in fact, clear similarities between structures at the two sites.

Definitions of three of the five classes of structures at Santa Cruz Bend refer to location relative to house rings as an aspect of inferences concerning their former function: Class I, one structure, communal structure (the so-called Big House; Mabry 1998a:210); Class II, two structures, integrative structures for extended family households, sleeping structures, or representing earlier or later occupations than the house groups; and Class III, five structures, specialized storage structures for the co-residents of house groups (Mabry 1998a:211-212).

In the case of the Class III Feature 32, only a 75-cm by 1.5-m test unit was excavated into it. It is placed in this class solely because a single large storage pit was (incompletely) revealed by the limited excavations, and–most importantly–the fact that it falls at the center of a possible ring of structures. Since the definition of this class of structures indicates they had "*more floor pits and higher total pit volumes than any other architectural class*" (Mabry 1998a:212, emphasis added), the great weight placed on position in perceived house rings is clearly revealed.

The inferred function of Class IV (five structures, storage facilities for residential groups) does not refer to location within perceived house rings. For the largest class of structures (Class V, 50 structures), only general characteristics of the structures are listed, and no inferences are presented concerning the function or functions of the class as a whole (Mabry 1998a:230). In the later discussion of site structure, however, *only* those members of Class V included in perceived house rings are classified as to function (habitation structures; Mabry 1998a:Figure 6.16). Thus, the location of structures relative to perceived house groups is applied selectively in creating the several classes of structures. For the largest class of structures, the only ones classified as to former function are those in perceived house rings.

Second, it is unclear how "techniques of construction" played a role in defining the several classes of structures. Since all structures were built within pits, and since size is largely independent of construction technique, the only evidence relevant to construction techniques is represented by the alignments of wall postholes (or lack thereof), floor grooves (or lack thereof), and any posthole patterns interpreted as having housed roof support posts. Arrangements of wall postholes are referred to in discussions of the single Class I structure (the Big House) and of the two Class II structures. In the latter case, the "closely spaced posts around the inside perimeter of the house pits" are a significant feature of construction in defining this two-member class (Mabry 1998a:212). However, one of the Class III structures (Feature 12), three of the Class IV structures (Features 85, 90, and 127), and at least one Class V structure (Feature 26) have similar arrangements of postholes. Three of the remaining four members of Class III and the other three structures in Class IV have neither posthole alignments nor grooves. As noted above, the fourth Class III structure (Feature 32) was only tested and no direct evidence for the nature of construction technique was recovered. The set of features included in the largest category, Class V, includes not only structures with alignments of postholes, but structures with floor grooves and structures which lack both posthole alignments and floor grooves. A "central roof support" (Mabry 1998a:212) is indicated for the Big House, and a possible wall-roof relationship is suggested for the two Class II structures, but no reference is made to the character of the roofs for the other three classes. Thus, it may be argued that evidence for techniques of construction was neither explicitly defined nor consistently applied in deriving the five classes of structures.

Finally, and most important for present concerns, time is not considered a potential source of architectural variation. Mabry notes that not all structures in the perceived house rings could have been contemporaneous and acknowledges the fact that overlapping membership in two or more of the rings indicates that not all of the perceived rings could have been contemporaneous (Mabry 1998a: 232). However, no real consideration is given to the possibility that architectural attributes might have varied in some systematic way over the span of the occupation. This possibility is explored below. First, an alternative typology of

architecture at both Santa Cruz Bend and Stone Pipe is offered. Second, evidence for a temporal relationship between the two structure types is presented. Finally, an alternative interpretation of site structure at Santa Cruz Bend is presented on the basis of this reconsideration of architectural variation.

AN ALTERNATIVE VIEW OF ARCHITECTURAL VARIATION AND SITE STRUCTURE AT SANTA CRUZ BEND AND STONE PIPE

Architectural Variation

The architectural typology offered here relies on morphological characteristics of individual structures and places emphasis on evidence for variable techniques of construction. Variation in construction techniques is represented by the simple presence or absence of encircling floor grooves or variably complete lines of wall postholes. Mabry argues that former alignments of interior wall postholes in structures where they were not observed may have been obscured by rodent activity "in some or all of them" (Mabry 1997:212). This inference is not supported by the available data. As will be shown below, structures with and without such features were involved in several cases of stratigraphic superposition. Selective and consistent destruction of postholes by rodents in one structure and not the other is not a plausible explanation in these cases. In addition, there are many more structures lacking grooves or alignments of postholes than there are structures having these features at both Santa Cruz Bend and Stone Pipe, and structures exhibiting the two construction modes were often found near one another (e.g., Features 4 and 5, 77 and 78, 85 and 95 at Santa Cruz Bend; Features 99 and 100 at Stone Pipe). Once again, selective obfuscation of postholes by rodents is not plausible.

Perhaps the most likely explanation for these basic differences is that–in the case of structures lacking postholes–either 1) the wall poles were simply jammed against the pit wall, bent over, and tied together at the top, held in place by tension and by horizontal stringers that connected them; or 2) the wall poles were simply leaned in toward the center and tied together tepee fashion (see Chapter 2; Mabry 1998a:212).

Evidence for the first of these two possible arrangements has been found at a site along the Gila River near Kearny. Radiocarbon dates on maize obtained from this site place it within the Late Cienega phase as defined for the Tucson Basin (Caven Clark, personal communication 1999) and thus, relatively contemporaneous with at least some of the features at Santa Cruz Bend and Stone Pipe. At this site, the walls of one structure were plastered with caliche-rich adobe after the poles were in place, leaving the impressions of the poles. The impressions were straight up-and-down against the pit walls, and no postholes were present beneath these vertical impressions, indicating that holes were not dug to anchor the posts. In the absence of the impressions, this would simply be a structure lacking a groove or an alignment of postholes.

Most of the structures at both Santa Cruz Bend and Stone Pipe can be readily separated into two groups on the basis of attributes argued to represent differing construction techniques and referred to here as Type 1 and Type 2. Type 1 structures have floor grooves, variably complete alignments of wall postholes, or both, indicating that the structural members for the walls were anchored via emplacement in excavated features. Type 2 structures lack floor grooves and continuous wall posthole alignments, indicating that wall poles were not so anchored.

Both types are subdivided into three groups depending upon the presence, absence, number, and morphology of intramural pits. Type 1a and Type 2a structures lack interior pits or have only small, shallow pits; Type 1b and Type 2b structures have a single, relatively large intramural pit; and Type 1c and Type 2c structures have two or more relatively large intramural pits. These subtypes are somewhat arbitrary and, as shown in Chapter 2, any given pit may not have been a feature of interior space over the entire use-life of the structure. They do, however, provide a general way to sort the two types in terms of the use of interior space, at least at some point during the use-life of each structure.

Sorting of structures into one of these two categories and their subtypes was accomplished only in cases of completely excavated structures or those that were sufficiently exposed to reveal the definitive presence or absence of the distinguishing attributes. Figure F.1 illustrates Type 1 structures; Figure F.2 illustrates Type 2 structures. Table F.1 lists the feature numbers of structures assigned to the respective types and subtypes; structures that could not be assigned to one of the subtypes and ambiguous features are also noted in this table. The Big House at Santa Cruz Bend (Feature 310) would fall into Type 2 as defined here. However, because of its obviously special character, this structure is not included in this type (see discussion below).

Several additional observations concerning differences between the two types may be offered. With few exceptions, Type 1 structures are generally round in shape and fairly regular in outline (see Figure F.1). In contrast, Type 2 structures appear to be less consistent and less regular in shape, and a number of them are clearly more oval or elongate (compare Figures F.1 and F.2). Several examples of Type 2 structures from Santa Cruz Bend have some combination of paired postholes and/or single postholes distributed around the interior margin of the pit or near it (see Figure F.2; Feature 107,

one isolate, two pairs; Feature 122, 5 isolates; Feature 139, one isolate, two pairs; Feature 201, one isolate, three pairs; Feature 5, two isolates, one pair). These tentative patterns may suggest a construction mode somewhat different from that represented in other Type 2 structures.

If we assume the amount and character of interior space relates to the manner in which individual structures were used, then characteristics of the respective subtypes may be used as a basis for general inferences about function. Either lacking intramural features or having only a few small ones, Types 1a and 2a may be inferred to have served as general habitation space. Types 1b and 2b both have a single, relatively large pit, but also have relatively large areas of usable floor space. In several Type 1b and 2b structures, the large pit is situated nearer one wall (Features 41, 111, 122, and 139 at Santa Cruz Bend and Feature 364 at Stone Pipe). If we assume that the pits were used primarily for storage, then these structures may have served a combined habitation-storage function. With their multiple pits, Types 1c and 2c have proportionally less available floor space. Following the logic applied by Mabry for his Class III structures (Mabry 1998a:212), a storage function might be inferred for these structures. However, a closer look at these two subtypes suggests an alternative interpretation (refer to Figures F.1 and F.2).

In the case of those structures having three or more pits, three of the pits occur in either a triangular arrangement (Features 5, 12, 13, 70, 100, and 102 at Santa Cruz Bend, and Features 97 and 134 at Stone Pipe) or in a linear arrangement across the approximate middle of the structure (Features 40 and 363 at Santa Cruz Bend). Although not completely excavated, Feature 1040 at the Clearwater site may represent a similar use of interior space involving a triangular arrangement (Diehl 1997a). In the case of structures having only two pits, they are always closely adjacent to one another and one of them is always near the wall of the structure (Features 1, 43, 6, 95, 112, and 127 at Santa Cruz Bend and Features 164 and 251 at Stone Pipe). In the cases of Feature 102 at Santa Cruz Bend and Feature 134 at Stone Pipe, it is plausible to reconstruct a sequence that involves two triangular arrangements or both a triangular and a linear one.

In all of these arrangements, variable amounts of usable floor space were present adjacent to the pits. In addition, the size and morphology of some pits in these structures do not necessarily support an inferred storage function. While storage pits are probably represented in all of them, other pits in the arrangements were relatively small and shallow, and several have a basin-shaped configuration. Thus, Types 1c and 2c may have not been used exclusively for storage; food processing and/or other activities were possibly carried out in these features as well.

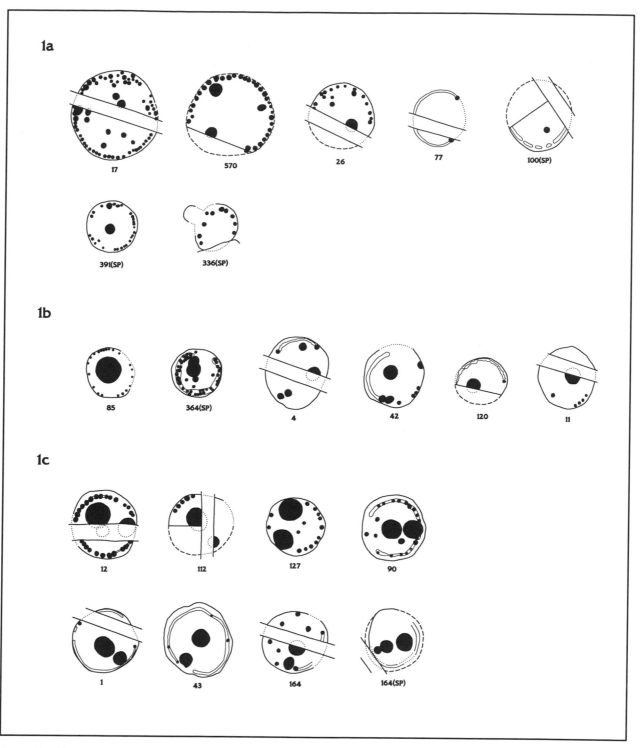

Figure F.1. Type 1 structures.

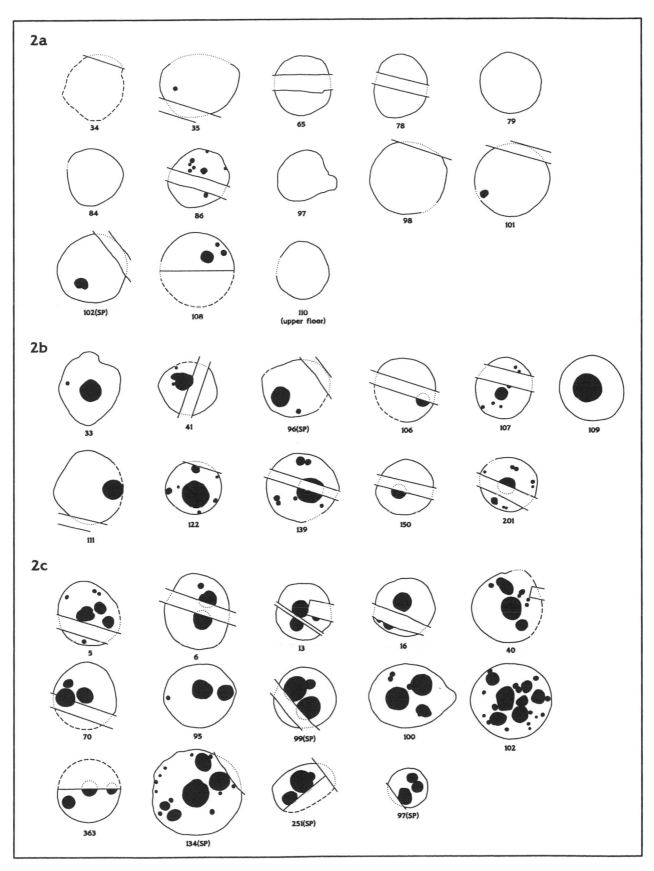

Figure F.2. Type 2 structures.

Table F.1. Alternative classification of structures at Santa Cruz Bend and Stone Pipe.

Type	Santa Cruz Bend Features	Stone Pipe Features
1a	1, 4, 42, 43, 120, 164	100, 164
1b	11, 12, 17, 26, 85, 112, 127, 570	336, 391
1c	90	364
1[a]		189
2a	(34), 35, 65, 77, 78, 79, 84, 86, 97, 98, 101, 110	16 (upper floor), (84), 102
2b	3, 33, 41, 106, 107, 109, 111, 122, 139, 150, 201	(93), 96
2c	5, 6, 13, 16, 40, 70, 95, 100, 102, 363	16 (lower floor), 97, 99, (134), 251
2[a]	108, 121, 124, 138, 186, 247, 339, 387	24, 45, 84, 93, 101, 103, 141, 143, 212, 214, 245

Note: Numbers in parentheses indicate ambiguous cases.
[a]Partially excavated structures not classified as to subtype.

While a sequential rather than contemporaneous use of pits is possible in all cases, the patterns reviewed above perhaps support the argument for contemporaneity and a use of interior space that contrasts markedly with that represented in the other structure subtypes.

Temporal Relationships

A number of reasons can be offered as to the source or sources of observed architectural variation described above. They might have resulted from the relative availability of building materials at the time of construction, the anticipated length of occupation of individual structures, or from attempts to subvert the deleterious effects of termites on the soft, buried wood. It is even possible that different cultural groups having different architectural traditions were responsible for the two groups of features. The outward appearance of the structures may have been virtually identical and the reason for employing one technique over another may have been simply a matter of ad hoc individual choice or style. All of these are plausible explanations, although none can be proven. It is clear, however, that different choices were made, and one of the more obvious possibilities is that the different construction techniques represent temporal variation. Two data sets are directly relevant to a consideration of potential temporal variation in construction techniques. The temporal relationships between the two structure types may be examined 1) in instances of demonstrated stratigraphic relationships involving the two structure types, and 2) with reference to radiocarbon dates associated with examples of the two types.

At Santa Cruz Bend, there were five cases of stratigraphic superposition involving the two types of structures. In each case, the *features having floor grooves or alignments of wall postholes were overlain by structures lacking these features*: Feature 65 overlay Feature 12 (Mabry and Archer 1997:51, Figures 2.15, 2.17); Feature 84 overlay Feature 85 (Mabry and Archer 1997:95,

Figure 2.40); Feature 41 overlay Feature 42 (Mabry and Archer 1997:77, Figures 2.30-2.31); Feature 108 overlay Feature 112 (Mabry and Archer 1997:128, Figures 2.59-2.60); and Feature 121 overlay Feature 120 (Mabry and Archer 1997:141, Figures 2.67-2.68). There was one example of superposition involving the two structure types at Stone Pipe, where the structure without wall postholes or a groove (Feature 141) once again overlay a structure having an interior alignment of wall postholes (Feature 189; Swartz and Lindeman 1997:350, Figure 4.37). In sum, in all cases of superposition of structures, Type 1 features are earlier and Type 2 features are later. In numerous cases, both Type 1 and Type 2 structures are intruded by extramural pits.

The sorting of structures into these two categories also comports quite well with associated radiocarbon dates from both sites. Table F.2 lists the structures and the radiocarbon dates obtained from them. As may be seen, there is only one date that violates the proposed ordering, a determination of 2180 ± 60 (B-81060) obtained from a sample from a pit within a Type 1 structure, Feature 90. However, this feature exhibited a relatively complex stratigraphy, and postabandonment disturbance of a floor assemblage was suggested (Mabry and Archer 1997:98-104). The structure fill also contained 22 Hohokam sherds, and the possibility of mixing with later deposits must be considered in assessing the radiocarbon date. Thus, Type 1 structures are assigned to the Early Cienega phase and Type 2 structures to the Late Cienega phase (see Chapter 11).

It should be noted that this temporal ordering does not preclude a sequence within the two groups, nor does it eliminate the possibility of earlier and later features at the site. Given the skewing of excavation toward the northeastern portion of the overall distribution exposed, the latter remains a distinct possibility. It is also acknowledged that this ordering may not be correct in each and every case. However, data reviewed above support this ordering, and it provides a reasonable basis for sorting most of the structures at both sites. This sorting is made use of in the temporal

Table F.2. Radiocarbon dates associated with Type 1 and Type 2 structures at Santa Cruz Bend and Stone Pipe (data from Mabry 1997:Table 1.2).

Feature	Site	Date	Sample Number
Type 1			
Feature 11.01	Santa Cruz Bend	2390 ± 60	B-67489
Feature 85.01	Santa Cruz Bend	2440 ± 50	B-81062
Feature 364 (fill)	Stone Pipe	2360 ± 50	B-81069
Feature 100 (fill)	Stone Pipe	2390 ± 50	B-81066
Feature 90.01	Santa Cruz Bend	2180 ± 60	B-81060
Type 2			
Feature 111.01	Santa Cruz Bend	2290 ± 60	B-81058
Feature 100.03	Santa Cruz Bend	2290 ± 60	B-81059
Feature 84 (fill)	Stone Pipe	2150 ± 60	B-81067
Feature 134.02	Stone Pipe	2250 ± 50[a]	B-81072[a]
Feature 110.01	Santa Cruz Bend	2010 ± 60	B-81061
Feature 99 (fill)	Stone Pipe	1720 ± 60	B-81065

[a]Date on wood charcoal; all others AMS dates on annual plants.

comparisons presented in Chapter 12; for purposes of those comparisons, it has been assumed that intramural features belong to the same interval as the structures in which they occurred.

In addition, it must be stated that this sorting cannot be generalized to the phases represented. As discussed in Chapter 2, almost all of the structures at Los Pozos had relatively complete alignments of wall postholes, and most of these structures were clearly constructed during the Late Cienega phase. Thus, architectural variation during the Early Agricultural period does not appear to represent a single, linear developmental sequence. Considerable variation in architecture has also been documented for the following Early Ceramic period (Gregory and Huckell 1998; Mabry 1998:212-216). These facts highlight two potentially related hypotheses that deserve attention in future research. The possibility that different cultural groups having differing architectural traditions were living along the Santa Cruz at the same time has already been mentioned. Another likely possibility is that multiple occupations representing variable group sizes, different levels of intensity, and/or variable lengths of time were responsible for the palimpsests of features at sites like Santa Cruz Bend, Stone Pipe, and Los Pozos.

Alternative Interpretations of Site Structure

Mabry's discussion of site structure at Santa Cruz Bend focuses on perceived rings of houses, an inner habitation zone, an outer zone of cooking and processing pits, and the role of the Big House and a possible associated plaza area (Mabry 1998a:231-233; Figure 6.16). Because of the narrow, linear portion of Stone

Pipe that was explored, little is said about site structure for that site. Sorting of structures by the typology presented above allows alternative interpretations of site structure that include both Santa Cruz Bend and Stone Pipe. Emphasis is placed on the intensively investigated portions of Santa Cruz Bend. The sets of structures identified and discussed below are referred to as house groups, identified on the basis of recurring combinations of different structure types and spatial relationships among individual features.

Plotting of Early Cienega phase structures (Type 1 structures) produces a relatively open pattern in the intensively investigated portion of the site (Figure F.3). Four possible house groups have been identified within this distribution. Each group consists of a pair of structures including one Type 1b and one Type 1c structure, and in each case there is also a third structure located closer to the pair than to any other structure assigned to this interval. In two cases, the third structure is a Type 2c feature (Groups 2 and 4), one is a Type 2a structure (Group 3), and one is a Type 2b structure (Group 1). These four groups of three structures each account for most of the Early Cienega phase features in that portion of the site where all structures were investigated. Two other structures, one Type 1a (Feature 26) and one Type 2c (Feature 164), are isolates, but may have been associated in the same manner with some combination of nearby unexcavated structures. The two large Type 1a structures (Mabry's Class II structures; Mabry 1998a:210-212) are also positioned well away from any other structures, and Feature 17 is located approximately equidistant from the four identified house groups and the isolated Feature 164. Mabry's inference that these two large structures represent specialized features (Mabry 1998a:212) is supported by these distributions.

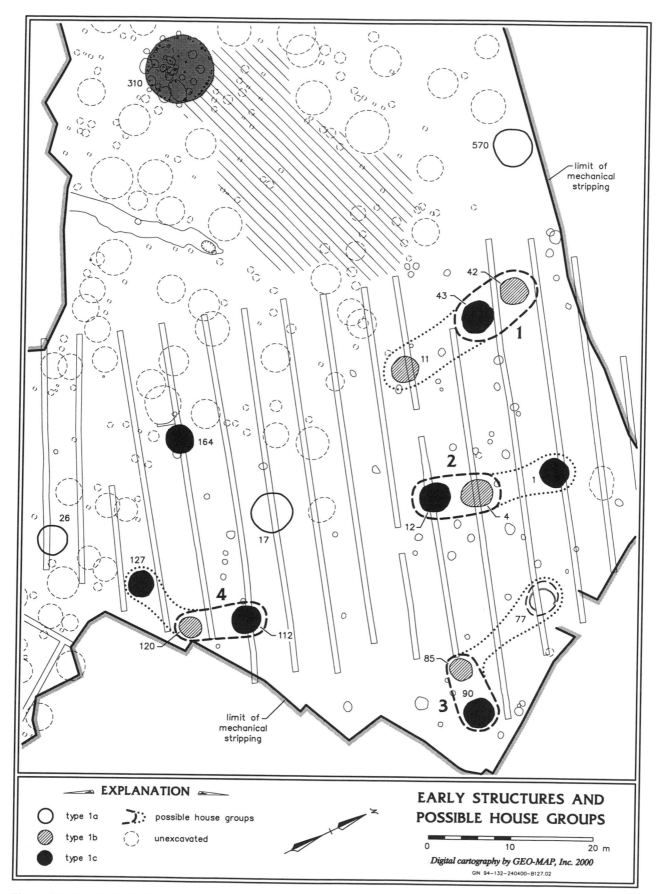

EXPLANATION

○ type 1a   ⟨⁚⟩ possible house groups

◍ type 1b   ◌ unexcavated

● type 1c

EARLY STRUCTURES AND
POSSIBLE HOUSE GROUPS

0   10   20 m

Digital cartography by GEO-MAP, Inc. 2000

GIN 94–132–240400–B127.02

Figure F.3. Possible Early Cienega phase house groups at Santa Cruz Bend.

Table F.3. Characteristics of possible Early Cienega phase house groups at Santa Cruz Bend.

House Group	Feature	Type	Effective Floor Area[a]	Population Estimate in Persons[b]	Total Pit Volume	Pit Volume-to-Floor Area Ratio	Distance to Nearest Structure in Cluster (m)
1	42	1b	4.9	2.1	.25	.051	5.3
	43	1c	6.8	3.0	.41	.060	5.3
	Subtotals		11.7	5.1	.66	.056	
	11(?)	1b	6.2	2.7	.31	.050	11.1
Totals			17.9	7.8	.97	.054	
2	4	1b	7.9	3.4	.51	.065	5.3
	12	1c	4.4	1.9	2.14	.486	5.3
	Subtotals		12.3	5.3	2.65	.215	
	1	1b	6.9	3.0	.25	.036	9.8
Totals			19.2	8.3	2.90	.151	
3	85	1b	3.2	1.4	.61	.191	5.7
	90	1c	5.2	5.7	.90	.173	5.7
	Subtotals		8.4	3.7	1.51	.180	
	77	1a	5.7	2.5	-	-	12.8
Totals			14.1	6.2	1.51	.107	
4	112[c]	1c	6.6	2.9	.20	.053	6.8
	120	1b	3.8	1.6	.10	.026	6.8
	Subtotals		10.4	4.5	.30	.029	
	127	1c	3.5	1.5	.77	.220	8.1
Totals			13.9	6.0	1.07	.077	

[a]Effective floor area is equal to the floor area minus the total area taken up by intramural pits.
[b]Following Cook's (1972) formula, population estimates for individual structures were derived by dividing the effective floor area by 2.3.
[c]Denotes partially excavated structure; question marks after type designations denote ambiguous subtype assignment.

Table F.3 lists several characteristics of each Early Cienega phase house group. This table shows that the distance between the structures making up the pairs, as well as that between the pairs and the associated third structure, are quite consistent in each case. The derived population estimates suggest that these house groups may represent the spatial domains of nuclear families.

The distribution of Late Cienega phase structures involves many more structures and is more complex (Figure F.4). Five complete house groups are identified in this distribution (Figure F.4), and Table F.4 presents quantitative characteristics for each group. At least one structure representing each of the three subtypes of features is present in each group, with Group 1 being the most elemental (Features 5, 33, and 35). In four of the five groups, there is only one Type 1b structure and one Type 1c structure, with the additional structures all being Type 1a features. Group 3 is the only one that varies from this pattern, having two Type 1c structures; one of these structures (Feature 13) is much smaller than the other (Feature 102).

As shown in Figure F.4, polygons have been created by connecting the approximate centers of all features in each group. In four of the five groups, a second, smaller polygon has been created to connect one of each structure type. The areas of these polygons serve as relative measurements of the spatial domains of the social groups represented by the house groups. As noted, there is only one polygon for House Group 1, but there are multiple alternatives for the smaller polygons in the other four groups. In three cases, there is only one option for the line between the Type 1b and 1c structures, and either two (Group 5) or three (Groups 2 and 4) options for the Type 1a structure. In the case of House Group 3, the presence of two Type 1c structures presents multiple alternative connections.

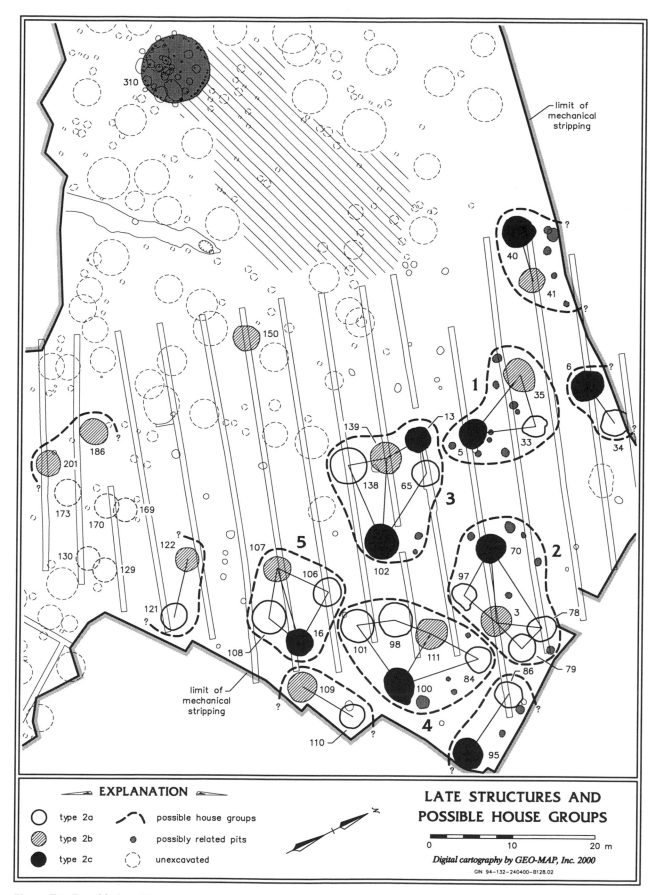

Figure F.4. Possible Late Cienega phase house groups at Santa Cruz Bend.

Table F.4. Characteristics of possible Late Cienega phase house groups at Santa Cruz Bend and Stone Pipe.

Site/ House Group	Feature	Type	Effective Floor Area[a]	Population Estimate in Persons[b]	Total Pit Volume	Pit Volume-to-Floor Area Ratio	Area of Associated Polygons (m²)
Santa Cruz Bend							
1	5	2c	7.47	-	.48	.064	
	33	2b	8.06	3.5	.44	.054	
	35	2a	8.90	3.9	-	-	
Totals			24.43	6.3-7.4	.92	.038	23.2
2	70	2c	7.92	-	.58	.073	
	3	2b	8.51	3.7	.29	.034	
	78	2a	6.10	2.6	-	-	
	Subtotals		22.53	6.3-6.4	.87	.039	25.0
	97	2a	4.00	1.7	-	-	
	79	2a	8.60	3.7	-	-	
Totals			35.13	11.7-11.9	.87	.025	47.4
3	102	2c	11.90	-	.84	.071	
	139	2b	8.99	3.9	.31	.034	
	138	2a	12.60	5.5	-	-	
	Subtotals		32.95	6.8-9.4	1.15	.035	25.5
	13	2c	6.32	2.8	.35	.055	
	65	2a	7.10	3.1	-	-	
Totals			46.37	7.6-15.3	1.50	.032	59.4
4	100	2c	9.00	-	1.13	.120	
	111	2b	10.40	4.6	.34	.032	
	84	2a	6.20	2.7	-	-	
	Subtotals		25.60	7.2-7.3	1.47	.057	21.2
	98	2a	10.90	4.7	-	-	
	101	2a	11.50	5.0	-	-	
Totals			48.00	17.0	1.47	.031	64.3
5	16	2c	6.70	-	.49	.073	
	107	2a	6.70	2.9	-	-	
	106	2a	6.69	2.9	-	-	
	Subtotals		19.09	5.8-8.3	.49	.026	23.03
	108[c]	2a(?)	11.50	5.0	-	-	
Totals			30.59	10.8-13.3	.49	.016	35.00
Stone Pipe							
1	251[c]	2c	4.79	-	.80	.167	
	245[c]	2a(?)	6.38	2.8	-	-	
	212[c]	2a(?)	11.40	5.0	-	-	
Totals			22.57	6.4-7.8	.80	.035	25.9
2	134	2c	15.10	-	1.85	.122	
	143[c]	2b(?)	10.20	4.4	.14	.014	
	84[c]	2a(?)	6.70	2.9	-	-	
	Subtotals		31.90	7.3	1.99	.062	27.7
	141[c]	2a(?)	7.46	3.3	-	-	
Totals			39.36	10.5-10.6	1.99	.051	45.7
3	134	2c	15.10	-	1.85	.122	
	24[c]	2b(?)	7.97	3.8	.71	.089	
	141[c]	2a(?)	7.46	3.3	-	-	
Totals			30.53	6.7-7.1	2.56	.083	22.9

[a]Effective floor area is equal to the floor area minus the total area taken up by intramural pits.

[b]Following Cook's (1972) formula, population estimates for individual structures were derived by dividing the floor area by 2.3. Ranges for estimates represent: 1) the sum of estimates for each structure; and 2) application of the formula to the summed floor area of all structures. Type 2c structures are excluded from population estimates (see text).

[c]Denotes partially excavated structure; question marks after type designations denote ambiguous subtype assignment.

The sets of three features selected to define these smaller polygons are somewhat arbitrary, but House Group 1 was used as a general model for this selection. As shown in Table F.4, the areas of the smaller polygons are quite similar; any of the other possible options would have produced areas of the *same scale*. Three possible house groups with similar characteristics have been identified at Stone Pipe (see Swartz and Archer 1997), and these polygons also reflect a similar spatial scale (Table F.4). The derived population estimates suggest that these house groups may represent the spatial domains of large nuclear families or small extended families.

Parts of other house groups at Santa Cruz Bend *may* be represented by six pairs of features. In four cases, other possible members of the groups would have been outside the stripped area of the site, while identified but unexcavated structures may have been associated with the other two (Features 129, 130, 16, 170, and 173).

Comparison of the population estimates provided in Tables F.3 and F.4 suggests that there was an increase in group size between the earlier and later occupations. The pit volumes and pit volume to floor area ratios given in these tables also suggest variation between the two intervals. While the absolute values for total pit volume per house group overlap substantially, the pit volume to floor area ratios show a substantial decrease between the early to the later groups. Further, those for the later house groups are much more internally consistent than those for the earlier groups. Assuming, as Mabry does, that total pit volume is a proxy for storage volume, then it would appear that there was less storage volume per person in the Late Cienega phase–at least for the groups of structures represented in the intensively investigated portion of the site.

The obviously specialized nature of the Big House (Feature 301) makes it an important aspect of any consideration of site structure. Unfortunately, due to right-of-way constraints, the feature was located in an area of the site where very few other features were investigated, and thus the temporal and spatial relationships between the Big House and other features are impossible to determine with confidence. Although Mabry places great emphasis on the centrality of the Big House within the overall distribution of features exposed at the site (Mabry 1998a:231), its centrality is time-dependent: whether or not this large feature occupied a central place in the settlement depends entirely upon which other features were present during the use-life of the structure. This is also true of the plaza and work areas identified by Mabry (1998a:231).

It is clear that the structure was not present throughout the occupation, since there were 14 extramural pits intruded into its fill, and since some sequence rather than contemporaneous use of all these intrusive features is indicated (Mabry and Archer 1997:165-173). While the general construction techniques represented would place the feature in the Early Cienega phase grouping defined above, it is often the case that such specialized constructions do not necessarily conform to the architectural styles of contemporaneous structures.

Absolute dating of this feature is also somewhat problematic. Two relevant radiocarbon dates were obtained, both of 2260 ± 60 b.p. (Mabry 1997:Table 1.2). One was from a sample from one of the shallow floor pits in the structure (Feature 301.01, B-81064) and the other from a pit that intruded into the fill of the large structure (Feature 406, B-81063). Given the numerous pits intruded into the fill of the structure, the possibility of contamination of the date from the floor pit must be considered. Given these data, an Early Cienega placement may be slightly favored. Once again, however, it is impossible to determine the spatial relationships between the Big House and the distribution of other features present during its use-life. It could have as easily been on the margins of that distribution, centrally located, or somewhere in between.

REFERENCES CITED

Abbott, R. Tucker
1974   *American Seashells: The Marine Mollusca of the Atlantic and Pacific Coasts of North America.* 2nd ed. Van Nostrand Reinhold, New York.

Adams, Jenny L.
1979   Groundstone from Walpi. In *Walpi Archaeological Project, Phase 2: Vol. 4. Stone Artifacts from Walpi,* Part II, by J. L. Adams and D. Greenwald, pp. 1-220. Museum of Northern Arizona, Flagstaff.

1988   Use-wear Analysis of Handstones Used to Grind Corn and Process Hides. *Journal of Field Archaeology* 15:307-315.

1989a   Experimental Replication of the Use of Ground Stone Tools. *Kiva* 54:3.

1989b   Methods for Improving Ground Stone Analysis: Experiments in Mano Wear Patterns. In *Experiments in Lithic Technology,* edited by D. S. Amick and R. P. Maudlin, pp. 259-276. BAR International Series 528. British Archaeological Reports, Oxford.

1993a   Mechanism of Wear on Ground Stone Surfaces. *Pacific Coast Archaeological Society Quarterly* 29(4):60-73.

1993b   Toward Understanding the Technological Development of Manos and Metates. *Kiva* 58:331-344.

1994   *The Development of Prehistoric Grinding Technology in the Point of Pines Area, East-Central Arizona.* Ph.D. dissertation, Department of Anthropology, University of Arizona, Tucson. University of Michigan Microfilms, Ann Arbor, Michigan.

1995a   The Ground Stone Assemblage: The Development of a Prehistoric Grinding Technology in the Eastern Tonto Basin. In *The Roosevelt Community Development Study: Vol. 1. Stone and Shell Artifacts,* edited by M. D. Elson and J. J. Clark, pp. 43-114. Anthropological Papers No. 14. Center for Desert Archaeology, Tucson.

1995b   Life History as a Framework for the Analysis of Ground Stone Artifacts. Paper presented at the 60th Annual Meeting of the Society for American Archaeology, Minneapolis.

1996a   *Manual for a Technological Approach to Ground Stone Analysis.* Center for Desert Archaeology, Tucson.

1996b   Refocusing the Role of Food Grinding Tools as Correlates for the Subsistence Strategies of Gatherers and Early Agriculturalists in the American Southwest. Paper presented at the 61st Annual Meeting of the Society for American Archaeology, New Orleans, 10-14 April.

1998   Ground Stone Artifacts. In *Archaeological Investigations of Early Village Sites in the Middle Santa Cruz Valley: Analyses and Synthesis,* Part I, edited by J. B. Mabry, pp. 357-422. Anthropological Papers No. 19. Center for Desert Archaeology, Tucson.

1999   Refocusing the Role of Food-grinding Tools as Correlates for the Subsistence Strategies in the U.S. Southwest. *American Antiquity* 64:475-498.

2001   Ground Stone Data Tables. In *The Early Agricultural Period Component at Los Pozos: Feature Descriptions and Data Tables,* by D. A. Gregory. Technical Report No. 99-4. Desert Archaeology, Inc., Tucson.

Adams, Karen R.
1988   *The Ethnobotany and Phenology of Plants in and Adjacent to Two Riparian Habitats in Southeastern Arizona.* Ph.D. dissertation, Department of Ecology and Evolutionary Biology, University of Arizona. University Microfilms, Ann Arbor, Michigan.

1994   A Regional Synthesis of *Zea mays* in the Prehistoric American Southwest. In *Corn and Culture in the Prehistoric New World,* edited by S. Johannessen and C. A. Hastorf, pp. 273-302. Westview Press, Boulder.

Adams, Kim, and Barbara S. Macnider

1992a *An Archaeological Assessment for the Rillito Loop, Santa Fe Pacific Pipeline, Tucson to Marana, Pima County, Arizona.* Archaeological Consulting Services, Ltd. Submitted to Santa Fe Pacific Pipeline. Copies available from Archaeological Consulting Services, Ltd., Tempe, Arizona.

1992b Archaeological Testing along the Rillito Loop, Santa Fe Pacific Pipeline, Tucson to Marana, Pima County, Arizona. Ms. on file, Archaeological Consulting Services, Ltd., Tempe, Arizona.

Aiken, M. J.

1990 *Science-based Dating in Archaeology.* Longman, London.

Aikens, C. Melvin

1970 *Hogup Cave.* Anthropological Papers No. 93. University of Utah Press, Salt Lake City.

1995 First in the World: The Jamon Pottery of Early Japan. In *The Emergence of Pottery: Technology and Innovation in Ancient Societies,* edited by W. K. Barnett and J. W. Hoopes, pp. 11-21. Smithsonian Institution Press, Washington, D.C.

de Alba Avila, Abraham

1983 Comparative Germination Ecology of *Sporobolus airoides* and *Hilaria mutica* from Mapimi Biosphere Reserve and Other Mexican and United States Locations. Unpublished Master's thesis, School of Renewable Natural Resources, University of Arizona, Tucson.

Allen, Wilma

1985 Prehistoric Features at Block 24-East. In *City of Phoenix Archaeology of the Original Townsite: Block 24-East,* edited by J. S. Cable, K. S. Hoffman, D. E. Doyel, and F. Ritz, pp. 41-84. Soil Systems Publications in Archaeology No. 8. Soil Systems, Inc., Phoenix.

Altschul, Jeffrey H.

1995 Introduction. *Kiva* 60:457-464.

Alvarez Palma, Ana Maria

1982 Archaeological Investigations at Huatabampo. In *Mogollon Archaeology: Proceedings of the 1980 Mogollon Conference,* edited by P. H. Beckett and K. Silverbird, pp. 239-250. Acoma Books, Ramona, California.

Archer, Gavin, and Andrea K. L. Freeman

1998 Architecture. In *Archaeological Investigations at the Wetlands Site, AZ AA:12:90 (ASM),* edited by A. K. L. Freeman, pp. 35-51. Technical Report No. 97-5. Desert Archaeology, Inc., Tucson.

Arnold, Dean E.

1985 *Ceramic Theory and Cultural Process.* Cambridge University Press, Cambridge, England.

Arroyo, Barbara

1995 Early Ceramics from El Salvador: The El Carmen Site. In *The Emergence of Pottery: Technology and Innovation in Ancient Societies,* edited by W. K. Barnett and J. W. Hoopes, pp. 199-208. Smithsonian Institution Press, Washington, D.C.

Baar, Sam W. IV

1996 *Interstate 10 Frontage Road Project: Results of Archaeological Testing, South of Speedway Parcel.* Technical Report No. 96-11. Center for Desert Archaeology, Tucson.

Bahr, Donald, Juan Smith, William S. Allison, and Julian Hayden

1994 *The Short, Swift Time of Gods on Earth: The Hohokam Chronicles.* University of California Press, Berkeley.

Barnett, William K., and John W. Hoopes (editors)

1995 *The Emergence of Pottery: Technology and Innovation in Ancient Societies.* Smithsonian Institution Press, Washington, D.C.

Bartlett, Katharine

1933 *Pueblo Milling Stones of the Flagstaff Region and Their Relation to Others in the Southwest: A Study in Progressive Efficiency.* Bulletin 3. Museum of Northern Arizona, Flagstaff.

Bass, W. M.

1987 *Human Osteology: A Laboratory and Field Manual.* 3rd ed. Special Publication No. 2. Missouri Archaeological Society, Columbia.

Bayham, Frank E.

1979 Factors Influencing the Archaic Pattern of Animal Exploitation. *The Kiva* 44:219-35.

1982 *A Diachronic Analysis of Prehistoric Animal Exploitation at Ventana Cave.* Ph.D. dissertation, Arizona State University. University Microfilms, Ann Arbor, Michigan.

Bayham, Frank E.
1986   The Picacho Reservoir Archaic Project. In *Prehistoric Hunter-Gatherers of South Central Arizona: The Picacho Reservoir Archaic Project*, edited by F. E. Bayham, D. H. Morris, and M. S. Shackley, pp. 1-15. Anthropological Field Studies No. 13. Office of Cultural Resource Management, Department of Anthropology, Arizona State University, Tempe.

Bayham, Frank E., and Pamela Hatch
1985   Archaeofaunal Remains from the New River Area. In *Hohokam Settlement and Economic Systems in the Central New River Drainage, Arizona*, edited by D. Doyel and M. D. Elson, pp. 405-33. Soil Systems Publications in Archaeology 4. Soil Systems, Inc., Phoenix.

Bayham, Frank E., and Donald H. Morris
1986   Episodic Use of a Marginal Environment: A Synthesis. In *Prehistoric Hunter-Gatherers of South Central Arizona: The Picacho Reservoir Archaic Project*, by F. E. Bayham, D. H. Morris, and M. S. Shackley, pp. 359-381. Anthropological Field Studies No. 13. Department of Anthropology, Arizona State University, Tempe.

1990   Thermal Maxima and Episodic Occupation of the Picacho Reservoir Dune Field. In *Perspectives on Southwestern Prehistory*, edited by P. E. Minnis and C. L. Redman, pp. 26-37. Westview Press, Boulder.

Behrensmeyer, A. K., K. D. Gordon, and G. T. Yanagi
1986   Trampling as a Cause of Bone Surface Damage and Pseudo-cutmarks. *Nature* 319:768-71.

Bennyhoff, James A., and Richard E. Hughes
1987   *Shell Bead and Ornament Exchange Networks between California and the Western Great Basin.* Anthropological Papers No. 64(2):79-175. American Museum of Natural History, New York.

Bequaert, Joseph C., and Walter B. Miller
1973   *The Mollusks of the Arid Southwest.* University of Arizona Press, Tucson.

Bernard-Shaw, Mary
1990a   *Archaeological Investigations at the Lonetree Site, AA:12:120 (ASM), in the Northern Tucson Basin.* Technical Report No. 90-1. Center for Desert Archaeology, Tucson.

1990b   Experimental Agave Fiber Extraction. In *Rincon Seasonal Occupation in the Northeastern Tucson Basin*, by F. W. Huntington and M. Bernard-Shaw, pp. 181-195. Technical Report No. 90-2. Institute for American Research, Tucson.

Binford, Lewis R.
1980   Willow Smoke and Dogs' Tails: Hunter-Gatherer Settlement Systems and Archaeological Site Formation. *American Antiquity* 45:4-20.

Bogucki, Peter
1995   The Linear Pottery Culture of Central Europe: Conservative Colonists? In *The Emergence of Pottery: Technology and Innovation in Ancient Societies*, edited by W. K. Barnett and J. W. Hoopes, pp. 89-97. Smithsonian Institution Press, Washington, D.C.

Bradfield, M.
1971   *The Changing Pattern of Hopi Agriculture.* Royal Anthropological Institute, Occasional Paper No. 30. Royal Anthropological Association of Great Britain and Ireland, Cambridge, England.

Bradley, Bruce A.
1980   *Excavations at Arizona BB:13:74, Santa Cruz Industrial Park, Tucson, Arizona.* CASA Papers No. 1. Complete Archaeological Service Associates, Oracle, Arizona.

Braun, David P.
1983   Pots as Tools. In *Archaeological Hammers and Theories*, edited by J. A. Moore and A. S. Keene, pp. 108-134. Academic Press, New York.

Brown, David E.
1994   Great Basin Conifer Woodland. In *Biotic Communities: Southwestern United States and Northwestern Mexico*, edited by D. E. Brown, pp. 52-57. University of Utah Press, Salt Lake City.

Brown, David E., and Charles H. Lowe
1994   Biotic Communities of the Southwest. Map supplement to *Biotic Communities: Southwestern United States and Northwestern Mexico*, edited by D. E. Brown. University of Utah Press, Salt Lake City.

Brugge, David M.
1961   History, Huki, and Warfare—Some Random Data on the Lower Pima. *The Kiva* 26(4):6-16.

Buikstra, J. E., and D. H. Ubelaker
1994   *Standards: For Data Collection from Human Skeletal Remains.* Research Series No. 44. Arkansas Archeological Survey, Fayetteville.

Burton, Jeffrey F., and Mary Farrell
1990   An Introduction to the Rock Art of Southeast Arizona. *Rock Art Papers* 6:1-16. Museum of Man, San Diego.

Cairns, Kellie M., and Richard Ciolek-Torrello
1998   Faunal Analysis. In *Early Farmers of the Sonoran Desert: Archaeological Investigations at the Houghton Road Site, Tucson, Arizona,* edited by R. Ciolek-Torrello, pp. 169-184. Technical Series 72. Statistical Research, Inc., Tucson.

Carr, M. E., B. S. Phillips, and M. O. Bagby
1985   Xerophytic Species Evaluated for Renewable Energy Resources. *Economic Botany* 39:505-513.

Castetter, Edward F., and Willis H. Bell
1935   *Ethnobiological Studies in the American Southwest: II. The Ethnobiology of the Papago Indians.* University of New Mexico Bulletin, Biological Series 4(3). University of New Mexico Press, Albuquerque.

1937   *Ethnobiological Studies in the American Southwest: IV. The Aboriginal Utilization of the Tall Cacti in the American Southwest.* University of New Mexico Bulletin, Biological Series 5(1). University of New Mexico Press, Albuquerque.

1942   *Pima and Papago Indian Agriculture.* University of New Mexico Press, Albuquerque.

Castetter, Edward F., and Ruth Underhill
1935   *Ethnobiological Studies in the American Southwest II. The Ethnobiology of the Papago Indians.* Bulletin No. 275. University of New Mexico, Albuquerque.

Childe, V. Gordon
1951   *Man Makes Himself.* New American Library of World Literature, London.

Ciolek-Torrello, Richard S.
1995   The Houghton Road Site, the Agua Caliente Phase, and the Early Formative Period in the Tucson Basin. *Kiva* 60:531-574.

Clark, Jeffery J.
1993a   *Interstate 10 Frontage Road Project, Miracle Mile Interchange to Speedway Blvd., Results of Archaeological Testing and a Plan for Data Recovery at AZ BB: 13:425 (ASM), Tucson, Pima County, Arizona.* Technical Report No. 93-9. Center for Desert Archaeology, Tucson.

1993b   *Interstate 10 Frontage Road Project, Prince Road to Miracle Mile Interchange: Results of Archaeological Testing and a Plan for Data Recovery.* Technical Report No. 93-3. Center for Desert Archaeology, Tucson.

Clark, John E., and Dennis Gosser
1995   Reinventing Mesoamerica's First Pottery. In *The Emergence of Pottery: Technology and Innovation in Ancient Societies,* edited by W. K. Barnett and J. W. Hoopes, pp. 209-221. Smithsonian Institution Press, Washington, D.C.

Close, Angela E.
1995   Few and Far Between: Early Ceramics in North Africa. In *The Emergence of Pottery: Technology and Innovation in Ancient Societies,* edited by W. K. Barnett and J. W. Hoopes, pp. 23-37. Smithsonian Institution Press, Washington, D.C.

Cobia, David W.
1978   Production Costs and Marketing. In *Sunflower Science and Technology,* edited by J. F. Carter, pp. 387-405. American Society of Agronomy, Madison, Wisconsin.

Cole, Sally J.
1992   *Katsina Iconography in Homol'ovi Rock Art, Central Little Colorado River Valley, Arizona.* Arizona Archaeologist No. 25. Arizona Archaeological Society, Phoenix.

Cook, Sherburne F.
1972   *Prehistoric Demography.* Modular Publications in Anthropology 16. Addison-Wesley Publishing Company, Reading, Massachusetts.

Cooke, Richard
1995   Monagrillo, Panama's First Pottery: Summary of Research, with New Interpretations. In *The Emergence of Pottery: Technology and Innovation in Ancient Societies,* edited by W. K. Barnett and J. W. Hoopes, pp. 169-184. Smithsonian Institution Press, Washington, D.C.

Coulam, Nancy J., and Alan R. Schroedl
1996 Early Archaic Clay Figurines from Cowboy and Walters Caves in Southeastern Utah. *Kiva* 61:401-412.

Cowgill, George L.
1990 Why Pearson's r is Not a Good Similarity Coefficient for Comparing Collections. *American Antiquity* 55:512-521.

Cressman, Luther S.
1943 Results of Recent Archaeological Research in the Northern Great Basin Region of South Central Oregon. *Proceedings* 86:236-237. American Philosophical Society, Philadelphia.

Crosswhite, Frank S.
1980 The Annual Saguaro Harvest and Crop Cycle of the Papagos with Reference to Ecology and Symbolism. *Desert Plants* 2(1):3-62.

Crown, Patricia L., and W. H. Wills
1995 Economic Intensification and the Origins of Ceramic Containers in the American Southwest. In *The Emergence of Pottery: Technology and Innovation in Ancient Societies*, edited by W. K. Barnett and J. W. Hoopes, pp. 241-254. Smithsonian Institution Press, Washington, D.C.

Culin, Stewart
1975 *Games of the North American Indians*. Reprinted. Dover Publications, New York. Originally published 1907, *Twenty-fourth Annual Report of the Bureau of American Ethnology*, Smithsonian Institution, Washington, D.C.

Curtis, James R.
1977 Prickly Pear Farming in the Santa Clara Valley, California. *Economic Botany* 31:175-179.

Czaplicki, Jon S., and Allen Dart
1984 Archaic Sites. In *A Class III Survey of the Tucson Aqueduct Phase A Corridor, Central Arizona Project*, edited by J. S. Czaplicki, pp. 36-60. Archaeological Series 165. Cultural Resource Management Division, Arizona State Museum, University of Arizona, Tucson.

Damon, P. E., J. C. Lerman, and A. Long
1978 Temporal Fluctuations of Atmospheric ^{14}C: Causal Factors and Implications. *Annual Review of Earth and Planetary Science* 6:457-494.

Damon, P.E., and T. W. Linick
1986 Geomagnetic-heliomagnetic Modulation of Atmospheric Radiocarbon Production. *Radiocarbon* 28:266-278.

Dart, Allen
1986 *Archaeological Investigations at La Paloma: Archaic and Hohokam Occupations at Three Sites in the Northeastern Tucson Basin*. Anthropological Papers No. 4. Institute for American Research, Tucson.

1989 *The Gunsight Mountain Archaeological Survey: Archaeological Surveys in the Valleys Southwest of Tucson, Arizona*. Technical Report No. 89-1. Center for Desert Archaeology, Tucson.

Davenport, Marietta A., John Hanson, and Lawrence Lesko
1992 The Rocks Remember . . . The Art of Snake Gulch. In *American Indian Rock Art* 18:65-70. American Indian Rock Art Research Association, El Toro, California.

Dean, Jeffrey S.
1991 Thoughts on the Hohokam Chronology. In *Exploring the Hohokam: Desert Dwellers of the Southwest*, edited by G. J. Gumerman, pp. 61-150. University of New Mexico Press, Albuquerque.

Deaver, William L., and Richard S. Ciolek-Torrello
1995 Early Formative Period Chronology for the Tucson Basin. *Kiva* 60:481-529.

Denton, G. H., and W. Karlen
1973 Holocene Climate Variations: Their Pattern and Probable Cause. *Quaternary Research* 3: 155-205.

DeVeaux, Jennie S., and Eugene B. Shultz Jr.
1985 Development of Buffalo Gourd (*Cucurbita foetidissima*) as a Semiaridland Starch and Oil Crop. *Economic Botany* 39:454-472.

Diehl, Michael W.
1996a *Archaeological Investigations at the Brickyard Site and the Tucson Pressed Brick Company, AZ BB:13:6*. Technical Report No. 96-13. Center for Desert Archaeology, Tucson.

1996b The Intensity of Maize Processing and Production in Upland Mogollon Pithouse Villages, A.D. 200-1000. *American Antiquity* 61:102-115.

Diehl, Michael W.

1997a *Archaeological Investigations of the Early Agricultural Period Settlement at the Base of A-Mountain, Tucson, Arizona.* Technical Report No. 96-21. Center for Desert Archaeology, Tucson.

1997b Excavation Methods, Feature Descriptions, and Preliminary Analyses. In *Archaeological Investigations of the Early Agricultural Period Settlements at the Base of A-Mountain, Tucson, Arizona*, by M. W. Diehl, pp. 22-52. Technical Report No. 96-21. Center for Desert Archaeology, Tucson.

1998 Macroplant Remains from Analyzed Flotation Samples at the Wetlands Site. In *Archaeological Investigations at the Wetlands Site, AZ AA:12:90 (ASM)*, edited by A. K. L. Freeman, pp. 229-247. Technical Report No. 97-5. Center for Desert Archaeology, Tucson.

2001 Macrobotanical Remains Data Tables. In *The Early Agricultural Period Component at Los Pozos: Feature Description and Data Tables*, edited by D. A. Gregory, pp. 131-152. Technical Report No. 99-4. Desert Archaeology, Inc., Tucson.

Diehl, Michael W., and Jennifer A. Waters

1997 Archaeobotanical and Osteofaunal Assessments of Diet Composition and Diversity. In *Archaeological Investigations of the Early Agricultural Period Settlements at the Base of A-Mountain, Tucson, Arizona*, by M. W. Diehl. Technical Report No. 96-21. Center for Desert Archaeology, Tucson.

Di Peso, Charles C.

1956 *The Upper Pima of San Cayetano del Tumacacori: An Archaeological Reconstruction of the Ootam of the Pimeria Alta.* Amerind Foundation Series No. 7. Amerind Foundation, Dragoon, Arizona.

Di Peso, Charles C., John B. Rinaldo, and Gloria J. Fenner

1974 Stone and Metal. In *Casas Grandes: A Fallen Trading Center of the Gran Chichimeca*, Vol. 7. Amerind Foundation, Series 9. Northland Press, Flagstaff, Arizona.

Dockstader, Frederick J.

1961 A Figurine Cache from Kino Bay, Sonora. In *Essays in Pre-Columbian Art and Archaeology*, by S. K. Lothrop and others, pp. 182-191. Harvard University Press, Cambridge, Massachusetts.

Doelle, William H.

1976 *Desert Resources and Hohokam Subsistence: The Conoco Florence Project.* Archaeological Series No. 103. Arizona State Museum, University of Arizona, Tucson.

1978 Hohokam Use of Nonriverine Resources. In *Discovering Past Behavior*, edited by P. Grebinger, pp. 245-274. Gordon and Breach, New York.

1980 *Past Adaptive Patterns in Western Papagueria: An Archaeological Study of Nonriverine Resource Use.* Ph.D. dissertation, University of Arizona. University Microfilms, Ann Arbor, Michigan.

Downs, James F.

1966 The Significance of Environmental Manipulation in Great Basin Cultural Development. In *The Current Status of Anthropological Research in the Great Basin: 1964*, edited by W. L. d'Azevedo, W. A. Davos, D. D. Fowler, and W. Suttles, pp. 39-56. Desert Research Institute, Reno, Nevada.

Downum, Christian E., Adrianne G. Rankin, and Jon S. Czaplicki

1986 *A Class III Archaeological Survey of the Phase B Corridor, Tucson Aqueduct, Central Arizona Project.* Archaeological Series 168. Cultural Resource Management Division, Arizona State Museum, University of Arizona, Tucson.

Eddy, Frank W., and M. E. Cooley

1983 *Cultural and Environmental History of Cienega Valley, Southeastern Arizona.* Anthropological Papers No. 43. University of Arizona Press, Tucson.

Eddy, Franklin W.

1958 A Sequence of Cultural and Alluvial Deposits in the Cienega Creek Basin, Southeastern Arizona. Unpublished Master's thesis, Department of Anthropology, University of Arizona, Tucson.

Eddy, John A.

1977 Climate and the Changing Sun. *Climate Change* 1:173-190.

Eighmy, J. L., and J. M. LaBelle

1996 Radiocarbon Dating of Twenty-seven Plains Complexes and Phases. *Plains Anthropologist* 41:53-69.

Ekholm, Gordon F.
1939   Results of an Archeological Survey of Sonora and Northern Sinaloa. *Revista Mexicana de Estudios Antropológicos* 3(1):7-10.

Elson, Mark D.
1994   Introduction. In *The Roosevelt Community Development Study: Vol. 1. Introduction and Small Sites*, by M. D. Elson and D. L. Swartz, pp. 1-12. Anthropological Papers No. 13. Center for Desert Archaeology, Tucson.

Elson, Mark D., and William H. Doelle
1987   *Archaeological Assessment of the Mission Road Extension: Testing at AZ BB:13:6 (ASM)*. Technical Report No. 87-6. Institute for American Research, Tucson.

Ensminger, Audrey H., M. E. Ensminger, James E. Konlande, and John R. K. Robson
1994   *Foods and Nutrition Encyclopedia*. 2nd ed. CRC Press, Boca Raton, Florida.

Erichsen-Brown, Charlotte
1979   *Medicinal and Other Uses of North American Plants: A Historical Survey with Special Reference to the Eastern Indian Tribes*. Dover Publications, New York.

Euler, Robert C., and Henry F. Dobyns
1983   The Ethnoarchaeology of Pai Milling Stones. In *Collected Papers in Honor of Charlie Steen, Jr.*, edited by N. L. Fox, pp. 253-267. Papers of the Archaeological Society of New Mexico No. 8. Albuquerque Archaeological Society Press, Albuquerque.

Ezzo, Joseph A., and William L. Deaver
1998   *Data Recovery at the Costello-King Site (AZ AA:12:503[ASM]), a Late Archaic Site in the Northern Tucson Basin*. Technical Series No. 68. Statistical Research, Tucson.

Fall, Sidi
1991   Induced Water Stress Effects on Grain Yield and Yield Components of Twelve Maize (*Zea mays* L.) Genotypes. Unpublished Master's thesis, Department of Plant Sciences, University of Arizona, Tucson.

Felker, Peter, and Robert S. Bandurski
1979   Uses and Potential Uses of Leguminous Trees for Minimal Energy Input Agriculture. *Economic Botany* 33:172-184.

Felker, Peter, G. H. Cannell, Peter R. Clark, Joseph F. Osborn, and Phyllis Nash
1981   Screening *Prosopis* (Mesquite) Species for Biofuel Production on Semi-arid Lands: Final Report to the U.S. Department of Energy for Period 1 April 1978 through 30 March 1981. Ms. on file, Special Collections, University of Arizona Library System, Tucson.

Ferg, Alan
1998a   Fired Clay Figurines and Beads. In *Archaeological Investigations at the Wetlands Site, AZ AA:12:90 (ASM)*, edited by A. K. L. Freeman, pp. 265-275. Technical Report No. 97-5. Desert Archaeology, Inc., Tucson.

1998b   Rare Stone, Fired Clay, Bone, and Shell Artifacts. In *Archaeological Investigations of Early Village Sites in the Middle Santa Cruz Valley: Analyses and Synthesis*, Part I, edited by J. B. Mabry, pp. 545-654. Anthropological Papers No. 19. Center for Desert Archaeology, Tucson.

Fish, Paul R.
1989   The Hohokam: 1,000 Years of Prehistory in the Sonoran Desert. In *Dynamics of Southwest Prehistory*, edited by L. S. Cordell and G. J. Gumerman, pp. 19-63. Smithsonian Institution Press, Washington, D.C.

Fish, Paul R., Suzanne K. Fish, and John Madsen
1990   Sedentism and Settlement Pattern Mobility Prior to A.D. 1000 in the Tucson Basin. In *Perspectives in Southwestern Prehistory*, edited by P. Minnis and C. L. Redman, pp. 26-91. Westview Press, Boulder.

Fish, Paul R., Suzanne K. Fish, John H. Madsen, Charles H. Miksicek, and Christine R. Szuter
1992   The Dairy Site: Occupational Continuity on an Alluvial Fan. In *The Marana Community in the Hohokam World*, edited by S. K. Fish, P. R. Fish, and J. H. Madsen, pp. 64-72. Anthropological Papers No. 56. University of Arizona, Tucson.

Fleming, J. E., and N. W. Galway
1995   Quinoa (*Chenopodium quinoa*). In *Cereals and Pseudocereals*, edited by J. T. Williams, pp. 3-83. Chapman and Hall, New York.

Flenniken, Jeffery J., and Terry L. Ozbun
1988   Experimental Analysis of Plains Grooved Abraders. *Plains Anthropologist* 33:37-52.

Ford, Richard I.
1968   *An Ecological Analysis Involving the Population of San Juan Pueblo, New Mexico.* Ph.D. dissertation, University of Michigan. University Microfilms, Ann Arbor, Michigan.

1981   Gardening and Farming before A.D. 1000: Patterns of Prehistoric Cultivation North of Mexico. *Journal of Ethnobiology* 1:6-27.

Fowler, Don D., and Catherine S. Fowler
1971   *Anthropology of the Numa: John Wesley Powell's Manuscripts on the Numic Peoples of Western North America, 1868-1880.* Smithsonian Contributions to Anthropology 14. Washington, D.C.

Freeman, Andrea K. L. (editor)
1998   *Archaeological Investigations at the Wetlands Site, AZ AA:12:90 (ASM).* Technical Report No. 97-5. Center for Desert Archaeology, Tucson.

Fritz, John H.
1974   The Hay Hollow Site Subsistence System, East Central Arizona. Unpublished Ph.D. dissertation, Department of Anthropology, University of Chicago, Chicago.

Fullington, Richard W.
1978   *The Recent and Fossil Freshwater Gastropod Fauna of Texas.* Ph.D. dissertation, North Texas State University. University Microfilms, Ann Arbor, Michigan.

Furlow, John J., and Richard S. Mitchell
1990   Betulaceae through Cactaceae of New York State. In *A Flora of New York State VIII*, Richard S. Mitchell, general editor. New York State Museum Bulletin No. 476. University of the State of New York, State Education Department, Albany.

Furst, Peter T.
1974   Ethnographic Analogy in the Interpretation of West Mexican Art. In *The Archaeology of West Mexico*, edited by B. Bell. West Mexican Society for Advanced Study, Ajijic, Jalisco, Mexico.

Galinat, Walton C.
1988   The Origins of Maiz de Ocho. *American Anthropologist* 90:682-683.

Gasser, Robert E.
1982   Hohokam Use of Desert Plant Foods. *Desert Plants* 3:216-234.

Gebauer, Anne Brigitte
1995   Pottery Production and the Introduction of Agriculture in Southern Scandinavia. In *The Emergence of Pottery: Technology and Innovation in Ancient Societies*, edited by W. K. Barnett and J. W. Hoopes, pp. 99-112. Smithsonian Institution Press, Washington, D.C.

Gifford, Edward W.
1936   The Northeastern and Western Yavapai. *University of California Publications in American Archaeology and Ethnology* 34:247-354. University of California Press, Berkeley.

1947   Californian Shell Artifacts. *University of California Anthropological Records* 9(1):1-132.

Gillespie, William B.
1987   Vertebrate Remains. In *The Archaeology of the San Xavier Bridge Site (AZ BB:13:14) Tucson Basin, Southern Arizona*, edited by J. C. Ravesloot, pp. 271-301. Anthropological Series 171. Cultural Resource Management Division, Arizona State Museum, University of Arizona, Tucson.

Gilman, Patricia A.
1983   Changing Architectural Forms in the Prehistoric Southwest. Unpublished Ph.D. dissertation, Department of Anthropology, University of New Mexico, Albuquerque.

1988   Sedentism/mobility, Seasonality, and Tucson Basin Archaeology. In *Recent Research on Tucson Basin Prehistory: Proceedings of the Second Tucson Basin Conference*, edited by W. H. Doelle and P. R. Fish, pp. 411-417. Anthropological Papers No. 10. Institute for American Research, Tucson.

Gilpin, Dennis
1994   Lukachukai and Salinas Springs: Late Archaic/Early Basketmaker Habitation Sites in the Chinle Valley, Northeastern Arizona. *Kiva* 60:203-218.

Gladwin, Harold S., Emil W. Haury, E. B. Sayles, and Nora Gladwin
1937   *Excavations at Snaketown: Material Culture.* Medallion Papers No. 25. Gila Pueblo, Globe, Arizona.

Glascock, M. D., and M. P. Anderson
1993   Geological Reference Materials for Standardization and Quality Assurance of Instrumental Neutron Activation Analysis. *Journal of Radioanalytical and Nuclear Chemistry* 174:229-242.

Glascock, Michael D.
1991   *Tables for Neutron Activation Analysis.* 3rd ed. University of Missouri Research Reactor Facility, Columbus.

Goudie, Andrew
1985   *The Nature of the Environment: An Advanced Physical Geography.* Basil Blackwell, London.

Govindaraju, K.
1989   1989 Compilation of Working Values and Sample Description for 272 Geostandards. *Geostandards Newsletter* 13 (special issue).

Grant, Campbell, James W. Baird, and J. Kenneth Pringle
1968   *Rock Drawings of the Coso Range.* Publication 4. Maturango Museum, China Lake, California.

Grayson, Donald K.
1984   *Quantitative Zooarchaeology.* Academic Press, New York.

Greenwald, Dawn M.
1988   Flaked Stone. In *Hohokam Settlement Along the Slopes of the Picacho Mountains,* Vol. 4, edited by M. Callahan, pp. 221-282. Museum of Northern Arizona Research Paper No. 35. Museum of Northern Arizona, Flagstaff.

Gregory, David A.
1993   *Excavations at AZ AA:2:62 (ASM), a Colonial and Sedentary Period Hohokam Settlement near Toltec, Pinal County, Arizona.* Cultural Resources Report No. 80. Archaeological Consulting Services, Ltd., Tempe, Arizona.

1995   *Interstate 10 Frontage Road Project, Ruthrauff Road to Prince Road: Results of Archaeological Testing and a Plan for Data Recovery at AZ AA:12:91 (ASM).* Technical Report No. 95-8. Center for Desert Archaeology, Tucson.

1996   New Issues in the Interpretation of Archaic Period Radiocarbon Dates. Paper presented at the Conference on the Archaic Prehistory of the North American Southwest, Maxwell Museum, University of New Mexico, Albuquerque.

1999   Data Integration and Synthesis. In *Excavations in the Santa Cruz River Floodplain: The Middle Archaic Component at Los Pozos,* edited by D. A. Gregory, pp. 85-124. Anthropological Papers No. 20. Center for Desert Archaeology, Tucson.

2001a   Architectural Features and Associated Deposits. In *The Early Agricultural Period Component at Los Pozos: Feature Description and Data Tables,* edited by D. A. Gregory, pp. 1-88. Technical Report No. 99-4. Desert Archaeology, Inc., Tucson.

2001b   Extramural Features and Associated Deposits. In *The Early Agricultural Period Component at Los Pozos: Feature Description and Data Tables,* edited by D. A. Gregory, pp. 89-102. Technical Report No. 99-4. Desert Archaeology, Inc., Tucson.

Gregory, David A. (editor)
1999   *Excavations in the Santa Cruz River Floodplain: The Middle Archaic Component at Los Pozos.* Anthropological Papers No. 20. Center for Desert Archaeology, Tucson.

Gregory, David A., and Sam W. Baar IV
1999   Stratigraphy, Chronology, and Characteristics of the Natural and Cultural Deposits. In *Excavations in the Santa Cruz River Floodplain: The Middle Archaic Component at Los Pozos,* edited by D. A. Gregory, pp. 13-32. Anthropological Papers No. 20. Center for Desert Archaeology, Tucson.

Gregory, David A., Andrea K. L. Freeman, and Gary A. Huckleberry
1999   Composite Stratigraphic Cross Sections. In *Excavations in the Santa Cruz River Floodplain: The Middle Archaic Component at Los Pozos,* edited by D. A. Gregory, pp. 125-142. Anthropological Papers No. 20. Center for Desert Archaeology, Tucson.

Gregory, David A., and Bruce B. Huckell
1998   Small, Round, and Stable: Early Agricultural Period Pithouse Architecture and Its Implications for the Rise of Long-Term Settlements in Southeastern Arizona. Paper presented at the 63rd Annual Meeting of the Society for American Archaeology, Seattle, Washington.

Gregory, David A., and Jonathan B. Mabry
1998   *Revised Research Design for the Archaeological Treatment Plan, Interstate 10 Corridor Improvement Project, Tangerine Road to the Interstate 19 Interchange.* Technical Report No. 97-19. Desert Archaeology, Inc., Tucson

Grey, D. C., and P. E. Damon
1970   Sunspots and Radiocarbon Dating in the Middle Ages. In *Scientific Methods in Medieval Archaeology,* edited by R. Berger, pp. 167-182. University of California Press.

Grove, Douglas Ruddell
1969   Yield and Various Agronomic Characters of Indian Corn (*Zea mays* L.) Cultivars in the Southwestern United States. Unpublished Master's thesis, Department of Agronomy, University of Arizona, Tucson.

Guernsey, S. J., and Alfred V. Kidder
1921   *Basketmaker Caves of Northeastern Arizona.* Papers of the Peabody Museum of American Archaeology and Ethnology No. 8(2). Harvard University, Cambridge.

Guernsey, Samuel J.
1931   *Explorations in Northeastern Arizona: Report on the Archaeological Fieldwork of 1920-1923.* Papers of the Peabody Museum of American Archaeology and Ethnology XII(1). Harvard University, Cambridge.

Hackbarth, Mark R.
1993   A Morphological and Functional Analysis of the SCFAP Pits. In *Classic Period Occupation on the Santa Cruz Flats: The Santa Cruz Flats Archaeological Project,* Part II, edited by T. K. Henderson and R. J. Martynek, pp. 513-40. Northland Research, Inc., Flagstaff, Arizona.

Halbirt, Carl D., and T. Kathleen Henderson (editors)
1993   *Archaic Occupation on the Santa Cruz Flats: The Tator Hills Archaeological Project.* Northland Research, Inc., Flagstaff, Arizona.

Halbirt, Carl D., Kurt E. Dongoske, and T. Kathleen Henderson
1993   Coffee Camp: A Late Archaic Site on the Santa Cruz Flats. In *Archaic Occupation on the Santa Cruz Flats: The Tator Hills Archaeological Project,* edited by C. D. Halbirt and T. K. Henderson, pp. 65-79. Northland Research, Inc., Flagstaff, Arizona.

Hampel, Joachim H.
1984   Technical Considerations in X-ray Fluorescence Analysis of Obsidian. In *Obsidian Studies in the Great Basin,* edited by R. E. Hughes, pp. 21-25. Contributions to the University of California Archaeological Research Facility No. 45. University of California, Berkeley.

Hanson, William R.
1954   Field Observations of Deer in the Prescott Study Area. In *Arizona Chaparral Deer Study.* Arizona Game and Fish Department. Federal Aid in Wildlife Restoration Project W-71-R-2:1-33.

Hard, Robert J.
1990   Agricultural Dependence in the Mountain Mogollon. In *Perspectives on Southwestern Prehistory,* edited by P. E. Minnis and C. L. Redman, pp. 135-149. Westview Press, Boulder.

Harden, M. L., and Reza Zolfaghari
1988   Nutritive Composition of Green and Ripe Pods of Honey Mesquite (*Prosopis glandulosa,* Fabaceae). *Economic Botany* 42:522-532.

Haury, Emil W.
1936   *The Mogollon Culture of Southwestern New Mexico.* Medallion Papers No. 20. Gila Pueblo, Globe, Arizona.

1940   *Excavations in the Forestdale Valley, East-Central Arizona.* Social Sciences Bulletin No. 12, Vol. 11(4). University of Arizona, Tucson.

1945   *The Excavation of Los Muertos and Neighboring Ruins in the Salt River Valley, Southern Arizona.* Papers of the Peabody Museum of American Archaeology and Ethnology No. 15(1). Harvard University, Cambridge, Massachusetts.

1950   *The Stratigraphy and Archaeology of Ventana Cave.* University of Arizona Press, Tucson.

1965a   Bone. In *Excavations at Snaketown: Material Culture,* by H. S. Gladwin, E. W. Haury, E. B. Sayles, and N. Gladwin, pp. 154-155. Reprinted. University of Arizona Press, Tucson. Originally published 1937, Medallion Papers No. 25. Gila Pueblo, Globe, Arizona.

1965b   Pottery. In *Excavations at Snaketown: Material Culture,* by H. S. Gladwin, E. W. Haury, E. B. Sayles, and N. Gladwin, pp. 169-229. Reprinted. University of Arizona Press, Tucson. Originally published 1937, Medallion Papers No. 25. Gila Pueblo, Globe, Arizona.

1965c   Shell. In *Excavations at Snaketown: Material Culture,* edited by H. S. Gladwin, E. W. Haury, E. B. Sayles, and N. Gladwin, pp. 135-153. Reprinted. University of Arizona Press, Tucson. Originally published 1937, Medallion Papers No. 25. Gila Pueblo, Globe, Arizona.

1976   *The Hohokam: Desert Farmers and Craftsmen. Excavations at Snaketown, 1964-1965.* University of Arizona Press, Tucson.

Haury, Emil W., and E. B. Sayles
1947   *An Early Pit House Village of the Mogollon Culture, Forestdale Valley, Arizona.* Bulletin 18(4). Social Science Bulletin No. 16. University of Arizona, Tucson.

Hayden, Brian
1995   The Emergence of Prestige Technologies and Pottery. In *The Emergence of Pottery: Technology and Innovation in Ancient Societies,* edited by W. K. Barnett and J. W. Hoopes, pp. 257-265. Smithsonian Institution Press, Washington, D.C.

Hegmon, Michelle
1988   The Risks of Sharing and Sharing as Risk Reduction: Interhousehold Food Sharing in Egalitarian Societies. In *Between Bands and States,* edited by S. A. Gregg, pp. 309-329. Occasional Papers No. 9. Center for Archaeological Investigations, Southern Illinois University Press, Carbondale.

Heidke, James M.
1989   Ceramic Analysis. In *Archaeological Investigations at the Redtail Site, AA:12:149 (ASM), in the Northern Tucson Basin,* by M. Bernard-Shaw, pp. 59-121. Technical Report No. 89-8. Center for Desert Archaeology, Tucson.

1990   Ceramic Analysis. In *Archaeological Investigations at the Lonetree Site, AZ AA:12:120 (ASM), in the Northern Tucson Basin,* by M. Bernard-Shaw, pp. 53-118. Technical Report No. 90-1. Center for Desert Archaeology, Tucson.

1991   Tortolita Red Attribute Analysis. In *Archaeological Testing at the Romero Ruin,* by D. L. Swartz, pp. 37-40. Technical Report No. 91-2. Center for Desert Archaeology, Tucson.

1993   Early Ceramic Period Pottery from Locus 2. In *Archaeological Testing of the Pima Community College Desert Vista Campus Property: The Valencia North Project,* by B. B. Huckell, pp. 101-111. Technical Report No. 92-13. Center for Desert Archaeology, Tucson.

1995   Ceramic Analysis. In *Archaeological Investigations at Los Morteros, a Prehistoric Community in the Northern Tucson Basin,* by H. D. Wallace, pp. 263-442. Anthropological Papers No. 17. Center For Desert Archaeology, Tucson.

1998   Early Cienega Phase Incipient Plain Ware and Tucson Phase Ceramics from the Wetlands Site. In *Archaeological Investigations at the Wetlands Site, AZ AA:12:90 (ASM),* edited by A. K. L. Freeman, pp. 187-203. Technical Report No. 97-5. Desert Archaeology, Inc., Tucson.

2001   Ceramic Containers: Coding Index and Comparative Data Tables. In *The Early Agricultural Period Component at Los Pozos: Feature Description and Data Tables,* edited by D. A. Gregory, pp. 115-130. Technical Report No. 99-4. Desert Archaeology, Inc., Tucson.

Heidke, James M., and Alan Ferg
1997   Pottery and Fired Clay Artifacts. In *Archaeological Investigations of the Early Agricultural Period Settlement at the Base of A-Mountain, Tucson, Arizona,* by M. W. Diehl, pp. 111-121. Technical Report No. 96-21. Center for Desert Archaeology, Tucson.

Heidke, James M., Christine E. Goetze, and Allen Dart
1994   Schuk Took Project Ceramics: Chronology, Formation Processes, and Prehistory of the Avra Valley. In *Archaeological Studies of the Avra Valley, Arizona: Excavations in the Schuk Took District: Vol. 2. Scientific Studies and Interpretations,* by A. Dart, pp. 11-76. Anthropological Papers No. 16. Center for Desert Archaeology, Tucson. Submitted to the Tohono O'odham Nation, Contract No. 8-CS-32-00380.

Heidke, James M., Elizabeth Miksa, and Michael K. Wiley
1998   Ceramic Artifacts. In *Archaeological Investigations of Early Village Sites in the Middle Santa Cruz Valley: Analyses and Synthesis,* Part II, edited by J. B. Mabry, pp. 471-544. Anthropological Papers No. 19. Center for Desert Archaeology, Tucson.

Heidke, James M., R. Jane Sliva, Deborah L. Swartz, and Jennifer A. Waters
1996   Artifact and Archaeobotanical Analyses. In *Limited Excavation at the Eastern Margin of the Hodges Site* by D. L. Swartz, pp. 15-39. Technical Report No. 96-6. Center for Desert Archaeology, Tucson.

Heidke, James M., and Miriam T. Stark
1996   Ceramic Container Technology in the Early Southwestern Farming Village: Inception, Adoption, and Intensification. Ms. on file, Center for Desert Archaeology, Tucson.

Heizer, Robert F., and Martin A. Baumhoff
1962　*Prehistoric Rock Art of Nevada and Eastern California.* University of California Press, Berkeley.

Hemmings, E. Thomas, M. D. Robinson, and R. N. Rogers
1968　Field Report on the Pantano Site (AZ EE:2:50). Ms. on file, Arizona State Museum Library, University of Arizona, Tucson.

Hill, Jane H.
1996　The Prehistoric Differentiation of Uto-Aztecan Languages and the Lexicon of Early Southwestern Agriculture. Paper presented at the 61st Annual Meeting of the Society for American Archaeology, New Orleans, 10-14 April.

Hitchcock, A. S.
1971　*Manual of the Grasses of the United States,* Vols. 1 & 2. Dover Publications, New York.

Hodge, Frederick W.
1920　*Hawikuh Bonework.* Indian Notes and Monographs 3(3). Museum of the American Indian, Heye Foundation, New York.

Hoffmeister, Donald E.
1986　*Mammals of Arizona.* University of Arizona Press, Tucson, and the Arizona Game and Fish Department, Phoenix.

Hoopes, John W.
1995　Interaction in Hunting and Gathering Societies as a Context for the Emergence of Pottery in the Central American Isthmus. In *The Emergence of Pottery: Technology and Innovation in Ancient Societies,* edited by W. K. Barnett and J. W. Hoopes, pp. 185-198. Smithsonian Institution Press, Washington, D.C.

Hoopes, John W., and William K. Barnett
1995　The Shape of Early Pottery Studies. In *The Emergence of Pottery: Technology and Innovation in Ancient Societies,* edited by W. K. Barnett and J. W. Hoopes, pp. 1-7. Smithsonian Institution Press, Washington, D.C.

Howard, Ann Valdo
1987　The La Ciudad Shell Assemblage. In *La Ciudad: Specialized Studies in the Economy, Environment, and Culture of La Ciudad,* edited by J. E. Kisselburg, G. E. Rice, and B. L. Shears, pp. 75-174. Anthropological Field Studies No. 20. Office of Cultural Resource Management, Arizona State University, Tempe.

Huckell, Bruce B.
1981　The Las Colinas Flaked Stone Assemblage. In *The 1968 Excavations at Mound 8, Las Colinas Ruins Group, Phoenix, Arizona,* edited by L. C. Hammack and A. P. Sullivan, pp. 171-200. Archaeological Series No. 154. Arizona State Museum, University of Arizona, Tucson.

1984　*The Archaic Occupation of the Rosemont Area, Northern Santa Rita Mountains, Southeast Arizona.* Arizona State Museum Archaeological Series No. 147(1). Cultural Resource Management Division, Arizona State Museum, University of Arizona, Tucson.

1987　Description of Investigated Sites. In *The Corona de Tucson Project: Prehistoric Use of a Bajada Environment,* by B. B. Huckell, M. D. Tagg, and L. W. Huckell, pp. 35-121. Archaeological Series 174. Cultural Resource Management Division, Arizona State Museum, University of Arizona, Tucson.

1988　Late Archaic Archaeology of the Tucson Basin: A Status Report. In *Recent Research on Tucson Basin Prehistory: Proceedings of the Second Tucson Basin Conference,* edited by W. H. Doelle and P. R. Fish, pp. 57-80. Anthropological Papers No. 10. Institute for American Research, Tucson.

1990　Late Preceramic Farmer-foragers in Southern Arizona: A Cultural and Ecological Consideration of the Spread of Agriculture into the Arid Southwestern United States. Unpublished Ph.D. dissertation, Arid Lands Resource Sciences, University of Arizona, Tucson.

1991　*Archaeological Testing for the Roger Road Waste Water Treatment Plant.* Technical Report No. 91-6. Center for Desert Archaeology, Tucson.

1993　*Archaeological Testing of the Pima Community College Desert Vista Property: The Valencia North Project.* Technical Report No. 92-13. Center for Desert Archaeology, Tucson.

1995　*Of Marshes and Maize: Preceramic Agricultural Settlements in the Cienega Valley, Southeastern Arizona.* Anthropological Papers No. 59. University of Arizona Press, Tucson.

1996　The Archaic Prehistory of the North American Southwest. *Journal of World Prehistory* 10: 305-373.

Huckell, Bruce B.
1998   Alluvial Stratigraphy of the Santa Cruz Bend Reach. In *Archaeological Investigations of Early Village Sites in the Middle Santa Cruz Valley: Analyses and Synthesis*, Part I, edited by J. B. Mabry, pp. 31-56. Anthropological Papers No. 19. Center for Desert Archaeology, Tucson.

Huckell, Bruce B., and Lisa W. Huckell
1984   Excavations at Milagro, a Late Archaic Site in the Eastern Tucson Basin. Ms. on file, Arizona State Museum, University of Arizona, Tucson.

Huckell, Bruce B., Lisa W. Huckell, and Suzanne K. Fish
1995   *Investigations at Milagro, a Late Preceramic Site in the Eastern Tucson Basin*. Technical Report No. 94-5. Center for Desert Archaeology, Tucson.

Huckell, Lisa W.
1993   The Shell Assemblage from Coffee Camp. In *Archaic Occupation on the Santa Cruz Flats: The Tator Hills Archaeological Project*, edited by C. D. Halbirt and T. K. Henderson. Northland Research, Inc., Flagstaff, Arizona.

1995a   Farming and Foraging in the Cienega Valley: Early Agricultural Period Paleoethnobotany. In *Of Marshes and Maize: Preceramic Agricultural Settlements in the Cienega Valley, Southeastern Arizona*, by B. B. Huckell, pp. 74-97. Anthropological Papers No. 59. University of Arizona, Tucson.

1995b   Paleoethnobotanical Analysis. In *Investigations at Milagro, a Late Preceramic Site in the Eastern Tucson Basin*, by B. B. Huckell, L. W. Huckell, and S. K. Fish, pp. 33-40. Technical Report No. 94-5. Center for Desert Archaeology, Tucson.

1998   Macrobotanical Remains. In *Archaeological Investigations of Early Village Sites in the Middle Santa Cruz Valley: Analyses and Synthesis*, Part I, edited by J. B. Mabry, pp. 57-148. Anthropological Papers No. 19. Center for Desert Archaeology, Tucson.

Hughes, Richard E., and Robert L. Smith
1993   Archaeology, Geology, and Geochemistry in Obsidian Provenance Studies. In *Scale on Archaeological and Geoscientific Perspectives*, edited by J. K. Stein and A. R. Linse, pp. 79-91. Geological Society of America Special Paper 283. Boulder, Colorado.

Hunter-Anderson, Rosalind L.
1986   *Prehistoric Adaptations in the American Southwest*. Cambridge University Press, Cambridge, England.

Hutira, Johna
1993   Pits, Pods, and Paradigms: Archaic Subsistence at Coffee Camp. In *Archaic Occupation on the Santa Cruz Flats: The Tator Hills Archaeological Project*, edited by C. D. Halbirt and T. K. Henderson, pp. 333-343. Northland Research, Inc., Flagstaff, Arizona.

Jackson, A. T.
1938   *Picture-Writing of Texas Indians*. Anthropological Papers Vol. 2. University of Texas, Austin.

James, Steven R.
1993   Archaeofaunal Analyses of the Tator Hills Sites, South-Central Arizona. In *Archaic Occupation on the Santa Cruz Flats: The Tator Hills Archaeological Project*, edited by C. D. Halbirt and T. K. Henderson, pp. 345-372. Northland Research, Inc., Flagstaff, Arizona.

1994   Hohokam Hunting and Fishing Patterns at Pueblo Grande: Results of the Archaeofaunal Analysis. In *The Pueblo Grande Project: Vol. 5. Environment and Subsistence*, edited by S. Kwiatkowski, pp. 249-318. Soil Systems Publications in Archaeology No. 20. Soil Systems, Inc., Phoenix.

Jenkins, Philip D., Frank W. Reichenbacher, Kristen Johnson, and Ann E. Gondor
1995   *Vegetation Inventory, Classification and Monitoring for Tonto National Monument, Arizona*. Technical Report No. 50. U.S. Department of the Interior, National Biological Service Cooperative Park Studies Unit, University of Arizona, Tucson.

Jennings, Jesse D.
1957   *Danger Cave*. Anthropological Papers No. 27. University of Utah Press, Salt Lake City.

Johnson, Alfred E.
1960   The Place of the Trincheras Culture of Northern Sonora in Southwestern Archaeology. Unpublished Master's thesis, Department of Anthropology, University of Arizona, Tucson.

Johnson, Duane L., and Mitra N. Jha
1993   Blue Corn. In *New Crops,* edited by J. Janick and J. E. Simon, pp. 228-230. John Wiley and Sons, New York.

Jones, K., and D. Madsen
1989   Calculating the Cost of Resource Transportation: A Great Basin Example. *Current Anthropology* 30:529-534.

Jones, Timothy W., Masa Tani, Kathy Cisco, and Wilson Hughes
1994   *Interstate 10 Frontage Road Project, Miracle Mile Interchange to Speedway Blvd.: Results of Archaeological Testing and a Plan for Data Recovery at AZ BB:13:110 (ASM) and AZ BB:13:159 (ASM), Tucson, Pima County, Arizona.* Technical Report No. 94-7. Center for Desert Archaeology, Tucson.

Kearney, Thomas H., and Robert H. Peebles
1973   *Arizona Flora.* University of California Press, Berkeley.

Keen, A. Myra
1971   *Sea Shells of Tropical West America: Marine Mollusks from Baja California to Peru.* 2nd ed. Stanford University Press, Palo Alto.

Kelly, Isabel T.
1978   *The Hodges Ruin: A Hohokam Community in the Tucson Basin.* Anthropological Papers No. 30. University of Arizona Press, Tucson.

Kelly, Robert L.
1983   Hunter-Gatherer Mobility Strategies. *Journal of Anthropological Research* 39:277-306.

1992   Mobility/Sedentism: Concepts, Archaeological Measures and Effects. *Annual Review of Anthropology* 21:43-66.

1995   *The Foraging Spectrum: Diversity in Hunter-Gatherer Lifeways.* Smithsonian Institution Press, Washington, D.C.

Kidder, Alfred Vincent
1932   *The Artifacts of Pecos.* Yale University Press, New Haven, Connecticut.

Kingery, David W.
1989   Ceramic Materials Science in Society. *Annual Review of Materials Science* 19:1-20.

Kisselburg, JoAnn E.
1993   The Tator Hills Ceramics: Perspectives on a Developing Technology. In *Archaic Occupation on the Santa Cruz Flats: The Tator Hills Archaeological Project,* edited by C. D. Halbirt and T. K. Henderson, pp. 279-304. Northland Research, Inc., Flagstaff, Arizona.

Kolber, Jane
1992   The Rock Art of the San Pedro River, Cochise County, Arizona. *American Indian Rock Art* 17:56-62. American Rock Art Research Association, San Miguel, California.

Ladd, Edmund J.
1979   Zuni Social and Political Organization. In *Handbook of North American Indians, Southwest* 9:482-491, edited by A. Ortiz. Smithsonian Institute, Washington, D.C.

Lancaster, James
1984   Groundstone Artifacts. In *The Galaz Ruin: A Prehistoric Mimbres Village in Southwestern New Mexico,* edited by R. Anyon and S. A. LeBlanc, pp. 247-262. University of New Mexico Press, Albuquerque.

Lancaster, Judith
1993   Chipped Stone Analysis for the Tator Hills Project. In *Archaic Occupation on the Santa Cruz Flats: The Tator Hills Project,* edited by C. Halbirt and K. Henderson, pp. 231-278. Northland Research, Inc., Flagstaff, Arizona.

Lathrap, Donald W.
1977   Our Father the Cayman, Our Mother the Gourd: Spinden Revisited, or a Unitary Model for the Emergence of Agriculture in the New World. In *Origins of Agriculture,* edited by C. A. Reed, pp. 713-751. Mouton, The Hague.

Layhe, Robert W.
1986   *The 1985 Excavations at the Hodges Site, Pima County, Arizona.* Archaeological Series No. 170. Arizona State Museum, University of Arizona, Tucson.

Lehmer, Donald J., and David T. Jones
1968   *Arikara Archaeology: The Bad River Phase.* River Basin Surveys, Museum of Natural History, Smithsonian Institution, Lincoln, Nebraska.

Lemonnier, Pierre
1986   The Study of Material Culture Today: Towards an Anthropology of Technical Systems. *Journal of Anthropological Archaeology* 5:147-186.

Li, Shen
1992 Nutritional and Chemical Properties of Sorghum, Rapeseed and Sunflower Pollens. Unpublished Master's thesis, Department of Nutrition and Food Science, University of Arizona, Tucson.

Lindsay, Alexander J. Jr., Richard Ambler, Mary Anne Stein, and Philip M. Hobler
1968 *Survey and Excavations North and East of Navajo Mountain, Utah, 1959-1962.* Bulletin No. 45. Museum of Northern Arizona, Flagstaff.

Lowe, Charles H.
1964 *The Vertebrates of Arizona.* University of Arizona Press, Tucson.

Lyman, R. Lee
1994 *Vertebrate Taphonomy.* Cambridge University Press, Cambridge, England.

Mabry, Jonathan B.
1990 *A Late Archaic Occupation at AZ AA:12:105 (ASM).* Technical Report No. 90-6. Center for Desert Archaeology, Tucson.

1993a *Interstate 10 Frontage Road Project, Results of Phase 1 Data Recovery at AZ AA:12:746 (ASM), Tucson, Pima County, Arizona.* Technical Report No. 93-13. Center for Desert Archaeology, Tucson.

1993b *Treatment Plan for Archaeological Resources within the Interstate 10 Corridor Improvement Project, Tangerine Road to the I-19 Interchange.* Technical Report No. 93-2. Center for Desert Archaeology, Tucson.

1997 Introduction. In *Archaeological Investigations of Early Village Sites in the Middle Santa Cruz Valley,* by J. B. Mabry, D. L. Swartz, H. Wöcherl, J. J. Clark, G. H. Archer, and M. W. Lindeman, pp. 1-8. Anthropological Papers No. 18. Center for Desert Archaeology, Tucson.

1998a Architectural Variability and Site Structures. In *Archaeological Investigations of Early Village Sites in the Middle Santa Cruz Valley: Analyses and Synthesis,* Part I, edited by J. B. Mabry, pp. 209-244. Anthropological Papers No. 19. Center for Desert Archaeology, Tucson.

1998b Conclusion. In *Archaeological Investigations of Early Village Sites in the Middle Santa Cruz Valley: Analyses and Synthesis,* Part II, edited by J. B. Mabry, pp. 757-792. Anthropological Papers No. 19. Center for Desert Archaeology, Tucson.

1998c Introduction. In *Archaeological Investigations of Early Village Sites in the Middle Santa Cruz Valley: Analyses and Synthesis,* Part I, edited by J. B. Mabry, pp. 1-30. Anthropological Papers No. 19. Center for Desert Archaeology, Tucson.

Mabry, Jonathan B. (editor)
1998 *Archaeological Investigations at Early Village Sites in the Middle Santa Cruz Valley: Analyses and Synthesis,* Parts I and II. Anthropological Papers No. 19. Center for Desert Archaeology, Tucson.

Mabry, Jonathan B., and Gavin H. Archer
1997 The Santa Cruz Bend Site, AZ AA:12:746 (ASM). In *Archaeological Investigations of Early Village Sites in the Middle Santa Cruz Valley,* by J. B. Mabry, D. L. Swartz, H. Wöcherl, J. J. Clark, G. H. Archer, and M. W. Lindeman, pp. 9-228. Anthropological Papers No. 18. Center for Desert Archaeology, Tucson.

Mabry, Jonathan B., and James P. Holmlund
1998 Canals. In *Archaeological Investigations at Early Village Sites in the Middle Santa Cruz Valley: Analyses and Synthesis,* Part I, edited by J. B. Mabry, pp. 283-298. Anthropological Papers No. 19. Center for Desert Archaeology, Tucson.

Mabry, Jonathan B., Deborah L. Swartz, Helga Wöcherl, Jeffery J. Clark, Gavin H. Archer, and Michael W. Lindeman
1997 *Archaeological Investigations of Early Village Sites in the Middle Santa Cruz Valley.* Anthropological Papers No. 18. Center for Desert Archaeology, Tucson.

McCarthy, J. J., and F. H. Schamber
1981 Least-squares Fit with Digital Filter: A Status Report. In *Energy Dispersive X-ray Spectrometry,* edited by K. F. J. Heinrich, D. E. Newbury, R. L. Myklebust, and C. E. Fiori, pp. 273-296. Special Publication No. 604. National Bureau of Standards, Washington, D.C.

McCulloch, Clay
1954 Three Bar Game Management Unit Observations of Game Species Other than Deer. In *Arizona Chaparral Deer Study*. Arizona Game and Fish Department. Federal Aid in Wildlife Restoration Project W-71R-2:1-6.

McDonald, Alison Meg
1992 Indian Hill Rockshelter and Aboriginal Cultural Adaptations in Anza-Borrego Desert State Park, Southeastern California. Unpublished Ph.D. dissertation, Department of Anthropology, University of California, Riverside.

McKittrick, Mary Anne
1988 *Surficial Geologic Maps of the Tucson Metropolitan Area*. Open-File Report 88-18. Arizona Geological Survey, Tucson.

Mahood, Gail A., and James A. Stimac
1981 Trace-element Partitioning in Pantellerites and Trachytes. *Geochemica et Cosmochemica Acta* 54:2257-2276.

Manson, James
1961 Seri Indian Figurines. *The Kiva* 26(4):30-33.

Manson, Joni L.
1995 Starčevo Pottery and Neolithic Development in the Central Balkans. In *The Emergence of Pottery: Technology and Innovation in Ancient Societies*, edited by W. K. Barnett and J. W. Hoopes, pp. 65-77. Smithsonian Institution Press, Washington, D.C.

Martin, Alexander C., and William D. Barkley
1961 *Seed Identification Manual*. University of California Press, Berkeley.

Martin, Paul S., and John B. Rinaldo
1950 Turkey Foot Ridge Site: A Mogollon Village, Pine Lawn Valley, Western New Mexico. *Fieldiana: Anthropology* 38(2). Field Museum of Natural History, Chicago.

Martin, Paul S., John B. Rinaldo, and Ernst Antevs
1949 Cochise and Mogollon Sites: Pine Lawn Valley, Western New Mexico. *Fieldiana: Anthropology* 38(1). Field Natural History Museum, Chicago.

Martin, Paul Sidney
1939 *Modified Basket Maker Sites, Ackmen-Lowry Area, Southwestern Colorado, 1938*. Anthropological Series 23(3). Field Museum of Natural History, Chicago.

1943 *The SU Site Excavations at a Mogollon Village, Western New Mexico, Second Season, 1941*. Anthropological Series 32(2). Publication 526. Field Museum of Natural History, Chicago.

Martin, Paul Sidney, John B. Rinaldo, and Eloise R. Baxter
1957 Late Mogollon Communities: Four Sites of the Tularosa Phase, Western New Mexico. *Fieldiana: Anthropology* 49(1). Field Natural History Museum, Chicago.

Martin, Paul Sidney, John B. Rinaldo, Elaine Bluhm, Hugh C. Cutler, and Roger Grange Jr.
1952 Mogollon Cultural Continuity and Change: The Stratigraphic Analysis of Tularosa and Cordova Caves. *Fieldiana: Anthropology* 40. Field Museum of Natural History, Chicago.

Matson, R. G.
1991 *The Origins of Southwestern Agriculture*. University of Arizona Press, Tucson.

1994 Anomalous Basketmaker II Sites on Cedar Mesa: Not So Anomalous After All. *Kiva* 60: 219-237.

Matthew, A. J., A. J. Woods, and C. Oliver
1991 Spots Before the Eyes: New Comparison Charts for Visual Percentage Estimation in Archaeological Material. In *Recent Developments in Ceramic Petrology*, edited by A. Middleton and I. Freestone, pp. 211-263. British Museum Occasional Papers No. 81. British Museum, London.

Mauldin, Raymond
1993 The Relationship between Ground Stone and Agricultural Intensification in Western New Mexico. *Kiva* 58:317-330.

Mayro, Linda L.
1985 Shell Artifacts. In *Excavations at the Valencia Site, A Preclassic Hohokam Village in the Southern Tucson Basin*, by W. H. Doelle, pp. 211-224. Anthropological Papers No. 3. Institute for American Research, Tucson.

Michelsen, R. C.
1967   Pecked Metates of Baja California. *Masterkey* 41(2):73-77.

Miksa, Elizabeth J., and Charles Tompkins
1998   Rock and Mineral Materials and Sources. In *Archaeological Investigations of Early Village Sites in the Middle Santa Cruz Valley: Analyses and Synthesis*, Part II, edited by J. B. Mabry, pp. 655-696. Anthropological Papers No. 19. Center for Desert Archaeology, Tucson.

Miksicek, Charles H.
1987   Formation Processes of the Archaeobotanical Record. In *Advances in Archaeological Method and Theory*, Vol. 10, edited by M. B. Schiffer, pp. 211-247. Academic Press, New York.

Mills, Peter R.
1993   An Axe to Grind: A Functional Analysis of Anasazi Stone Axes from Sand Canyon Pueblo Ruin (5MT765), Southwestern Colorado. *Kiva* 58:393-413.

Minnis, Paul E.
1981   Seeds in Archaeological Sites: Sources and Some Interpretive Problems. *American Antiquity* 46:143-151.

1989   Prehistoric Diet in the Northern Southwest: Macroplant Remains from Four Corners Feces. *American Antiquity* 54:543-563.

1991   Famine Foods of the Northern American Desert Borderlands in Historical Context. *Journal of Ethnobiology* 11:231-257.

Minturn, Penny Dufoe, Lorrie Lincoln-Babb, and Jonathan B. Mabry
1998   Human Osteology. In *Archaeological Investigations of Early Village Sites in the Middle Santa Cruz Valley: Analyses and Synthesis*, edited by J. B. Mabry, pp. 739-756. Anthropological Papers No. 19. Center for Desert Archaeology, Tucson.

Monasterio, Roberto E. Maurer Ortiz
1981   Effect of Timing and Amount of Irrigation and Drought Stress Conditioning in Corn (*Zea mays* L.). Unpublished Ph.D. dissertation, Department of Agronomy, University of Nebraska, Lincoln.

Montgomery, F. H.
1978   *Seeds and Fruits of Plants of Eastern Canada and Northeastern United States*. University of Toronto Press, Toronto.

Moore, A. M. T.
1995   The Inception of Potting in Western Asia and Its Impact on Economy and Society. In *The Emergence of Pottery: Technology and Innovation in Ancient Societies*, edited by W. K. Barnett and J. W. Hoopes, pp. 39-53. Smithsonian Institution Press, Washington, D.C.

Morris, Donald H.
1990   Changes in Groundstone Following the Introduction of Maize into the American Southwest. *Journal of Anthropological Research* 46:177-194.

Morris, Earl H.
1927   *The Beginnings of Pottery Making in the San Juan Area: Unfired Prototypes and the Wares of the Earliest Ceramic Period*. Anthropological Papers No. 28. Museum of Natural History, New York.

Morss, Noel
1954   *Clay Figurines of the American Southwest*. Papers of the Peabody Museum of American Archaeology and Ethnology 49(1). Harvard University, Cambridge, Massachusetts.

Morton, Julia F.
1963   Principal Wild Food Plants of the United States Excluding Alaska and Hawaii. *Economic Botany* 17:319-330.

Moser, Edward, and Richard S. White
1968   Seri Clay Figurines. *The Kiva* 33:133-154.

Myerhoff, Barbara G.
1974   *Peyote Hunt: The Sacred Journey of the Huichol Indians*. Cornell University Press, Ithaca, New York.

Nabhan, Gary Paul
1983   Papago Fields: Arid Lands Ethnobotany and Agricultural Ecology. Unpublished Ph.D. dissertation, Arid Lands Resources Committee, University of Arizona, Tucson.

1985   *Gathering the Desert*. University of Arizona Press, Tucson.

Negrín, Juan
1975   *The Huichol Creation of the World*. E. B. Crocker Art Gallery, Sacramento, California.

Nesbitt, Paul
1938   *Starkweather Ruin: A Mogollon-Pueblo Site in the Upper Gila Area of New Mexico, and Affiliative Aspects of the Mogollon Culture.* Publications in Anthropology, Bulletin 6. Logan Museum, Beloit College, Beloit, Wisconsin.

Ng, Timothy J.
1993   New Opportunities in the Cucurbitaceae. In *New Crops,* edited by J. Janick and J. E. Simon, pp. 538-546. John Wiley and Sons, New York.

Ortner, D. J., and W. G. J. Putschar
1985   *Identification of Pathological Conditions in Human Skeletal Remains.* Smithsonian Contributions to Anthropology No. 28. Smithsonian Institution Press, Washington, D.C.

Owen, Roger C.
1956   Some Clay Figurines and Seri Dolls from Coastal Sonora, Mexico. *The Kiva* 21(3-4):1-11.

Oyuela-Caycedo, Augusto
1995   Rocks Versus Clay: The Evolution of Pottery Technology in the Case of San Jacinto 1, Columbia. In *The Emergence of Pottery: Technology and Innovation in Ancient Societies,* edited by W. K. Barnett and J. W. Hoopes, pp. 133-144. Smithsonian Institution Press, Washington, D.C.

Parker, Kittie F.
1990   *An Illustrated Guide to Arizona Weeds.* University of Arizona Press, Tucson.

Parry, W., and R. Kelly
1986   Expedient Core Technology and Sedentism. In *The Organization of Core Technology,* edited by J. Johnson and C. Morrow, pp. 285-304. Westview Press, Boulder.

Pearsall, Deborah M.
1989   *Paleoethnobotany: A Handbook of Procedures.* Academic Press, New York.

Plog, Fred T.
1974   *The Study of Prehistoric Change.* Academic Press, New York.

Pollard, Helen P.
1997   Recent Research in West Mexican Archaeology. *Journal of Archaeological Research* 5:345-384.

Popper, Virginia S.
1988   Selecting Quantitative Measurements in Paleoethnobotany. In *Current Paleoethnobotany,* edited by C. Hastorf and V. S. Popper, pp. 53-71. University of Chicago Press, Chicago.

Reed, Mickey Lynn
1988   The Effect of Moisture Stress and Salinity on Germination and Growth of Grain Amaranth, *Amaranthus cruentus* and *Amaranthus hypochondriacus.* Unpublished Master's thesis, Department of Plant Sciences, University of Arizona, Tucson.

Rehder, Harald A.
1981   *The Audubon Society Field Guide to North American Seashells.* Alfred A. Knopf, New York.

Reid, Jefferson, and Stephanie Whittlesey
1997   *The Archaeology of Ancient Arizona.* University of Arizona Press, Tucson.

Rice, Prudence M.
1987   *Pottery Analysis: A Sourcebook.* University of Chicago Press, Chicago.

Roberts, Frank H. H. Jr.
1929   *Shabik'eshchee Village: A Late Basketmaker Site in Chaco Canyon, New Mexico.* Bulletin No. 92. Bureau of American Ethnology, Washington, D.C.

1931   *The Ruins at Kiatuthlanna, Eastern Arizona.* Bulletin No. 100. Bureau of American Ethnology, Washington, D.C.

Robinson, R. G.
1978   Production and Culture. In *Sunflower Science and Technology,* edited by J. F. Carter, pp. 89-143. American Society of Agronomy, Madison, Wisconsin.

Rodríguez, Camilo
1995   Sites with Early Ceramics in the Caribbean Littoral of Columbia: A Discussion of Periodization and Typologies. Translated by Renée M. Bonzani. In *The Emergence of Pottery: Technology and Innovation in Ancient Societies,* edited by W. K. Barnett and J. W. Hoopes, pp. 145-156. Smithsonian Institution Press, Washington, D.C.

Roosevelt, A. C.
1995 Early Pottery in the Amazon: Twenty Years of Scholarly Obscurity. In *The Emergence of Pottery: Technology and Innovation in Ancient Societies*, edited by W. K. Barnett and J. W. Hoopes, pp. 115-131. Smithsonian Institution Press, Washington, D.C.

Roth, Barbara J.
1983 *Archaeological Survey in the Eastern Tucson Basin, Saguaro National Monument, Rincon Mountain Unit, Cactus Forest Area.* Publications in Anthropology No. 22. U.S. Department of the Interior, National Park Service, Western Archeological and Conservation Center, Tucson.

1988 Recent Research on the Late Archaic Occupation of the Northern Tucson Basin. In *Recent Research on Tucson Basin Prehistory: Proceedings of the Second Tucson Basin Conference*, edited by W. H. Doelle and P. R. Fish, pp. 81-86. Anthropological Papers No. 10. Institute for American Research, Tucson.

1992 Sedentary Agriculturalists or Mobile Hunter-Gatherers? Recent Evidence of the Late Archaic Occupation of the Northern Tucson Basin. *Kiva* 57:291-314.

1995a Late Archaic Occupation of the Upper Bajada: Excavations at AZ AA:12:84 (ASM), Tucson Basin. *Kiva* 61:189-207.

1995b Regional Land Use in the Late Archaic of the Tucson Basin: A View from the Upper Bajada. In *Early Formative Adaptations in the Southern Southwest*, edited by B. J. Roth. Monographs in World Archaeology No. 5. Prehistory Press, Madison, Wisconsin.

Roth, Barbara June
1989 Late Archaic Settlement and Subsistence in the Tucson Basin. Unpublished Ph.D. dissertation, Department of Anthropology, University of Arizona, Tucson.

Russell, Frank
1975 *The Pima Indians.* Reprinted. University of Arizona Press, Tucson. Originally published 1908, *Twenty-sixth Annual Report of the Bureau of American Ethnology, 1904-1905*, pp. 1-390. Smithsonian Institution, Washington, D.C.

Rye, Owen S.
1981 *Pottery Technology: Principles and Reconstruction.* Manuals on Archaeology No. 4. Taraxacum Press, Washington, D.C.

Sayles, E. B.
1941 Archaeology of the Cochise Culture. In *The Cochise Culture*, by E. B. Sayles and E. Antevs, pp. 1-30. Medallion Papers No. 29. Gila Pueblo, Globe, Arizona.

1945 *The San Simon Branch, Excavations at Cave Creek and in the San Simon Valley I: Material Culture.* Medallion Papers 34. Gila Pueblo, Globe, Arizona.

1983 *The Cochise Cultural Sequence in Arizona.* Anthropological Papers No. 42. University of Arizona Press, Tucson.

Sayles, E. B., and Gladys Sayles
1948 The Pottery of Ida Redbird. *Arizona Highways* January:28-31.

Schaafsma, Polly
1980 *Indian Rock Art of the Southwest.* University of New Mexico Press, Albuquerque.

Schamber, F. H.
1977 A Modification of the Linear Least-squares Fitting Method which Provides Continuum Suppression. In *X-ray Fluorescence Analysis of Environmental Samples*, edited by T. G. Dzubay, pp. 241-257. Ann Arbor Science Publications, Ann Arbor, Michigan.

Schiffer, Michael B.
1982 Hohokam Chronology: An Essay on History and Method. In *Hohokam and Patayan: Prehistory of Southwestern Arizona*, edited by R. H. McGuire and M. B. Schiffer, pp. 299-344. Academic Press, New York.

1987 *Formation Processes of the Archaeological Record.* University of New Mexico Press, Albuquerque.

1992 *Technological Perspectives on Behavioral Change.* University of Arizona Press, Tucson.

Schiffer, Michael B., and James M. Skibo
1987 Theory and Experiment in the Study of Technological Change. *Current Anthropology* 28: 595-622.

Schlanger, Sarah H.
1990 Artifact Assemblage Composition and Site Occupation Duration. In *Perspectives on Southwestern Prehistory*, edited by P. E. Minnis and C. L. Redman, pp. 103-121. Westview Press, Boulder.

Schott, Michael J.
1992   Radiocarbon Dating as a Probabilistic Technique: The Childers Site and Late Woodland Occupation in the Ohio Valley. *American Antiquity* 57:202-230.

Schroeder, Albert H.
1982   Historical Overview of Southwestern Ceramics. In *Southwestern Ceramics: A Comparative Review*, edited by A. H. Schroeder, pp. 1-26. Arizona Archaeologist No. 15. Arizona Archaeological Society, Phoenix.

Shackley, M. Steven
1986   Lithic Technology and Mobility Strategies at Picacho. In *Prehistoric Hunter-Gatherers of South Central Arizona: The Picacho Reservoir Project*, edited by F. E. Bayham, D. H. Morris, and M. S. Shackley, pp. 109-156. Anthropological Field Studies 13. Arizona State University, Tempe.

1988   Sources of Archaeological Obsidian in the Southwest: An Archaeological, Petrological, and Geochemical Study. *American Antiquity* 53:752-772.

1990   Early Hunter-gatherer Procurement Ranges in the Southwest: Evidence from Obsidian Geochemistry and Lithic Technology. Unpublished Ph.D. dissertation, Department of Anthropology, Arizona State University, Tempe.

1992   The Upper Gila River Gravels as an Archaeological Obsidian Source Region: Implications for Models of Exchange and Interaction. *Geoarchaeology* 7:315-326.

1995   Sources of Archaeological Obsidian in the Greater American Southwest: An Update and Quantitative Analysis. *American Antiquity* 60: 531-551.

1996a   Elko or San Pedro? A Quantitative Analysis of Late Archaic Projectile Points from White Tanks, Yuma County, Arizona. *Kiva* 61:413-432.

1996b   Range and Mobility in the Early Hunter-gatherer Southwest. In *Early Formative Adaptations in the Southern Southwest*, edited by B. J. Roth, pp. 5-16. Monographs in World Archaeology 25. Prehistory Press, Madison, Wisconsin.

1998   An Energy Dispersive X-ray Fluorescence (EDXRF) Analysis of Obsidian Artifacts. In *Archaeological Investigations of Early Village Sites in the Middle Santa Cruz Valley: Analyses and Synthesis*, Part 2, edited by J. B. Mabry, pp. 857-864. Anthropological Papers No. 19. Center for Desert Archaeology, Tucson.

Shum, Dee Ann, and Edward B. Jelks, editors
1962   *Handbook of Texas Archaeology: Type Descriptions.* Bulletin 4. Texas Memorial Museum, Austin.

Silsbee, Joan M.
1958   Determining the Source of California *Olivella* Shells. In *Papers in California Archaeology*, pp. 10-11. Reports of the University of California Survey No. 41. University of California, Berkeley.

Simms, Steven R.
1987   *Behavioral Ecology and Hunter-Gatherer Foraging.* An Example from the Great Basin. BAR International Series 381, Oxford, England.

Slawson, Laurie V.
1990   *The Terminal Classic in the Tucson Basin, Rabid Ruin, a Late Tucson Phase Hohokam Settlement.* Southwest Cultural Series No. 10. Cultural and Environmental Systems, Inc., Tucson.

Sliva, R. Jane
1995   A Life History Approach to the Analysis of Lithic Assemblages from Early Agricultural Communities in the Santa Cruz Drainage, Arizona. Paper presented at the 60th Annual Meeting of the Society for American Archaeology, Minneapolis.

1997   Flaked Stone Artifacts. In *Archaeological Investigations of the Early Agricultural Period Settlement at the Base of A-Mountain, Tucson, Arizona*, edited by M. W. Diehl, pp. 72-96. Technical Report No. 96-21. Center for Desert Archaeology, Tucson.

1998a   Flaked Stone Artifacts. In *Archaeological Investigations at Early Village Sites in the Middle Santa Cruz Valley: Analyses and Syntheses*, Part I. edited by J. B. Mabry, pp. 299-356. Anthropological Papers No. 19. Center for Desert Archaeology, Tucson.

Sliva, R. Jane

1998b   The Flaked Stone Assemblage. In *Archaeological Investigations at the Wetlands Site, AZ AA:12:90 (ASM)*, edited by A. K. L. Freeman, pp. 147-163. Technical Report No. 97-5, Center for Desert Archaeology, Tucson.

1999   Flaked Stone Artifacts. In *Excavations in the Santa Cruz River Floodplain: The Middle Archaic Component at Los Pozos*, edited by D. A. Gregory, pp. 33-46. Anthropological Papers No. 20. Center for Desert Archaeology, Tucson.

2000   Temporal, Spatial, and Functional Variability in the Flaked Stone Assemblage. In *Tonto Creek Archaeological Project: Artifact and Environment Analyses: Vol. 2. Stone Tool and Subsistence Studies* (draft), edited by J. J. Clark, pp. 487-534. Anthropological Paper No. 23. Center for Desert Archaeology, Tucson.

2001   Flaked Stone Data Tables. In *The Early Agricultural Period Component at Los Pozos: Feature Description and Data Tables*, edited by D. A. Gregory, pp. 103-106. Technical Report No. 99-4. Desert Archaeology, Inc., Tucson.

Smiley, Francis E.

1994   The Agricultural Transition in the Northern Southwest: Patterns in the Current Chronometric Data. *Kiva* 60:165-189.

Smiley, Terah, Henry F. Dobyns, Bonnie Jones, and James T. Barter

1953   San Jose de Tucson, Its History and Archaeological Exploration. Ms. on file, Arizona State Museum Library Archives (Folder A-271), University of Arizona, Tucson.

Smith, G. E. P.

1938   *The Physiography of Arizona Valleys and the Occurrence of Groundwater*. Technical Bulletin No. 77. College of Agriculture, University of Arizona, Tucson.

Snow, Charles E., and William T. Sanders

1954   The Durango Skeletons. In *Basketmaker II Sites near Durango, Colorado*, by E. H. Morris and R. F. Burgh, pp. 89-92. Publication 604. Carnegie Institution of Washington, Washington, D.C.

Speth, John D.

1983   *Bison Kills and Bone Counts*. University of Chicago Press, Chicago.

Spier, Leslie

1928   *Havasupai Ethnography*. American Museum of Natural History, New York.

1933   *Yuman Tribes of the Gila River*. University of Chicago Press, Chicago.

Stallknecht, G. F., and J. A. Schulz-Schaeffer

1993   Amaranth Rediscovered. In *New Crops*, edited by J. Janick and J. E. Simon, pp. 211-218. John Wiley and Sons, New York.

Steenbergh, Warren F., and Charles H. Lowe

1983   *Ecology of the Saguaro III: Growth and Demography*. Scientific Monograph Series No. 17. National Park Service, U.S. Department of the Interior, Washington, D.C.

Stephen, Alexander M.

1936   *Hopi Journal of Alexander M. Stephen*, edited by E. Clews Parson. Columbia University Press, New York.

Steward, Julian H.

1938   *Basin-Plateau Aboriginal Sociopolitical Groups*. Bulletin No. 120. Smithsonian Institution, Bureau of American Ethnology, Washington, D.C.

Stuiver, M., and T. F. Brazunias

1988   The Solar Component of the Atmospheric ^{14}C Record. In *Secular Solar and Geomagnetic Variations in the Last 10,000 Years*, edited by F. R. Stephenson and A. W. Wofendale, pp. 245-266. Kluwer, Dordrecht, the Netherlands.

Stuiver, M., T. F. Brazunias, B. Becker, and B. Kromer

1991   Climatic, Solar, Oceanic and Geomagnetic Influences on Late-Glacial and Holocene Atmospheric $^{14}C/^{12}C$ Change. *Quaternary Research* 35:1-24.

Stuiver, Minze, and P. J. Reimer

1987   CALIB: Radiocarbon Calibration Program, 1987. Quaternary Isotope Laboratory, University of Washington, Seattle.

1993   Extended ^{14}C Data Base and Revised CALIB 3.0 ^{14}C Age Calibration Program. *Radiocarbon* 35:215-230.

Suess, H. E.
1961 Secular Changes in the Concentration of Atmospheric Radiocarbon. In *Problems Related to Interplanetary Matter*, pp. 90-95. Nuclear Science Series Report No. 33, Publication 845. National Academy of Sciences-National Research Council, Washington, D.C.

1986 Secular Variations of Cosmogenic ^{14}C on Earth: Their Discovery and Interpretation. *Radiocarbon* 28:259-266.

Sutherland, Kay, and Paul P. Steed
1974 The Fort Hancock Rock Art Site Number One. *The Artifact* 12:1-64.

Swartz, Deborah L.
1995 An Archaeological Survey for Mining Activity South of Patagonia, Arizona. Letter Report No. 95-106. Desert Archaeology, Inc., Tucson.

1997a *Archaeological Investigations for the I-10/I-19 Interchange Focused on the Julian Wash Site, AZ BB:13:17 (ASM)*. Technical Report No. 97-8. Center for Desert Archaeology, Tucson.

1997b *Further Archaeological Testing at the Eastern Margin of the Hodges Ruin, AZ AA:12:18 (ASM)*. Technical Report No. 97-11. Center for Desert Archaeology, Tucson.

Swartz, Deborah L., and Michael W. Lindeman
1997 The Stone Pipe Site, AZ AA:13:425 (ASM). In *Archaeological Investigations of Early Village Sites in the Middle Santa Cruz Valley*, by J. B. Mabry, D. L. Swartz, H. Wöcherl, J. J. Clark, G. H. Archer, and M. W. Lindeman, pp. 281-418. Anthropological Papers No. 18. Center for Desert Archaeology, Tucson.

Szuter, Christine
1989 Hunting by Prehistoric Horticulturalists in the Southwest. Unpublished Ph.D. dissertation, Department of Anthropology, University of Arizona, Tucson.

Szuter, Christine R., and Frank E. Bayham
1995 Faunal Exploitations during the Late Archaic and Pioneer Periods in South-Central Arizona. In *Early Formative Adaptations in the American Southwest*, edited by B. J. Roth, pp. 65-105. Monographs in World Archaeology No. 5. Prehistory Press, Madison, Wisconsin.

Tagg, Martyn D.
1994 Projectile Points of East-Central Arizona: Forms and Chronology. In *Middle Little Colorado River Archaeology: From the Parks to the People*, edited by A. T. Jones and M. D. Tagg, pp. 87-147. Arizona Archaeologist No. 27. Arizona Archaeological Society, Phoenix.

Taylor, R. E.
1987 *Radiocarbon Dating: An Archaeological Perspective*. Academic Press, Orlando.

Teles, Francisco F. F.
1977 Nutrient Analysis of Prickly Pear (*Opuntia Ficus Indica*, Linn). Unpublished Ph.D. dissertation, Committee on Agricultural Biochemistry and Nutrition. University of Arizona, Tucson.

Thiel, J. Homer
1995 *Rock Art in Arizona*. Technical Report No. 94-6. Center for Desert Archaeology, Tucson. Submitted to Arizona State Parks, State Historic Preservation Office, Phoenix.

1998 Faunal Remains. In *Archaeological Investigations of Early Village Sites in the Middle Santa Cruz Valley: Analyses and Synthesis*, edited by J. B. Mabry, pp. 165-208. Anthropological Papers No. 19. Center for Desert Archaeology, Tucson.

Turner, Ellen Sue, and Thomas R. Hester
1987 *A Field Guide to the Stone Artifacts of Texas Indians*. Texas Monthly Press, Austin.

Turner, Raymond M., and David E. Brown
1994 Sonoran Desertscrub. Reprinted. In *Biotic Communities: Southwestern United States and Northwestern Mexico*, edited by D. E. Brown, pp. 181-221. University of Utah Press, Salt Lake City. Originally published 1982 as *Desert Plants* 4(1-4):181-221, Boyce Thompson Southwestern Arboretum, Superior, Arizona.

Underhill, Ruth M.
1938 *Singing for Power: The Song Magic of the Papago Indians of Southern Arizona*. University of California Press, Berkeley.

1939 *Social Organization of the Papago Indians*. Contributions to Anthropology, Vol. 30. Columbia University Press, New York.

Underhill, Ruth M.
1946　*Papago Indian Religion.* Columbia University Press, New York.

Upham, Steadman, R. S. MacNeish, W. C. Galinat, and C. M. Stevenson
1987　Evidence Concerning the Origin of Maiz de Ocho. *American Anthropologist* 89:410-418.

Upham, Steadman, R. S. MacNeish, and C. M. Stevenson
1988　The Age and Evolutionary Significance of Southwestern Maiz de Ocho. *American Anthropologist* 90:683-684.

U.S. Department of Agriculture
1974　*Seeds of Woody Plants in the United States.* USDA Handbook No. 450. Forest Service, U.S. Department of Agriculture, Washington, D.C.

Varien, Mark D., and Barbara J. Mills
1997　Accumulations Research: Problems and Prospects for Estimating Occupation Span. *Journal of Archaeological Method and Theory* 4:141-191.

Vitelli, Karen D.
1995　Pots, Potters, and the Shaping of Greek Neolithic Society. In *The Emergence of Pottery: Technology and Innovation in Ancient Societies,* edited by W. K. Barnett and J. W. Hoopes, pp. 55-63. Smithsonian Institution Press, Washington, D.C.

Vokes, Arthur
1984　The Shell Assemblage of the Salt-Gila Aqueduct Project Sites. In *Hohokam Archaeology along the Salt-Gila Aqueduct, Central Arizona Project: Vol. 8. Material Culture,* edited by L. S. Teague and P. L. Crown, pp. 465-502. Archaeological Series No. 150. Arizona State Museum, University of Arizona, Tucson.

1998a　Shell Artifacts. *Archaeological Investigations at Early Village Sites in the Middle Santa Cruz Valley: Analyses and Synthesis,* Part I, edited by J. B. Mabry, pp. 438-467. Anthropological Papers No. 19. Center for Desert Archaeology, Tucson.

1998b　Shell Material from the Wetlands Site. In *Archaeological Investigations at the Wetlands Site, AZ AA:12:90 (ASM),* edited by A. K. L. Freeman, pp. 249-264. Technical Report No. 97-5. Desert Archaeology, Inc., Tucson.

de Vries, H.
1958　Variations in Concentration of Radiocarbon with Time and Location on Earth. *Proceedings, Nederlandsche Akademie van Wetenschappen,* Series B 61.1.

Wallace, Henry D.
1995　Decorated Buffware and Brownware Ceramics. In *The Roosevelt Community Development Study: Vol. 2. Ceramic Chronology, Technology, and Economics,* edited by J. M. Heidke and M. T. Stark, pp. 19-84. Anthropological Papers No. 14. Center for Desert Archaeology, Tucson.

1996　*Archaeological Assessment of a Portion of the Knapp Parcel Southeast of the Confluence of the Rillito and Santa Cruz Rivers, Tucson, Arizona.* Technical Report No. 96-2. Center for Desert Archaeology, Tucson.

Wallace, Henry D., James M. Heidke, and William H. Doelle
1995　Hohokam Origins. *Kiva* 60:575-618.

Wallace, Henry D., and James P. Holmlund
1986　*Petroglyphs of the Picacho Mountains, South Central Arizona.* Anthropological Papers No. 6. Institute for American Research, Tucson.

Warner, Jesse E.
1994　An Introduction to Figures Representing a Double Entity. *American Indian Rock Art* XIV:127-148. American Rock Art Research Association, San Miguel, California.

Waters, Jennifer A., and Helga Wöcherl
2001　Faunal Remains Data Tables. In *The Early Agricultural Period Component at Los Pozos: Feature Description and Data Tables,* edited by D. A. Gregory, pp. 157-164. Technical Report No. 99-4. Desert Archaeology, Inc., Tucson.

Welch, Joseph M.
1960　A Study of Seasonal Movements of White-tailed Deer (*O. virginianus couesi*) in the Cave Creek Basin of the Chiricahua Mountains. Master's thesis, University of Arizona, Tucson.

Wellman, Kevin D.
1994　*Archaeological Survey of the Saguaro National Monument, 1994: The Saguaro Land Acquisition and Trails Inventory.* Publications in Anthropology No. 65. U.S. Department of the Interior, National Park Service, Western Archeological and Conservation Center, Tucson.

Wetterstrom, Wilma E.
1976   *The Effects of Nutrition on Population Size at Pueblo Arroyo Hondo.* Ph.D. dissertation, University of Michigan. University Microfilms, Ann Arbor, Michigan.

Whalen, Michael E.
1994   Turquoise Ridge and Late Prehistoric Residential Mobility in the Desert Mogollon Region. University of Utah Anthropological Papers No. 118, Salt Lake City.

Whalen, Michael E., and Patricia A. Gilman
1990   Introduction to Transitions to Sedentism. In *Perspectives on Southwestern Prehistory*, edited by P. E. Minnis and C. L. Redman, pp. 71-74. Westview Press, Boulder.

Wheat, Joe Ben
1955   *Mogollon Culture Prior to A.D. 1000.* Memoirs No. 82. American Anthropological Association, Menasha, Wisconsin.

Wheat, Margaret M.
1967   *Survival Arts of the Primitive Paiutes.* University of Nevada Press, Reno.

White, Theodore E.
1953   A Method of Calculating the Dietary Percentage of Various Food Animals Utilized by Aboriginal Peoples. *American Antiquity* 18:396-98.

Whittlesey, Stephanie M.
1995   Mogollon, Hohokam, and O'otam: Rethinking the Early Formative Period in Southern Period. *Kiva* 60:465-480.

Wilcox, David R.
1986   The Tepiman Connection: A Model of Mesoamerican-Southwestern Interaction. In *Ripples in the Chichimec Sea: New Considerations of Southwestern-Mesoamerican Interactions*, edited by F. J. Mathien and R. H. McGuire, pp. 134-154. Southern Illinois University Press, Carbondale and Edwardsville.

Wilke, Philip J., Meg McDonald, and L. A. Payen
1986   *Excavations at Indian Hill Rockshelter, Anza-Borrego Desert State Park, California, 1984-1985.* UCRARU #772, Archaeological Research Unit, University of California, Riverside.

Williams, J. T., and D. Brenner
1995   Grain Amaranth (*Amaranthus* species). In *Cereals and Pseudocereals*, edited by J. T. Williams, pp. 129-186. Chapman and Hall, New York.

Williams, Patrick T.
1976   Grass Production Changes with Mesquite (*Prosopis juliflora*) Reinvasion in Southern Arizona. Unpublished Master's thesis, School of Renewable Natural Resources, University of Arizona, Tucson.

Wills, Wirt H.
1988   Early Agriculture and Sedentism in the American Southwest: Evidence and Interpretations. *Journal of World Prehistory* 2:445-488.

1995   Archaic Foraging and the Beginning of Food Production in the American Southwest. In *Last Hunters–First Farmers: New Perspectives on the Prehistoric Transition to Agriculture*, edited by T. D. Price and A. B. Gebauer, pp. 215-242. School of American Research Press, Santa Fe.

Winter, Joseph C.
1973   The Distribution and Development of Fremont Agriculture: Some Preliminary Interpretations. *American Antiquity* 38:439-451.

Wöcherl, Helga
1998   Extramural Pits. In *Archaeological Investigations of Early Village Sites in the Middle Santa Cruz Valley: Analyses and Synthesis*, Part 1, edited by J. B. Mabry, pp. 245-282. Anthropological Papers No. 19. Center for Desert Archaeology, Tucson.

Wöcherl, Helga, and Jeffery J. Clark
1997   The Square Hearth Site, AZ AA:12:745 (ASM). In *Archaeological Investigations of Early Village Sites in the Middle Santa Cruz Valley*, by J. B. Mabry, D. L. Swartz, H. Wöcherl, J. J. Clark, G. H. Archer, and M. W. Lindeman, pp. 229-280. Anthropological Papers No. 18. Center for Desert Archaeology, Tucson.

Woodbury, George, and Edna Woodbury
1935   *Prehistoric Skeletal Remains from the Texas Coast.* Medallion Papers XVIII. Gila Pueblo, Globe, Arizona.

Woodbury, Richard
1954 *Prehistoric Stone Implements of Northeastern Arizona.* Papers of the Peabody Museum of American Archaeology and Ethnology Vol. 34. Harvard University, Cambridge.

Woodbury, Richard B., and Ezra B. W. Zubrow
1979 Agricultural Beginnings, 2000 B.C.-A.D. 500. In *Southwest,* edited by A. Ortiz, pp. 43-60. *Handbook of North American Indians, Vol. 9,* W. C. Sturtevant, general editor. Smithsonian Institution, Washington, D.C.

Wormington, H. Marie
1944 *Ancient North America.* 2nd ed. Popular Series No. 4, edited by Alfred M. Bailey. Museum of Natural History, Denver.

Wright, Katherine I.
1994 Ground-stone Tools and Hunter-Gatherer Subsistence in Southwest Asia: Implications for the Transition to Farming. *American Antiquity* 59:238-263.

Wright, Mona K.
1993 Simulated Use of Experimental Maize Grinding Tools from Southwestern Colorado. *Kiva* 58:345-355.

Yellen, John E.
1977 *Archaeological Approaches to the Present: Models for Reconstructing the Past.* Academic Press, New York.

Young, D., and Douglas Bamforth
1990 On the Macroscopic Identification of Used Flakes. *American Antiquity* 55:403-409.